THE
25th
DIVISION
IN FRANCE
AND FLANDERS

BY LIEUT.-COL. M. KINCAID-SMITH

PUBLISHED BY
THE NAVAL & MILITARY PRESS

PART I.

THE following pages do not pretend to be more than the very briefest sketch of the operations in which the 25th Division was engaged from time to time on the Western Battle Front.

Raised during the later months of 1914 the Division proceeded to France in September, 1915, and was soon employed on a defensive sector of the line south of Ypres. In November, 1915, the 76th Brigade left the Division and was replaced by the 7th Brigade.

During the period covered by this record, the Division has played its part with distinction in the battles of the Somme, July to November, 1916 ; Messines, June, 1917 ; and Ypres, August, 1917. In the intervening periods it has been employed in various defensive sectors of the British front with very short intervals for rest and training.

Its boldness and dash in offensive operations, its tenacity in holding whatever it may have captured, and its efficient administrative arrangements for the feeding, clothing, general comfort and entertainment of the men, have earned for the Division a reputation high amongst the British Armies in France.

In recognition of their services officers and men of the Division have received :—

2 V.C.
1 K.C.B.
3 C.M.G.
65 D.S.O.
259 M.C.
173 D.C.M.
781 Military Medals.
8 Meritorious Service Medals.
308 Mention in Despatches.

Many members of its staff have been promoted to more responsible positions, and no less than four of its Battalion Commanders, Lt.-Col. C. E. Bond, C.M.G., D.S.O., Border Regt.; Lt.-Col. A. B. Forman, D.S.O., R.A.; Lt.-Col. Johnstone, D.S.O., M.C., Cheshire Regt. ; and Lt.-Col. W. K. Evans, D.S.O., Cheshire Regt. ; have become Brigadier Generals in other Divisions.

The losses of the Division have been very heavy :—270 officers killed (including Lt.-Col. W. S. Brown, Wilts Regt. ;

Lt.-Col. W. B. Gibbs, D.S.O., Worcester Regt. ; Lt.-Col. H. Brassey, S. Lancs. Regt., Lt.-Col. R. L. Aspinall, D.S.O., Cheshire Regt. ; and Lt.-Col. H. T. Cotton. D.S.O., S. Lancs. Regt.), 858 officers wounded, 3,683 other ranks killed, 17,947 other ranks wounded ; 44 officers and 2,337 other ranks missing, of whom the great majority are believed to have been killed.

The good feeling that exists between the infantry, the Divisional Artillery and all other combatant and administrative services, is a striking proof of the mutual confidence within the Division. To this confidence is undoubtedly due the development of the fine *esprit de corps* which characterises all units of the Division and which has been so largely responsible for its success.

Space unfortunately does not permit of a full and detailed account of the many acts of gallantry and devotion to duty which have received recognition by well merited decorations and promotions. Many equally gallant have fallen whose names and deeds remain unrecorded except in the memories of their comrades. Full justice can hardly be done here to a subject so vast and vivid, but it is hoped that something of the energy, zeal and the fortitude of all ranks may be realised by a perusal of these pages. They form a simple record of splendid achievements and those historic events with which the Division has been associated. To many they will in time to come serve to recall thrilling experiences with the 25th Division in France and Flanders—memories of days, sometimes wearisome, but never altogether lacking the consciousness and satisfaction of work well done.

M. K.-S.

BAPAUME,

8th February, 1918.

Since the above was written, other chapters have been added dealing with the momentous events of 1918, in which the 25th Division was engaged. After a short period in the defensive sector of Bethune, towards the end of 1917 the Division was transferred to the Somme. With the IVth Corps, in front of Bapaume, it fought the most glorious fight of its career and withstood in brilliant fashion the great German attack on the 21st March. Within three weeks the Division was again called upon to oppose a strong attack along the river Lys when its battalions suffered heavy casualties, including several of their most experienced commanding officers : followed by a brilliant counter-attack at Kemmel and the recapture of the village the 26th April. Arriving in Champagne the beginning of May, the Division had had no time to absorb large numbers of reinforcements, and in its exhausted, untrained and unwelded state was in no fit condition to withstand the overwhelming attack along the Aisne the 27th May.

In recognition of their services officers and men of the Division have received since Christmas, 1917—

2 V.C.'s.	81 D.C.M.'s
3 C.M.G.'s.	513 Military Medals.
26 D.S.O.'s.	41 Meritorious Service Medals.
145 M.C.'s	52 Mention in Despatches.

The losses during this period have been heavy, including 102 officers killed, 361 wounded, 187 missing ; 942 other ranks killed, 6,461 wounded, and 7,320 missing.

Withdrawn from the line the middle of June all ranks of the Division heard with feelings of deepest regret that owing to scarcity of reinforcements the regular battalions, 3rd Worcesters, 1st Wilts and 2nd South Lancashires would be transferred to other Divisions, and the 9th L. North|Lancs, 8th Borders, 10th Cheshires, 11th Cheshires, 4th South Staffords and 11th Lancashire Fusiliers would be ultimately disbanded to feed their sister units.

A sad day of parting for old friends who together had so often experienced both the joy of victory as well as the bitterness of defeat. All, however, whether regular battalions or new Service battalions, soon to be nothing but a name, carrying with them the very best wishes of the few who remained behind—all alike proud to know that the greatest and most splendid achievements of these gallant units would for ever be associated with the records of the 25th Division

M. K.-S.

ROYON,
   15th July, 1918.

NOTE.—Full totals of rewards and casualties sustained by the Division will be found on page 307.

To face page 5].

MAJOR-GENERAL SIR GUY BAINBRIDGE, K.C.B.

25th DIVISION.

Battle Order, 1st July, 1916, and subsequent changes.

COMMANDER..	..	MAJOR-GENERAL SIR E. G. T. BAINBRIDGE, K.C.B.
A.D.C. ..	..	Capt. Hon. G. St. V. Harris, M.C.
A.D.C. ..	..	Capt. J. A. Reiss.
G.S.O. 1 ..	..	Lt.-Col. E. M. Birch, D.S.O.
		Lt.-Col. C.H. L. Nicholson, D.S.O. 12.1.17.
		Lt.-Col. R. T. Lee, D.S.O. 16.12.17.
G.S.O. 2 ..	..	Major H. J. Davis.
		Major H. S. J. Adair, D.S.O. 15.7.16.
		Major J. M. Hamilton, D.S.O. 24.1.17.
		Major E. K. B. Furze, D.S.O., M.C. 24.10.17.
		Major G. R. Dubs, M.C. 28.4.18.
G.S.O. 3 ..	..	Capt. E. N. E. Hitchins, M.C.
		Capt. J. H. Bradney. 10.2.17.
		Capt. W. K. M. Leader, M.C. 1.9.17.
		Capt. C. de L. Gaussen, R.E. 6.6.18.
A.A. and Q.M.G.	..	Lt.-Col. R. F. Legge, D.S.O.
		Lt.-Col. Hon. E. P. J. Stourton, D.S.O. 3.5.18.
D.A.A.G. ..	..	Major P. L. W. Powell, D.S.O.
		Major J. S. Fulton, M.C. 11.12.16.
D.A.Q.M.G...	..	Major J. C. B. Robinson, D.S.O.
		Major R. W. Cooper, M.C. 13.2.18.
A.D.M.S. ..	..	Colonel H. I. Pocock, C.M.G., R.A.M.C.
		Colonel H. N. Dunn, C.M.G., D.S.O., R.A.M.C. 23.3.17.
D.A.D.M.S...	..	Major H. A. Emmerson, D.S.O., R.A.M.C.
		Capt. J. E. Hepper, R.A.M.C. 10.11.16.
		Major T. E. Dun, M.C., R.A.M.C. 6.9.17.
D.A.D.V.S. ..	..	Major W. Ludgate, D.S.O.
		Major G. D. Norman, A.V.C. 4.12.17.
D.A.D.O.S. ..	..	Capt. R. Roberts (killed).
		Capt. A. J. Sturton. 22.7.16.
		Capt. J. S. Stewart-Wallace. 20.6.17.
		Capt. A. C. H. Eagles, M.C. 23.4.17.
A.P.M. ..	..	Capt. Sir F. V. L. Robinson, Bt., M.C.
S.C.F. ..	..	Rev. Major L. G. Dickenson, D.S.O.
H.Q., R.A.		
COMMANDER	..	Brig.-Gen. B. R. KIRWAN, C.M.G., R.A.
		Brig.-Gen. K. J. Kincaid-Smith, C.M.G., D.S.O., R.A. 27.10.16.
Bde. Major	..	Major B. L. Duke, D.S.O., R.A.
		Capt. N. M. McLeod, D.S.O., M.C., R.A. 16.4.17.
Staff Captain	..	Capt. Sir J. FitzGerald, Bt., M.C.
		Capt. M. F. Horton, M.C., R.A. 29.10.17.

Staff Lieut. ..	Lieut. J. de C. Murray, R.A.	
	Lieut. L. V. Caldwell, M.C., R.A.	26.2.17.
	Lieut. E. J. Hassard, R.A.	16.8.17.
	Lieut. G. A. Keay, R.A.	20.11.17.

H.Q., R.E.

COMMANDER ..	Lt.-Col. C. R. DOBBS, R.E.	
	Lt.-Col. R. S. Done, D.S.O., R.E.	30.8.16.
Adjt.	Lieut. J. A. Ross, R.E.	
	Capt. C. A. Butcher, M.C., R.E.	1.1.17.
O.C. 25th Div. Sig. Co.	Major E. de W. H. Bradley, M.C.	

112th Brigade R.F.A. .. Lt.-Col. B. A. B. Butler.
Lt.-Col. A. B. Forman, D.S.O.
16.10.16.
Lt.-Col. E. V. Sarson, D.S.O.
(Missing). 7.8.17.

110th Brigade R.F.A. .. Lt.-Col. J. P. Hawksley, D.S.O.,
R.A. (Killed).
Lt.-Col. J. de V. Bowles, D.S.O.,
R.A. 12.5.17.
Lt.-Col. H. R. Phipps, D.S.O.,
R.A. 5.3.18.
Lt.-Col. S. C. R. Willis, D.S.O.,
R.A. 13.6.18.

111th Brigade R.F.A. .. Colonel E. H. R. J. Cloete.

113th Brigade R.F.A. .. Lt.-Col. F. F. Lambarde, D.S.O.

Divl. Ammn. Column .. Colonel A. H. Block.
Lt.-Col. C. S. Hope-Johnson.
12.2.17.

H.Q., T.M. Group .. .. Lieut. P. M. Chaworth-Musters.
M.C., R.A. (Killed).
Capt. L. V. Caldwell, M.C.
17.8.17.
Capt. G. D. Williams, M.C.
21.3.18.

105th Field Coy. R.E. .. Major R. Walker. (Died of
wounds).
Major F. W. Richards, M.C.,
R.E. (Wounded). 27.10.17.
Major J. W. Lloyd, R.E.
(Wounded and Prisoner of
War). 21.4.18.
Capt. F. H. Ridge, R.E. 29.5.18.

106th Field Coy. R.E. .. Major N. T. Fitzpatrick, D.S.O.,
M.C., R.E.
Major C. G. Lynam, M.C., R.E.
27.10.17.

130th Field Coy. R.E. .. Capt. G. F. T. Oakes. (Died of
wounds).
Major R. K. A. Macaulay, D.S.O.

Major P. H. Thorne, M.C. 15.3.18.
Major F. E. Musgrave, M.C.
18.5.18.

75th Field Ambulance ..	Lt.-Col. H. A. Davidson, D.S.O., R.A.M.C.
76th Field Ambulance ..	Lt.-Col. A. B. Hinde, R.A.M.C. Lt.-Col. W. Tyrrell, D.S.O., M.C., R.A.M.C. 15.3.17.
77th Field Ambulance ..	Lt. Col. H. B. Kelly, D.S.O. Lt.-Col. H. H. Lesson, M.C. 15.6.18.
6th S. Wales Borderers (Pioneers). ..	Lt.-Col. E. V. O. Hewett, C.M.G., D.S.O. Lt. - Col. N. T. Fitzpatrick, D.S.O., M.C., R.E. (Wounded) 27.10.17. Major L. C. W. Deane, D.S.O., M.C. (Killed). 14.4.18. Major W. L. Crawford, D.S.O. 2.6.18.
25th Bn. Machine Gun Corps..	Lt.-Col. J. D Deane-Drummond, D.S.O., M.C. (Wounded). Lt.-Col. W. T. Raikes, M.C. 21.4.18.
H.Q., Divl. Train	Lt.-Col. F. J. L. Howard, D.S.O. L.-Col. F. S. Atkinson. 25.1.18. Lt.-Col. F. B, Lord, D.S.O. 25.5.18.
Senior Supply Officer	Major F. H. Bush, D.S.O.

7th INFANTRY BRIGADE.

COMMANDER ..	Brig.-Gen. C. E. HEATHCOTE. Brig.-Gen. C. C. Onslow, C.M.G., D.S.O. 31.8.16. Brig.-Gen. C. J. Griffin, C.M.G., D.S.O. (Wounded) 12.8.17. Brig.-Gen. C. J. Hickie. 9.6.18.
Brigade Major ..	Major A. C. Johnston, D.S.O., M.C. Capt. E. K. B. Furze, D.S.O., M.C. 28.8.16. Capt. R. P. Perrin M.C. (Killed). 10.5.18. Capt. R. M. Burmann, M.C. (Killed) 9.6.18.
Staff Captain ..	Capt. M. G. Douglas, M.C. Capt. S. Hawkins, M.C. (Killed). 20.11.16.
8th N. Lancs Regt. ..	.. Lt.-Col. G. B. Marriott, D.S.O.
10th Cheshire Regt. ..	.. Lt.-Col. S. J. Jervis, D.S.O.
1st Wilts Regt. ..	.. Lt.-Col. W. L. Brown (Killed).
3rd Worcester Regt. ..	.. Lt.-Col. G. M. E. Davidge (Wounded).
7th Machine Gun Coy. ..	Capt. J. A. Rutherford (Killed).

74th INFANTRY BRIGADE.

COMMANDER ..	Brig.-Gen. G. A. ARMITAGE.	
	Brig.-Gen. H. K. Bethell, D.S.O.	14.10.16.
	Brig.-Gen. H. M. Craigie-Halkett, D.S.O.	
		1.1.18.
Brigade Major ..	Major H. N. S. Fargus.	
	Capt. E. C. de R. Martin, M.C.	23.7.16.
	Major Hon. W. E. Guinness, D.S.O.	26.2.17.
	Capt. W. B. Bagshaw, M.C.	14.5.18.
Staff Captain ..	Capt. G. C. S. Hodgson.	
	Capt. J. C. O. Marriott, D.S.O., M.C.	4.10.16.
	Capt. W. P. White, M.C.	23.4.18.
2nd R. Irish Rifles ..	.. Lt.-Col. L. C. Sprague.	
9th L. N. Lancs Regt.	.. Lt.-Col. C. B. Messiter, D.S.O.	
11th Lancashire Fusiliers ..	Lt.-Col. L. G. Bird, D.S.O.	
13th Cheshire Regt. ..	.. Lt.-Col. L. H. K. Finch, D.S.O.	
	(Wounded).	
74th Machine Gun Coy.	.. Capt. C. F. Jerrard.	

75th INFANTRY BRIGADE.

COMMANDER ..	Brig.-Gen. N. F. JENKINS.	
	Brig.-Gen. E. St. G. Pratt, D.S.O.	10.7.16.
	Brig.-Gen. H. B. D. Baird, C.M.G., D.S.O.	
		1.12.16.
	Brig.-Gen. H. T. Dobbin, D.S.O.	24.2.18.
	Brig.-Gen. C. C. Hanney, D.S.O.	12.5.18.
	Brig.-Gen. A. A. Kennedy, C.M.G.	9.6.18.
Brigade Major ..	Major E. N. Snepp.	
	Capt. G. le Q. Martell, D.S.O., M.C., R.E.	
		20.7.16.
	Capt. K. F. D. Gattie, D.S.O., M.C.	28.9.16.
	Capt. W. K. Innes, D.S.O., M.C. (Wounded).	
		12.5.18.
Staff Captain ..	Capt. L. F. Urwick.	
	Capt. K. Dykes, M.C. (Wounded)	25.10.16.
	Capt. N. L. Tunbridge, M.C.	28.11.17.
8th S. Lancs Regt. ..	.. Lt.-Col. H. E. Brassey (Killed).	
2nd S. Lancs Regt. ..	.. Lt.-Col. H. T. Cotton, D.S.O.	
	(Killed).	
8th Border Regt. ..	.. Lt.-Col. C. E. Bond, C.M.G., D.S.O.	
11th Cheshire Regt. ..	.. Lt.-Col. R. L. Aspinall, D.S.O.	
	(Killed).	
75th Machine Gun Coy.	.. Capt. R. Cochrane.	

NOTE.—All profits from the sale of this book will be devoted towards the cost of the stone memorial to be erected to the 25th Division in the market square of Bailleul or its vicinity.

CHAPTER I.

The Somme.

IN the Spring of 1916, British troops took over from the French Army most of the line from Arras to the Somme.

The German position, naturally very strong, had been strengthened by every sort of military device during the 18 months previous to the summer of 1916. Established along the higher ground it gave the enemy excellent observation over our lines and preparations for the attack. Numerous and extremely well-made dugouts had been built throughout their front line system for the protection and comfort of the German troops and for the protection of the machine guns and their detachments during bombardment.

The front consisted of a strong front line system, with firing, support and reserve trenches. These made a perfect labyrinth of fortifications, connected up by well-built communication trenches and often with long underground tunnels leading to small manholes where snipers could be concealed. Behind, a less strong intermediate line covering the field batteries and still further behind a third strongly-wired and fortified defensive position. From front to rear the three systems covered in depth six to seven miles of country; in addition there were many fortified villages, woods and strong points dotted about in commanding positions, which offered the most determined resistance to any advance, and were only captured after the heaviest fighting.

In the section of assault, the German line running from north to south covered Gommecourt, followed the high ground in front of Serre and Beaumont Hamel and crossed the Ancre to the north-west of Thiepval. It then ran in front of Thiepval, the villages of Ovillers and La Boiselle and about 1¼ miles east of Albert, where it left the sector with which the 25th Division was concerned.

On the 1st July the 4th Army attacked with five Army Corps. From just north of the Ancre to Authuille lay the Xth Corps, and east of Albert the IIIrd Corps. On the 2nd July the battle area from the Albert–Bapaume Road northwards passed under the control of the 5th Army.

The third week in June the 25th Division, which had been training west of St. Pol, moved south to the 4th Army. At the commencement of the battle it lay round Warly about four miles behind the front line, together with the 12th Division in 4th Army Reserve.

The following day the 7th Brigade moved into Xth Corps, and proceeded to Aveluy Wood, and was held in Corps Reserve, the 75th Brigade to Martinsart, and together with the 105th Field Coy., R.E., two companies of the S. Wales Borderers, and 75th Field Ambulance, was placed under the orders of the 32nd Division in the front line. The attack by the Xth Corps had made a certain amount of headway opposite Ovillers and had resulted in the capture of a small portion of the Leipzig salient. Further north the 36th Division made one of the most brilliant advances of the war, taking the whole of their objectives in scheduled time. Owing to the failure of the attacks on their flanks and on other parts of the line, the ground gained was gradually lost by them and by the relieving troops after their withdrawal from the battle. Much the same state of affairs existed north of the Ancre. The same evening the 75th Brigade was ordered to Aveluy Wood and to deliver an attack on the Thiepval Spur from the direction of Authuille at 3 a.m. the next day, 3rd July. The operation was planned in conjunction with an attack by the VIIIth Corps against the enemy's line north of the Ancre River, whilst the 49th Division were to attack the line south of the river as far as the Thiepval Spur and the 12th Division to attack Ovillers and the defences immediately to the north of the village.

During the night 2nd/3rd July, however, the proposed attack by the VIIIth Corps and the 49th Division on the left was cancelled, and that by the 75th Brigade postponed till 6 a.m., whilst the 12th Division attacked at 3 a.m. according to the original plan. The latter, however, failed to reach their objectives. At 6 a.m. the artillery barrage lifted from the German front line and the 75th Brigade went forward with the 11th Cheshire under Lt.-Col. R. L. Aspinall on the right, 8th Borders, Lt.-Col. C. E. Bond, in the centre, and the 2nd S. Lancs., Lt.-Col. Cotton, on the left, with the 8th S. Lancs., Lt.-Col. H. Brassey, in reserve.

The assembly of the assaulting troops had been carried out with some difficulty owing to the heavy shelling of all approaches and communication trenches. Lack of knowledge of the ground increased the difficulties, but in spite of this the battalions were ready at the appointed moment of attack. The four companies of the Cheshires, under Capt. J. Batson, Capt. Nicholson, Capt. Abel and Capt. Murray, the 8th Borders with A, B, C, and D Cos., commanded respectively by Capt. Bishop, Major Birt, Capt. Miller and Capt. Coxon, and the 2nd S. Lancs., with A, B, C, and D Coys., commanded by Capt. Gates, Capt. Rathbone, Capt. Blair, and Capt. Whitaker respectively, suffered very heavy casualties, and were met by heavy flanking machine-gun fire and never reached their objectives. Lt.-Col. Aspinall was killed. In the centre the Borders were more successful, but were unable, owing to pressure on their flanks, to maintain themselves in the German front line-for more than 1½ hours. Of the Battalion, 2nd Lieut. Gordon, 2nd Lieut. Aldous, 2nd Lieut. Curteis, and 2nd Lieut. Foss were killed. Capt. Parker, R.A.M.C., was awarded the D.S.O. for his work on this occasion. Being badly enfiladed by machine guns and heavy shell fire from Thiepval and beyond, they were forced to retire to their original line. The failure of the operation can be largely attributed to the lack of time for reconnaissance, previous preparation, and the lack of co-ordination between artillery and infantry plans.

During the night 3rd/4th July, the Division relieved the 32nd Division in the line, with the 7th Brigade on the right and the 75th Brigade on the left. The 74th Brigade at the same time moved from Warly to Bouzincourt. The next night, 4th/5th July, the 75th Brigade was withdrawn to Aveluy Wood, the 7th Brigade extending its front to the north, in touch with the 12th and 49th Divisions on its right and left respectively.

At 7 p.m. the 5th July, the Wilts attacked about 500 yards of the main German trench of the Leipzig Redoubt. After an intense bombardment of one minute by artillery and trench mortars, C and D Coys. under Capt. G. B. Russell and Capt. R. L. Knubley went forward, A and B Coys., under Lieut. Gosden, and Lieut. Snelgar being in support. C Coy. was entirely successful but D Coy. gained only part of their objective owing to heavy machine gun fire. Lt.-Col. W. S. Brown and Capt. Hales fell early in the attack, when Capt. Ogilvie took command of the Battalion. A and B Coys., Worcester Regt., under Capt. T. G. Parkes and 2nd Lieut. T. Percy, were sent up to reinforce and did splendid work. At 1.15 a.m. the following night, the enemy commenced a very heavy bombing attack on the captured trench but were successfully beaten off and arrangements were made for another assault at 9.30 a.m. the morning of the 7th July. A hurricane bombardment of one minute again preceded the advance. Good shooting was made by the 7th Brigade T.M. Battery under Capt. Harrison, and also by battalion snipers, who' had been pushed forward during the night. These men were very successful and with steel nosed bullets managed to silence an enemy machine gun on the left flank.

At 9.30 a.m. A, B and C Coys. went forward to the attack, and in a few minutes had captured the German trench, the whole of the garrison being either killed or captured. At 1.30 p.m. the enemy opened a heavy bombardment causing many casualties. In spite of the shelling, bad weather conditions and the difficulties of consolidation, the position was held with the greatest determination. At this juncture A and B Coys., 3rd Worcesters, under Capt. T. G. Parkes and 2nd Lieut. Percy, now relieved C Coy. of the Wilts. The same evening the Worcesters, under Lt.-Col. Davidge, assisted by one company N. Lancs., took over the line. The method and arrangements for the attack were well conceived and energetically carried out, and its success was no doubt largely due to the surprise effected by our infantry following close up behind a sudden and intense barrage. Casualties were heavy, the Wilts. losing 26 officers and about 400 men killed and wounded ; the Worcesters, 5 officers and 140 men killed and wounded.

On the 5th July the 74th Brigade was detached and joined the 12th Division, taking over a sector of the line in the village of La Boisselle, which had been captured the previous day by the 19th Division. On the morning of the 7th, it participated in an attack by the 12th Division on Ovillers and the trenches to the right across the Pozieres Road. The attack was carried out by the 9th N. Lancs., Lt.-Col. Messiter, and 13th Cheshires, Lt.-Col. Finch, with the 2nd R. Irish Rifles, Lt.-Col. Sprague, and the 11th Lancs. Fusiliers, Lt.-Col. Bird, in support. The attacking battalions after an intense bombardment from massed artillery of all calibres moved forward at 8.5 a.m. and successfully reached their first objectives after heavy fighting. Mainly owing to the heavy losses great difficulty was experienced in reaching the second objectives the same day, but during the night of the 7th/8th and the following morning bombing parties eventually established themselves in the enemy's line just south of the Pozieres Road. That evening strong patrols of the R. Irish Rifles and 11th Lancs. Fusiliers were pushed forward and succeeded in getting on another 600 yards. C Coy., Lancs. Fusiliers, under Capt. Metcalfe, was forced to bear the brunt of a heavy counter-attack the morning of the 9th July against overwhelming odds, and held their ground although at the end only six men were left.

The night of the 7th/8th July, the 49th Division extended its front southwards and relieved the 7th Brigade, which was now withdrawn to Aveluy Wood. The night of the 10th/11th the 7th Brigade relieved the 74th Brigade on the right of the 75th Brigade. The 8th July Divisional Headquarters moved to Henincourt and the following day the 25th Division took over the front held by the 12th Division, with the 19th and 32nd Divisions on its right and left respectively. The line now consisted of trenches in the south-west corner of Ovillers and astride the Pozieres Road.

Up to this time the 74th and 75th Brigades with the Divisional artillery had been constantly working under other Divisions, an arrangement unsatisfactory at the best. With its units working under a strange staff, divisional cohesion becomes seriously impaired ; all mutual understanding and confidence which is so vitally necessary for the efficient and energetic execution of an offensive operation, will soon cease to exist. From the 9th July onwards, the Division worked as a whole.

On 12th July, the Divisional Headquarters moved from Henincourt to a camp near Senlis and the same day attacks were made northwards towards Ovillers by the 7th and 75th Brigades. The 7th Brigade failed to reach their objectives, but the 75th Brigade was more successful. The Borders formed up under cover of darkness and drove the enemy from the front line fire trench without much difficulty. The capture of the communication trenches was a more difficult matter and progress was very slow. A Coy., 2nd S. Lancs., under Lieut. Powell, managed to get a footing in the outskirts of the village after stubborn resistance and in spite of heavy counter-attacks gradually extended their hold on the enemy's trenches. Casualties were heavy. The next day A Coy. 8th S. Lancs., relieved the 2nd S. Lancs. and further progress was made by bombing attacks when Colonel Brassey was unfortunately killed by a sniper. The night of the 15th/16th the 74th Brigade relieved the 7th Brigade and the following morning by repeated bombing attacks some further advance was made. The Borders attacked from their recently captured trench, but were met with exceedingly heavy and accurate machine-gun fire. B and D Coys. under Lieut. Thomson and Lieut. Stewart, managed to get within 50 yards of the enemy's trench but were eventually forced to retire.

Neither Brigade was fully successful, but their attack undoubtedly drew off the enemy's attention and enabled the Warwickshires of the 48th Division to move across the open to the east and reach a position behind the Oviller's garrison without much difficulty. Close fighting with bombing parties and rifle grenades continued all day during the 16th when the remnants of the Oviller's garrison finally surrendered to parties of the R. Irish Rifles and 11th Lancs. Fusiliers. Both German and British casualties had been very heavy in this locality. The defences were composed of a perfect labyrinth of trenches, dugouts and well protected machine gun emplace-ments which the garrison of Prussian Guard Fusiliers defended with the utmost determination.

Immediately to the south repeated attacks had resulted in the capture of Contalmaison, quickly followed on the 14th July by successful attacks on Byzantins le Petit and Delville Wood.

During the night 16th/17th July the Division was relieved by the 48th Division and next day moved to Beauval and neighbourhood for a short period of rest.

From the 23rd July to the 10th August, the Division held a sector of the line from the River Ancre northwards. During this period it took no part in actual offensive operations, but was able to give material assistance by means of artillery and machine gun fire to the troops attacking south of the Ancre. A great deal of work was accomplished in digging new forward assembly trenches for use later on by troops attacking Beaumont Hamel and the German defences south of the Ancre. Deep dugouts for the men, brigade and bat-talion headquarters were also put in hand. This work was carried on under conditions of very great difficulty owing to heavy shell fire and trench mortars. A new type of poison gas shell was also used for the first time.

Between the 7th and 10th August the Division was relieved by troops of the 6th and Guard's Divisions and moved back to Bus les Artois and neighbourhood for short rest and training.

The 18th August, divisional headquarters moved up to Hedauville, and the 7th Brigade relieved the 146th Brigade in the sector which included portions of the Leipzig Salient captured from the enemy early in July.

The 19th August the 74th Brigade took over from the 147th Brigade the line immediately south of the Ancre, whilst the following day the 75th Brigade proceeded to Aveluy Wood in divisional reserve.

The 21st August a very successful local attack was carried out by the 7th Brigade. In conjunction with the Gloucester Regt. 48th Division, who were responsible for the main attack on the right, the 1st Wilts attacked eastwards and captured important points in the enemy's front and support line of the Leipzig Redoubt. The attack was completely successful and about 63 prisoners were captured and 50 Germans killed. It was carried out by C Coy., under Capt. G. D. Brown. Our casualties were small during the attack, but a considerable number were sustained during the heavy bombardment of the captured trench later on.

The operation was chiefly remarkable for the fact that a " push pipe mine " was used for the first time by this Division. The mine had been laid under the German block in their old communication trench. It was exploded as our troops advanced and resulted not only in destroying the enemy's block, but also in forming a means of communication which was afterwards improved into a communication trench. Although of a subsidiary and minor character, the attack had been most carefully prepared and its successful execution reflected the greatest credit on the troops engaged.

The 23rd August the Division extended its front southwards, the 3rd Worcesters, 7th Brigade, relieving the left battalion of the 48th Division. Two days later the 7th Brigade delivered an attack with the Wilts and Worcesters on the main Hindenburg trench. During the day the heavy artillery carried out a bombardment of the line to be attacked as well as trenches and communication trenches in the neighbourhood in such a way as not to attract undue attention to the particular objective. At 4.10 p.m. the 25th August an intense artillery barrage was put down on the Hindenburg trench and a rolling barrage in front of it. Under cover of this the

Wilts and Worcesters advanced and assaulted the position. The attacking companies of the Wilts, A, B and D, were under 2nd Lieut. W. J. Ross, Capt. B. S. Macklin, and Capt. L. H. Horncastle, with C Coy., Capt. G. D. Brown in close support. Two companies of 8th L. N. Lancs., were utilised to garrison the original German front line. The whole objective was captured except a small portion on the left where strong opposition was met with in very broken ground and very little progress was made. At 4.12 p.m. two " push mines " had been exploded and A Coy. of the Wilts advanced down them to the enemy's trench. B and D Coys. of the Wilts with the Worcesters on the right advanced across the open at 4.14 p.m. The attack was carried out in three waves, the number of men employed being approximately one man per yard of the objective. Our casualties were small and over 150 German prisoners were captured and a number killed. In addition a batch of about 100 German prisoners were caught and killed by their own artillery barrage. The attack undoubtedly came as a surprise to the enemy, and its success was largely due to the fact that the troops advanced well up under the artillery barrage which was most effective in every way. They were materially assisted by a smoke barrage near Thiepval Wood which was designed to draw the enemy's fire in its direction and which undoubtedly succeeded in its object. Heavy bombing went on all day on the left sector and very little further progress was made. The whole of the Leipzig Salient was heavily shelled during the afternoon of the 25th August, causing many casualties.

It had been intended to relieve the Wilts and L. N. Lancs. during the evening of the 25th August, as the former battalion had suffered heavy casualties during the preceding two days. The relief, however, could not take place as the Germans appeared to be massing for a counter-attack about 6.30 p.m., but if intended it was stopped by our artillery which at once put down a very effective barrage. Unfortunately both the Wilts and Worcesters suffered heavy casualties owing to the absence of dugouts and the lack of protection in the captured Hindenburg trench. This trench had been so badly knocked about by our heavy artillery before the attack and could not at once be effectively consolidated after its capture.

The 26th August the 7th Brigade was relieved by the 75th Brigade, with the exception of the 8th L. N. Lancs.

who were placed at the disposal of the 75th Brigade in order to attack the small pocket of Germans who were still holding on to a small portion of the Hindenburg trench on our left. The belief that the remnants of the enemy's garrison was demoralised through want of food and water and therefore likely to surrender was unfounded.

An attack by D Coy., 8th L. N. Lancs., under Capt. Cash with Lieut. May and Lieut. Copeman was made at 6 p.m. The information as to the condition of the garrison of this strong post called the "Wunderwurk" turned out to be incorrect and the enemy were very much more numerous and better prepared for resistance than had been expected. The first wave succeeded in entering the enemy's position but though reinforced by a second and third wave the N. Lancs. were unable to maintain themselves and were finally forced to retire to their original line, both Capt. Cash and Lieut. May being killed.

The 26th August the 74th Brigade was relieved by troops of the 49th Division and the same afternoon the 8th S. Lancs. endeavoured to carry by assault a section of the enemy's defences on the Thiepval Spur. The attack was launched at 4 p.m. after most careful preparation and supported by an intense bombardment with artillery and trench mortars. The attacking waves succeeded in reaching their objective but were unable to maintain themselves and consolidate the position and were finally forced to retire to their original line.

The 29th August the 7th Brigade relieved two brigades of the 48th Division in the Ovillers sector and on the 31st August the 8th Borders of the 75th Brigade which was then holding the eastern end of the Hindenburg trench was relieved by the 10th Cheshires, 7th Brigade, and withdrawn to Bouzincourt for rest.

Preparations were completed for an attack northwards up the Thiepval Spur in conjunction with an attack by the 29th Division north of the Ancre. South of the river the attack was to be carried through by the 49th Division on our left against Thiepval Spur and by the 4th Australian Division on our right against Mouquet Farm. The 1st Wilts and 3rd Worcesters were placed at the disposal of the 75th Brigade for this operation. The attack was launched at 5.10 a.m. on the 3rd September by the Wilts and Worcesters and the

2nd S. Lancs. The position had been carefully marked out by tapes during the night as well as the general line of advance across " No Man's Land." Unfortunately all three battalions taking part in the operation failed to reach their objectives and were forced to retire to their original positions. Casualties were very heavy indeed, including Col. Gibbs of the Worcesters, and Lt.-Col. Cotton, of the S. Lancs., who were both killed. Large numbers of wounded remained out in No Man's Land throughout the day and were got in later, mainly owing to the indefatigable work of Capt. Hughes, R.A.M.C. The battalions were relieved in their sector during the afternoon by the 11th Cheshires and 8th S. Lancs., and on the 7th September the Division was finally relieved by the 11th Division and moved back about 20 miles to a rest camp near Abbeville for a short period of rest and training. The Division remained in rest for upwards of three weeks, when its move forward on 25th September to the forward area commenced.

On the 26th September the 74th Brigade was sent up in 'buses and remained in corps reserve during the attack on Thiepval. The Brigade then took over a sector of the line immediately south of the Ancre. A small and successful enterprise was carried out by D Coy., 11th Lancs. Fusiliers against a small salient of the enemy's line known as the " Pope's Nose," in connection with an attack by the 18th Division on the Schwaben Redoubt and the trenches north of Thiepval. The 30th September the 7th Brigade, Brig.-Gen. Onslow, and 75th Brigades, Brig.-Gen. Pratt, relieved the brigades of the 11th Division on its right and the 74th Brigade was also relieved and moved back to Bouzincourt to divisional reserve. During the previous fortnight Thiepval had been captured and the British held a line approximately east and west along the Thiepval Spur. As far as the right sector of the divisional front was concerned, we had observation over the Grandcourt Valley, but in the left sector from Stuff Redoubt westwards, the Germans were on the crest of the ridge. As regards Stuff Redoubt itself, though we held the southern part, the northern end was still in their hands. Preparations were then made to capture the northern face and the higher ground just north of Stuff Redoubt as early as possible and to push forward posts so as to have observation over the whole of the Grandcourt Valley. With this end in view new communication trenches were dug and as far as possible deep dugouts for the assaulting troops. A spell of bad weather necessitated the postponement of the attack, but on the 9th October the northern end of the redoubt was successfully carried by assault by the 10th Cheshires at 12.35 p.m.

Most careful preparations were made for the attack and under cover of an intense barrage the first objective was reached at 12.42 p.m. D and B Coys. under 2nd Lieut. Wilson and Capt. Simmons, with C and A Coys. under 2nd Lieut. Evans and Major Trestrail in support and reserve were responsible for this excellent piece of work.

Although unsuccessful in reaching the high ground immediately north of Stuff Redoubt, the battalion had every reason to be proud of its fine performance. Its casualties were comparatively slight and the operation yielded four officers and 123 German prisoners with 50 to 60 killed. In the evening the enemy counter-attacked but were successfully repulsed by artillery and machine gun fire.

The 10th October the 8th L. N. Lancs., 7th Brigade, relieved the 10th Cheshires and preparations were made for a further attack on the high ground called " The Mounds " just north of the Stuff Redoubt.

In the meantime another determined attempt by the Germans to recapture Stuff Redoubt was successfully beaten off. By the use of special " Storm Troops " the enemy succeeded in gaining a footing at one point in the line, but were speedily ejected and suffered considerable casualties.

The attack was finally carried out by A and B Coys. of the 8th L. N. Lancs. at 2.46 p.m., although at 2.40 p.m. just before our attack was timed to begin, the Germans put down a heavy barrage on our position. This was carried out by A and B Coys. under Capt. Shields, with Lieut. Bolton and Lieut. Turner. The distance to be covered was roughly 200 yards, but the left party, under Lieut. Alford, had further to go before reaching their objective. The artillery was most effective and the men kept well up to the barrage. It was afterwards learnt from prisoners that the enemy had observed our troops preparing to advance, but the German officer in command, however, appears to have thought that no attack was contemplated and to have ordered the enemy's artillery to stop firing by 2.40 p.m.

When our barrage was put down at 2.46 p.m., the enemy's barrage had died down and our troops gained their objective with but slight casualties. This fine piece of work resulted in the capture of one officer and 100 German prisoners as well as several machine guns, and also gave us the required observation all along the ridge with the line of observation posts pushed forward beyond the crest.

In view of a possible further advance which was subsequently ordered, work on communication trenches and forward dumps was pushed on. The 16th October the 39th Division extended their front as far as Stuff Dedoubt, with the 75th, Brig.-Gen. Pratt, and 74th Brigades, Brig.-Gen. Bethel, on its right. Each brigade held a line of about 1,000 yards and was given a battalion of the 7th Brigade to assist with working parties, so as to allow troops detailed for the attack to be well rested.

The attack on Stuff and Regina Trench originally ordered for the 19th October was postponed on account of bad weather until the 21st October. At 12.6 p.m. the attack was launched together with the 18th Division on the right and the 39th Division on the left. The distance from our line to Stuff and Regina Trenches varied considerably fron 200 yards to 500 yards, which was the longest distance to be traversed by our assaulting troops.

Very careful arrangements were made for the bombardment of the enemy's line of trenches, all known strong points and machine gun emplacements. The rolling barrage by the divisional artilleries of the 11th, 19th, and 25th Divisions, covering the Division, was most effective. All worked admirably. At 12.6 p.m. the troops of the 74th and 75th Brigades moved out under cover of the barrage.

Owing to the weakness of the battalions of the 74th Brigade, the assault was carried out by three battalions in the front line, going forward in three waves.

The Lancs. Fusiliers, Lt.-Col. Bird, on the right, 9th L. N. Lancs., Lt.-Col. Messiter, in the centre, and the 13th Cheshires, Lt.-Col. Hall, on the left, with the 2nd R. Irish Rifles, Lt.-Col. Sprague, and 1st Wilts, Lt.-Col. Williams, in support; A, B, C and D Coys., Lancashire Fusiliers, were commanded by Lieut. W. I. Edwards, 2nd Lieut. R. K. Beswick, Capt. J. C. P. E. Metcalfe and Lieut. R. F. Mackinnon; 9th L. N. Lancs., with their four Coys. commanded by 2nd Lieut. G. B. Wardle, 2nd Lieut J. Motherwell (killed), 2nd Lieut. G. C. Filey (killed) and 2nd Lieut. H. Dobbyn (wounded). All the Battalions kept well up to the rolling barrage and reached their objectives without much difficulty, but some stiff fighting took place in Regina Trench. On the left of the brigade the 13th Cheshires, when nearly all their officers became casualties, slightly lost direction and consequently a considerable gap was left between their left and the 8th Borders, some of whom had also overshot their objectives and lost touch. The 75th Brigade attacked with the 8th Borders, Lt.-Col. Bond, on the right, the 8th S. Lancs. in the centre, and 2nd S. Lancs., Lt.-Col. Craigie-Halkett, on the left, with the 11th Cheshires, Lt.-Col. Evans, in reserve. A, B, C, and D Coys. of the Borders were commanded by Lieut. Slater, Capt. Watson-Thomas, Capt. T. D. Miller, and Capt. J. E. Stewart, respectively ; 2nd S. Lancs., with A, B, C, and D Coys. commanded by 2nd Lieut. Milligan, 2nd Lieut. Nevill, 2nd Lieut. Snowden, and 2nd Lieut. Hatch ; the 11th Cheshires, with four companies commanded by Capt. Ellington, Lieut. McKerrow, Capt. Nares and 2nd Lieut. Curwen.

Ten minutes after the attack was launched, German prisoners were being sent back across " No Man's Land," and dugouts in their front and support lines were bombed and cleared out. The party of the Borders who went forward about 100 yards beyond the objective towards Grandcourt, damaged some light forward guns and brought back 150 prisoners. Meanwhile some Germans were still holding out in the angle formed by Regina and a communication trench.

The 2nd S. Lancs. were equally successful in their attack and at 1.25 p.m. a contact aeroplane dropped a message from which it appeared that most of the objective had been gained, but that some of our troops had gone too far and that there was a gap of some 300 yards between the Borders and the 74th Brigade. The situation here was soon cleared up by bombing parties and the 75th Brigade, Stokes mortar battery, under Lieut. Hibbert. A remarkably fine piece of work. The S. Wales Borderers and 106th Field Coy., R.E., did extremely good work in pushing through a communication trench up to the new front line immediately after dark.

Touch was gained with the divisions on either flank and by 4 p.m. it was certain that the whole objective had been gained.

The success of these operations was largely due to the careful and thorough preparation for the attack, the excellent artillery preparation and the increased confidence with which the troops advanced close up under the artillery barrage.

Seven hundred and thirty-one Germans were captured, including five officers as well as 19 machine guns and three larger field guns.

The following day and during the night 22nd/23rd October, the division was relieved and moved back to the neighbourhood of Doullens.

Before leaving the 5th Army, in which it had been fighting with but short intervals for four months, units of the division were inspected by the C.-in-C. and the following message was received from the Army Commander :—

> " It is with great regret that the Commander of the Reserve Army bids farewell to Major-Gen. Bainbridge and the 25th Division. This Division has the proud distinction of having served longer in the Somme battle than any other in the Army. During the past four months it has been successful in many engagements, has taken many prisoners and has inflicted very heavy losses upon the enemy. These successes are due to good leadership and sound organisation in the higher ranks. and to a spirit of cheerfulness, courage, and resolution in the junior ranks, officers and men. It has every reason to be proud of these achievements and this spirit."

The following are a list of those who received rewards for services during the operations, with details of some of the more notable acts of gallantry for which the award was granted :—

Lieut. R. B. B. Jones, 8th L.N. Lancs. Regt. (Killed in action.)

For most conspicuous bravery at Vimy. He was holding with his Platoon a crater recently captured from the enemy. About 7.30 p.m. the enemy exploded a mine 40 yards to his right, and at the same time put a heavy barrage of fire on our trenches, thus isolating the Platoon. Then they attacked in overwhelming numbers.

Lieut. Jones kept his men together, steadied them by his fine example, and shot no less than 15 of the enemy as they advanced, counting them aloud as he did so, to cheer his men.

When his ammunition was expended he took a bomb, but was shot through the head while getting up to throw it.

His splendid courage had so encouraged his men, that when they had no more ammunition or bombs they threw stones and ammunition boxes at the enemy.

Finally the Platoon was practically annihilated, with the exception of several wounded men, who crawled away under cover of darkness.

Awarded . . . . **V.C.**

Major A. Anderton, R.F.A.

For conspicuous gallantry in carrying out skilful reconnaissances on 7th, 9th and 11th July, 1916, in Ovillers and Mash Valley, and in bringing back valuable information as to the situation of our infantry and enemy dispositions. To accomplish this he frequently went through trenches not occupied by our infantry and across the open under rifle and machine-gun fire, and on more than one occasion was instrumental in preventing patrols of our own infantry firing on each other.

Awarded.........M.C.

No. 63660 Corporal S. Broughton, R.F.A.

For conspicuous gallantry and devotion to duty on 17th July, 1916. Keeping the telephone wire mended from battery to observation post under very heavy gun and machine-gun fire.

Awarded.........D.C.M.

No. 65164 C.S.M. F. Brown, 106th Field Coy., R.E.

For good example and determined leading when a new communication trench was dug up to Regina Trench, the night after its capture on 21st October, 1916. The trench was taped out and dug under continuous shell fire. C.S.M. Brown materially assisted the completion of this important work by his fine example, energy and determination.

Awarded.........D.C.M.

2nd Lieut. E. D. Birnie, 8th Border Regiment.

For gallant conduct on 21st October in the attack on Regina Trench He took charge of a bombing attack against a strong party of the enemy still holding out after the trench had been occupied. He set a fine example of coolness and courage by getting up on the parapet and sniping while his men were bombing, and shot at least eight Germans. The whole party about 60 strong very soon surrendered to him.

Awarded.........M.C.

No. 6/16769 Pte. Berry, 6th S. Wales Borderers.

A gap had been cut in the communication between Stuff and Sowaben Redoubts. The Germans saw the gap and determined to do all in their power to prevent it getting mended during the night.

The gap was kept under continuous fire from field guns and volunteers were called for, and amongst the first to come forward was Pte. Berry. He inspired the party throughout the work, which was finished in spite of all opposition.

Awarded.........M.M.

No. 8261 C.S.M. W. C. Field, 2nd S. Lancashire Regt.

This warrant officer came out with the original B.E.F. in August, 1914, and served continuously with the battalion. At Thiepval on 3rd September, 1916, he displayed exceptional gallantry and initiative when his company officers had all been put out of action, rallying his company with admirable coolness and resource under extremely heavy fire. He did excellent work in the trenches during the whole winter.

Awarded .... **D.C.M.**

No. 6/16401 Sergt. W. H. Goodman, 6th S. Wales Borderers.

This N.C.O.'s platoon was detached from the remainder of the company and was working under a heavy enemy bombardment in the neighbourhood of Zollern Redoubt. When the men were all under cover, Sergt. Goodman walked a distance of two or three hundred yards through the thickest part of the barrage and reported to his company commander the position of his platoon.

Awarded .... **M.M.**

No. 41949 Sergt. A. E. Howson, R.A.M.C.

For conspicuous bravery while attending wounded under heavy shell fire at Mailly-Maillet, September, 1916.

For conspicuous gallantry whilst in charge of stretcher-bearers during the battle of Messines, June, 1917.

Awarded .... **M.M. and Bar.**

Capt. H. L. G. Hughes, R.A.M.C., attd. 1st Wilts Regt.

On the 6th July, 1916, in the Leipzig Salient for most conspicuous gallantry and devotion to duty. In broad daylight and although subjected to heavy rifle-fire, this officer went out between the trenches into the open and bandaged and tended seven wounded men. He was compelled to lie in an exposed spot for $1\frac{1}{2}$ hours under heavy rifle fire, and part of the time during an intense bombardment. At nightfall this officer led out a party in spite of an intense bombardment and safely brought back the seven wounded men.

By this most gallant action the lives of these seven men were most undoubtedly saved.

Awarded .... **D.S.O.**

No. 8495 Sergt. J. Hillings, 1st Wilts Regt.

On the 7th July, 1916, at the Leipzig Salient during the capture of an enemy trench, this N.C.O. displayed the finest qualities of bravery and coolness under intense shell fire. This N.C.O. was Acting Company Sergeant-Major. His company commander and company officers were killed very early, and he took command of the company. Under very heavy shell fire he encouraged his men, supervised the erection of blocks and the general consolidation of the trench with such marked ability that it was held in spite of frequent attempts on the part of the enemy to bomb the company out of it.

Awarded .... **Bar to D.C.M.**

Lieut. T. H. Harrison, 130th Field Company, R.E. (Wounded.)

This officer was in charge of a party making a bomb stop after the capture of Stuff Redoubt by the 10th Cheshires on 16th October, 1916. This block was repeatedly blown down by hostile trench mortars till the party had become casualties except Lieut. Harrison and one sapper. Observing some of the enemy getting over a road block, he drove them off with his revolver. Going back for more men he eventually completed the bomb stop, after 13 hours, although wounded himself early in the day.

Awarded..........M.C.

T./Lieut.-Col. P. S. Hall, 13th Cheshire Regt.

During the short time he has been in command of a battalion he has, by his personal example and initiative, created a fine soldierly spirit throughout all ranks. He has shown conspicuous ability as a leader in all situations.

Awarded..........D.S.O.

No. W/1036 L.-Corpl. J. Hulme, 13th Cheshire Regt.

During the advance on the German trenches near Ovillers on the 7th July, 1916, he rendered first-aid and brought in Lt.-Col. L. H. K. Finch. The medical officer reported that but for this devotion the colonel would have lost his life, owing to a severed artery. Whilst bringing in the colonel this corporal attended to two other wounded men in a shell hole.

Awarded..........M.M.

Capt. F. G. Lescher, R.A.M.C.

For leading the bearer division and co-ordinating the work of clearing the regimental aid posts at Leipzig Salient, making frequent explorations under heavy fire — August, 1916.

While in command of the bearer division at Messines Ridge, 7th and 8th June, 1917, he made frequent searches for wounded under heavy shell fire, and generally co-ordinated the work of clearing cases.

Awarded..........M.C. and Bar.

No. 16313 C.S.M. T. Lines, 10th Cheshire Regt.

This warrant officer on the Vimy Ridge in May, 1916, when all the officers of his company had become casualties, took command of the company, and by building blocks he succeeded, with great gallantry, in holding up the enemy who had attacked the front line trenches. During the attack on Stuff Redoubt he showed absolute disregard for personal danger, and was the first to enter the enemy trenches, himself killing several Germans who were defending the trench.

Awarded..........D.C.M.

No. 15003 Sergt.-Major T. Lewis, 8th S. Lancs. Regt. (Wounded.)

During the taking of Regina Trench on 21st October, the bombing officer was wounded early. This warrant officer took his men along the top, thus putting the enemy at a disadvantage, bombed them out of dug-outs several hundred yards in front of the furthest line to which the brigade had advanced, and killed a considerable number by rifle fire. He then consolidated and held a block.

Awarded..........D.C.M.

No. 52004 Sergt. J. M. Mahon, R.F.A. (W/25 T.M. Battery).

For gallantry and devotion to duty at Zollern Redoubt on the Somme on 14th-15th October, 1916.

Awarded.........M.M.

Capt. J. C. P. E. Metcalfe, 11th Lancashire Fusiliers.

On the evening of the 15th July, 1916, when his company was holding a portion of a trench near Pozieres taken the previous evening, the position was attacked by a largely superior enemy force preceded by an artillery bombardment, which caused very heavy casualties. The enemy attacked on both flanks. Capt. Metcalfe collected the un- wounded men near him, numbering six, and placed them in a large shell hole from which they continued to fire " rapid " on the advancing enemy. Seeing that the enemy had forced their way through the right flank, he ordered his party to fall back on the supporting trench. They started under a very heavy rifle and machine-gun fire and five of the party fell. Capt. Metcalfe and one sergeant succeeded in reaching the communication trench, where they joined a party of the 2nd Royal Irish Rifles and assisted in checking the enemy's advance and re- organising the defence. This officer has on many occasions shown great coolness and determination, noticeably during operations carried out by this battalion on the Vimy Ridge.

Awarded.........M.C.

No. 16453 Corpl. G. Marsden, 11th Cheshire Regt.

At Thiepval on 3rd July, 1916, for great determination and initiative in re-organising and leading his company when all officers and other N.C.Os. had become casualties.

Awarded.........D.C.M.

No. 9253 A./R.S.M. E. Nicholson, 2nd S. Lancashire Regt.

For extreme coolness and devotion to duty at Thiepval on 3rd Sep- tember, 1916. On three consecutive occasions he rallied his men and assaulted the enemy trenches. He had been stunned previously by a shell burst, but stuck to his men until forced back by shell fire. This warrant officer was brought to notice for devotion to duty at Thiepval on 3rd July, 1916, and again at Ovillers on the 14th July, 1916, and was already in possession of the D.C.M.

Awarded.........M.C.

Lieut. F. J. Oatts, 10th Cheshire Regt.

At Vimy Ridge in May, 1916, when the enemy attacked our front line trenches, this officer showed great gallantry and resource. His behaviour during the enemy bombardment and the attack was mag- nificent, and his prompt action with a machine gun was largely instru- mental in holding up the enemy. He also entered a dug-out which was being heavily shelled and was on fire, in order to rescue three officers who were believed to be still inside.

Awarded.........M.C.

No. 6/14537 C.S.M. P. J. O'Neil, 6th S. Wales Borderers.
(Wounded.)

The company was detailed to establish communication between Hessian and Regina Trenches. During heavy shelling the party was dispersed and sustained many casualties. Although wounded himself, Sergt.-Major O'Neil collected the remainder of the men and insisted on remaining there until all of them were at work. All this took place under heavy enemy barrage fire.

Awarded..........D.C.M.

No. 60040 Sergt. J. Paddock, 25th Divl. Signal Coy.

This N.C.O. behaved with great gallantry and endurance at Regina Trench. For a week previous to the battle he was continuously mending the line running from Mouquet Farm to Zollern Redoubt, which was the centre of the enemy's barrage zone, and on the day of the attack by 24 hours' continuous work he succeeded in keeping the lines through to battalion headquarters in Hessian Trench.

Awarded..........M.M.

No. 3/15209 Pte. Paddock, 6th S. Wales Borderers. (Killed.)

Whilst consolidating Stuff Redoubt, Pte. Paddock volunteered to go over and bring in a wounded officer. There was a heavy fire on from machine and field guns, and in spite of it all Pte. Paddock went over, found the wounded officer, carried him back and had almost regained the trench when he was hit and killed.

Pte. Paddock had displayed great bravery and coolness on many occasions, and he was an excellent man in every way.

No. 52744 Pte. J. C. Robinson, 11th Cheshire Regt.

On the 3rd September, 1916, after an attack by the 7th Brigade, this stretcher-bearer saw a wounded man lying in front of the enemy wire. Pte. Robinson voluntarily brought in this man in daylight and in full view of the enemy.

Awarded..........M.M.

No. 6951 Pte. J. Skelhorn, 11th Lancashire Fusiliers.

During the attack on 21st October, 1916, on Regina Trench, right half company was held up by heavy rifle fire from a portion of the trench in front. Pte. Skelhorn was with the left half, which had gained its objective. In order to create diversion, Pte. Skelhorn, with great promptitude and dash, led a bombing attack against the enemy's flank. This he pressed home till a great number of the enemy were killed and wounded, and the remainder surrendered.

Awarded..........M.M.

2nd Lieut. R. Strong, 8th Border Regt.

During the attack on Regina Trench on 21st October, seeing that some of our men had gone beyond their objective and were in our own barrage, he went out and succeeded in getting some of them back.

Later, hearing that there was a gap in the trench still held by the enemy, he at once organised a party, made a block, and held it with a Lewis gun until reinforcements arrived about an hour afterwards. At night he went out with a small patrol and captured a patrol of 12 fully armed Germans. His conduct throughout was admirable and set a fine example.

Awarded..........**M.C.**

No. 1793 Bombdr. W. Williams, R.F.A.

For gallantry and devotion to duty. Owing to enemy shelling lines to "A" Battery, the wire was constantly cut. This N.C.O., together with another signaller, laid a wire in full view of the enemy across the open to an old enemy gun pit in No Man's Land, a distance of about 100 yards from the front line. The gun pit was the only place from which it was possible to observe for important wire cutting in front of Regina Trench. The two signallers were soon observed by the enemy and shelled, but they continued to keep in touch with the battery until ordered to retire.

Awarded..........**M.M.**

No. 8/15815 Corpl. E. Waugh, 8th Border Regt.

On 3rd July, south of Thiepval, this N.C.O. was first across No Man's Land with his squad of bombers, and made several subsequent journeys to the German front trench. He rallied his men in the trench when he found that the battalion was retiring, bombed the enemy as long as possible, and was last to leave the German trench.

Awarded..........**D.C.M.**

No. 14767 C.S.M. Wood, 8th S. Lancs. Regt.

This warrant officer showed great gallantry on many occasions during the Somme offensive, especially at Ovillers on 8th July, 1916, when he was instrumental in capturing an enemy machine gun, and again in August at the Leipzig Redoubt, when on two different occasions his courageous conduct was the cause of successful actions by our troops.

Awarded..........**D.C.M.**

Awards and Honours.

BAR TO D.S.O.

Capt. H. L. G. Hughes .. .. R.A.M.C., attd. 1st Wilts Regt.

D.S.O.

Capt. G. S. Briscoe	3rd Worcester Regt.
Lt.-Col. L. G. Bird	11th Lancashire Fusiliers.
Lieut. (T./Capt.) G. W. Calverley	2nd Royal Irish Rifles.
2nd Lieut. M. A. Callaghan ..	11th Lancashire Fusiliers.
Lieut. H. L. G. Hughes	R.A.M.C., attd. 1st Wilts Regt.

2nd Lieut. A. Harrison	8th L. N. Lancs. Regt.
Major(T./Lt.-Col.) E. V. O. Hewett	6th S. Wales Borderers.
Major (T./Lt.-Col.) P. S. Hall ..	W. Yorks Regt., attd. 13th Cheshire Regt.
Lieut. J. Mould	3rd Worcester Regt.
Major (T./Lt.-Col.) G. B. Marriott	8th L. N. Lancs. Regt.
Lt.-Col. C. B. Messiter ..	9th L. N. Lancs. Regt.
Lieut. (T./Capt.) S. S. Ogilvie	1st Wilts Regt.
Lieut. S. Ramsay	8th L. N. Lancs. Regt.
T./Capt. G. B. Russell	1st Wilts Regt.
Lt.-Col. A. J. Richardson.. ..	8th S. Lancs Regt.
Major F. G. Wynne	8th L. N. Lancs Regt.

BAR TO MILITARY CROSS.

T./Capt. A. Anderton	R.F.A.
2nd Lieut. (T./Capt.) J. B. Barron	3rd Worcester Regt.
Capt. J. H. Hibbert	8th S. Lancs Regt. attd. 75th T.M. Battery.
Lieut. B. J. Macklin	1st Wilts Regt.
Capt. E. R. S. Prior	8th S. Lancs Regt.
Capt. P. R. Shields	8th L. N. Lancs Regt.

MILITARY CROSS.

T./Capt. A. Anderton	R.F.A.
2nd Lieut.(T./Capt.) W. M. Austin	1st Wilts Regt.
2nd Lieut. E. R. Alford	8th L. N. Lancs. Regt.
2nd Lieut. (T./Capt.) J. B. Barron	3rd Worcester Regt.
18107 B.S.M. F. G. Batchelor ..	R.F.A.
Capt. J. H. Bayley	R.A.M.C.
Capt. C. C. Beatty	75th Field Ambulance.
2nd Lieut. G. D. Brown	1st Wilts Regt.
2nd Lieut. P. L. Bolton	8th L. N. Lancs Regt.
2nd Lieut. C. L. Blair	106th Field Co Coy. R.E.
2nd Lieut. E. D. Birnie	8th Border Regt.
Lieut. E. S. Bissell..	77th Field Ambulance.
2nd Lieut. R. K. Beswick ..	11th Lancs Fusiliers.
Lieut. C. M. Brenan	25th Divnl. Signal Coy., R.E.
2nd Lieut. E. C. Clegg	1st Wilts Regt.
Lieut. M. Christie-Murray ..	R.F.A.
C.S.M. J. P. Cliff	9th L. N. Lancs. Regt.
Lieut. H. D. Copeman	8th L. N. Lancs. Regt.
Capt. A. G. Clark	76th Field Ambulance.
2nd Lieut. (T./Lieut.) S. J. S. Cox	3rd Worcester Regt.
2nd Lieut. (T./Capt.) J. D. Deane-Drummond	8th M.G. Squadron.
Capt. The Rev. M. S. Evers ..	attd. 9th L. N. Lancs Regt.
Capt. N. T. Fitzpatrick	106th Field Coy., R.E.
2nd Lieut. H. J. Goss	10th Cheshire Regt.
2nd Lieut. J. Gilroy	9th L. N. Lancs Regt.
Capt. G. L. Grimsdale	8th S. Lancs Regt.
2nd Lieut. (T./Capt.) L. H. Horncastle	1st Wilts Regt.

2nd Lieut. T. Higgins	.. ..	130th Field Coy., R.E.
Capt. T. W. Hart ..	.. ..	Chaplains' Dept., attd. 76th Field Ambulance.
2nd Lieut. O. M. Hills	.. ..	10th Cheshire Regt.
Lieut. T. H. Harrison	.. ..	130th Field Coy., R.E.
Capt. W. G. Haslam	.. ..	13th Cheshire Regt.
2nd Lieut. A. L. Jenner	.. ..	7th M.G. Coy.
2nd Lieut. G. M. Jones	.. ..	E. Kent attd. 9th L. N. Lancs.
2nd Lieut. W. S. Knowles	..	3rd Worcester Regt.
Lieut. C. E. L. Lyne	.. ..	R.F.A.
2nd Lieut. L. H. Lanham..	..	9th L. N. Lancs. Regt.
Capt. F. G. Lescher	.. ..	77th Field Ambulance.
2nd Lieut. W. R. Loader..	..	R.F.A.
Capt. J. C. P. E. Metcalfe	..	11th Lancs. Fusiliers.
2nd Lieut. C. F. Melling	.. ..	11th Lancs. Fusiliers.
2nd Lieut. W. McEwan	.. ..	2nd S. Lancs Regt.
Capt. T. D. Miller ..	.. ..	8th Border Regt.
2nd Lieut. N. Mathieson	.. ..	1/2 W. R. Field Company.
2nd Lieut. D. G. Le May	.. ..	8th Border Regt.
Lieut. (T./Capt.) C. Mumford	..	6th S. Wales Borderers.
2nd Lieut. D. Mac,kinnon	..	130th Field Coy., R.E.
Capt. R. G. McElney	..	77th Field Ambulance.
Capt. E. C. de R. Martin	..	2nd Y. L. I., Bde. Major 74th Brigade.
Capt. W. McFarlane	..	R.A.M.C.
2nd Lieut. J. H. Mumford	..	R.F.A.
9253 C.S.M. E. Nicholson	..	2nd S. Lancs. Regt.
2nd Lieut. R. Nevill	..	2nd S. Lancs. Regt.
2nd Lieut. G. P. O'Donovan	..	3rd Worcester Regt.
Capt. H. G. Oliver	..	76th Field Ambulance.
Lieut. G. W. Penruddocke	..	1st Wilts Regt.
2nd Lieut. W. A. L. Poundal	..	2nd S. Lancs. Regt.
Capt. E. R. S. Prior	.. ..	8th S. Lancs. Regt.
2nd Lieut. R. C. Perry	..	3rd Worcester Regt.
2nd Lieut. S. E. Rumsey	..	6th S. Wales Borderers.
Capt. K. L. Spiers	.. ..	3rd Worcester Regt.
Sergt. E. Smart ..	.. ..	8th Border Regt.
Lieut. P. R. Shields	..	8th L. N. Lancs. Regt.
T./Capt. J. A. Simmonds	..	10th Cheshire Regt.
2nd Lieut. R. Strong	..	8th Border Regt.
2nd Lieut. C. R. Tattam	..	2nd S. Lancs. Regt.
Lieut. E. Turner ..	..	8th L. N. Lancs. Regt.
Capt. H. S. Turner	..	76th Field Ambulance.
T./Lieut. L. de Velly	..	Z/25 T.M. Batty.
T./ 2nd Lieut. G. D. Williams	..	X/25 T.M. Batty.
2nd Lieut. W. A. Wilson	.. ..	10th Cheshire Regt.

BAR TO D.C.M.

2650 Sergt. H. Fearnihough	..	8th L. N. Lancs. Regt.
Sergt. G. B. Hillings	.. ..	1st Wilts Regt.
6975 Sergt. A. Loveday	.. ..	1st Wilts Regt.
15464 Sergt. J. A. Tinsley	..	8th L. N. Lancs. Regt.

D.C.M.

1109 R.S.M. W. P. Ahearn	..	13th Cheshire Regt.
63660 Corpl. S. Broughton	..	R.F.A.
1786 Corpl. J. G. Burton ..	..	Y/25 T.M. Battery.
Pte. F. Banner	..	3rd Worcester Regt.
Sergt. F. G. Bowtell ..	..	74th Bde. M.G. Coy
19767 Pte. J. H. Baillache	..	1st Wilts Regt.
15126 Sergt. T. Barnes ..	..	8th L. N. Lancs. Regt.
65164 C.S.M. F. Brown ..	..	106th Field Coy., R.E.
6/17361 C.S.M. H. Brooke	..	6th S. Wales Borderers.
A/Sergt. J. G. Carroll ..	..	13th Cheshire Regt.
Sergt. G. Caldicote.. ..	..	2nd S. Lancs. Regt.
Sergt. F. Champion ..	..	2nd S. Lancs. Regt.
Pte. E. Chandler	..	8th S. Lancs. Regt.
17706 Sergt. W. H. Douglas	..	8th L. N. Lancs. Regt.
L./Corpl. H. Eden ..	..	2nd S. Lancs. Regt.
2105 Sergt. W. Evans ..	..	2nd S. Lancs. Regt.
Pte. W. Frost	..	13th Cheshire Regt.
6180 C.S.M. G. F. Filor ..	..	1st Wilts Regt.
8505 Sergt. W. Fidler ..	..	1st Wilts Regt.
12650 Corpl. H. Fearniough	..	8th L. N. Lancs Regt.
23807 Sergt. C. F. Francis	..	R.F.A.
Sergt. H. T. Groves ..	..	Z/25 T.M. Batty.
Pte. B. Guest	..	1st Wilts Regt.
17675 Pte. W. Heyes ..	..	2nd S. Lancs Regt.
33896 Batty. Sgt.-Major F. Howes		R.F.A.
32532 Sergt. W. Holsgrove	..	10th Cheshire Regt.
16895 Sergt. G. E. Hutchinson	..	8th L. N. Lancs. Regt.
3215 Pte. (L/Cpl.) E. Humphries		8th L. N. Lancs. Regt.
5651 C.S.M. T. J. Higgins	..	11th Lancs Fusiliers.
8490 Sergt. G. B. Hillings	..	1st Wilts Regt.
8298 Sergt. F. Jowett ..	..	3rd Worcester Regt.
29521 Pte. T. Killgallon ..	..	8th L. N. Lancs. Regt.
14494 Pte. H. Kivell ..	..	11th Cheshire, att. 25th Div. Sig. Coy., R.E.
15003 Sergt. T. Lewis ..	..	8th L. N. Lancs. Regt.
Corpl. D. M. Mansell ..	..	1st Wilts Regt.
Pte. W. Mullings	..	1st Wilts Regt.
Corpl. G. Marsden ..	..	11th Cheshire Regt.
10547 Pte. G. W. Milsom ..		1st Wilts Regt.
9327 Sergt. L. McCormick	..	2nd S. Lancs .Regt.
9649 L./Corpl. (A./Sgt.) E. Morris		9th L. N. Lancs. Regt.
23377 Pte. T. McDermott	..	74th Bde. M.G. Coy.
15253 Pte. T. Nuttall ..	..	8th L.N. Lancs· Regt.
Pte. N. Nelson	..	9th L. N. Lancs. Regt.
7903 Sergt. A. Owen ..	..	11th Lancs. Fusiliers.
6/14537 C.S.M. J. P. O'Neil	..	6th S. Wales Borderers.
Sergt. C. Price	..	3rd Worcester Regt.
Corpl. J. Parker	..	2nd S. Lancs. Regt.
14320 A/C.S.M. W. Powell	..	8th L. N. Lancs. Regt.
4285 Sergt. W. Pasquill ..	..	8th L. N. Lancs. Regt

18306 Sergt. H. Royle	10th Cheshire Regt.
15676 Pte. (L.-Corpl.) W. Shenton	3rd Worcester Regt.
6/14547 R.S.M. T. Shermer	6th S. Wales Borderers.
12762 Pte. C. Speakman	8th L. N. Lancs. Regt.
Sergt. W. G. Thomas	2nd Hants. attd. 1st Wilts.
15464 Sergt. J. A. Tinsley	8th L. N. Lancs Regt.
18083 Sergt. J. Taylor	7th M. G. Coy.
22498 Corpl. B. Vine	1st Wilts Regt.
L.-Corpl. W. White	11th Lancs. Fusiliers.
Corpl. E. Waugh	8th Border Regt.
10667 Pte. (L./Corpl.) G. Woolford	1st Wilts Regt.
7010 C.S.M. J. W. Wynne	10th Cheshire Regt.
45948 L.-Corpl. H. Watson	25th Signal Coy., R.E.
12376 B.S.M. J. Wilson	R.F.A.

BAR TO MILITARY MEDAL.

8870 Pte. F. Evans	1st Wilts Regt.
15772 Corpl. J. Holgate	10th Cheshire Regt.
7939 Pte. S. Miles	1st Wilts Regt.
8781 Pte. (L.-Corpl.) S. Reynolds	1st Wilts Regt.

MILITARY MEDAL.

L.-Corpl. T. Anderson	1st Wilts Regt.
73790 Corpl. V. Addison	R.F.A.
Pte. H. Allen	3rd Worcester Regt.
Pte. R. Ambler	10th Cheshire Regt.
10900 Sergt. W. Ashbrooke	10th Cheshire Regt.
14275 L.-Sergt. W. G. Awbery	8th S. Lancs. Regt.
66243 2nd Corpl. J. Armstrong	106th Field Coy., R.E.
18057 Pte. G. Aslatt	13th Cheshire Regt.
Pte. J. Bell	1st Wilts Regt.
L.-Corpl. W. Birch	1st Wilts Regt.
L.-Corpl. J. Bird	1st Wilts Regt.
L.-Corpl. W. Bradley	3rd Worcester Regt.
Pte. J. Brewer	8th S. Lancs. Regt.
67474 Gunner Bellis	R.F.A.
56662 Gunner T. Bee	R.F.A.
8963 Corpl. J. F. Bridges	1st Wilts Regt.
21691 Pte. C. Braddock	1st Wilts Regt.
15511 Pte. (L.-Corpl.) S. Boardman	8th L. N. Lancs. Regt.
12213 Pte. H. Burton	8th L. N. Lancs. Regt.
23031 Pte. F. C. Beynon	1st Wilts Regt.
65507 Sapper A. L. Baker	106th Field Coy., R.E.
65283 Sapper F. Barber	106th Field Coy., R.E.
66459 Sapper A. C. Barnard	105th Field Coy., R.E.
67008 2nd Corpl. W. Barker	130th Field Coy., R.E.
39410 Pte. F. H. Burgess	77th Field Ambulance.
57307 Sergt. J. Barnett	77th Field Ambulance.
6/16769 Pte. A. Berry	6th S. Wales Borderers.
3657 Pte. A. Bee	11th Lancs Fusiliers.
15562 Corpl. N. Broughton	9th L.N. Lancs. Regt.
Pte. A. Clewley	3rd Worcester Regt.

Pte. G. Cooper	3rd Worcester Regt.
Pte. G. T. Cain	13th Cheshire Regt.
9619 Pte. R. J. Crowe	1st Wilts Regt. attd. 7th T. M. Batty.
17161 Pte. J. H. Cosgrove	8th S. Lancs. Regt.
21280 Pte. A. Carver	8th Border Regt.
10409 Pte. H. Conway	1st Wilts Regt.
7459 Sergt. J. Crook	11th Lancs. Fusiliers.
17504 Sergt. T Crosbyy	8th L. N. Lancs. Regt.
15790 Pte. F. Cartwright	8th L. N. Lancs. Regt.
65047 2nd Corpl. J. Cowan	105th Field Coy. R.E.
6/17433 Pte. H. Corbett	6th S. Wales Borderers.
14889 Pte. W. Cunliffe	9th L. N. Lancs. Regt.
Sergt. G. Davies	2nd R. Irish Rifles.
Sergt. J. W. Downie	8th Border Regt.
29556 Pte. F. A. Drever	8th S. Lancs. Regt.
7659 Pte. P. Dempsey	2nd S. Lancs. Regt.
9927 Sergt. L. Doel	1st Wilts. Regt.
13384 Pte. J. Done	10th Cheshire Regt.
17055 Sergt. T. Daniels	8th S. Lancs. Regt.
10341 Pte. B. Davies	2nd S. Lancs. Regt.
6/16925 Corpl. W. Davies	6th S. Wales Borderers.
2567 L.-Sergt. J. Devaney	9th L. N. Lancs. Regt.
8870 Pte. F. Evans	1st Wilts Regt.
18846 Pte. (L.-Corpl.) G. H. Etchells	10th Cheshire Regt.
27076 Pte. H. Ellison	8th L. N. Lancs. Regt.
6/17154 Corpl. J. Elsdon	6th S. Wales Borderers.
302 Sergt. G. Ellis	13th Cheshire Regt.
Pte. W. Frost	1st Wilts Regt.
L.-Corpl. C. French	1st Wilts Regt.
L.-Corpl. J. W. Foster	13th Cheshire Regt.
Pte. J. Freeman	2nd S. Lancs. Regt.
10004 Sergt. C. Flack	3rd Worcester Regt.
14484 Sergt. C. Foote	8th S. Lancs. Regt.
65638 Corpl. J. Foley	106th Field Coy. R.E.
16530 Sergt. S. Foster	9th L. N. Lancs. Regt.
Corpl. G. Gibbs	1st Wilts Regt.
8/15142 L.-Corpl. N. Greig	8th Border Regt.
33533 Corpl. H. Gleave	10th Cheshire Regt.
17897 Pte. E. Gibbons	10th Cheshire Regt.
22320 Corpl. D. W. Goodwin	2nd S. Lancs. Regt.
59338 Sapper F. Garside	106th Field Coy. R.E.
6/11305 Sergt. J. Gibbin	6th S. Wales Borderers.
6/16884 Pte. W. Griffiths	6th S. Wales Borderers.
6/16401 Sergt. W. H. Goodman	6th S. Wales Borderers.
47257 2nd Corpl. J. W. Goodwin	25th Divnl. Signal Coy. R.E.
4359 Pte. P. Garry	11th Lancs. Fusiliers.
Sergt. H. Holmes	8th L. N. Lancs. Regt.
L.-Corpl. J. Hulme	13th Cheshire Regt.
Sergt. R. Hayes	13th Cheshire Regt.
L.-Corpl. W. H. Hyde	8th Border Regt.
4235 Sergt. H. Horrocks	8th L. N. Lancs. Regt.

15219 Pte. G. W. Hutchinson .. 8th S. Lancs. Regt.
1780 Pte. T. Heenigan .. .. 2nd S. Lancs. Regt.
41949 Sergt. A. Howson .. .. 76th Field Ambulance.
39748 Pte. A. V. Hunt .. .. 77th Field Ambulance.
14782 Corpl. J. Hetherington .. 8th Border Regt.
14475 L.-Corpl. H. Huxtable .. 8th S. Lancs. Regt.
49402 Pte. M. Hodgson .. .. 10th Cheshire Regt.
35524 Pte. J. Haseltine .. .. 10th Cheshire Regt.
13774 L.-Corpl. I. Hough .. 10th Cheshire Regt.
6931 Corpl. T. Hayes .. .. 1st Wilts Regt.
36750 Pte. N. Humphries.. .. 10th Cheshire Regt.
8/14774 L.-Corpl. S. Huddart .. 8th Border Regt.
65025 Sapper T. Hunt .. .. 105th Field Coy. R.E.
66304 Sapper G. Hutchings .. 105th Field Coy. R.E.
39213 Sergt. J. Ingram .. .. 77th Field Ambulance.
17757 Pte. (L.-Corpl.) H. C. Jeffries 1st Wilts Regt.
16129 Corpl. R. J. Jones .. 2nd S. Lancs. Regt.
6/17285 Sergt. A. T. Jones .. 6th S. Wales Borderers.
6/17074 L.-Corpl. W. Judkins .. 6th S. Wales Borderers.
48981 Pte. W. James .. .. 77th Field Ambulance.
Sapper D. James .. .. .. 25th Divnl. Signal Coy. R.E.
12944 Pte. E. Johnston .. .. 10th Cheshire Regt.
13878 Pte. J. Kelly .. .. 10th Cheshire Regt.
6/16917 Pte. D. Keohane .. 6th S. Wales Borderers.
6/17432 Pte. G. Kew .. .. 6th S. Wales Borderers.
47267 Sapper J. Kerr .. .. 25th Divnl. Signal Coy. R.E.
Pte. J. W. Little .. .. 8th Border Regt.
15003 L.-Corpl. T. Lewis .. .. 8th S. Lancs. Regt.
42244 Pte. G. Leyland .. .. 76th Field Ambulance.
41759 Pte. J. Leigh .. .. 76th Field Ambulance.
94246 2nd Corpl. A. W. Locock .. 130th Field Coy. R.E.
17999 Pte. R. Leather .. .. 8th L. N. Lancs. Regt.
1739 L.-Corpl. J. H. Lomax .. 2nd S. Lancs. Regt.
6/16327 L.-Corpl. G. Lehou .. 6th S. Wales Borderers.
Pte. S. Miles .. .. .. 1st Wilts Regt.
13184 L.-Corpl. A. Mathers .. 10th Cheshire Regt.
L.-Corpl. J. Mason.. .. .. 9th L. N. Lancs. Regt.
66820 Gunner E. Munns .. .. R.F.A.
15074 Pte. J. Mann .. .. 8th L. N. Lancs. Regt.
16207 Pte. J. Mather .. .. 8th L. N. Lancs. Regt.
13738 Pte. T. McGarr .. .. 8th L. N. Lancs. Regt.
14587 Sergt. S. Moss .. .. 8th S. Lancs. Regt.
39127 Pte. C. Mountfield .. .. 77th Field Ambulance.
13259 Pte. P. Moore .. .. 11th Cheshire Regt.
16453 Sergt. G. Marsden .. .. 11th Cheshire Regt.
9362 Sergt. J. McCamley .. .. 2nd R. Irish Rifles.
52004 Sergt. J. McC. Mahon .. W/25 T. M. Batty.
15633 Pte. W. Massey .. .. 8th S. Lancs. Regt.
57219 2nd Corpl. A. Moore .. 105th Field Coy. R.E.
65224 Sapper A. J. Mitchell .. 105th Field Coy. R.E.
6/17188 Pte. F. Moore .. .. 6th S. Wales Borderers.
6795 L.-Corpl. R. Mowbray .. 74th M. G. Coy.

10344 Corpl. R. Milne	2nd S. Lancs. Regt.
27125 L.-Corpl. M. Morris ..	13th Cheshire Regt.
L.-Corpl. G. Noble..	1st Wilts Regt.
15470 L.-Corpl. G. New	8th S. Lancs. Regt.
95412 Spr. (A/L.-Corpl.) W. H. Nichols	130th Field Coy. R.E.
Sergt. W. Payne	11th Lancs. Fusiliers.
Pte. J. Polglaze	2nd S. Lancs. Regt.
14738 Pte. T. Paice	1st Wilts Regt.
1828 Pte. W. Pollard ..	R.H.G., 8th M.G.S.
18771 L.-Corpl. G. W. Potts ..	2nd S. Lancs. Regt.
8957 Corpl. E. H. Poolman ..	1st Wilts Regt.
13606 Pte. H. Pollitt ..	8th L. N. Lancs. Regt.
15626 L.-Corpl. T. Parkinson ..	8th S. Lancs. Regt.
18917 Pte. S. Pilsbury	8th S. Lancs. Regt.
12587 Pte. G. Pugsley	2nd S. Lancs. Regt.
58904 Sapper J. Phillips	106th Field Coy. R.E.
57201 Corpl. J. Potter	105th Field Coy. R.E.
6/16946 Pte. E. Price	6th S. Wales Borderers.
6/16409 Pte. F. Perrins	6th S. Wales Borderers.
39392 Pte. E. W. Plummer ..	77th Field Ambulance.
60040 Corpl. J. Paddock	25th Divnl. Signal Coy. R.E.
11602 Pte. W. C. Pinegar ..	10th Cheshire Regt.
6/17437 L.-Corpl. A. J. Quinton	6th S. Wales Borderers.
Corpl. G. A. Reading	2nd R. Irish Rifles.
Pte. B. Roberts	11th Lancs. Fusiliers.
Corpl. T. Raine	8th Border Regt.
Pte. F. Roberts	8th Border Regt.
8781 Pte. (L.-Corpl.) S. Reynolds	1st Wilts Regt.
10982 Pte. C. Robbins	3rd Worcester Regt.
38415 Sergt. W. A. Riley ..	75th Field Ambulance.
1869 Pte. W. Roulston	2nd S. Lancs. Regt.
8/13748 Pte. E. Robinson ..	8th Border Regt.
65063 Sergt. R. Rye	130th Field Coy. R.E.
66673 Gunner J. Ryle	R.F.A.
6/19223 Sergt. J. Ransom ..	6th S. Wales Borderers.
Pte. J. Sharpe	1st Wilts Regt.
L.-Corpl. D. Smith	1st Wilts Regt.
Pte. M. Sullivan	3rd Worcester Regt.
Pte. F. Scott	7th M. G. Coy.
Pte. E. Slade	2nd S. Lancs. Regt.
13711 Sergt. C. Stoner	3rd Worcester Regt.
10639 Pte. J. Sellars	3rd Worcester Regt.
5613 Corpl. C. Smith	1st Wilts Regt.
9129 Pte. (L.-Corpl.) A. Sheen ..	1st Wilts Regt.
11123 Pte. (L.-Corpl.) H. Slade ..	1st Wilts Regt.
17249 Pte. F. Sharpe	3rd Worcester Regt.
10451 Pte. T. Schofield	8th L. N. Lancs. Regt.
7714 Sergt. A. Stevens	10th Cheshire Regt.
14732 Sergt. W. Speed	10th Cheshire Regt.
19418 Pte. W. Schofield	2nd S. Lancs. Regt.

10931 L.-Corpl. J. Seddon	2nd S. Lancs. Regt.
18527 Sergt. T. Sanders	2nd S. Lancs. Regt.
5721 Sergt. G. Saul	8th Border Regt.
95059 Sapper A. Sampson	130th Field Coy. R.E.
6/14547 C.S.M. T. Shermer	6th S. Wales Borderers.
37966 Pte. J. Scatcherd	74th M. G. Coy.
6951 Pte. Skelhorne	11th Lancs. Fusiliers.
39499 Pte. H. L. Settle	11th Lancs. Fusiliers.
23755 Pte. J. W. Sutcliffe	9th L. N. Lancs. Regt.
Pte. H. Thomas	11th Lancs. Fusiliers.
Pte. W. Tidman	8th Border Regt.
1375 Corpl. W. Truelove	1/2 W. R. Field Coy. R.E.
70360 L.-Corpl. J. Tinham	25th Divnl. Signal Coy. R.E.
10212 Corpl. T. M. Todhinter	2nd S. Lancs. Regt.
24418 L.-Corpl. L. Thomas	130th Field Coy. R.E.
6/17567 L.-Corpl. A.J. Thomas	6th S. Wales Borderers.
82338 Pte. H. Tomlinson	76th Field Ambulance.
50781 Pte. J. Taylor	76th Field Ambulance.
47738 Sapper W. Taylor	25th Divnl. Signal Coy. R.E.
30485 Pte. R. Vallance	75th Field Ambulance.
L.-Corpl. H. F. Wiltshire	1st Wilts Regt.
Pte. J. Webster	13th Cheshire Regt.
Pte. A. White	11th Cheshire Regt.
L.-Corpl. F. Wallace	8th Border Regt.
25489 Pte. A. Wood	3rd Worcester Regt.
6056 Corpl. W. Wilding	3rd Worcester Regt.
16252 Pte. J. W. Woodhead	8th Border Regt.
39227 Pte. T. Whiston	76th Field Ambulance.
13848 Pte. F. Woods	10th Cheshire Regt.
9260 Pte. A. G. Whitehead	1st Wilts Regt.
14844 Pte. W. Wixey	8th S. Lancs. Regt.
15288 Pte. R. Whalley	8th S. Lancs. Regt.
47255 Sergt. A. Warham	25th Divnl. Signal Coy. R.E.
58033 2nd Corpl. A. Waugh	106th Field Coy. R.E.
6/17169 Sergt. J. Whitehouse	6th S. Wales Borderers.
6/16329 Sergt. A. Williams	6th S. Wales Borderers.
4924 Pte. G. H. Walls	13th Cheshire Regt.
14885 Pte. P. Williams	13th Cheshire Regt.
18186 Pte. F. Wilkinson	10th Cheshire Regiment.
Pte. W. Yelton	8th Border Regt.

New Year Honours, 1917.

C.M.G.

Colonel H. I. Pocock .. .. A.D.M.S., 25th Division.
Col. and T./Brig.-Gen. E. St. G. 75th Infantry Brigade.
    Pratt

MAJOR-GENERAL.

T./Major-General E. G. T. Bain- Commanding 25th Division.
    bridge.

BREVET COLONEL

Lt.-Col. and T./Brig.-Gen. B. R. G.O.C., R.A.
    Kirwan (Brevet-Lieut-Colonel)
Major and T./Lt.-Col. B. A. B. R.F.A.
    Butler

BREVET MAJOR.

Capt. N. T. Fitzpatrick .. .. 106th Field Coy., R.E.

D.S.O.

Major, Brevet Lt.-Col., T./Brig.-
    General G. A. Armytage .. 7th Infantry Brigade—K.R.Rifles.
T./Major A. H. D. Britton .. A.S.C.
T./ Major H. F. Bush .. .. A.S.C.
Major B. L. Duke .. .. Bde.-Major, H.Q., R.A.
Major (T./Lt.-Col.) H. A. Davidson 75th Field Ambulance.
Capt. M. G. Douglas .. .. Staff Capt., 7th Brigade, H.A.C
Major H. H. A. Emerson .. D.A.D.M.S., 25th Division.
Capt., (T./Lt.-Col.) L. H. K. Finch 13th Cheshire Regt.
Lt.-Col. F. J. L. Howard .. .. O.C., Divnl. Train, A.S.C.
Major (T./Lt.-Col.) H. B. Kelly .. 77th Field Ambulance.
Major (T./Lt.-Col.) R. F. Legge .. A.A., and Q.M.G., 25th Division.
Major C. P. MacLellan .. .. R.G.A.
Capt. W. N. Parker .. .. R.A.M.C., attd. 8th Borders.

MILITARY CROSS.

Lieut. and Q.M. J. Bowyer .. 11th Lancs Fusiliers.
Lieut. W. E. L. Brown .. .. 10th Cheshire Regt.
T./Capt. F. R. Barry .. .. R.F.A.
Major D. D. H. Campbell.. .. R.F.A.
T./Capt. E. C. Choinier .. .. 6th S. Wales Borderers.
Capt. C. R. Chambers .. .. 8th S. Lancs. Regt.
Capt. A. B. Cheeves .. .. R.A.M.C.
T./Lieut L. C. W. Deane .. .. 6th S. Wales Borderers.
T./Lieut. A. P. Evershed .. .. R.F.A.
7768 C.S.M. W. Evans .. .. 3rd Worcester Regt.
Capt. N. T. Fitzpatrick .. .. 106th Field Coy., R.E.
Capt. J. C. Holmes .. .. 25th Divnl. Signal Coy., R.E.

(12064) B 3

Capt. (T./Major) G. E. S. Hodgson	Staff Capt., 74th Brigade.
Lieut. S. Hawkins	H.A.C., 7th Brigade.
Capt. C. F. Hill	11th Cheshire Regt.
T./Capt. K. Kennard	A.S.C.
2nd Lieut. W. E. Mason	8th L. N. Lancs. Regt.
Lieut. W. P. Moss	2nd Royal Irish Rifles.
Capt. F. J. J. Ney	Sanitary Section.
Capt. G. S. Norman	2nd Royal Irish Rifles.
5653 R.S.M. S. J. Parker ..	1st Wilts Regt.
Capt. M. Perrin	9th L. N. Lancs. Regt.
Captain Sir F. V. L. Robinson, Bt.	A.P.M.
Lieut. (T./Capt.) F. W. Richards	106th Field Coy., R.E.
Capt. A. B. Raffie	R.A.M.C.
T./Capt. A. Safford	A.S.C.
Capt. J. E. Stewart	8th Border Regt.
Capt. L. F. Urwick	3rd Worcester Regt.
Lieut. H. B. Wall	105th Field Coy., R.E.

DISTINGUISHED CONDUCT MEDAL.

3847 C.S.M. J. Anderson ..	8th L. N. Lancs Regt.
18112 Sergt. P. Brophy ..	7th M.G. Coy.
63836 A/Corpl. J. E. G. Crow ..	R.F.A.
45550 Sergt. H. Edgar ..	25th Divnl. Signal Coy., R.E.
8/15143 Sergt. J. C. Grant ..	8th Border Regt.
17907 Sergt. W. E. Jackson ..	11th Cheshire Regt.
10/16313 C.S.M. T. Lines ..	10th Cheshire Regt.
14512 Sergt. F. Morrow ..	3rd Worcester Regt.
9865 Corpl. A. Prankard ..	2nd S. Lancs Regt. attd. 75th T.M. Batty.

MERITORIOUS SERVICE MEDAL.

S365573 S.Q.M.S. A. E. Mirfin ..	A.S.C., attd. D.H.Q.
16447 Sergt. T. Walsh ..	8th L. N. Lancs attd 7th T.M. Batty.

MENTION IN DESPATCHES.

Major H. S. Adair	G.S.O. 2, 25th Division.
66293 L./corpl. J. Armstrong ..	106th Field Co., R.E.
10/10900 Sergt. W. Ashbrooke ..	10th Cheshire Regt.
15481 Pte. A. Atherton	8th L. N. Lancs Regt.
Lieut. N. P. Bailey	75th M.G. Coy.
87018 Driver J. Blezard	R.F.A.
T./Capt. E. Beadon	A.S.C.
T3/027894 Corpl.A. S. Benbow ..	A.S.C.
Capt. H. Bayley	R.A.M.C.
2120 Corpl. (A./Q.M.S.) W. M. Burnett	42nd Sanitary Section.
37307 Sergt. J. Barnett	R.A.M.C.
Lt.-Col. H. E. Brassey	8th S. Lancs Regt.
Lt.-Col. E. W. Birch	G.S.O. 1, 25th Division.

T./Major A H. D. Britton	A.S.C.
T /Major H. H. F. Bush	A.S.C.
18112 Sergt. P. Brophy	7th M.G. Coy.
T./Lt.-Col. L. G. Bird	11th Lancs Fusiliers.
Lieut. C. A. G. Campion	H.Q., 111th Brigade.
171121 Bombdr. A. P. Craven	R.F.A.
52019 Sergt. F. Carr	R.F.A.
Lieut. R. M. Cox	6th S. Wales Borderers.
6/14720 R.S.M. E. Casey	6th S. Wales Borderers.
T./Lieut. R. G. Chittenden	A.S.C.
T./Major A. F. S. Caldwell	8th L. N. Lancs Regt.
2nd Lieut. (T./Lieut.) S. J. S. Cox	3rd Worcester Regt.
8484 Sergt. G. Chilton	11th Lancs Fusiliers.
Lt.-Col. H. T. Cotton	2nd S. Lancs Regt.
Major (T./Lt.-Col.) R. J. Done	C.R.E. 25th Division.
71775 Sergt. E. Dale	R.F.A.
51398 Sergt. D. J. Davies	A.D.M.S. Office.
18062 Sergt. W. F. Dyer	7th M.G. Coy.
Lieut. J. Dawson	8th Border Regt.
Major B. L. Duke	Bde. Major, H.Q., R.A.
Capt. M. G. Doulgas	Staff Capt. 7th Brigade.
T./Lieut. H. S. Edwards	A.S.C.
Major J. Evans	R. I. Fus., attd. Royal Irish Rifles.
Major (T./Lt.-Col.) W. K. Evans	Manchester Regt., attd. 11th Cheshire Regt.
T./Captain W. J. Fergusson	A S.C.
Capt. H. W. Foster	2nd Royal Irish Rifles.
8476 Sergt. W. Foden	11th Lancs Fusiliers, attd. 74th T.M. Batty.
Capt. N. T. Fitzpatrick	106th Field Coy., R.E.
T./Capt. R. Ganley	11th Lancs Fusiliers.
Major T./Lt.-Col. W. B. Gibbs	3rd Worcester Regt.
S4/232705 Sergt. G. A. Griffin	A.S.C.
Capt. G. L. Grimsdell	8th S. Lancs Regt.
Major (T./Lt.- Col.) J. P. Hawksley	R.A.
T./Lieut. A. E. Hansen	R.F.A.
Corpl. J. H. Hayes	R.F.A.
65050 Sergt. E. Hodgson	105th Field Coy., R.E.
14855 Sergt. S. Howcroft	9th L. N. Lancs Regt.
W/773 L./Corpl. H. Higgins	13th Cheshire Regt.
8/14772 C.S.M. E. Higham	8th Border Regt.
15047 Sergt. E. Heathcote	11th Cheshire Regt.
15194 Pte. T. Handley	8th S. Lancs Regt.
18794 Pte. W. Humphreys	8th S. Lancs Regt., attd. 75th T.M. Batty.
Lt.-Col. F. J. L. Howard	A.S.C.
51397 Sergt. C. H. Jefferson	R.E., attd. D.H.Q.
8114697 Pte. S. R. Jenkinson	8th Brigade, attd. D.H.Q
T./Lieut. T. M. Illingworth	R.F.A.
89138 Bombdr. E. H. Jeffreyt	R.F.A.
30623 Sergt.-Major J. R. Ivins	77th Field Ambulance.
10537 Corpl. W. Jackson	1st Wilts Regt.

Major F. B. Knyvett	R.F.A.
Lieut. H. D. Kay	11th Cheshire Regt.
2nd Lieut. W. R. Loader ..	R.F.A.
60593 Bombdr. R. Lieper.. ..	R.F.A.
1444 Bombdr. C. Langley.. ..	R.F.A.
Lieut. E. H. V. Leach	2nd Royal Irish Rifles.
14634 C.S.M. C. Lowth	11th Cheshire Regt.
Capt. and Bt. Major R. A. A. Mac-	130th Field Coy., R.E.
aulay	
T./Capt. N. S. MacDonnell ..	R.F.A.
T./Lieut. W. G. Mackay	R.F.A.
Capt. (T./Lt.-Col.) G. B. Messiter..	9th L. N. Lancs Regt.
Lieut. T. J. Neale	6th S. Wales Borderers.
Capt. A. F. Noble	10th Cheshire Regt.
Capt. G. F. F. Oakes	130th Field Coy., R.E.
6/14537 C.S.M. P. J. O'Niel ..	6th S. Wales Borderers.
Lieut. and T./Major S. S. Ogilvie	1st Wilts Regt.
8964 Corpl. F. Olive	11th Lancs Fusiliers.
Capt. W. N. Parker	R.A.M.C.
57201 Corpl. Potter	105th Field Coy., R.E.
Lieut. J. A. Palmer	1st Wilts Regt.
14315 Corpl. W. Pollard	74th M.G. Coy.
Major J. P. B. Robinson	D.A.Q.M.G., 25th Division.
Lieut. C. G. Radcliffe	R.A.
Lieut. G. F. W. Reed	8th Border Regt.
45759 Corpl. W. F. Rayner ..	R.F.A.
T./Lieut. T. A. Ross	C.R.E. Office.
Lieut. W. H. Reynolds	11th Lancs Fusiliers.
52744 Pte. J. C. Robinson ..	11th Cheshire Regt.
8198 C.S.M. T. Ross	2nd S. Lancs Regt.
563 Pte. C. H. Stevens	R.A.M.C.
11533 Pte. C. Sheppard	1st Wilts Regt.
1041 L./Corpl. E. Sorrell	2nd S. Lancs. Regt.
5184 C.SM. J. W. Tingey ..	3rd Worcester Regt.
Capt. H.C. Townsend	95th Inf. Brigade.
S4/c84640 A./Sergt. F. Wilkinson	A.S.C.
Q.M., Hlon. Major A. Whitty ..	3rd Worcester Regt.
Lieut. W. F. Waite	11th Lancs Fusiliers.
Major W. H. M. Wienholt ..	9th L. N. Lancs Regt.
19959 L./Corpl. W. Weston ..	8th S. Lancs Regt.

CHAPTER II.

Ploegsteert.

ON the 28th October and following days, the 25th Division entrained at Doullens for Caestre in the Second Army Area. The divisional artillery remained for another fortnight in action on the Somme. When they eventually rejoined the Division the end of November, they had been continuously in action on the Somme from the 5th July to the 22nd November, 1916.

The 31st October, Divisional Headquarters moved to Bailleul and 7th (Brig.-Gen. Onslow), 74th (Brig.-Gen. Bethel), and 75th (Brig.-Gen. Baird) Brigades took over the Ploegsteert Sector. With a frontage of about 6,000 yards, the line extended from the River Lys on the right, to Hill 63 on the left, which was later on taken over by the Ulster Division, when St. Ives became the northern boundary of the Divisional Front.

From the beginning of January, the defence of the line was entrusted to two Brigades with one in reserve, and this arrangement enabled each brigade in turn to be withdrawn for a fortnight to reserve billets round Bailleul.

The Sector now held by the 25th Division during the winter months was a comparatively quiet one. There had been but few changes in the actual trench lines since the original fighting in Ploegsteert Wood in November, 1914.

Garrisoned by various divisions through the two years 1915 and 1916, it had not been the scene of any offensive actions by either side. Its trench system was breast work, which suffered considerably from enemy trench mortars and artillery, but especially the former.

During the three and a half months from the beginning of November, 1916, to the middle of February, 1917, when the Division moved back for a short rest, a very great deal of work was done in improving its defensive possibilities and initiating a new system of defence by machine guns. Also improvements were made to better the condition of the troops in the front and support lines, as well as the camps and horse l nes in the back area.

The administrative arrangements in the D vision for the provision of baths, laundries and entertainments for the men, were carried through in a most highly efficient manner. The Pierrot Troupe, then in its infancy, rapidly gained in popularity amongst the Troops, and under the direction of Capt. Ney and Sergt. Fowler, provided many thousands of men with an enjoyable evening's performance at Bailleul and the surrounding camps. During offensive operations its services, together with the divisional orchestra and band, were always at the disposal of the brigades to help with entertainments and concerts during their short intervals of rest. The following year at Bethune, the troupe attracted and developed further talent from the Division, and during its visit to the London Music Halls at Xmas, 1917, its performances earned the high approval of the theatrical world.

A Divisional School with Lt.-Col. Kincaid-Smith as Commandant and Capt. P. J. Goodman as Adjutant was started at Meteren in November, 1916, for the instruction of junior officers and N C.O's. for the 25th Division. Along with its special st class s for instruction in "signal;" under Lieut. Belcher, hand grenades under Lieut. Reed (killed), and musketry under Capt. Jeffares (killed), the Divisional School achieved considerable success not only on educational lines but also in the cultivation of a strong Divisional esprit de corps, and in some respects was the pioneer of a system afterwards to be found throughout the Army. Lectures by speakers from other Units on semi-military topics were always much appreciated, and it was astonishing how much talent was d scovered amongst the students themselves.

No incident of special mention occurred during the 14 weeks spent in this sector of the line, though several raids on the enemy's trenches were carried out with varying success.

On Xmas Day, 1916, General Baird's Brigade organised a raid in the neighbourhood of the "Birdcage," a strongly fortified system opposite Ploegsteert Wood and forming a useful salient to the enemy's defensive front line. Lieut. Knowles and Lieut. Wright, 11th Cheshire Regt., with 40 men successfully entered the German trenches and identified the German division on our front. Many German casualties were claimed by the raiding party.

Some weeks later a large daylight raid was carried through by the 7th Brigade on the 17th February. The 10th Cheshires and 1st Wilts participated in this operation.

Gaps in the wire had been previously cut by trench mortars. On the right, Lieut. K. Wait and 2nd Lieut. Filor, 1st Wilts, with 100 men, 1st Wilts successfully entered the enemy's trenches at 10 a.m. in three parties.

Their advance was covered by snipers who had been pushed forward before daylight into " No Man's Land," and who did excellent work in silencing the enemy machine guns. Consequently practically no casualties were experienced before entering the enemy's trenches. Very few Germans were found, and of these 15 were killed.

Corpl. Mock, 1st Wilts, though wounded, persisted in carrying on, and his gallant conduct, for which he afterwards received the D.C.M., set a fine example to the men under his command. Unfortunately, a few casualties occurred on the return journey to our trenches.

Further to the left, Capt. Appleton, with 2nd Lieut. Rowe, awarded the M.C., subsequently killed in action, 2nd Lieut. Nichols, wounded, 2nd Lieut. Manning, died of wounds, and 205 men of the 10th Cheshires, went forward in several parties across " No Man's Land " at 10.40 a.m. They succeeded in killing some 50 Germans and started on the return journey with 10 prisoners, of whom eight were killed by fire from a German machine gun. Some casualties occurred on returning to our own front line, but most of these were fortunately very slight.

Excellent work was done by sappers of the 106th Field Coy. R.E., attached to the raiding parties in destroying dugouts, machine-gun emplacements, and trench material.

On the other hand the enemy put through several raids of a similar character. Their raid on the 22nd January, 1917, after a preliminary bombardment by a large concentration of trench mortars and artillery must be mentioned. The enemy raiding parties came over about 4.50 p.m., just before dusk and succeeded in entering our front line system at two points held by the 11th Lancs. Fusiliers.

These were, however, driven back by immediate counter attack and at other points the German raiding parties were dispersed by Lewis gun fire.

The 24th February, the Division was withdrawn from the line and moved back to the excellent training area in the neighbourhood of St. Omer, where every advantage was taken of the opportunity for musketry and field firing practice.

The 21st March the Division was transferred to the 2nd Anzac Corps, and at once moved up into Corps Reserve in the Merris and Caestre area with the Divisional Headquarters at Merris. A week later the Division relieved the New Zealand Division in the Wulverghem sector, where work was at once commenced in view of the coming offensive. Large working parties were supplied by Units of the Division for road making, cable burying and the construction of shelters, and bcml-proof dugouts.

The 30th April, the 25th Division was once more withdrawn frcm the line to the Corps reserve area, where it remained until tl e 11th May, when it again relieved the New Zealand Division in the Wulverghem sector, with Divisional Headquarters at Ravelsberg, one and a half miles east of Bailleul.

During these weeks several small raids were organised; aerial and artillery activity increased along the whole front and was promptly followed by corresponding activity on the part of the Germans.

On this sector, the Division had the good fortune of holding the actual line allotted to it in the approaching battle for the Messines-Wystchaete Ridge, and was thus able to reap the fruits of the hard work of the technical troops, pioneers and working parties from the units of the Division, in the general preparations for the attack.

The following are a list of those who received rewards for services during the operations, with details of some of the more notable acts of gallantry for which the award was granted :—

2nd Lieut. W. Aitchinson, R.F.A., Y/25 T.M. Battery.

This officer was in charge of two 2″ T.M.'s opposite Messines on the evening 19th May, 1917. His mortars were under heavy shell fire and half his detachment had become casualties. He kept his men in hand and continued firing until the allotted time was finished, though one emplacement received two direct hits. His absolute coolness and indifference to danger undoubtedly inspired his men to accomplish an exceptionally fine performance. On previous occasions 2nd Lieut. Aitchinson has shown great gallantry and devotion to duty.

Awarded..........M.C.

No. 18719 L.-Corpl. H. Mock, 1st Wilts Regt.

On the occasion of the daylight raid carried out by this Battalion on February 17th, 1917, this N.C.O. displayed the utmost gallantry. He was severely wounded in the leg while crossing " No Man's Land," but nevertheless effected an entry into the enemy's trench, and with his bombing squad inflicted several casualties upon the enemy and organised the erection of a block. It was only when he had seen his party back into our own line, that he allowed himself to be attended to. Throughout the operation he set a magnificent example.

Awarded............,D.C.M.

No. 1796 Gunner J. Wilkinson, R.F.A.

For conspicuous gallantry and devotion to duty at Neuve Eglise, When gunpit and ammunition were set in flames by hostile fire, regardless of danger he successfully extinguished same.

Awarded.........D.C.M.

10483 Sergt. H. Wood, 10th Cheshire Regt.

During a daylight raid at St. Yves in February, 1917, this N.C. O., after the order to withdraw had been given, saw a wounded man lying in the enemy wire. He at once rushed back, and under heavy M.G. fire picked him off the wire and carried him half way across to " No Man's Land " to a shell hole, where he fell exhausted. The wounded man was brought in after dark.

Awarded.........M.M.

Honours and Awards.

BAR TO MILITARY CROSS.

Capt. J. H. Hibbert   ..   ..   8th S. Lancs. Regt.

MILITARY CROSS.

2nd Lieut. W. Aitchison   ..   ..   Y/25 T.M. Batty.
2nd Lieut. W. F. Bryden ..   ..   8th S. Lancs. Regt.
2nd Lieut. J. W. Davies   ..   ..   8th S. Lancs. Regt.
Lieut. L. E. Faber   ..   ..   195th M.G. Coy.
2nd Lieut. G. F. Filor   ..   ..   1st Wilts Regt.
2nd Lieut. G. Greenhill   ..   ..   3rd Worcester Regt.
Lieut. A. J. B. Hudson   ..   ..   3rd Worcester Regt.
2nd Lieut. J. A. Knowles   ..   11th Cheshire Regt.
2nd Lieut. C. O. Rich   ..   ..   1st Wilts Regt.
2nd Lieut. H. W. W. Rowe   ..   10th Cheshire Regt.
Lieut. G. Wait   ..   ..   ..   1st Wilts Regt.

DISTINGUISHED CONDUCT MEDAL.

7176 Corpl. W. Beckett	.. ..	2nd R. Irish Rifles.
13236 Corpl. R. Cook	.. ..	10th Cheshire Regt.
28536 Pte. D. Hall	.. ..	11th Lancs. Fusiliers.
17516 Corpl M. Howard	.. ..	8th S. Lancs. Regt.
52459 Pte. J. Kenny	.. ..	10th Cheshire Regt.
18719 L.-Corpl. H. Mock	.. ..	1st Wilts Regt.
31183 Sergt. A. J. Montell	..	R.G.A.X/25 T. M. Batty.
44125 Pte. T. R. Slack	.. ..	10th Cheshire Regt.
12084 Pte. A. Wheeler	.. ..	1st Wilts Regt.
1796 Gunner J. Wilkinson	..	R.F.A.

BAR TO MILITARY MEDAL.

66799 Sapper C. H. Hensby	..	25th Signal Co., E.R.

MILITARY MEDAL.

14691 Pte. J. Austin	.. ..	11th Cheshire Regt.
13034 Pte. E. J. Blyth	.. ..	1st Wilts Regt.
29829 Pte. W. Burroughs	..	1st Wilts Regt.
52019 Gunner F. Carr	.. ..	R.F.A.
756 Pte. C. Cheyold	.. ..	1st Wilts Regt.
15422 Pte. G. Cadman	.. ..	8th S. Lancs. Regt.
6350 Sergt. J. Casson	.. ..	3rd Worcester Regt.
6/17449 Corpl R. Coombes	..	6th S. Wales Borderers.
13905 Sergt. H. Farrington	..	11th Cheshire Regt.
40169 Pte. (L.-Corpl.) W. Fisher ..		3rd Worcester Regt.
Pte. W. J. French	.. ..	195th M.G. Coy.
L.-Corpl. J. Golder	.. ..	195th M.G. Coy.
40187 Pte. Gower ..	.. ..	3rd Worcester Regt.
17799 A/Bmbdr. W. J. Houlden ..		R.F.A.
10683 Pte. H. Jones	.. ..	10th Cheshire Regt.
12946 Pte. E. Johnson	.. ..	10th Cheshire Regt.
41670 Pte. (A/Sergt.) T. A. Johnson	.. ..	76th Field Ambulance.
63067 Corpl. A. G. Kelman	..	R.F.A.
36172 L.-Corpl. J. Langford	..	10th Cheshire Regt.
6/17284 Sergt. J. H. Lewis	..	6th S. Wales Borderers.
434 Corpl. A. P. Maloney ..	..	6th E. Kent attd. 7 T.M. Batty.
5470 Sergt. G. New	.. ..	8th S. Lancs. Regt.
39618 Sapper R. Smith ..	..	R.E.
8700 Sergt. F. Selley	.. ..	1st Wilts Regt.
14459 Pte. G. Stickler	.. ..	8th S. Lancs. Regt.
52655 Pte. A. Trickey	.. ..	11th Cheshire Regt.
52464 Pte. T. Taylor	.. ..	11th Cheshire Regt.
33024 Pte. E. Toomey	.. ..	1st Wilts Regt.
11408 L.-Corpl. G. Tall	..	1st Wilts Regt.
64502 Gunner S. Trafford	..	Y/25 T.M. Battery.
1793 Bmdr. W. Williams	..	R.F.A.
10483 Sergt. H. Wood	..	10th Cheshire Regt.
15209 Corpl. C. Woodall	..	10th Cheshire Regt.
47243 Sergt. A. K. Young	..	25th Div. Sig. Co. R.E.

Birthday Honours and Awards, June, 1917.

BREVET LIEUT.-COLONEL.

Major (T/Lt.-Col.) R. F. Legge ..   A.A. Q.M.G., 25th Division
Major (T/Lt.-Cl.) O. H. L. Nichol-
son   ..   ..   G.S.O.I., 25th Division

BREVET MAJOR.

Capt. (T/Lt.-Col.) E. C. de R. Martin   11th Lancs Fusiliers

D.S.O.

Rev. Major L. G. Dickenson ..	S.C.F., 25th Division
Major (T/Lt.-Col.) R. J. Done ..	C.R.E., 25th Division
Bt.-Major (T/Lt.-Col.) A. C. Johnston	3rd Worcs, commdg. 10th Cheshire Regt.
Major F. B. Knyvett	R.F.A.
Lieut. J. C. O. Marriott	S.C., 74th Brigade
Lt.-Col. (T/Brig.-Gen) C. C. Onslow	Commanding 7th Inf. Bde.
Major J. R. B. Robinson	D.A.Q.M.G., 25th Division
Major W. H. M. Wienholt ..	9th L. N. Lancs.

MILITARY CROSS.

T/Lieut. C. L. Blair	106th Field Coy. R.E.
Capt. E. de W. H. Bradley ..	K.O.Y.L.I., 25th Divnl. Signal Coy.
Capt. J. H. Bagley	76th Field Ambulance
Q.M. and Hon. Lieut. B. Bartholomew	9th L. N. Lancs Regt.
Lieut. E. T. Caparn	106th Field Coy. R.E.
Chaplain G. M. Evans	C.F.
Capt. Sir J. P. G. M. Fitzgerald, Bt.	S.C., 25th Divnl. Arty.
2nd Lieut. P. J. Goodman ..	2nd South Lancs Regt.
2nd Lieut. A. T. Griffiths ..	1st Wilts Regt.
Capt. Hon. G. St. V. Harris ..	A.D.C.
T/Capt. D. C. Lyell	8th Border Regt.
Lieut. G. W. Nowell-Usticke ..	Z/25 T.M. Batty.
2nd Lieut. T. G. Parkes	3rd Worcester Regt.
2nd Lieut. W. G. Round	3rd Worcester Regt.
Lieut. W. H. Reynolds	11th Lancs Fusiliers
Capt. G. H. Stead	74th T. M. Batty.

D.C.M.

8261 Sergt. (A/C.S.M.) W. C. Field	2nd S. Lancs Regt.
11842 R.S.M. S. Harvey	11th Cheshire Regt.
6/17437 Sergt. A. J. Quinton ..	6th S. Wales Borderers

MILITARY MEDAL.

10583 Rfn. H. Quigley	2nd R. Irish Rifles
44135 Rfn. H. Quarterman ..	2nd R. Irish Rifles

MERITORIOUS SERVICE MEDAL.

51397 Sergt. C. H. Jefferson   ..   R.E.
5712 Sergt. C.G. Journeaux   ..   A.O.C.

MENTION IN DESPATCHES.

Capt. B. Auret	R.F.A.
Sergt. A. R. Ackland	25th Signal Co.
6/16459 Sergt. C. E. Bourne ..	6th S. Wales Borderers
14882 Pte. H. Braddock	10th Cheshire Regt.
8692 Corpl. J. Bastable	3rd Worcs Regt. attd. 7th T. M. Batty.
Lt.-Col. (T/Br.-Gen.) H. K. Bethell	Commanding 74th Brigade
18080 Sergt. T. Barber	9th L. N. Lancs Regt.
Lieut. K. M. Bourne	2nd S. Lancs Regt.
7310 Sergt. W. Bickley	3rd Worcester Regt.
Lieut. T. C. Bennett	75th M. G. Coy.
Lt.-Col. B. A. Butler	R.F.A.
Capt. E. S. Brittain	R.F.A.
T/2nd Lieut. F. W. Cooper ..	105th Field Coy. R.E.
6/14720 R.S.M. E. Casey	6th S. Wales Borderers
24171 Pte. W. Curbishley.. ..	10th Cheshire Regt.
Major (T/Lt.-Col.) H. M. Craigie-Halkett	9th L. N. Lancs Regt.
Major W. G. Constable	11th Lancs Fusiliers
8795 L.-Corpl. G. Choules ..	2nd S. Lancs Regt.
2nd Lieut. H. S. Coppock ..	8th S. Lancs Regt.
Capt. A. G. Carpenter	11th Cheshire Regt.
2nd Lieut. A. R. Cunningham ..	8th S. Lancs Regt., attd. 75th T.M. Btty.
Major D. D. H. Campbell.. ..	R.F.A.
04697 L.-Corpl. (A/Sergt.) D. E. Durrant	A.O.C.
2nd Lieut. (T/Lieut.) W. H. Densham	X/25 T. M. Btty.
Lieut. (T/Capt.) J. D. Deane-Drummond	8th L. N. Lancs Regt., Divnl. M. G. Officer
Capt. H. V. Dean	R.F.A.
8/14432 Sergt. J. Escolme ..	8th Border Regt.
Lt.-Col. A. D. Forman	R.F.A.
Lieut. P. A. Foy	Signal Coy. R.E.
Capt. J. Forrest	Mobile Vety. Section
Capt. E. K. B. Furze	Bde.-Major 7th Brigade
Capt. (T/Lt.-Col.)L. H. K. Finch ..	13th Cheshire Regt.
Q.M. and Hon. Capt. H. W. Foster	2nd R. Irish Rifles
1427 C.S.M. C. E. Fubby	13th Cheshire Regt.
26184 L.-Corpl. C. Finn	2nd S. Lancs Regt., attd. 75th T. M. Btty.
Major (T/Lt.-Col.) H. R. Goodman	2nd R. Irish Rifles
Capt. K. F. D. Gattie	Bde.-Major 75th Inf. Brigade
8/14445 L.-Corpl. J. Gibson ..	8th Border Regt.
Capt. (Bt.-Major) J. M. Hamilton	G.S.O.2
56495 Sergt. W. J. Hogg	105th Field Coy. R.E.

Capt. A. H. Huycke	75th Field Ambulance
2nd Lieut. (T/Capt.) A. Harrison	8th L. N. Lancs., attd. 7th T. M. Batty.
16651 C.S.M. C. H. Holland ..	9th L. N. Lancs Regt.
9044 Sergt. C. H. Hall	2nd S. Lancs Regt.
Capt. S. O. Jones	R.F.A.
Lt.-Col. (T/Brig.-Gen.) K. J. Kincaid-Smith	C.R.A., 25th Division
T/Lieut. (A/Capt.) S. B. Keast ..	130th Field Coy. R.E.
6/16908 Corpl. R. King	6th S. Wales Borderers
Capt. (T/Lt.-Col.) T. M. H. Kincaid-Smith	Res. of Off.Lancers, attd. 1st Wilts.
19702 Pte. A. E. Kay	3rd Worcester Regt.
Major (T/Lt.-Col.) R. F. Legge ..	A.A. and Q.M.G. 25th Division
Major W. Ludgate	A.D.V.S.
18059 Sergt. E. C. Light	7th M. G. Coy.
35 R.Q.M.S. C. Laycock	13th Cheshire Regt.
2nd Lieut. E. B. K. Lloyd ..	2nd R. Irish Rifles
T/Lieut. E. J. C. Maddison ..	7th M. G. Coy.
Capt. E. C. de H. Martin ..	Bde. Major, 74th Brigade
2nd Lieut. P. J. Murphy	2nd R. Irish Rifles
Capt. N. F. Marriott	74th M. G. Coy.
Lieut. E. C. Mogridge	74th M. G. Coy.
6727 C.S.M. W. Martin	74th M. G. Coy.
Capt. W. H. McKerrow	11th Cheshire Regt.
10416 Pte. (L.-Corpl.) H. Marsh ..	75th M. G. Coy.
Capt. (T/Major) E. P. Nares ..	13th Cheshire Regt.
Lt.-Col. (T/Br.-Gen.) C. C. Onslow	Commanding 7th Brigade
Lieut. (T/Capt.) J. C. Owen ..	6th S. Wales Borderers
Lieut. H. D. H. Padwick ..	9th L. N. Lancs Regt.
6670 Sergt. W. Parry	2nd S. Lancs Regt.
Lieut. G. E. Pilkington	10th Cheshire Regt.
2nd Lieut. J. B. Poultney ..	8th S. Lancs Regt.
10271 R.Q.M.S. J. Quinn ..	3rd Worcester Regt.
Lieut. J. A. Reiss	Camp Commandant, 25th Divn.
2nd Lieut. (T/Capt.) J. Reader ..	1st Wilts Regt.
T/2nd Lieut. W. J. E. Ross ..	1st Wilts Regt.
27710 Pte. S. Reeves	3rd Worcester Regt.
2nd Lieut. J. L. Robbins ..	10th Cheshire Regt.
35220 Pte. T. Rudd	10th Cheshire Regt.
Major E. L. Roddy	Ches. Regt., attd. 2nd R.I.R.
15505 L/Cpl. D. Salked	8th K.O.R.L.
Lieut. W. B. Solly	3rd Lancs Fus., attd. 74th T.M. Battery.
14663 L.-Corpl. G. Stamper ..	8th Border Regt.
T/Lieut. J. R. Taylor	1st Wilts Regt.
Capt. T. J. C. C. Thompson ..	4th R.I.F., attd. 2nd R.I.R.
6/17058 Sergt. J. Wilkinson ..	6th S. Wales Borderers
T/Lieut. (A/Q.M.) H. Webber ..	1st Wilts Regt.
23254 Sergt. R. Williams ..	3rd Worcester Regt.
12995 Corpl. J. Wilson	10th Cheshire Regt.
17799 Pte. E. Williams	8th S. Lancs Regt.
3953 Bmbdr. G. Webb	R.F.A.

CHAPTER III.

Messines.

O N the 7th June, 1917, the 2nd Army attacked with three Army corps the Germans defences along the line of hills from Messines to Wytschaete. The capture of this line by the British Troops was necessary before any attack could be developed further north and to the east of Ypres. In addition to their possession of the higher ground, which gave them excellent observation both to the east and over the Ypres Salient, the Germans held a position of great natural strength. This they fortified with line upon line of trenches, together with concrete machine gun emplacements, strong points, and numerous dugouts for the protection of their troops.

The front of attack allotted to the 25th Division extended from the Wulverghem–Messines Road to the Wulverghem–Wytschaete Road.

The New Zealand Division attacked on the right and the 36th Division on the left of the 25th Division respectively.

The objective of the 25th Division lay in front of the village of Wulverghem and comprised the strip of ground with a front of about 1,200 yards on the German front line to a depth of about 3,000 yards but narrowing towards the top of Messines Ridge to about 700 yards. A short forward slope followed by a descent into the Steenebeek Valley. The stream, about 4 feet wide, ran through marshy ground in winter, but fairly dry in summer except for occasional pools, and presenting no natural obstacles unless stiffened by the aid of military science.

From this point the ground rises steeply, flanked on either side by Hell Farm and Sloping Roof Farm, with Four Huns Farm, Chest Farm, Middle Farm on the crest of the ridge, and Lumms Farm a little further on to our left front. These farms, both naturally and tactically strong points, had been converted by military science into positions of immense strength and importance, impregnable to all but overwhelming heavy artillery.

Even with the mass of guns at our disposal for the bombardment of these strong points, the garrison, though dazed and shaken, were able to put up a good resistance for an appreciable period.

Along this line of advance, which was considerably deeper than the ground to be covered by the New Zealand Division on our right flank, there lay nine distinct lines of enemy trenches to be stormed and captured.

For the task of preparing the Wulverghem sector for the capture by the 25th Division of their objectives, the technical troops consisted of the 105th Field Coy., R.E., 106th Field Coy., R.E., and the 130th Field Coy., R.E., commanded by Major C. G. Lynam, Major N. T. Fitzpatrick, M.C., and Major R. K. A. Macauley, D.S.O., respectively, and the 6th Battalion South Wales Borderers (Pioneers), commanded by Lt.-Col. E. V. O. Hewitt, C.M.G., D.S.O. Work commenced about 12th April to 31st April, when the Division was withdrawn from the line. It was resumed about 11th May and continued until the eve of the attack when the whole programme was completed.

During these periods the Pioneers were employed on road-making, dugouts, tunnelled dugout for Reserve Brigade Headquarters, and the constructions of communication trenches.

The 106th and 130th Field Coys., R.E., supervised the R.E. preparations on the right and left sub-sectors respectively, and departmental works in the back area, and the preparation of artillery positions, until about 18th May, when the 105th Field Coy., which up to then had been employed elsewhere, chiefly on the construction of heavy artillery emplacements, took over from the 106th Field Coy., R.E., the R.E. work for battery positions.

The construction of the first line assembly trench was a notable piece of work. Working parties of the 7th Infantry Brigade dug their trench in three hours on the night of 30th/31st May, including communication trenches and wiring. The trench was roughly 150 yards from the enemy front line and was so sited that the garrison of each length of it would face directly towards the portion of enemy line required to assault. The taping of the operation was shared equally by 106th and 130th Field Coys., R.E. The last two days before the attack were used to put final touches, including the placing of bridges and ladders for the use of assaulting troops. At noon on 6th June all trenches were reported to be in good order. During the whole of this period of preparation, infantry worked with the technical troops on the scale of one battalion daily to each sub-sector and another 200 men daily for work on artillery positions and another 120 men daily from the R.A.M.C. for work on medical preparations. In this case the men were working against time and the task was only completed thanks to the unremitting toil of the technical troops, combined with the hard work and keenness of the infantry working parties, who knew that their work was in no small measure contributing to the defeat of the enemy.

Previous experience has conclusively proved that to keep up an efficient telephone system during offensive operations, all cable must be buried at least 7 feet. Where it was impossible to get the full depth the route was strengthened by piling up broken bricks and earth on the top of the trench. During the preliminary bombardment the enemy shelled the buried cable route area considerably, getting no less than 50 direct hits without doing any damage.

The labour involved in the carrying out of this work was very great. For six weeks roughly 400 men working six hours a day were employed in burying cable on the divisional front of attack. It covered roughly 13,000 yards with an average of 45 circuits in each cable route. One of the most important items in the many preparations for the attack, the time and labour expended in this way was fully justified.

During the fortnight previous to the attack the field artillery allotted to the 25th Division gradually arrived and the groups were formed.

Gun platforms, shelters and command posts were being prepared and camouflaged. Precautions were taken to conceal the number of guns from the enemy, and only 75 per cent. were allowed to open fire at any given time before zero hour. The " N " Group (Guards Divisional Artillery) occupied forward positions and were silent except for registration until the moment of attack.

Excellent work was performed during this period by the trench mortars in the destruction of the enemy front and support lines, wire and trenches, under Capt. P. M. Chaworth-Musters, M.C., as well as by the heavy trench mortar battery commanded by Capt. J. P. Creagh. The former fired an average of about 100 rounds per day per mortar and the heavy about 20 rounds per day per mortar in spite of more than one direct hit on their emplacements. Something like a record must have been created by these trench mortar batteries in firing 1,250 60-lb. bombs from the 2-inch trench mortars in one day, besides 108 9.45-inch bombs.

A great deal of work was necessary in the preparation of shrapnel-proof emplacements for the machine guns.

Mule pits to hold two mules each were dug in close proximity to each battery and proved invaluable. These eight mules were used to carry up ammunition immediately behind the batteries when they moved forward. Each mule made three trips carrying 2,000 rounds of S.A.A. per trip.

The offensive line on 6th June was held by the 2nd Battn. S. Lancs. Regt., and two Companies of the 8th Battn. Border Regt., 75th Infantry Brigade. These were relieved during the afternoon of the 6th by companies of the 7th and 74th Infantry Brigades and withdrawn to their assembly positions. Under cover of darkness on the night 6th/7th June the brigades marched into their assembly positions. This was reported fully complete by 1.30 a.m. and proved an operation of some difficulty in the dark.

THE ATTACK.

At 1.30 a.m. the Division was assembled in its order of battle with the 74th Infantry Brigade on the right, 7th Infantry Brigade on the left, and the 75th Infantry Brigade in Reserve.

74TH INFANTRY BRIGADE ...	Brig.-Gen. H. K. BETHELL.
2nd Battn. R. Irish Rifles	Lt.-Col. H. R. Goodman.
13th Battn. Cheshire Regt.	Lt.-Col. L. H. K. Finch, D.S.O.
9th Battn. L. N. Lancs. Regt.	Lt.-Col. H. M. Craigie-Halkett.
11th Lancs. Fusiliers ...	Lt.-Col. E. C. de R. Martin, M.C.

7TH INFANTRY BRIGADE ...	Brig.-Gen. C. C. ONSLOW, C.M.G., D.S.O.
3rd Battn. Worcester Regt.	Lt.-Col. P. R. Whalley.
8th Battn. L. N. Lancs. Regt.	Lt.-Col. G. B. Marriott, D.S.O.
10th Battn. Cheshire Regt.	Major J. A. Howell, M.C.
1st Wiltshire Regt. ...	Lt.-Col. A. E. Williams.
75TH INFANTRY BRIGADE ...	Brig.-Gen. H. B. D. BAIRD, D.S.O.
11th Battn. Cheshire Regt.	Lt.-Col. W. K. Evans, D.S.O.
8th Battn. Border Regt....	Lt.-Col. W. H. Birt.
2nd S. Lancs. Regt. ...	Lt.-Col. D. L. Maxwell.
8th Battn. S. Lancs. Regt.	Lt.-Col. J. B. Allsopp.

The 25th Division was supported by the following field artillery under Brig.-Gen. K. Kincaid-Smith, C.M.G., D.S.O. :

	18 Pdr.	4.5-in. Howitzers.
25th Divisional Artillery	36	12
2nd N.Z. Army F.A. Brigade ...	18	4
34th Army F.A. Brigade	18	6
93rd Army F.A. Brigade	18	—
Guards Divisional Artillery ...	36	12
	126	34

They were divided into five groups :—

" A " Group, Lt.-Col. A. B. Forman, D.S.O. ... ... 30 guns.
" B " Group, Lt.-Col. I. de V. Bowles, D.S.O. ... ... 30 guns.
" C " Group, Lt.-Col. F. B. Sykes, D.S.O. 30 guns.
" D " Group, Lt.-Col. C. F. P. Parry, D.S.O. ... ... 22 howitzers.
" N " Group, Lt.-Col. H. B. Bethell,⎰ 36 guns.
D.S.O. ... ...⎰ 12 howitzers.

The attack opened at early dawn at 3.10 a.m. and in addition to the intense clouds of dust and smoke which obscured all view except in the immediate neighbourhood, there was a slight ground mist. This ground mist retarded the approach of full dawn and has given some of those taking part in the attack the impression that it might with advantage have been delayed some 10 to 15 minutes. In spite of this, direction was fairly well maintained by the majority.

At the exact moment a mine was exploded in the south-western edge of the divisional objectives at Ontario Farm, another about a mile to the north under the Spanbroekmolen and others at varying distances along the Army front attacked.

The whole of the artillery supporting the Division opened fire simultaneously as the mine went up —

　126　18-pounders.
　33　4.5-inch howitzers.
　72　heavies (34 of which were for counter battery work),

and in addition an Army Group of heavy artillery covering the Army front.

Briefly the plan of attack was for the two leading battalions of both brigades to capture all enemy trenches up to the Steenebeek. For one battalion of both brigades to move up in artillery formation immediately behind the rear waves of the leading battalions, to pass through them in leap-frog system and to capture the further objective. The remaining battalion of each brigade to leave the assembly position at 3.40 a.m. and to gradually close upon the leading battalion. At 4.5 a.m. one battalion of the reserve Brigade (75th Infantry Brigade) to leave its assembly position, gradually close up to the battalions of the leading brigades, pass through them in the leap-frog system and capture the next line of trenches by 7.10 a.m.

As the artillery opened fire the whole line along our 1,200 yards front, 8th Battn. L. N. Lancs. Regt., 3rd Battn. Worcester Regt., 2nd Battn. R. Irish Rifles, and 13th Battn. Cheshire Regt. left their trenches. Moving forward across the 130 yards of No Man's Land behind the creeping barrage of 60 guns, they entered the German trenches at once. Simultaneously a standing barrage of 24 18-pounder guns and 36 4.5-inch howitzers had opened on the further line with another 36 18-pounder guns on the line Occur–Sloping Roof Farm–Hell Farm Spur. Six 18-pounder guns were allotted to deal with Ozone Alley.

In addition, 20 6-inch howitzers opened on suspected machine gun emplacements on the Hell Farm–Sloping Roof Farm Spur, and 8 8-inch howitzers on strong points further to the rear.

From left to right 8th Battn. L. N. Lancs. Regt., with B and A Coys. in front, D and C Coys. behind, under the command of Capt. C. H. Hadley, Lieut. S. Andrews, Capt. Tindal Atkinson, and Lieut. Tollett respectively. The 3rd Battn. Worcester Regiment, with B and C Coys. in front, A and D Coys. behind, under the command of Lieut. Hudson, Capt. Mason, Capt. Birch Jones and Capt. McDonald respectively. The 13th Battn. Cheshire Regt., with C and D Coys. in front and A and B Coys. behind, under the command of Lieut. Pigot, Capt. Thomas, Lieut. Gilderall, and Capt. Moir respectively. The 2nd Battn. R. Irish Rifles, with D, C, and B Coys. in front and A Coy. behind, commanded by Lieut. Fry, Lieut. Anderson, Capt. Thompson and Capt. McEwen respectively.

The line swept on at 3.17 a.m., the rear waves of the 8th Battn. L.N. Lancs. Regt. and 3rd Battn. Worcester Regt. had captured the enemy support line, pushing on to the next line where a few prisoners were taken in dugouts. Two machine guns were secured by the 13th Battn. Cheshire Regt., and four more by the 2nd Battn. R. Irish Rifles.

The enemy's barrage came down on our old front line at 3.14 a.m., but caused very few casualties, as by this time the leading battalions on the left were clear of this area.

The 10th Battn. Cheshire Regt. left their assembly position just behind the rear waves of the 8th Battn. L. N. Lancs. Regt. and 3rd Battn. Worcester Regt. Passing through the latter, the four companies, A, B, C, and D, 10th Battn. Cheshire Regt., commanded respectively by Capt. D. C. Fry, Lieut. L. W. G. Owen, Capt. S. F. Morgan, and Lieut. C. Cheetham, moved on to their objectives.

Very little opposition was encountered except at one point about 80 yards south of the south-west corner of L'Enfer Wood. Here the Germans were ejected without much difficulty, leaving 50 prisoners and eight machine guns in our hands. In the meantime 3rd Battn. Worcester Regt. were reformed and set to dig a support trench and a communication trench from the right of October Trench westwards as soon as October Reserve had been captured. A party assisted in the capture of a strong point immediately west of Middle Farm and along with the 10th Battn. Cheshire Regt. secured a considerable number of prisoners and machine guns in the south-west corner of L'Enfer Wood.

At 3.40 a.m. the 1st Battn. Wiltshire Regt., A, B, C, and D Coys., commanded by Capt. R. F. Hayward, Lieut. Rowe, Lieut. Turner and Lieut. Taylor respectively, left their assembly trenches in artillery formation and passing through the leading battalions advanced against their first objective. The only opposition encountered in this operation was from a party of 16 of the enemy with a machine gun, which were in a strong concrete dugout at the northern end of the trench. Those not killed were taken prisoner and the machine gun put into action against the enemy. Some more prisoners and two machine guns were also secured in Four Huns Farm and the neighbouring trenches. At this stage there was a gap between the left of the 1st Battn. Wiltshire Regt. and the right battalion of the adjacent Division, and as our men were suffering from machine gun fire from Lumms Farm on our left flank, immediate action was taken and Major Ogilvie, with a company of the 1st Battn. Wiltshire Regt. and parties collected in the vicinity from 10th Battn. Cheshire Regt., 8th Battn. Border Regt., 11th Battn. Lancs. Fusiliers, 8th Battn. S. Lancs. Regt., and other battalions, captured or killed the whole garrison of 40 men. A line of posts was then established east of Lumm Farm, shell holes consolidated and a fighting patrol sent out. These discovered a small party of Germans in a farm in front who were soon dealt with, leaving two more machine guns in our hands.

Away on the right the 9th Battn. L. N. Lancs. Regt. and the 11th Battn. Lancs. Fusiliers had left the assembly positions in artillery formation immediately behind the rear waves of the two leading battalions of their brigades. The four companies, A, B, C, and D of the 9th Battn. L. N. Lancs. Regt., commanded by Capt. Laurie, Lieut. Pollitt, Capt. Godfrey and Lieut. Lanham respectively, and the four companies, A, B, C, and D of the 11th Battn. Lancs. Fusiliers, commanded by Major Munday, Lieut. Sharp, Capt. Ward and Lieut. Hadfield respectively. Unfortunately, the enemy's barrage caught the carrying parties of their leading companies, causing some casualties ; however, passing through the leading battalions, the two battalions advanced across the

Steenebeek which was found to be dry and to present no serious obstacle.

The 11th Battn. Lancs. Fusiliers got two machine guns, but little resistance was met with until the German support line was reached, when 9th Battn. L. N. Lancs. Regt. and 11th Battn. Lancs. Fusiliers each took two more machine guns. The latter met with stiff resistance at Middle Farm, where A Coy. carried out a turning movement in support of a frontal attack by C Coy. The 13th Battn. Cheshire Regt. and 2nd Battn. R. Irish Rifles had meanwhile been re-organised and taken over a portion of the front line. Seeing that Middle Farm was still causing trouble, Capt. Thompson with B Coy., 2nd Battn, R. Irish Rifles, reinforced and by working round the right flank, assisted in the capture of that strong point, which was found to contain four machine guns. The garrison did not wait for our infantry to attack but left their four machine guns and bolted. On the capture of their final objective, the 9th Battn. L. N. Lancs. Regt. and 11th Battn. Lancs. Fusiliers pushed forward outposts and consolidated a line of shell holes in advance of their new position.

West of the Steenebeek very little opposition had been met. The garrisons were mostly killed by our artillery fire and those who were left readily surrendered. The few who refused were quickly disposed of with the bayonet. Owing to the poor light, clouds of dust and smoke from the intensity of the artillery fire, great difficulty was experienced in keeping direction and in identifying the enemy trench lines which had been in many places obliterated by our bombardment. This lead to some confusion and intermingling by units with others on their flanks, and numbers of men lost touch for the moment with their own battalions.

The objectives allotted to Gen. Baird's Brigade were :—

A line about 2,400 yards from our original front line and a further line about 850 yards beyond and running north from Despagne Farm.

The 8th Battn. S. Lancs. Regt. and the 11th Battn. Cheshire Regt. were employed for the attack on these lines respectively.

The 8th Battn. Border Regt. were in Brigade Reserve and held in readiness to assist in consolidation, whilst the 2nd Battn. S. Lancs. Regt. were kept in Divisional Reserve and held in readiness for the work of carrying up stores. At

4.5 a.m. the 8th Battn. S. Lancs. Regt., A, B, C and D Coys., commanded by Capt. Ross, Capt. Kimber, Lieut. Bryden, and Capt. Case respectively, left their assembly trench and advanced in artillery formation. They passed through the troops of the 7th and 74th Infantry Brigades, who were consolidating according to programme. Very little opposition was met with and the Battalion soon gained its objective. Some prisoners and four machine guns were captured.

The 11th Battn. Cheshire Regt. left their assembly positions at 6.50 a.m., A, B, C and D Coys., commanded by Lieut. Clist, Capt. Williams, Capt. Knowles, and Capt. Nicholson respectively, to attack the further line. The 8th Battn. Border Regt. left at ·7 a.m., A, B, C, and D Coys,, commanded by Lieut. Healy, Capt. P. H. Coxon, Capt. J. Dawson and Lieut. Johnson respectively, to assist in consolidation.

The former pushed on towards their objective, meeting with opposition from a small party of Germans in a strong point. This was, however, left to and dealt with by two platoons of 8th Battn. Border Regt., who quickly captured the whole party.

Up to the October Support Trench, the New Zealand Division had been echeloned in front of our line, owing to the very much greater depth of the trench system to be captured by the 25th Division, but from this point onwards the two Divisions advanced simultaneously along with the 36th Division on the left. Connection was established with the 36th Division at Lumms Farm and on the right with the 1st New Zealand Brigade, New Zealand Division. A trench was rapidly dug and consolidated, gaps in the line held by the 8th Battn. S. Lancs. Regt. filled up, and small parties of men who had got mixed with other units reformed and re-organised to meet any counter-attack. On the left Capt. Dawson, with C Coy., 8th Battn. Border Regt., did good work in the organisation and consolidation of a portion of the new front line, whilst a small party of men of D Coy. of the same battalion along with two tanks helped to capture a gun and several prisoners.

At 8.30 a.m. the 11th Battn. Cheshire Regt., who had advanced steadily in their line of platoon columns at 50 paces interval with their leading sections, extended to form a line of skirmishers, reached their objective, a line running north from Despagne Farm. The constructions of posts was at once put in hand, a platoon of the 8th Battn. Border Regt. being sent up to construct posts on each flank of the 11th Battn. Cheshire Regt. During the advance the battalion captured four field guns and one machine gun, and a good piece of work was done by our machine guns under Major Drummond in knocking over two enemy gun teams which were trying to get away with their guns.

The completion of this work may be said to have ended the first phase of the battle. Messines and the ridge had been captured in one hour and 40 minutes. In the words of the Commander-in-Chief's despatch, " The position assaulted was one of very great natural strength, on the defence of which the enemy had laboured incessantly for nearly three years. Its possession, overlooking the Ypres Salient, was of the greatest tactical and strategical value to the enemy. The excellent observation he had from this position added enormously to the difficulty of our preparation for the attack and ensured to him ample warning of our intentions."

The use of machine guns throughout the battle was most satisfactory. Those under the Divisional Machine Gun Officer, Major J. Deane Drummond, did excellent work in overhead indirect barrage fire, which was reported most satisfactory and effective both by our own troops and by prisoners. Of the two sections left with each Brigade, the majority were sent well forward with the infantry, supported the attack and strengthened the various lines to be consolidated. When the line was finally taken and consolidated, 12 machine guns moved forward to positions east of Messines–Wytschaete Road, to put a protective barrage in front of our outpost line. These did extremely good work and assisted later on to beat off the counter-attack on the 11th Battn. Cheshire Regt.

ARTILLERY WORK.

In every case the creeping and standing barrages opened fire on their respective targets according to a most carefully arranged time-table and programme, which had been worked out in co-operation with and to meet the needs of the infantry and their estimated rates of advance. This naturally varied according to the nature of the obstacle and resistance expected.

In no case was any alteration in the artillery time-table asked for or required by the assaulting infantry, a valuable proof of the skill with which the whole scheme had been prepared.

The Brigades in each case reported that the artillery shooting was marvellously accurate and the lifts very well timed. No difficulty was experienced in keeping men well up to the barrage, and but few casualties resulted from our own artillery fire.

The standing barrages advanced from one trench system to more distant targets in such a way as to ensure that all trenches within 1,500 yards of the infantry were kept under continuous fire. Targets for the 4.5-inch, 6-inch, and 8-inch howitzers were changed directly the infantry reached points within 300 yards of their fire. The 18-pounder standing barrages remained on their various objectives till the creeping barrage arrived, then leap-frogged over other barrages to more distant lines. The creeping barrages meanwhile formed a protective barrage to cover points where the infantry were consolidating.

In the isolated cases of casualties reported from our own artillery fire, thorough investigation points to the probability that this fire was enfilade fire from the south, where the enemy were known to have a large number of guns concentrated in the neighbourhood of Deulemont and Warneton. It is also extremely difficult to determine the direction of the fire from the German high-velocity gun.

At 4.50 a.m. the guns in forward positions (Guards Divisional Artillery) had taken up the creeping barrage and at 7 a.m. the 112th Brigade R.F.A., were ordered to advance to positions in the neighbourhood of our old front trench system. These batteries were in action by 11 a.m., and took part in the creeping barrage to cover the attack by the 4th Australian Division at 3.10 p.m.

Unfortunately, one battery commander, Major Campbell and his battery staff, who had ridden on to reconnoitre gun positions, were all killed by a shell near Middle Farm, somewhat delaying a further advance of his battery which had been contemplated. The 110th Brigade R.F.A., were also ordered to advance, and came in to action near the 112th Brigade R.F.A.

The work of the F.O.Os., Lieut. Densham, Lieut. Gooding, Lieut. Hayton, and Lieut. Patterson, was invaluable, along with Lieut. L. V. Caldwell, Divisional R. A. Intelligence

Officer. It is of a particularly arduous nature and requires a clear head and a stout heart, and is usually performed by a junior officer. The F.O.Os. followed up the advance of the infantry and established O.Ps. near Four Huns Farm and Middle Farm. The view proved very disappointing owing to hedges and clumps of trees which obstructed the view from ground O.Ps. In spite of this, good work was done and much appreciated.

COUNTER-ATTACK, 1.45 p.m.

It had always been considered probable that the enemy, if driven out of his main positions, would do his best to regain possession of the ridge and that a counter-attack might be expected on our line of posts through Despagne Farm. This attack began to develop towards mid-day. German troops which had been reported earlier in the day as collecting about Gardelieu were at 12.15 p.m. reported as advancing towards our line. At 1 p.m. the 11th Battn. Cheshire Regt. again reported enemy advancing and hostile batteries in action at Delporte and Deconinck Farm. At 1.45 p.m. the expected counter-attack was delivered against posts of the Cheshires up the Blauwepoort Beek by about 600 of the enemy advancing in four waves, but was beaten off by 2.8 p.m. with heavy casualties by rifle, Lewis gun, machine gun and artillery fire.

SECOND PHASE.

About this time the 4th Australian Division were crossing the Messines–Wystschaete Road in artillery formation to prepare for their attack on Owl Trench and Odious Trench, roughly 500 yards beyond the 11th Battn. Cheshire Regt.'s line of posts.

This attack was timed to start at 3.10 p.m., delivered by two Brigades of the 4th Australian Division in line along the combined fronts of the 25th and New Zealand Divisions. At the exact moment the Australian Brigades advanced under cover of the artillery barrage, and at 4.15 p.m. a message was received that the attack appeared to have been successful and all objectives reached. Unfortunately the 12th Australian Infantry Brigade on the left appears to have pushed too far up north, thus leaving a considerable gap between their right flank and the 4th Australian Infantry Brigade.

In this gap and to the west were several enemy strong points and concrete blockhouses which offered strong resistance and could not be taken without further artillery bombardment. News, however, from the front line was very scanty, and there was at the time no reliable information as to the exact situation and position of the line held by the Australian troops. Meanwhile a reorganisation of the troops was effected, so that the 8th Battn. S. Lancs. Regt. were responsible for the southern half and the 8th Battn. Border Regt. for the northern half, both for consolidation and defence. During the night 7th 8th and following morning there was intermittent shelling of our line and at 6 p.m. the same evening a message was received that a counter-attack was moving up the valley from the south-east and artillery assistance was required. A protective barrage was accordingly put down and was apparently successful in holding the enemy to his trenches. A little later at 8.30 p.m. a heavy enemy barrage came down on our line of posts rolling back towards the Black Line, resulting in some casualties to our troops. Later on the same evening some confusion was caused by the 12th Australian Infantry Brigade bringing round a battalion from their left to fill the gap existing between their right flank and the 14th Australian Infantry Brigade. This attempt to straighten and connect up their line was not successful, and Gen. Holmes, G.O.C., 4th Australian Division, decided to make a fresh attack with artillery preparation on the strong points and portions of Odd and Owl Trenches still held by the enemy. Brig.-Gen. Baird's Brigade was also relieved by Brig.-Gen. Onslow's Brigade. The attack was carried out at 9 p.m. on the 10th June by the 50th and 52nd Battns. of the 13th Australian Infantry Brigade and was completely successful, about 100 Germans being killed and several machine guns captured.

Between 7 and 9 p.m. the enemy heavily shelled our line in rear of the Australians and along Messines Ridge, causing several casualties in this Brigade.

It had originally been intended to relieve the 52nd Australian Battn. by the 7th Infantry Brigade, but owing to the fighting continuing all night nothing could be done. The following night. 10th/11th, the 9th Corps extended their front about 700 yards to the south and the 32nd Brigade, 11th Division, took over that portion of the line.

Difficulty had been anticipated in the employment of Tanks on the front of the 25th Division, owing to the marshy nature of the ground on the line of the Steenebeek. This proved well founded as three out of the four allotted to the Division were ditched before crossing the enemy's front line in the initial attack. The fourth, commanded by 2nd Lieut. Woodcock, got safely through. The four others detailed for the subsequent attack on the further line overcame the difficulties of the journey and were of some use to the 11th Battn. Cheshire Regt. and 8th Battn. Border Regt., though little opposition was encountered. The Tank commanded by Lieut. Tuit materially assisted the latter with its machine gun fire in the capture of the position and some prisoners. The high percentage of casualties sustained by their personnel are a sufficient indication of the difficulties of their work.

The three Field Coys. R.E., and the 6th Battn. S. Wales Borderers (Pioneers) were held in Divisional Reserve, with the exception of the 106th Field Coy. R.E., who were detailed to assist the 75th Brigade in the consolidation of the new forward positions. Certain definite tasks were allotted to these troops dependent on the successful progress of the attack.

For three weeks prior to the 7th June the 6th Battn. S. Wales Borderers (Pioneers) were well employed in the revetment of the various communication trenches, construction of light trench tramways and repair of roads in the Wulverghem sector. The day of the attack two companies, A and C, with a strength of about 150 men each, commanded by Major Ellis and Capt. Owen respectively, had been detailed to clear and make good the Wulveghem–Messines Road, so that it might be available for guns and wheeled traffic as soon as possible. These two companies were detained by heavy shelling on the forward slope of the road, but shortly after 5 a.m. work had commenced and in spite of continuous shelling was carried on until late in the afternoon. By then the road was open to traffic to within 300 yards of Messines.

The other two companies, B and D, commanded by Capt. Cox and Capt. Reed-Kellett, worked on the extension of the Fort Pinkie Trench Tramway across No Man's Land in the direction of Messines, completing the same day about 400 yards of track.

The casualties to the battalion of seven officers wounded and one officer gassed, 10 other ranks killed and 61 other ranks wounded, show the trying conditions under which this highly important work was so well carried out. The work of the 106th Field Coy. R.E. was invaluable throughout the day.

One section of the 105th Field Coy. R.E. cleared a forward route to enable guns to advance from Boyle's Farm. The remainder of the company made tracks through our own trenches, and through the captured enemy's country, to be first of all practicable for mules and later for wheeled transport. These sections went forward at 4.30 a.m. to start work according to the programme. No. 1 Section with the help of 50 men of the Pioneer Battn. experienced some heavy shelling in the Steenebeek Valley, but the track was practicable for limbered wagons by 10.30 a.m. A dump for consolidating material was formed at Sloping Roof Farm, where Capt. Wall, R.E., was able to bring 12 wagon loads, the first load of wire and pickets arriving at 2 p.m., a very fine performance indeed.

The 130th Field Coy. R.E. assisted the 7th and 74th Infantry Brigades to construct communication trenches, working westwards towards our old line. The company moved forward at 7.10 a.m., when Major Macauley, D.S.O., laid out and started work on two communication trenches, afterwards known as Bob and Pip Avenues. Work was continued on these communication trenches by infantry working parties during the night.

The 106th Field Coy. R.E. was earmarked to assist the 75th Infantry Brigade for consolidation of the captured line. Three sections of the company moved forward in rear of the 8th Battn. Border Regt., one being kept in reserve but was very soon ordered up for work on the right flank. The company built two strong points and dug a continuous trench as far as possible.

During the minor operations 14th/15th June and subsequent days, much good work was done by the Field Coys. R.E., in siting, digging and consolidating a continuous trench system, including front and support lines, along the newly captured line and laying out and constructing communication trenches, machine guns positions and strong points.

The mule pack transport for taking forward quickly wire and tools for consolidation was of great value, though most of the material actually used the first night, 7th/8th, was carried forward by a battalion of infantry.

C

The whole of the arrangements for communication were under the supervision of Major E. de W. H. Bradley, M.C., K.O.Y.L.I., O.C. Divisional Signal Coy., with Brigade Signal Officers, 7th Infantry Brigade, Lieut. Pullen ; 3rd Battn. Worcester Regt., 74th Infantry Brigade, Lieut. W. H. Reynolds ; 11th Battn. Lancs. Fusiliers, 75th Infantry Brigade, Lieut. Haynes, 1st Wiltshire Regt., Royal Artillery, Capt. Foy, R.E.

The Brigade forward parties were under :—

> 7th Infantry Brigade, Lieut. Holdaway, 10th Battn. Cheshire Regt. ;
>
> 74th Infantry Brigade, Lieut. Ashburner, 11th Battn. Lancs. Fusiliers ;
>
> 75th Infantry Brigade, Lieut. Marsden, 2nd Battn. S. Lancs. Regt.

The communications may be said to have worked extremely well, and without any avoidable hitch throughout the operations. In no case was any buried cable broken by shell fire. Later on, during the advance, cable communication was only maintained by gallantry on the part of the linemen who worked unceasingly at a very difficult and lonely job under incessant fire.

A large mine was laid almost under Ontario Farm. The work was only completed and the mine ready to fire at 12 noon 6th June. This had been, owing to natural condition, a most difficult operation, and was only put through by great effort on the part of officers and other ranks of the 171st Tunnelling Coy. R.E.—Capt. Thornton, R.E., the officer in charge, was responsible for the successful termination of the scheme. The mine was successfully exploded at 3.10 a.m. on 7th June. One of the effects of the mine was to destroy the garrison or at least a large part of it, in the enemy salient, it is confidently believed.

A great deal of work was performed in the preparation of tunnelled dugouts for brigade and battalion headquarters, and no damage was done, although several received direct hits.

The full complement of chaplains were present during the battle, though somewhat differently distributed than had been the case during trench warfare or earlier operations.

> Rev. M. G. Evans accompanied troops of the 7th Infantry Brigade.

Rev. M. S. Evers accompanied troops of the 74th Infantry Brigade.

Rev. H. C. Townsend accompanied troops of the 75th Infantry Brigade.

These remained with the troops of their respective brigades throughout the battle, moving freely about amongst the men in the front line, wherever they felt their presence was giving assistance. The Commanding Officers spoke in the highest terms of their courage, calmness and helpfulness. On many occasions during this long and strenuous day, their presence gave encouragement to both officers and men.

A chaplain was also allotted to each regimental aid post, the advanced dressing station and corps main dressing station.

These were able to do equally good work in administering to the wounded, and helped in much needed ways to make more comfortable the inevitable casualties in the wake of the advance. Their presence and sympathetic help on such occasions was gratefully appreciated by all ranks.

To augment the means of getting forward supplies of all kinds to the fighting troops and to diminish the harassing work of carrying parties, a pack transport company under Capt. Finch, A.S.C., was formed from within the Division to do the work after zero hour. The company of 300 pack animals was organised in five convoys, each under an officer :—

Lieut. Green, 13th Cheshires.
Lieut. Shamier, Royal Artillery.
2nd Lieut. T. H. Richards, 6th Battn. S. Wales Borderers.
Lieut. Brown, 1st Battn. Wiltshire Regt.
Lieut. Crothers, 8th Battn. Border Regt.

Each convoy of 60 animals was organised into three gangs of 20 men and 20 animals each.

During the battle and subsequent days, stores of all kinds, including food, water, munitions and consolidating material, were pushed forward to Brigade and Battalion Headquarters by means of this pack transport company, which proved absolutely invaluable for the work.

All administrative arrangements were excellent. No hitch of any sort occurred at any time. An issue of rum was supplied actually in the assembly trenches to all troops taking part in the attack. Every man's water bottle was filled with a mixture of cold tea and lemon and an extra meal of hot soup and meat was supplied at the place of concentration between 7 and 9 p.m. before moving up to the assembly trenches. Rations were conveyed by pack animals instead of by limber and the full ration was issued the whole time. Too much credit cannot be given to the regimental first line transport for the prompt delivery of these rations to their respective units even in the front line.

During the attack of the 75th Infantry Brigade on the night 14th/15th June, Lieut. Crothers was able to take his convoy to the forward line within two or three hours of the commencement of the attack.

Large quantities of water rations, ammunition, grenades, and R.E. stores were carried up in this way, including 5,000 rounds 4.5-inch ammunition.

The trophies captured included :—

> 1 5.9-inch howitzer.
> 3 4.2-inch howitzers.
> 4 77 mm. field guns.
> 48 machine guns.
> 4 trench mortars.
> 1 electric lighting set,

together with many other miscellaneous articles.

Total number of prisoners captured :—

Officers.		Other ranks.
11	...	580 unwounded.
8	...	372 wounded.

These comprised men from many different regiments, but the large majority were Bavarians.

The collection and concentration of gun ammunition for the 18-pounders and 4.5-inch howitzers (divisional artillery) began about 14 days before the battle.

The expenditure of gun ammunition from 1st to 10th June by the 126 18-pounder guns and 34 4.5-inch howitzers :—

18-pounder	...	...	...	142,564
4.5-inch howitzers	...	...		38,500

The actual capture of the objective was in every case carried out with very few casualties, but the subsequent enemy shelling resulted in heavy losses. The enemy's artillery barrage was well timed and remarkably accurate in searching our successive and freshly consolidated lines. His heavy guns took a daily toll of casualties amongst the carrying parties, working parties, and other services in the back areas ; 90 per cent. of the total casualties were caused by shell fire, and only the remaining 10 per cent. by machine gun and rifle fire. Bombs and rifle grenades were hardly used at all by either side.

No less than 24 Company Commanders and their successors became casualties during the attack.

The total casualties were :—

	Killed.		Wounded.		Missing.
Officers ...	27	...	117	...	1
Other ranks...	501	...	2,265	...	141

It is impossible to give too much praise to the medical officers and the stretcher-bearers, in their work in front line and behind. At no time was there any congestion of wounded cases, and between 3 a.m. and midnight on the 7th June 1,549 cases of the 25th Division were conveyed to the Corps Main Dressing Station, giving an average of 73 per hour. This does not include the troops of other Divisions, who also passed through our dressing stations.

OPERATION OF 14TH-15TH JUNE.

It was decided to carry out a further attack and advance our line about 800 yards beyond the line then held by the 2nd Anzac Corps. To the 25th Division was allotted a front of attack of about 1,500 yards between the Blauweportbeek to the north and La Douve River to the south.

The 75th Infantry Brigade moved up from their camp near Neuve Eglise the evening of 12th June and proceeded to relieve the 14th Battn. Australian Infantry in their line and forward posts. The relief was completed before daybreak, the 8th Borders on the left and 2nd S. Lancs. on the right. During the afternoon of the following day, 13th June, the O.C., 8th Border Regt., not being satisfied with the report sent in by his patrols, proceeded to make a personal reconnaissance assisted by Lieut. Anderson and three men, and established the fact that the enemy were holding Les Quatre Rois Cabt, Steignast Farm and the Puits. Coming suddenly on to a small party of Germans in a trench behind some trees, Lieut. Anderson was unfortunately shot owing to the safety catch of his rifle being secured, but the remainder of the party were quickly disposed of by L.-Corpl. Robinson and Ptes. Bell and Livesay, a very creditable performance.

During the night of the 13th, much good work was done in the preparation of communication trenches and the improvement of the existing trench, but it was considerably interfered with by the heavy barrage which was put down by the enemy probably in anticipation of a further attack.

The assembly of the two battalions for the attack was completed by 6.30 p.m. Carried out in broad daylight, men being dribbled up in twos and threes behind hedges, this operation showed good leading by company officers and excellent discipline of other ranks. Snipers caused casualties to the men assembled behind the hedges, but the real significance of the movement was not detected by the enemy. From first to last this was an excellent piece of work and reflects great credit on all concerned.

At 7.30 p.m. the line moved forward under a creeping barrage in conjunction with the New Zealand Division on the right. On the left the 8th Battn. Border Regt., A, B, and D Coys. in front, C Coy. in support, commanded by Lieut. K. Strong, Capt. P. H. Coxon, Lieut. J. Duggan and Capt. J. Dawson, and on the right the 2nd S. Lancs. Regt., with A, B, and D Coys. in front and C Coy. in support, commanded by Capt. T. C. Weston, Capt. R. Neville, Lieut. H. E. House and Capt. McEwen respectively. Owing to our standing barrage falling practically on to the objective simultaneously with our advance, the enemy were unable to retreat, and in 25 minutes all the line of our objectives Fme. de la Croix—Les Quatre Rois Cabt—Gapaarde—Deconinck Farm had been gained. The enemy were found lying mostly in shell holes and improvised trenches which were quickly cleared. One or two wired strong points gave some trouble, but they were quickly outflanked, leaving several machine guns and some prisoners in our hands. The New Zealanders were equally successful, and gained their objectives without much loss or difficulty. Five minutes after the line moved forward to the attack, the enemy's barrage of 4.2's and 5.9's came down on our old front line in rear, and again about 9 p.m. the enemy's barrage came down with great intensity lasting for about half-an-hour in rear of our front line, and causing some casualties. During the night the battalions energetically consolidated and wired the posts to be ready in the event of any counter-attack.

During the night 22nd/23rd, the Division was finally withdrawn from this sector of the line, and on the 24th moved back for a well-earned rest to the Bomy Area, south of St. Omer.

The following are a list of those who received awards for services during the operations, with details of some of the more notable acts of gallantry for which the award was granted:—

2251 Pte. W. Ratcliffe, 2nd S. Lancs. Regt.

On the 14th June, 1917, during the advance at Messines, this man discovered a party of the enemy with a machine gun which was firing into our flank, and although a stretcher bearer, he voluntarily rushed the position singlehanded, killed the crew of the gun and brought the latter to our lines, afterwards opening fire with it, thus preventing many casualties and greatly assisting the operations in progress.

Awarded . . . . **V.C.**

14563 R. Sergt.-Major A. Barnes, 8th S. Lancs. Regt.

During the operations 7th—9th June, 1917, this warrant officer conducted himself with conspicuous gallantry, and under very heavy shell fire organised and got up a big supply of S.A.A., and saw it personally taken to each Company. He set a very fine example to the whole Battalion and showed great devotion to duty. This warrant officer showed gallantry also on many occasions in the Somme battle and at Ypres.

Awarded . . . . **D.C.M.**

2nd Lieut. M. L. Bernstein, 11th Lancashire Fusiliers (died).

This officer commanded his platoon with great skill and dash throughout the attack, especially in the capture of Swayne's Farm. He was wounded while waiting for the barrage to lift off October support, but led his men in and with them captured 30 Germans. He afterwards helped to re-organise until sent to the Dressing Station by his Company Commander about two hours later.

Awarded . . . . **M.C.**

12893 Pte. F. Brown, 8th Bn. Border Regt.
16232 Corpl. H. Carter, 8th Bn. Border Regt.

During the attack on Messines Ridge on June 7th, 1917, these two men had reached their objective and were hard at work consolidating, when they noted a hostile battery in action about the point o.27.a.25.45. At this moment they observed one of our tanks going across their front in an Easterly direction from the farm at o.26.d.8.8. They rushed over to the tank and called the tank officer's attention to the hostile guns and when the tank moved off to attack the position, they followed close behind. On getting closer the tank fired a broadside at the Battery and Corporal Carter and Private Brown immediately charged the position by themselves. By this time the gun team had retired to their dugout, but on two rifle shots being fired into the dugout by Pte. Brown, the team (7 in all—2 being wounded by the rifle shots) came out and surrendered themselves to Corpl. Carter and Pte. Brown, who then took possession of a helio and the gun, marking the latter, " Corpl. Carter, Pte. Brown, 8th Border Regt." This done the two men proceeded by themselves to another gun pit immediately north of the first one. Here Corpl. Carter was knocked senseless by a cylindrical stick bomb, and Pte. Brown continued on by himself and took this gun team (6 in all) prisoners. Thinking he might do more good work in this direction, Pte. Brown endeavoured to mount a stray Anzac cavalry horse, but the animal being wounded, he was unable to manage it, and returned to his Company. Corpl. Carter soon recovered and also returned.

Awarded.........**D.C.M.**
Awarded.........**D.C.M.**

Sergt. Conway, 1st Wilts Regt.

On the 7th June, 1917, during the assault on the Messines Ridge, this N.C.O. showed the greatest gallantry. Perceiving that the attack on the right of the Battalion had been hung up by a concrete post, this N.C.O. rushed with two others to assault it from the flank. In spite of heavy rifle and machine gun fire, he persisted in his attack, bombing with such skill and accuracy that the hostile garrison was killed. Unless this N.C.O. had shewn an absolute disregard of personal safety, the hostile post would probably have held up the attack for several hours.

Awarded.........**D.C.M.**

Sergt. Cook, Pioneer Sergt. 1st Wilts Regt.

On the 7th June, 1917, in storming the Messines Ridge, for most noteworthy gallantry.

This N.C.O., in spite of heavy machine gun fire and only supported by a mere handful of men, assaulted and carried two strongly fortified farms, capturing about 45 prisoners and 4 machine guns, at a most critical moment of the battle. This great success was almost entirely due to the magnificent example of dash, daring and initiative set by this N.C.O. His demeanour inspired all concerned.

Awarded.........**D.C.M.**

2nd Corpl. W. J. Cooper, 105th Field Coy. R.E.

On June 5th and 6th, this N.C.O. was engaged in making a forward track through our trenches. The track was heavily shelled several times each day, causing many casualties, but he displayed great courage and resolution in keeping his party continuously at work. This track was of much use on 7th June, 1917, for getting forward guns and supplies.

On the night 13th—14th June, 1917, with Lieut. F. M. Cooper, R.E., near Bethlehem Farm, he displayed great courage in taping out a trench under heavy shell fire.

He had been previously recommended for gallantry in the Leipsig Redoubt operations.

Awarded . . . .**M.M.**

14490 Sergt. R. Chorlton, 9th L.N. Lancs. Regt.

During the attack on Messines Ridge he took charge of his platoon after his officer had been wounded and led his men with wonderful coolness and dash, thereby inspiring great confidence in his men. The courageous manner in which he tackled a M.G. Emplacement was beyond all praise, and he succeeded in clearing about 20 of the enemy from their position. His services throughout the engagement were invaluable as was also the example to the men under his charge.

Awarded . . . .**M.M.**

7759 Rifleman J. Curtin, 2nd R. Irish Rifles.

During the attack on and capture of Messines-Wytschaete Ridge on June 7th, this Rifleman, having lost touch with his Company, collected 4 other men, went on and attacked a German machine gun in action. He killed 2 Germans working the gun and captured it, and by prompt action on his own initiative, undoubtedly saved another Battalion, that was then attacking, many casualties.

Awarded . . . .**D.C.M.**

23141 Corpl. G. Currell, 3rd Worcester Regt.

This N.C.O. was wounded while crossing No Man's Land, but still carried on and took his Lewis Gun Team to a position in advance of where the Battalion was consolidating, where he was again badly wounded, but he refused to leave his post. He eventually fainted and was carried back to the aid post.

Awarded . . . .**D.C.M.**

Capt. H. V. Dean, R.F.A.

For very gallant conduct and continuous good work when acting as Commander of 6 gun Battery during operations at Messines, June, 1917. His exceedingly good work both when observing and in obtaining information from the advanced posts was of the greatest value. He was frequently exposed to heavy fire, but always carried out his work.

Awarded . . . .**M.C.**

Sergt. William Devo, R.F.A.

On the Messines Ridge on the night of June 12th, when his Battery was being heavily shelled, an ammunition dump in a gun pit caught fire. Sergt. Devo at once rushed to the pit with water, calling to the other men to bring more. As the water seemed to have little effect, Sergt. Devo climbed on the blazing pile of ammunition and proceeded to beat out the flames with two canvas buckets. By his cool daring act, this N.C.O. saved about 300 rounds of ammunition and probably his gun.

Awarded..........D.C.M.

No. 45500 Sergt. H. Edgar, 25th Divisional Signal Section.

For coolness in collecting and leading his party which had been scattered by the hostile barrage, when in charge of a Brigade Forward Signalling Station. It was owing to his personal example that communications were successfully maintained. He had previously gained the D.C.M. on the Somme at the Leipzig Salient.

Awarded..........M.M.

40658 Sergt. H. Goodwin, R.A.M.C.

For conspicuous gallantry and devotion to duty in June, 1917, during the Battle of Messines. He showed the utmost fearlessness and untiring energy in supervising the collection of wounded from various parts of the battlefield, doing magnificent work under heavy fire of every description. He refused to be relieved until all wounded had been brought in.

Awarded..........D.C.M. and Bar.

No. 57008 Corporal J. Gray, R.F.A. (Killed.)

On 7th June, 1917, just before Zero Hour this N.C.O. went continually backwards and forwards along Snipe Avenue and Trench under very heavy shell fire laying his battery telephone wires. On the advance he accompanied his battery commander to Four Huns Farm and carried messages safely through the German barrage on four occasions. He was afterwards killed at Ypres.

Awarded..........D.C.M.

62860 Gunner F. Hodges, R.F.A., Y/25 T.M. Battery. (Wounded.)

Whilst marching through Armentieres about 11 a.m. on 15th June, 1917, with eleven other N.C.O.'s and men under an officer, Gunner Hodes, together with five men and the officer, was wounded. Athough severely wounded in the arm, he did his utmost to get the others into a place of safety. It was not until all the other men had been removed and dressed that Gunner Hodges disclosed the fact that he also had a serious wound and was in urgent need of assistance. His gallant conduct inspired the men and was instrumental in saving further casualties.

Awarded..........M.M.

65363 A./2nd Corporal J. Harfield, 130th Field Coy. R.E.

For gallantry on many occasions particularly on June 7th, 1917, when assisting to superintend the digging of a C.T. west of Middle Farm (Messines Ridge).

After the work was disorganised by enemy shells he showed great coolness in reorganising the work and set a fine example in determination and energy.

Awarded..........M.M.

10571 L./Corpl. J. Holt, 2nd S. Lancs. Regt.

For conspicuous gallantry and initiative at Messines on 14th June, 1917, when in several instances the attack was temporarily checked, he brought his Lewis Gun into action and dispersed the enemy, contributing largely towards the success of the operations.

Awarded..........D.C.M.

30482 Pte. W. Ingram, 13th Cheshire Regt. (Wounded.)

During the attack on and capture of Messines Ridge on June 7th, 1917, this man by his fearless and resolute conduct did much to give drive to that section of the attack in which he was. He was wounded in the hand but carried on, capturing at one time a Machine Gun and crew of 3 men.

Awarded..........D.C.M.

No. 48981 Pte. W. James, R.A.M.C.

This man did splendid work in removing wounded from Regina Trench after its capture on 21/10/17.

For guiding parties of stretcher bearers on three occasions through heavy shell fire at Messines on June 7th and 8th, 1917.

Awarded..........M.M. and Bar.

41670 Sergt. T. A. Johnson, R.A.M.C. (Died of wounds.)

For conspicuous gallantry when in charge of a working party constructing an A.D.S. near Wulverghem. He rescued wounded under shell fire and himself died of wounds received at the same time. May, 1917.

Awarded..........M.M.

601 Sergt. W. Lamb, 75th Machine Gun Company.

This N.C.O. was in charge of a gun team during the attack on Messines Ridge, June 7th, 1917. Soon after reaching his objective the whole of his team were put out of action by heavy hostile shell fire. He continued to serve his gun for a considerable period till his Section Officer was able to reorganise his section and send extra men to Sergt. Lamb. This N.C.O. has on every occasion, when he has been in action, displayed remarkable courage and reliability.

Awarded..........D.C.M.

No. 17284 Sergt. J. H. Lewis, 6th S. Wales Borderers.

A few days before the Messines attack, a gas shell penetrated a dug-out in which this N.C.O. and 14 men were living. The majority of the men were gassed before they had time to adjust their respirators. Sergt. Lewis was on the point of putting on his respirator when he noticed that the respirator of one of the wounded men had been broken, so he put his own respirator on the wounded man and just managed to get him out of the gas, when he was gassed himself.

Awarded.........M.M.

14364 Coy. Sergt.-Major C. Louth, 11th Cheshire Regiment.

For exceptional judgment and dash in clearing parties of the enemy out of shell holes and gun emplacements during the advance on 7/6/17. Throughout the operation is he set a splendid example by his devotion to duty.

Awarded.........D.C.M.

A./Capt. I. N. Mason, 3rd Worcester Regt. (Wounded.)

Capt. Mason was wounded early in the battle, but he refused to leave his Company until they had reached their final objective, where he collapsed from exhaustion and was carried back to the Aid post.

Awarded.........M.C.

31183 Sergt. A. J. Montell, R.G.A., X/25 T.M. Battery. (Wounded.)

In action opposite Messines on the 6th June, 1917, about midday, Sergt. Montell was badly shaken by a premature from the 2 in. Trench Mortar he was in charge of. He, nevertheless, continued to fire the gun until he was wounded by a second premature. In spite of this he attempted to carry on again, but found that his gun was too badly damaged by the second explosion to continue firing.

Sergt. Montell had served with this Battery at the front for over 18 months. He has consistently set a remarkable example to the rank and file and by his excellent work when out of the line.

Awarded.........D.C.M.

2nd Lieut. A/Capt.) A. R. Moir, 13th Cheshire Regt.

For conspicuous gallantry and devotion to duty. During an attack he handled his company with great coolness and ability, capturing and holding all objectives with skill and deliberation. His services were of great value afterwards in reorganising the battalion.

Awarded.........M.C.

2nd Lieut. A. W. H. Sime, 75th Machine Gun Company.

This officer took charge of 7 guns in the most advanced point of the infantry attack on the Messines Ridge, June 7th, 1917. He displayed great initiative, got two of his guns into action immediately the "line of posts" was formed, and was instrumental in putting out of action two enemy teams of six horses each, who were attempting to recover field guns, with the result that the guns had to be left behind by the retreating enemy.

Awarded.........M.C.

No. 19206 A/Corpl. A. Tildesley, 9th L.N. Lancs. Regt.

During the attack on Messines Ridge this N.C.O. did good work during the attack pushing well forward with only one man, using his Lewis Gun with good effect and inflicting severe losses on the enemy, Awarded . . . .**D.C.M.**

Capt. T. J. C. C. Thompson, 2nd Royal Irish Rifles. (Wounded.)

During the attack on and capture of Messines-Wytschaete Ridge on June 7th, this officer led his company with very great dash and secured all his objectives west of the Steenebeek. The 9th Loyal N. Lancs. then passed through his battalion against their objectives. Heavy rifle and machine gun fire opened from the Ridge in the neighbourhood of Middle Farm. Captain Thompson on his own initiative immediately took his own men forward and got on the flank of the Farm and took 40 prisoners, thus rendering its capture by the 9th Loyal N. Lancs. easier. This officer's company had originally a difficult task of its own to do, and distinguished itself by its dash throughout the attack. This was largely due to the personality and gallant behaviour of its Commander at all times and on all occasions. This officer was severely wounded whilst entering the Brigade's last objective, October Support. Awarded . . . .**D.S.O.**

Corpl. Watson, 25th Divnl. Signal Section. (Killed in action.)

This N.C.O. throughout the battle behaved in a most gallant manner During and after the attack on June 14th, he was mending lines outside a battalion headquarters, which were continuously heavily shelled, for 24 hours without once coming under cover, although frequently advised to do so. He was finally killed at his duty.

No. 6/42241 Pte. W. Wells, 6th S. Wales Borderers.

This man set a most noteworthy example of devotion to duty under the most trying circumstances.

On the second day of the Battle of Messines, this man was acting as a stretcher bearer to his Company, which was working on the Wulverghem-Messines Road. He remained at his post at the entrance to Messines Village the whole day, displaying the greatest coolness under heavy and continuous enemy fire. Wherever there were casualties this man was to be found doing his job.

Awarded . . . .**M.M.**

Honours and Awards, Messines Ridge, 1917

VICTORIA CROSS.

2251 Private W. Ratcliffe.. .. 2nd S. Lancs. Regt.

BAR TO D.S.O.

Major (T./Lt.-Col.) W. K. Evans 11th Cheshire Regt.

D.S.O.

Major (A./Lt.-Col.) C. W. H. Birt	8th Border Regt.
Major (T./Lt.-Col.) H. M. B. Craigie Halkett	H.L.I., attd. 9th L. N. Lancs.
Capt. K. F. D. Gattie	Bde.-Major, 75th Brigade.
Major (A./Lt.-Col.) H. R. Goodman	2nd Royal Irish Rifles.
Major J. A. Howell	10th Cheshire Regt.
T./Major J. D. Deane-Drummond	25th Divnl. M.G. Officer.
Capt. T. J. C. C. Thompson ..	4th Royal Irish Rifles, attd. 2nd Royal Irish Rifles.
Lt.-Col. A. E. Williams	4th Royal Warwickshire Regt., Commanding 1st Wilts Regt.

BAR TO MILITARY CROSS.

Lieut. (T./Capt.) R. F. J. Hayward	1st Wilts Regt.
Capt. F. G. Lescher	R.A.M.C.
2nd Lieut. J. H. Mumford ..	R.F.A.
Capt. R. Nevill	2nd S. Lancs. Regt.

MILITARY CROSS.

2nd Lieut. H. B. Brown	1st Wilts Regt.
T./2nd Lieut. B. Bebbington ..	R.F.A.
Capt. A. Birch-Jones	3rd Worcester Regt.
2nd Lieut. J. Brady	13th Cheshire Regt.
2nd Lieut. M. L. Bernstein ..	11th Lancs. Fusiliers.
Lieut. K. M. Bourne	2nd S. Lancs. Regt.
Capt. R. M. Cox	6th S. Wales Borderers.
2nd Lieut. L. F. Clist	11th Cheshire Regt.
2nd Lieut. R. J. Cholmeley ..	13th Cheshire Regt.
2nd Lieut. A. Craven	2nd S. Lancs. Regt.
2nd Lieut. A. P. Cunningham ..	8th S. Lancs. attd. 75th T.M. Batty.
Lieut. C. W. Curry	75th M.G. Coy.
Capt. P. H. Coxon	8th Border Regt.
2nd Lieut. P. F. Crothers ..	8th Border Regt.
2nd Lieut. (T./Lieut.) L. V. Caldwell.	H.Q., 25th Divnl. Artillery.
T./Lieut. F. W. Cooper	105th Field Coy. R.E.
T./Lieut. H. V. Dean	R.F.A.
Capt. J. Dawson	8th Border Regt.
2nd Lieut. T. C. Eckenstein ..	2nd S. Lancs. Regt.
2nd Lieut. A. Ferguson	2nd S. Lancs. Regt.
Lieut. E. B. Haynes	25th Divnl. Signalling Coy. R.E.
T./Lieut. J. S. Hayton	R.F.A.
Lieut. E. H. Hill	1st Wilts Regt.
2nd Lieut. B. Harris	8th S. Lancs. Regt.
2nd Lieut. F. M. H. Jones ..	3rd Worcester Regt., attd. 8th Borderers.
T./Lieut. (A./Capt.) S. B. Keast ..	130th Field Coy., R.E.
T./Capt. F. R. Laurie	9th L. N. Lancs. Regt.
T./Lieut. P. Mackinnon	130th Field Coy. R.E.

T./Lieut. F. E. Musgrave	130th Field Coy., R.E.
2nd Lieut.(A./ Capt.) I. N. Mason	3rd Worcester Regt.
T./Capt. A. R. Moir	13th Cheshire Regt.
2nd Lieut. J. M. Marsh	9th L. N. Lancs Regt.
Capt. and Adjut. W. H. McKerrow	11th Cheshire Regt.
Capt. R. le B. Nicholson	11th Cheshire Regt.
2nd Lieut. L. W. G. Owen	10th Cheshire Regt.
2nd Lieut. J. H. Pickersgill	10th Cheshire Regt.
T./ 2nd Lieut J. M. Paterson	R.F.A.
2nd Lieut. E. C. S. Parsons	1st Wilts Regt.
2nd Lieut. J. Rossiter	75th M.G. Coy.
Sergt.-Major L. J. Richardson	76th Field Ambulance.
Capt. J. Stephenson	R.A.M.C.
2nd Lieut. R. Swayne	1st Wilts Regt.
2nd Lieut. T. B. Storrell	8th S. Lancs Regt.
2nd Lieut. A. W. H. Sime	75th M.G. Coy.
Capt. (A./Major) G. Sumpter	R.F.A.
2nd Lieut. G. R. Turner	1st Wilts Regt.
Capt. E. Talbot	8th S. Lancs Regt.
Lieut. J. R. Taylor	1st Wilts. Regt.
2nd Lieut. G. R. Tanner	1st Wilts Regt.
T./Lieut. J. W. Vaughan-Williams	105th Field Coy. R.E.
T./Capt. M. A. Ward	11th Lancs Fusiliers.
T./Capt. W. A. Williams	9th King's Liverpools.
2nd Lieut. C. Wright	11th Cheshire Regt.
2nd Lieut. C. W. Warwick	8th Border Regt.
2nd Lieut. J. H. B. Young	10th Cheshire Regt.
Lieut. R. A. Young	2nd Royal Irish Rifles.

BAR TO D.C.M.

2105 Sergt. W. Evans	2nd S. Lancs Regt.

DISTINGUISHED CONDUCT MEDAL.

14780 C.S.M. J. H. Airey	10th Cheshire Regt.
5622 C.Q.M.S. (A./C.S.M.) G. Barnes	1st Wilts Regt.
18266 Pte. G. W. Barnes	1st Wilts Regt.
49939 L./Corpl. A. Barnes	13th Cheshire Regt.
14563 A./R.S.M. A. Barnes	8th S. Lancs Regt.
33267 Pte. E. E. Beach	8th Border Regt.
12893 Pte. F. Brown	8th Border Regt.
27963 Pte. T. Bell	8th Border Regt.
1978 L./Corpl. W. J. Bridge	2nd S. Lancs Regt.
23141 Corpl. G. Currell	3rd Worcester Regt.
10409 Sergt. H. Conway	1st Wilts Regt.
6416 Sergt. F. G. Cook	1st Wilts Regt.
10422 Sergt. J. Collins	10th Cheshire Regt.
9397 Corpl. (A./Sergt.) P. Conlan	2nd Royal Irish Rifles.
7759 Rfn. J. Curtin	2nd Royal Irish Rifles.
16232 Corpl. H. Carter	8th Border Regt.
18289 Pte. A. W. Dean	1st Wilts Regt.

16694	Sergt. W. Devo	R.F.A.
18484	B.S.M. R. Earle	R.F.A.
12361	Sergt. J. W. F. Forrest	3rd Worcester Regt.
14156	Sergt. S. Fletcher	11th Cheshire Regt.
57008	Corpl. J. Gray	R.F.A.
40658	Sergt. H. Goodwin	76th Field Ambulance.
14447	Pte. W. Garroway	8th Border Regt.
10329	Corpl. R. P. Harwood	1st Wilts Regt.
14884	L./Corpl. A. P. Hogarth	8th Border Regt.
14772	C.S.M. E. Higham	8th Border Regt.
10571	Pte. (L./Corpl.) J. Holt	2nd S. Lancs Regt.
10863	Pte. C. Jasper	3rd Worcester Regt.
40482	Pte. W. Ingram	13th Cheshire Regt.
41669	Sergt. C. C. Johnstone	76th Field Ambulance.
622	L./Corpl. W. Little	13th Cheshire Regt., attd. 74th T.M. Batty.
14634	C.S.M. C. Lowth	11th Cheshire Regt.
6961	Sergt. W. Lamb	75th M.G. Coy.
25319	A./Corpl. J. B. Mann	9th L. N. Lancs Regt.
15108	Pte. J. Mack	11th Lancs Fusiliers.
17628	A./Corpl. W. Mallin	2nd S. Lancs Regt.
8895	C.S.M. S. McCrea	2nd Royal Irish Rifles.
8971	C.S.M. J. W. Nolan	11th Lancs Fusiliers.
12587	Pte. G. Pugsley	2nd S. Lancs Regt.
12079	Corpl. T. Reid	8th S. Lancs Regt.
23903	L./Corpl. W. Robinson	8th Border Regt.
30334	L./Corpl. J. Swash	11th Cheshire Regt.
11327	Sergt. W. A. Thomas	10th Cheshire Regt.
19204	Corpl. A. Tildsley	9th L. N. Lancs Regt.
14678	Corpl. J. Tremble	8th Border Regt.
17525	Pte. J. Turner	2nd S. Lancs Regt.
14714	Sergt. S. Whitney	10th Cheshire Regt.

BAR TO MILITARY MEDAL.

8963	Sergt. J. F. Bridges	1st Wilts Regt.
14484	Sergt. C. Foote	8th S. Lancs Regt.
47257	2nd Corporal J. W. Goodwin	25th Divnl. Signalling Co., R.E.
41949	Sergt. A. E. Howson	R.A.M.C.
48981	Pte. W. James	R.A.M.C.

MILITARY MEDAL.

59595	Sergt. A. R. Ackland	25th Divnl. Signalling Coy., R.E.
71908	Gunner A. E. Alcock	R.F.A.
4289	Sergt. J. Alexander	195th M.G. Coy.
15451	Pte. A. Atherton	8th L. N. Lancs Regt.
4996	Sergt. J. Ashley	11th Lancs Fusiliers.
12805	Pte. A. R. Bayliff	8th Border Regt.
9713	Corpl. P. Blythe	11th Lancs Fusiliers.
14178	Sergt. H. Barnes	11th Cheshire Regt.
60601	Corpl. E. Barham	R.F.A.

134178 A./2nd Corpl. C. Baxter ..	130th Field Coy., R.E.
92457 Corpl. R. Belsten	R.F.A.
60891 Corpl. T. Brinkley	105th Field Coy., R.E.
60028 Corpl. A. Bradley	25th Divnl. Signalling Coy., R.E.
45954 2nd Corporal C. Brown ..	25th Divnl. Signalling Coy., R.E.
6047 Pte. (L./Corpl.) G. Bumstead	1st Wilts Regt.
13258 Corpl. A. Bate	3rd Worcester Regt.
27038 Sergt. A. Broster	8th L. N. Lancs Regt.
11748 Pte. W. Bannister	10th Cheshire Regt.
14521 Pte. (A./Corpl.)J. Bowden	7th T.M. Batty.
19200 Sergt. J. Brown	9th L. N. Lancs. Regt.
14862 Corpl. W. Bateson	8th Border Regt.
17552 Corpl. W. Booth	2nd S. Lancs Regt.
2562 Pte. J. Brown	2nd S. Lancs Regt.
10300 L./Corpl. T. Baxter ..	8th S. Lancs Regt.
15005 Pte. J. Brindle	8th S. Lancs Regt.
28375 L./Corpl. C. W. Braithwaite	11th Cheshire Regt.
37334 Corpl. (L./Sergt.) F. Booth	75th M.G. Coy.
72462 Bombdr. T. A. Boul ..	R.F.A.
138404 Gunner W. Bannister ..	R.F.A.
24288 Pte. J. Blucoe	9th L. N. Lancs Regt., attd. 74th T.M. Batty.
765 Pte. T. Broster	13th Cheshire Regt.
34159 L./Corpl. J. Brown ..	9th L. N. Lancs Regt.
8692 Corpl. J. Byrne	9th L. N. Lancs Regt.
29686 Pte. W. Buckley	9th L. N. Lancs Regt.
8946 Pte. F. A. Black	R.A.M.C.
66123 Pte. E. S. Buckley ..	R.A.M.C.
3489 Pte.E. Chadwick	2nd S. Lancs Regt.
76796 Gunner J. F. Clare	R.F.A.
34391 Corpl. R. Clayton	195th M.G. Coy.
6819 Corpl. C. Chalcroft	74th M.G. Coy.
92560 Pte. G. Chapman	11th Cheshire Regt.
5459 Pte. C. E. Clack	1st Wilts Regt.
6/17449 Corpl. R. Coombes ..	R.F.A.
19905 Pte. L.-Corpl. H. Cornfield	3rd Worcester Regt.
17054 Corpl. D. Cook	3rd Worcester Regt.
23818 Pte. H. Chilton	8th L. N. Lancs. Regt.
378 Sergt. G. Cobley	13th Cheshire Regt.
7995 Sergt. G. Caldicott	2nd S. Lancs. Regt.
10203 L.-Corpl. H. V. Carter ..	2nd S. Lancs. Regt.
12208 Pte. G. Clayton	8th S. Lancs. Regt.
16972 L.-Corpl. F. Crilly	8th S. Lancs. Regt.
18260 Corpl. S. Catterall	75th T.M. Battery.
27872 Pte. H. Capstick	2nd S. Lancs. Regt.
65613 2/Corpl. W. J. Cooper ..	105th Field Co., R.E.
80078 Sergt. C. A. Curtis	Essex Yeo., attd. 74th Bde. H.Q.
9679 L.-Corpl. H. Coquard ..	11th Lancs. Fusiliers.

14490 Sergt. R. Chorlton ..	.. 9th L. N. Lancs. Regt.
40549 Rifleman J. P. Caithness ..	.. 2nd Royal Irish Rifles.
5111 Rifleman J. Caldwell	.. 2nd R. Irish Rifles.
7163 Sergt. J. J. Crosier ..	.. 2nd R. Irish Rifles.
M2/082625 Pte. H. P. Creasley	.. A.S.C. M.T., attd. 76th Field Ambulance.
M1/07776 Corpl. E. R. Cooper	.. A.S.C., M.T., attd. 76th Field Ambulance.
883 Corpl. H. Davies	.. 2nd S. Lancs. Regt.
43007 Gunner J. Daley ..	.. R.F.A.
14531 L.-Corpl. W. Davies	.. 8th S. Lancs. Regt.
14929 Sergt. A. Dykes	.. 8th S. Lancs. Regt.
24996 Driver E. Dale ..	.. R.F.A.
86904 2/Corpl. H. Duggan	.. 25th Divl. Sig. Co., R.E.
70146 Pte. E. S. Dalley ..	.. R.A.M.C.
21684 Pte. C. Davies	.. 10th Cheshire Regt.
18025 Sergt. L. Dunn	.. 11th Cheshire Regt.
30275 Pte. F. Dewsnup ..	.. 8th Border Regt.
27012 Sergt. T. Driver ..	.. 11th Cheshire Regt.
49482 L.-Corpl. H. Dood ..	.. 11th Cheshire Regt.
47245 A/Sergt. R. Demay	.. 25th Divl. Sig. Co., R.E.
152137 Gunner G. Dolan ..	.. R.F.A.
45550 Sergt. H. Edgar ..	.. 25th Divl. Sig. Co., R.E.
16530 L.-Sergt. W. D. Evans	.. 10th Cheshire Regt.
3/38 Corpl. P. C. A. Evans	.. 1st Wilts, Regt.
7672 Pte. A. Eastwood ..	.. 11th Lancs. Fusiliers.
34502 Sergt. J. Edmunds	.. 25th D.A.C.
9427 L.-Corpl. W. English	.. 2nd S. Lancs. Regt.
8476 Sergt. W. Fowden ..	.. 11th Lancs. Fusiliers.
81204 Pte. H. Ferguson ..	.. R.A.M.C.
8083 Sergt. E. C. Fletcher	.. 1st Wilts Regt.
315161 Pte. A. French ..	.. 1st Wilts Regt.
8526 L.-Corpl. A. Farrell ..	.. 2nd Royal Irish Rifles.
8821 Corpl. J. Faragher ..	.. 11th Lancs. Fusiliers.
30656 L.-Sergt. J. Fisher	.. J. Fisher.
68286 Gunner G. F. Facey	.. R.F.A.
4972 Pte. H. Fairclough ..	.. 13th Cheshire Regt.
11349 L.-Corpl. T. Gibbons	.. 8th S. Lancs. Regt.
33648 A/Sergt. W. Gee ..	.. A.S.C.
47750 Sergt. J. E. Gass ..	.. 25th Divl. Sig. Coy. R.E.
14887 L.-Corpl. J. T. Garrahy	.. 105th Field Coy. R.E.
12729 Sapper G. Gillham	.. 25th Divl. Sig. Co. R.E.
31500 Sergt. F. G. Gooch ..	.. 25th Divl. Sig. Coy. R.E.
9757 Corpl. C. Grearson ..	.. 1st Wilts Regt.
18524 Pte. L.-Corpl. L. Griffin	.. 1st Wilts Regt.
6770 Rifleman T. Gamble	.. 2nd R. Irish Rifles.
16915 Pte. J. Ganderton ..	.. 2nd S. Lancs. Regt.
6922 Sergt. B. Gunn ..	.. 75th M.G. Coy.
16985 L.-Corpl. G. Greenall	.. 11th Cheshire Regt.
82696 Fitter E. J. Griffin	.. R.F.A.
8721 L.-Corpl. T. Gallaway	.. 2nd R. Irish Rifles.
49299 Sergt. T. Grinshaw	.. 13th Cheshire Regt.

24439 Pte. H. Gobbold	13th Cheshire Regt.
M2/022126 Sergt. W. M. Green	A.S.C., M.T.
55278 Pte. J. R. Hamer	195th M.G. Coy.
5826 L.-Corpl. T. Hodgkinson	11th Lancs. Fusiliers.
65363 A/2/Corpl. J. Harfield	130th Field Coy. R.E.
39768 Pte. W. T. Harwood	R.A.M.C.
22236 Pte. L.-Corpl. C. Hall	1st Wilts Regt.
29898 Corpl. J. F. Horler	1st Wilts Regt.
23224 Pte. L.-Corpl. W. Hagger	3rd Worcester Regt.
25281 Pte. W. Hackney	10th Cheshire Regt.
50841 Pte. J. E. Holt	10th Cheshire Regt.
23435 Pte. H. Holliwood	11th Lancs. Fusiliers.
5556 Pte. I. Hunter.	8th Border Regt.
14768 Sergt. C. Hyde	8th Border Regt.
31051 Pte. A. Hodkinson	8th S. Lancs. Regt.
34703 L/Corpl. T. Hadfield	11th Cheshire Regt.
18029 Pte. E. J. Hine	11th Cheshire Regt.
1675 Pte. W. Heyes	2nd S. Lancs. Regt.
52605 Pte. W. Horrells	11th Cheshire Regt.
24515 Sergt. H. Hughes	11th Cheshire Regt.
11243 Pte. J. Heywood	8th Border Regt.
14872 L.-Cpl.C. A.S. Hainsworth	8th Border Regt.
17675 Pte. F. Hodges	Y/25 T.M. Battery.
8615 Sergt. J. F. Haslam	11th Lancs. Fusiliers.
19123 Sergt. W. Helm	9th Lancs. Regt.
43035 L.-Corpl. D. J. James	R.A.M.C.
75531 Pte. E. A. Jones	R.A.M.C.
9065 Pte. C. Inchley	1st Wilts Regt.
8293 Sergt. W. Johnson	3rd Worcester Regt.
14979 Pte. A. Jones	10th Cheshire Regt.
8037 Rifleman E. Johnson	2nd R. Irish Rifles.
17936 L.-Corpl. A. Jones	11th Cheshire Regt.
34 Corpl. W. J. Joynson	13th Ches. attd. 74th T.M. Batty.
76716 Pte. G. L. Jolly	R.A.M.C.
29825 Corpl. G. Kitcher	1st Wilts Regt.
996 Corpl. J. H. Keggan	13th Cheshire Regt.
5915 Rifleman J. Kavanagh	2nd R. Irish Rifles.
5357 Rifleman H. Kernahan	2nd Royal Irish Rifles.
134404 Driver A. Kellett	A.S.C.
14325 Pte. F. Leeson	8th Border Regt.
15003 Sergt. T. Lewis	8th S. Lancs. Regt.
74330 Sapper A. Lawson	25th Divl. Sig. Co., R.E.
95384 Sergt. I. B. Law	130th Field Coy. R.E.
9983 Pte. E. W. Leftly	1st Wilts Regt.
12017 Sergt. C. L. Lewis	1st Wilts Regt.
29778 Pte. F. Lloyd	9th L.N. Lancs. Regt.
35573 Pte. A. V. Lock	11th Lancs. Fusiliers.
1573 Corpl. J. Loughran	2nd S. Lancs. Regt.
12802 L.-Sergt. B. Lowery	2nd S. Lancs. Regt.
35289 Pte. S. Lewis	8th S. Lancs. Regt.
6/17284 Sergt. J. H. Lewis	6th S. Wales Borderers.
36628 Pte. A. Lyons	8th S. Lancs. Regt.

18536 Pte. G. H. Livesey	.. ..	8th Border Regt.
20901 Pte. W. Langton	.. ..	8th Border Regt.
8470 L.-Corpl. W. McLeod	..	2nd S. Lancs. Regt.
6/17210 Corpl. T. Maiden	.. ..	6th S. Wales Borderers.
50559 Pte. R. Marriott		R.A.M.C.
17960 Sergt. T. McGuire	..	R.A.M.C.
35959 Pte. J. B. Moss	..	R.A.M.C.
74 Pte. D. Mullin	.. ..	R.A.M.C.
8901 Sergt. T. Marks		1st Wilts Regt.
8425 Pte. F. Moran	..	3rd Worcester Regt.
9362 L./Corpl. M. McNulty	..	2nd Royal Irish Rifles.
30049 Pte. T. Mergerson	..	9th L. N. Lancs Regt.
24095 L./Corpl. L. Moss	..	13th Cheshire Regt.
14330 Sergt. H. Mason	..	2nd S. Lancs. Regt.
17395 Pte. D. Misell		2nd S. Lancs. Regt.
12766 Pte. F. McLoughlin		2nd S. Lancs. Regt.
29181 L./Corpl. W. F. Moulder	..	74th M.G. Coy.
14820 Pte. W. Miller		9th L. N. Lancs. Regt.
41846 Pte. W. H. Mancey		R.A.M.C.
41760 Pte. W. Marsh	..	R.A.M.C.
8848 Rfn. W. McIlwraith		2nd Royal Irish Rifles.
67026 Sergt. J. Miller	..	130th Field Coy., R.E.,
40335 Pte. W. A. Morley	..	R.A.M.C.
10791 Rfn. W. McGate	..	2nd Royal Irish Rifles.
44420 A./Sergt. A. Neale	..	130th Field Coy., R.E.
57236 Corpl. J. Nixon	..	R.E.
13029 Pte. H. Northrop	..	11th Cheshire Regt.
57205 Sapper E. J. O'Shea		R.E.
40690 Pte. S. Oldham	..	R.A.M.C.
8005 Sergt. J. O'Shea	..	2nd Royal Irish Rifles.
15765 Sergt. G. Ousby	..	8th Border Regt.
28632 L./Corpl: J. Ostler	..	13th Cheshire Regt.
59150 L./Corpl. H. H. O'Connor		R.A.M.C.
43108 Sergt. A. Porter	.. ..	105th Field Coy., R.E.
33212 Pte. A. Pearce	.. ..	1st Wilts Regt.
30131 Pte. A. L. Peacre	.. ..	1st Wilts Regt.
7427 Sergt. S. Pearce	.. ..	1st Wilts Regt.
42646 Corpl. L. G. Phillipson	..	7th M.G. Coy.
14560 A./C.S.M. L. Pritchard	..	8th S. Lancs. Regt.
52661 Pte. W. Pimblott	..	11th Cheshire Regt.
32699 Pte. W. Prestner	..	11th Cheshire Regt.
2088 Pte. J. Price	.. ..	2nd S. Lancs. Regt.
545702 Pte. (A./Sergt.) H. Rayner		R.A.M.C.
16656 Pte. A. Rushton	..	9th L. N. Lancs. Regt.
437 Corpl. T. Robinson	..	13th Cheshire Regt.
40002 Pte. C. A. Rosser	..	11th Lancs Fusiliers.
2251 Pte. W. Ratcliffe	..	2nd S. Lancs. Regt.
14549 L./Corpl. W. Rae	..	8th Border Regt.
1869 L./Corpl. W. Roulston	..	2nd S. Lancs. Regt.
7053 A./ Corpl. T. Robertson	..	11th Lancs. Fusiliers.
7311 Sergt. J. Riley	.. ..	2nd Royal Irish Rifles.
14663 L./Corpl. G. Stamper	..	8th Border Regt.

107162 Sapper G. H. Smith	..	R.E.
120995 Gunner H. Shillock	..	R.F.A.
65178 Sergt. W. Saunders	..	105th Field Coy., R.E.
65249 L./Corpl. G. Shepherd	..	105th Field Coy., R.E.
563 Pte. G. H. Stevens	..	R.A.M.C. attd. 1st Wilts.
28757 Pte. J. Speed	..	3rd Worcester Regt.
17620 Pte. F. Stanley	..	8th L. N. Lancs. Regt.
18121 Pte. (L./Corpl.) G. Stevenson		7th M.G. Coy.
39225 Sergt. C. E. Smith	..	R.A.M.C.
33229 Pte. A. W. Slade	..	9th L. N. Lancs. Regt.
13733 L./Corpl. R. Sorley	..	9th L. N. Lancs. Regt.
34748 Pte. R. T. Stroud	..	9th L. N. Lancs. Regt.
5964 Sergt. S. Scott	..	8th Border Regt.
12124 L./Corpl. G. Seddon		8th Border Regt.
19677 Pte. W. Stewart	..	2nd S. Lancs. Regt.
29657 Pte. R. Suter	..	2nd S. Lancs. Regt.
15233 Sergt. G. Smith	..	8th S. Lancs. Regt.
6972 Pte. J. S. Schofield	..	75th M.G. Coy.
6909 Pte. (L./Corpl.) E. Simpson	..	75th M.G. Coy.
16861 L./Corpl. J. Smith	..	11th Cheshire Regt.
73155 Sergt. A. E. Saunders	..	R.F.A.
44269 Pte. (L./Corpl.) A. W. Spencer		11th Cheshire Regt.
17971 Pte. R. Sparks	..	13th Cheshire Regt.
6770 Corpl. E. Simpson	..	74th M.G. Coy.
58627 L./Corpl. J. W. Todd	..	195th M.G. Coy.
61397 Corpl. S. Tutton	..	R.F.A.
400073 Corpl. R. Tierney	..	R.A.M.C.
19356 Pte. (L./Corpl.) B. E. Telling		1st Wilts Regt.
49579 Pte. R. Templeton	..	13th Cheshire Regt.
26659 Sergt. (A./C.S.M.) W. Tinkler.		11th Lancs. Fusiliers.
5854 L./Corpl. W. Troughton	..	8th Border Regt.
14505 Sergt. T. Taylor	..	8th S. Lancs. Regt.
5830 Sergt. G. Turner	..	11th Lancs. Fusiliers.
990 L./Corpl. J. Taylor	..	13th Cheshire Regt.
67215 Gunner R. Vaughan	..	R.F.A.
17844 Pte. H. Victor	..	8th S. Lancs. Regt. attd. 75th M.G. Coy.
74288 Driver R. C. Williams	..	R.F.A.
16704 Pte. S. Wilcox	..	11th Cheshire Regt.
95672 Sapper B. Wright	..	130th Field Coy., R.E.
6/42241 Pte. W. Wells	..	6th S. Wales Borderers.
38978 Sergt. R. Watts	..	R.A.M.C.
29833 Pte. (L./Corpl.) S. Ward	..	1st Wilts Regt.
10786 Pte. (L.Corpl.) L. A. Williams		1st Wilts Regt.
29771 Pte. H. Wiltshire	..	1st Wilts Regt.
32325 Pte. R. J. Witt	..	1st Wilts Regt.
7832 Corpl. A. Witts	..	1st Wilts Regt.
14883 Sergt. A. T. Webster	..	10th Cheshire Regt.
098 Corpl. W. H. Woods	..	2nd Royal Irish Rifles.

273812 Pte. G. Walsh	..	..	74th M.G. Coy.
21581 Pte. S. Wright	..	..	8th Border Regt.
14799 Sergt. E. Wilkinson		..	8th Border Regt.
44270 Pte. H. Whitby	..	..	11th Cheshire Regt.
525 Pte. B. Whyte..	..	..	11th Cheshire Regt.
17856 Pte. S. Woodward	..	..	11th Cheshire Regt.
173308 Gunner C. D. Withers		..	R.F.A.
49583 Pte. J. Watson	..	..	13th Cheshire Regt.
14642 Sergt. F. Whittle	..	..	9th L. N. Lancs Regt.

CHAPTER IV.

Ypres, 24th June to 10th September, 1917.

YPRES AND WESTHOEK RIDGE.

A S soon as the attack and capture of the Messines and Wystchaete Ridge had been successfully accomplished on the 7th June and the following days, preparations were made for the main offensive east and north of Ypres. On the 10th June, the 5th Army took over command from Boesinghe to the north with the IInd, XIXth, XIVth and XVIIIth Corps.

The 25th Division which had been resting round Bomy, 15 miles south of St. Omer since the 24th June, moved up on the 7th and 8th July by route march and bus to Ypres, and the IInd Corp's forward area, with the exception of the 74th Brigade (Brig.-Gen. Bethel), which remained in the training area for another fortnight.

The divisional artillery on its withdrawal from the battle front at Messines, marched direct on the 6th July to the Ypres area and at once commenced work on preparing gun positions and transporting ammunition. The work of the Divisional Ammunition Column was a remarkable performance. Between 8th and 13th July, the Divisional Ammunition Column carried up 17,445 rounds (389 wagon loads) to the battery positions along roads and tracks which were seldom free from enemy shell fire. On one night alone, the 11th/12th July, 64 wagon loads containing 7,000 rounds of ammunition were driven up and all reached their destination except seven wagon loads which were destroyed by enemy shell fire.

The 105th and 130th Field Coys. R.E., under Major Lynam, M.C., and Major Macaulay, D.S.O., had been engaged for some weeks on preparing gun positions, shell-proof machine gun emplacements, brigade and battery headquarter dugouts, dressing station, aid posts, water supply, storage, and other work. Large working parties from the 75th Brigade were now supplied to relieve men of the 8th Division for work with the tunnelling companies and other technical troops, and by this means a great deal of hard work was accomplished in the necessary preparations for the coming attack. The R. Irish Rifles who were also detached from the 74th Brigade for work in the front area, carried through a very useful piece of work in the construction of a new diversion road between Withnies Cabaret, 1½ miles south of Ypres Station, and the plank road known as Warneton Road.

This was finished in five days, a record performance. The work involved cutting through the dry bed of the canal and the Ypres–Menin Railway. It was fascined throughout, and proved of the utmost value in avoiding the heavily shelled area known as Shrapnel Corner, and its neighbourhood near Ypres.

On the 8th July, the Divisional Headquarters moved to Busseboom, 7 miles south south-west of Ypres. The 7th Brigade relieved the Brigades of the 8th Division in the left sector of the IInd Corps front on the 9th/10th July, and the G.O.C., 25th Division, took over command of the sector from the 8th Division the following day. The 16th July the 7th Brigade was relieved by the 75th Brigade in the front line, and on the 22nd/23rd Brigades of the 8th Division again took over the left sector of the IInd Corps front from the 25th Division, and the G.O.C., 8th Division, assumed command on 24th July.

During the previous fortnight there were no incidents of special importance on the Divisional front. Aerial and artillery activity increased as the date fixed for the attack approached, but work went on steadily, though working parties were considerably hampered by the splendid observation afforded the enemy from their dominating positions east of Ypres, as well as the continuous shelling by gas shells. In spite of this it was found that infantry carrying parties were able to take up rations by day instead of by night with very much greater rapidity and at the same time they suffered fewer casualties.

Preparations were completed by the 26th July, but the attack was postponed for a few days, and it was not until the morning of the 31st July at 3.50 a.m. that the 5th Army, with the IInd, XIXth, XIVth, and XVIIIth Corps delivered its assault on the German main line defences.

On the right of the 5th Army, the 2nd Army made a subsidiary attack with the Xth Corps, and on its left the 1st French Army advanced its right in conformity with the British advance.

The front of the 5th Army attack extended from the Zillebeeke-Zandvoorde Road to Boesinghe inclusive, a distance of about 7½ miles. The IInd Corps attacked with the 24th Division, 30th Division, and 8th Division in the line supported by the 18th Division in the centre and the 25th Division on the left in Corps reserve. Their front was supported by numerous field and heavy batteries, and tanks.

On the greater part of the front, especially north of the Ypres-Roulers Railway, the resistance of the German defence was quickly overcome and good progress made, but along the IInd Corps front, in the difficult country east of Ypres, determined opposition was encountered.

In their advance south of the Ypres-Roulers Railway, the 30th and 8th Divisions were engaged in very heavy and continuous fighting on both sides of the Menin Road, and after the capture of the German first line system, our troops were held up in front of the two small woods known as Inverness Copse and Glencorse Wood, and the strongly fortified position known as Stirling Castle, which crowned the ridge, but on the left, units of the 8th Division continued their advance and reached the outskirts of the village of Westhoek.

The 7th and 75th Brigades of the 25th Division moved up from their place of assembly at the Belgian Chateau at 8.30 a.m., the 31st July, and were held in readiness about 2,000 yards in rear of the assaulting troops. As, however, that attack was unexpectedly held up on the right, the Brigades of the 25th Division were not called upon to undertake the *role* previously assigned to them and to pass through the 8th Division and to carry on the advance.

The 74th Brigade, less one battalion, the 13th Cheshires, was placed at the disposal of the Chief Engineer, IInd Corps, for work on roads and water supply, together with the 6th S. Wales Borderers (Pioneers) and the 106th and 130th Field Coys. R.E. These troops proved invaluable during the subsequent days in opening up communication with the forward line, digging communcation trenches, laying mule tracks and consolidation of the new front line generally.

The afternoon of the 1st August, the 7th and 75th Brigades relieved the 8th Division in the front line and held the sector

until the 4th August, when they were in turn relieved by the
74th Brigade. The division now held the Westhoek Ridge
and Bellewaarde Ridge, with the 74th Brigade in the front
line, the 75th Brigade in support at Ypres, and the 7th
Brigade in reserve west of Ypres. Owing to the incessant
rain and bad weather conditions, the troops in the front line
were, during the next few days, relieved every 48 hours, and
at the same time preparations were energetically pushed
forward for another attack on the German line of defences
along Inverness Copse, Glencorse Wood, and the Westhoek Ridge. The capture of these positions was most
important in order to give observation to the east and south
east.

To complete the capture of the Westhoek Ridge was the
task allotted to the 74th Brigade (under Brig.-Gen. H. K.
Bethell). On the right the 55th and 54th Brigades of the 18th
Division had as their objectives the capture of the Inverness
Copse and Glencorse Wood.

The 74th Brigade attacked with all four battalions in the
front line, along a front of about 2,000 yards, with its left
flank on the Ypres-Roulers Railway. The 13th Cheshires,
Lt.-Col. L. H. K. Finch,D. S.O., the 2nd R.I. Rifles, Major
Rose, the 9th L.N. Lancs, Major Wienholt, D.S.O., and the
11th Lancs. Fusiliers, Lt.-Col. E. C. de R. Martin, M.C.

By vigorous patrolling, most of the ground comprising the
objective of the 11th Lancs. Fusiliers was already won before
the battle.

The assembly of the assaulting troops was complete by
3.25 a.m. 10th August. At 4.25 a.m. the whole line moved
forward to the attack and were well clear of our line when
the enemy's barrage came down a few minutes later. From
right to left, the 13th Cheshires, with its four Companies
under the command of Capt. A. Payne, wounded, and succeeded by Lieut. Huffan, Lieut. L. E. M. Green, M.C.,
Captain W. C. Wilkinson, killed, and succeeded by 2nd
Lieut. Silcock, who afterwards died of wounds. The 2nd
Battn. R.I. Rifles, with A, B, C, and D Coys. under the
command of Capt. J. B. McArevey, M.C., Capt. R. T.
Jeffares, Capt. T. McAlindon, M.C., and Lieut. S. V. Morgan,
afterwards killed. The four companies of the 9th L.N.
Lancs, commanded by Capt. W. F. Lowdon, Capt.
E. V. Green, M.C., killed, and succeeded by 2nd Lieut.

A. L. Kemp, Lieut. H. J. Priestland, wounded, and succeeded by 2nd Lieut. McCarthy, and Capt. H. Everett, respectively, and the 11th Lancs. Fusiliers, with A, B, C, and D Coys., under the command of Capt. T. Rufus, Capt. R. K. Beswick, M.C., Lieut. G. A. Keir, and Capt. G. A. Potts.

The supporting artillery of five brigades R.F.A. opened simultaneously and throughout the day replied with great promptitude to all signals for assistance against numerous attempted counter attacks.

The attack was a complete success in every way and notwithstanding some severe fighting, particularly on the right, the whole Brigade was firmly established on its objectives by 5.30 a.m. Several strong points, " pill boxes " and fortified houses garrisoned with machine guns, offered considerable opposition, but were quickly rushed and captured by assaulting troops. One rather more important fortified post in front of the 13th Cheshires held up the attack for some little time, but was eventually reduced by a well organised and vigorous assault in which two Stokes mortars, under Captain Solly, played an important part.

The Irish Rifles rushed Westhoek, together with the two strong points, and took the garrison before the enemy realised they were being attacked. The N. Lancs advanced in three waves. The first company was held up by a strong point which they quickly surrounded, and captured a machine gun and its detachment. The battalion had many casualties from snipers, especially on the right flank. German aeroplanes also flew low and fired on any bodies of troops moving in the open.

The 11th Lancs. Fusiliers captured several machine guns and a good many prisoners. The whole garrison of one strong point about 38 men, was killed whilst trying to escape.

From first to last the plans and their execution reflected the greatest credit on all concerned. The progress of the troops was in exact accordance with the time table previously laid down. The artillery support was excellent and all along the line the assaulting troops reported that the artillery shooting was wonderfully accurate and the barrage remarkably effective. The administrative arrangements allowed of no hitch—the pack transport was well organised and boldly used—food, water, ammunition, consolidating material and all necessary stores reached the fighting troops with a minimum of delay and the carrying parties supplied by the supporting battalions worked with untiring energy. Signal communication under the Brigade Signal Officer, Lieut. Reynolds, was excellent and throughout the day it was found possible, in spite of the difficult circumstances, to maintain direct communication by means of daylight lamps with all battalions in the front line with the exception of the 11th Lancs.Fusiliers. Runners, had, as usual, a particularly difficult task, which they performed with the greatest gallantry and despatch.

Private Seel, 9th L.N. Lancs Regt., whilst carrying a message from Brigade Headquarters, was badly wounded by a shell in both legs and head. In spite of his wounds, this runner crawled on through the heavy bombardment and succeeded in delivering his despatches. He afterwards received the D.C.M.

The medical arrangements for the evacuation of the wounded were excellent and with the experience learnt at Messines gave the most complete satisfaction to the units of the Brigade.

Casualties were severe—12 officers, 146 other ranks, killed, and 35 officers, 998 other ranks wounded, with over 100 other ranks missing, of whom the majority were killed. Of these the 13th Cheshires suffered most severely, losing 19 officers and 395 other ranks, including Lt.-Col. Finch and Major Nares, both wounded.

Consolidation was actively pressed on under cover of the protective barrage, but owing to the difficulties encountered by the 18th Division against Glencorse Wood, our right was somewhat unduly exposed. Enemy snipers and machine guns, safely concealed in the wood, caused considerable trouble and a certain number of casualties. It was therefore found impossible to dig at once a continuous line or to provide working parties for digging communication trenches. During the day the 106th and 130th Field Coys. R.E. worked with the greatest energy under the most trying circumstances and continuous shell fire.

Three battalions of the 7th Brigade, the 1st Wilts, Worcesters and 10th Cheshires, were placed at the disposal of General Bethell, 74th Brigade, to be used if the necessity arose. The Worcesters gave close support to the 13th Cheshires, and eventually Lt.-Col. Whalley, 3rd Worcesters, assumed command of the residue of the 13th Cheshires.

The 10th Cheshires also moved forward in close support to the Westhoek Ridge, whilst the 1st Wilts were retained in reserve, suffering many casualties from shell fire.

Throughout the 10th August and the night of the 10th/11th several determined enemy counter-attacks were made on our new positions. In nearly every case timely information was got through to the Artillery by either S.O.S. Signal, daylight lamps, pigeons, or runners, and the attacking forces were broken up in their assembly positions.

On one occasion at 7.15 p.m., the 10th August, the S.O.S. signal being obscured by smoke, the situation to the front of the 11th Lancs. Fusiliers became somewhat critical, but the German troops were driven back by machine guns, Lewis guns and rifle fire. The men of all units used their rifles with great effect, and events proved the extreme value of the musketry and field firing practices which had been so energetically carried out in the training areas, whenever the Division had been out of the line.

Machine guns were at all times made the fullest use of, both in barrage fire and in close support of the infantry. Two machine guns, which were pushed well forward by Major Deane-Drummond, 25th Division Machine Gun Officer, alone fired 10,000 rounds during the day and rendered invaluable assistance in enfilading counter-attacks and breaking up enemy concentration.

The 11th/12th August, the 75th Brigade relieved units of the 74th Brigade in the new line and the following nights the 56th and 8th Divisions took over the right and left sectors respectively of the Divisional front. At 10 a.m., 14th August, the G.O.C., 25th Division, handed over command, and on the 17th and following days, Divisional Headquarters moved back to Steenwoorde and the Division was withdrawn to the Steenwoorde and Eecke area.

The 7th Brigade followed on the 23rd August, whilst the 6th S. Wales Borderers (Pioneers) were left for work in the front line under the Chief Engineer, 2nd Corps.

The 25th Divisional Artillery were withdrawn on the 23rd August for a short rest to 30th August, when they again went forward and came into action in their former positions.

On the 30th August, the 7th Brigade moved up once more to Ypres, followed on the 1st September by the 74th and 75th Brigades, and the Division took over on the following day, the portions of the Front held by the 23rd and 47th Divisions. This sector now comprised Westhoek Ridge and trenches in front of Glencorse Wood and Stirling Castle.

Heavy and continuous fighting had taken place in the immediate neighbourhood with varying success, but it had not been possible in all cases to maintain the ground won previously by the 8th and 56th Divisions. The Divisional front was now held by two brigades, with one in support and much work was done in consolidation and improvement of the existing defences during the next few days.

The 9th September, the 25th Division was finally relieved by the 47th Division, and the G.O.C., 47th Division, assumed command the following day.

Divisional Headquarters moved to 1st Army area, in the neighbourhood of Bethune, and units of the Division proceeded to the same area by route march on the 10th September and following days.

The following is a list of those who received awards for services during the operations, with details of some of the more notable acts of gallantry for which the award was granted.

Lieut. W. Atkinson, R.F.A., 25th D.A.C. (Died of wounds.)

This officer supervised the filling up of gun positions with ammunition from July 8th to July 13th, 1917 (5 consecutive nights) in the vicinity of Zillebeeke. The entire work was admirably carried out—invariably under heavy shell fire—and the full amount of ammunition delivered 3 days in advance of the time allowance for the purpose.

On the night 12th—13th July, he was mainly responsible for the organisation and supervision of an ammunition convoy—consisting of 64 wagons and 384 animals—which came under a very heavy barrage of enemy fire, involving casualties to the extent of 16 personnel and 44 animals.

His conduct was equally commendable at Messines Ridge action, and he has consistently shown the greatest coolness and daring in the performance of his duties when under shell fire.

On the night 17th—18th July, this officer was in charge of an ammunition convoy, which suffered 7 casualties, including himself. He died of wounds on 19th July, and never lived to receive the Military Cross which had been previously awarded to him.

Awarded . . . . M.C.

No. 134178 A./Corporal C. Baxter, 130th Field Coy. R.E.

For gallant conduct on many occasions, including the following :—

On the night 2nd/3rd August, 1917, on the Westhoek Ridge, he worked for three hours under heavy and continuous shell fire, taping support trenches and assisting infantry working parties to dig them.

On the night 7th/8th August, 1917, on the Westhoek Ridge, he taped out a C.T. required by the Infantry holding the line, to facilitate assembly for the attack on 10th August, 1917, and met working parties from a new formation and put them on to the work.

On the 10th August, 1917, he took part in the final attack on the Westhoek Ridge. When his officer was killed and his party disorganised by shell fire, he collected and re-organised them, carried the wire to the new front line and returned for more.

Awarded . . . . **Bar to M.M.**

22423 Sergt. F. Borkin, R.F.A.

For great resource and coolness when bringing up his gun and other transport to the position near L'Ecole, Ypres, on the night 15th/16th July, 1917. When one of the vehicles was damaged and had to be abandoned, he took up the remainder and then returned with parts to replace those damaged and brought the wagon to the position. All this was under very heavy shell fire and extremely difficult conditions. This N.C.O. was killed 2 weeks later.

Awarded . . . . **D.C.M.**

66014 Private P. S. Cross, R.A.M.C.

At Ypres on August 10th this man went through a heavy barrage to get to cases at R.A. post on Bellewaarde Ridge, and carried cases back under heavy shell fire.

Awarded . . . . **M.M.**

Lieutenant W. H. Densham, R.F.A.

The Battery position of A/110 near Ypres was heavily shelled on July 20th, 1917. The shelling ignited four gun pits, six ammunition dumps and the camouflage netting, covering the position. Immediately the fire broke out, Lieut. Densham gathered together a party of men and led them to the burning pits and dumps. The personal example he set the men and his organisation of the party was such that the fires were extinguished in spite of heavy shelling by the enemy, and exploding ammunition in the dumps. The initiative displayed by this officer and his prompt action undoubtedly saved four guns from being put out of action, and a large quantity of ammunition from destruction.

Awarded . . . . **M.C.**

50799 Pte. E. Duddles, 11th Cheshire Regt.

This man acted as a Company Stretcher Bearer during the operations on the Westhoek Ridge on the 31/7/17 to 4/8/17 and carried out his duties with conspicuous gallantry. On the 31/7/17 he volunteered to go out and bring in a badly wounded officer. On the 4/8/17 he continued to carry a stretcher case, although he had been wounded and his right arm shattered by a shell splinter. Both these acts were carried out under intense enemy shelling. Pte. Duddles displayed complete personal disregard of danger, thus encouraging the other stretcher bearers working with him.

Awarded . . . . **D.C.M.**

14476 L.-Corpl. T. Durham, 8th S. Lancs. Regt.

During the operation on the Westhoek Ridge on 3/8/17, on two separate occasions this N.C.O. went out in front of our line alone to bring in wounded during daylight under heavy machine gun and sniper's fire, but was unable to drag them out of the mud, but at night with a party of three more, he rescued them. On another occasion during daylight he crawled out alone and reconnoitred five old gun emplacements 350 yards in front, bringing back most valuable information.

Awarded . . . . **M.M.**

W/1232 Sergt. J. Fisher, 13th Cheshire Regt.

Recommended for gallantry and leadership. On August 10th, 1917, during the attack on and capture of Westhoek Ridge, when all the officers of his Company had become casualties, he took over command of his Company, and by his fearless example, inspired his men to consolidate their position in spite of a severe enemy barrage.

Later on in the day, when ordered, he withdrew his Company from their advanced position and showed great initiative in consolidating the Battalions on the left Flank.

Awarded . . . . **D.C.M.**

31900 Pte. A. Flewitt, 2nd S. Lancashire Regt.

For conspicuous bravery and devotion to duty on 2nd August, 1917. A section of trench occupied by his Company was blown in, killing an officer and burying a number of men. Pte. Flewitt, at great personal risk and under heavy shell fire, rushed to the spot and worked until all had been extricated. He then volunteered to carry men to the dressing station under fire, returning afterwards to help in repairing the damaged trench. He was a splendid example to the men of his Company, of presence of mind and devotion to duty.

Awarded . . . . **M.M.**

6/17476 Pte. L. Frayne, 6th S. Wales Borderers. (Wounded.)

During the attack on Westhoek Ridge this man was given an important report to carry back to the report centre. Pte. Frayne had already been wounded and on his way to the report centre he was buried three times and blinded in one eye by a splinter. In spite of his wounds and the barrage, Pte. Frayne carried on without even waiting to have his wounds dressed and delivered the report. He showed great determination and bravery.

Awarded . . . . **D.C.M.**

63013 Gunner G. Grant, R.F.A.

For extreme gallantry in rescuing a man under intense shell fire at Ypres.

Awarded . . . . **D.C.M.**

2nd Lieut. H. P. Grenier, 11th Lancashire Fusiliers.

On 7th August, 1917, when the Battalion was in action on Westhoek Ridge, this officer successively seized and occupied an advanced post about 300 yards in front of the left Battalion sector. On 10th August, after the attack on the Black Line, the enemy made two attempts to rush his post. He beat off both attacks, killing 48 of the enemy with his Lewis guns and Rifle Sections at close range. At 6.30 p.m. on 10th August, he observed a Battalion of the enemy massing in the wood in Hanebeer Valley, and got information back to Headquarters. Later in the evening when the enemy counter-attacked the Westhoek Ridge, his men with a Vickers gun also caused the enemy severe loss by enfilade fire.

He held his post for four days under trying circumstances.

Awarded . . . . **M.C.**

14542 A./C.S.M. R. Gilbertson, 9th L. N. Lancs. Regt.

During the attack on Westhoek Ridge on 10th August, 1917, this N.C.O. led a storming party attacking a strong point which was captured with its garrison of 2 officers and 12 men.

Throughout the attack he led his men with absolute disregard of danger, and himself accounted for several of the enemy. During the consolidation he was invaluable to his Company officer and in the counter-attack which followed, his coolness and control of the rifle fire gave confidence to every one and the repulse of the enemy was due mainly to his organisation of our defence.

Awarded . . . . **D.C.M.**

66896 Gunner J. R. Hill, R.F.A.

For conspicuous gallantry and devotion to duty at Ypres on 31st July, 1917, in trying to maintain communication by visual signalling when all other means had failed. When he found he could not get through by this means, he acted as runner, repeating his journey three times, although the shell fire was intense. Throughout the day he was invaluable to the F.O.O. by reason of his pluck and energetic support.

Awarded . . . . **D.C.M.**

1081 Sergt. F. Hall, D.C.M., 11th Lancs. Fusiliers.

On Westhoek Ridge on 10/8/17, this N.C.O. went with his platoon to capture two enemy strong points. His platoon officer was killed, but he continued and captured two machine guns and 52 prisoners. In one strong point where 38 enemy had been captured, they later resisted, blew up the captured machine gun, killed a Lewis gun team and attempted to escape. He with his men killed them all. He himself was wounded. He behaved throughout with extraordinary gallantry.

Awarded . . . . **M.M.**

Captain N. G. Hay-Will, 11th Cheshire Regt.

For conspicuous courage and leadership during the operations on Westhoek Ridge from 31/7/17 to 6/8/17, and 11/8/17 to 14/8/17

During these periods, Captain Hay-Will commanded his company, which was holding an advanced position on the Westhoek Ridge, with great ability under extremely bad weather conditions and continual heavy shelling. Under these trying conditions Captain Hay-Will showed the greatest coolness and cheerfulness and set a fine example to his men. On the 12/8/17 and 13/8/17, Captain Hay-Will in the absence of his Commanding Officer took command of the Battalion which had just taken over a line of Battle Outposts. Under heavy shell fire, and constantly exposed to hostile machine gun and rifle fire, this officer personally reconnoitred the whole of his Battalion sector and obtained information of great value regarding our own and the enemy's disposition. The information obtained was absolutely essential for the successful co-operation of the artillery in repelling hostile counter-attacks which developed during that period.

Awarded . . . . M.C.

41669 Sergt. C. C. Johnstone, R.A.M.C.

For conspicuous gallantry and devotion to duty. He entered an ammunition dump that was under heavy shell fire in search of wounded. With heroic disregard for his personal safety he removed and dressed a number of wounded men. He then went to a building that was ablaze and rescued two more. As he got clear of the building it collapsed, exploding the ammunition stored inside. He personally saved several lives that without his presence of mind must have been sacrificed, and his absolute fearlessness and devotion cannot be too highly praised.

Awarded . . . . D.C.M.

A./Major W. G. Mackay, R.F.A.

For continuous good work and frequent acts of gallantry during the operations at Messines and Ypres in 1917. This officer did very valuable F.O.O. and Liaison work and frequently exposed himself to great danger in order to have the most thorough knowledge of the situation.

Awarded . . . . M.C.

No. 9619 Pte. A. B. Mills, 1st Wilts. Regt.

This man in the line at Railway Wood, east of Ypres, during a heavy hostile bombardment on the night of July 18th, was twice blown over by a shell and buried. At the time he was doing duty at a Lewis gun post, and the remainder of the team were wounded by the shells. On each occasion of being buried, he struggled up on to his feet again and opened fire with his gun, thus setting a magnificent example to those about him.

Awarded . . . . M.M.

Capt. W. McFarlane, M.C., R.A.M.C., attd. 11th Lancs. Fusiliers.

From 6th August to 11th August, 1917, on Westhoek Ridge, this officer in spite of very severe shelling, made daily rounds to aid posts established by him with all Companies and moved freely to all centres where his services could be of assistance.

His coolness under fire, his absolute disregard of danger, his cheerfulness under all circumstances and his constant devotion to his work which was always most ably carried out, not only resulted in the promptest alleviation of the wounded and their successful evacuation but also set the finest possible example to all ranks, inspiring confidence and courage under very trying circumstances.

His work on the Messines Ridge in June, 1917, was of the same high standard.

Awarded . . . . Bar to M.C.

13733 L./Corpl. R. McSorley, 9th L. N. Lancs. Regt.

At Westhoek Ridge on the 10th August, 1917, this N.C.O., showing absolute disregard for danger, brought down wounded men from exposed positions, and dressed them under continuous shell and rifle fire.

During enemy counter-attack he took charge of a Lewis gun of which the team had been knocked out and was thereby of great assistance in repelling the attack.

After consolidation this N.C.O. was continually bringing in and attending to wounded in very exposed places, and under heavy sniping fire. He evacuated all wounded in an excellent manner, and his example and coolness made the stretcher-bearers one of the finest parties of men of the day.

Awarded . . . . D.C.M.

Lieut. (A./Capt.) J. B. McArevey, 2nd Royal Irish Rifles.

While the Battalion was holding the line, previous to the attack on Westhoek Ridge, this officer was indefatigable in work of consolidation in keeping the men fit, cheery and alert, especially during the time when the enemy was shelling the line. He organised his Company for the attack on Westhoek in an excellent manner, and though time was limited, every man knew his job. He showed great judgment in selecting the men for the difficult operation of storming the dug-outs at Westhoek, capture of which was essential for the success of the advance. He led his Company in the attack with great dash and skill, and on reaching the objective, quickly got them in hand and commenced consolidating. He worked under most tiring conditions on August 11th, all his officers and N.C.O.'s with the exception of one Lance-Corporal, having become casualties.

Awarded . . . . M.C.

8722 L./Corpl. T. McTeague, 2nd Royal Irish Rifles. (Wounded.)

During the attack on Westhoek on August 19th, 1917, this N.C.O. showed great courage, dash and initiative. Whenever any signs of resistance was offered in his line of advance, he immediately rushed to the danger. He set to flight and captured two pickets of the enemy. His example was truly magnificent and inspired all around him. After reaching the objective he carried an important message back to the Battalion headquarters. While crossing the enemy barrage, he was wounded ; nevertheless he delivered safely the message. Instead of getting his wound dressed at the time, he immediately returned to his company and remained at duty doing excellent work for the remainder of the operation.

Awarded .... **D.C.M.**

T./Major E. P. Nares, 13th Cheshire Regiment. (Wounded.)

For conspicuous gallantry and devotion to duty. When nearly all the officers of his battalion had become casualties, he rendered invaluable service to his commanding officer in planning the assembly arrangements of his battalion, which subsequently took and held all its objectives in spite of having lost 60 per cent. of its men. It was due to the example set by these two officers that the ground was maintained against many determined hostile counter-attacks, and after Major Nares had successfully established communication with other units on either flank he was very severely wounded whilst returning to report to his commanding officer. His gallantry and devotion to duty deserved the highest praise.

Awarded .... **M.C.**

58358 Corpl. R. P. Roberts, 195th Machine Gun Coy.

On the 8th August, 1917, near Kit and Kat, a Vickers gun team of 5 men were buried by shell fire. Under heavy fire, Corpl. Roberts, unaided, went to the assistance of the team and dug out the men buried and assisted the men who were only wounded.

On the 10th August, 1917, at a position south-east of Frezenberg, when in charge of a Vickers gun in an advanced isolated post he showed exceptional powers of leadership and gallantry. Despite heavy sniping fire and shelling, he kept his gun in action for 24 hours, inflicting heavy casualties on a large party of the enemy advancing towards Hanebeke Wood from the direction of Anzac. Later, finding he could obtain a better field of fire by moving forward to an exposed position, he did not hesitate to do so. He has always shown exceptional bravery.

Lt.-Col. Martin, Commanding 11th Bn. Lancashire Fusiliers, also commended this man.

Awarded .... **M.M.**

6/42289 Pte. Reacher, 6th S. Wales Borderers.

This man was a stretcher bearer and did most excellent work on the Warrington and Menin roads. Both of these roads were regularly shelled throughout the day and night and the working parties suffered very heavily. At all times Pte. Reader went about his work of tending the wounded, absolutely regardless of himself. One particularly bad morning on the Menin Road all work was stopped and the parties were withdrawn, but Pte. Reader stayed on devoting himself to the wounded. He was killed on the Bellewarde Ridge whilst dressing a wounded man. His record is one of tremendous gallantry and devotion to duty.

Awarded .... **M.M.**

10453 Pte. W. Swanborough, 1st Wilts Regt. (Wounded.)

This man while doing duty as a runner on the night 3rd/4th August, 1917, displayed the utmost gallantry and devotion to duty. He was carrying a message from battalion headquarters to the Brigade Forward Station when he was severely wounded by a heavy shell which broke both his arms and injured his legs. In spite of the great pain which he was suffering, he succeeded in reaching the Brigade Station by crawling and was able to deliver the message. The moment he had done this he fainted from exhaustion.

Awarded . . . . M.M.

Lieut. R. Strong, M.C., 8th Border Regt.

For exceptional bravery and consistent devotion to duty as Intelligence Officer during a particularly severe tour of duty in the front line, 5th/9th September, 1917. This officer went out on patrol on three successive nights across exceedingly difficult country and obtained valuable information as to the location and strength of the enemy's advanced posts. On the night 8th/9th September he stood in an exposed position under a very heavy enemy bombardment, and was thus able to keep his C.O. informed as to the situation, not only on his own front, but also on those of neighbouring units.

Awarded . . . . Bar to M.C.

32012 Sergt. Tyer, 2nd S. Lancashire Regiment.

For conspicuous gallantry and devotion to duty on 3rd August, 1917, when in charge of a platoon. Several officers were casualties, and there were no stretcher bearers available. He at great personal risk made several journeys with wounded men through a heavy barrage.

Awarded . . . . M.M.

7608 Sergt. G. Tucker, 3rd Worcester Regt.

This N.C.O., who was acting Coy.-Sergt.-Major, showed great coolness and gallantry under intense shell fire in organising the defence of his company and assisting his Company Commander in every respect. He also did excellent work in digging out men who had been buried by shells.

Awarded . . . . D.C.M.

2nd Lieut. A. W. Vint, 3rd Worcester Regt.

On Westhoek Ridge this officer was in command of " C " Company which was supporting the 13th Cheshire Regt., when he was told to attack a strong point which was holding up the left flank of the battalion. He showed great initiative and gallantry and with a few men attacked the strong point, capturing many prisoners.

Awarded . . . . M.C.

T./Lieut. J. W. Vaughan-Williams, 105th Field Coy., R.E.

On 8th, 10th and 12th August, when constructing a plank road near Hell Fire Corner, he was heavily shelled several times each day.

His party was scattered several times, but he immediately rallied them, and by his determination, leadership and infectious coolness, kept them steadily at work in spite of further shelling.

Awarded . . . . **M.C.**

21581 Pte. S. Wright, M.M., 8th Border Regt.

On 4th August, during operations in front of Ypres, Pte. Wright was one of a stretcher party in charge of Pte. Langley. His disregard of personal danger enabled him to assist Langley when he was buried, and in getting the stretcher case through the heavy enemy barrage to the Aid Post. He has throughout the operations shown the greatest daring and has been outstanding in his fearless behaviour.

Awarded . . . . **Bar to M.M.**

Honours and Awards, Ypres, 1917.

BAR TO D.S.O.

Capt. T/Lt.-Colonel L. H. K. Finch   13th Cheshire Regt.
Major W. H. M. Wienholt   ..   9th L. N. Lancs. Regt.

DISTINGUISHED SERVICE ORDER.

Bt. Lt.-Col., T/Brig.-Gen. H. K.
   Bethell   ..   ..   Commanding 74th Inf. Bde.
Major, Hon. W. E. Guinness   ..   Bde. Major 74th Bde.
Bt. Major T/Lt.-Col. E. C. de R.
   Martin   ..   ..   11th Lancs. Fusiliers.
Capt. T/Lt.-Col. W. Tyrrell   ..   76th Field Ambulance.
Major T/Lt.-Col. P. R. Whalley   ..   3rd Worcester Regt.

BAR TO MILITARY CROSS.

Capt. J. H. E. Dean   ..   ..   13th Cheshire Regt.
Lieut. W. H. Reynolds   ..   ..   25th Div. Signalling Coy., R.E.
Lieut. R. Strong   ..   ..   ..   8th Border Regt.
Rev. Capt. M. S Evers   ..   ..   C. F., attd. 9th L. N. Lancs.
Capt. W. McFarlane   .   ..   R.A.M.C., attd. 11th Lancs. Fus.

MILITARY CROSS.

2nd Lieut. W. Atkinson   ..   ..   25th D.A.C.
2nd Lieut. H. V. Barrett   ..   ..   R.F.A.
2nd Lieut. H. K. Banks   ..   ..   R.F.A.
2nd Lieut. A. Brewer   ..   ..   3rd Worcester Regt.
T/Lieut. C. F. Bilson   ..   ..   105th Field Coy., R.E.
T/Lieut. A. C. R. David   ..   ..   R.F.A.
Lieut. W. H. Densham   ..   ..   R.F.A.
T/Capt. H. Everit   ..   ..   ..   9th L. N. Lancs. Regt.
Capt. P. A. Foy   ..   ..   ..   25th Div. Signalling Co., R.E.
2nd Lieut. F. J. B. Gardner   ..   R.F.A.

Lieut. L. E. M. Green	13th Cheshire Regt
2nd Lieut. H. P. Grenier	11th Lancs. Fusiliers.
2nd Lieut. G. W. Hughes	13th Cheshire Regt.
2nd Lieut. W. O. Holmes	9th L N. Lancs. Regt.
Capt. N. G. Hay-Will	11th Cheshire Regt.
2nd Lieut. G. W. Hawkins ..	8th Border Regt.
Lieut. W. J. Ishister	R.A.M.C.
Lieut. D. Jenkins	6th S. Wales Borderers.
Lieut. R. S. Kennedy	R.A.M.C.
2nd Lieut. J. Kane-Smith ..	R.F.A.
2nd Lieut. M. C. Kay	R.F.A.
Capt. W. F. Lowdon	9th L.N. Lancs. Regt.
Capt. G. E. Lindsay	R.A.M.C.
2nd Lieut. T. F. McCarthy ..	9th L.N. Lancs. Regt.
2nd Lieut. T. McAlindon	2nd R. Irish Rifles.
Lieut. J. B. McArivey	2nd R. Irish Rifles.
T./Capt. (A./Major) W. G. MacKay	R.F.A.
Capt. E. P. Nares	13th Cheshire Regt.
Capt. J. I. O'Sullivan	R.A.M.C.
Capt. A. Reid-Kellett	6th S. Wales Borderers.
2nd Lieut. A. E. A. E. Reid ..	R.F.A.
Capt. R. de R. Rose	2nd R. Irish Rifles.
2nd Lieut. J. H. Richards.. ..	6th S. Wales Borderers.
Lieut. J. C. Shepherd	R.F.A.
Capt. W. B. Solly	11th Lancs. Fusiliers.
Capt. J. Stephenson	R.A.M.C.
2nd Lieut. A. W. Vint	3rd Worcester Regt.
2nd Lieut. T. C. Wallis	2nd R. Irish Rifles.
2nd Lieut. R. S. Walsh	2nd R. Irish Rifles.
2nd Lieut. O. W. Waldron ..	74th M.G. Coy.
Lieut. T. C. D. Watt	R.A.M.C., attd. 10th Cheshire Regt.

BAR TO D.C.M.

40658 Sergt. H. Goodwin	76th Field Ambulance.

DISTINGUISHED CONDUCT MEDAL.

Adjutant R. M. G. Ammann ..	H.Q., 75th Infantry Bde.
17804 C.Q.M.S. W. H. Batchelor	10th Cheshire Regt.
24223 Sergt. F. Borkin	R.F.A.
925165 Gunner N. Browne ..	R.F.A.
28110 L.-Corpl. E. Boon	13th Cheshire Regt.
4951 Sergt. G. Bellis	2nd R. Irish Rifles.
50799 Pte. E. Duddles	11th Cheshire Regt.
6/17476 Pte. L. Frayne	6th S. Wales Borderers
1232 Sergt. J. Fisher	13th Cheshire Regt.
29812 Pte. D. Godson	3rd Worcester Regt.
14542 Sergt. R. Gilbertson ..	9th L.N. Lancs. Regt.
63013 Gunner G. Grant	R.F.A.
67012 Bdr. S. A. Hatt	R.F.A.
66892 Gunner J. Hill	R.F.A.

1188 Sergt. J. Lally	13th Cheshire Regt.
20887 Sergt. C. Lanbourne	74th M.G. Coy.
63141 Sergt. H. Macmilian	R.F.A.
13733 L.-Corpl. R. McSorley	9th L. N. Lancs. Regt.
8722 L.-Corpl. T. McTeague	2nd R. Irish Rifles.
925127 Sergt. H. C. Norris	R.F.A.
2004 Sergt. F. Robinson	11th Lancs. Fusiliers.
43895 Sergt. J. Ronald	74th M.G. Coy.
25330 Private T. F. Seel	9th L. N. Lancs. Regt.
7608 Sergt. G. Tucker	3rd Worcester Regt.
6436 L.-Corpl. J. Wright	2nd R. Irish Rifles.
47243 Sergt. A. K. Young	25th Divnl. Signalling Coy. R.E.

BAR TO MILITARY MEDAL.

134178 A/Corpl. C. Baxter	130th Field Coy. R.E.
47750 Sergt. J. E. Gass	25th Divnl. Signal Coy.
15008 Pte. J. G. Harvey	3rd Worcester Regt.
213184 Pte. (L.-Corpl.) A. Mathers	10th Cheshire Regt.
95412 L.-Corpl. W. H. Nicholls	130th Field Coy. R.E.
60040 Sergt. J. Paddock	25th Divnl. Signalling Coy. R.E.
2088 Pte. J. Price	2nd S. Lancs. Regt.
6/17437 Sergt. A. J. Quinton	6th S. Wales Borderers.
12258 Sergt. W. O. Smith	R.F.A.
1041 A./Corpl. E. Sorrell	2nd S. Lancs. Regt.
28581 Pte. S. Wright	8th Border Regt.

MILITARY MEDAL.

20750 Driver W. Armstrong	25th D.A.C.
82679 Gunner J. Austin	R.F.A.
91049 L.-Corpl. R. Adamson	130th Field Coy. R.E.
66762 Sapper J. Austin	25th Divl. Signal Coy.
18387 Sergt. A. Anderson	9th L. N. Lancs. Regt.
32975 Pte. G. Ainsworth	13th Cheshire Regt.
7795 Rifleman J. Atkinson	2nd R. Irish Rifles.
25986 Pte. W. Brooke	13th Cheshires attd. 74th T.M. Batty.
95926 Sergt. H. Breeze	105th Field Coy. R.E.
146543 Sapper F. Bott	105th Field Coy. R.E.
65253 A./Corpl. P. J. B. Bowsher	130th Field Coy. R.E.
123178 A./Corpl. E. Baxter	R.E.
38027 Pte. E. Brownhill	R.A.M.C.
8709 Sergt. R. Buncle	3rd Worcester Regt.
35562 Corpl. J. Batley	9th L. N. Lancs. Regt.
49943 Pte. F. Brandreth	13th Cheshire Regt.
27465 Pte. J. Briars	13th Cheshire Regt.
200540 Sergt. E. Blythe	13th Cheshire Regt.
10763 L.-Corpl. W. Bostock	13th Cheshire Regt.
304 Corpl. M. Banon	13th Cheshire Regt.
8272 Pte. W. Boyd	11th Lancs. Fusiliers.
4948 Rfn. E. Bartaby	2nd Royal Irish Rifles.
4753 Sergt. R. Bevan	2nd Royal Irish Rifles.
30217 Pte. J. Black	8th Border Regt.

12896 Pte. J. W. Brown	..	8th Border Regt.
75990 Driver D. Curtis	..	25th D.A.C.
6/16973 Pte. F. Carter	..	6th S. Wales Borderers.
6297 Sergt. C. W. Coleman	..	1st Wilts Regt.
40458 Pte. F. W. L. Cross	..	R.A.M.C.
66014 Pte. D. S. Cross	..	R.A.M.C.
47262 Sapper G. Curry	..	25th Divnl. Signalling Coy.
40827 Pte. H. Coles	..	3rd Worcester Regt.
35515 L.-Corpl. T. F. Cox	..	3rd Worcester Regt.
25441 Pte. J. Chorlton	..	9th L. N. Lancs. Regt.
24277 L.-Corpl. T. Cross	..	9th L. N. Lancs. Regt.
5717 Pte. R. Costello	..	2nd Royal Irish Rifles.
4981 L.-Corpl. L. Clarke	..	2nd Royal Irish Rifles.
43023 Rfn. T. Courtney	..	2nd Royal Irish Rifles.
29803 Pte. A. Corless	..	2nd S. Lancs. Regt.
24248 Sergt. F. Cross	..	11th Cheshire Regt.
49864 Pte. J. Craven	..	11th Cheshire Regt.
52562 Pte. H. Clarke	..	11th Cheshire Regt.
37191 Sergt. H. Dillon	..	25th D.A.C.
94254 A./2nd Corpl. G.T. Dymock		130th Field Coy. R.E.
65075 Sapper J. Dore	..	130th Field Coy. R.E.
81323 Pte. G. Dickson	..	R.A.M.C.
39779 Sergt. G. Davis	..	3rd Worcester Regt.
29774 Pte. W. Davies	..	9th L. N. Lancs. Regt.
15984 Sergt. H. Dixon	..	9th L. N. Lancs. Regt.
51035 Pte. J. Daly	..	13th Cheshire Regt.
14719 Pte. J. W. Dood	..	13th Cheshire Regt.
7860 C.Q.M.S. J. Dixon	..	2nd S. Lancs. Regt.
32054 Pte. H. Day	..	8th S. Lancs. Regt.
14476 L.-Corpl. T. Durham	..	8th S. Lancs. Regt.
925060 Gunner G. H. Donovan		R.F.A.
60203 L.-Corpl. J. Evason	..	105th Field Coy. R.E.
21403 Corpl. G. T. Edwards	..	8th Border Regt.
34054 Pte. R. Evers	..	3rd Worcester Regt.
34523 Pte. E. Elphick	..	9th L. N. Lancs. Regt.
49201 Pte. A. G. Evans	..	13th Cheshire Regt.
22410 Sergt. J. Eddleston	..	8th S. Lancs. Regt.
15129 Corpl. W. Ellwood		8th Border Regt.
73928 Pte. J. Fraser	..	R.A.M.C.
35022 Pte. J. Foster	..	R.A.M.C.
537 Pte. T. Fitzpatrick	..	13th Cheshire Regt.
37599 Pte. W. Freeman	..	11th Lancs. Fusiliers.
12150 Pte. W. Fowler	..	11th Lancs. Fusiliers.
5937 Rfn. T. Fay ..	..	2nd Royal Irish Rifles.
31900 Pte. A. Flewitt	..	2nd S. Lancs. Regt.
23801 Gunner R. Graham	..	R.F.A.
22399 Sergt. C. Grime	..	9th L. N. Lancs. Regt.
54048 Sapper E. Green	..	130th Field Coy. R.E.
5294 Pte. J. Griffen	..	11th Lancs. Fusilliers.
6771 Sergt. F. Green	..	74th M.G. Coy.
67205 Sergt. R. Gray	..	R.F.A.
2755 Pte. S. Gates	..	2nd S. Lancs. Regt.
17570 Pte. E. Graham	..	8th Border Regt.

57114 Driver W. Hurst	..	..	R.F.A.
6/17016 Pte. J. Horrobin		..	6th S. Wales Borderers.
47777 Sergt. C. Hollamby		..	25th Divnl. Signals.
P.3 Sergt. S. H. Hallaway			M.M.P.
4536 Rfn. T. Hall	..	..	2nd Royal Irish Rifles.
41663 Pte. J. Horrocks	..	..	R.A.M.C.
39820 Pte. J. Hammond	..	..	3rd Worcester Regt.
27828 Pte. J. Hewitson		..	9th L. N. Lancs. Regt.
12820 Pte. C. Horan	..	..	9th L. N. Lancs. Regt.
23527 Pte. H. Horton	..	..	9th L. N. Lancs. Regt.
265856 Pte. S. Holland	..	..	13th Cheshire Regt.
49980 Pte. H. Horton	..	..	13th Cheshire Regt.
51037 Pte. T. Hunt	..	..	13th Cheshire Regt.
26155 Pte. J. E. Hamlett		..	13th Cheshire Regt.
31328 Pte. J. Hodson	..	..	11th Lancs. Fusiliers.
235203 Pte. E. Howarth	..	..	11th Lancs. Fusiliers.
1081 Sergt. F. Hall	..	..	11th Lancs. Fusiliers.
7005 Pte. H. Harrop	..	..	11th Lancs. Fusiliers.
4084 Pte. T. Hopwood	..	..	11th Lancs. Fusiliers.
32245 Pte. R. J. Hardwick		..	11th Lancs. Fusiliers.
9861 Pte. W. T. Hart	..	..	11th Lancs. Fusiliers.
42617 Rfn. S. Hoffman	..	..	2nd Royal Irish Rifles.
49979 Pte. E. Horsfield	..	..	13th Cheshire Regt.
8779 Corpl. A. J. Hemmett		..	2nd S. Lancs. Regt.
995 Corpl. (L.-Sergt.) J. Hughes	..		2nd S. Lancs. Regt.
59746 Driver G. Hazlett	..	..	R.F.A.
14765 Corpl. J. D. Hayhurst		..	8th Border Regt.
30215 Sergt. I. Hodgson	..	..	8th Border Regt.
9044 C.Q.M.S. C. H. Hall		..	2nd S. Lancs. Regt.
198875 2nd Corporal H. W. Jackson			25th Divnl. Signals.
65147 Corpl. J. B. Jones	..	..	105th Field Coy. R.E.
66763 Sapper E. Jones	..	..	25th Divnl. Signals.
7780 Corpl. J. Joll	..	..	11th Lancs. Fusiliers.
1517 Pte. J. Jackson	..	..	8th S. Lancs. Regt.
20960 Private R. James	..	..	11th Cheshire Regt.
45552 Sergt. T. Kenworthy		..	25th D.A.C.
79193 Pte. T. B. Kersey	..	..	R.A.M.C.
10892 Corpl. H. Kay	..	..	9th L. N. Lancs. Regt.
11385 Pte. W. Kerr	..	..	11th Cheshire Regt.
22988 L.-Corpl. G. Kingsbury		..	8th Border Regt.
6782 Rfn. P. Killeen	..	..	2nd Royal Irish Rifles.
10758 Sergt. E. Lingard	..	..	10th Cheshire Regt.
41444 Sergt. G. Langley	..	..	R.F.A.
6/25921 Pte. F. Lipyeart	..	..	6th S. Wales Borderers.
65278 2nd Corpl. R. B. Lindsay			105th Field Coy. R.E.
67695 Sapper H. A. Lowe		..	25th Divnl. Signalling Coy.
26164 Pte. A. Leek	..	..	3rd Worcester Regt.
49991 Pte. R. Lee	..	..	13th Cheshire Regt.
50270 Pte. J. Lee	..	..	13th Cheshire Regt.
62914 L.-Corpl. S. T. Luke		..	74th M. G. Coy.
31591 Pte. E. Lea	..	..	2nd S. Lancs. Regt.
23294 Pte. E. Langley	..	..	8th Border Regt.
T4/045736 Corpl. G. Martin		..	25th Divnl. Train, A.S.C.

9619 Pte. A. B. Mills	1st Wilts Regt.
105338 Pte. F. Messenger ..	R.A.M.C.
90941 Driver W. Morrison ..	105th Field Coy. R.E.
74119 Pte. E. Manning	R.A.M.C.
13664 Pte. W. Martin	3rd Worcester Regt.
29764 Pte. J. W. Mason	9th L. N. Lancs. Regt.
14563 Pte. J. Mills	9th L. N. Lancs. Regt.
10411 Rfn. J. McDermott ..	2nd Royal Irish Rifles.
7674 L.-Sergt. A. Macfarlane ..	2nd Royal Irish Rifles.
17628 Pte. (A.-Corpl.) W. Mallin	2nd S. Lancs. Regt.
19714 Pte. T. Mitchell	2nd S. Lancs. Regt.
36031 Pte. W. J. Martin	8th S. Lancs. Regt.
13856 Pte. W. Mumford	8th Border Regt.
24315 L./Corpl. F. Moreton ..	11th Cheshire Regt.
15979 Pte. D. McGivering ..	11th Cheshire Regt.
11892 Corpl. R. Morton	11th Cheshire Regt.
185556 Gunner E. T. A. Murga-troyd	R.F.A.
3414 Corpl. H. McLoughlin ..	2nd S. Lancs. Regt.
14718 Pte. A. Nichols	8th S. Lancs. Regt.
24483 L.-Corpl. R. Newby ..	13th Cheshire Regt.
2967 Pte. S. Nesbit	2nd S. Lancs. Regt.
26078 Sergt. A. Nelson	8th Border Regt.
9814 Pte. H. Orr	11th Lancs. Fusiliers.
43952 Rfn. W. Otway	2nd Royal Irish Rifles.
6781 Rfn. M. O'Gara	2nd Royal Irish Rifles.
19214 Pte. R. M. Owen	11th Lancs. Fusiliers.
6/16899 Pte. J. Price	6th S. Wales Borderers.
29823 Pte. (L.-Corpl.) J. Postans	1st Wilts Regt.
48908 Sapper E. Perris	25th Divnl. Signal Coy.
71737 Gunner J. Pinkney.. ..	R.F.A.
103469 Sapper G. H. A. Phipps ..	105th Field Coy. R.E.
29951 Driver R. Parkinson ..	105th Field Coy. R.E.
33276 Pte. W. Ponger	3rd Worcester Regt.
3259 L./Corpl. W. Portlock ..	9th L. N. Lancs. Regt.
3/34667 Pte. H. Parker	13th Cheshire Regt.
18525 Pte. G. A. Pemberton ..	13th Cheshire Regt.
50001 L./Corpl. T. Pemberton ..	13th Cheshire Regt.
63628 Driver J. S. Penfold ..	25th D.A.C.
11109 Rfn. N. Preston	2nd Royal Irish Rifles, attd. 74th T.M. Batty.
17681 Pte. E. Phillips	11th Cheshire Regt.
15057 Sergt. W. Prestidge ..	2nd S. Lancs. Regt.
66979 Driver F. Robinson ..	R.F.A.
6/42289 Pte. F. Reacher	6th S. Wales Borderers.
14998 Pte. T. Roberts	8th S. Lancs. Regt.
46829 Sergt. W. Ryan	105th Field Coy. R.E.
8404 Sergt. E. Rogers	1st Wilts Regt.
27891 Pte. B. J. Rider	9th L. N. Lancs Regt.
8792 L.-Corpl. J. Read	9th L.N. Lancs. Regt.
34047 Sergt. D. Robinson ..	9th L. N. Lancs. Regt.
49219 L./Corpl. J. Rogers.. ..	13th Cheshire Regt.
5219 Rfn. J. Roberts	2nd Royal Irish Rifles.

5121 Corpl. T. Roberts	.. ..	2nd Royal Irish Rifles, attd. 74th T.M. Batty.
37271 Corpl. W. Rawlings	..	2nd S. Lancs Regt.
16529 Pte. G. Ronson	..	11th Cheshire Regt.
10049 L.-Corpl. J. Roxby	..	11th Cheshire Regt.
58358 Corpl. R. Roberts	.. ..	195th M.G. Coy.
96631 A./Bombdr. S. Scarfe	..	25th D.A.C.
56163 Sergt. H. Stokes	..	25th D.A.C.
6/16753 Pte. G. Sargent	..	6th S. Wales Borderers.
12258 Sergt. W. O. Smith	..	R.F.A.
90433 A./Bombdr. E. Stanhope	..	R.F.A.
7385 Sergt. E. A. Sadler	..	1st Wilts Regt.
10453 Pte. W. Swansborough	..	1st Wilts Regt.
54201 Corpl. J. A. Sharples	..	25th Divnl. Signalling Coy., R.E.
6/16757 Sergt. J. Sheppard	..	6th S. Wales Borderers.
P.4606 Pte.(A./Sergt.) B.J. Spencer		M.M.P.
42032 Pte. R. A. Scott	..	R.A.M.C.
545158 Pte. (A./Sergt.) C. Snell	..	R.A.M.C.
27578 L.-Corpl. L. Symons	..	1st Wilts. Regt.
13349 Corpl. W. Scott	..	9th L. N. Lancs. Regt.
34609 Pte. A. E. Storkey	..	9th L. N. Lancs. Regt.
290733 Pte. A. Smith	..	13th Cheshire Regt.
13151 Sergt. H. Smith	..	11th Lancs. Fusiliers.
9996 L.-Corpl. F. Sheridan		2nd R. Irish Rifles.
6928 Rifleman J. Smyth	..	2nd R. Irish Rifles.
3/1525 Rifleman W. H. Salt	..	2nd R. Irish Rifles.
8593 L.-Corpl. G. Sinclair	..	2nd R. Irish Rifles.
3/8582 Corpl. J. Smith	..	2nd R. Irish Rifles.
15207 Corpl. S. Swindells	..	8th S. Lancs. Regt.
7104 L.-Corpl. J. Smyth	..	2nd R. Irish Rifles.
19651 Pte. S. Smith	..	2nd S. Lancs. Regt.
32012 Sergt. R. Tye	..	2nd S. Lancs. Regt.
90125 L.-Corpl. E. Tucker	..	105th Field Coy., R.E.
51459 Sapper R. Thompson	..	25th Divnl. Signal Coy.
34687 Pte. T. Tamplin	..	3rd Worcester Regt.
30023 Pte. D. Thornton	..	9th L.N. Lancs. Regt.
885 Corpl. F. Thomas	..	13th Cheshire Regt.
265544 Pte. J. Timlin	..	13th Cheshire Regt.
5334 L.-Corpl. F. Trotter	..	11th Lancs. Fusiliers.
9647 Q.M.S. J. J. Turner	..	2nd R. Irish Rifles.
32270 Pte. J. Thompson	..	8th S. Lancs. Regt.
24891 Pte. G. Telford	..	8th Border Regt.
128775 A./2/ Corpl. J. J. Wright	..	R.E.
47292 Corpl. A. Whitlow	..	R.A.M.C.
6/17153 Corpl. A. Williams	..	6th S. Wales Borderers.
6466 Sergt. G. Wood	..	1st Wilts Regt.
30025 Pte. J. Whittle	..	9th L.N. Lancs. Regt.
5854 Sergt. I. Wainman	..	11th Lancs. Fusiliers.
6720 Sergt. Whelan	..	2nd R. Irish Rifles.
235102 Pte. J. H. Wheatley	..	2nd S. Lancs. Regt.
9927 Sergt. J. Walsh	..	2nd R. Irish Rifles.
14798 Pte. T. Wileman	..	8th S. Lancs. Regt.
7179 Sergt. A/C.S.M. W. Young	..	11th Lancs. Fusiliers.

25th Division.

SUMMARY OF CASUALTIES SUFFERED BY THE DIVISION DURING OPERATIONS FROM 10th OCTOBER, 1915, TO 31st DECEMBER, 1917.

Unit.	Officers.			Other Ranks.		
	K.	W.	M.	K.	W.	M.
110th Brigade, R.F.A. ..	5	19	—	38	157	—
111th Brigade, R.F.A. ..	—	7	—	2	58	—
112th Brigade, R.F.A. ..	4	22	1	48	222	1
113th Brigade, R.F.A. ..	—	7	—	11	36	—
D.A. Column	—	1	—	11	74	—
T.M. Batteries	7	25	—	53	197	4
Royal Engineers	7	24	—	58	361	8
25th Signals	1	—	—	7	27	1
7th Brigade—						
8th N. Lancs. Regt. ..	16	53	4	307	1376	154
10th Cheshires	10	77	4	321	1458	313
1st Wiltshires	23	63	3	230	1467	186
4th S. Staffs.	—	2	—	6	24	—
7th M.G. Coy.	5	14	—	29	110	1
74th Brigade—						
13th Cheshires	28	68	3	293	1458	415
9th N. Lancs. Regt. ..	21	57	1	322	1423	113
11th Lancs. Fusiliers ..	20	47	2	306	1182	142
3rd Worcesters	28	40	7	239	1587	108
74th M.G. Coy. ..	4	9	—	32	144	12
75th Brigade —						
11th Cheshires	13	50	5	195	931	224
8th Borders	19	48	2	228	1232	137
2nd S. Lancs. Regt. ..	14	47	5	294	1131	153
8th S. Lancs. Regt. ..	12	59	5	279	1093	173
75th M.G. Coy. ..	2	5	....	23	138	4
6th S.W.B's. (Pioneers)	4	40	—	81	533	13
195th M.G. Coy. ..	1	6	—	15	96	—
2nd R. Irish Rifles ..	23	59	2	222	1321	175
25th Train				..	16	....
H.Q. and other Units ..	....	6	....	11	20	....
R.A.M.C.	3	3	....	16	59	
225th Emp. Coy.	..	..	....	1	6	
Salvage	—	—	....	....	2	—
Total	270	858	44	3683	17949	2337

Officers.

ABSTRACT OF CASUALTIES FROM 10th OCTOBER, 1915, TO 31st DECEMBER, 1917.

10th Cheshire Regt.

Killed.

Capt. A. F. Noble.
Capt. W. M. Langdon.
Capt. N. C. R. Merry.
2nd Lieut. G. F. Oliver.
2nd Lieut. R. Walter.

2nd Lieut. J. C. Manning.
2nd Lieut. G. W. Hastings.
Lieut. H. W. W. Rowe.
Capt. C. F. Ellerton.
2nd Lieut. W. E. Langster.

Wounded.

2nd Lieut. G. W. Holmes.
2nd Lieut. J. G. Wood.
2nd Lieut. C. T. Wilson.
Lieut. J. G. Wood.
2nd Lieut. J. A. Wardle.
2nd Lieut. K. S. Withers.
Capt. W. G. Haslam (2) .
Lieut. H. J. E. Wade.
2nd Lieut. L. W. G. Owens (2).
Lt.-Col. G. D. Broughton.
2nd Lieut. B. D. R. Sunderland.
2nd Lieut. J. A. Fidders.
Lieut. G. E. Pilkington (2).
Major Menzies.
2nd Lieut. J. G. Glover.
2nd Lieut. E. Martin.
2nd Lieut. C. G. Hampson.
2nd Lieut. A. V. Ley.
Lieut. G. C. Lowry.
2nd Lieut. A. M. Hutber.
2nd Lieut. S. Barton (2).
2nd Lieut. M. W. Seagrove.
2nd Lieut. C. G. Turner.
2nd Lieut. D. C. Evans (2).
Capt. R. T. Frost.
Lieut. J. A. Simmonds.
Lieut. G. W. Holmes (2).
Capt. P. E. Pollexfen.
Lieut. R. Aldersay.
Lieut. J. A. Simmons (2).
2nd Lieut. H. E. Dummer.
2nd Lieut. W. Hunter.
2nd Lieut. D. C. Evans (2).
2nd Lieut. W. A. Wilson.
2nd Lieut. O. M. Hills.

T./Major J. A. Howell.
2nd Lieut. W. N. Nicholls.
2nd Lieut. C. V. W. Bles.
Lieut. B. S. Murray.
Capt. S. F. Morgan.
2nd Lieut. W. H. Maybury.
2nd Lieut. R. C. Shau.
2nd Lieut. H. V. Chamberlain (2).
2nd Lieut. L. Wilson.
2nd Lieut. T. E. Storrs.
2nd Lieut. W. Hesketh. (Died.)
2nd Lieut. J. T. Cole (2).
2nd Lieut. H. Pumphrey.
2nd Lieut. G. H. Stone.
2nd Lieut. A. J. Webster.
2nd Lieut. J. H. B. Young (2).
Lt.-Col. A. C. Johnston.
Lieut. J .F. Oatts.
2nd Lieut. E. H. Simpson.
Capt. A. C. Meredith.
Lieut. H. W. W. Rowe.
2nd Lieut. F. Hague.
Lieut. W. E. L. Brown.
2nd Lieut. H. M. Owen.
Capt. (A./Lt.-Col.) W. E. Williams. (Middx. Regt.)
Capt. W. H. Wilkinson.
Lieut. R. S. F. Cooper.
2nd Lieut. C. J. Watson.
Capt. H. H. Gamble.
2nd Lieut. C. G. J. Thomas (attd. from 1st Wilts. Regt.).
2nd Lieut. W. Sowerbutts.

NOTE.—Figures after names indicate number of times wounded.

Missing (Believed killed in action).

2nd Lieut. L. B. G. Young.
2nd Lieut. H. J. Goss.

2nd Lieut. F. Harris.
2nd Lieut. S. H. Thrift.

8th L.N. Lancs Regt.

Killed.

Capt. G. E. C. Clarke.
2nd Lieut. G. R. Kewley (11th Battn. attd.).
2nd Lieut. E. J. Nicholls.
Rev. A. H. O'Sullivan.
Lieut. G. Ashworth.
A./Capt. E. S. Underhill.
2nd Lieut. E. S. Williams.
Lieut. R. B. B. Jones, V.C.

Capt. S. Ramsay.
A./Major T. M. Foote.
2nd Lieut. H. Y. Emerson.
2nd Lieut. H. Day.
Capt. A. N. Faulkner.
Lieut. C. C. Howard.
2nd Lieut. W. G. Everard.
2nd Lieut. Pringle.

Wounded.

2nd Lieut. P. Walsh. (Died.)
2nd Lieut. S. Ramsey.
Lieut. R. B. B. Jones.
Capt. W. Furness.
2nd Lieut. H. J. Priestland.
2nd Lieut. C. E. F. Everett.
Capt. T. M. Foote.
Lieut. F. Gregory.
Lieut. L. T. Taylor. (Died.)
2nd Lieut. W. O. G. Whitehead.
2nd Lieut. W. V. Brunger.
2nd Lieut. R. D. Muir.
2nd Lieut. T. W. Devenport.
Lieut. P. Walsh. (Died.)
2nd Lieut. T. White. (Died.)
Major F. G. Wynne.
Capt. O. H. Hadley.
Capt. H. D. Bennett.
Lieut. H. Haworth.
2nd Lieut. W. H. Grimshaw.
2nd Lieut. A. Summer.
Lieut. P. R. Shields.
2nd Lieut. C. M. White.
2nd Lieut. T. F. Coade.
Capt. R. J. Cash
2nd Lieut. G. G. Hardy.
2nd Lieut. A. M. Fairweather.

2nd Lieut. E. M. Bonner.
2nd Lieut. H. D. Copeman.
2nd Lieut. L. B. Panchand.
2nd Lieut. E. A. Holden.
2nd Lieut. P. L. Bolton.
2nd Lieut. A. Kendal.
2nh Lieut. F. Smith.
2nd Lieut. H. P. Hill
    (9th Manchesters).
Lieut. J. S. Hill.
A./Capt. F. Smith.
2nd Lieut. B. Rowe.
Capt. O. H. Hadley.
Lieut. A. H. Chaworth-Musters.
2nd Lieut. F. C. Flood.
2nd Lieut. W. Ibbotson.
2nd Lieut. H. Brown.
2nd Lieut. F. C. Hood.
Capt. C. F. Tindall-Atkinson.
2nd Lieut. J. P. Knight.
Lieut. A. Sumner.
2nd Lieut. A. M. Fairweather.
2nd Lieut. R. V. Gilliat.
2nd Lieut. H. Hield.
A./Lt.-Col. A. F. S. Caldwell.
2nd Lieut. T. M. Taylor.
2nd Lieut. R. O. Weber. (Died.)

Missing (Believed Killed).

2nd Lieut. L. C. Tatam.
Lieut. G. E. Cash.

Lieut. S. H. May.
2nd Lieut. S. D. Appleby.

1st Battn. Wiltshire Regt.

Killed.

Lieut. E. E. Brown.
Lt.-Col. W. S. Brown.
Capt. A. H. Hales.
Lieut. G. W. H. Norman.
Lieut. L. A. H. B. Morris.
Lieut. D. W. Gosden.
2nd Lieut. J. S. Hayward.
2nd Lieut. E. Butler.
2nd Lieut. R. D. Martin.
2nd Lieut. C. D. Pigott.
2nd Lieut. H. L. H. Du Boulay.
2nd Lieut. R. E. E. Skyme.
2nd Lieut. D. S. Sharp.

Lieut. N. G. B. King.
2nd Lieut. S. F. G. Jones.
2nd Lieut. J. D. Wood.
Capt. H. F. B. Turner.
2nd Lieut. W. R. Maybrook.
2nd Lieut. J. B. Starkey.
2nd Lieut. D. C. B. Gumbling.
Lieut. H. F. B. Turner.
2nd Lieut. R. W. Bird.
Lieut. G. H. W. Holman.
Lieut. E. Butler.
Lieut. C. P. J. Brooke.
2nd Lieut. E. P. Barton.

Wounded.

2nd Lieut. W. M. Austin.
Lieut. E. R. Millard.
2nd Lieut. K. C. Nicholls.
Lieut. E. E. Brown.
2nd Lieut. H. C. Clark.
2nd Lieut. W. J. E. Ross (2)
Lieut. G. W. Penruddocke.
2nd Lieut. K. A. McKelvey.
2nd Lieut. A. E. Carleton.
2nd Lieut. J. A. Richard.
2nd Lieut. E. J. Troughton.
2nd Lieut. G. T. Sands.
2nd Lieut. I. M. Stockbridge.
2nd Lieut. G. Cartwright.
2nd Lieut. R. J. Taylor (2).
2nd Lieut. J. M. Bales.
2nd Lieut. J. T. Snelgar.
2nd Lieut. R. J. A. Palmer (Died).
2nd Lieut. S. E. Terry.
Capt. R. L. Knubley (Died).
Lieut. E. C. Clegg.
2nd Lieut. P. E. Petter.
2nd Lieut. E. H. Butler.
2nd Lieut. F. M. Strawson.
2nd Lieut. L. H. Watkinson.
T/Lt.-Col. S. S. Ogilvie (2).
2nd Lieut. C. J. Jefferies.
2nd Lieut. B. W. Bidwell (2).
2nd Lieut. L. G. Sherwood.

2nd Lieut. B. P. Hannam (2).
2nd Lieut. H. E. Jackson.
Lieut. P. P. Legg.
Lieut. J. H. F. Ramsden.
2nd Lieut. L. E. Neal.
Capt. E. M. Gingell.
2nd Lieut. J. R. Illingworth.
2nd Lieut. F. V. Magrini.
2nd Lieut. C. H. G. Thomas.
Lieut. E. G. White.
Lieut. F. B. Adams.
2nd Lieut. J. J. Widdowson (Died).
2nd Lieut. J. W. Gunning.
2nd Lieut. H. W. Awdry.
2nd Lieut. L. G. Lewis.
2nd Lieut. C. L. Usher.
Capt. G. B. Russell.
Lieut. C. Sainsbury (Died).
2nd Lieut. G. R. Tanner.
Lieut. H. Webber.
2nd Lieut. B. H. Stribling.
2nd Lieut. H. Clarke.
2nd Lieut. G. F. Filor.
2nd Lieut. G. B. Hillings.
Major C. L. Blew.
A/Capt. J. Reader.
2nd Lieut. S. H. White.
Capt. A. Mostyn Robinson.
Capt. R. F. Hayward.

3rd Worcestershire Regt.

Killed.

2nd Lieut. H. A. Jennings.
2nd Lieut. W. N. Wevell.
2nd Lieut. J. D. W. McMichael.
Lieut. J. M. Johnston, R.A.M.C.
2nd Lieut. B. V. Williams.
2nd Lieut. K. L. Hallyward.
2nd Lieut. S. J. Knott.
2nd Lieut. S. F. Fell.
2nd Lieut. A. L. Langford.
Lieut. G. G. Barnes.
2nd Lieut. W. L. Perks.
Lt.-Col. W. B. Gibbs.
Capt. J. Mould.
Capt. H. King.
2nd Lieut. H. Ginn.
2nd Lieut. P. J. Holliwell.
2nd Lieut. R. W. Powell.

Lieut. F. W. Ferrell.
2nd Lieut. R. S. Jones.
2nd Lieut. H. C. Bernard.
2nd Lieut. T. W. Leeby.
2nd Lieut. R. G. Cook.
Lieut. A. J. B. Hudson.
A/Capt. S. J. P. MacDonald.
Lieut. L. Piper.
2nd Lieut. H. L. Brampton.
Lieut. C. Greenhill.
Rev. G. M. Evans, C.F.
Capt. H. G. Willis, R.A.M.C.
Lieut. V. M. Goddard.
2nd Lieut. A. C. G. Alford.
2nd Lieut. A. R. Ping.
2nd Lieut. J. M. Metcalfe.

Wounded.

Capt. O. L. V. de Wesselow, R.A.M.C.
Capt. T. P. Muspratt.
2nd Lieut. R. W. B. Vinter.
2nd Lieut. S. J. P. MacDonald.
2nd Lieut. W. S. Knowles.
2nd Lieut. F. A. Reading.
2nd Lieut. R. J. Thomson.
2nd Lieut. T. Cruwys.
2nd Lieut. F. Percy.
2nd Lieut. E. G. Morgan.
Lieut. W. P. Wilson (2).
Lt.-Col. G. M. C. Davidge.
2nd Lieut. A. E. Fryer.
2nd Lieut. H. U. Richards.
2nd Lieut. J. Killby.
2nd Lieut. T. C. Tall.
T/Major G. S. Briscoe.
Capt. K. Spiers.
Capt. J. B. Barrow.

2nd Lieut. E. L. Lazarus (2).
2nd Lieut. R. S. Knowles.
2nd Lieut. M. P. Atkinson.
Major H. F. T. Fisher.
Capt. A. F. Birch Jones.
2nd Lieut. F. M. H. Jones. (Died.)
2nd Lieut. R. J. R. MacKenzie.
2nd Lieut. S. T. Dixon.
2nd Lieut. A. V. P. Rowlands.
A/Capt. I. N. Mason.
2nd Lieut. C. E. S. Brimmell.
2nd Lieut. E. M. Dodd.
2nd Lieut. A. W. Vint.
2nd Lieut. G. P. Brettell.
2nd T. Randle. (Died).
2nd Lieut. A. S. Kemp.
Lieut. C. L. de C. Hinds.
A/Capt. T. H. Little.
Lieut. W. N. Brettell.

Missing.

2nd Lieut. A. E. Fryer.

2nd Lieut. E. H. Jones.

4th S. Staffordshire Regt.

Wounded.

2nd Lieut. W. S. J. Williamson.

2nd Lieut. F. G. Dolman.

7th Machine Gun Coy.

Killed.

Capt. J. A. Rutherford.
2nd Lieut. R. W. Bird.
2nd Lieut. F. Luvis.

Lieut. L. D. Fanshawe.
2nd Lieut. S. A. West.

Wounded.

2nd Lieut. E. D. Oakes.
2nd Lieut. E. R. Leary.
2nd Lieut. R. C. Streathfield.
Lieut. N. V. Allway.
2nd Lieut. S. G. S. Lovell (2).
Lieut. G. A. Ramsey.

Lieut. E. J. C. Maddison.
2nd Lieut. D. H. Evans.
Lieut. T. S. Fay.
T/Major A. D. Spark (2).
Lieut. C. B. Bridge (N. Lancs.).
2nd Lieut. F. H. Lawford.

11th Lancashire Fusiliers.

Killed.

2nd Lieut. A. M. Stephens.
Capt. W. J. H. Leete.
2nd Lieut. E. H. Jewell.
2nd Lieut. R. Barrett.
2nd Lieut. A. K. MacFarlane.
2nd Lieut. W. F. Baker.
Lieut. A. F. C. R. Dunn.
2nd Lieut. C. R. Rowley.
2nd Lieut. J. C. Kay.
Capt. R. Ganley.

Lieut. R. F. Mac-Kinnon.
2nd Lieut. A. H. Bradbeer.
Lieut. G. L. Butler.
Lieut. and Qmr. J. Bowyer.
2nd Lieut. J. W. Stanley.
2nd Lieut. H. W. Almon.
2nd Lieut. J. Harrison.
Capt. and Adjut. W. J. Edwards.
2nd Lieut. G. M. Carruthers.
2nd Lieut. E. R. Rushmore.

Wounded.

2nd Lieut. H. E. Tee.
Lieut. H. H. Scott, R.A.M.C.
Capt. A. N. Jewell.
Capt. E. Munday.
Lieut. H. H. Fowkes.
2nd Lieut. H. M. Bellamy.
2nd Lieut. T. W. Willson
   (K.O.S.B. attd.).
2nd Lieut. A. McDougall.
Lieut. L. N. Holden. (Died.)
2nd Lieut. C. F. Melling.
Capt. P. D. Ward.
2nd Lieut. G. F. P. Smale.
2nd Lieut. W. F. Waite.
2nd Lieut. R. H. Stubbs.
2nd Lieut. J. F. Glendinning.
2nd Lieut. M. A. Callaghan.
2nd Lieut. W. L. Grey.
2nd Lieut. S. O. Hetherington.
   (Died.)
2nd Lieut. W. Morris.
2nd Lieut. R. P. F. Ashburner.
Capt. P. D. Ward. (Died).
2nd Lieut. L. R. Huxtable.

Capt. J. C. P. E. Metcalfe.
Capt. H. H. Fowkes.
Capt. V. H. Kempson.
2nd Lieut. E. Robinson.
2nd Lieut. H. W. J. Lermit.
2nd Lieut. C. A. Saunders.
2nd Lieut. J. A. Nathan.
2nd Lieut. T. J. Kershaw. (Died.)
2nd Lieut. J. M. McFarlane.
Lieut. C. C. Hadfield.
2nd Lieut. E. E. Sharp.
2nd Lieut. H. Bagguley.
2nd Lieut. G. F. P. Smale.
2nd Lieut. H. Radcliffe.
2nd Lieut. M. L. Bernstein.
   (Died.)
Lt.-Col. E. C. de R. Martin.
2nd Lieut. E. Kendall.
2nd Lieut. R. P. F. Ashburner.
2nd Lieut. W. G. Trimingham.
2nd Lieut. L. Smith.
2nd Lieut. J. W. Swan.
2nd Lieut. A. J. Caton.
2nd Lieut. F. M. Atkins.

2nd Lieut. S. Rowson.   2nd Lieut. J. Adamson.
(Believed killed.)   (Prisoner.)

2nd Royal Irish Rifles.

Killed.

Lieut. M. MacKenzie, R.A.M.C.   Capt. E. W. V. Leach.
2nd Lieut. C. H. W. Darling, 3rd   2nd Lieut. W. J. S. Tydd (Con-
  Royal Irish Rifles.   naught Rangers).
2nd Lieut. C. H. Wale.   2nd Lieut. M. J. McDonnell.
2nd Lieut. H. W. D. Stone (4th   2nd Lieut. S. J. V. O'Brien.
  Connaught Rangers).   2nd Lieut. W. Dobbie.
2nd Lieut. Mitchell.   Lieut. E. Brown.
2nd Lieut. J. Watson.   2nd Lieut. P. J. McKee.
2nd Lieut. W. W. Vernon.   Capt. R. J. Jeffares.
Capt. W. A. Smiles.   Lieut. S. V. Morgan.
2nd Lieut. J. Leckey.   Lieut. A. B. Ross.
2nd Lieut. J. F. Stein.   2nd Lieut. D. J. Healey.
2nd Lieut. C. R. Cooney.   *Lieut. W. C. Hill.*

Wounded.

Lieut. J. A. Stewart.   2nd Lieut. P. E. Murray.
2nd Lieut. G. J. Jenkinson.   2nd Lieut. P. Windle.
Lieut. E. V. Q. Leach.   Capt. D. H. Kelly.
2nd Lieut. A. H. Broomfield.   2nd Lieut. T. H. Gallaway.
2nd Lieut. H. W. O'Rielly.   2nd Lieut. F. R. Fowler.
Lieut. A. E. Workman.   2nd Lieut. J. J. Daly (Leinster
2nd Lieut. H. Phillips.   Regt.).
Capt. D. B. de A. Borcherds.   2nd Lieut. H. Elphick.   (Died.)
2nd Lieut. P. E. Murray.   Capt. T. J. C. C. Thomson (2).
2nd Lieut. H. E. White.   Lieut. R. J. Tuckett.
Lieut. A. Massey.   2nd Lieut. S. A. Bell.
2nd Lieut. T. H. Gray.   2nd Lieut. E. J. Williams.
2nd Lieut. T. H. Jenkinson.   2nd Lieut. J. W. Hougham.
Lieut. T. J. C. C. Thomson.   2nd Lieut. E. J. Williams.
Capt. G. S. Norman.   2nd Lieut. L. J. Ricks.
Lieut. W. P. Moss.   2nd Lieut. P. McMahon.   (Died).
2nd Lieut. Sharkey.   2nd Lieut. W. E. Caldwell.
2nd Lieut. White.   2nd Lieut. H. Marshall.
Capt. H. R. H. Ireland.   2nd Lieut. H. C. Mallett.
Lieut. W. P. Moss.   2nd Lieut. R. S. H. Noble.
Lieut. W. C. MacConnell.   (Died).   2nd Lieut. S. Mercer.
2nd Lieut. P. MacMahon.   2nd Lieut. F. C. Knox.
2nd Lieut. C. Weir.   2nd Lieut. B. J. Murphy.
2nd Lieut. C. E. Wilson.   2nd Lieut. R. Carruthers.
2nd Lieut. J. L. MacLoughlin.   2nd Lieut. P. D. Alexander.
2nd Lieut. D. O. Turpin.   2nd Lieut. R. S. Walsh.
Lieut. C. F. Wilkins.   Capt. R. T. Jeffares.
2nd Lieut. T. E. Barton.   2nd Lieut. C. Rule.
2nd Lieut. C. V. Smylie.   2nd Lieut. A. J. Lennox.
2nd Lieut. J. M. Clarke.

Missing.

2nd Lieut. T. E. Barton.   2nd Lieut. A. Davison.

9th L.N. Lancashire Regt.

Killed.

Lieut. C. C. Yates.
Capt. A. O. Trefusis.
2nd Lieut. R. W. K. Reid.
2nd Lieut. W. S. J. Stevens.
Capt. C. W. F. Finch-Noyes.
2nd Lieut. G. C. Tiley.
Capt. R. D. Robinson.
2nd Lieut. C. Lunt.
2nd Lieut. S. R. F. Empey.
2nd Lieut. M. C. Perks.
Lieut. E. H. Kann, attd, R.F.C.

Lieut. R. Willis.
Capt. W. J. Henderson.
2nd Lieut. W. S. B. Harrison.
2nd Lieut. T. H. S. Bullough.
2nd Lieut. J. Moses.
2nd Lieut. S. A. Talbot.
2nd Lieut. J. E. Motherwell.
Capt. E. U. Green.
2nd Lieut. H. (H. Swift.
2nd Lieut. C. R. Sedley-Brown.
2nd Lieut. G. Bate, attd. R.F.C.

Wounded.

Capt. W. H. M. Wienholt.
2nd Lieut. R. D. Robinson.
Lieut. J. D. Crichton.
2nd Lieut. F. C. Happold.
Lieut. C. C. Yates.
2nd Lieut. C. W. Sayers.
2nd Lieut. C. F F. Everett (8th Battn.).
Lieut. H. N. Stokoe.
2nd Lieut. M. C. Parker.
2nd Lieut. W. A. Dundas
2nd Lieut. C. N. C. Williams.
Major R. M. Everett.
2nd Lieut. W. B. Gillingham.
2nd Lieut. F. Stephenson.
2nd Lieut. N. E. Hazel.
Lieut. E. W. Taylor.
2nd Lieut. J. P. Oliver.
2nd Lieut. H. Dobbin.
2nd Lieut. T. Davenport.
Lieut. M. W. Nolan.
Lieut. G. R. Sharpe.
2nd Lieut. R. L. Brock.
2nd Lieut. H. J. Shipp (2).
2nd Lieut. R. Hay.
2nd Lieut. A. Cross.
2nd Lieut. R. C. S. Stark.
2nd Lieut. H. J. Priestland.
2nd Lieut. F. G. Edge. (Died.)

2nd Lieut. T. G. Skingley.
2nd Lieut. H. J. Charles.
Lieut. J. H. Pullin. (Died.)
Lieut. C. P. Gillies. (Died.)
Lieut. F. G. Laurie.
Lieut. L. F. Jenkins.
Capt. A. C. Hay.
2nd Lieut. E. U. Green.
Capt. H. H. M. Smith.
Lieut. W. F. Loudon.
Lieut. R. D. Robinson.
2nd Lieut. B. J. Edward.
2nd Lieut. H. Rodwell. (Died.)
2nd Lieut. E. F. Sonnenthal.
2nd Lieut. E. B. R. Colles (2nd Royal Irish Rifles).
Capt. O. S. Darby-Griffiths.
2nd Lieut. F. Mitchell.
2nd Lieut. H. Lewis.)
2nd Lieut. W. L. Kirkham. (Died.)
2nd Lieut. M. C. Perks.
Lieut. L. H. Lanham.
2nd Lieut. T. Pollitt.
2nd Lieut. T. Sefton.
2nd Lieut. T. H. Elkington.
2nd Lieut. J. D. Howarth. (Died.)
2nd Lieut. A. G. W. Ferguson.
2nd Lieut. W. O. Holmes.
2nd Lieut. W. Leggatt.

Missing.

Lieut. L. F. Jenkins, R.F.C.

13th Cheshire Regt.

Lieut. G.C. White.
2nd Lieut. E. H. Bates.
2nd Lieut. A. Gould.
Lieut. and A./Adjt. W. E. Davy.
Lieut. F. A. Somerset.
Capt. F. G. Hall.
2nd Lieut. H. F. Stevenson.
2nd Lieut. D. A. Stewart.
2nd Lieut. C. M. Bellis.
2nd Lieut. R. R. Newstead.
2nd Lieut. H. H. Maxwell.
2nd Lieut. R. J. Roberts.
Major L. Kerwood.
2nd Lieut. J. O'Callaghan.

2nd Lieut. A. E. Dicken.
2nd Lieut. B. H. Shaw.
Lieut. D. W. Ellis.
2nd Lieut. W. G. Curry.
2nd Lieut. E. S. McCullagh.
2nd Lieut. W. Harrington.
A,/Capt. C. W. R. Mountain.
A./Capt. W. O. Wilkinson.
Major J. C. Metcalfe.
2nd Lieut. A. E. Cotton.
2nd Lieut. D. S. Webb.
2nd Lieut. G. P. Green.
2nd Lieut. J. P. Storrs.
2nd Lieut. P. B. Silcock.

Wounded.

2nd Lieut. A. H. Cooper.
Capt. E. C. W. Arend.
Lieut. E. C. Kendall.
2nd Lieut. W. G. Roche.
2nd Lieut. R. J. R. Farrow.
Capt. J. J. E. Quier.
Capt. A. Jordan.
2nd Lieut. C. W. Tatham.
2nd Lieut. F. B. Whitehead.
2nd Lieut. R. J. Cholmeley (2).
Capt. W. Porter.
2nd Lieut. H. T. W. Oswell.
2nd Lieut. J. Horne.
Major J. M. Reeves.
Lieut. C. A. Oliver.
2nd Lieut. E. R. Bruce.
Lt.-Col. L. H. K. Finch (2).
Capt. J. H. E. Dean.
Capt. L. I. L. Ferguson.
2nd Lieut. G. M. Rooker.
2nd Lieut. W. A. Bridge.
2nd Lieut. R. Grant.
2nd Lieut. F. J. Currie.
2nd Lieut. R. S. Hellier.
Capt. T. H. McArthur.
2nd Lieut. R. U. Bennett.
Major H. Platten.
2nd Lieut. F. W. Harvey.
2nd Lieut. R. J. Roberts.
Major R. W. Gray.
2nd Lieut. H. H. Davies.
2nd Lieut. L. L. Crisp.
2nd Lieut. W. A. Malone (2)

Lt.-Col. P. S. Hall.
Capt. and A./Adjt. W. R. Corfield.
2nd Lieut. W. W. Underwood.
2nd Lieut. W. T. Shannon.
2nd Lieut. A. Burgess.
2nd Lieut. J. W. Kendrick.
2nd Lieut. D. Jones.
2nd Lieut. A. E. Beith.
2nd Lieut. D. Jones (5th Welsh
  Regt.).
2nd Lieut. C. R. Snape.
A/Capt. H. W. Thomas.
2nd Lieut. T. Phillipson.
2nd Lieut. F. N. Gilderdale.
2nd Lieut. J. Brady.
2nd Lieut. G. R. Montague.
Lieut. and A./Adjt. L. L. Green.
2nd Lieut. F. T. West.
2nd Lieut. F. C. Dale.
2nd Lieut. A. Scott.
2nd Lieut. F. W. Richardson.
2nd Lieut. T. Lloyd.
2nd Lieut. J. D. Miln.
A./Capt. A. R. Moir.
Major E. P. Nares.
2nd Lieut. W. E. Shaw.
2nd Lieut. E. J. Cross.
2nd Lieut. L. E. M. Green.
2nd Lieut. W. Skelton.
A./Capt. A. Payne.
2nd Lieut. J. J. A. Tempest.
Lt.-Col. J. Harrington.

Missing.

Capt. C. C. Patterson. (Believed killed). 2nd Lieut. W. A. Malone. (Prisoner.)

2nd. Lieut. C. C. L. Walsh.

74th Machine Gun Coy.

Killed.

Lieut. R. Faraday.
2nd Lieut. A. F. M. Berkerley.

2nd Lieut. W. Bowler.
2nd Lieut. K. G. Williams.

Wounded.

2nd Lieut. B. M. Tyson.
Lieut. C. A. Robinson.
Lieut. R. Gardner.
2nd Lieut. R. L. Parton.
Lieut. R. J. Davies.

2nd Lieut. T. Clark.
2nd Lieut. W. N. Gallway.
2nd Lieut. W. L. Johnson.
A./Capt. Gillis. (Died.)

8th S. Lancashire Regt.

Killed.

Lieut. W. Newcombe.
Capt. R. A. Rickett.
2nd Lieut. F. G. Woodhouse.
Lt.-Col. Brassey.
Lieut. A. E. Daniels.
2nd Lieut. J. B. Poultney.

Capt. J. A. J. Baylis.
Lieut. W. H. Kember.
2nd Lieut. E. J. S. Solomon.
Lieut. E. H. Lomax.
2nd Lieut. R. T. P. Morgan.
Lieut. T. B. Howell.

Wounded.

2nd Lieut. C. B. Smedley.
Lieut. J. D. Graham.
2nd Lieut. S. G. T. Earle.
Lieut. N. D. Morris. (Died.)
Major J. G. Harding.
2nd Lieut. J. H. Darlington.
2nd Lieut. E. A. Daniels.
2nd Lieut. J. R. Beall.
2nd Lieut. H. D. McKay.
Capt. C. R. Chambers.
2nd Lieut. R. M. Trevethan.
2nd Lieut. A. L. Rougetel.
2nd Lieut. E. A. C. McCulluck.
2nd Lieut. J. W. Pryor.
2nd Lieut. A. W. Ferguson.
Lieut. G. R. Oliphant.
2nd Lieut. E. W. Lane.
2nd Lieut. S. K. Watson.
Capt. J. A. J. Baylis.
2nd Lieut. G. F. Peers.
2nd Lieut. S. F. Martin.

Capt. G. L. Grimsdell.
2nd Lieut. W. E. Ward.
2nd Lieut. C. R. Bayley (2).
2nd Lieut. W. J. Turner.
2nd Lieut. E. Kershaw.
2nd Lieut T. G. Tickner. (Died.)
Lieut. N. L. Ross.
2nd Lieut. A. P. Cunningham.
2nd Lieut. A. V. Marlor.
Lieut. W. H. Kember.
Capt. A. Reade.
Capt. O. S. Hooper.
2nd Lieut. K. H. O. R. Sadgrove.
2nd Lieut. T. E. Davies.
2nd Lieut. H. T. Fielding.
2nd Lieut. J. Negropontie. (Died.)
2nd Lieut. R. Bickerstaffe.
2nd Lieut. B. Harris.
Major J. McCarthy-O'Leary.
2nd Lieut. H. Fenton.
2nd Lieut. R. A. Bigham.

2nd Lieut. H. W. Marsden.
2nd Lieut. J. E. H. Hill.
2nd Lieut. D. H. Wilkinson (2).
2nd Lieut. S. P. Wilson.
2nd Lieut. H. J. Wenn.
2nd Lieut. F. Buckler.
2nd Lieut. H. G. L. Golding.
Lt.-Col. J. B. Allsopp.

2nd Lieut. C. E. Peck (2nd Battn.).
2nd Lieut. J. W. Davies.
2nd Lieut. S. Mullock.
Capt. G. R. Kew.   (Died.)
2nd Lieut. H. Coppock.
Lieut. Jones.
2nd Lieut. Boret.

Missing (Believed Killed).

2nd Lieut. Peacocke.
2nd Lieut. G. Cumming.
Lieut G. Appleby.

Capt. E. C. Jarvis.
2nd Lieut. H. Dickie.

2nd S. Lancashire Regt.

Killed.

2nd Lieut. T. Beven.
Capt. A. M. Blair.
Lieut. C. W. Castle.
2nd Lieut. J. L. W. Collinson.
2nd Lieut. H. W. Cotterill.
Lieut. E. G. Fletcher.
2nd Lieut. N. C. Hatch.
Lt.-Col. H. T. Cotton.
A/Capt. A. W. Gates.

2nd Lieut. N. Howarth.
2nd Lieut. R. Jones.
2nd Lieut. F. Littler.
Lieut. R. K. Powell.
Lieut. W. C. C. Winchester.
A/Capt. C. P. Winterbottom.
2nd Lieut. C. G. Withers.
2nd Lieut. A. E. Grieve.
2nd Lieut. C. M. Skottowe.

Wounded.

2nd Lieut. R. G. Ash-Moody.
2nd Lieut. J. W. F. Agabeg.
2nd Lieut. E. F. Brooks.
2nd Lieut. J. I. Blackburne.
2nd Lieut. W. T. Brown.
2nd Lieut. C. W. Castle.
2nd Lieut. W. O. Cobbett.
2nd Lieut. A. Craven.
2nd Lieut. D. I. Dawbarn.
2nd Lieut. T. C. Eckenstein.
2nd Lieut. W. Edwards.
Major B. Evans.
2nd Lieut. N. E. Evans. (Died.)
2nd Lieut. A. L. G. Everett.
2nd Lieut. W. G. Fletcher.
2nd Lieut. E. S. Fox.
2nd Lieut. G. Gething.
2nd Lieut. T. Hodson.
2nd Lieut. T. Hopewell.
2nd Lieut. E. Harrison.
T/Capt. F. A. Holden (2).
2nd Lieut. S. S. Jones (2).
2nd Lieut. G. R. Kew.

2nd Lieut. L. W. Larsen.
2nd Lieut. G. F. Langford.
2nd Lieut. L. A. Macreight.
T/Capt. W. McEwan.
Major D. L. Maxwell.
2nd Lieut. D. D. McMahon.
2nd Lieut. H. W. Mirehouse.
2nd Lieut. R. Nevill.
2nd Lieut. J. F. Newton.
2nd Lieut. J. G. O'Brien.
2nd Lieut. C. E. Peck.
2nd Lieut. W. A. L. Poundal.
2nd Lieut. J. B. Poultney.
2nd Lieut. F. L. Roe.   (Died.)
Capt. C. A. Rathbone.
2nd Lieut. J. Roughley.
2nd Lieut. H. R. Stone.
2nd Lieut. W. A. Wassner.
Capt. C. P. Whitaker.
Lieut. F. D. Wright.
2nd Lieut. H. B. Whingates (2).
   (Died.)

Missing.
2nd Lieut. F. P. Warren.

11th Cheshire Regt.

Killed.

Lt.-Col. R. L. Aspinall.
2nd Lieut. J. C. Chandler.
2nd Lieut. P. H. Salisbury.
2nd Lieut. A. J. S. Anderson.
2nd Lieut. K. W. L. Scott.
2nd Lieut. C. F. S. Rhodes.
2nd Lieut. E. R. Thomas.

Capt. R. Mallinson.
Capt. G. E. Martin.
2nd Lieut. G. W. Watson.
2nd Lieut. T. C. Morgan.
2nd Lieut. S. R. Duncanson.
2nd Lieut. A. Peake.

Wounded.

Lieut. K. G. H. Ford. (Died.)
Lieut. B. E. Taylor.
Lieut. S. W. Vickers.
2nd Lieut. G. G. Bushe. (Died.)
Capt. R. C. B. Nicholson.
Capt. C. Lloyd.
Capt. J. Batson.
2nd Lieut. G. Twigg.
2nd Lieut. P. B. Worrall.
2nd Lieut. A. H. Bowley.
2nd Lieut. A. Handcock.
2nd Lieut. M. F. Dames.
2nd Lieut. P. P. Mallinson.
2nd Lieut. J. Brady.
2nd Lieut. J. Sweet.
Lieut. G. E. Martin.
2nd Lieut. H. E. Dewar. (Died.)
Capt. C. F. Hill.
2nd Lieut. H. Pomeroy.
2nd Lieut. A. P. Hamilton.
2nd Lieut. A. F. Young.
2nd Lieut. G. E. Barton.
Capt. N. B. Ellington.
2nd Lieut. B. G. L. Hickey.
2nd Lieut. A. G. Carpenter.

2nd Lieut. C. F. S. Rhodes.
2nd Lieut. K. P. Hall.
2nd Lieut. H. Holland.
2nd Lieut. D. W. Hughes.
2nd Lieut. W. M. Snell.
Lieut. J. A. Knowles.
2nd Lieut. H. W. Balance.
2nd Lieut. T. C. Morgan.
2nd Lieut. R. Latham.
2nd Lieut. R. Paul.
2nd Lieut. B. Molyneux.
2nd Lieut. S. C. Stevens.
2nd Lieut. P. R. Digby.
2nd Lieut. C. Potts. (Died.)
2nd Lieut. C. Blyth.
2nd Lieut. A. G. Carpenter.
Capt. J. Batson.
2nd Lieut. K. P. Hall.
2nd Lieut. F. A. Lawson.
2nd Lieut. H. W. Tooker.
2nd Lieut. T. B. Curtis.
2nd Lieut. R. Jones.
Lieut. A. W. Pocock.
Lieut. H. D. Kay.
Capt. V. L. Yates.

Missing (believed killed).

Capt. T. Murray.
Capt. J. L. W. H. Abell.
Lieut. W. A. C. Dowse.

2nd Lieut. L. L. B. Dunlop.
2nd Lieut. E. C. Lacey.

8th Border Regt.

Killed.

2nd Lieut. D. J. Gordon.
2nd Lieut. G. H. Foss.
2nd Lieut. L. Curtis.
2nd Lieut. A. E. Aldous.
Capt. W. G. Cassells.
2nd Lieut. J. M. Hall.
Lieut. F. W. H. Renton.
Capt. T. D. Miller.
2nd Lieut. W. P. Watson-Thomas.
2nd Lieut. E. Healey

2nd Lieut. W. A. Bell.
2nd Lieut. W. H. Anderson.
2nd Lieut. W. F. J. Lait.
2nd Lieut. R. Smith.
2nd Lieut. H. S. Langworth.
Capt. J. C. C. Barnes.
Capt. T. McCulloch.
2nd Lieut. T. Donohue.
2nd Lieut. F. M. H. Jones (3rd
  Worcester Regt.).

Wounded.

Lieut. A. G. Wingate-Gray (3).
Capt. A. O. Bishop (2).
2nd Lieut. J. P. Edgar (2).
2nd Lieut. J. F. Hinksman.
2nd Lieut. J. N. Brown.
Capt. P. H. Coxon
Major C. W. H. Birt (2).
Lieut. N. M. Saunders.
2nd Lieut. V. R. McKay.
2nd Lieut. T. W. Gruby. (Died.)
2nd Lieut. S. D. Withers.
2nd Lieut. F. L. Clark.
Lieut. G. C. Hutton.
2nd Lieut. J. E. K. Bell. (Died.)
2nd Lieut. J. K. Rhodes. (Died.)
Capt. T. S. Wilkinson.
2nd Lieut. D. D. Low.
2nd Lieut. M. Keys. (Died.)
Lieut. J. I. Wood (2).
Lieut. R. E. Parkinson.
Capt. J. D. Graham.

2nd Lieut. J. Turner.
2nd Lieut. A. D. Lewis.
2nd Lieut. A. Wilson.
Lieut. F. Parmenter.
2nd Lieut. F. N. Allen.
2nd Lieut. D. G. Le May.
Lieut. G. F. W. Reed.
Lieut. E. S. Phillips. (Died.)
Capt. J. E. Stewart (2).
Capt. J. Dawson.
2nd Lieut. J. H. Johnson.
2nd Lieut. G. R. Bott.
A./Capt. C. King.
2nd Lieut. A. J. Bentley (2).
2nd Lieut. G. W. Hawkins.
2nd Lieut. J. W. A. Allen.
2nd Lieut. J. Duggan.
Capt. F. J. G. Smith.
2nd Lieut. J. S. Kamester.
Capt. H. S. Turner, R.A.M.C.

Missing.

Lieut. A. Warren. (P. of W. Died).

2nd Lieut. J. W. Robson (prisoner of war).

75th Machine Gun Coy.

Killed.

Lieut. J. L. H. Fraser.

2nd Lieut. P. Pountney.

Wounded.

2nd Lieut. R. A. Lumb.
2nd Lieut. H. Johnson. (Died.)
Lieut. T. C. Bennett.

2nd Lieut. H. S. Ward.
2nd Lieut. A. Arkle.

195th Machine Gun Coy.

Killed.

Lieut A. E. G. Lewis (Essex Regt.).

Wounded.

2nd Lieut. A. Robertson.
Lieut. B. R. B. Jones.
2nd Lieut. P. Masterman-Smith.

Lieut. R. C. Pollock.
Lieut. A. O. Fairgreive.
Lieut. A. J. Dick.

110th Brigade, R.F.A.

Killed.

Lt.-Col. J. P. V. Hawkesley.
Lieut. H. O. Marks.
A./Major C. C. Gordon.

2nd Lieut. J. I. Watson.
Lieut. J. H. Mumford.

Wounded.

2nd Lieut. W. H. Densham.
Capt. G. Sumpter.
Lieut. C. F. L. Lyne.
2nd Lieut. J. C. P. Magwood.
Lieut. L. H. Garnett.
Capt. D. R. MacDonald.
Lieut. H. D. Woodsend.
Major F. B. Knyvett (3).
Lieut. J. J. L. Hollington.

2nd Lieut. G. A. Keay.
2nd Lieut. A. B. Laxton. (Died.)
Lieut. J. F. Parker.
2nd Lieut. E. S. Harrison.
Lieut. J. C. Shepherd.
Lieut. J. F. Parker.
2nd Lieut. J. Kane-Smith.
Capt. C. A. G. Campion.

111th Brigade, R.F.A.

Wounded.

Capt. W. A. D. Edwards.
2nd Lient. W. L. Dennis.
2nd Lieut. S. C. Shead.
Lieut. G. H. Woodman.

Lieut. E. M. Watts.
2nd Lieut. W. R. Loader.
2nd Lieut. L. R. Ravald.

112th Brigade, R.F.A.

Killed.

Capt. B. Aurett.
2nd Lieut. W. J. Dunlop.

Major D. D. H. Campbell.
2nd Lieut. C. V. C. Berry.

Wounded.

Lieut. Chaworth-Masters.
Capt. B. Aurett.
2nd Lieut. F .C. Letts.
Lieut. M. Christie-Murray. (Died.)
Lieut. C. Kennedy.
Lieut. S. A. Lange.
2nd Lieut. T. S. Thomson.
T./Major C. H. David.
2nd Lieut. W. L. Wilson.
2nd Lieut. G. M. Fraser.
2nd Lieut. J. D. V. Radford.

2nd Lieut. W. R. Gwathmey.
2nd Lieut. K. L. Ironside.
2nd Lieut. S. Williams.
2nd Lieut. R. S. Dempster.
2nd Lieut. D. Young.
Major W. G. MacKay.
2nd Lieut. M. C. Kay.
2nd Lieut. J. M. Moresby-White.
A./Major W. G. MacKay.
2nd Lieut. F. J. B. Gardner.
2nd Lieut. E. Persse.

Missing.

2nd Lieut. H. G. E. Durnford. (Prisoner.)

113th Brigade, R.F.A.

Wounded.

Major F. B. Knyvett (5).
2nd Lieut. H. T. Jennings.
2nd Lieut. G. W. Stobart.

2nd Lieut. S. W. Harris.
2nd Lieut. D. R. MacNeil.
Lieut. W. Miller.

Trench Mortar Batteries.

Killed.

2nd Lieut. J. L. Burke.
2nd Lieut. A. E. Hampson.
2nd Lieut. J. T. Halstead.
Lieut. W. C. Hill (Royal Irish Rifles).

2nd Lieut. M. C. Perks.
2nd Lieut. A. J. S. Doveren.
2nd Lieut. D. J. Healey (Royal Munster Fusiliers).
Capt. R. M. Chaworth-Masters.

Wounded.

2nd Lieut. Stainforth.
2nd Lieut. L. A. C. De Velly (2).
2nd Lieut. Menzies.
Capt. G. V. Dudley.
Capt. D. W. Reid.
Lieut. E. C. G. Clarke.
Capt. O. Lloyd.
Lieut. H. Burke.
2nd Lieut. F. J. G. Hedges.
Lieut. G. D. Williams.
T./Capt. J. E. Hibbert.
2nd Lieut. O. Mansdorp.

2nd Lieut. T. R. A. Duncan.
2nd Lieut. W. Aitchison.
A./Capt. F. W. Richards.
2nd Lieut. T. B. Kilpin. (Died.)
2nd Lieut. Arkwright.
2nd Lieut. R. E. Symington.
Capt. G. H. Stead.
Lieut. C. G. Turners.
2nd Lieut. E. G. L. Marshall.
A./Capt. W. B. Solly.
2nd Lieut. T. G. S. Kingsley.
2nd Lieut. W. J. Voss.

Royal Engineers.

Killed.

Lieut. Harris.
Lieut. J. M. Thornton.
2nd Lieut. D. C. Aldin.
2nd Lieut. S. F. Weeks.

2nd Lieut. K. M. Priestman.
Lieut. C. L. Blair.
2nd Lieut. J. M. McKay.

Wounded.

2nd Lieut. R. V. Alexander.
2nd Lieut. T. H. Upton.
Lieut. G. K. Scott.
Lieut. Wall.
2nd Lieut. R. R. Reid. (Died.)
Capt. G. F. F. Oakes. (Died.)
Lieut. J. F. A. Readman.
2nd Lieut. E. T. Caparn.
Lieut. C. G. Carson.
Lieut. T. Higgins. (Died.)
2nd Lieut. P. Mackinnon.
Major R. Walker. (Died.)

Lieut. T. H. Harrison.
2nd Lieut. G. T. Higgins.
2nd Lieut. T. A. N. Bent.
2nd Lieut. A. B. Gladwell.
2nd Lieut. T. H. Locke.
Lt.-Col. R. J. Done.
2nd Lieut. A. Elliott.
Lieut. P. MacKinnon.
2nd Lieut. T. A. E. Ledbury.
Lieut. S. B. Keast.
2nd Lieut. A. A. Price.
Lieut. C. F. Bilson.

Divisional Ammunition Column.

Wounded.

2nd Lieut. W. Atkinson.

Divisional Signal Coy.

Killed.

Lieut. E. B. R. Scott.

R.A.M.C.

Killed.

Lieut. M. W. Loy.
Lieut. J. M. C. Johnston.

Lieut. A. B. Ross.

Wounded.

Lieut. F. C. D. Watt.
Capt. A. D. Willis.

Capt. H. S. Turner.

37th Mobile Veterinary Section.

75th Brigade Headquarters.

Wounded.

T./Capt. H. Dykes.

7th Infantry Brigade Headquarters.

Wounded.

Brig.-Gen. C. Gosling.

Other Units.

Wounded,

Lieut. Gray (9th Entrenching Battn.).
Rev. Capt. W. G. Harris, attd. 11th Cheshires.

Rev. Capt. J. E. Ward, attd. 8th Border Regt.

6th S. Wales Borderers.

Killed.

2nd Lieut. G. H. Jones.
2nd Lieut. N. Griffiths.

2nd Lieut. H. Kent.
2nd Lieut. B. F. Kerley.

Wounded.

2nd Lieut. S. Evans.
2nd Lieut. W. G. T. Edwards.
2nd Lieut. B. S. Marshall.
Capt. E. Ll. Lloyd.
2nd Lieut. E. C. Amos.
2nd Lieut. S. Evans.
Major S. C. Morgan.
Capt. F. B. Thomas (2).
2nd Lieut. T. G. Evans.
2nd Lieut. J. L. Evans.
2nd Lieut. W. S. Renwick (3).
Lieut. R. L. Eskell.
Capt. E. C. Choinier.
2nd Lieut. R. H. Jones.
2nd Lieut. G. J. March.
2nd Lieut. B. N. Seden.
Lieut. M. C. Ede.
Capt. C. Mumford.

2nd Lieut. W. A. Cox.
Lt.-Col. E. V. O. Hewett.
2nd Lieut. D. P. Joss.
2nd Lieut. A. D. Roberts.
2nd Lieut. G. Jacob.
2nd Lieut. C. W. H. Salter.
2nd Lieut. A. G. Pearce.
2nd Lieut. E. W. S. Kite.
Major G. A. Renwick.
2nd Lieut. L. Petts.
2nd Lieut. D. C. Brook.
2nd Lieut. J. H. Davies.
2nd Lieut. R. A. Jury.
2nd Lieut. W. H. Hanna (2).
Major G. S. Crawford. (Died.)
Major A. Reid-Kellett (2).
2nd Lieut. H. Davies.

CHAPTER V.

Bethune.

THE 25th Division for about three weeks, subsequent to its arrival in the 1st Corps Area, South of Bethune, had an excellent opportunity for re-organisation and training, of which the fullest advantage was taken.

During its stay here a most successful fete was organised for the whole Division at Allouagne. The organising committee under Lt.-Col. Legge, A.A. and Q.M.G., assisted by Capt. Ney, and Capt. Pomeroy fully deserved the loud praises heard on all sides. The fete included a horse show, sports and side shows of every description, which were much appreciated by the men who had just come out of the line, after three months hard fighting. Several previous attempts had been made to organise a fete of this description, but in each case before the preparations were complete, sudden orders to move had prevented its taking place. This time, however, in glorious weather a most successful day was spent reminiscent of Olympia and Blackpool at its best.

The beginning of October the Divisional Artillery went into action for a few days under the 11th Division in Lieven to the South-West of Lens and Brig.-Gen. Baird's Brigade, the 75th, was moved in the same direction to be ready in the event of an offensive taking place. The intention to use the 25th Division in this sector was changed and on the 4th October, the Brigades took over the Givenchy sector from the 2nd Division in the XIth Corps Area with Divisional Headquarters at Locon, 2½ miles north of Bethune.

All three Brigades were in the line, with two Battalions in front and one in support and one in reserve, respectively; 7th Brigade on the right with 75th, and 74th Brigades in the centre and left respectively. The line held was approximately 8,000 yards with the La Bassee Canal running almost through the centre of the 75th Brigade sector. Givenchy was the dominating position of the whole line with the Aubers Ridge on the left front. Givenchy itself had been captured by the 1st Corps in the early days of 1915, and was now about a mile inside the British Line. For 2½ years the front had remained unchanged. An immense amount of labour had been expended in strengthening and improving the system of trenches with tunnels, deep dug-outs for machine guns and their detachment and strong fortified posts. All this was well repaid by the successful defence which the 55th Division were enabled to put up against the strong German attack the following April. In all probability it is no exaggeration to say that the Givenchy sector was the best and most scientifically defended portion of the whole British front.

At the Ferme-du-Roi a few hundred yards across the Canal north of Bethune a most successful Divisional Reinforcement Camp was established. Here all men going and returning from leave and courses were assembled, bathed, and given fresh clothing if required; classes of instruction for N.C.Os. were organized under Major Munday, Capt. Goodman, M.C., and Lieut. Naylor : all reinforcements remained for two days, visited the Gas School to test their gas masks before being despatched to their units and in every way the institution proved of the greatest convenience to the Division. Situated within the Divisional Area and close to the railhead it had none of the disadvantages of a Corps Reinforcement Camp, which later on were wisely abolished.

During the seven weeks in which the Division was holding this front, nothing of importance occurred to put on record. No operations of any magnitude were undertaken and the work of the units in the line consisted in denying " No Man's Land " to the enemy by means of active patrolling every night. A few prisoners were taken, and the Battalions likewise had slight losses whilst carrying out these tactics ; the enemy was also kept on the alert by constant heavy concentrations of medium and heavy trench mortar fire assisted on one occasion by a Portuguese medium trench mortar battery.

The Portuguese Division was now holding the sector on our left and all through November fresh Portuguese Battalions were serving under our Brigades for training purposes and to gain experience. On various occasions prisoners gave information about intended raids, but only in two cases did any actual raid take place. The Battalions however were kept constantly on the alert and much annoyance and inconvenience was caused by the enemy's cunning tactics.

The night of the 10th December a raid was repulsed by the 4th South Staffords who lay in wait for the enemy outside the front line trench in " No Man's Land " and at the same time escaped the bombardment on the trenches behind them.

The middle of October the 2nd Battalion Royal Irish Rifles to the regret of the whole Division left the 25th Division to join their countrymen of the 36th Irish Division. The Battalion was replaced by the 4th Battn. South Staffordshire Regt., which although recently raised and fresh from England soon gained experience and was able to give an excellent account of itself in the fighting the following March.

Great success during its stay at Bethune was achieved by the Pierrot Troupe who were installed at the Municipal Theatre. Their daily performances gave the greatest pleasure to thousands of men of all units within reach, and the employment in this manner of a few talented men, some professionals, some amateurs, was amply justified by their cheering effect on the troops during the winter months. The importance of providing good wholesome entertainment of this description for the troops in competition with the estaminets cannot be over-estimated. Towards the end of November slight shelling and bombing by night of Bethune commenced and to everybody's regret the Municipal Theatre was destroyed by a shell which narrowly escaped the Pierrot Party of another Division just about to commence a rehearsal.

The 20th November the Cambrai attack down south had taken place making a deep salient 6 miles across its base and resulting in the capture of 10,000 German prisoners. After the German counter-attack on the south-eastern corner of the salient had neutralised the original British success, the 25th Division just relieved in the line by the 42nd Division was ordered to entrain for the Somme area.

The 1st of December and the following days the 25th Division entrained at Bethune and Choques and arrived at Achiet le Grand 3 miles north-west of Bapaume during a spell of bitter winter weather. Soon after its arrival in the IVth Corps area the 25th Division relieved the 3rd Division in the Quéant sector due south of Bullecourt with Divisional Headquarters at the Monument, 1 mile north of Bapaume.

The line about 6,000 yards was held with two Brigades in front with one Brigade, in reserve. On the right the right sector of the IVth Corps was held by the 51st Division and on our left we were in touch with the 59th Division of the VIth Corps. The front line in this sector consisted of a series of disconnected posts, with very few communication trenches. The Division now spent all its energies in digging a continuous front system with several strong belts of wire, communication trenches, and reserve lines. Owing to the very cold and frosty weather digging was extremely difficult, but in spite of this good results were obtained. Unfortunately, when the frost broke the trenches collapsed and for several days were quite impassable. During these few days all movement by troops of both sides was more or less above ground and in full view of one another.

The Corps line between Vaulx and Monchy, which afterwards proved of such great value during the German attack, was rapidly developed. Machine gun defences with pits were established in depth along the front of the forward areas " No Man's Land " varied in width up to a thousand yards or more and during the few weeks very little contact was made with the enemy. Very few casualties were sustained though enemy aeroplanes were very active at night, bombing the various camps and ammunition dumps. On one occasion the 198th Coy. A.S.C. lost a large number of horses from the effect of one bomb, after which the horses were distributed at night in scattered groups so as to minimize as far as possible the effect of an exploding bomb.

Between the 1st and 16th February a campaign was organised within the Division to encourage investment in War Savings Certificates. The scheme included a Prize Fund in which purchasers of War Savings Certificates were entitled to one 5 franc ticket for each investment in one War Savings Certificate. Great assistance was given by the Director of Army Printing G.H.Q. who supplied several thousand circulars and leaflets for distribution amongst the troops. At the end of the campaign it was found that no less than 16,496 and 34,699 War Savings Certificates, or a total of 51,195, had been purchased by Officers and other ranks respectively in the Division, representing a total investment of about £40,000. About 450 Officers and 10,000 other ranks made investments. The Officers' Prize Fund totalled £780 and was distributed by lot amongst 42 prize winners ; the prizes ranging from two prizes of 125 War Savings Certificates each, down to 25 prizes of 10 War Savings Certificates each.

For other ranks the Prize Fund totalled £2,398 which was distributed by lot amongst 896 prize winners with prizes ranging from two prizes of 250 War Savings Certificates each, down to 600 prizes of one War Savings Certificate. Lt.-Col. H. M. Craigie-Halkett and 2nd-Lieut. Cole were the fortunate winners of the two large prizes in the Officer's draw, with Pte. Mills, 10th Cheshire Regt. and Pte. Lane, 8th Border Regt., the winners in the draw for the other ranks.

All prizes were paid in War Savings Certificates representing a further investment of £3,178 or a total investment by the Division of £42,156. The campaign was undertaken with the idea of encouraging saving amongst all ranks and of creating a large number of investors. All units contributed equally to the success of the campaign, though the artillery and the 4th South Staffords closely followed by the 8th Border Regt., were actually the largest investors.

The second week in February the 8th South Lancashire Regt., 8th Loyal North Lancashire Regt., and 13th Cheshire Regt., were disbanded and their personnel absorbed in their sister battalions. This new policy of disbanding battalions led to the disappearance of units which had gained a high reputation in the Division. Unfortunately, owing to the scarcity of reinforcements, the policy was inevitable as being the only method of keeping the other battalions up to strength.

The 13th February, the 25th Division was relieved in the line by the 6th Division and withdrew to Achiet-le-Petit area about 4 miles north-west of Bapaume.

Honours and Awards, New Year, 1918.

K.C.B. (MILITARY DIVISION).

Major-General E. G. T. Bainbridge   Comdg. 25th Division.

C.M.G.

Bt. Lt.-Col. (T/Brig.-Gen.) H. B. D.
Baird   ..   ..   ..   Comdg. 75th Infantry Brigade.
Col. H. N. Dunn, D.S.O. ..   ..   A.D.M.S. 25th Division.

BREVET COLONEL.

Lt.-Col. (T./Brig. Gen) K. J.
Kincaid-Smith, C.M.G., D.S.O. C.R.A., 25th Division.

BREVET LIEUT.-COLONEL.

Major (T/Lt.-Col.) H. M. Craigie-
Halkett ..   ..   H.L.I., attd. L.N. Lancs.

BREVET MAJOR.

Capt. (T/Lt.-Col.) L. H. K. Finch   13th Cheshire Regt.

HON. LT.-COLONEL.

Q.M. and Hon. Major A. Whitty .. 3rd Worcester Regt.

TO BE GRANTED NEXT HIGHER RATE OF PAY UNDER THE PROVISIONS OF THE ROYAL WARRANT.

Q.M. and Hon. Lieut. T. W.
Bennett ..   ..   8th Border Regt.

D.S.O.

T/Major (A/Lt.-Col.) A. F. S. Cald-
well ..   ..   9th L.N. Lancs. Regt.
Capt. and Bt. Major N. T. Fitz-
patrick ..   ..   R.E.
Capt. E. K. B. Furze   ..   ..   Queen's Regt.,Bde.Major 7th Bde.
Major W. Ludgate   ..   ..   D.A.D.V.S. 25th Divn.
Major N. M. McLeod   ..   ..   Brig. Maj. H.Q.R.A.
T/Major (A/Lt.-Col.) E. R. S. Prior 8th S. Lancs. Regt.
Major (A/Lt.-Col.) E. V. Saison .. R.F.A.
Capt. (T/Lt.-Col.) W. Tyrrell .. R.A.M.C.
Lt.(T/Capt.and Adjt.) C.F.Wilkins R.Irish Rifles.
Major D.C. Wilson   ..   ..   R.F.A.

BAR TO D.S.O.

T/Major (A/Lt.-Col.) S. S. Ogilvie.. 1st Wilts. Regt.
Bt. Major (T/Lt.-Col.) A. C. Johnston 10th Cheshire Regt.

MILITARY CROSS.

Capt. B. F. Bartlett	R.A.M.C.
T/Capt. E. Beadon	25th Divnl. Train A.S.C.
T/Capt. and Adjt. J. R. Beall	8th S. Lancs. Regt.
Lieut. G. G. R. Bott	8th Border Regt.
Capt. and Adjt. R. J. Cash	8th L.N. Lancs. Regt.
Chaplain B. Conway	C.F., 4th Class
T/Capt. T. E. Craik	K.O.Y.L.I., attd. M.G. Coy.
2nd Lieut. J. Grellis	8th Border Regt.
2nd Lieut. W. L. P. Dobbin	2nd R. Irish Rifles.
Lieut. (T/Capt.) A. C. H. Eagles	D.A.D.O.S., 25th Divn.
Q.M. and Hon. Capt. H. W. Foster	2nd R. Irish Rifles.
Capt. J. S. Fulton ..	Lancs. Fusiliers, D.A.A.G., 25th Divn.
14704 R.S.M. W. Lightfoot	8th Border Regt.
T/Capt. (A/Major) C. G. J. Lynam	R.E.
Capt. G. A. Potts ..	11th Lancs. Fusiliers.
Lieut. C. G. Radcliffe	R.F.A.
T/Lieut. (A/Capt.) F. A. Reading..	3rd Worcester Regt.
Lieut. W. W. Scott-Moncrieff	25th Signal Coy., R.E.
Capt. (A/Major) W. Swinton	R.F.A.
T/Lieut. (A/Capt.) W. S. Syme	Cheshire Regt.

THE DISTINGUISHED CONDUCT MEDAL.

1886 Bdr. A. H. Bayliss ..	R.F.A.
43358 Sergt. L. Dawe	R.F.A.
45939 C.Q.M.S. F. W. Holt	25th Div. Signal Coy., R.E.
8365 R.S.M. E. Irving	G. Gds., attd. Lancs. Fusiliers.
9880 C.S.M. A. O'nions	South Lancs.
6/17063 C.S.M. W. H. Ricketts	6th South Wales Borderers.
17823 Corpl. S. S. Rogers ..	R.F.A., attd. T.M. Batty.
36727 R.S.M. A. Wileman	Northants, attd. 9th L.N. Lancs.

THE MERITORIOUS SERVICE MEDAL.

S/33206 L.-Corpl. A. L. Bale	Divnl. H.Q.
51398 Q.M.S. D. J. Davies	Divnl. H.Q.
53556 T/S.M. F. A. Harvey	R.A.H.Q.
14697 Pte. S. R. Jenkinson	8th Border Regt., attd. D.H.Q.
3513 Sergt. F. Lester	3rd Worcester Regiment.
39854 S.M. F. Miller	R.A.M.C.
46522 Sergt. C. S. Saunders	25th Signal Coy. R.E.
108298 A/R.S.M. G. H. Wheller ..	H.Q., R.E., D.H.Q.
Sergt. Pipe ..	9th L. N. Lancs.

MENTION IN DESPATCHES.

Major (T/Lt.-Col.) J. B. Allsopp ..	8th S. Lancs. Regt.
15312 Driver F. Allen	R.F.A.
13792 Sergt. J. Airey	L.N. Lancs. Regt.
Lieut.-Col. C. W. H. Birt ..	8th Border Regt.

3843 R.Q.M.S. C. Asher	L.N. Lancs. Regt.
Bt. Lt.-Col. (T/Brig.-Gen.) H. K. Bethell	Comdg. 74th Infantry Bde.
Capt. (T/Major) E. de W. H. Bradley	K.O.Y.L.I., 25th Signal Coy., R.E.
2nd Lieut. W. H. Belcher ..	25th Divnl. Sig. Coy., R.E.
Major (A/Lt.-Col.) J. de V. Bowles	R.F.A.
Capt. J. M. Bayley	R.A.M.C.
Q.M. and Hon. Capt. S. T. Boast	2nd S. Lancs. Regt.
14591 A/Sergt. S. Bancroft ..	Cheshire Regt.
T/Major (A/Lt.-Col.) A. F. S. Caldwell	9th L. N. Lancs. Regt.
Lieut. C. A. G. Campion	R.F.A.
Lieut. S. E. Chamier	R.F.A.
T/Capt. F. W. Clarke	6th S. Wales Borderers.
2nd Lieut. J. W. R. Campbell ..	3rd Worcester Regt.
58004 A/Sergt. G. Cockburn ..	R.A. Div. H.Q.
6/16470 Sergt. (A/C.S.M.) T. Chattington	6th S. Wales Borderers.
Lt.-Col. (T/Colonel) H. N. Dunn ..	R.A.M.C.
Lieut. D. D. P. Evans	R.F.A.
17066 Sergt. E. Eldred	R.F.A.
Capt. and Bt. Major N. T. Fitzpatrick	R.E.
Capt. E. M. B. Furze	Bde. Major 7th Bde.
Bt. Major (T/Lt.-Col.) L. H. K. Finch	13th Cheshire Regt.
T/Capt. R. G. Finch	Divnl. Train.
71505 A/Sergt. J. R. Forsyth ..	R.A.
22846 Pte. (L.-Corpl.) W. Ferris ..	Wiltshire Regt.
Capt. C. A. Godfrey	L.N. Lancs. Regt.
Eev. H. V. Gill	C. F., attd. R,I. Rifles.
Lt.-Col. C. J. Griffen	Comdg. 7th Infantry Bde.
Captain H. Goodman	R.A.M.C.
2nd Lieut. W. H. Hanna	S. Wales Borderers.
Capt. (Bt. Major) J. M. Hamilton	G.S.O.2, 25th Division.
Major, Hon. Lt.-Col.(A./Lt.-Col.)C. S. Hope-Johnstone	R.F.A.
T./Lieut. (A./Capt.)A. E. Hansen	R.F.A.
Lieut. (T. Capt.) S. Hawkins ..	Staff Capt., 7th Brigade.
Lieut. (A./Capt. and Adjt.) P. W. Hargreaves	3rd Worcester Regt
2nd Lieut. (A./Capt.) M. Hardman	3rd Worcester Regt
T./Lieut. J. L. J. Hughes ..	Cheshire Regt.
3470 Sergt. J. Hulme	South Lancs. Regt.
13722 L./Corpl. G. H. Hornby ..	M.G. Corps.
Lieut. (A./Capt.) T. M. Illingworth	R.F.A.
36623 S.M. J. R. Ivins	R.A.M.C.
Capt. J. H. Jones	A.V.C.
Capt. R. T. Jeffares	Royal Irish Rifles.
Capt. F. J. J. Ney	6th S. Wales Borderers and Empl. Coy.

Major (T./Lt.-Col.) H. B. Kelly ..	R.A.M.C.
Lieut. and Q.M. W. H. D. King ..	L.N. Lancs Regt.
Major W. Ludgate	D.A.D.V.S., 25th Division.
2nd Lieut. W. H. J. Lermit ..	11th Lancs Fusiliers.
Major (Bt. Lt.-Col.) R. F. Legge ..	A.A.Q.M.G., 25th Division.
Lieut. (T./Capt.) T. Lynch ..	R.F.A.
80937 Sergt. W. S. Lewis ..	R.E.
Major N. M. McLeod	Bde. Major, H.Q., R.A.
Capt. S. F. Morgan	Cheshire Regt.
2nd Lieut. J. M. Mackay	R.E.
Capt. (Bt. Major) R. K. A. Macauley	R.E.
Lieut. E. J. C. Maddison	M.G. Corps.
Capt. J. C. O. Marriott ..	Staff Capt., 74th Brigade.
Lieut. E. Marquis	Cheshire Regt., attd. T.M. Batty.
Major E. Munday	11th Lancs Fusiliers.
2nd Lieut. P. Murphy	Royal Irish Rifles.
Capt. (A./Lt.-Col.) D. L. Maxwell	S.H. Yeo., attd. 2nd South Lancs
46827 Sergt. W. J. Mayne ..	R.E.
66752 Gunner W. T. Metcalfe ..	R.F.A.
W/116 C.Q.M.S. W. Martin ..	Cheshire Regt.
2319 Pte. J. Matthews	South Lancs Regt.
Bt. Lt.-Col. O. R. L. Nicholson ..	G.S.O. 1, 25th Division.
Capt. A. H. Noycke	R.A.M.C.
Capt. (T./Major) E. P. Nares ..	13th Cheshire Regt.
90889 Sergt. W. W. Nutley ..	R.E.
2689 C.Q.M.S. T. B. Newton ..	South Lancs Regt.
Lieut., T./Major, (A/Lt.-Col.) S. S. Ogilvie	1st Wilts Regt.
Capt. J. C. Owen	6th S. Wales Borderers.
T./Major (A./Lt.-Col.) E. R. S. Prior	8th South Lancs Regt.
2nd Lieut. E. G. Pullan	3rd Worcester Regt.
T./Capt. G. E. Pilkington.. ..	10th Cheshire Regt.
Lieut. H. D. H. Padwick ..	L.N. Lancs Regt.
2nd Lieut. H. Pomeroy	Cheshire Regt., attd. Emp. Coy
P797 L.-Corpl. J. Petch	M.M.P.
54209 Sergt. H. L. Pennington ..	25th Divnl. Signal Coy., R.E.
6/17619 Sergt. D. G. Parker ..	S. Wales Borderers.
12050 Sergt. H. Plant	Cheshire Regt.
31536 Pte. S. Phill;ps	S. Lancs Regt.
Major J. P. B. Robinson	D.A.Q.M.G., 25th Division.
T./Lieut. W. L. Rowe	1st Wiltshire Regt.
2nd Lieut. W.J. E. Ross	1st Wiltshire Regt.
2nd Lieut. G. W. Round	3rd Worcester Regt.
Capt. (A./Major) R. de R. Rose ..	2nd Royal Irish Rifles.
15412 Corpl. J. Radley	S. Lancs Regt.
15450 Pte. J. P. Rochell	S. Lancs Regt., attd. D.H.Q.
Major (A./Lt.-Col.) E. V. Sarson ..	R.F.A.
Chaplain W. P. Smith	C.F., 4th Class.
65190 Sergt. A. J. Stephens ..	R.E.
10443 Driver A. Sims	R.F.A.

10451 Sergt. T. Schofield	L. N. Lancs. Regt.
16919 Sergt. J. Skelton	Cheshire Regt.
563 Pte. C. H. Stevens	R.A.M.C., attd. Wilts Regt.
7356 Pte. A. Smith	Wilts Regt., attd. Signal Section.
17120 Pte. S. Smith	South Lancs. Regt.
Capt. (T./Lt.-Col.) W. Tyrrell	R.A.M.C.
2nd Lieut. W. G. Trimmingham	Lancs. Fusiliers.
T./Capt. H. S. Turner	R.A.M.C., attd. Border Regt.
8776 A./R.S.M. F. Taylor	Cheshire Regt.
9767 Sergt. J. Tynan	Lancs. Fusiliers.
2nd Lieut. W. J. Voss	R.F.A., T.M.B.
Major D. C. Wilson	R.F.A.
Lieut. (T./Capt. and Adjt.) C. F. Wilkins	Royal Irish Rifles.
Lieut. (A /Capt.) S. A. Webb	R.F.A.
T./Capt. G. W. H. Whelon	Divnl. Train.
Lieut. H. P. White	Cheshire Regt.
2nd Lieut. (A./Capt.) J. T. Wood	Wilts Regt.
Lieut. G. F. Wolff	Royal Welsh Fusiliers, attd. M.G. Corps.
Lieut. (A/Capt.) H. M. Wilkinson	Cheshire Regt.
33953 Bombdr. G. Webb	R.F.A.
5526 Sergt. J. Walker	Border Regt.
65096 Sapper J. Yates	R.E., attd. Divnl. Emp. Coy.
2nd Lieut. W. H. Marsden	S. Lancs. Regt.

French Honours and Awards.

LEGION D'HONNEUR (OFFICIER).

Major-Gen. E. G. T. Bainbridge   Commanding 25th Division.

LEGION D'HONNEUR (CHEVALIER).

Major (T./Lt.-Col.) R. F. Legge ..   A.A. and Q.M.G., 25th Division.

CROIX DE GUERRE. (OFFICERS).

Lieut. J. D. Deane-Drummond	8th L. N. Lancs. Regt.
Capt. H. L. G. Hughes	R.A.M.C., attd. 1st Wilts Regt.
Lt.-Col. (T./Brig.-Gen.) C. O. Onslow	Commanding 7th Infantry Brigade.
Lieut. J. F. Kulp	Officier Int., 25th Division.

CROIX DE GUERRE (OTHER RANKS).

8275 Corpl. (A./Sergt.) F. Elliott	2nd Royal Irish Rifles.
3215 Pte. (L./Corpl.) J. E. Humphries	8th L. N. Lancs. Regt.
14634 C.S.M. C. Lowth	11th Cheshire Regt.
8198 C.S.M. T. Ross	2nd S. Lancs. Regt.
65036 Sapper R. Royall	105th Field Coy., R.E.

MEDAILLE MILITAIRE.

18080 Sergt. T. Barber .. .. 9th L. N. Lancs. Regt.
882 Sergt. G. H. Jordan .. .. R.F.A.
65140 Sergt. H. May .. .. 105th Field Coy., R.E
10806 Pte. (L./Corpl.) F. Oldfield 10th Cheshire Regt.

Russian Honours and Awards.

ORDER OF ST. ANNE, 3rd CLASS.

Lt.-Col. E. M. Birch .. .. G.S.O.I., 25th Division.

CROSS OF ST. GEORGE, 4th CLASS.

15153 Pte. T. Nuttall .. .. 8th L. N. Lancs. Regt.

MEDAL OF ST. GEORGE, 1st CLASS.

4918 R.S.M. T. V. W. Roberts .. 2nd S. Lancs. Regt.

MEDAL OF ST. GEORGE, 3rd CLASS.

5822 Rfn A. Mills .. .. .. 2nd Royal Irish Rifles.

MEDAL OF ST. GEORGE 4th CLASS.

64173 Gunner B. Beddow .. R.F.A.

Belgian Honours and Awards.

CHEVALIER DE L'ORDRE DE LA COURONNE.

Lieut. (A/Capt.) C. A. Godfrey .. 9th L.N. Lancs. Regt.

DECORATION MILITAIRE.

68154 Sergt. H. W. Freeman .. R.G.A.

Italian Decorations.

SILVER MEDAL FOR MILITARY VALOUR.

T/Lieut. (A/Capt.) H. D. Woodsend R.F.A.

BRONZE MEDAL FOR MILITARY VALOUR.

19628 Pte. H. Hutchinson, .. 8th L.N. Lancs. Regt.
8484 Sergt. G. Chilton .. .. 11th Lancs. Fusiliers.
14767 C.S.M. G. T. Wood .. .. 8th S. Lancs. Regt.

Belgian Decorations.

DECORATION MILITAIRE.

66190 Sergt. J. A. Stephens   ..   R.E.

BELGIAN CROIX DE GUERRE.

3847 C.S.M. J. Anderson ..	L.N. Lancs. Regt.
46708 Driver R. Buttar ..	25th D.A.C.
14882 L.-Sergt. H. Braddock	Cheshire Regt.
9297 C.S.M. S. Byron ..	Worcester Regt.
46204 Pte. L. Burn ..	Cheshire Regt.
14286 Pte. W. Beard ..	S. Lancs. Regt.
16353 Pte. E. Condliffe ..	Lancs. Fusiliers.
Capt. F. W. Clarke ..	6th S. Wales Borderers.
T3/O28993 C.S.M. A. A. Cooper ..	A.S.C.
Capt. K. Dykes	Staff Capt. 75th Brigade.
10337 Pte. G. Everitt ..	Machine Gun Coy.
16936 Corpl. G. H. Hodgkins ..	Trench Mortar Batty.
66030 Sergt. E. Hodgson ..	R.E.
T./Capt. S. Hawkins ..	Staff Capt. 75th Brigade.
16631 C.S.M. E. Holland ..	Loyal N. Lancs. Regt.
1346 Pte. G. Hartless ..	S. Lancs. Regt.
14174 Corpl. G. Hughes ..	S. Lancs. Regt.
52SR/91359 C.S.M. C. Hewett ..	A.S.C.
39123 Sergt. G. Ingram ..	R.A.M.C.
3520 Pte. J. Jamieson ..	R.A.M.C.
19702. L.-Sergt. A. E. Kay ..	Worcester Regt.
32874 Sergt. W. H. Lea ..	Cheshire Regt.
66752 Gunner W. T. Metcalfe ..	R.F.A.
Capt. J. C. C. Marriott ..	Staff Capt. 74th Brigade.
6/14330 C.Q.M.S. H. Malley ..	Border Regt.
39834 Sergt.-Major F. Miller ..	R.A.M.C.
L/16510 Bdr. R. Naylor ..	R.F.A.
63603 Pte. C. H. Nicholson ..	M.G. Coy.
Capt. F. J. J. Ney ..	6th S. Wales Borderers.
25420 Corpl. J. O'Connell..	Borders., attd. T.M.B.
4283 C.S.M. W. Pasquill ..	11th Lancs. Fusiliers.
54209 Sergt. H. L. Pennington ..	25th Division Sig. Co., R.E.
Capt. J. A. Reiss	Camp Commandant, 25th Division
63220 Pte P. Rudd ..	Cheshire Regt.
6863 C.Q.S.M. W. J. C. Roberts ..	Worcester Regt.
563 A/Corpl. C. H. Stevens ..	R.A.M.C., attd. Wilts Regt.
12662 Sergt. R. M. Tyler, ..	Worcester Regt.
T./Lt.-Col. W. Tyrell ..	R.A.M.C.
TS/1464 Far.S. Sergt. C. P. Thorpe	A.S.C.

M2/O90837 Corpl. H. D. G. Whit-
combe .. .. A.S.C.
108298 Conductor G. H. Weller .. H.Q., R.E.
91088 Driver F. E. Weale .. R.E.
6466 Sergt. G. Wood .. .. Wilts. Regt.
6881 Sergt. T. A. Williams .. M.G. Coy.
6/17494 Corpl. R. Whitehead .. 6th S. Wales Borderers.
6/25520 Pte. W. H. Walters .. 6th S. Wales Borderers.
22563 Sergt. C. Whiting .. .. M.G. Coy.

CHAPTER VI.

Battle of Bapaume, 21st March, 1918.

THE 25th Division had been withdrawn from the line in the middle of February and lay in IVth Corps reserve round Achiet, a few miles north-west of Bapaume. The whole Division was provided with excellent huts of the Nissen type, and during the few weeks following its withdrawal from the line a great deal of work was done in the improvement of the various camps and in building stables and horse lines for the Artillery and A.S.C.

At the time, the British line held by the VIth, IVth and Vth Corps, ran approximately north and south from about 4 miles east of Arras, covering the important main road from Arras to Bapaume and the main railway from Arras to Bapaume and Albert.

Following the high ground east of Croisilles-Bullecourt the line crossed at right angles the elongated spurs and valleys which radiated in a north-easterly direction from the ridge on which stood the ruins of Bapaume. In the valleys the remains of the small villages of Louverval, Morchies, Lagnicourt, Noreuil, Vaulx Vraucourt, with Demicourt, Boursies, Doignies, Beaumetz, and Beugny on the higher slopes.

With the exception of one small portion the German line was situated on the extremities of the main spurs giving him excellent command of the valleys, making the selection of our battery positions a matter of some difficulty. Further south the line crossed the main Bapaume-Cambrai Road east of Beaumetz, covering Boursies and Demicourt and then left the sector with which the 25th Division and IVth Corps were concerned.

The front of the IVth Corps was held by the 51st and 6th Divisions, in touch with the 17th Division, Vth Corps on the right ; and the 59th Division VIth Corps on the left. The 19th and 47th Divisions were in reserve to the Vth Corps, with the 25th Division and 41st Division in reserve to the IVth Corps and VIth Corps respectively.

The sectors allotted to the 51st and 6th Divisions were approximately 6,000 yards each and were held with three Brigades in the line. Each Brigade had two battalions in the line and one in reserve, giving a battalion frontage of about 1,500 to 1,600 yards. The Battalions were disposed in depth along a front line lightly held with small posts and Lewis guns, with a support and main battle defence line in the rear. Machine guns were placed in groups in depth on either side of the main line of defence.

At the distance of three thousand yards from this first system was a second or Corps line of defence, and about 3,000 yards in rear a third or Army Line of defence. Both of these trench lines were fairly well protected with wire defences but were unprovided with communication trenches to connect the different systems.

During the early days of March rumours grew more active as to the imminence of the much advertised German offensive, and on the 12th March, the 74th Brigade was moved up into close support of the 51st Division, just north-west of Fremicourt, and for the next few days was busily employed in burying cable back through its Brigade H.Q. Later on this line rendered valuable service. The 75th Brigade was also moved up to Biefvillers, north-west of Bapaume, so that along with the 74th Brigade they might be conveniently placed to deliver counter-attacks on prominent strategical points should the enemy succeed in penetrating our lines.

The spurs at Demicourt, Doignies, Louverval, Lagnicourt, on the immediate front of the IVth Corps, with the Hermies Ridge on our right and the Longatte-Noreuil Spurs on the left, were the important tactical features which had been given to troops of the 25th Division as objectives in a counterattack should the necessity arise.

Later on events moved too rapidly for this plan to materialise and owing to the exigencies of the military situation Brigades and Battalions of the Division were used piecemeal to reinforce the 51st and 6th Divisions. In fact, from the opening phases of the battle up to a time six days later, when the Division was finally withdrawn, it was fighting continuously under strange Commanders and a strange Staff. To a Division full of Esprit de Division, no more cruel fate could have been reserved than the manner in which it was unavoidably used throughout the battle.

Reports from spies, deserters, and other sources clearly indicated that the attack might be expected any time after 17th March, but it was only on the 19th that aeroplane reconnaissance and photographs disclosed large numbers of fresh German batteries on our immediate front.

It had been intended that the 25th Division should relieve the 6th Division in the left Sector of the IVth Corps front, but owing to the probability of a German attack the relief was postponed.

At 5 a.m. March 21st, the camps were awakened by heavy artillery fire on the whole Corps front, at the same time the enemy's heavy artillery bombarded the railheads, supply depots, dumps and camps in rear, to which our guns replied vigorously.

Orders were at once sent out for all units to get their breakfast and be ready to move.

7TH INFANTRY BRIGADE	Brig.-Gen. C. J. GRIFFEN, D.S.O.
10th Battn. Cheshire Regt.	Lt.-Col. W. E. Williams.
1st Battn. Wiltshire Regt.	Lt.-Col. S. S. Ogilvie, D.S.O.
4th Battn. S. Staffs. Regt.	Lt.-Col. C. W. Blackhall.
74TH INFANTRY BRIGADE ...	Brig.-Gen. H. K. BETHELL, D.S.O.
11th Battn. Lancs. Fusiliers	Lt.-Col. E. C. de R. Martin, D.S.O., M.C.
9th Battn. L.N. Lancs. Regt.	Lt.-Col. H. M. Craigie-Halkett, D.S.O.
3rd Battn. Worcester Regt.	Lt.-Col. P. R. Whalley, D.S.O.
75TH INFANTRY BRIGADE ...	Brig.-Gen. H. T. DOBBIN, D.S.O.
8th Bn. Border Regt. ...	Lt.-Col. W. H. Birt, D.S.O.
2nd Bn. S. Lancs. Regt. ...	Lt.-Col. J. B. Allsopp, D.S.O.
11th Bn. Cheshire Regt. ...	Lt.-Col. G. Darwell, M.C.
25th Battn. M.G. Corps ...	Lt.-Col. J. D. Deane-Drummond, D.S.O., M.C.

Soon after 8 a.m. orders were issued to the 75th Infantry Brigade to move forward about 4 miles from its camp at Biefvillers to the Favreuil Area. By 9.30 a.m. the Brigade was clear of Bihucourt and at 11.30 a.m. was in position, ready for any emergency, in close support of the Brigades of the 6th Division, under whose command they now acted. The 74th Brigade was at the same time placed under the orders of the 51st Division, and the 7th Brigade moved up from their camp at Achiet le Grand to the neighbourhood of Fremicourt and went into IVth Corps reserve. The 110th and 112th Brigades R.F.A. moved forward and passed under the command of the 6th and 51st Divisions, respectively.

At about 11.30 a.m. information was received that the Germans had launched their great attack, and in many cases were through our first, second and main defence lines. Information was scanty and reliable news was difficult to obtain, but it was evident that the attack along the whole Corps front and also on our right and left had been delivered in great force.

As far as can be judged ten German Divisions (4th, 119th 3rd Guard Reserve, 20th, 195th, 17th, 39th, 1st Guard Reserve, 5th Bavarian and 33rd Divisions) attacked the IVth Corps front, thus giving each German Division a frontage of about 1,200 yards. The method of attack was several succeeding waves of infantry, with light machine guns in front, followed by heavy machine guns with the rear waves. Behind the rear Brigades of each Division came Field Artillery in column formation. In some cases, as many as eight waves could be seen advancing at the same time, very little if any extension between the men in each wave. The waves or lines of attacking infanty succeeded one another at about 20 yards interval, and in rear of the last wave came larger bodies of troops in artillery formation.

To our men, the attacking waves of German troops gave the impression of troops at close order drill. This formation was kept up notwithstanding their appalling losses from our rifle, Lewis gun, and machine gun fire at ranges from 700 down to 200 yards.

The dry ground was of very great assistance to the attacking force in helping the movement of guns, horses, transport and troops. The weather was all that an attacking force could have wished for. The heavy mist during the early morning undoubtedly enabled the assaulting troops, not only to get well up to their assembly positions, but almost up to our own wire defences without discovery from our front outpost line or from aeroplanes, and gave them partial security from Artillery long-range rifle, and machine gun fire. The forcing of our line proved that parallel lines of trenches, however gallant their defenders, were no efficient substitute for the perfect labyrinth of trenches, such as formed the original German line on the Somme and which were only captured at such heavy sacrifice and cost during the summer and autumn of 1916. These German lines of defence were linked up to a depth of several miles with switches giving flank defence, and provided with deep dugouts and concrete machine gun emplacements or "pillboxes" for the machine guns and their detachments during bombardment, and were further strengthened by converting farms, villages and other outstanding positions into strong points or redoubts.

All three Brigades were quickly in action. Towards midday it became apparent that the situation was becoming serious and that the enemy had not only forced his way through our front defensive system but in places was in the second or Corps line.

The 74th Brigade was at once moved forward by the 51st Division with orders to place itself astride the Bapaume-Qambrai Road, the 11th Lancashire Fusiliers south of the road A, B, C and D companies commanded by Capt. T. Rufus, Capt. H. W. S. Lermit, wounded, then 2nd Lieut. E. E. Sharp, Lieut. G. A. Keir, wounded, then Lieut. J. A. Nathan, and Capt. H. C. Stead, wounded, then 2nd Lieut. N. E. Ward. The 9th L.N. Lancs. Regt., to the north of the road, A, B, C and D Companies commanded by 2nd Lieut. E. M. Scott, Capt. J. D. Crichton (killed), Capt. R. C. L. Keays, and Capt. H. Everett, with the 3rd Battn. Worcesters, A, B, C and D Companies commanded by Lieut. F. G. Elliott (killed), and succeeded by 2nd Lieut. W. H. Parker, Capt. J. M. Lett (killed) and succeeded by Capt. E. Lattey, 2nd Lieut. W. V. Shaw, and Capt. S. V. P. Parsons, about 1,000 yards behind in support. Whilst returning to his machine guns from Brigade Headquarters, Capt. G. F. Wolff, Commanding B Company, 25th Battn. M.G. Corps, was killed. The portion of the Corps line held by the 51st Division to their immediate front was, however, still intact.

About 6 p.m., owing to a reported breach in the Corps line about Vaulx Wood, the 3rd Worcesters were ordered to dig themselves in, along small lengths of trenches 30 to 40 yards long for their platoons, placed in echelon to the west of Morchies. This work was assisted by the 130th Field Company R.E., and one Company of the 6th Battn. S.W. Borderers.

Soon after the arrival of the 75th Brigade at Favreuil, about 11.0 a.m. 21st March, the G.O.C. 6th Division ordered the 8th Borders up to reinforce the 16th Brigade of his Division to assist in holding the Corps line Vaulx-Morchies, or if possible to counter-attack up the Noreuil Valley. The 2nd S. Lancs. came under the orders of the Brigadier of the 71st Brigade, 6th Division, with orders to hold the Corps line from Vaulx Wood, south-east, and for the moment the 11th Cheshires were kept in Divisional Reserve.

About mid-day definite news arrived that the front line system of the IVth Corps had been broken through by the German attack, and that they were advancing in large numbers with artillery in column formation up the valley south of Lagnicourt. The 11th Cheshires were then, with eight machine guns of D Company, 25th Battn. M.G. Corps, placed at the disposal of the Brigadier, 71st Brigade, 6th Division, to assist if required in re-establishing the Corps Line. The 2nd S. Lancs. who about 4 p.m. were established, along with elements of the 16th Brigade in the Corps line resisted all enemy attacks.

Continuous waves of German infantry came on to the attack but in every case were repulsed with heavy losses. " D " Company, 2nd S. Lancs., which had been left to form a defensive flank on the high ground above Vraucourt rejoined the Battalion during the night. As the enemy were observed to be attacking in thick masses up the Noreuil Valley, and also towards Vaulx Wood from the direction of Lagnicourt, the 8th Borders were ordered to counter-attack to the north of Vaulx Wood as far as the Vaulx-Morchies line. A, B, and C with D Coys. in support, commanded by Capt. Birnie, Lieut. Reed, 2nd Lieut. Allan, and Lieut. Duggan—Capt. Dove, commanding D Coy. had been killed by a shell earlier in the day ; Lieut. Reed was also badly wounded and died soon after. Each Company attacked in depth and the Battalion advanced in good formation and reached the Vaulx-Morchies line north of Vaulx Wood by 3.10 p.m. The enemy were driven back and this position of the Corps line was now secured ; later they appeared to be getting round the left flank from the direction of Noreuil and D Coy. of the 8th Borders was ordered up to the sugar factory at Vraucourt to form a defensive flank to the left. Lieut. Bell with Sergt. Bowman and Pte. Stewart did excellent work when sent forward to reconnoitre. Later on in the afternoon, Lieut. Bell was wounded and Pte. Stewart killed. Lieut. Bell received a bar to his M.C. and Sergt. Bowman the D.C.M.

The same afternoon the 7th Brigade was moved up from its camp at Achiet le Grand to a camp at Fremicourt, and held in IVth Corps reserve. The three Battalions of the Brigade now took over the third or Army line of defence along a front from about 1,000 yards south of Fremicourt on the Bapaume-Fremicourt main road to a point about 1,000 yards north of Beaugnatre on the Bapaume-Beugnatre Road.

The 10th Cheshires on the left, A, B, C, and D Coys. commanded by 2nd Lieut. R. S. Bell, Lieut. E. B. Petty (killed 23rd March succeeded by 2nd Lieut. H. H. Bootman), Capt. G. W. J. Cole, and Capt. G. E. Pilkington.

The 1st Wilts on the centre with A, B, C and D Coys., commanded by Capt. E. F. J. Hayward, Lieut. G. R. Tanner, Capt. G. B. Russell, and Lieut. W. Holmes, and the 4th S. Staffs on the right with A, B, C, and D Coys. commanded by Capt. J. M. Edgar (killed) succeeded by 2nd Lieut. H. Guiton, 2nd Lieut. H. L. Bell (wounded) succeeded by 2nd Lieut. A. E. Collins, 2nd Lieut. O. H. Mason, and Capt. L. G. Carr.

The 1st Wilts had suffered from long-range shelling before leaving their camp at Achiet, otherwise casualties were comparatively slight. By dusk the Brigade was well established in their new line and working hard to improve their defences.

The position up to the evening of the 21st March was very favourable. The Corps line of defence was intact except in places at Vaulx Wood and Maricourt Wood, where the enemy had effected a lodgement, and the casualties throughout all units of the Division had been comparatively slight.

The night of the 21st-22nd March was mainly spent in re-organising along the Corps line, and getting ready for the battle next day. Enemy shelling began early, soon after dawn, and by 7.30 a.m. the first attack was well on its way all along the line. Before 8 o'clock, the enemy had gained an entrance into the trench on the right of the Borders, and pushing on took possession of Vaulx Wood. Thus early in the fight their positions in the Vaulx-Morchies line was enveloped from three sides, but for five hours, B, A, and C Coys. of the Borders under Capt. Birnie maintained their position against heavy odds. Lieuts. Dowdell, Mcavish, T and Warwick fell early in the fight, and later 2nd Lieut. J. B. Fryer. Capt. Birnie excelled as a fighting officer and leader and was indefatigable. in organising the defence. He afterwards received the D.S.O. together with 2nd Lieut. Oakden for their services. As the morning wore on attack after attack was beaten off and the Borders remained secure in possession of the line.

Good work was done by Sergt. Macdonald, L/Cpl. Stee, Pte. Varty, and Pte. Westbrook, with the Lewis guns. Sergt. Taylor, when all the officers of B Coy. had become casualties, took command of B Coy., reorganised them, and during lulls in the battle produced a piccolo on which he played popular tunes to put new life into the weary men. Sergt. Ives took charge of A Coy. later on, and with Corp. Pickup, did splendid work in reorganising and encouraging the men. All three N.C.Os. received the D.C.M. Sergt. Crayson, Corpl. Wise, Corpl. Carr, Corpl. Sewell and Corpl. Burkin did excellent work in bombing attacks, and Pte. Lawless and Pte. Porter as battalion runners never once failed in their duty. The former displayed the greatest courage in carrying an urgent message over ground swept by machine gun fire, though five other runners had already become casualties in former attempts to do the journey—Pte. Jones, Pte. Langley, M.M., Pte. Routledge, Pte. Crone, Pte. Bailey, Pte. Todkill, Pte. Wright, M.M., and Pte. Singleton as stretcher bearers were conspicuous for their disregard of danger in bringing in the wounded. L.-Cpl. Duckworth in charge of carrying parties and " Tump Lines " kept up a steady supply of ammunition. L.-Cpl. Johnston and Pte. Kelly Battalion signallers, Pte. Lawrence and Pte. Ferguson in charge of the ammunition column, all received well-earned decorations. 2nd Lieut. Allan commanded his Company with great ability and received the M.C.

At about 10 a.m., 200 men of the 16th Brigade, 6th Division, under Major Colling, attempted to counter-attack on Vaulx Wood. This counter-attack was held up by machine gun fire after it had gone a few hundred yards. Vaulx Wood was soon afterwards cleared of the enemy by artillery fire but it was impossible to pass through it. Verbal orders were now received to form a defensive flank on the eastern outskirts of Vaulx. D Coy. was ordered on to the western edge of the village, the remnants of A, B, and C Coys. were divided into two parties one of which was detailed to keep touch with the troops on the left.

By dusk and after most other troops had withdrawn, the remainder of the 8th Borders were ordered to fall back to the Army line where they came into touch with the 1st Wilts. and were then re-organised. The sector of the Corps line behind Vaulx Wood and Marricourt held by the 2nd S. Lancs., was heavily attacked after daybreak on the 22nd. Parties of the enemy succeeded in entering the trench at several points but were soon driven out. Heavy fighting went on all the morning up to about 5 p.m. In order to conform to a movement on the right a retirement became necessary to the new line about 1,000 yards in rear to which the remnants of the Battalion was now withdrawn. During the fighting two Officers had been killed, four wounded and seven were missing. Capt. Nicholson, M.C., won the D.S.O., for the fine leadership he displayed in command of his company, successfully beating off repeated attacks with great slaughter. Capt. Wilkinson and 2nd Lieut. Woodcock gained the Military Cross for their excellent work. Sergt. Brandon distinguished himself in command of his platoon ; Cpl. Binns, Pte. Walker and Pte. Morley did wonderfully good work with Lewis guns near Morchies. Sergt. Deveney and Cpl. Smith, M.M., successfully covered the retirements with their Lewis guns ; Sergt. Lieversley, when all officers had become casualties, commanded his company with great ability and with Pte. Evanson and Pte. Taylor all won decorations.

The 11th Cheshires from the 75th Brigade late on the night of the 21st, were placed at the disposal of the Brigadier of the 18th Brigade, 6th Division. A and C Coys. during the early morning of the 22nd dug and occupied a line south-west of Morchies. B Coy. dug and took up a position from the north-west corner of Chauffers Wood, whilst D Coy. was kept in reserve for the present in order to counter-attack if required. At 3.30 in the afternoon, D Coy. took a position in rear of the Corps line with a post in Morchies and at 5 p.m., when the enemy broke through the Corps line north of Maricourt A and C Coys. counter-attacked with 24 tanks. This counter-attack was successful for the moment in driving back the Germans and inflicting heavy casualties. 2nd Lieut. Woodwarp

gallantly led a bombing counter-attack and with Lieut.
Edwards and Lieut. Beckett won the Military Cross for their
services in command of their companies. Cpl. Ashton and
Sergt. Broadfoot rendered splendid service in reorganising
their men and received the D.C.M. Pte. Birchall and Pte
Bury coolly went out into " No Man's Land " to collect unused
ammunition from casualties for their Lewis guns. Cpl.
Bates, Sergt. Griffiths and Sergt. Horridge led their platoons
with great ability and L.-Cpl. Cockshoot, L.-Cpl. Cullen and
Cpl. Turner did excellent work with their Lewis guns. Pte.
Brindle, Pte. Roberts, M.M., and Pte. Turner as Battalion
runners, Pte. Kay and Pte. Thomas in their attention to the
wounded under heavy fire were conspicuous for their gallantry
and all received decorations which they richly deserved.

Later on in the afternoon the Corps line was broken through
away on the right and the Battalion was withdrawn to conform
with the gradual retirement on the right. During these
operations the 11th Cheshires acted under the order of Brig.-
Gen. H. K. Bethell, D.S.O., Commanding 74th Infantry
Brigade.

At about 10 a.m., 22nd March, the 3rd Worcesters extended
their left flank with B and C Coys. along the north side of
Maricourt Wood and towards Vaulx Wood, where heavy attacks
were taking place. From these positions they were able
to inflict heavy casualties on persistent enemy attacks throughout the day.

At about 4.30 p.m., the 3rd Worcesters were ordered to
commence the withdrawal of two Companies. At the moment,
owing to a fresh German attack, only C Coy. could retire, but
later on, at about 7 p.m., A, C and D Coys. with elements of the
51st Division held the line about 1,000 yards north-east of
Beugny to cover the withdrawal of other troops. 2nd Lieut.
Parker commanded the Company covering the retirement
with great ability and with Capt. Hargreaves received the
Military Cross. Pte. Jones, Pte. Tuffin and Pte. Robinson
gained the Military Medal for their splendid work as stretcher
bearers, remaining behind to bring along the wounded whenever retirements were ordered. Sergt. Gardner, D.C.M.,
M.M., remained behind in Morchies and covered the withdrawal with three Lewis guns. L.-Cpl. Raybould with a small
patrol captured a German machine gun and its detachment.
L.-Sergt. Forrester, L.-Cpl. Hawkins and Pte. Reynolds

showed great coolness in covering the retirement, whilst Pte. Sellars, M.M., as Battalion runner, did excellent work and all received the Military Medal.

The 11th Cheshires during the evening fell back on a line about 500 yards in advance of, and parallel to, the 3rd Worcesters. Of this Battalion two Companies it is feared never received the order to retire and were left gallantly fighting until swept away by the German avalanche.

From mid-day onwards, owing to reports received of the enemy massing astride the Bapaume-Cambrai Road, the 9th L.N. Lancs. were moved gradually up to reinforce the 6th Black Watch and 7th Gordons in that part of the Corps line immediately north of the Bapaume-Cambrai Road. The Germans were continually pressing on in large numbers and very heavy casualties were inflicted on them by the 9th L.N. Lancs. and other troops in this portion of the line. About 4 p.m. a small party of the enemy with machine guns broke through on the left of the 9th L.N. Lancs. and with, their numbers steadily increasing, the line north of the Bapaume-Cambrai Road became untenable ; Major F. M. King had been killed and many other officers and other ranks had become casualties when the O.C. 9th L.N. Lancs. decided to withdraw to the right and to line the south side of the Bapaume-Cambrai Road with a view to a counter-attack on those of the enemy behind his line, but before this could be organised and carried out it was found that Germans had also broken through south of the road. This increased their difficulties so much that by 5.30 p.m., most of the men were casualties and the remainder were successfully withdrawn in small parties to this new position.

The 9th L.N. Lancs. then moved south of the road, throwing back a defensive flank to face northwards in touch with the 6th Seaforths, 51st Division, in the Corps line south of the road. This Battalion sent another Company to reinforce the defensive flank of the 9th L.N. Lancs., and the position was held until midnight when orders were received to withdraw from this portion of the line. The remainder of the Battalion then took up a position on the south side of Beaumetz facing north until the following morning, 23rd, when orders were received to withdraw to Fremicourt. " D " Coy. during the first withdrawal became detached from the Battalion and joined the 11th Lancashire Fusiliers with whom they

remained throughout the fighting during that day.   Lieut.
Brown and 2nd Lieut. Short led their men with great ability
and 2nd Lieut. Swift, for his excellent work in charge of the
Battalion signallers, received the Military Cross. Sergt.
Schofield, Sergt. Cowap and Sergt. Phillips received the D.C.M.
for their exceptional coolness and courage when leading their
platoons to reinforce the Corps line east of Morchies.   L.-Sergt.
Jones and Pte. Llewellyn did fine work with their Lewis guns.
Pte. Grew as a Battalion runner and Pte. Barnes, Pte. Livesay,
Pte. Lowe, Pte. Glease and L.-Cpl. Goodwin were all conspicuous for their bravery and disregard of danger in attending
to and bringing in wounded.   Cpl. Atherton was responsible
for rations reaching men in the front line and all received the
Military Medal.

During the 22nd/23rd the 3rd Worcesters were withdrawn
to Fremicourt, and the 11th Cheshires were at 4 p.m., on the
morning of the 23rd also instructed to withdraw as soon as
relieved. The 11th Lancaster Fusiliers, still in position south
of the Bapaume-Cambrai Road north of Beaumetx, were
now left holding the point of the salient much threatened from
the south.   During the 22nd they had suffered chiefly from
low flying aeroplanes, which came over apparently to observe
their positions, and inflicted casualties by machine gunfire.
During the fighting of the 22nd "A" and "D" Coys. of the
11th Lancs. Fus. withdrew from their positions and took
up positions south of the Bapaume-Cambrai Road in rear
of "B" and "C" Coys. Two machine guns of B Coy.,
25th Batt., Machine Gun Corps, were reinforced during the
night 22nd/23rd by five machine guns of C Coy., 25th
Batt., Machine Gun Corps, under Major Burn, and the
whole were placed in depth south of the Bapaume-Cambrai
Road.   During the night patrols of the 11th Lancs. Fusiliers under Lieut. Biffer, captured a German officer and
five O.Rs., killing several others in patrol fighting. At 5.30
a.m., just as dawn was beginning to show, the attack
began from the north-west.   At 6.15 a.m., A and D Coys.
were compelled to fall back, in conformity with the retirements of troops of the 18th Brigade on their left, to positions
south of and parallel with the Bapaume-Cambrai Road.
At 7 a.m., an attack on B and C Coys. began from Beaumetz
from the south-east and by 8 a.m., German machine guns had
worked round to the right flank when Major Massey ordered

a withdrawal to a line running north-west. By 9 a.m. the Battalion had fallen back to the west of Beugny. This position was untenable owing to the position of enemy machine guns in Lebucquiere on the right flank and at 11.30 a.m., the remains of the Battalion began a withdrawal to Fremicourt passing south of Beugny. In this fight, lasting over six hours, the 11th Lancs. Fusiliers lost nearly half their numbers. Major Massey had been wounded and Capt. Potts took over command of the Battalion.

There is no doubt that the seven machine guns with them inflicted very heavy casualties on the enemy, who were continually pressing on in close formation and offered splendid targets. Capt. Rufus set a fine example in command of his Company, Lieut. Keir showed great ability in covering the retirement and received the Military Cross. C.S.M. Haslam, M.M. when his Company was attacked on both flanks did excellent work in controlling the men. Pte. Helm, Pte. Mackereth, Sergt. O'Neill, Sergt. Waynman, M.M., and Sergt. Rossner, M.M., were conspicuous for their courage in bringing in the wounded under very heavy fire. L./Corpl. Rauth, Sergt. Ritchie and Sergt. Doleman handled their men with great ability. Pte. Deakin and L./Corpl. Eastwood, M.M., did excellent work with their Lewis guns. All received decorations which they richly deserved, in addition to Pte. Ashworth (Battalion signaller) and Corpl. Tomlinson for his excellent work in command of his platoon.

The position along the whole Corps front was still favourable: the gradual withdrawal from the Corps line was rendered necessary in order to conform with the retirement of the Corps and Army on our right, the whole pivotting on the left of the Third Army in front of Arras. Time after time this necessitated the withdrawal of companies and bodies of troops firmly entrenched and perfectly able to maintain themselves and inflict heavy casualties on the dense masses of the enemy who were always pushing their way forward with the greatest energy. The 3rd or Army Line in front of Fremicourt-Beugnatre-Sapignies-Behagnies-Ervillers was now held throughout, and during the night 23rd/24th a withdrawal took place of all troops in front of that line. The 74th Infantry Brigade, 3rd Worcesters, 9th Loyal N. Lancs, and 11th Lancs. Fusiliers, together with the 11th Cheshires, were ordered to concentrate at Bihucourt, near Achiet. This march of about four miles was completed about 4.30 p.m., 23rd, and the whole Brigade assembled between Biefvillers and Bihucourt. During the retirement the contents of the canteens at Achiet and Bapaume were much appreciated by our troops. Large quantities of cigars, cigarettes and tinned goods were distributed, nothing being allowed to fall into the enemy's hands. Orders were issued at 10 p.m., 24th, for the 74th Infantry Brigade to be prepared to assemble on a line about 1,000 yards north of Biefvillers, and parallel with the Bapaume-Achiet main road.

Away on the left the 8th Borders and 2nd S. Lancs., 75th Infantry Brigade, had withdrawn during the late afternoon of the 22nd to the 3rd or Army Line, and were now in touch with the 1st Wilts., 7th Brigade. These were relieved soon after midnight by troops of the 41st Division and rejoined their transport at about 4 a.m., 23rd, near Sapignies. Although very tired the troops by 4 p.m., were well dug in along the line on the spur covering Sapignies, and Behagnies. They were reinforced by the 6th South Wales Borderers, 105th, 106th, and 130th Field Coys. R.E., and a composite battalion of the Divisional " B " Teams under Major Weinholt, D.S.O. By the evening the line had been rendered more secure and the whole force was entrenched in three lines of trenches with wire defences along the front. The 120th and 121st Brigades, 40th Division, VIth Corps, were in advance on the left with the 122nd Brigade in advance on the right. The situation remained quiet except for some shelling of Sapignies and heavy shelling on the Sapignies-Mory Road. Shortly after midnight, Major Prior, 11th Cheshires, reached 75th Brigade H.Q., and about 2 a.m., the remains of the 11th Cheshire Regt., which now numbered less than 100 O.Rs., reached their transport lines. During the morning of the 23rd, the Composite Battn. of the B Teams were split up and sent back to their own units. At about dusk the 11th Cheshires went up to the 75th Brigade Group on the new line and dug a position on the extreme right with the right thrown back so as to get in touch with the 5th Entrenching Battn., under Col. Finch.

The Brigade Group held their line in front of Sapignies Behagnies until relieved by a Brigade of the 42nd Division about 3.30 a.m. on the 25th. During the night parties of another Division fell back in disorder on this line. Two men who were adding to the confusion and endeavouring to cause panic were at once shot by Sergt. Evans, 2nd S. Lancs, and afterwards were found to be German soldiers. By 6 a.m. the 25th, the 75th Brigade had reached its new position east of Logeast Wood and a line was at once dug with the 11th Cheshires on the right, in touch with the 7th Brigade, 8th Borders in the centre, and the 2nd S. Lancs on the left, and by the afternoon a strong defensive line had been established. Throughout the day the position was intermittently shelled with 5.9-in. During the afternoon a successful counter-attack was made by tanks against the enemy each side of Achiet. This succeeded in checking and driving the enemy back.

We must now follow the fortunes of the 7th Brigade, who with the 10th Cheshires on the left, 1st Wilts on the centre, and 4th South Staffords on the right, had established themselves in the 3rd or Army line, the evening of the 21st March, and during that night and the following day did much to improve the trenches. After the withdrawal from the 2nd or Corps Line many stragglers from various units were collected and organised for purposes of defence. The night of 22nd/23rd was fairly quiet in this sector except for intermittent shelling and the time was spent in organising and improving the position for the battle next day.

At 9.30 a.m., the 23rd March, the enemy attempted a surprise attack on the left, taking in part of the left Company front. This attack was swept away by rifle and Lewis gun fire at 200 yards range. About 2 p.m. the enemy artillery opened out with a heavy bombardment along the whole Brigade front and support lines. At 3.15 p.m. the enemy attacked with large masses of men in four waves. The attack was completely broken by rifle and Lewis gun fire, and not a wave reached our wire. A second attack was launched later during the afternoon but was repulsed with great slaughter. Having failed in this attack the enemy withdrew to some dead ground about 150 yards east of our wire and dug themselves in. Lieut.-Col. S. S. Ogilvie, D.S.O., in command of the 1st Wiltshire Regt., won the rare distinction of a second bar to his D.S.O. for his fine leadership throughout the battle.

During the night 23d/24th the 7th T.M. Battery under Capt, Cecil with Lieut. Tinley, Pte. Ludgate, 4th South Staffords, Pte. Robinson, L./Cpl. Palmer and Cpl. Ockwell, 1st Wilts.

did excellent work and all received decorations. Capt. Petty, 10th Cheshire was killed and Capt. Hayward was wounded. Capt. Hayward greatly distinguished himself and afterwards received the V.C. Though slightly wounded on the morning of the 21st he insisted on taking his Company into action. On the 23rd he was badly wounded in the arm but remained in command of his Company encouraging his men and organising the defence until he was again badly wounded in the head. Pte. Badcock and Pte. Phillips, 1st Wilts, did remarkably fine work as runners through the heaviest machine gun fire and shelling during the 23rd/24th March, for which they received the D.C.M. and M.M., respectively. Pte. Brown, Sergt. Pearce, M.M., and Pte. Chilcott showed great bravery in bringing in the wounded. Cpl. Woolford, in command of his post, beat off three attacks and Cpl. Spruels, when all other N.C.O.'s had become casualties, handled his men with great ability. Pte. Titchener, Sergt. Feltham, L./Cpl. Britten as linesman and Cpl. Mustoe, in charge of the pack transport, all distinguished themselves and received the M.M. Major Bartlett, M.C., R.A.M.C., and Capt. Hughes, D.S.O., R.A.M.C., deliberately attended the wounded in the open in spite of very heavy machine gun fire until wounded themselves; Lieut. Thomas set a splendid example in command of his platoon, and all received the Military Cross. With the 10th Cheshires Capt. Cole commanded his Company with great ability and with Lieut. Evans, Capt. Meredith and Lieut. Montague received the Military Cross for their excellent work during the battle. Sergt. Boden and Sergt. Jones reorganised and led their men with great dash. During the withdrawal L./Cpl. Hamlett, M.M., and L./Cpl. Hughes displayed great bravery in covering the retirement of the other troops, also Cpl. Roberts, L./Cpl. Seddon and Pte. Wrench with their Lewis guns. Sergt. Leonard in charge of the battalion signallers, Pte. Broster, M.M., as battalion runner, and L./Cpl. Lindley in command of carrying parties and "Tump Lines," all distinguished themselves and won well-earned decorations.

The general position on the evening of the 23rd was satisfactory along the IVth Corps front. The 3rd or Army line was intact. Two heavy attacks had been repulsed with great slaughter and fresh British Divisions were about to relieve the tired troops who had withstood the first shock of the German attack. The confidence of the men was unbroken and their moral as high as ever.

The morning of the 24th the 4th South Staffords were relieved by a Battalion of the 62nd Division and retired to a position between Fremicourt and Beugnatre, from which position they were able to cover later in the afternoon the retirement of other troops from the 3rd or Army line. Capt. Oldham went forward with a Lewis gun from where he was able to inflict heavy casualties on the enemy : Major Charrington did good work in command of a composite Company of the 7th Brigade, and Capt. Nicholls, R.A.M.C., was conspicuous in his attention to the wounded under heavy fire. All these officers received the Military Cross. C.S.M. Clowsley, Sergt. Hare and Cpl. Vaughan, when their officers had become casualties, reorganised and led their men with great energy and dash ; Pte. Fernley, Cpl. Gibbons, Pte. Fox, Pte. Hill and Pte. Hoare showed great bravery in looking after the wounded under heavy fire. Pte. Adams, Pte. Tolley, Pte. Birch, Pte. Drabble and Pte. Foster all distinguished themselves as runners and received decorations.

The morning of the 24th the enemy opened with a heavy bombardment, much of the fire being directed by hostile aeroplanes. On this particular sector the absence of any British aeroplanes materially assisted the enemy, and short-shooting by our own artillery caused some casualties amongst our troops. By mid-day the enemy were again observed massing east and south-east of Vaulx, presumably for another attack.

At about 3 p.m., the troops on the right began to withdraw and soon after the 1st Wilts and 10th Cheshires began their retirement, covered by the 4th South Staffords, from a position across the Bapaume-Fremicourt Road.

As the withdrawal began the enemy delivered a third attack ; this was beaten off from the front, but the 1st Wilts suffered heavily from machine gun fire as they retired up the forward slopes of the ridge. The 10th Cheshires withdrew gradually to a line south-east of Beugnatre where touch was kept with the 4th South Staffords on the right. Capt. Edgar, 4th South Staffords, was killed during the afternoon. The enemy was still coming on in large numbers but was made to pay a heavy price for every yard of his advance. 2nd Lieut. Bates was invaluable and received the D.S.O. for his work. Capt. Carr remained behind each time until his Company had taken up a new position, inflicting heavy losses on the enemy with his Lewis gun. 2nd Lieut. Bell also did wonderfully good work with his Lewis guns and won the M.C. Sergt. Tilley did splendid work collecting and organising stragglers. After dark the remains of the 1st Wilts and 10th Cheshires were collected at Bihucourt and marched to a camp on the Achiet-Bucquoy Road. The majority of the officers, including all four Company Commanders, had by this time become casualties. This withdrawal was rendered necessary by the gradual retirement of the Corps on our right to conform with the movement of the Vth Army, otherwise there is no doubt that our troops could have perfectly well maintained themselves for a considerable time in the positions from which they repulsed attack after attack on the 23rd. Meanwhile the 4th South Staffords, who had covered the retirement of the other troops on their front, suffered severely when forced to withdraw. About 8 p.m., the 24th, the Battalion dug itself in about 400 yards east of Bief-villiers on the right of the 74th Brigade. During the shelling on the following morning Col. Blackall was killed and Col. Finch, who had previously commanded the 13th Cheshires in the 74th Brigade, now took over the Battalion. The South Staffords had only joined the Division from England in October, 1917, and, except for periods in the defensive lines, this was its first experience of a modern battle.

Divisional Headquarters in the afternoon of the 24th moved from Achiet le Petit to a camp on the Achiet-Bucquoy Road and on the following day, the 25th, to Pusieux in the morning and to Fonquevillers in the afternoon.

The 74th Brigade, which after its withdrawal, had concentrated at Bihucourt near Achiet by 4.30 p.m. on the 23rd, was ready to move off the following morning at 5 a.m. At midday orders were issued for the Brigade to dig themselves in along the front just west of Biefvillers crossing the Bapaume-Achiet main road and prolonged south as far as Grevillers.

This line was to be held to support the 75th Brigade, Field Companies and 6th South Wales Borderers who were covering Sapignies and Behagnies. At 8 a.m., March 25th, the Brigade front was quiet; on the left flank the 11th Lancs. Fusiliers were in position 2,000 yards west of Favreuil, the right flank in touch with the 51st Division at the cross roads a mile west of Grevillers. About 8.30 a.m. the enemy occupied Biefvillers in considerable strength and the 11th Lancs. Fusiliers and Loyal North Lancs. withdrew by stages to a position east of Bihucourt astride Bapaume-Achiet main road. During the afternoon the withdrawal continued, but by 5 p.m. on the 25th a Brigade of a fresh Division (62nd) had come up and were digging in east of Achiet le Petit and thence joining up with the line held by the 75th Brigade east and south-east of Logeast Wood. Later on the same evening the whole Brigade was withdrawn through the troops of the 62nd Division and assembled in a field near 74th Brigade Headquarters immediately west of Bucquoy. The last of the Brigade reached this place about 11.20 p.m. and after being given hot food moved up to Biez Wood where they spent the night. At the same time the 75th Brigade commenced to withdraw from their position east and south-east of Logeast Wood about 8 p.m. Pusieux was reached about 1 a.m. the 26th and after a short rest and a hot meal a start was made to dig another defensive position covering Pusieux from the south-east. This was held by 2nd South Lancs. in touch with the 62nd Division on the left, Borders in the centre, and the 11th Cheshires on the right. Information was extremely scanty as to the situation away on the right and at 4 a.m. the Brigade was again ordered to withdraw and to concentrate north of Gommecourt. This position was reached about 6.30 a.m. and at 10 a.m. the Brigade moved into an old German trench east of Gommecourt. The 7th Brigade, who after their withdrawal from the third or Army line, concentrated in a camp west of Achiet le Petit on the Bucquoy Road. At 7.30 a.m. on the morning 25th the Brigade had dug a slit trench east and south-east of Logeast Wood, with the South Staffords on the right, 10th Cheshires in the centre, and 1st Wilts on the left. At dusk, in conformity with the withdrawal of the other Brigades, the Battalions retired across country to the Achiet-Bucquoy Road, and then down the road to Bucquoy. On the morning of the 26th the 7th Brigade took up an outpost position south of Gommecourt Wood but later moved to new positions east of Gommecourt. At 9.30 a.m. the 74th Brigade took up a position from the north-east corner of Gommecourt Wood through Pigeon Wood facing south-east, with the 9th Loyal North Lancs. on the right, 11th Lanc. Fusiliers on the left. The 75th Brigade moved into support further to the weat. Late that night, at 11 p.m. 26th, orders reached the three Brigades to withdraw from their positions and assemble west of Fonquevillers on the Souastre Road and from there to concentrate at Couin.

During the last two days much uncertainty had been caused by rumours started by German agents in British uniform with the object of creating confusion and panic amongst the retiring troops. Appalling congestion of traffic amongst the transport was caused by individuals repeating these rumours regarding the approach of the enemy, rumours which in all cases were totally unfounded. In every situation there is always a touch of comedy and the fighting units of the Division heard with some amusement of the occasion when servants, drivers, and everybody who had a rifle, were lined up west of Souastre to withstand an attack from an imaginary enemy from the south.

Divisional Headquarters on the 26th moved to Pommier, and on the 27th to Couin, where the Brigades of the Division had concentrated during the early hours of the morning and were subsequently joined by their transport. At 2.30 p.m. the Division marched by Brigades to bivouac at Puchevillers where they arrived before nightfall. The following morning Divisional Headquarters moved to Berneuil, and the Brigades marched to the area south of Doullens.

Since the opening hours of the battle on the 21st March the Battalions had fought, without a moment's rest; they had dug innumerable new positions and trenches, and finished on 27th and 28th by marching 36 miles in 36 hours, a remarkably fine performance. The losses had been heavy and many retirements were ordered when the troops were perfectly secure and able to repulse any attacks the Germans could have made against them. These retirements during daylight were, and always will be, extremely costly and should be avoided whenever possible. Several parties, unfortunately, must never have received their orders to retire; they fought to the last and were eventually engulfed in the German advance. A retirement in the face of overwhelming odds, especially when rendered necessary to conform with large swinging movements, and in the face of an enemy energetically pushing their advantage, must always be the supreme test of the discipline and training of the troops. That the retirement was successfully carried out is the greatest proof of their value. To quote the words of the Commander-in-Chief in his official despatch :—

"The 25th Division was in close support when the German attack opened and was at once sent into battle in the neighbourhood of the Bapaume-Cambrai Road. Though constantly attacked it was not dislodged from any position by the enemy's assault. When withdrawn from the Somme fighting the spirit of the Division was exceptionally high. It has since been heavily engaged in the Lys Battle and has again performed distinguished service."

One of the brightest and not the least important feature of the battle and the retirement was the fact that in no case were the men without ammunition or food, though unfortunately there was little opportunity for cooking. This reflects the greatest credit on the administrative arrangements and also on the regimental transport in their successful efforts to keep the men supplied with rations.

MACHINE GUN BATTALION.

The work of the Machine Gun Battn. was invaluable throughout the battle. Previously, each Brigade had its own Machine Gun Company, but in February the Companies had been formed into a Machine Gun Battn. for the Division, and Lt.-Col. J. D. Deane-Drummond, D.S.O., M.C., the Divisional Machine Gun Officer, took over the command. The fact that the Division was in reserve to the entire Corps front at the commencement of the battle rendered any close co-operation of the Battalion impossible and during the four days the Companies of the Machine Gunners were attached to and supporting troops of the 6th, 51st, 41st and 19th Divisions. Casualties were heavy but not more so than was to be anticipated when every officer and man went into battle with the instructions and intentions that except under direct orders no one was to retire. Two officers were killed : Capt. G. F. Wolff and Lieut. R. A. Colley ; eleven were wounded and seven missing, of whom the majority are believed to have become casualties, and about 300 other ranks became casualties. In every case during the fighting the positions occupied on the second and third lines of defence were maintained until the Infantry retired ; on several occasions guns were maintained in forward positions until practically surrounded, and inflicted very heavy casualties on the enemy before being destroyed.

B Coy., under the command of Capt. G. F. Wolff, took up positions supporting the 51st Division, east and south-east of Beaumetz. All four sections during the three days fighting were offered splendid targets by the enemy as they advanced time after time to the attack. Early on the 23rd, three guns of No. 2 Section did great execution in breaking up the enemy in massed formation moving to the attack along the Cambrai Road towards Beaumetz. Gradually, nearly all the guns were knocked out by the enemy machine gunfire and shelling. Pte. Moorcroft greatly distinguished himself carrying messages across ground swept by machine gunfire and received the M.M.

D Coy., commanded by Capt. Ashcroft, concentrated with the 75th Brigade at Favreuil and were then despatched to the Vaulx-Morchies Line. Two days later Lieut. Souter took over the Company which he commanded with great ability ; 2nd Lieut. Hind, with two machine gunners in position north-west of Morchies and later in front of Beugny, beat off the enemy with heavy casualties and received the M.C. for their services. Sergt. Brown, Cpl. Burnett, M.M., Sergt. Whiting, and L.-Cpl. Bretherton did splendid work with their guns, and all received well-earned decorations. C Coy., under the command of Major R. C. W. Burn, had its 16 guns holding strong posts along the IVth Corps front. Of these 14 were knocked out by shell fire during the fighting of the 21st. Nine new guns were sent up the same night and were able to give splendid support to the 11th Cheshires and 11th Lancs. Fusiliers when attacked the next day. On the 24th all the guns were again knocked out. Lieut. Syme with four guns north-west of Doignies did very good work and only managed to get away with three survivors of the four machine gun teams. Pte. Craddock, the sole survivor of one gun team, greatly distinguished himself at this place. Lieut. Bentley with No. 4 Section though cut off and without Infantry support repulsed all enemy attempts to advance south of Doignies from 3 p.m. to dusk. Cpl. Simpson, M.M., in charge of a machine gun detachment south of Lagnicourt, Cpl. Tigwell, Pte. Atkinson, and Sergt. Williams with two guns south of Moreuil, especially distinguished themselves and received the M.M.

A Coy. under the command of Major A. M. Bellingham assembled with the 7th Infantry Brigade and did not come into action the first day of the battle, but on the following days rendered splendid service in breaking up the enemy attacks as they advanced in the open against the 3rd or Army Line held by the 1st Wilts., 10th Cheshires, and Highlanders of the 51st Division. Sergt. Beddow, Cpl. Needle, L.-Cpl. Mellor showed great gallantry in covering the retirement of the Infantry ; Pte. Page. as a runner, and Pte. Chesters, L.-Cpl. Davies, Pte. Parker, Pte. Pladdys and Dr. Ingley thoroughly deserved the decorations awarded them. Cpl. Myers did wonderful work the morning of the 24th with three machine guns until the whole of the gun teams were knocked out, he himself being wounded. Guns of No. 4 Section, under Lieut. Maddison, got fine targets down the Cambrai Road and at a range of 200 yards mowed down the enemy attacking in close formation. The majority of the guns of this Company, as with the other Companies, were eventually all destroyed. At the end of the first three days, out of the 64 guns belonging to the Battalion only 15 were got back. Testimony was received from all sources as to the effective work done by these guns until the machine guns themselves were destroyed by shell fire or the detachments became casualties. Too much praise cannot be given to the 25th Battn., Machine Gun Corps for their gallant behaviour throughout the battle and it may be said without exaggeration that the wonderful tenacity displayed by all ranks was the backbone of the successful defence of this portion of the British front. Scarcity of ammunition in the later stages of the battle forced the machine gunners to be rather more economical in their fire, and in some cases only to engage large bodies of the enemy.

ROYAL ENGINEERS AND 6th SOUTH WALES BORDERERS.

The Technical Troops of the Division were the 105th, 106th, and 130th Field Coys. R.E., Commanded by Major F. W. Richards, Major C. W. Lynam, and Major Thorpe, respectively, and 6th South Wales Borderers (Pioneers) Commanded by Lt.-Col. N. T. Fitzpatrick, D.S.O., M.C., R.E.

Prior to the attack the three Field Coys. were working under the Chief Engineer of the Corps on the Bapaume and Vaulx defences and one Company of the Pioneers was finishing an elaborate dugout system for Divisional Headquarters in Favreuil Wood. Later on this dugout proved of the very greatest value to other Divisional and Brigade Headquarters during the battle. The morning of the 21st Sapper Dunham and L.-Cpl. Swallow, 105th Field Coy., R.E., won a M.M.

or their bravery in harnessing horses and getting the wagons away under heavy shelling. The afternoon of the 21st the three Coys., with the Pioneers under the C.R.E. (Lt.-Col. R. J. Done, D.S.O.), were ordered to dig and improve the third or Army line across the Beugnatre-Longatte Road. By 11 p.m., that night these troops were well dug in, two Companies of the 6th S.W. Borderers holding 1,000 yards north of the Beugnatre-Longatte Road in touch with the 40th Division on the left. The 105th and 106th Field Coys., R.E., were holding the ground between Beugnatre-Vaulx and Beugnatre-Longatte Roads, in touch with the 10th Cheshires (7th Brigade) on the right, later joined by the 130th Field Coy. About 9 p.m., the 22nd, troops of the 41st Division, relieved the Field Companies and Pioneers who retired to a camp between Bihucourt and Sapignies. The following morning the Pioneers were shelled out of their camp and, together with the three Field Coys., were placed under the Command of the 75th Infantry Brigade to dig in and hold a position covering Sapignies and Behagnies; during the night wire was put up in front of this line of trenches. On the 24th the three Field Coys. and Pioneers were ordered back to take up a position from West of Achiet le Grand to east of Logeast Wood. Two Companies of the Pioneers, however, remained in front of Sapignies and were on the morning of the 25th heavily engaged with the enemy. Though surrounded on three sides they managed to withdraw to the high ground west of Sapignies and one and a half companies of Pioneers under Major Deane later on assisted in the counter-attack which drove the enemy out of Bihucourt. For his fine work he received the D.S.O. Lieut. Pearce in command of an isolated Lewis gun post, Lieut. Petts and Lieut. Davies won the M.C., for their fine leadership during the fighting. Sergt. Evans, Sergt. Green, L./Sergt. Johnson, Sergt. Lander, Pte. Pearce, Pte. Jones and Pte. Halliday for their gallantry all received well-earned decorations. Of the Sappers, Sergt. Foley, M.M., and Sergt. Saunders, 106th Field Coy., R.E., handled their men with great ability and received the M.M. The 105th and 106th Field Coys., R.E., and one and a half companies of Pioneers dug in along the front of Logeast Wood. Late in the afternoon of the 25th the three Field Coys. and the 6th S.W.B.'s withdrew to Fonquevillers. Major Richards, 105th Field Coy., R.E., and Capt. Caparn, 106th Field Coy., were wounded during

F

the afternoon whilst reconnoitring a new defensive line, and were succeeded in command of the Field Coys. by Lieuts. Ridge and Ellen.

On the 26th the 106th and 130th Field Coys. took up a position north-east of Hannescamp and late that night moved back to the Couin area. Pte. Atherton, Pte. Harroben, M.M., Pte. Reynolds as stretcher bearers and Pte. Waters, Pte. Howells, and Pte. Swain as runners were conspicuous for their gallantry throughout. Sapper Baldwin, 106th Field Coy., R.E., as cyclist orderly was most reliable in delivering messages under most difficult circumstances. All thoroughly deserved the decorations awarded them.

During the whole of the fighting the three Field Coys. and S.W. Borderers were necessarily used as Infantry and not for Technical Duties. Had the Division been in command of the front line no doubt the destruction and demolition of roads, bridges, etc., would have been assigned to them, but they were not required for this purpose : during the retirement the R.E. and Pioneers dug and held positions to prevent a break-through by the enemy at threatened points : The first time between Vaulx and Beugnatre and next on the Sapignies-Behagnies line behind Mory, then between Achiet and Logeast Wood and later in front of Hannescamp. The R.E. casualties were not heavy, only four officers being wounded and 40 casualties amongst the other ranks. Of the Pioneers the casualties were comparatively slight, one officer killed and four wounded. During the five days these troops dug and manned at least five different lines of trenches and one company marched as much as 87 miles.

ARTILLERY.

The Divisional Artillery previous to the 21st March, was out of the line with the remainder of the Division. When the battle began the 112th Brigade at once reported to Headquarters 51st Division and came under the orders of the 51st Divisional Artillery.

112TH BRIGADE, R.F.A.				Lt.-Col. E. V. Sarson, D.S.O.
A/112	...	...	...	Major W. Swinton, M.C.
B/112	...	...	...	Major H. T. Vincent.
C/112	...	...	...	Major W. E. Mackay, M.C.
D/112	...	...	...	Major G. Sumpter, M.C.

All four Batteries were quickly in action in reserve positions about 300 yards south-east of Beugny against the enemy advancing east of Beaumetz, down the Bapaume-Cambrai Road. Considerable losses were caused amongst the horses in their wagon lines from the fire of long-range guns. Observation was good and during the night and most of the 22nd, the Batteries continued to answer repeated calls for assistance against concentrations of the enemy advancing along the main Bapaume-Cambrai Road who were engaged and dispersed. A body of cavalry, concentrating along the Bapaume-Cambrai Road was engaged and dispersed in confusion, and continued attacks near Beaumetz were beaten off. Cpl. Robertson and Driver Rose, D/112, won the M.M. for excellent work in maintaining a visual signal station under heavy fire on the Cambrai Road until forced to retire with the infantry. Lieut. Ironside D/112, and 2nd Lieut. Paterson, M.C., B/112, 2nd Lieut. Ross B/112, established O.P.'s under heavy fire and received the M.C. for their gallantry. These officers kept up uninterrupted communication during the day and it was mainly owing to their efforts that the batteries were enabled to break up enemy concentrations and inflict heavy casualties. When the counter-attack with tanks took place in the afternoon of the 22nd, A and B Batteries turned on with direct observation from their battery positions to engage enemy reinforcements coming up against this counter-attack. These guns did great execution; the guns of B Battery driving off some of the enemy who were attacking our tanks. The afternoon of the 22nd, the Batteries were withdrawn in succession to positions east of Bancourt. D Battery remained in position till after dark and was able to carry out most effective shooting on the Bapaume-Cambrai Road. About mid-day the 23rd, the Batteries again retired in succession : Major W. Swinton was wounded, but on the whole casualties were comparatively slight. Gunner Brown, Gunner Jinks and Driver Taylor, A/112 distinguished themselves by successfully defending a signal station during the German attack near Beugny. Capt. Hansen, Commanding C/112 also did excellent work throughout the fight.

On the 24th, the Batteries continued to engage the advancing enemy though the valley in which the Batteries were placed was heavily shelled. About mid-day a further retirement began to positions west of Thilloy and later on east of Grevillers. The retirement was carried out in succession C, D, B and A Batteries, Lieut. Murchon covering the retirement of D Battery by coming into action against the advancing infantry at close range. B Battery suffered casualties in men and horses from shell fire as the guns were limbering up and a good many were caused by enemy machine gun fire at this point. Most effective shooting at masses of the enemy moving from Irles on Miraumont had been possible, and during the further retirement Major Sumpter with a 4.5 howitzer of D Battery did great execution at close range. Sergt. Agnew D/112 and Sergt. Dale A/112 also brought their guns into action with open sights and displayed great gallantry in covering the retirement of the infantry. Gunner Bannister B/112 maintained a Signal Station and kept touch with his Battery under very heavy fire and Saddler Cpl. Smith was conspicuous for his bravery in attending to and bringing in wounded. The following morning the Brigade occupied a position southeast of Puisieux. All received decorations.

On the 26th the Brigade came into action south-west of Fonquevillers, but by this time several guns of the Battery were out of action from defects and enemy shell fire, though during the retirement it was never found necessary to abandon any guns to the enemy—B Battery, 112th Brigade, were fortunately able to reinforce themselves with a 60-pounder, whose personnel had apparently become casualties. From now on they were supporting troops of the New Zealand Division who had come up on the right of the IVth Corps. During the whole of these four days the fighting had been continuous, the batteries had been in action without rest and keeping up a continuous rate of fire. Great credit is due to the drivers, who never for one moment failed to keep the guns supplied with ammunition ; they worked practically all day and all night in transporting and bringing the ammunition up to the guns. A few days later, near Riencourt, Gunner Bloomfield, B/112, and Bombdr. Oates, D/112, repaired wires and kept up communications under heavy fire. All these received decorations for their gallantry, and also Major Mackay, M.C., commanding C/112, for his excellent work throughout the operations.

The 110th Brigade early on the 21st marched from their camp at Ablainzeville to an assembly point west of Sapigny–

Bapaume main road and came under the orders of the 6th Divisional Artillery.

110TH BRIGADE, R.F.A.	...		Lt.-Col. H. R. PHIPPS, D.S.O.
A/110	...	...	... Major A. Anderton, M.C. (died of wounds).
B/110	...	...	... Major A. L. Harman, M.C.
C/110	...	...	... Major D. C. Wilson, M.C.
D/110	...	...	... Major A. P. Evershed.

A and C Batteries came into action south-west of Vaulx, from which position they were able to do effective shooting against the enemy. A continuous rate of fire was kept up all night, and on the afternoon of the 22nd a strong attack by the enemy was successfully broken up by B Battery. In the afternoon of the 22nd enemy massing in Maricourt Wood and also in Vaulx Wood were successfully engaged, and at 9.30 p.m. on the 22nd the batteries were ordered to retire to positions behind the 3rd or Army Line of Defence. 2nd Lieut. Battersby A/110 and Lieut. Pritchard B/110 did splendid work as F.O.O. in the outpost line. 2nd Lieut. Watson A/110 retired his guns by sections and kept up the fire of his battery with great ability. Capt. Watts C/110 set a fine example to the men in bringing up the teams through heavy shelling so that his Batteries were able to change their positions quickly. Sergt. Cheese C/110, Sergt. Gardiner C/110, and L./Cpl. Tooth A/110 maintained the fire of their guns with great gallantry. Driver Fitzgerald, Johnson, Nixon, Robinson, Williams and Myatt A/110 displayed great gallantry as gun team drivers of the Section left behind to cover the retirement of the rest of the Battery near Beugny. L./Bombr. Yeoman A/110 and Gunner Ball A/110 were excellent in keeping up Battery communication and Cpl. Swindles C/110 repaired lines under heavy fire. Early the 23rd the positions were heavily shelled by the enemy and about noon a further retirement in succession took place. Lieut. A. J. Cunningham, C Battery, was killed at this position. Just before dark the Batteries were ordered to retire to a position further to the rear. Good shooting had been done during the 23rd and 24th, though great difficulty was experienced in maintaining a line up to the F.O.O. as it was continually cut in many places by the enemy's shell fire. The 24th the Batteries retired round the outskirts of Bapaume and took up a position east of Bihucourt.   Batt.-Sergt.-Major Cobden B/110 showed great skill in maintaining the supply of ammunition for his Battery when the officers had become casualties.   Bombr. Hyett D/110 was conspicuous for his bravery in attending to wounded under heavy fire, and all received decorations.

On the 25th the Batteries came into action near Achiet-le-Grand, retiring later on to the left of Achiet-le-Petit, and later again in the evening to a position at Essars.   The morning of the 27th the positions were heavily shelled and a good many casualties to men and horses were sustained.   Later the Batteries took up a position west of Quesnoy Farm, where they remained until the morning of the 29th, when the Brigade was transferred along with the 112th Brigade to the New Zealand Division.   A few days later Bombr. Parry and Bombr. Reith A/110 distinguished themselves in successfully getting up ammunition under heavy fire.   Driver Butler D/110, Driver Clegg A/110, and Cpl. Marshall D/110 set a fine example to the men.   All these received decorations which they richly deserved, as well as Major Anderton, commanding A/110 a second bar to his M.C. for his coolness and gallantry throughout the operation.   In spite of the persistent shelling by the enemy the Brigades were extremely fortunate in sustaining comparatively few casualties.   The drivers, who were indefatigable in getting the ammunition up to the guns, were also lucky in this respect.   The work of F.O.Os. was extremely arduous and constant changes of positions increased the difficulties in getting communication through to the batteries from the Front Line.   Visual communication was very necessary and in many cases was effectively used.

The work of the Heavy Trench Mortar Battery was most excellent.   Bombr. Hill and Bombr. Rowley, Y.25 T.M. Battery won the D.C.M. and M.M. respectively, on the 22nd March near Hermies—though enfiladed by machine guns the Battery continued firing after the Infantry had retired and only when surrounded were the guns blown up and the crews retired.

SIGNAL COMMUNICATIONS.

The signal communications under the command of Major E. de W. Bradley, M.C., were most effective throughout the fighting ; Lieuts. Pullan, Reed and Belcher being responsible for the communications of the 7th, 74th, and 75th Brigades, respectively. The 7th and 74th Brigades maintained almost continuous telephone communication with their Battalions ; the 74th by means of the buried route which they themselves had dug a few days before the battle, and the 7th Brigade from their position in the Army Line of defence by cable over ground. Signal communication of the 75th Brigade was somewhat more difficult, as the Battalions were detached and sent to reinforce troops of other brigades. Sapper Hogarth and Pte. Leavey, in charge of a Visual Signal Station ; Sapper Dingle and Cpl. Taylor as linesmen, also Pte. Milner and Pte. Senior were all conspicuous for their bravery in taking messages to the Battalions of the 7th Brigade. Sergt. Gass, M.M., of the 74th Brigade Signal Section was invaluable in maintaining communication between the Brigade Headquarters and the Battalions of the 74th Brigade.

The Brigade Forward Stations were in all cases worked until their Battalions were ordered to retire. Unfortunately the 74th Brigade forward party under Sergt. Paddock remained too long and the whole party became casualties. Visual communications were used extensively by both brigades. Lieut. Belcher and Lieut. Rendle received the M.C. for their excellent work throughout the battle. Sapper Allen and Sapper Turner laid a line near Vaulx under heavy fire ; L./Cpl. Pinchbeck in charge of the Divisional Forward Exchange was excellent ; Pte. Meade, Cpl. Stanbury and Sapper Wakeford as motor cyclists never failed to deliver messages entrusted to them. All these received decorations for their services.

Wireless was also used extensively ; a (wireless) set was erected at Divisional Headquarters and was in constant communication with the Brigades ; this eventually proved of the greatest value in intercepting messages and helped to keep the General Staff informed as to the events along the whole Corps front. Sapper Simpson in charge of the wireless received the M.M. Although the Brigades of the Division were constantly on the move yet telephone communication was opened as quickly as possible. The work of the linesmen was most severe, and great praise is due to them for the way they performed their duties.

SUPPLIES.

During the whole of the fighting the greatest credit is due to the Divisional Train, A.S.C., and to the Senior Supply

Officer, Major Bush, in their efforts to keep the Division supplied with rations. The morning of the 21st, the Supply Railhead was at Achiet-le-Grand and the Divisional Train was loading direct by horse transport. From a very early hour in the morning the Railway Station was heavily shelled and it became impracticable to proceed with the loading of the wagons; these were parked on arrival in the neighbouring fields and later on during a lull in the shelling the loading was resumed. For the next three days the supply railhead for the Division moved back to Miraumont. A certain amount of difficulty was caused by the fact that the Brigades were so split up in order to reinforce other Divisions: the difficulty of finding transport lines which were continually moving was also very great. Congestion of the roads delayed the wagons, but in no case was it found impossible to deliver the supplies to the various units and re-filling points. The late evening of the 25th the Divisional Train was moved back as far as Authie, which meant considerable distances to be covered by the supply wagons each day. On the 27th, the 199th, 200th and 201st Coys., A.S.C., under Capt. Kennard, Capt. Finch, and Capt. Fenner moved to Puchevillers and on the 28th to the Canaples area where each Company was located with its own Brigade group. During the whole of the period covering the retirement the distances were very great and proved a severe strain on both men and horses. The work was continuous, but all proved equal to the task.

CASUALTIES AND MEDICAL ARRANGEMENTS.

The 75th, 76th, and 77th Field Ambulances commanded by Lt.-Col. Davidson, D.S.O., Lt.-Col. Tyrell, D.S.O., and Lt.-Col. Kelly, D.S.O., all of whom received a bar to their D.S.O. for their distinguished services, were at Achiet and south of Beugny when the battle commenced.

75th and 77th Field Ambulances became responsible for clearing casualties of the 7th and 74th Brigades to the Corps Main Dressing Station at Beugny, whilst the 76th Field Ambulance looked after the 75th. Brigade with its Main Dressing Station at Favreuil. This arrangement lasted for two days though continuous shelling made it sometimes necessary to change the location of the advanced dressing station to less exposed positions. On one occasion during the retirement the 77th Field Ambulance was attacked by four enemy aeroplanes and during the night, 23rd/24th March, bombs were dropped killing two and wounding four other ranks of the medical personnel, besides destroying many of the horses and a couple of wagons.

During the battle the casualties in the Division were severe, but not more than was to have been expected with such continuous and heavy fighting.

	Killed.		Wounded.		Missing.
Officers ...	34	...	105	...	40
Other ranks...	284	...	1,391	...	1,548

The treatment and evacuation of the wounded was only carried on under great difficulties. Heavy and continuous shelling of the back areas and the main roads made it impossible at times for motor ambulances to reach the advanced dressing stations and bring away all stretcher cases, consequently of these a few were left behind and fell into German hands. This must inevitably happen during a retirement, and that so large a number of serious cases were brought back to the Regimental Aid Posts and successfully evacuated, is a remarkable proof of the fine skill and devotion to duty displayed by the Battalion Stretcher Bearers, personnel of the Aid Posts and Advanced Dressing Stations throughout. The Battalion Medical Officers worked unceasingly, and of these Capt. R. G. McElney was killed. Capt. Kennedy, M.C., Major Lescher, M.C., and Capt. Stevenson, M.C., all received bars to their M.C. for their bravery in attending to wounded in the open under heavy fire. Pte. Allen, 76th Field Ambulance, showed great presence of mind when the Dressing Hut was destroyed ; Pte. Graydon i/c of an Aid Post south of Vaulx ; Sergt. Lechmere, A.S.C., M.T., as Motor Cyclist Orderly ; Sergt. Boxall, Pte. Hodgson, Pte. Vallance, 75th Field Ambulance, Pte. Oliver and Pte. Paul, 77th Field Ambulance and Cpl. Trolley, 76th Field Ambulance, all won decorations for their self-sacrifice and disregard of danger in attending to and bringing in wounded under heavy fire.

The following are a list of those who received rewards for services during the operations, with details of some of the more notable acts of gallantry for which the reward was granted :—

Capt. R. F. J. Hayward, M.C., 1st Wiltshire Regt. (Wounded.)

The 21st, 22nd and 23rd March, 1918, near Fremicourt for the most conspicuous gallantry in action.

This officer, while in command of a Company, displayed almost superhuman powers of endurance, and consistent courage of the rarest nature. In spite of the fact that he was buried, wounded in the head, and rendered deaf on the 21st, and again had his arm shattered on the morning of the 23rd he refused to go down even though he received a third serious injury to his head on the afternoon of the 23rd, until he collapsed from sheer physical exhaustion.

Throughout the whole of this period, the enemy were attacking his Company front without cessation and this officer continued the whole time to move across the open from one trench to another with absolute disregard of his personal safety, concentrating entirely on reorganising his defences and encouraging his men.

It was entirely due to the magnificent example of ceaseless energy of this officer that many most determined attacks upon his portion of the trench system failed entirely.

Awarded . . . . **V.C.**

Major A. Anderton, M.C., A Battery, 110th Brigade, R.F.A.

Near Beugy on 22nd March, 1918, the Battery was in action. Owing to the retirement of our Infantry, it was left exposed. This Officer stopped the last lot of infantry passing the guns, led them to the crest under heavy machine gun fire, deployed them, showed them targets, and directed their fire, showing the utmost coolness and initiative, Encouraged by his fine example the Infantry (100 men) held the ridge, and thus enabled the Battery to retire by sections in an orderly manner.

Major Anderton continued to control the fire of the Battery and retired his last Section only when the enemy were 600 yards away.

Awarded . . . . **Second Bar to M.C.**

No. 13672 Corpl. J. Ashton, 2nd South Lancashire Regt.

For conspicuous gallantry. During the enemy attack on the Vaulx-Morchies line on the 22nd March, this N.C.O. showed fine qualities of initiative. When the enemy had penetrated our line, he organised and led a bombing squad and rounded up this party of the enemy, and after inflicting heavy casualties on them brought back four prisoners.

He set a fine example to the rest of his Company, and his brave action undoubtedly saved the situation at a critical moment.

Awarded . . . . **D.C.M.**

No. 27225 Pte. G. Badcock, 1st Wiltshire Regt.

From the 21st to the 26th March, 1918, in the trenches north-east of Fremicourt, for most conspicuous gallantry.

This Private acted as Battalion runner and as such volunteered again and again to carry messages 400 yards over exposed ground swept by machine gun fire. On one occasion in particular he volunteered to carry a message through the heaviest possible machine gun barrage when it appeared absolutely impossible for anyone to pass through it, and succeeded in safely delivering his message, thereby giving the most vital information to a Company Commander in the front line. His determination, courage and untiring energy were beyond all praise. By his gallant action he was very largely instrumental in enabling the Battalion when ordered so to do, to evacuate the position, and thus avert complete destruction.

Awarded..........**D.C.M.**

No. 78018 Gunner A. Ball, A Battery, 110th Brigade, R.F.A.

On the 22nd March, 1918, near Beugny he showed great courage and devotion to duty as telephone man with the Observing Officer, on the front of a hill exposed to heavy shell and machine gun fire from enemy. Men fell round him and our Infantry had to pass him, but he kept up communication with the Battery and thus passed all orders. His coolness was remarkable.

Awarded..........**M.M.**

On 5th April, 1918, at Courcelies au Bois as signaller at the O.P. when all wires were cut by heavy shelling, Gunner Ball volunteered to bring back a message through the barrage and did so. Returning to O.P. he found the F.O.O. severely wounded and with another man carried him back, though exhausted. Though ordered to rest, he went out several times to mend wires in the villages, heavily shelled. When the Battery Commander was mortally wounded, this man was the first to help him. Later when a new F.O.O. went out, he volunteered to accompany him, though actually unfit to walk even a few hundred yards. It is by the exceptional courage of such signallers and linesmen that Batteries are able to deal with new targets in battle, as otherwise no news comes through.

Awarded..........**D.C.M.**

2nd Lieut. C. Bates, 4th South Staffordshire Regt. (Wounded.)

On the 23rd March, near Beugny, he went forward alone some 300 yards in front of our line, through a heavy barrage, to a commanding position, and lay there in the open under heavy fire for three hours, noting the dispositions of the enemy and sending back information. He then returned and altered the disposition of the platoon in such a manner that he succeeded in holding up the enemy for the remainder of the day, in spite of his persistent efforts to attack in front and to turn the flanks. He was twice wounded, but insisted on remaining with his Command and kept them cheerful and confident. When eventually he withdrew his Command on the following day, he was instrumental in saving what might have been a nasty situation near Fremicourt, as the enemy was pressing heavily, but on his arrival he quickly sized up the situation and got a Lewis gun into position on the railway embankment and remained firing it himself until all available ammunition was exhausted. He was then able to withdraw, as his action had put a stop to the enemy's attempt to advance in that vicinity.

Awarded..........**D.S.O.**

Capt. E. D'Arcy Birnie, M.C., 8th Border Regt. (Wounded.)

This officer was commanding A Coy. of the 8th Borders and when we counter-attacked in the Vaulx-Morchies line on the afternoon 21st March, 1918, he took charge of the three Companies in the line and re-organised. Early in the morning 22nd March, 1918, the enemy attacked in force and effected an entrance into trenches on our right and secured Vaulx Wood, leaving our right flank in the air. Although enveloped on three sides this officer led attack after attack against enemy bombing parties and for five hours kept large forces of the enemy at bay. Twice he dispersed strong attacks of the enemy coming from the direction of Lagnicourt and while the men were engaged bombing the enemy out of our trenches, Capt. Birnie (who is a marksman) took up a position on the parapet and accounted for over 100 of the enemy with his own rifle. Finally when his position became untenable owing to lack of bombs, he successfully withdrew his men to the Vaulx-Fremicourt Road, later pushing up to the Vaulx-Morchies Road and establishing touch with troops of the 71st Brigade on our right, seven hours after touch had been lost.

He was badly wounded late in the afternoon 22nd March, 1918, and it is mainly due to his efforts that the enemy advance in our portion of the line was so long retarded. Throughout all Capt. Birnie displayed exceptional skill and bravery in the face of immense odds.

Awarded.........D.S.O.

No. 25197 Sergt. H. A. Brandon, 11th Cheshire Regt.

Near Morchies on 23rd March, 1918, this N.C.O.'s Platoon was holding a position on the right flank of the Battalion and was practically isolated from the remainder of his Company. His Platoon Officer was wounded early in the day and Sergt. Brandon commanded the Platoon with the utmost coolness and bravery. He held on to his position until nearly surrounded and finally, when ordered to withdraw, successfully extricated his Platoon under heavy machine-gun fire.

Awarded..........D.C.M.

No. 18327 Corpl. A. Burnett, M.M., D Coy., 25th Battn. Machine Gun Corps.

On 21st March, 1918, at 4.15 p.m. this corporal was in charge of two Vickers guns near Vaulx. He volunteered and went along with his Section Officer to choose positions to enable fire to be brought to bear on the Bois de Vaulx, being under direct enemy machine gun fire. An hour later he wen ou. alone to find two Corps machine gun positions, in which he was successful, the whole time being under heavy fire. On 22nd March, 1918, at 9.15. a.m. he saw the left flank exposed after the Infantry had retired and the enemy were coming over the crest. He immediately took one of his guns to a position to cover the flank and was successful in holding up the enemy's advance for a considerable time until they had worked round and nearly surrounded him and were within 30 yards, two of his gun team being killed. At all times he has shown exceptional gallantry.

Awarded.......D.C.M.

No. 16670 Sergt. A. W. Cheese, C Battery, 110th Brigade, R.F.A.

Near Beugny on 22nd March, 1918, the Battery was heavily shelled. He showed great gallantry and disregard for his own safety in maintaining the fire of his gun in spite of casualties, and by his example inspired courage in all. Every day to the 28th March his conduct was the same.

Awarded..........**M.M.**

No. 15851 Sergt. W. Cowap, 9th Loyal North Lancs. Regt.

During the advance of his Company to reinforce the Corps line east of Morchies on the 22nd March, this N.C.O. showed the greatest coolness, courage and ability, in directing and collecting his men under heavy fire, and on reaching the line, collected ammunition organised his men and directed fire. He later successfully carried a message through the barrage, when the Battalion was in danger of being surrounded. Throughout the day this N.C.O.'s cheerfulness and utter disregard of danger was most pronounced.

Awarded..........**D.C.M.**

Major L. C. W. Deane, M.C., 6th South Wales Borderers (Pioneers).

For conspicuous gallantry, good leadership, and great endurance during the operations about Sapignies and Bihucourt between 21st and 28th March, 1918.

Major Deane was ever to the front in every operation displaying in every case an entire disregard of personal safety, a very quick and accurate appreciation of the ever changing tactical situation, and the most cool and determined leadership.

At a most critical period opposite Bihucourt Wood on the afternoon of the 25th, Major Deane organised a counter-attack which he led himself thereby checking the enemy advance.

Major Deane did splendid work throughout the operations.

Awarded..........**D.S.O.**

7672 L.-Corpl. A. Eastwood, M.M., 11th Lancashire Fusiliers.

On 22nd March, 1918, west of Beaumetz-les-Cambrai, this N.C.O. showed conspicuous bravery throughout the enemy's attack. He was in charge of a Lewis Gun Section. When the line was withdrawn, although in danger of being cut off by the enemy, he refused to retire until he had fired his last Lewis gun magazine into the enemy, and thereby considerably held up the attack.

Awarded..........**Bar to M.M.**

No. 18622 Sergt. A. G. Gardner, D.C.M., M.M., 3rd Worcester Regt.

On the 22nd March, 1918, at Morchies, this N.C.O. was in command of three Headquarters Lewis guns. When our troops were ordered to withdraw, he remained behind with his guns and for some time prevented the enemy entering Morchies. He then withdrew to a position just outside Morchies and again prevented the enemy from advancing, thus covering the withdrawal of our troops.

Awarded..........**Bar to M.M.**

No. 47750 Sergt. J. E. Gass, M.M. and Bar, 25th Divl. Signal Coy., R.E.

During the operations in the vicinity of Morchies, and later near Biefvillers and Achiet-lePetit, 21st and 27th March, this Brigade Signalling Sergeant showed much initiative and was indefatigable in his efforts to maintain communication. Not once during the three stages of withdrawal was there a failure to speak to every Battalion on the 'phone. He was continuously under shell fire, but by his cheerfulness and disregard of danger, he set a splendid example to his Section, who worked magnificently. In more than one case, the successful withdrawal of our troops was entirely due to the splendid telephonic communications.

Awarded..........**D.C.M.**

Sergt. S. Graydon, R.A.M.C., 76th Field Ambulance. (Wounded.)

When in charge of No. 3 Relay Post on the evening of 22nd March, 1918, in Sunken Road, south of Vaulx, the Post received a direct hit, wounding four stretcher bearers and Sergt. Graydon. This N.C.O. with great gallantry got the wounded men away, arranged another Post and hearing that the Regimental Aid Post, for which he was responsible, had changed its position, though severely wounded in the thigh, he set out in search of it, through a heavy barrage and located it, and got his men in touch with it. He then made his way back over the open, reported the circumstances at the dressing station, and then collapsed. A fine example of devotion to duty.

Awarded..........**D.C.M.**

No. 28513 Sergt. F. G. Hare, 4th South Staffordshire Regt.

On 23rd March near Fremicourt, as platoon Sergeant and later as acting C.S.M. he displayed great courage and coolness in leading his men through several barrages and heavy machine-gun fire, keeping them well under control the whole time.

Awarded..........**M.M.**

L.Corpl. J. E. Hamlett, M.M., 10th Cheshire Regt.

On the 23rd March near Fremicourt, when the front line had received orders to withdraw, this N.C.O. rendered splendid work in the support line. He covered the line that was withdrawing with the greatest skill, and remained in action at his post until he was satisfied that a new line had been formed behind him.

There is no doubt that the gallantry and skill of this N.C.O. enabled the line to withdraw under the best conditions possible.

He set a splendid example to all around him.

Awarded..........**Bar to M.M.**

No. 725155 Bombr. W. Hill, Y-25 M. T.M. Battery, R.F.A.

This N.C.O. showed great gallantry and devotion to duty on 22nd March, 1918, near Hermies. He worked his mortar for over an hour while the position was being heavily shelled and enfiladed by a machine gun. After he had been firing for three-quarters of an hour the Infantry were given orders to retire, as they were being outflanked, but he continued firing until he saw the enemy almost behind him. He then destroyed his gun and withdrew to the Infantry.

Awarded . . . . **D.C.M.**

No. 21955 Pte. B. Hodgson, R.A.M.C., 75th Field Ambulance.

During the forenoon of the 23rd of March, 1918, in company with No. 30485 L.-Corpl. R. Vallance, R.A.M.C., and the Orderly of the M.O. i/c 11th Lancs. Fusiliers, he went forward through a heavy barrage at a time when the enemy were attacking and brought back the second in command of the 11th Lancashire Fusiliers who was seriously wounded and lying in front of the main body of the Battalion. The Battalion was retiring and this squad was under continuous machine-gun fire, but he helped to carry this officer along the Battalion front to a flank where assistance could be got for him.

Awarded . . . . **M.M.**

No. 6/16760 Pte. W. Holliday, 6th S. Wales Borders (Pioneers).
(Died of wounds.)

For conspicuous gallantry and devotion to duty. On the morning of the 25th March, Pte. Holliday was one of a Lewis Gun Team posted in a gap in the front line about 800 yards east of Sapignies. Small parties of Highland Light Infantry were withdrawing through the Sapignies line under very heavy machine-gun fire which caused many casualties.

One wounded man of the Highland Light Infantry was abandoned about 200 yards in front of Pte. Holliday's Post. He at once went out to him, dressed him, and carried him safely back to Behagnies under very heavy machine-gun barrage. Pte. Holliday rejoined the team again through heavy fire. Pte. Holliday's team fought the gun, doing great execution from two positions and finally withdrew under orders from higher authority when the Germans were on three sides.

Pte. Holliday showed magnificent courage and great coolness throughout 11 hours continuous action.

Awarded . . . . **D.C.M.**

No. 62319 L. Corpl. G. Leavey, 7th Brigade Signals (25th Divl. Signal Coy., R.E.).

For most conspicuous gallantry and devotion to duty during the Fremicourt operations 21st-28th March. For three of these days he was in charge of the Brigade Forward Station. During this period he maintained continuous telegraphic and visual communication with three Battalions under very heavy shell fire, and the most exhausting circumstances.

It was by his magnificent personal example in mending lines and manning visual stations under heavy shell fire that Brigade Headquarters was always able to speak and send messages to its Battalions, and obtain the most valuable information regarding massing of enemy troops, &c.

Later, when the Brigade was ordered to withdraw, this N.C.O. waited until all the Infantry had passed through him, and sending the men who were with him back, he sent a message to Brigade Headquarters explaining the situation, and then destroyed his instruments.

Awarded.........D.C.M.

No. 24381 Sergt. G. Lievesley, 11th Cheshire Regt.

On 22nd March, 1918, after the enemy attacked and practically surrounded the Company at a point about 1,500 yards in front of Beugny and 300 yards on the left of the sugar refinery on the Bapaume-Cambrai Road. In the absence of all the officers this N.C.O. displayed great determination and ability in taking charge of the Company. He conducted the withdrawal of the Company in an orderly manner, displaying great coolness under very heavy machine-gun and shell fire. This N.C.O. has been recommended on previous occasions. He has been in every action the Battalion has taken part in.

Awarded.........D.C.M.

No. 11884 Sergt. J. Macdonald, 8th Border Regt.   (Wounded.)

On the morning of the 22nd March, at Vaulx Wood, when the enemy was advancing, Sergt. MacDonald took up a Lewis gun which had lost its team, got out of the trench and went forward with it, firing from his shoulder. He then got his gun into position and continued to fire it until he was badly wounded. By this prompt action and bravery he beat off the attack and kept the enemy from entering his trench.

As Platoon Sergeant he led his men with great skill and showed great courage throughout the 21st and 22nd, and was a fine example to all ranks.

Awarded.........M.M.

No. S4/158590 Corpl. A. V. Martin, 25th Divl. Train, A.S.C.

On 22nd and 23rd March, 1918, this N.C.O. was issuer in charge of advanced supply dump at Bapaume remaining on duty until last moment.

He was under continual shell fire and showed great coolness and courage, completing such issues as were required.

Awarded.........M.M.

Capt. G. G. Meredith, 10th Cheshire Regt.

During the period that the Battalion was in occupation of defensive positions in the vicinity of Vaulx from 21st to 27th March, this Officer displayed the greatest courage and gallantry.

Whilst acting second in Command he showed excellent judgment and on the afternoon of the 23rd of March, when occupying a forward position, he obtained much useful information regarding the progress of the attack, which assisted the Commanding Officer very materially.

Immediately after the third enemy attack, this Officer went round the whole of the front line and cleared up the situation and helped it in the reorganisation and set a splendid example to the men under heavy rifle and machine-gun fire.

On the 24th, when the Battalion received orders to withdraw, this Officer showed the greatest contempt for his own personal safety, organising new lines of defence.

Throughout the whole operations, this Officer by his gallantry and quickness of action saved many critical situations, and rendered invaluable services to the Battalion.

Awarded..........M.C.

No. 37956 Pte. E. W. Oliver, R.A.M.C., 77th Field Ambulance.

Near Fremicourt on the Bapaume-Cambrai Road, this man showed great bravery as a stretcher bearer from 21st to 26th March, especially on 24th March. He was out collecting cases under heavy shell fire. After collecting several he found a badly wounded man and there being no more men available he put this man on a wheel-barrow and brought him in, although shells were bursting round him. He did not wait for any rest or food but started out again with some more stretcher bearers.

Awarded..........M.M.

No. 74333 Bombdr. J. Parry, A Battery, 110th Brigade, R.F.A.

On 5th April, 1918, at Courcelles au Bois as mounted Orderly at gun line, he brought ammunition thrice under very heavy shelling, showing great coolness and initiative. One gun detachment being all casualties, he then collected some men and kept up S.O.S. fire though without cover and still under heavy fire, thus setting a very fine example to all, and helping to defeat the enemy attack.

Awarded..........M.M.

No. 27094 Sergt. E. Phillips, 9th Loyal North Lancs. (Wounded.)

On 22nd March when his Company were reinforcing the Corps line east of Morchies, this N.C.O. showed great coolness and valour in leading his platoon, and afterwards the company through the barrage On reaching the line, he collected all the men in the vicinity and taking them under control set them a magnificent example. He then took up a position on the parapet and personally accounted for a great quantity of the enemy before being wounded. The service he performed was of inestimable value.

Awarded..........D.C.M.

Lieut. E. C. Pritchard, B Battery, 110th Brigade, R.F.A.

On the 22nd March, 1918, near Favreuil he went as F.O.O. to our outpost line (very lightly held). By his excellent observations he turned fire on to the advancing enemy and inflicted heavy casualties. He kept the wire to the battery going all day under heavy shell fire.

On 24th March near Sapignies the battery was heavily shelled. He showed great coolness and gallantry in controlling the fire, walking from gun to gun and setting a fine example to all.

Awarded . . . . **M.C.**

No. 27336 Pte. W. Reynolds, 3rd Worcester Regt.

On the 22nd March, 1918, at Morchies, this man was in command of a Lewis gun team, when his company was outflanked and nearly cut off. He covered the withdrawal of his Company with his gun, showing great determination and coolness. He then withdrew his gun and team through a barrage. It was greatly due to his efforts that the Company was successfully withdrawn.

Awarded . . . . **M.M.**

Capt. T. Rufus, 11th Lancashire Fusiliers.

On 23rd March, 1918, west of Beaumetz-les-Cambrai, this Officer's Company was very heavily attacked at 5.30 a.m. This attack was beaten off by fire. Subsequently when outflanked and ordered to retire he rallied his men under very heavy machine-gun fire, showing a marked disregard for danger. It was entirely due to his splendid example that the enemy was held up in this vicinity for two hours.

Awarded . . . . **M.C.**

2nd Lieut. A. W. H. Sime, M.C., C Coy., 25th Battn. Machine Gun Corps.

This officer showed exceptional gallantry, initiative, and devotion to duty during the action north-west of Doignies on the 21st and 22nd March, 1918. He was in charge of four Vicker's machine guns. On the night of the 21st, being suspicious of enemy movement near his guns, he organised a patrol and finding a party of enemy within 15 yards he and the party captured a prisoner which he sent to Headquarters 6th Battn. Black Watch, and killed the remainder. Later the same night, he captured another prisoner.

On the morning of the 22nd the left flank being unprotected he moved his gun to exposed positions which were under heavy machine-gun fire and sniping, and succeeded in checking the enemy advance inflicting very heavy casualties. On the same morning, he and a Corporal captured another prisoner with maps showing objective. This man he sent to the same Battalion Headquarters. About midday on the 22nd the enemy commenced digging in about 100 yards from the gun position and for 1½ hours was prevented from doing so by the action of this Officer with machine guns and rifle grenades. At about 5 o'clock in the afternoon the enemy succeeded in surrounding both flanks and the friendly troops having evacuated the Corps line which was behind the guns, he remained for about 30 minutes and when all ammunition was used and the enemy within about 75 yards, the Officer, who was the sole survivor of the gun and had been firing by himself for about one hour, put the gun, which had already been damaged, out of action and succeeded in escaping with the sole survivor of the other gun, and reported to superior Officer at Beetroot Factory, Bapaume-Cambrai Road.

Awarded . . . . **D.S.O.**

Major G. Sumpter, M.C., D Battery, 112th Brigade, R.F.A.

For repeated acts of gallantry in the fighting east of Bapaume between 22nd and 25th March.

On 22nd this officer established and maintained an O.P. near Baumetz-les-Cambrai under very heavy shell fire and carried out valuable reconnaissances.

On 23rd he performed a similar service near Delsaux Farm. On 24th he covered the retirement of the infantry on Puisieux, brought a gun into action with open sights in immediate rear of the infantry and did great execution among the advancing enemy. Has shown exceptional gallantry throughout.

Awarded..........**Bar to M.C.**

No. 46370 L.Corpl. L. Swallow, 105th Field Coy., R.E.

At Iebuquiere on 21st March, 1918, L.Corpl. Swallow volunteered to return to his section's camp, from which they had been shelled out, in order to get the wagons away. This he contrived to do, packing up the section's equipment, and loading up the wagons under continuous and heavy shell fire, and thereby saving the equipment from capture by the enemy.

Awarded..........**M.M.**

No. 17525 L.Corpl. J. Turner, D.C.M., 2nd South Lancashire Regt.

For conspicuous gallantry. On the morning of the 22nd March, in front of Vaulx when our position was attacked, this N.C.O. fired his Lewis gun until his pinion broke. He then with great presence of mind crawled to the nearest Lewis gun post of the Battalion on his flank and got a new pinion and fired his gun until the troops were ordered to withdraw. He was the last to withdraw, and undoubtedly his coolness in action saved the lives of many of his comrades. When he withdrew he brought back his gun and set a magnificent example to the rest of the company.

Awarded..........**M.M.**

No. 222952 Sapper A. Wakeford, 25th Divisional Signal Coy.

On the afternoon of 21st March this Despatch Rider showed the greatest courage and determination in reaching the 74th Brigade Headquarters near Morchies with vitally important orders although a heavy barrage was being maintained on the Bapaume-Cambrai Road.

On 25th March he again carried an important Order to a Battalion of the 185th Brigade through heavy shell fire.

During the operations of 21st to 28th March, he was almost continuously on duty with his machine, carrying his despatches promptly to their destinations despite the exceptional difficulties the condition of the roads presented.

Awarded..........**M.M.**

No. 66991 Driver W. J. Williams, A/110th Brigade, R.F.A.

For conspicuous courage and coolness on 22nd March, 1918, near Beugny. As the gun team driver of the section left behind to cover the retirement of the rest of the battery he remained a very short way from their guns, under heavy fire from the enemy guns, machine guns and aeroplanes. Our infantry retired past them and the enemy was drawing nearer. It was due to his fine behaviour that the guns were got safely away.

On 23rd March, 1918, near Vaulx the enemy broke through our line. The guns were ordered to retire, and the idea of the men at the moment was that the enemy were right up to our guns. This driver again behaved splendidly and limbered up in fine and orderly manner.

Awarded . . . . **M.M.**

Awards for Battle of Bapaume, 21st March to 29th March, 1918.

VICTORIA CROSS.

Lieut. (A./Capt.) R. F. J. Hayward, 1st Wilts. Regt.
M.C.

SECOND BAR TO D.S.O.

Lieut. (A./Lt.-Col.) S. S. Ogilvie, 1st Wilts. Regt.
D.S.O.

BAR TO D.S.O.

Bt. Lt.-Col. H. M. Craigie-Halkett, H.L.I. Commdg. 9th L.N.L.
D.S.O.

Major (T/Lt.-Col.) H. A. Davidson, 75th Field Amb.
D.S.O., R.A.M.C.

Major Hon. W. E. Guinness, D.S.O. .. Suffolk Yeo., Bde. Major 74th
        Brigade.

Major (T/Lt.-Col.) H. R. Kelly, D.S.O., 77th Field Amb.
R.A.M.C.

Capt. (T/Lt.-Col.) W. Tyrrell, D.S.O., 76th Field Amb.
R.A.M.C.

D.S.O.

2nd Lieut. C. Bates .. .. .. 4th South Staffords.
Capt. E. D'Arcy Birnie, M.C. .. .. 8th Border Regt.
T/Capt. (A./Major) L. C. Deane, M.C... 6th S.W. Borderers.
Major (A/Lt.-Col.) C. W. H. Birt .. 8th Bn. Border Regt.
Lieut. (A/Major) F. G. Massey, M.C... 2nd New Zealand R. Bde.
        (attd. 11th Lancs. F.).
Capt. R. le B. Nicholson, M.C... .. 11th Cheshire Regt.
2nd Lieut. T. H. Oakden .. .. 8th Border Regt.
2nd Lieut. A. W. H. Syme, M.C. .. 25th Battn. M. Gun Corps.

SECOND BAR TO M.C.

Capt. (A/Major) F. G. Lescher, M.C. .. 77th Field Ambulance.
Lieut. (A/Major) A. Anderton, M.C. .. A/110th Bde., R.F.A.

BAR TO M.C.

2nd Lieut. R. Bell, M.C. .. .. 8th Battn. Border Regt.
T/Capt. R. S. Kennedy, M.C., 76th Field Ambulance.
R.A.M.C.
2nd Lieut. J. M. Paterson, M.C. .. B/112th Bde., R.F.A.
Capt. (A/Major) J. Stephenson, M.C., 75th Field Ambulance.
R.A.M.C.
Capt. (A/Major) G. Sumpter, M.C. .. D/112th Bde., R.F.A.
Major B. Bartlett, M.C., R.A.M.C. .. Attd. 1st Wilts.

MILITARY CROSS.

2nd Lieut. J. W. A. Allen	8th Border Regt.
2nd Lieut. M. C. Battersby	A/110th Bde., R.F.A.
Lieut. W. A. Beckett	2nd South Lancs.
Lieut. W. H. Belcher	Army Signals R.E.
2nd Lieut. H. L. Bell	4th South Staffords.
2nd Lieut. F. Bentley	25th Battn. M. Gun Corps.
2nd Lieut. F. Brown	9th L.N. Lancs. Regt.
Capt. L. G. Carr..	4th South Staffords.
2nd Lieut. (A/Capt.) L. H. Cecil ..	11th K.R.R.C., attd. 7th T.M. Battery.
T/Capt. G. W. J. Cole	10th Cheshire Regt.
Capt. (A/Major) C. E. W. Charrington	4th South Staffords.
T/Lieut. H. Davis	6th South W. Borderers.
Lieut. L. F. Edwards	2nd Battn. South Lancs.
Lieut. H. G. Evans	3rd R. West Kents, attd. 10th Cheshires.
T/Lieut. (A/Capt.) A. E. Hansen ..	C/112th Bde., R.F.A.
Lieut. (A/Capt.) P. W. Hargreaves ..	3rd Worcesters.
2nd Lieut. A. H. Hind	25th Battn. M. Gun Corps.
T/Capt. H. L. G. Hughes, D.S.O., R.A.M.C.	Attd. 1st Wilts.
T/Lieut. K. L. Ironside	D/112th Bde., R.F.A.
Lieut. G. A. Keir	11th Lancs. Fus.
Lieut. E. J. C. Maddison	25th Battn. M. Gun Corps.
T/Capt. G. C. Meredith..	10th Cheshire Regt.
Lieut. G. R. Montague	10th Cheshire Regt.
Capt. F. C. Nicholls, R.A.M.C. ..	Attd. 4th South Staffords.
Capt. R. D. O. Oldham	4th South Staffords.
2nd Lieut. W. H. Parker	3rd Worcester Regt.
T/Lieut. A. G. Pearce	6th S.W. Borderers.
2nd Lieut. W. L. Petts..	6th S.W. Borderers.
Lieut. E. C. Pritchard	B/110th Bde., R.F.A.
2nd Lieut. M. E. Ross	D/112th Bde., R.F.A.
Capt. T. Rufus	11th Lancs. Fus.
2nd Lieut. H. Short	9th L.N. Lancs.
T/Lieut. C. W. Soutar	25th Battn. M. Gun Corps.
2nd Lieut. W. Swift	13th Cheshire Regt. (attd. 9th L.N.L.).
T/Lieut. C. H. G. Thomas	1st Wilts. Regt.
Lieut. H. Tinley..	1st Wilts. Regt.
2nd Lieut. (A/Capt.) J. W. Watson ..	A/110th Bde., R.F.A.
Capt. H. M. Watts	C/110th Bde., R.F.A.
Lieut. (A/Capt.) H. M. Wilkinson ..	11th Cheshire Regt.
2nd Lieut. F. T. Woodcock	11th Cheshire Regt.
2nd Lieut. L. Woodward	2nd Battn. South Lancs.

D.C.M.

67143 Sergt. Agnew	D/112 Bde., R.F.A.
13672 Corpl. J. Ashdon	2nd South Lancs.
27225 Pte. G. Badcock	1st Wilts.

15919 Sergt. R. F. Bowman	..	8th Borders.
25197 Sergt. H. A. Brandon	..	11th Cheshires.
10837 Sergt. W. Broadfoot	..	2nd South Lancs.
17337 Corpl. A. Burnett, M.M.		25th Battn. M.G. Corps.
20153 C.S.M. S. Clowsley	..	4th Battn. South Staffords.
47565 B.S.M. A. J. Cobden	..	B/110 Bde., R.F.A.
15851 Sergt. W. Cowap..	..	9th Loyal North Lancs.
15315 Pte. F. C. Craddock	..	25th Battn. M.G. Corps.
47750 Sergt. J. E. Gass, M.M.	..	25th Divl. Signal Co.
42939 Pte. (A/Sergt.) S. Graydon	..	76th Field Ambulance.
8615 C.S.M. J. Haslam, M.M. ..	..	11th Lancashire Fusiliers.
725155 Bdr. W. Hill	..	Y/25 Trench Mortar Battery.
6/16860 Pte. W. Holliday	..	6th S.W. Borderers.
30468 Sergt. J. Ives	..	8th Borders.
16930 Sergt. T. Jones ..	..	10th Cheshires.
62310 Pte. (L./Corpl.) G. Leavey	..	25th Divl. Signal Co.
24381 Sergt. G. Lieversley	..	11th Cheshires.
4866 Pte. J. J. MacCreth	..	11th Lancashire Fusiliers.
11345 Corpl. A. Ockwell	..	1st Wilts (attd. 7th T.M.B.).
11018 L./Corpl. J. Palmer	..	1st Wilts (attd. 7th T.M.B.).
27049 Sergt. E. Phillips	..	9th L.N. Lancs.
27376 Corpl. G. Pickup..	..	8th Borders.
10451 Sergt. Schofield ..	..	9th L.N. Lancs.
10575 Sergt. W. A. Taylor	..	8th Borders.
6967 Corpl. A. Tigwell ..	..	25th Battn. M.G. Corps.
12005 Sergt. A. Titley ..	..	4th South Staffords.
21563 Sergt. C. Whiting	..	25th Battn. M.G. Corps.
78018 Gnr. A. H. Ball ..	..	A/110 Bde., R.F.A.

SECOND BAR TO M.M.

21481 Pte. S. Wright (M.M. Bar)	..	8th Borders.

BAR TO M.M.

W/765 Pte. T. Broster, M.M. ..	..	10th Cheshires.
7672 L./Corpl. A. Eastwood, M.M.	..	11th Lancs. Fusiliers.
15638 Sergt. J. Foley, M.M.	..	106th Field Coy., R.E.
18622 Sergt. A. Gardner, D.C.M., M.M.		3rd Worcesters.
26155 Pte. (L.-Corpl.) J. E. Hamlet, M.M.		10th Cheshires.
6/15016 Pte. J. Hoprobin, M.M.	..	6th S. W. Borderers.
23294 Pte. F. Langley, M.M. ..	..	8th Borders.
7427 Sergt. S. Pearce, M.M. ..	..	1st Wilts.
14998 Pte. T. Roberts, M.M. ..	..	2nd South Lancs. (attd. 75th Bde., Signals).
4002 Pte. C. Rosser, M.M.	..	11th Lancs. Fusiliers
6906 Corpl. E. Simpson, M.M...	..	25th Battn. M.G. Corps.
16861 Corpl. J. Smith, M.M. ..	..	11th Cheshires.
10639 Pte. J. O. Sellars, M.M...	..	3rd Worcesters.
30485 Pte. (A./L.-Corpl.) R. Valence, M.M.		75th Field Ambulance.
5854 Sergt. I. Waineman, M.M.	..	11th Lancs. Fusiliers.
86684 L./Bdr. A. J. Yeoman, M.M.	..	A/110 Bde., R.F.A.

M.M.

48986 Pte. A. Adams	4th South Staffords.
313141 Spr. F. Allen	25th Divl. Signals.
4166 Pte. (A./L.-Corpl.) W. Allen ..	76th Field Ambulance.
14489 Corpl. J. Atherton	9th L.N. Lancs.
6/17111 Pte. J. Atherton	6th S.W. Borderers.
71511 Pte. W. Atkinson	25th Battn. M.G. Corps.
37372 Pte. W. Ashworth	11th Lancs. Fusiliers.
153731 Spr. J. G. Caldwell	106th Field Coy., R.E.
26460 Pte. J. Bailey	8th Borders.
87018 Gnr. A. Ball	A/110 Bde., R.F.A.
13489 Pte. G. Barnes	9th L.N. Lancs.
66791 Gnr. J. Bannister	B/112 Bde., R.F.A.
53365 Sergt. W. G. Beddow	25th Bn. M.G. Corps.
10031 Pte. B. Beasley	1st Wilts (attd. Bde. Signals).
18815 Corpl. J. Bates	2nd South Lancs.
30539 S.-Sergt. F. G. Boxall	75th Field Ambulance.
15525 Sergt. G. Boden	2nd South Lancs.
27889 Sergt. H. J. Brown	25th Battn. M.G. Corps.
45701 Gnr. N. Brown	A/112 Bde., R.F.A.
18880 Pte. W. Brown	1st Wilts.
8716 L.-Corpl. F. Britten	1st Wilts.
36960 Pte. R. Birch	4th South Staffords.
52517 Corpl. R. M. Binns	11th Cheshires.
26871 Pte. W. Birchall	2nd South Lancs.
37338 Pte. G. Brindle	2nd South Lancs (attd. 75th Bde. Signals).
6/15458 Pte. S. Burston	6th S.W. Borderers.
100835 Dvr. M. Butler	D/110th Bde., R.F.A.
12235 Corpl. J. W. Burkin	8th Borders.
30329 Pte. J. T. Bury	2nd South Lancs.
55289 L.-Corpl. J. Bretherton ..	25th Battn. M.G. Corps.
9644 Corpl. P. Carr	8th Borders.
15091 Sergt. M. Crayston	8th Borders.
16670 Sergt. A. W. Cheese	C/110th Bde., R.F.A.
82315 Pte. B. Chesters	25th Battn. M.G. Corps.
17920 Pte. A. Crawford	25th Div. Signals.
25171 Pte. J. H. Crone..	8th Borders.
29764 Pte. G. Chilcott	1st Wilts.
114585 Dvr. P. Clague	A/110th Bde., R.F.A.
27222 L.-Corpl. G. Cocskhoot	2nd South Lancs.
329821 L.-Corpl. A. L. Cullen	2nd South Lancs.
71775 Sergt. E. Dale	A/112th Bde., R.F.A.
7174 L.-Corpl. C. A. Davies	25th Battn. M.G. Corps.
38968 Pte. H. Drabble	4th South Staffords.
13755 Pte. G. Deakin	11th Lancs. Fusiliers.
56481 Corpl. J. H. Demol	25th Div. Signals.
14407 Corpl. J. Deveney	11th Cheshires.
255003 Spr. H. Dingle	25th Div. Signals.
9699 Sergt. C. Dolman	11th Lancs. Fusiliers.
16233 L.-Corpl. B. Duckworth ..	8th Borders.
524878 Spr. C. Dunham	105th Field Coy., R.E.

13086 Sergt. R. Dux	..	9th L.N. Lancs.
9/3670 Sergt. A. J. Evans	..	6th S.W. Borderers.
243216 Pte. T. Evanson	..	11th Cheshires.
6792 Sergt. A. Feltham..	..	1st Wilts.
5622 Pte. H. Ferguson ..	..	8th Borders.
31963 Pte. E. Fearnley..	..	4th South Staffs.
62847 Dvr. T. Fitzgerald	..	A/110th Bde., R.F.A.
15352 L.-Corpl. Forrester	..	3rd Worcesters.
203588 Pte. H. Foster ..	..	4th South Staffords
39330 Pte. I. L. Fox	..	4th South Staffords.
114585 Dvr. P. Clegg ..	..	A/110 Bde., R.F.A.
153730 Spr. J. G. Baldwin	..	106th Field Coy., R.E.
1728 Sergt. W. R. Gardiner	..	C/110th Bde., R.F.A.
30667 Corpl. S. Gibbons	..	4th South Staffs.
90958 Corpl. H. Gilman	..	106th Field Coy., R.E.
16308 Sergt. R. Griffiths	..	2nd South Lancs.
37581 Pte. W. Glease ..	..	9th L.N. Lancs.
25296 L.-Corpl. G. H. Goodwin	..	9th L.N. Lancs.
44495 Sergt. T. Green ..	..	6th S.W. Borderers.
17460 Pte. H. Grew	..	9th L.N. Lancs.
39821 L.-Corpl. V. Hawkins	..	3rd Worcesters.
28513 Sergt. F. J. Hare	..	4th South Staffords.
34714 Pte. G. G. Helm ..	..	11th Lancs. Fusiliers.
40123 Pte. S. Hill	..	4th South Staffords.
5934 Sergt. W. Horridge	..	2nd South Lancs.
26153 Pte. G. Hoare ..	..	4th South Staffords.
21935 Pte. B. Hodgson..	..	75th Field Ambulance.
46401 Spr. A. Hogarth ..	..	25th Div. Signals.
31151 Pte. J. Howells ..	..	6th S.W. Borderers.
57790 Bdr. A. H. Hyett	..	D/110th Bde., R.F.A.
9655 Pte. (L.-Corpl.) R. Hughes	..	10th Cheshires.
5470 Sergt. J. Hulme ..	..	2nd South Lancs.
86285 Dvr. J. Ingley ..	..	25th Battn. M.G. Corps.
224390 Gnr. J. Jinks ..	..	A/112 Bde., R.F.A.
6/43342 L.-Sergt. A. Johnson ..	..	6th S.W. Borderers.
103297 Dvr. W. E. Johnson ..	..	A/110th Bde., R.F.A.
15153 Pte. J. R. Jones ..	..	8th Borders.
6/19038 Pte. T. Jones ..	..	6th S.W. Borderers.
15012 Pte. T. Jones ..	..	3rd Worcesters.
12895 L.-Sergt. W. Jones	..	9th L.N. Lancs.
15597 L.-Corpl. T. Johnson	..	8th Borders.
19747 Pte. J. Kay	..	2nd South Lancs.
34067 Pte. P. H. Keane	..	9th L.N. Lancs.
14509 Pte. J. Kelly ..	..	8th Borders.
6/17176 Sergt. W. Lander	..	6th S.W. Borderers.
202149 Pte. G. Lawless..	..	8th Borders.
18388 Pte. R. Lawrence	..	8th Borders.
M2/020775 Corpl. (A/Sergt.) Lechnere.	B.	A.S.C. (attd. 77th F.A.).
24589 Sergt. E. Leonard	..	10th Cheshires.
16903 Pte. T. Lewis ..	..	11th Cheshires.
30292 Pte. J. Llewelyn..	..	9th L.N. Lancs.
50115 L.-Corpl. F. Lindley	..	10th Cheshires.

30305 Pte. A. H. Livesay	..	..	9th L.N. Lancs.
19176 Pte. M. Lowe	..	..	9th L.N. Lancs.
10790 Pte. J. Ludgate ..	..	..	10th Cheshires (attd. 7th T.M.B.).
4866 Pte. J. J. MacKerth	..	..	11th Lancs. Fusiliers.
11884 Sergt. J. MacDonald	..	..	8th Borders.
638 Pte. F. Milliner	..	..	6th R.W. Kents (attd. 7th Bde. Signals).
666309 Corpl. R. J. Marshall	..	..	D/110th Bde., R.F.A
77599 Dvr. W. Myatt ..	..	..	A/110th Bde., R.F.A.
34205 Corpl. J. F. Meall	..	..	25th Div. Signals (M.T. Coy.).
46541 L.-Corpl. J. R. Miller	..	..	25th Battn. M.G. Corps.
141246 Pte. C. Morcrott	..	..	25th Battn., M.G. Corps.
7321 Corpl. G. Mustoe ..	..	..	1st Wilts.
50830 Pte. A. L. Morley	..	..	11th Cheshires.
83191 Dvr. J. T. Nixon..	..	..	A/110th Bde., R.F.A.
18160 Corpl. P. Needle..	..	..	25th Battn. M.G. Corps.
37958 Pte. E. Oliver ..	..	..	77th Field Ambulance.
8862 Sergt. F. O'Neill ..	..	..	11th Lancs. Fusiliers.
3900 Pte. A. W. Parker	..	..	25th Battn. M.G. Corps.
60060 Pte. W. J. Caul ..	..	..	77th Field Ambulance.
11018 Pte. (L.-Corpl.) J. Palmer	..		1st Wilts (attd. T.M.B.).
74303 Bdr. J. Parry	..	..	A/110th Bde., R.F.A.
14135 Pte. J. Page	..	..	25th Battn. M.G. Corps.
6/17578 Pte. A. Pearce ..	..	..	6th S.W. Borderers.
13602 Pte. T. Phillips ..	..	..	1st Wilts.
313157 L.-Corpl. G. Pinchbeck	..		25th Div. Signals.
30198 Pte. G. Porter ..	..	..	8th Borders.
25221 Pte. C. J. Pladdys	..	..	25th Battn. M.G. Corps.
3296 L.-Sergt. J. W. Ratcliffe..	..		9th L.N. Lancs.
344 L.-Corpl. A. Rauth..	..	..	11th Lancs. Fusiliers.
17895 Corpl. Raybould..	..	..	3rd Worcesters.
6/17529 Pte. W. Reynold	..	..	6th S.W. Borderers.
27336 Pte. Q. W. Reynolds	..	..	3rd Worcesters.
8875 Sergt. R. W. Ritchie	..	..	11th Lancs. Fusiliers.
36717 Corpl. J. Roberts	..	..	10th Cheshires.
1094 Pte. S. Robinson ..	..	..	10th Cheshires (attd. 7th T.M. Battery).
7718 Corpl. G. Robertson	..	..	D/112th Bde., R.F.A.
42865 Pte. W. Robinson	..	..	3rd Worcesters.
37920 Dvr. W. Robinson	..	..	A/110th Bde., R.F.A.
45910 Dvr. H. Rose ..	..	..	D/112th Bde., R.F.A.
14792 Pte. G. Routledge	..	..	8th Borders.
120859 Bdr. A. D. Rouley	..	..	Y/25 Med. T.M.B.
65178 Sergt. W. Sanders	..	..	106th Field Coy. R.E.
35000 Pte. (L.-Corpl.) F. Seddon	..		10th Cheshires.
32272 Corpl. J. Sewell ..	..	..	8th Borders.
13749 Pte. W. Senior ..	..	..	10th Cheshires (attd. 7th Bde. Signals).
152284 Spr. J. Simpson	..	..	25th Div. Signals.
27434 Pte. H. Singleton	..	..	8th Borders.
24645 Corpl. J. Slee ..	..	..	8th Borders.

52584 Pte. W. A. Southam	11th Cheshires (attd. 75th Bde. Signals).
13295 Sdr./Corpl. W. Smith	D/112th Bde., R.F.A.
9737 Corpl. W. Spruels	1st Wilts.
54201 Corpl. A. Scanbury	25th Div. Signals.
260318 Pte. W. Swaine..	6th S.W. Borderers.
46370 L.-Corpl. L. Swallow	105th Field Coy. R.E.
L/16490 Corpl. G. W. Swindles	C/110th Bde., R.F.A.
313146 Corpl. J. W. Taylor	25th Div. Signals.
24288 Dvr. J. Taylor	A/112th Bde., R.F.A.
41432 Corpl. J. W. Tomlinson..	11th Lancs. Fusiliers.
5913 Pte. W. Titchener..	1st Wilts.
2960 Pte. H. Todkill	8th Borders.
92876 Corpl. (A-Sergt.) G. Trolley	76th Field Ambulance
67725 L.-Bdr. W. A. Troth	A/110th Bde., R.F.A.
39164 Pte. E. G. Tuffin	3rd Worcesters.
43026 Spr. T. Turner	25th Div. Signals.
38443 Pte. Z. Tolley	4th South Staffords.
35826 Corpl. A. Tolley ..	4th South Staffords
244212 Pte. T. B. Taylor	11th Cheshires.
1806 Pte. T. Taylor	11th Cheshires.
32125 Pte. C. Thomas ..	2nd South Lancs.
17525 L.-Corpl. J. Turner, D.C.M.	2nd South Lancs.
32125 Pte. P. Turner ..	2nd South Lancs. (attd. 75th Bde. Signals).
36695 Corpl. T. W. Vaughan ..	4th South Staffords.
13589 Pte. J. Varty	8th Borders.
50707 Pte. A. Walker ..	11th Cheshires.
222950 Spr. A. Wakeford	25th Div. Singls.
17080 Pte. S. Waters	6th S.W. Borderers.
17436 L.-Sergt. R. D. Wheeler	6th S.W. Borderers.
11058 Pte. W. Westbrook	8th Borders.
16026 Pte. A. Wrench ..	10th Cheshires.
21036 Corpl. H. Wise ..	8th Borders.
86991 Dvr. W. J. Williams	A/110th Bde., R.F.A.
6881 Sergt. T. A. Williams	25th Battn. M.G. Corps.
29539 Corpl. H. Woolford	1st Wilts.
71945 Bdr. D. E. Reith	A/110th Bde., R.F.A.

25th Division.

Unit.	Officers.			Other Ranks.		
	K.	W.	M.	K.	W.	M.
D.H.Q.	1	..	..	..	..	..
7th Inf. Brigade—						
10th Cheshires	1	11	1	20	118	88
4th S. Staffs.	4	9	1	26	150	69
1st Wilts...	5	11	3	34	83	294
7th T.M.B.	..	2	..	..	9	6
74th Inf. Brigade—						
11th L. Fus.	1	11	3	19	145	86
3rd Worcs.	4	2	..	16	112	44
9th L.N.L.	5	11	1	17	113	215
74th T.M.B.	..	..	..	..	3	2
75th Inf. Brigade—						
11th Cheshires	..	4	13	18	8	330
8th Borders	5	6	2	32	167	46
2nd S. Lancs.	2	4	7	25	125	191
75th T.M.B.	..	..	..	..	1	..
6th S.W. Bord.	1	3	..	8	32	4
25th M.G. Battn.	2	11	7	24	113	163
Royal Artillery—						
110th Brigade	1	5	1	19	35	..
112th Brigade	1	8	..	19	43	4
Royal Engineers—						
105th F. Coy.	..	2	..	1	8	..
106th F. Coy.	..	1	..	4	16	..
130th F. Coy.	..	2	..	1	8	..
R.A.M.C.—						
75th F. Amb.	..	..	..	..	6	6
76th F. Amb.	..	..	..	..	9	..
77th F. Amb.	1	..	1	1	5	1
Attd. 1st Wilts.	..	2	..	..	..	..
Total	34	105	40	284	1391	1549

STATEMENT OF OFFICER CASUALTIES FROM
21st MARCH TO 28th MARCH, 1918.

D.H.Q.

Killed.

Lieut. J. L. Robbins.

10th Cheshire Regt.

Killed.

Lieut. E. E. Petty.

Wounded.

Capt. G. W. L. Cole	2nd Lieut. J. W. Wynne.
Capt. G. E. Pilkington.	2nd Lieut. O. H. Thomas.
2nd Lieut. S. A. White.	2nd Lieut. R. S. Bell.
2nd Lieut. H. J. Willis.	2nd Lieut. R. D. McWilliam.
2nd Lieut. T. S. Ward.	Lieut. J. H. Pichersgill, M.C.
2nd Lieut. K. W. Boothman.	

Missing.

2nd Lieut. J. Bostock.

4th South Staffs. Regt.

Killed.

Lt.-Col. C. E. Blackhall.	Capt. C. E. Holdsworth.
Capt. J. H. Edgar.	2nd Lieut. J. B. Small.

Wounded.

Capt. R. D. Oldham.	2nd Lieut. W. J. Amos.
2nd Lieut. S. J. Davies.	2nd Lieut. R. C.Acherley.
2nd Lieut. H. L. Green.	2nd Lieut. W. C. Hand.
2nd Lieut. H. L. Sell.	2nd Lieut. A. C. Bull.

Missing.

2nd Lieut. S. Dolphin.

1st Wilts. Regt.

Killed.

2nd Lieut. G. T. Morley, M.M.	Lieut. H. W. Gibson.
2nd Lieut. A. V. S. Grant.	2nd Lieut. G. R. Tanner, M.C. (died).
2nd Lieut. J. W. Gunning.	Capt. S. F. Terry.

Wounded.

Capt. R. F. J. Hayward, M.C. (2)	Lieut. E. H. Hill, M.C.
Capt. G. B. Russell, D.S.O.	2nd Lieut. W. R. Holmes.
2nd Lieut. E. T. Burry.	2nd Lieut. J. J. Riddle.
2nd Lieut. L. V. K. Wyatt.	2nd Lieut. J. G. King.
2nd Lieut, H. Clarke.	2nd Lieut. E. S. C. Parsons.

Missing.

Lieut. F. J. London.	2nd Lieut. S. C. Smith.

7th T.M. Battery.

Wounded.

Lieut. H. Tinley.

2nd Lieut. A. H. Parsons

11th Lancashire Fusiliers.

Killed.

2nd Lieut. H. J. Lockley.

Wounedd.

Major F. G. Massey, M.C.
Capt. H. C. Stead.
Capt. H. W. J. Lermit.
Lieut. L. R. Huxtable.
Lieut. J. H. Briffa.
2nd Lieut. J. W. Swan.

2nd Lieut. T. Wood.
2nd Lieut. T. Rohester.
2nd Lieut. H. Sutcliffe.
2nd Lieut. C. Clarke.
Lieut. G. H. Keir.

Missing.

2nd Lieut. C. E. Sharp.

2nd Lieut. J. Porteous.

3rd Worcesters.

Killed.

Capt. J. M. Lett.
Lieut. F. G. Elliott.

Lieut. D. G. Hemus.
2nd Lieut. A. Houghton.

Wounded.

2nd Lieut. C. Latham.

2nd Lieut. W· R. Dixon.

9th L.N. Lancs. Regt.

Killed.

Major F. M. King.
Capt. J. D. Crichton.
2nd Lieut. W. D. James.

2nd Lieut. R. A. Tait (died).
2nd Lieut. L. A. Kemp.

Wounded.

2nd Lieut. F. Brown.
2nd Lieut. H. Short.
Lieut. R. V. Reid (d. of w.)
Capt. H. Everett, M.C.
Lieut. T. B. Harker-Thomas.
2nd Lieut. F. N. Scott.

2nd Lieut. J. F. Hepburn.
2nd Lieut. A. Hughes.
2nd Lieut. H. S. A. Brien.
2nd Lieut. J. Rudyard.
2nd Lieut. W Swirt.
Capt. R. E. O. Keays.

Missing.

2nd Lieut. G. Holt (wounded).

11th Cheshire Regt.

Wounded.

Capt. H. V. Leonard, M.C.
Capt. R. le B. Nicholson, M.C.

2nd Lieut. W. Ryden.
2nd Lieut. J. C. Lugg.

Missing.

2nd Lieut. A. H. D. Dutton.
2nd Lieut. R. S. Coode.
2nd Lieut. F. K. J. Trayes
2nd Lieut. E. F. Byron.
2nd Lieut. J. W. Foster.
2nd Lieut. G. F. Miller.
2nd Lieut. G. F. Piggott.

2nd Lieut. H. H. Owen.
Lieut. W. A. Williams, M.C.
Lieut. W. M. Parry.
Lieut. E. C. Dixon.
Lieut. A. H. Kissack.
2nd Lieut. W. R. Jones.

8th Border Regt.

Killed.

2nd Lieut. C. W. Warwick, M.C.
2nd Lieut. E. G. Dowell, M.C.
2nd Lieut. H. MacTavish.

Capt. C. B. Dove.
Lieut. L. F. W. Reed.
2nd Lieut. J. P. Fryer.

Wounded.

Capt. E. D'A. Birnie, M.C. (Died.)
2nd Lieut. H. E. Sandwell.
2nd Lieut. W. E. Lightfoot.

2nd Lieut. T. H. Oakden.
Lieut. A. E. Gandolfo.
2nd Lieut. R. Bell, M.C.

Missing.

2nd Lieut. F. W. Fentiman (wounded and missing).

2nd South Lancs. Regt.

Killed.

Capt. J. Boast, M.C.
Lieut. S. Franks.
2nd Lieut. L. G. Marthews.

2nd Lieut. Z. Sones.
Lieut. L. A. Macreight.

Wounded.

Lieut. G. M. Walton.
Lieut. (A/Capt.) W. A. Wassner.

Lieut. D. D. McMahon.
2nd Lieut. P. L. Adamson.

Missing.

Lieut. G. Case.
Lieut. K. H. O'R. Sadgrove.
(Prisoner of war.)

Lieut. A. C. Gosden. (Prisoner of war.)
2nd Lieut. L. Woodward.

6th S.W. Borderers.

Killed.

2nd Lieut. S. N. Hillier.

Wounded.

Lieut. A. G. Pearce.
Lieut. W. H. Hanna.

2nd Lieut. H. L. Thomas.

25th Divl. Artillery.
110th Brigade, R.F.A.

Killed.

Lieut. A. J. Cunningham.

Wounded.

Major A. Anderton, M.C. (d. of w.)
Lieut. E. C. Pritchard.
2nd Lieut. F. Keay.

2nd Lieut. A. A. E. Coward.
2nd Lieut. A. E. W. Walder.
Lieut. W. H. Densham, M.C.
(d. of w.).

Missing.
2nd Lieut. J. C. P. Magwood.

112th Brigade, R.F.A.

Wounded.

Major W. Swinton, M.C.
Lieut. F. E. H. Bostock.
2nd Lieut. A. E. Swain.
2nd Lieut. E. Gordon.

2nd Lieut. D. W. Milne.
Lieut. E. W. C. A. Rendle.
Lieut. J. C. Shepherd.
Capt. T. M. Illingworth.

105th Field Coy., R.E.

Wounded.

Major F. W. Richards.

2nd Lieut. A. Elliott, M.C.

106th Field Coy., R.E.

Wounded.
Capt. E. T. Caparn, M.C.

130th Field Coy., R.E.

Wounded.
2nd Lieut. H. Thomson.

R.A.M.C.

Wounded.

Major R. F. Bartlett (attd. 1st Wilts.).

Capt. H. L. G. Hughes, D.S.O.
(attd. 1st Wilts.).

77th Field Ambulance.

Killed.
Capt. R. G. McElrey.

Missing.
Capt. W. Arnott.

25th Battn. M.G. Corps.

Killed.

Lieut. R. A. Colley.

Capt. G. F. Wolff.

Wounded.

Major R. O. W. Burn.
2nd Lieut. O. W. Waldron.
Capt. G. S. Duckworth.
Capt. D. J. G. Dixon (Gas).
Lieut. S. J. Curtis.
Lieut. J. Young.

2nd Lieut. T. C. C. Stanfield.
2nd Lieut. S. M. Elliott.
2nd Lieut. E. W. Potts.
2nd Lieut. J. Rossiter.
2nd Lieut. W. H. Cooper.

Missing.

2nd Lieut. V. L. Manning (wounded).
Major L. E. Faber. (Prisoner of war.)
Lieut. W. D. Lawson. (Prisoner of war.)

2nd Lieut. F. C. Rhodes. (Prisoner of war.)
Lieut. J. MacD. Laing. (Wounded.)
Capt. A. Woods. (Prisoner of war.)
2nd Lieut. Bentley. (Wounded and prisoner of war.)

CHAPTER VII.

Battle of the Lys, 9th April, 1918.

THE 30th and 31st March, 1918, the 25th Division entrained at Doullens and Canaples for Caestre, in the 2nd Army Area, where they joined the Australian Corps, which was itself relieved a few days later by the IXth Corps. The Division at once took over the Ploegsteert sector from the 2nd Australian Division. The line, about 7,000 yards along, lay in front of Ploegsteert Wood, in touch with the 19th Division on the left at the River Douve, and then following the River Lys round to the north-west of Armentieres, where the line linked up with the 34th Division.

On the right of the Divisional sector for about 6,000 yards the German trenches lay on the far side of the River Lys; in front of Deulemont and Warneton they crossed to the British side of the river and then curved round the lower ground in front of Messines and Wytschaete, held by troops of the 19th Division. The river itself was about 20 feet wide, easily bridged by temporary structures capable of carrying troops across. The defences in this particular sector of our lines were extremely weak, and but little time remained to improve them. The 2nd or Corps Line of Defence was poor and, in addition, little or no attempt had been made to prepare other substantial systems of defence in the rear. The policy as to their construction was still under consideration when the attacked was launched. The Division, however, without waiting for any decision began to strengthen the defence at what was known as the " Grey Farm Line " about 1,500 yards behind the front line. At the moment, however, no attack was imminent in the opinion of the Higher Command.

The Division, which had lost more than half of its fighting strength in the Battle of Bapaume, was much benefited by its two days' rest during its entrainment for the north. Reinforcements were now rapidly arriving, and in four or five days the Battalions were practically up to strength. These reinforcements, largely composed of the 19 year old class, who had been training for the last nine months in England, were most excellent material, but the absence of older men suitable for promotion to N.C.Os.' rank was, in some units, a serious disadvantage. A proportion under 19 years of age were wisely kept back for another two or three months' training. It is a thousand pities that they should have been sent from England at all. Owing to age and physique some of these immature boys were quite incapable of carrying the weight and doing the work required of an infantry soldier in the line : their presence in the ranks rendered them a danger to their units. To use them at the time was only a waste of those who might later on, with proper training and physical development, have become valuable reinforcements for the Army.

The policy of keeping B teams of officers, instructors, and N.C.Os. with a proportion of expert signallers, bombers, machine gunners, &c., out of the opening phases of the battle, had proved extremely useful. When Battalions suffered heavy casualties these B Teams formed a nucleus, and a solid stiffening for the new reinforcements. On the present occasion, however, the attack came so unexpectedly on this sector of the line that it was not possible to withdraw these B Teams from the Battalions before the fighting began. But it must not be forgotten that this was not the Division that entered the battle and fought so well, on 21st March, 1918. With only a leavening of the old Division, several weeks hard training were necessary to enable officers to get to know their men, to absorb their reinforcements and for the whole to become a useful fighting force. Unfortunately it was not possible to give the Division this necessary period of training behind the line, and along with other Divisions in much the same state, the 25th Division was placed in what was supposed would be a quiet sector for at least an appreciable time.

Many changes had also taken place in the Higher Commands of the Division. Brig.-Gen. H. K. Bethell, Commanding 74th Infantry Brigade, since October, 1916, now received command of the 66th Division and was succeeded by Lt.-Col, H. M. Craigie-Halkett, from the 9th Loyal N. Lancashire Regt. Brig.-Gen. Dobbin, who recently had been appointed to the command of the 75th Brigade, was succeeded by Brig.-Gen. O. R. Hanney. Lt.-Col. R. F. Legge, D.S.O., who had

been with the Division from its early days, first as D.A.A. &
Q.M.G., and since June, 1916, as A.A. & Q.M.G., received well-
deserved promotion on the Staff. An extremely energetic
and capable Administrative Staff Officer whose activities
were manifest in many directions and whose loss was felt
throughout the Division.

The divisional sector about 7,000 yards, between the River
Lys to the River Douve, was held with the 75th Brigade
on the right and the 7th Brigade on the left, the 74th
Brigade being in Divisional Reserve. Three machine gun
companies held positions along the sector. The two Field
Companies, R.E., were employed one on each sector of the
line and the third was digging a second or Corps line from
Gasometer Corner to Despirre Farm, about 1,500 yards behind
the front line.

7TH BRIGADE ...	...	Brig.-Gen. H. J. GRIFFIN, D.S.O.
1st Wilts.... ...	...	Lt.-Col. S. S. Ogilvie, D.S.O.
10th Cheshires ...	...	Lt.-Col. W. E. Williams.
4th South Staffs.	...	Lt.-Col. L. H. K. Finch, D.S.O.
74TH BRIGADE ...	...	Brig.-Gen. H. M. CRAIGIE-HALKETT, D.S.O.
11th Lancs. Fusiliers	...	Lt.-Col. E. C. de R. Martin, D.S.O., M.C.
3rd Worcesters ...	...	Major R. F. Traill.
9th L. N. Lancs.	...	Lt.-Col. W. H. M. Wienholt, D.S.O.
75TH BRIGADE ...	...	Brig.-Gen. R. HANNEY, D.S.O.
8th Borders ...	...	Lt.-Col. W. H. Birt, D.S.O.
2nd S. Lancs. ...	...	Lt.-Col. J. B. Allsopp.
11th Cheshires ...	...	Lt.-Col. G. Darwell, M.C.

At 11 a.m., 9th April, news was received at the Divisional
Headquarters that the Germans had made a vigorous attack
soon after daybreak on the British line south of Armentières
as far as Givenchy, the sector held by the Portuguese and
troops of the XVth Corps. At the same time the 34th Division
in front of Armentieres was heavily shelled with mustard gas.

G 2

The enemy appeared to have quickly gained possession of Fleurbaix, Laventie, and the whole British lines of defence nearly as far south as Givenchy. They at once pushed on west and north-west through Estaires and Bac-St.-Muir towards Merville and Steenwerck. To meet this menace on our right flank the 74th Brigade, 25th Division was ordered about mid-day to move to Steenwerck to be at the disposal of the 34th Division, XVth Corps. At 1 p.m., the Brigade started and by 4 p.m. was in touch with the enemy south of Steenwerck. At this moment the Germans had already penetrated as far as Croix du Bac. Here the 9th L. N. Lancs. were held up by machine gun fire, and at about 6.30 p.m. Lt.-Col. W. H. M. Wienholt, in command, had his horse shot under him in the village and he, himself, was wounded; Major Nares then took over the command of the Battalion. The 3rd Worcesters had meanwhile made good the northern bank of the Lys and were in touch with the 34th Division on their left. The 11th Lancs. Fusiliers, in the centre, pushed their line forward but did not succeed in forcing the enemy south of Croix du Bac. Owing to the importance of driving the enemy south of the Lys before daylight, a counter-attack was organised at 2 a.m. the morning of the 10th.

The counter-attack was launched at 3 a.m., with the 9th L. N. Lancs. on the right, 11th Lancs. Fusiliers in the centre, and the 3rd Worcesters on the left. The 9th L. N. Lancs. attacked with A, B, C Companies in front and D Company in support, commanded by Capt. Loudon, Lieut. Edwards, 2nd Lieut. J. G. Barrett, succeeded by Capt. Hartley, and Capt. F. Smith (wounded), succeeded by 2nd Lieut. Ridyard. The 11th Lancs. Fusiliers, with A, B, C and D Companies commanded by Capt. Rufus (killed), succeeded by 2nd Lieut. Timson, Captain Beswick, Capt. Ward (wounded) succeeded by Capt. Garland, and Major Munday (wounded) succeeded by Capt. Hudson. The 3rd Worcester Regiment attacked with A Company, commanded by Capt. Reading (wounded) succeeded by 2nd Lieut. Armstrong; B Company, commanded by Capt. Lattey; C Company, commanded by Lieut. Giles (wounded), succeeded by 2nd Lieut. Stevens; D Company, commanded by Capt. Brewer (wounded), succeeded by 2nd Lieut. Bomber (killed).

The first attack at 3 a.m. failed to dislodge the enemy, who were in some force with numerous machine guns in and around the village of Croix du Bac. Capt. Hartley won a Military Cross for the gallant way in which he re-organised and led his Company in the counter attack, and also Lieut. Wilson and Lieut. Brittorous. Lc./Corpl. Diggle, L./Corpl Dodd and L./Corpl. Lake received the Military Medal for their fine work in command of their men. Lieut. Edward, of the 9th N. Lancs., with his Company beat off two attacks, but was badly wounded and missing during the counter-attack in the early morning of the 10th. A further attack was organised for 4.30 a.m., and this time the 9th L.N. Lancs. went straight through the village and established themselves on the north bank of the River Lys. Further to the left, the Brigade was less successful, with the result that the 9th L.N. Lancs. found themselves under enfilade machine gun fire, and suffered heavy casualties. About 7 a.m. the Battalion was forced to withdraw from the river bank. At 9 a.m. the Brigade was ordered to make a further attempt to drive the enemy across the river. But by this time the Germans were firmly established on the northern bank with large reinforcements of infantry and machine guns. About 10.30 a.m. the enemy began to get round the left flank of the 11th Lancs. Fusiliers, and by 3.30 p.m. they had succeeded in working round both sides of Steenwerck, more especially on the east of the village. Lt.-Col. R. Martin, D.S.O., M.C., Commanding 11th Lancs. Fusiliers, whilst engaged in street fighting was taken prisoner and Major Beswick took over Command of the Battalion. For the moment the position was somewhat critical, but a new line was success-fully formed from Pont de Pierre through Steenwerck Station, in touch with the 88th Brigade on the left and the 40th Divi-sion to the right, under whose orders the Brigade was now placed.

2nd Lieut. Ackerley, 11th Lancs. Fusiliers, did excellent work with his platoon and beat off two German counter-attacks with great slaughter. C.-S. M. Abbott during one counter-attack went further than anybody and set a wonderful example to the men. Corpl. McConnell did very good work, Pte. Foulder, Pte. Lord and Pte. Stebbings were conspicuous by their work as stretcher bearers. All thoroughly deserved the decorations awarded to them. Of the 3rd Worcester Regt., Sergt. Cook, M.M., displayed great gallantry during the re-tirement. Pte. Aldsworth, Pte. Bennett, Pte. Lewis and

Pte. Owen, for their work as stretcher bearers under most difficult circumstances, and Pte. Taylor and Pte. Wells all won Military Medals.

During the 9th April, whilst the 74th Brigade was with some difficulty holding its ground to the south, there had been no indication that the enemy were preparing to attack the Divisional front. Aerial observation on the 9th April reported nothing unusual. Patrols during the night 9/10th only reported a certain amount of extra wagon movement around Pont Rouge. The night and morning were thick and misty and gave ample opportunity to the enemy to assemble his men and also to bring up pontoons and bridging material quite close to the river bank without being seen. Some gas shelling took place between 2 a.m. and 3 a.m., and at 5 a.m. very heavy artillery fire was opened along our front with high explosives and gas. At 5.40 a.m., covered by a heavy blanket mist, the Germans effected a crossing of the river and attacked our lines.

The 75th Brigade had the 8th Borders on the right with A, B, C and D Coys., commanded by 2nd Lieut. J. W. A. Allan, Capt. P. H. Coxon, Capt. A. J. Bentley and Capt. J. Dawson, and the 11th Cheshires on the left with the four companies commanded by Capt. W. S. Syme (wounded), Capt. Barton (killed), Lt. H. R. Wall and Lieut. J. A. Snape, and the 2nd S. Lancs. in support with their companies, commanded by Capt. K. M. Bourne, Capt. T. Sweet-Escott, 2nd Lieut. J. Acheson and Capt. S. B. Schwabe. The 7th Brigade on the left had the 1st Wilts on its right with A, B, C and D Coys., commanded by Capt. Smith, Capt. Thomas, Capt. Waite and Capt. Priestley, and the 4th Staffords on the left with companies commanded by Capt. Barlow (died of wounds), succeeded by Lieut. Guiton, Capt. Kelsey, 2nd Lieut. Mason, and Capt. Carr respectively. The 10th Cheshires in support with four companies commanded by Capt. Dean, Capt. Cheetham, Lieut. Huffam and Lieut. Gadsdon.

The 11th and 38th Army Brigades R.F.A., and the 2nd Brigade of the New Zealand R.F.A., supported the 25th Division.

Owing to the employment of the 74th Brigade south of Steenwerck the Divisional sector was left without any reserve and it became necessary once more to use the three Field Companies R.E. and the Pioneer Battalion as a Divisional Reserve.

At 5.40 a.m. the 19th Division on the left reported the S.O.S. signal on our left sector and here all attacks were successfully repulsed. On the right sector small parties of the enemy managed to penetrate our thinly held line on each flank of the right battalion, and at places where close connection should have been maintained with the troops on either flank. These small parties were quickly reinforced in the misty weather and spread up north-west behind the 8th Borders and 11th Cheshires. The 8th Borders Battalion Headquarters was soon over-run but managed to effect a retirement. Two companies of the 11th Cheshires were subsequently surrounded and cut off. Attacked from all sides they were eventually captured.

The first intimation reaching Divisional Headquarters at 6.10 a.m. was to the effect that the enemy were already through Le Touqet moving into Ploegsteert Wood and along to the river. Events now moved rapidly and at 8.30 a.m. German troops were moving along the road from Ploegsteert Village to Hyde Park Corner, endeavouring to cut off any British troops east of the wood. By 1 p.m., they were reported to be in the southern end of Ploegsteert Wood. The 2nd South Lancashire Regiment with the Pioneer Battalion and the three Field Companies R.E. were at once ordered to counter-attack. The attack south of Armentieres and the retirement of our troops had drawn away the 74th Brigade the preceding day. The absence of any other supporting troops, outside the Royal Engineers and Pioneer Battalion, made the situation extremely difficult and gave but little hope of being able to effectively restore the line. The 9th Cheshires from the 56th Brigade, 19th Division, at Nieppe were placed at the disposal of the G.O.C., 75th Brigade, and the 1/5th K.S.L.I., of the 56th Brigade, was also sent to the 7th Brigade. These battalions rendered invaluable assistance throughout the six days' hard fighting, whilst attached to the Division.

About mid-day the 34th Division withdrew to a line west of Armentieres with orders to link up with the 75th Brigade at Vanne, and during the afternoon the 75th Brigade Headquarters withdrew to Les Trois Rois, on the Neuve Eglise-Nieppe Road. Meanwhile, the Germans had penetrated Ploegsteert Wood, and small parties were in possession of the southern part of the wood. The 2nd New Zealand Brigade, R.F.A., who had a battery of Howitzers in Ploegsteert Wood, fought their guns up to the last moment when the guns were blown up and rendered useless.

At 6 p.m., a counter-attack by troops of the 75th Brigade, which had been due to take place for some hours, commenced, two companies of the 10th Cheshires co-operating by driving south from Ploegsteert Wood. The attack was carried out by the 9th Cheshires on the right, the 105th, 106th, and 130th Field Companies R.E., and the 6th South Wales Borderers in the centre, and two companies of the 2nd S. Lancs. on the left. This counter-attack at first achieved a certain amount, but it was eventually held up by machine-gun fire from Ploegsteert Village. Lt.-Col. J. D. Deane-Drummond, commanding the 25th Battalion Machine Gun Corps, co-operated on the left of the 2nd S. Lancs., with about 200 Machine Gunners acting as Infantry ; whilst leading his men he was wounded. Lieut. Bryden, 2nd S. Lancs., did excellent work with his company during the counter-attack, as well as Sergt. Rimmer, Corporal Hailey, L. Corpl. Kirkham, and Pte. Cooper, of whom the latter showed great courage as a battalion runner. All received decorations.

The situation, in the evening of the 10th, along the Corps and Divisional front, was causing some anxiety, but it was not critical. The 7th Brigade had resisted all attacks on the left sector of the Divisional front and were firmly established on a line about 1,000 yards north and east of Ploegsteert Wood ; though small parties of the 10th Cheshires and Germans were mixed up in the wood. With their multiplicity of light machine guns the enemy managed to dribble small parties through our lightly held line without being detected owing to the misty weather. These parties often managed to create confusion by opening fire from positions behind our line, making a pretence of force which they did not possess. A small gap of about 500 yards existed in the line behind Ploegsteert Wood, between Grand Monque Farm and Hyde Park Corner. This gap was filled up about 3 a.m. on the 11th by a company of the Shropshires who were in touch with the 147th Brigade at Nieppe. The greater portion of the Hill 63, an important hill dominating the valley beyond, was still in our hands. The 88th Brigade of the 19th Division, who were de-bussing south of Bailleul, came under the orders of the G.O.C. 25th Division and at once counter-attacked the enemy in La Creche. This attack was successful and the Brigade by the evening of the 10th was established in Steenwerck Station, and along the railway.

The original attack on the 9th Corps front had been carried out by five German Divisions, with two in support. Though the strength of the attacking forces was comparatively small, yet it must be remembered that the British line was here held by divisions all of which had taken part in the severe fighting down south, and who had had but little time to absorb large numbers of reinforcements. In addition, many of the battalions had lost their senior officers. From the moment of their initial success the Germans, however, began to bring up as rapidly as possible fresh and new Divisions, and on the 12th April, the famous Alpine division made its appearance on the 25th Divisional sector.

At about 8 a.m., 11th April, German troops were seen massing opposite Grey Farm and the reserve line, and at 11 a.m., a strong German attack developed west of Ploegsteert Wood, on the front of both Brigades. About 11.15 a.m., the line held by the 75th Brigade near Romarin was broken. By 11.30 a.m., small parties of Germans with light machine guns reached Red Lodge, and by mid-day the attack on the 7th Brigade increased in intensity. By 3 p.m., troops of the Division were back on the Army Line east of Neuve Eglise with the 7th Brigade still holding the east of Ploegsteert Wood and round Hill 63. The Brigade was then ordered to retire to a position on the high ground west of Neuve Eglise, falling back north of Hill 63, and covered on its retirement by companies of the 10th Cheshires from positions on the high ground east of the wood. This Battalion was in support to the 7th Brigade and stationed in the " Catacombs," a vast series of tunnelled dug-outs excavated in the western side of Hill 63, where ample room existed for 1,000 men. A Coy. was holding Hill 63, and at daybreak on the 11th, B, C, and D Coys. were sent to take up previously reconnoitred positions east of Ploegsteert Wood.

During the afternoon, about 5 p.m., the Germans gradually closed round the "Catacomb" dug-outs. Casualties were heavy throughout the three Battalions of the Brigade during the withdrawal and it is feared that few of those actually in the front line trench managed to get away. Throughout the morning they had steadily held their ground against all frontal attacks, but realised that the enemy were gradually creeping round both flanks, increasing the difficulties of a retirement during daylight. Lieut. Bates, 4th South Staffords, won the Military Cross, in addition to his D.C.M. and D.S.O., for his fine leadership. After dark, Capt. Carr, 4th South Staffords, managed to withdraw his company of the Staffords practically through the German lines without a single casualty. This retirement was a remarkable piece of work and was entirely due to the skilful leading by its Company Commander. Capt. Carr received a bar to his M.C., but subsequently died of wounds received a few days later at Kemmel ; 2nd Lieut. Fairie, in command of his platoon, L./Corpl. Coppock and Pte. Moore were conspicuous for their good work. Pte. Barty showed great courage as a runner, and Pte. Tate as linesman was untiring in repairing broken lines under heavy fire throughout the fighting. All thoroughly earned their decorations.

Two companies of the Wilts, who had held Zambuk post against all attacks during the 10th and 11th, were also enabled to reach their new position near Neuve Eglise, by the skilful leadership of their Company Commander, Capt. Priestley. This officer had been severely wounded early on the 10th but refused to leave his Company. Capt. Cecil, of the 7th T. M. Battery, did useful work with his guns. Of the 10th Cheshires, C.S.M. Trowbridge, when all officers were casualties, showed great initiative and leadership, Sergt. Goodwin and Corporal Perrin with their Lewis guns, and R.S.M. Greenhalgh were conspicuous for their gallantry.

Lt.-Col. S. S. Ogilvie, Commanding 1st Wilts., and Lt.-Col. Williams, Commanding the 10th Cheshires, and Lt.-Col. F. K. H. Finch, Commanding 4th South Staffords, who were in the " Catacombs " dug-out with their Battalion Headquarters, were all either captured or killed. Later on it was learned that they were prisoners of war in German hands. These Officers were a very great loss to the 7th Brigade. Lt.-Col. S. S. Ogilvie had enlisted in the 1st Wiltshire Regiment in August, 1914. Coming out to France in November 1914, he had served continuously in every rank with the Battalion, up to the present time. In June, 1915, he received a Commission and in August, 1917, was appointed to the Command of the Battalion, and in all probability would have received further advancement.

The 100th Brigade, 33rd Division, was now placed at the disposal of the G.O.C., 25th Division. About 7 p.m., two

Battalions of the Brigade took up positions on the Army Line south-east of Neuve Eglise to about Romarin. The night of the 11/12th was quiet on the Divisional front except for a small attack against the 148th Brigade, which was driven off. The line now ran, roughly, north and south in front of Neuve Eglise, with the 75th Brigade on the right, the 100th Brigade in the centre and the 148th Brigade on the left, the 7th Brigade being in support, west of the Village. Two Batteries of Motor Machine Guns were supporting the centre in the vicinity of Kortipyp.

2nd Lieut. Foulkes, 2nd S. Lancs., won the M.C. for his good work during the German attack on Ploegsteert. Pte. Brady, L./Corpl. Didsbury, Sergt. P. Graff, L./Corp. Latham, Serg.. Tonkin, and Sergt. Wilkinson, 2nd S. Lancs., were all conspicuous for their gallantry during the retirement from Le Bizet and the attack on Ploegsteert. Of the 11th Cheshires, Sergt. Bertenshaw, when all officers had become casualties, took Command of his Company with great ability, L./Corpl. Atkinson, Corpl. Pearson in command of their platoons; L./Corpl. Bradshaw, Pte. Bearchill, L./Corpl. Costello for work with their Lewis guns all thoroughly deserved their Military Medals. As runners Pte. Babington, Pte. Maylor, Pte. Widdows and Pte. Christian, for his gallantry in attending and bringing in wounded, also received the Military Medal.

Lt.-Col. Birt, D.S.O., 8th Border Regt., won a bar to his D.S.O. for his fine leadership and great personal courage when in command of his battalion. Capt. Bentley, Lieut. Duggan, and Lieut. Strong, M.C., all received the M.C. for their services during the battle. C. S. M. Gent, when officers had become casualties, took command of his company which he led with great ability, and also Sergt. Crayston, M.M., received decorations. The two cooks, Pte. McGuinness and Pte. Stafford, and Pte. George of the Sanitary Squad won Military Medals for their capture of a German aeroplane and its pilot, which was forced to descend and would have got away again had it not been for the enterprise of these three men. Pte. Jones, M.M., and Pte. Todkill, M.M., were conspicuous throughout for their courage as stretcher bearers, and both received a bar to their Military Medals.

At 8 a.m., 12th April, the enemy attacked heavily all along the front, as well as to the right and left of the Divisional Sector. The 148th Brigade repulsed all attacks, but on the right the 100th Brigade and the 75th Brigade were forced to retire and the enemy got through the line at Kortipyp. The K.R.Rs. of the 100th Brigade suffered heavy casualties at this point.

During the attack and subsequent retirement, Lieut. Bourne, M.C., of the 2nd S. Lancs., won a bar to his Military Cross for the skilful way in which he handled his men. Pte. Bimpson and Pte. Misel, M.M., as runners and Pte. Watkins as stretcher bearer, were conspicuous for their gallantry. Corporal Morris, 2nd S. Lancs., and Cpl. O'Connell, 8th Border Regt., did excellent work with the Trench Mortar Battery. L./Corpl. Bray, Sergt. Graham, and Pte. Hewitt, 8th Borders, distinguished themselves with their Lewis guns, and the latter managed to knock out two German machine guns. All these were decorated with the Military Medal, as well as Pte. W. D. Jones, 8th Borders, for his gallantry as a runner.

Owing to the report that the enemy had broken through into Bailleul from the south, the 7th Brigade with 12 machine guns were moved at about 4 p.m. to a position near the asylum, just north of Bailleul. This report proved to be incorrect and the Brigade moved back to a position about Crucifix Corner. Major A. Reade, M.C., led a counter-attack at Crucifix Corner, killing about 60 Germans, and received a D.S.O. for his gallant leadership throughout the fighting. Of the 10th Cheshire Regt., Sergt. Wilson performed wonderful work with his five Lewis guns : Pte. Bailey, Pte. Dunbeben, Pte. Wiggins as runners and Pte. Bradbury as signaller were excellent. Of the 1st Wilts, Sergt. Bridges, M.M., and C. S. M. Pearce, M.M., both received the D.C.M., for their bravery and fine example to the men ; Pte. Burry and Pte. Tovey distinguished themselves as signallers, mending wires and keeping up communications ; whilst Lieut. H. A. Brown, M.C., was invaluable in Command of his Company at Crucifix Corner. Lieut. Miller, 4th South Staffords, did excellent work with his Company ; Pte. Spencer, with his Lewis gun, and Pte. Rose, 4th South Staffs, as a runner, all received decorations thoroughly well earned.

The Army Line of defence, which was in front of Dranoutre, joining up with the Kemmel defences, was now held, as far as the 25th Divisional sector was concerned, by a hastily organised composite force under Brig.-Gen. Wyatt. To these were added men of the three Field Companies, R.E., and about 200 North

Lancs., under Major Nares. On their left was the 2nd Corps Cyclist Battalion, and further behind, the XXIInd Corps Cavalry Regt. In front of Neuve Eglise a line was held by two Battalions of the 148th Brigade, with the 2nd Wiltshire Regt.. 102nd Brigade, on their right and in touch with the 19th Division on the left. The 75th Brigade being established on the rising ground south-west of Neuve Eglise with its Battalion Headquarters at Crucifix Corner.

About 6 p.m., on the 13th, two battalions of the 71st Brigade (6th Division) reached Dranoutre by 'bus and came under the orders of the 25th Division. The third Battalion of the Brigade arrived the following morning. Two battalions went into the line the same night, 13/14th, along a line astride the Neuve-Eglise-Dranoutre Road and then along the railway, linking up on the left with the 19th Division and on the right with a portion of the 100th and 75th Brigades.

During the morning the Germans had got possession of the south and south-west corners of the village of Neuve Eglise and were gradually dribbling in reinforcements with light machine guns. A counter-attack by troops of the 100th and 148th Brigades was organised and by mid-day the village was completely cleared of the enemy and remained in our hands until the troops were finally withdrawn before daybreak on the 15th.

The Divisional Artillery, who had remained in action with the New Zealanders after the withdrawal of the 25th Division from the Somme front, left Doullens on the 10th to rejoin the Division. Marching up east of Hazebrouck, the batteries now came into action on the 13th behind the 34th Division.

During the night 13/14th, the 74th Brigade, which had gradually retired in touch with the 101st Brigade on the right and 88th Brigade on the left, was now established along the high ground east of Bailleul. On the 13th, during the German attack at Mont de Lille, Capt. Lattey and 2nd Lieut. Stephens, 3rd Worcester Regt., organised a successful counter-attack and received the Military Cross. L./Corpl. Sprugg and L./Corpl. Wallis did excellent work with their Lewis guns ; L./Corpl. Gray, Sergt. Duffill and L./Corpl. Hawkesley distinguished themselves by mending lines under heavy fire and keeping up communications ; all received the Military Medal, and Sergt. H. Smith the D.C.M., for their gallant conduct throughout the fighting.

The enemy lost no time in following up the withdrawal of the Brigade to the new line, and the outpost line on the Bailleul-Armentieres Road was soon driven in. At 9.30 a.m., the enemy opened a heavy bombardment and at 11.30 a.m., advanced to the attack. Late in the afternoon parties of the enemy succeeded in reaching the high ground, but were immediately counter-attacked by a party of N. Lancs. under 2nd Lieut. Downing, in conjunction with some men of the 3rd Worcesters and 11th Lancs. Fusiliers. About 30 Germans were killed, several machine guns captured and the remainder put to flight. 2nd Lieut. Ward, 11th Lancs. Fusiliers, with a few stragglers charged and cleared the crest of the hill, and C.S.M. Crote, 9th L.N. Lancs., received a D.C.M., and Corpl. Elliman, 3rd Worcs., a Military Medal for his excellent work during the counter-attack. Major Nares, M.C., Commanding the 9th L.N. Lancs., and Lieut. Marsh, M.C., Adjutant received a D.S.O. and bar to the Military Cross, respectively, for their good work with the battalion. Pte. Bromley, Pte. Kay, Pte. Prescott as stretcher bearers, Pte. Cobbold, Pte. Parker, Pte. Hayward, 9th L.N. Lancs., and Pte. Pennifold, 11th Lancs. Fusiliers, as runners all thoroughly deserved the Military Medal awarded them, also Pte. Wilson, 3rd Worcesters, for attending and bringing in the wounded at Mont de Lille

During the early hours of the following morning, the 15th, the 74th Brigade was relieved by the 176th Brigade. About 8 p.m., the 14th, the enemy attacked the high ground east of Bailleul and also endeavoured to reach the town from the south; this attempt was unsuccessful. On the high ground east of Bailleul the 7th Brigade not only beat off the attack but organised a counter-attack, when Major Reade, 10th Cheshires, succeeded in capturing a large number of prisoners and machine guns. The Command of the Divisional sector passed to the G.O.C. 49th Division, the afternoon of the 14th, and as far as possible, the 7th and 75th Brigades were relieved from the front line. The fighting strength of the 7th and 75th Brigades was now roughly 600 men. With the 1st Wilts all the officers had become casualties and their total strength was about 100 men. With the 74th Brigade the position was somewhat better, but the troops of the whole Division were sadly in need of rest.

The morning of the 15th, Mont de Lille and the high ground east of Bailleul, as well as the town of Bailleul, were captured by the German attack. Up to this time the enemy had been confined to the low ground south of Bailleul and the range of hills known as Ravelsberg with Mont de Lille and Crucifix Corner as the point. With the capture of these positions the whole line was forced to retire, involving the surrender of the town of Bailleul itself.

When relieved, the 74th Brigade, who had been continuously under the 34th Division, holding Mont de Lille, went back to rest a few miles behind, near St. Jeans Cappel. There they dug a line which later on became the front line during the retirement on the following day, the 15th. The 7th and 75th Brigades were also relieved the night of the 14/15th by the 49th Division and went back to Boeschepe on the slopes of Mont des Cats.

When the enemy delivered their attack on the morning of the 15th on Ravelsberg and the high ground to the east, the 74th Brigade were at once put into the line which they had helped to dig about two miles in rear. The 7th and 75th Brigades, greatly reduced in strength, were formed into a composite battalion and placed under the Command of Brig.-Gen. Griffin, 7th Brigade.

The loss of the high ground east of Bailleul early the morning of the 15th necessitated retirement of the whole line back to previously prepared positions covering St. Jeans Cappel-Dranoutre and then linking up with the defensive lines round Kemmel. Neuve Eglise had been evacuated before daybreak on the 15th. There was no attack on the line during the 16th, but during the day two French Divisions with two Cavalry Divisions moved up towards the front line on either flank of the IXth Corps. The two French Cavalry Divisions, who had marched 125 miles in three days, were looking remarkably fresh and the British troops were extremely relieved at the approach of much needed assistance. The units of the Division had been continuously fighting for five days and nights against overwhelming odds. The enemy, though perhaps not numerically superior at the commencement of the battle, had been able to bring up fresh Divisions with which to attack our tired troops. In the evening of the 16th and the following morning the 133rd French Division attacked the enemy north-east of Meteren, with some success. Further north the 19th Division drove the Germans back from the slopes of Kemmel, as far as Wytschaete.

About 11 a.m., on the 16th, the 7th and 75th Brigades as a composite unit moved up from Boeschepe and went into Corps reserve under the G.O.C. 34th Division. Later on in the afternoon they moved forward as far as Woolfoek, south of Mont Noir.

By the 17th April, the situation was relieved of all anxiety. The 133rd French Division, on the right, with the 6th French Cavalry Division held the line from Meteren eastwards, in touch with the 34th Division about 2,000 yards behind Mont de Lille, and covering St. Jeans Cappel; these again were in touch with the 49th Division, covering Dranoutre and the 19th Division holding the line of the Kemmel defences. The 7th and 75th Brigades with machine guns were in the support line with the 34th Division, with the 74th Brigade, also under the 34th Division, holding a portion of the line south of St. Jeans Cappel. Capt. Hutson and Lieut. Stelfox, 11th Lancs. Fusiliers, organised a most successful counter-attack, at Haegerdoorne. Pte. Fearnside, 9th L.N. Lancs., with his Lewis gun, and Corporal Jones, Corporal Glover, 9th L.N. Lancs., Pte. Jobber, Pte. Joll, M.M., 11th Lancs. Fusiliers, all won the Military Medal for their gallantry throughout the battle.

On the night of the 17/18th, the 7th and 75th Brigades rationed and assembled near Abeele ; on the 18/19th, the three Field Companies, R.E., and 6th S. Wales Borderers were withdrawn, and on the 20/21st the 74th Brigade was relieved and the Division marched to Poperinghe-Proven area and came into 2nd Army Reserve.

Kemmel.

After four days of comparative quiet, the Germans opened a bombardment at about 7.10 p.m., the evening of the 23rd, and later attacked the French on Kemmel Hill. French troops were holding the sector comprising Kemmel and the Kemmel defences in touch with the 22nd Corps on their right. The German attack failed, and up to the morning of the 24th the line was unbroken. About 5 p.m., on the same afternoon a second bombardment commenced. This increased in intensity and from 8.30 p.m., the whole line was subjected to a very heavy bombardment until daylight on the 25th. During the night, Kemmel Hill was deluged with gas shells, and at daybreak the enemy launched a heavy attack all along this portion of the line. Between Kemmel and Wytschaete, in the neighbourhood of the junction of the French with the 22nd Corps, the enemy was successful and by 9 a.m., the 25th, the Germans had succeeded in pushing forward about 1,000 yards in front of Kemmel Village. This success menaced our whole line, and at 11.30 a.m. a message was received from 8th Corps that the 25th Division must be ready to support the 22nd Corps. By 5 p.m. the 7th, 74th, 75th Brigades had arrived in the Reninghelst area. All B Teams, together with the three Field Companies R.E. and the 6th S.W.Bs., remained for the present near Proven. During the morning information was rather vague and reports were contradictory as to the extent of the success achieved by the German attack, but during the afternoon it became apparent that the enemy had established themselves both on Kemmel Hill and in Kemmel Village.

The 25th Division now came under the orders of the 2nd French Cavalry Corps and a counter-attack was organised for the following morning in conjunction with French troops. At 3 a.m., the 26th, the counter-attack started ; the 74th Brigade on the right, the 7th Brigade on the left, with the 75th Brigade in support. On the right the 3rd Worcs., with A, B, C, D Coys., commanded by 2nd Lieut. Pickles. 2nd Lieut. H. E. Hatwood, Capt. E. V. P. Parsons (wounded), succeeded by Lieut. G. U. Duffield, and Capt. Hardman (wounded), succeeded by 2nd Lieut. A. E. Draggins (killed). The 9th Loyal North Lancs., with four Companies commanded by Capt. A. Sumner, Capt. L. C. Rice (wounded), succeeded by Lieut. L. Bolton, Lieut. A. E. Bulling and Capt. Leverson (wounded) succeeded by 2nd Lieut. J. Draper, and the 11th Lancs. Fusiliers, in support with A, B, C, and D Coys., commanded by Capt. Newman, Lieut. Ward, Capt. Gowland and Lieut. Nathan. On the left the 10th Cheshires, A, B, C, and D Coys., commanded by 2nd Lieut. Willmore (killed), 2nd Lieut. Rutherford, Capt. Webb (killed), Lieut. Cotterill and 2nd Lieut. Ralston (wounded). The 4th S. Staffords with A, B, C and D Coys., commanded by Lieut. Guiton, 2nd Lieut. Moorcroft (wounded), succeeded by 2nd Lieut. Mason, Lt. Miller, and Capt. Carr (wounded), succeeded by 2nd Lieut. Hawkins. The 1st Wilts, in support with A, B, C, and D Coys., commanded by Lieut. Anderson, 2nd Lieut. Howe, 2nd Lieut. Turnbull and Capt. Priestley.

Owing to the uncertainty of the exact position held by the enemy, Officer patrols were sent out by both brigades to learn the exact situation both as regards the enemy's line and also the line held by the French and troops of the 49th and 9th Divisions, on their left. These patrols were successful in clearing up what was a somewhat obscure situation and, before midnight, final orders for the counter-attack had been issued and all arrangements made for the barrage. To carry out the counter-attack the two Brigades of Artillery of the 38th Division were placed under the G.O.C. 25th Division. By midnight all arrangements were complete, also as regards co-operation of 'the 38th French Division on the right and the 49th Division on the left. Unfortunately soon after midnight it began to rain and by 3 a.m. there was a heavy downfall which soaked men to their skins and made the going very heavy for our troops over the bad ground.

At 3 a.m. the Brigades advanced to the attack at 25 yards per minute, each with two Battalions in the front line and the remaining companies in reserve and support respectively. The flooded state of the Kemmel Beck proved a serious obstacle to the advance and made it difficult for the troops to keep up with the barrage. The enemy who were holding the line on the railway with light machine guns were either captured or driven back, and at 4.55 a.m., the 3rd Worcs. reached their first objective with very few casualties. The 9th L.N. Lancs. were equally successful and altogether about 50 prisoners and several machine guns were captured by the 74th Brigade. On the left the 7th Brigade went forward with the 10th Cheshires and 4th S. Staffords in front and the 1st Wiltshire Regt. in support. Each battalion had two companies in front and two companies in reserve and support respectively. During the early morning the fog was very heavy and some difficulty was experienced in keeping directions, but by 5 a.m., the battalions of the 7th Brigade had successfully reached their objectives and were established east of the Kemmel Beck. Another 40 or more prisoners with machine guns were captured. About three platoons of the 3rd Worcs. and 9th L.N. Lancs, entered Kemmel Village and another party of 11th Lancs. Fusiliers, 9th L.N. Lancs., and 3rd Worcesters under Capt. Newman, 11th Lancs. Fus., pushed on ahead. Here Capt.

Newman became a casualty and 2nd Lieut. M. D. Walker, 11th Lancs. Fusiliers, took the party right through the village and some distance beyond into the open country, where a small and dilapidated strong point was re-occupied. During the day Lt.-Col. Cade, D.S.O., M.C., 1st Wilts, Lt.-Col. J. E. Stewart, M.C., 4th South Staffs, were both killed and Lt.-Col. A. Reade, 10th Cheshire Regt., was wounded. These Officers were a great loss to their units and to their Brigades, as it was largely owing to their leading and actual presence at the head of their battalions that the attack met with so great a success. The operation, however, was spoiled owing to a portion of the Division on the left being unable to capture Rossignol Wood, leaving a dangerous gap on our left flank. On the right of the 25th Division very little progress was made at all, with the result that by 8 a.m., it was apparent that the position of our troops in front of Kemmel Beck formed a dangerous salient and at 9 a.m. both Brigades withdrew to the line of the Kemmel Beck. By 12 noon, the line held by the 74th Brigade ran along the railway with a second line about 400 yards in rear ; on their left the 7th Brigade in touch with machine gun battalion of the 19th Division, and the 147th Brigade, 49th Division, still further to the left. During the afternoon the whole line was consolidated and the battalions re-organised throughout.

With the 74th Brigade, Capt. Underhill commanded the 3rd Worcesters with great dash, and Lieut. Doherty, M.O.R.C., U.S.A., attached to the battalion, was conspicuous for his gallantry in attending to the wounded under heavy fire. Both these officers won the Military Cross for their services. Sergt. Kay did good work with a captured German machine gun ; Pte. McFarland with his Lewis gun, Pte. Bullivant, Pte. Lamport and Pte. Roberts as runners ; Pte. Cotterill as a stretcher bearer, and Sergt. Pugh, for his excellent work with his company, all won well deserved decorations. Of the 11th Lancs. Fusiliers, Pte. Blackburn and L./Corpl. Corlett did wonderfully good work with their Lewis guns ; L./Corpl. Dugdale and Corpl. Greaves led rushes on German machine guns ; Pte. Nicholas as a runner and Pte. Brocklehurst, Pte. Oliver, and Pte. Tabrum for their work as stretcher bearers all received the Military Medal. Sergt. Stourbridge and Pte. Murphy, 9th L.N. Lancs., pushed on in front of the main attack and alone captured or killed about 20 Germans ; Corpl.

Newnham, Sergt. Rowe, and L./Corpl. Watson showed great ability in re-organising their men after the attack and all won the Military Medal.

On the left with the 7th Brigade, Lieut. Walker, 10th Cheshires, won the M.C. for his personal reconnaissance before the attack when he succeeded in gaining valuable information as to the situation ; Major Simmonds, M.C., won the D.S.O. for the gallant manner in which he led the battalion after Lt.-Col. Reade was wounded. Pte. Ingram crawled out as a sniper and was most effective ; Corp. Jones, Pte. Mellor, Pte. Morris and Pte. Ashley were conspicuous for their bravery in attending to and bringing in the wounded under heavy fire, and L./Corpl. Gee all thoroughly deserved the M. Medals awarded them. L./Corpl. Colbourne, 1st Wilts., was excellent with his Lewis gun, and Corpl. Cole, after the senior N.C.Os. had become casualties, led his platoon with great ability. Pte. Kitchener as a runner and Pte. Barker and L./Corpl. Taylor were most noticeable for their gallantry as stretcher bearers. L./Corpl. Clare, in charge of the stretcher beareis, set a fine example and exercised a good steadying influence with the men. All received the Military Medal. With the 4th S. Staffords, Lieut. Miller, who took Command of the battalion when all other senior officers had become casualties and showed great leadership and initiative, and 2nd Lieut. Woolleys who pushed on with a small party and captured two German machine guns with their crew, received the D.S.O. and M.C., respectively. Pte. Taylor was conspicuous for his gallantry as a runner and Pte. Forsbury and Pte. Stevens as stretcher bearers all won well earned decorations.

Casualties had been comparatively slight throughout the advance, but in the withdrawal from the line of the railway, battalions had suffered more heavily. Later on, the following message was received from the Commander-in-Chief :—

" Please congratulate the 25th Division upon their very gallant counter-attack at Kemmel Village on the morning of the 26th instant. The courage, enterprise, and resolution shown on this occasion after so many days of heavy fighting both on the Lys front and south of Arras reflect the highest credit upon all ranks."

At 11.30 a.m., the previous morning, orders had arrived for the Division to hold itself in readiness to move to the support of the 22nd Corps. It had then been necessary to collect the men from working parties in other districts ; to withdraw the B Teams from the battalions, and to march more than eight miles to a position of assembly and through country which was being heavily shelled. During the late evening it had again been necessary to get all information as to the exact situation of the line by means of " Officer Patrols " and at 3 a.m. in the morning the troops delivered the counter-attack with conspicuous success over 3,000 yards of very difficult country ; about 180 prisoners and several machine guns being captured.

During the night 26/27th, the 7th Brigade was withdrawn from the line, being relieved by troops of the 147th Brigade, 49th Division. The Divisional sector now comprised one Brigade front, which included the La Clytte-Kemmel road, with the 7th Brigade in support and the 75th in reserve. During the afternoon of the 27th, the 75th Brigade relieved the 7th Brigade in support, and during the early morning of the 28th, the 75th Brigade took over the line from the 74th Brigade. The night was quiet and the relief was carried out without any difficulty. During the night 27/28th the 105th and 106th Field Companies, R.E. and two Companies of the 6th S. Wales Borderers dug and wired a trench between the front line and La Clytte. The following night this trench was improved and more wire put out.

During the 28th, intelligence reports indicated that an attack might be expected along the whole front with Ypres as the objective. Owing to the importance of La Clytte and the high ground to the west two Companies of the R.E., two Companies of the 6th S.W.B., and one Company of the Machine Gun Battalion were detailed for the special purpose of the defence of La Clytte under the French Commander of that sector. At 6 p.m., orders were issued to the 7th and 74th Brigades to be ready to move at half an hour's notice, should the attack develop. Later on in the afternoon a German concentration was reported opposite Zellebeke and in the Wytschaete area. Every preparation was made to meet the attack and at 3.5 a.m., on the morning of the 29th, the enemy's bombardment commenced. The 7th and 74th Brigades were ordered to stand to in case their assistance should be required. On several occasions during the early morning the enemy attempted to launch their attack against the line held by the 75th Brigade, but on each occasion the attack was broken up by artillery and machine gun fire. The 8th Borders were especially successful in repulsing all attempts to get near their line. The attack was equally unsuccessful along the front of the 22nd Corps and the 38th and 39th French Divisions. During the morning a report was received that Mont Rouge and Mont Vidiauge had been captured, two important strategical points on our line. This, however, was inaccurate and in no case were the enemy successful in penetrating the French or British front except at one isolated point between Scherpenberg and La Clytte, from which they were quickly ejected.

Of the 8th Borders, Lieut. Williams beat off four attacks with his platoon and 2nd Lieut. Darwell gained most valuable information with a patrol. Both these officers received the Military Cross. Pte. Bell did useful work in bringing up ammunition during the attack ; Pte. Roberts, Military Medal, as a runner and Pte. Gelling and Pte. Hird as stretcher bearers were all conspicuous for their gallantry and received the Military Medal. Capt. Schwabe, 2nd S. Lancs., led his company during the German attack with great ability ; Pte. Hooper as a scout, Pte. Derby as a runner and Pte. Collins and Pte. Nevitt as stretcher bearers were most noticeable and thoroughly deserved the decorations awarded them. Sergt. Wildgoose, 11th Cheshires, displayed cool leadership with his company ; Pte. Facey and Pte. Rees were conspicuous for their gallantry in attending to and bringing in wounded under heavy fire ; also Pte. Strachan as a runner and L./Corpl. Cheshire as a linesman, for his success in mending lines and keeping up communications under very difficult circumstances. All received decorations.

Casualties to the 75th Brigade had been comparatively light, 5 officers, including Lt.-Col. Birt, and 65 other ranks ; of 2nd S. Lancs., 2 officers and 5 other ranks : and the 11th Cheshires, 4 officers and 60 other ranks. During the whole of the afternoon of the 29th small parties of the enemy were seen dribbling back and presented good targets to the Artillery. On the evening of the 30th at about 8 p.m. the 2nd S. Lancs. took part in a minor operation, with French troops on their right, to straighten out the line. Their attack was successful, but as they found themselves in a dangerous salient they were forced to retire. No doubt the enemy attempted to attack early the 1st and again the morning of 4th May, but on both occasions were unable to move forward ; the artillery fire, both of British and French, being very skilfully worked and extremely heavy.

During the 2nd of May the line was comparatively quiet. The 75th Brigade was relieved by the 7th Brigade during the night of 1/2nd May, and the following night the 74th Brigade was relieved by the 114th Brigade of the 49th Division. Throughout the 3rd of May the Artillery was very active and at 7 p.m. heavy shelling started on the French front. No enemy attack took place either that night or next morning, though it appeared probable from intelligence sources that an attack was intended. Early the 4th May the 7th Brigade was relieved by the 15th French Regiment, and the following day the Division concentrated in an area about 10 miles west of Poperinghe.

MACHINE GUN BATTALION.

The 9th April, the 25th Battalion Machine Gun Corps under Lt.-Col. J. D. Deane-Drummond, D.S.O., had A Coy., commanded by Major Billingham and C Coy., commanded by Capt. Syme on the fronts of the 7th and 75th Brigades respectively, with D Coy. in reserve, commanded by Capt. Soutar. About noon half of B Coy. under Major Courtauld, M.C., proceeded with the 74th Brigade to Steenwerck, and the following day the remainder of the Coy. moved to Red Lodge. Although the Battalion had experienced heavy losses during the battle of Bapaume both in machine guns and personnel, yet its numbers had by this time been made up and the fighting spirit of all ranks was excellent. As during the battle round Bapaume, the Machine Gun Battalion was invaluable, and only when nearly surrounded were the machine guns blown up and the detachment retired. Of the officers, Capt. Ashcroft, Lieut. Brutton and Lieut. Weldrick were killed, 15 others were wounded and 11 reported missing.

About 5.30 p.m., 10th April, Lt.-Col. J.D. Deane-Drummond co-operated on the left of the counter-attack against Ploegsteert with about 200 details of the battalion acting as Infantry; unfortunately the former was wounded whilst trying to rush a German machine gun; a fine fighter himself, Col. Drummond had by his energy, determination and powers of organisation been invaluable to the Machine Gun Battalion and the Division. He now received the rare distinction of a second bar to his D.S.O. Major Bellingham showed great ability and leadership during the counter-attack and with 2nd Lieut. Dyson received the Military Cross for their services. Pte. Mabson and Corpl. Simson greatly distinguished themselves with B Coy. attached to the 74th Brigade. Held up by a German machine gun they rushed the house where it was located, killed the machine gun crew and disabled the gun. L./Corpl. Blake, Corpl. Burnett, D.C.M., M.M., and C.S.M. Goodwin all showed the greatest bravery in holding up the enemy advance and covering the retirement of the Infantry with their machine guns during the battle on the 10/11th April. All these N.C.Os. won the D.C.M., which they richly deserved. Corpl. Leggett did good work in command of a signal station at Ploegsteert and Corpl. Cotterill in successfully maintaining communications under most difficult circumstances. L./Corpl. Jones was conspicuous with his machine gun, Pte. James and Pte. Scouller attended to and brought in wounded under very heavy fire. Corpl. Hilson did wonderful good work with his machine gun on 13th April at Kemmel. At La Clytte on the 29th Pte. Atkins, Pte. Graham, Pte. Hughes, Sergt. Taylor, Sergt. Smith, Sergt. Lewis, Sergt. Pearce and Sergt. Graham were conspicuous for their bravery and determination with their machine guns and succeeded in inflicting very heavy losses on the attacking infantry. L./Corpl. Greenhalgh, Pte. Parr and Pte. Taylor as runners never once failed to deliver the messages entrusted to them. All these N.C.Os. and men were subsequently awarded the Military Medal for their Services.

. R.E. AND PIONEERS.

On arrival in the Ploegsteert area, the 105th, 106th, and 130th Field Companies R.E. and 6th S. Wales Borderers, (Pioneers) were under the Command of Major J. W. Lloyd, Capt. Cator, during the absence of Major Lynam, on leave, and Major P. H. Thorne, with Lt.-Col. N.T. Fitzpatrick in Command of the Pioneer Battalion A great deal of work was found to be necessary; the 106th and 130th Field Companies R.E. were employed on the right and left Brigade sectors including a line of concealed Battle posts running from in front of Ploegsteert Wood to the River Douve ; the 105th Field Company R.E. was working on a new corps line some 2,000 yards behind the

ront system of defence, and the Pioneer Battalion commenced the construction of dug-outs for Divisional Battle
Headquarters.

The morning of the 9th April, owing to the dispatch of the
74th Brigade to assist the 34th Division on our right, the
25th Division was left without any reserve troops except the
Field Companies R.E. and the Pioneers. These were at once
placed under the 75th Brigade to form a defensive flank from
Vanne along the line of the River Lys. During the night 2nd
Lieut. Armstrong, 105th Field Company R.E., with one section
reconnoitred the bridges on our front and found that all
preparations were complete for their demolition with sappers
attending to the charges. He received the M.C. for his work
on this occasion.

The following day, after the Germans, under cover of the
dense fog, had managed to cross the river the Field Companies
R.E. and S.W. Borderers, under Lt.-Col. N. T. Fitzpatrick,
were ordered to counter-attack along with 9th Cheshire
Regiment and two Companies 2nd S. Lancs.

At 5.30 p.m., following a Machine Gun Barrage and short
Trench Mortar barrage, the attack went forward in short rushes.
A, C and D Coys. S. Wales Borderers under Major Pearson,
Capt. Owen, and Capt. Jenkins respectively. The whole
line was immediately met with sweeping machine gun fire both
from Ploegsteert and the neighbourhood of Le Bizet.
Casualties were heavy, but the attack pushed forward in a
most determined manner to within 200 yards of the Village,
when, owing to enfilade fire, the remnants of the attacking
troops were compelled to fall back. Capt. Owen and
Capt. Jenkins were both wounded, being succeeded by
Lieut. Amos and Lieut. Hanna. The Field Companies
R.E. and 6th S. Wales Borderers now occupied a position
between Regina Camp and Dou Dou Farm. This line
was heavily shelled all night and at about 10 a.m. the
following morning they were slowly withdrawn back to the
Army Line of Defence east of Romarin, and later, to about
half a mile west of the village. Capt. Cator, R.E., who had
become separated with a few men of the 105th Field Coy.
R.E., was shortly afterwards killed. At 2 p.m. the S. Wales
Borderers attempted to recapture Romarin ; this attempt
was unsuccessful and also a second attempt at 4 p.m. met with
no better result. At dusk the line fell back and dug in with

the S. Lancs. of the 75th Brigade on the left and the remnants of the Field Companies R.E. on the right.

The fighting had been very severe and continuous for 40 hours. As on the Somme the assistance of these Technical troops was required in a crisis. They all did remarkably well ; though to use skilled Technical troops in this way is not economical or to be recommended and it would probably be better value to employ them as well as the Pioneers on digging back lines rather than as Infantry pure and simple.

Of the S. Wales Borderers, Major Pearson, M.C., was invaluable throughout the fighting and received the D.S.O. for his services ; 2nd Lieut. Kennedy, 2nd Lieut. Saxon, 106th Field Coy., Lieut. Cecil and Capt. Stickler, 6th S. Wales Borderers, won the Military Cross for their fine leadership and initiative when in command of their men, and a few days later Lieut. Ellen, 105th Field Coy., R.E. Capt. Mann, R.A.M.C., received the Military Cross for his devoted attention to the wounded, and Corpl. Bishop, Pte. Cassidy, L./Corpl. Davies, Pte. Gallent and Pte. Thomas of the S. Wales Borderers the Military Medal for their gallant conduct as stretcher bearers.

Sergt. Sanders, M.M., 106th Field Coy. R.E., was conspicuous for his gallant conduct throughout these operations ; Sergt. Foley, M.M., 106th Field Coy. R.E., distinguished himself by the cheerful manner in which he encouraged the men of his section ; several times he won his bet that he would drop three Bosches in five shots at 200 yards ; his success undoubtedly encouraged others to do the same. These N.C.Os., together with Sergt. Barker, M.M., 130th Field Coy. R.E., and Sergt. Pearson, 6th S. Wales Borderers, received the D.C.M. for their good work. Sergt. Chattington, S. Wales Borderers, Sapper Barwick, Sapper Bradley, C.S.M. Breeze, M.M., Corpl. Burles, Corpl. Henderson, Corpl. Hudgeton, L./Corpl. Wilson, Sapper Thwaites, Corpl. Tingen, all of the 106th Field Coy. R.E. L./Corpl. Harding, Corpl. Jopling, Sergt. Miller, L./Corpl. Turner, Corpl. Mogridge, Corpl. Croucher, 130th Field Coy. R.E., and Pte. Maybury, S. Wales Borderers, all won Military Medals by their gallantry and fine example to all ranks during a most trying time. Corpl. Fellows, S. Wales Borderers, took command of a platoon when his senior N.C.Os. had become casualties ; L.-Corpl. Poole, 105th Field Coy. R.E., used his Lewis gun with marked ability, and on several occasions covered the retirement of his comrades ; he was also instrumental in bringing down an enemy aeroplane. As runners, Pte. Lewis, Pte. Martin, and Pte. Young, S. Wales Borderers, Sapper James, Sapper Moir, Sapper Jones, 130th Field Coy. R.E., Sapper Morgan, 106th Field Coy. R.E., Sapper Burgess, 105th Field Coy. R.E., showed the greatest gallantry in delivering messages through heavy fire. Sapper Davey, Sapper Freeman, 106th Field Coy. R.E., managed to get rations to the men of their unit in the front line under exceptionally difficult circumstances, and all thoroughly deserved the Military Medal awarded them.

At 2 p.m., 12th April, 1918, the portion of the line held by the Pioneers and remnants of the R.E. Companies on the right of the 75th Brigade was attacked after heavy artillery bombardment and the troops gradually withdrew to the general line of the Kortypyp Road which was held all night. At 6 a.m. the following morning, the 13th April, the line was again attacked and gave way on the right, the R.E. Companies and S. Wales Borderers being forced back to the high ground east of Crucifix Corner. Those of the S. Wales Borderers who fell back to Neuve Eglise were later on in the evening transferred to Crucifix Corner.

Meanwhile 140 details of the R.E. had been collected from the transport lines and were sent on the evening of the 12th April to a position north of Bailleul under Major Lloyd and the following day joined Gen. Wyatt's force in the Army line of defence in front of Dranoutre.

The position here was heavily shelled all night and the following morning, the 14th, Lieut.-Col. N. T. Fitzpatrick, D.S.O., M.C., commanding the 6th S. Wales Borderers, was severely wounded. This officer had been a tower of strength throughout the fighting, and the battalion owed much to his leadership and powers of organisation. Major Deane succeeded to the command.

At 6 p.m. the Germans attacked the position at Crucifix Corner in force but were beaten back with heavy casualties. Sergt. Green, S. Wales Borderers, won a bar to his Military Medal for the initiative and gallantry he displayed during the fight. The S. Wales Borderers and about 30 R.E.'s were relieved during the night, 14th/15th, after five days' continuous fighting, during which the former had lost no less than 16 officers and 380 other ranks.

The 15th was a comparatively uneventful day for the remainder of the R.E.'s with Gen. Wyatt's force in front of Dranoutre which two days later became the front line. Lieut. Rice, 106th Field Coy. R.E., and Lieut. Cooper, did a fine piece of work when the Ravelsberg ridge in front of their position was captured during the day; going forward to ascertain the situation they collected some 50 stragglers, and with this small body of troops they delivered a most successful counter-attack, filled a dangerous gap, and were able to cover the retreat of other units.

Sergt. Hodgson, 105th Coy., and Sapper Dovaston, 106th Field Coy. R.E., were conspicuous for their good work on this occasion; the latter shot one by one the entire crew of an enemy machine gun. Sergt. Horrod, 106th Field Coy. R.E., managed to deliver rations under very difficult circumstances, and all received the Military Medal.

At 7.15 a.m. 17th April, 1918, the line in front of Dranoutre was heavily attacked after a terrific bombardment. Our artillery barrage was excellent and the attack was beaten off with great slaughter by machine guns and rifle fire. Lieut. Cooper, 105th Coy. R.E., who had displayed the utmost gallantry on all occasions, attempted to rush a German machine gun by himself and was unfortunately killed. He was a great fighter and his death was a great loss to his unit. Sapper Gibbs, Sapper Lack, L./Corpl. Thomas, 130th Coy. R.E., L./Corpl. Harley, 106th Field Coy. R.E., L./Corpl. Sayles, Corpl. Smart, 105th Field Coy. R.E., all received the Military Medal for their services, and Sapper Townend, motor cyclist orderly, for the highly efficient manner in which he carried out his duty, often under heavy shelling and rifle fire.

The 18th April, the position was again heavily bombarded, and the night 18th/19th April, the Field Companies were finally relieved from the line. Casualties had been severe during these seven days fighting, 5 officers and 123 other ranks.

Between the 25th April and the 4th May, whilst the Division was operating round Kemmel, the Field Companies and S. Wales Borderers were employed on second line defences, wiring and improving the trenches and strengthening Battalion and Brigade Headquarters.

ARTILLERY.

After the withdrawal of the 25th Division from the Battle of Bapaume and its departure for Flanders, the Divisional Artillery remained in action with the New Zealand Division between Hebeturne and Mailly-Mailles. The line had become stationary by this time, and the New Zealand troops carried out several successful minor operations, including an attack on the 30th March, when they captured many prisoners and 109 machine guns. On the 5th April, during a heavy German bombardment Major Anderton, commanding " A " Battery, 110th Brigade, and Lieut. W. H. Densham, were both severely wounded, and died almost immediately. These officers had greatly distinguished themselves during the recent fighting and were a great loss to the Division.

The 7th April the Divisional Artillery was relieved and moved back to St. Pol a few days later. Leaving his two brigades to follow on by road the C.R.A. Brig.-Gen. Kincaid-Smith, arrived at 25th Division Headquarters on the 9th April, and at once took charge of the 11th, 2nd New Zealand, and 38th Army Field Artillery Brigades, covering the 25th Division front, reinforced later on by the 149th Brigade R.F.A.

The 10th April, when the German attack developed on the 25th Division front, the 84th Battery fought their guns until the enemy closed round, when all the guns were blown up. During the day the brigades withdrew to new positions as the infantry gradually fell back. On the 13th April, and the following days, the brigades were heavily engaged round Neuve Eglise ; after the enemy had successfully gained a footing on the high ground north east of Bailleul the guns were withdrawn under cover from the Ravelsberg Ridge. Later on when the 34th French Division finally relieved the British 25th and 49th Divisions, the 154th French Division came in alongside the 34th French Division and the 11th, 38th, and 2nd New Zealand Brigades R.F.A. were grouped under the French Commander. Lieut.-Col. Hood, commanding the 38th Army Brigade was decorated with the Croix de Guerre with silver stars, on the field of battle for his artillery support and defence of Mont Rouge. He was killed almost immediately afterwards.

The 13th April, the Divisional Artillery arrived in the neighbourhood and at once came into action west of Bailleul under the orders of the 33rd Division.

110th Brigade R.F.A.		Lt.-Col. H. R. PHIPPS, D.S.O.
A/110	... ...	Major J. Watson, M.C.
B/110	... ...	Major A. L. Harman, M.C.
C/110	... ...	Majoɪ D. C. Wilson, D.S.O.
D/110	... ...	Major A. P. Evershed, M.C.
12th Brigade R.F.A.	...	Lt.-Col. E. V. SARSON, D.S.O.
A/112	... ...	Major S. O. Jones, M.C.
B/112	... ...	Major H. T. Vincent.
C/112	... ...	Major W. E. Mackay, M.C.
D/112	... ...	Major G. Sumptor, M.C.

From this position the Brigades were shortly moved to the southern slopes of Mont des Cats, covering Meteren and the British line south of the village.

The line had now become fairly stationary, but the German pressure was still strong. On their immediate front the batteries were instrumental in breaking up several German attacks and for the first week the enemy shelling and counter-battery work was very severe. Major Jones, A/112th Brigade R.F.A., gained his Military Cross by his fine leadership during most trying times at his battery position near Mont des Cats. Bty.-Sergt.-Major Howes, A/112th Brigade, also received a bar to his D.C.M. for the fine example he set on the same occasion, and L.-Bomb. Dyer, Gnr. Ingles, and Gnr. Pinknay, all of the A/112th Brigade R.F.A., won Military Medals for their gallantry in collecting the wounded and getting them away to a place of safety. L.-Bomb. Blackwell and Bty.-Q.M.S. Looney, both of C/112th Brigade R.F.A., gained Military Medals for their good work. In B/110th Brigade R.F.A. Sergt. Crew, Corpl. Warren and Sergt. Smith all won Military Medals for their good work with their batteries near Meteren and Dvr. Cooper for the admirable manner in which he managed to get rations up to his battery. With the D.A.C., Bomb. Orford distinguished himself in conveying wounded to the Field Ambulance under heavy shelling.

On the 23rd April, 1918, Brig.-Gen. Kincaid-Smith handed over command of the Brigades which he had temporarily directed, to the C.R.A., 154th French Division, and the following day took over command of the 25th Division Artillery

and the 113th Army Field Artillery Brigade, forming the
left group covering the 1st Australian Division, holding the
base of the salient which had been made by the German advance
west of Armentières.

The batteries remained for the next few days in action
north of Fletre, and extreme activity was displayed by the
artillery on both sides. The 28th April the German artillery
opened a heavy bombardment on our left, but no infantry
attack developed ; the same occurred the following morning
whilst the Germans were delivering their unsuccessful assault
on the French and British line, from Locre to Zillebeke.

The following week the 110th and 112th Brigades were
withdrawn and entrained at Arques along with the 25th
Division for Champagne.

COMMUNICATIONS.

In the first stages of the battle buried routes proved of
the greatest value. On the right sector of the Divisional
front the 75th Brigade were soon out of touch with their
forward station owing to its being off the buried route ; on
the left with the 7th Brigade, communications worked well
during both the 10th and 11th to its battalions, through the
exchange, although the enemy had overrun many of the
test points behind it. When communication was finally
interrupted the forward party, although almost entirely
surrounded, succeeded in getting back.

On the 12th a forward station was opened at Locre Chateau
which successfully handled the communications of the 7th,
74th and 75th, 100th, 101st, 71st, and 176th Brigades, and
Gen. Wyatt's force. Some difficulty was experienced in maintaining telephonic communication to battalions, but in most
cases a line was kept through the centre of the Brigade Area
to a forward office. A chain of linemen's posts was established
along such lines, and the forward office usually became the
combined headquarters of all those battalions.

L.-Cpl. Bangay, though wounded, carried on with his work,
Sapper Milnes and L.-Cpl. Liddell all showed great courage
in mending lines under heavy fire ; Cpl. Carr, in charge of
artillery communications. Sergt. Edgar, D.C.M., M.M.,
won a bar to his D.C.M. for his continuous good work. Though
twice blown up and gassed, he stuck to his work in charge of

the advanced Bde. Signal Station during the Kemmel operations, and succeeded in keeping communication through to the battalions and back to Brigade Headquarters. L.-Cpl. Wells gallantly laid and maintained a line during the German attack on the British front on the 28th, and Sapper Aspinall and Sapper Pigg were conspicuous for their disregard of danger whilst repairing broken lines. Corpl. Willoughby, motor cyclist, never failed to deliver messages entrusted to him. All these N.C.Os. and men were awarded the Military Medal, which they richly deserved.

Visual signalling was very little used owing to the misty weather which prevailed nearly all through the battle. Wireless stations were erected and in communication throughout, but were not made much use of, as the cables were able to handle all the work. A power and amplifier station in La Basse Ville was in continuous communication with a station in St. Ives, until the troops were withdrawn from the latter place on the 11th. Pte. Bromage received the Military Medal for his excellent work in charge of this station. Although the enemy were all round, he stayed on till the last moment, and then got away with the most important parts of his instrument.

MEDICAL ARRANGEMENTS AND CASUALTIES.

The work of the 75th, 76th, and 77th Field Ambulances was particularly arduous during the time the Division was in action from the 9th April onwards. The 76th Field Ambulance under Lt.-Col. Tyrrell, D.S.O., with its headquarters at Pont de Chelle, was responsible for clearing casualties of the 74th Bde. when it moved to Steenwerck. As the line withdrew the Field Ambulance moved to Outtersteene, Fletre, and later to Godeersvelde, where large numbers of the 34th, 40th, 29th, and 28th Divisions were dealt with.

During the severe fighting round Steenwerck, and Croix de Bac, Pte. Bissmire, Pte. Chiltern, Pte. Pears and Pte. Whittle, of the 76th Field Ambulance, greatly distinguished themselves by their gallantry in attending and bringing in wounded under heavy fire when the regimental stretcher bearers were fully occupied. A few days later Pte. Middlemass, M.T., A.S.C., and Pte. James, 76th Field Ambulance, did remarkably well in making an extemporised bridge under heavy shell fire in order to get their motor ambulance full of wounded to its destination. All these thoroughly deserved their decorations as well as Capt. Chance, R.A.M.C., 76th Field Ambulance, who won the Military Cross for the gallant manner in which he re-organised and led his bearer squads under heavy fire.

When the attack developed, the morning of the 10th April, along the Divisional front, the 75th and 77th Field Ambulances, under Lt.-Col. Davidson, D.S.O., and Lt.-Col. Kelly, D.S.O., were responsible for clearing casualties of the 7th and 75th Brigades. As the line fell back the main dressing stations were successively withdrawn to Westhof Farm, to Berthen, and on the 11th April, to Haegedoorne. Heavy shelling of the main roads and back areas made it extremely difficult at times for the motor ambulances to bring casualties to a place of safety. Pte. Dawson, M.T., A.S.C. did excellent work with his car, and succeeded in getting many loads of wounded away before the road became quite impassable. In no case were any wounded who reached the Regimental Aid Posts allowed to fall into the enemy's hands. That this was possible is entirely due to the wonderful courage displayed by the regimental stretcher-bearers, and R.A.M.C. personnel, who had tended wounded and brought them in to safety often under the heaviest fire. Pte. Cross, M.M., 75th Field Ambulance, won the D.C.M. for conspicuous bravery in bringing in wounded under heavy machine gun fire, whilst Pte. Hall, 75th Field Ambulance, Pte. Fray, and Pte. Cragg, 77th Field Ambulance, also gained the Military Medal. Sergt. Ingram, 77th Field Ambulance, gained the D.C.M., for his exemplary conduct throughout the six days' fighting.

Casualties were extremely heavy amongst the medical officers and the personnel of the three Field Ambulances. Capt. Kennedy, R.A.M.C., 76th Field Ambulance, was killed at Mont Noir. Capt. Oliver, R.A.M.C., Capt. Williams, R.A.M.C., and Capt. McLean, were wounded, and six other medical officers were missing, of whom three were believed to have been taken prisoners with the Battalion Headquarters of the 1st Wilts, 4th South Staffords, and 10th Cheshires.

162 officers, and 3,923 other ranks were dealt with by the Field Ambulances between the 9th and the 22nd April, of whom about half belonged to other Divisions.

(12064)   H

From the 25th April to the 4th May, the Field Ambulances were responsible for clearing casualties from the Brigades in the counter-attack on Kemmel on the 26th April, and also during the unsuccessful attack by the Germans on the French and British line on the 29th April. During this period the Field Ambulances with their headquarters at Vanschier Farm on the Reninghelst-Poperhinge Road, dealt with 49 officers and about 1,000 other ranks. Unfortunately a tent sub-division, with two horse ambulances of the 75th Field Ambulance was almost destroyed on the switch road, west of Poperhinge. Two shells alone causing casualties to R.A.M.C. personnel of 11 killed and 15 wounded. Capt. Huycke, R.A.M.C., 75th Field Ambulance, received the Military Cross for the great gallantry he displayed in organising advanced dressing stations under very heavy shell fire. The 4th May the Field Ambulances were finally relieved by ambulances of the 32nd French Division.

The following are a list of those who received rewards for services during the operations with details of some of the more notable acts of gallantry for which the award was granted : —

Sergt. J. Bertenshaw, 11th Cheshire Regt.

On the 10th April, 1918, during the operations in the neighbourhood of Ploegsteert Wood, this N.C.O. showed exceptional gallantry and initiative in a counter-attack by organising the men around him and pushing forward. When his position become untenable and he was ordered to withdraw, he successfully withdrew his men and personally carried two wounded men to cover under heavy fire. Later when all his officers had become casualties, he took command and successfully maintained his position until relieved. He set an example, and acted with cool precision and determination throughout the fighting.

Awarded .... D.C.M.

Lieut.-Col. C. W. H. Birt. D.S.O., 8th Border Regt. (Wounded.)

For conspicuous gallantry and devotion to duty throughout the operations in the Ploegsteert and Neuve Eglise sectors from 10th to 16th April.

This officer, by his great personal courage and magnificent example to his men, repeatedly saved the situation at most critical times. His presence on the spot in the front line during the greater part of the time enabled him to keep such a grasp on his men, and to control the situation in his part of the line in such a manner as to ensure the steady carrying out of any withdrawal that became necessary. This was particularly the case when his battalion was holding a line near Le Bizet in front of Oosthove Farm, and the troops on his flanks were forced back by the enemy. Col. Birt covered their withdrawal, and succeeded in extricating his battalion from an untenable position, re-establishing it on a line in the rear.

Awarded .... **Bar to D.S.O.**

No. 72528 L.-Corpl. A. E. F. Blake, 25th Battn. M.G. Corps.

On the 10th April, 1918, near Le Bizet, this N.C.O. showed great gallantry and initiative when in command of a gun team. When all his men became casualties he continued to fire the gun until all the ammunition was expended, and being then surrounded blew up the gun and tripod and fought his way back to our lines, effectively using his revolver. By this action he held up the Boche attack for over three hours.

He has always behaved in a most gallant manner.

Awarded .... **D.C.M.**

No. 64610 Bomb. F. G. Blackwell, " C " Btry., 112th Brigade, R.F.A.

On April the 13th near Meteren, this N.C.O. volunteered to run out a line, which was constantly broken by shell fire, to an O.P. under a very heavy barrage and kept the line in repair while the battery was registered.

Again, on the 17th, near Mont Des Cats, when his battery position was being heavily shelled and the signaller working a lamp to the O.P. had been wounded, this N.C.O. got a new lamp working, and continued to keep in communication with the O.P. under heavy shell fire.

Awarded .... **M.M.**

Lieut. K. M. Bourne, M.C., 2nd South Lancashire Regt.

For conspicuous gallantry on the 12th April at Neuve Eglise when our line was attacked, this officer displayed the highest qualities of bravery and endurance. When the line had been broken on his right he at once formed a defensive flank, and it was owing to his fine leadership that the first attack was held up on his company front. When the second attack materialised, and when compelled to withdraw, he organised a steady retirement and inflicted great loss on the enemy at a very critical time which proved invaluable to other units concerned.

His example of fearlessness under very adverse conditions inspired his men with the greatest confidence.

Awarded .... **Bar to M.C.**

No. 29819 Corpl. H. E. Cole, 1st Wiltshire Regt.

On the morning of the 26th April, during the counter-attack on Kemmel, this N.C.O. in the absence of a platoon officer or senior N.C.O.'s, led his platoon into action in a most capable and gallant manner, showing great initiative.

On having to withdraw, owing to an exposed flank, he re-organised his platoon and withdrew in perfect good order under intense artillery and machine-gun fire.

His behaviour throughout these operations was magnificent, and the example he set to his men was excellent in every way.

Awarded .... M.M.

No. 6847 L./Corpl. A. Corlett, 11th Battn. Lancashire Fusiliers.
(Died.)

On the night of the 25/26th April, during the counter-attack on Kemmel-Village, this N.C.O. seeing that the battalion on his right was held up by a nest of enemy machine guns and suffering heavy casualties, he took out a Lewis Gun Section and took up a position from which he brought flanking fire on enemy machine guns and compelled them to withdraw. In taking up this position he was badly wounded, but continued to encourage his men until exhausted. He and his section came under very heavy machine-gun fire, and although four of the section, including himself, were wounded, he succeeded in clearing away the obstacle, so enabling the next battalion to advance.

Awarded .... D.C.M.

No. 39678 Pte. A. J. Cotterell, 3rd Battn. Worcester Regt.

Near La Clytte on 27th April, 1918, this man was acting as stretcher-bearer, and displayed great devotion to duty and utter disregard of personal danger. When going out with three other bearers to fetch in a wounded man, they were heavily sniped, two being killed and the other wounded. Pte. Cotterell having bound his fellow stretcher-bearers, succeeded in reaching the wounded man, whom he dressed and brought to safety.

Awarded .... M.M.

Lieut. F. W. Cooper, M.C., 105th Field Coy. R.E. (Killed.)

During the periods 21st March to 28th March and 9th to 17th April, 1918, when the 25th Division was heavily engaged with the enemy, Lieut. Cooper's conduct was a consistent example of gallant and brave bearing in face of the enemy. A conspicuous example was on the 10th April, 1918, near Le Bizet. This officer went out on patrol with a sergeant of his company, to get information badly needed on account of the dense fog. The sergeant was severely wounded. Lieut. Cooper took him on his back and crawled 150 to 200 yards with him under very heavy fire of machine guns, and succeeded in bringing him to a place from where he could be rescued, thus saving his life.

Near Ravelsberg, on the 15th April, 1918, seeing a party of our troops being surrounded by the enemy, he collected and organised a party of 50 stragglers, personally bringing necessary ammunition to them under heavy fire ; only he and one man of the carrying party remaining unwounded. He then delivered a successful counter-attack which enabled our troops to be withdrawn.

Again, near Dranoutre, on the 17th April, 1918, when the enemy succeeded in establishing a forward machine gun close to and enfilading Lieut. Cooper's position, without waiting for assistance Lieut.

Cooper attempted to rush it single handed. He got to within a few yards of it, but was killed by a sniper hidden in a shell hole close to it.

. . . .

No. 40458 Pte. F. W. L. Cross, M.M., R.A.M.C. 75th Field Ambulance.

On the morning of April 11th, 1918, near Petit Munque Farm, a party of stretcher-bearers with a wounded man came under machine gun and rifle fire during an enemy attack. Two of the bearers being hit, the wounded man was placed behind a farm house, and Pte. Cross then crawled out under intense rifle and machine-gun fire and dragged in one of them. Accompanied by Sergt. Baldwin, R.A.M.C., 75th Field Ambulance, he went out to bring in the other, but the sergeant was hit. Pte. Cross dragged in the second wounded man, then went out again and helped the sergeant to cover.

After a counter-attack Pte. Cross went for more bearers and evacuated all the cases from behind the farm, which was then held as an outpost.

His conduct throughout was magnificent.

Awarded . . . . D.C.M.

Lt.-Col. J. D. Deane-Drummond, D.S.O., M.C., 25th Battn. M.G. Corps. (Wounded.)

For conspicuous gallantry and determination.

On April 10th, 1918, the Germans having penetrated into Ploegsteert Wood and Village, a counter-attack was ordered, but as it was slow in developing Lt.-Col. Deane-Drummond visited the Commanding Officers of the units concerned and got a move on. He took part in the attack, leading 200 machine gunners armed with rifles. In the wood his party was stopped by a German machine gun. He therefore rushed the gun with a couple of men, but these were wounded, and when within 20 yards of the gun it was turned on to him, but he killed the No. 1 with a rifle bullet, the rifle jammed as he was re-loading, and the No. 2 succeeded in wounding Lt.-Col. Deane-Drummond very severely. The latter, however, rolled into a shell hole and took on the gun, with his rifle putting the gun and team out of action, thus allowing his men to proceed.

Awarded . . . . Bar to D.S.O.

No. 45530 Sergt. H. Edgar, D.C.M., M.M. and Bar, 25th Div. Signal Coy., attd. 7th Bde., Signal Section.

For conspicuous gallantry throughout the operations, Mont Kemmel, on April 26th, 1918.

This N.C.O. was in charge of a signal detachment at Advanced Bde. H.Q., during this period, and was responsible for keeping communications by wire through to battalions and back to rear Bde. H.Q. For two days this N.C.O. was in the forward area mending lines which had been broken by the very heavy shelling during which time he had no rest and remained in the open mending the lines, refusing to take cover although being twice blown up by shells, and gassed.

II 3

Later, he remained in the main street of the village that was being barraged, keeping the line through to Brigade.

This total disregard of personal danger and control over the men with him were beyond praise. It was entirely due to his courage that lines were kept through, and important messages were able to be delivered to and from battalions.

Awarded .... **Bar to D.C.M.**

No. 241660 Pte. D. Fearnside, 9th Loyal North Lancs. Regt.

At Mont de Lille, during a counter-attack on the 17th April, he pushed forward with a Lewis gun and opened fire on a body of the enemy who were threatening our right flank, and from an exposed position dispersed them, inflicting very heavy casualties. Throughout the whole of the operations he showed remarkable courage and initiative, and his coolness under heavy artillery and machine gun fire was a notable example for all.

Awarded .... **M.M.**

No. 13563 Pte. W. Forsbury, 4th South Staffordshire Regt.

On 26th April, 1918, Pte. Forsbury was in charge of a squad of stretcher bearers during the attack on Kemmel Village. When the main body were forced to withdraw, Pte. Forsbury remained behind and succeeded in bringing in a number of wounded men, but for his gallantry and coolness under fire, these men would undoubtedly have been taken prisoner.

Awarded .... **M.M.**

No. 5069 C. S. M. Gent, J. M. J., 8th Battn. Border Regt.

For conspicuous gallantry, leadership and devotion to duty. On April 10th, when all the officers of his company had become casualties, he took command and re-organised it at Ploegsteert. He remained in command four days, fighting a rearguard action the whole time. His magnificent example of courage and coolness against overwhelming odds inspired his men to a stubborn resistance and they were able by taking up strong positions in succession to inflict heavy casualties on the enemy. The gallant action of this W.O. during the whole period was the means of reducing the casualties in his own company and of checking the advance of immensely superior numbers of the enemy.

Awarded .... **D.C.M.**

No. 44495 Sergt. T. Green, M.M., 6th South Wales Borderers.

At Ravelsberg on the 14th April, 1918, the enemy put down a heavy barrage on the outpost line held by this N.C.O. Seeing his men falling back he ran out, rallied them, and led them back to the advanced shell hole line. Later, seeing that his men would become casualties, he withdrew to another line; taking his men forward again as soon as the barrage lifted, he immediately filled a gap at a critical point.

The courage and initiative displayed by this N.C.O., together with his ready grasp of the situation throughout the operations, were invaluable.

Awarded .... **Bar to M.M.**

No. 33896 Battery Sergt.-Major F. Howes, " A " Battery, 112th Brigade, R.F.A.

On April 17th this W.O. was at the battery position near the Mont Des Cats when the battery was subjected to a heavy shelling, causing some 22 casualties.

He walked up and down the battery and by his personal example steadied the men who were much shaken, and kept the gunners firing at their posts.

Shortly afterwards the forward wagon lines were shelled and many casualties. This W.O. ran over at once and superintended the evacuation of the remaining horses, though salvoes were falling round.

He thereby saved many casualties.

Awarded .... Bar to D.C.M.

No. 39213 Staff-Sergt. J. Ingram, M.M., Croix de Guerre, R.A.M.C., 77th Field Ambulance.

As bearer-sergeant throughout the offensive, April 10th-15th, 1918. In the early hours of the morning April 13th, he organised parties to search for wounded men who had been buried in the debris of a house at the corner of Ravelsberg-Waterloo and Clapham Roads, digging out two men and assisting others under very heavy shell fire, and then assisted in dressing their wounds.

During the six days he did most exemplary work and showed great bravery, keeping in touch with the regimental stretcher bearers day and night, and thus greatly assisting in getting away many very badly wounded men.

Awarded .... D.C.M.

No. 20482 Pte. W. Ingram, 10th Cheshire Regt.

For conspicuous gallantry in action at Kemmel on 26th April, 1918. This man showed initiative. He crawled out alone under heavy machine gun fire and lay in the open for two hours sniping an enemy post that was very troublesome.

He showed great coolness, bravery and disregard of personal danger.

Awarded .... M.M.

Major S. O. Jones, " A " Battery, 112th Brigade, R.F.A.

On the 17th April, near the Mont Des Cats, when his battery position was being heavily shelled, causing 22 casualties, this officer showed the greatest gallantry in superintending the removal of the wounded and in keeping his battery in action during a most trying time.

His coolness and courage were an example to all ranks.

Awarded .... M.C.

No. 14830 L./Corpl. W. Kirkman, 2nd South Lancashire Regt.

For conspicuous gallantry during the counter-attack on Ploegsteert on the 10th April, whilst in charge of a Lewis gun section.

This N.C.O. controlled his team with exceptional skill and bravery. When four of his section had become casualties, he worked his gun single handed, although subjected the whole time to extremely heavy machine gun fire.

When forced to withdraw he exhibited great skill in the selection of positions for his gun, which he kept in action throughout and undoubtedly used to the best advantage, thereby enabling the remainder of his platoon to extricate itself with the least possible loss.

Awarded . . . . **M.M.**

No. 30255 Sergt. L. Lee, 25th Divisional Train, A.S.C.

On the evening of the 25th April, 1918, when in charge of a supply section of No. 2 Coy. 25th Divl. train returning from Reninghelst, came under severe shell fire, resulting in two horses being killed and one badly wounded. By his coolness and presence of mind kept the men and horses of his section together, succeeded in recovering the derelict wagon and brought them safely in, the whole being under continuous shell fire.

Awarded . . . . **M.M.**

No. 313154 L./Corpl. W. Liddell, 25th Divisional Signal Coy., R.E.

On the 13th April, 1918, near Meteren, when a strong enemy attack was developing, communications between the Brigade and Batteries broke down owing to the intensity of enemy shell fire.

This N.C.O., regardless of personal risk, went out and repaired the line and remained out for over four hours, maintaining telephonic communication between the Brigade and its batteries at a most critical time and vital period.

Awarded . . . . **M.M.**

No. 27595 Pte. J. Maylor, 11th Cheshire Regt.

During the operations on the 10th April in the neighbourhood of Ploegsteert, this man was selected to carry an important message to Battalion H.Q. This he accomplished under heavy machine gun fire and had to pass through a barrage. He returned with orders and again went to Battalion H.Q. During the whole day communication was maintained between his company and Battalion Commander by this man continually under fire. He never failed to find either H.Q., although both were constantly moving. His devotion to duty and courage were beyond praise, and the result of his work was invaluable.

Awarded . . . . **M.M.**

No. 032977 Pte. W. H. Middlemass, A.S.C. (M.T.), attd. 76th Field Ambulance.

While driving a motor ambulance loaded with wounded along the Berthen-Boeschepe Road on the evening of the 16th April, 1918, the road was being searched by enemy gun fire. An ammunition lorry was set on fire and blocked the road. With ready wit and great gallantry Pte. Middlemass, with the car orderly, collected planks and stakes and extemporised a parapet bridge over the ditch opposite the burning lorry. Using this he was just able to rush his car past the lorry.

Awarded . . . . **D.C.M.**

Lieut. A. B. Miller, 4th South Staffordshire Regt.

For conspicuous gallantry and leadership in the attack near Kemmel in the early morning of the 26th April.

After all the senior officers of the battalion had become casualties and things were critical, he immediately assumed command, re-organised and led the battalion with great dash and determination, killing a large number of the enemy and taking about 70 prisoners.

When the withdrawal became absolutely necessary owing to both flanks being exposed, and to enfilade machine gun fire from Kemmel Hill, he formed defensive flanks, organised his force to give mutual covering fire, and so got back to our front line in perfect order.

His prompt action and brilliant organisation and leadership made what was on the verge of being a failure a brilliant success.

Awarded .... **D.S.O.**

No. 31600 Bomb. J. Orford, 25th D.A.C. No. 2 Section.

Near Meteren on the night 24th/25th April, 1918, Bomb. Orford was in charge of three wagons (six mule teams) which were returning empty and were ordered to pick up Australian wounded and convey them to the field ambulance. The convoy was subjected to heavy shell fire on the road, and it was owing to the N.C.O.'s great coolness and his splendid example that the wounded were safely handed over to the field ambulance. One driver was wounded and three animals were killed.

Awarded .... **M.M.**

Major N. G. Pearson, M.C., 6th S.W. Borderers (Pioneers).

During the operations around Ploegsteert-Neuve Eglise and Ravelsberg from the 9th to 15th April, 1918, this officer was of great value. Throughout the operations he showed exceptional courage and coolness in the handling of his men.

He organised several minor counter-attacks and personally led them in the fighting around Romarin Village.

He carried out many daring reconnaissances by night and was able to send back valuable information. His cheerful spirit and courageous example did much to all around him on many critical occasions.

He did very fine work throughout the period.

Awarded .... **D.S.O.**

No. 71737 Gnr. J. Pinkney, M.M., " A " Battery, 112th Bde., R.F.A.

On April 17th, 1918, near the Mont Des Cats, when his battery position was being heavily shelled, this gunner showed great gallantry in collecting wounded and getting them away to a place of safety under heavy fire.

Awarded .... **Bar to M.M.**

No. 23742 Pte. H. Prescott, 9th Loyal North Lancs. Regt.

This man showed great bravery and devotion to duty during the whole of the fighting from 9th to 20th April, 1918. During a heavy bombardment on the 17th April at St. Jans Cappel, when acting as stretcher bearer, he dressed wounded in the open and carried them back to a place of safety. Through his courage and determination, he undoubtedly saved the lives of many of his comrades.

Awarded . . . . **M.M.**

No. 169214 L./Corpl. W. D. Poole, 105th Field Coy. R.E.

At Dou Dou Farm, on 11th April, 1918, whilst in charge of a Lewis gun, by his initiative and skilful handling of his gun he was instrumental in bringing down E.A. During the whole of the attack this N.C.O. showed marked ability and on several occasions covered his comrades' withdrawal and brought his gun safely to a new position and at once got into effective action in spite of continuous heavy enemy shell and machine gun fire. His example had a fine effect on the morale of his comrades under very trying circumstances.

Awarded . . . . **M.M.**

No. 22100 Pte. W. Powell, 25th Battn. M.G. Corps.

At La Clytte, on May 3rd, 1918. During an extremely heavy enemy bombardment a defective round jammed in the barrel and stopped the gun firing. Pte. Powell, who was No. 1 on the gun, without any hesitation, ran a distance of 700 yards through a most intense barrage, procured a new barrel, came back through the barrage, fitted the barrel in the gun, and carried on firing, causing heavy casualties.

Awarded . . . . **M.M.**

No. 10890 Corpl. P. W. Puddick, 1st Wiltshire Regt.

In the vicinity of Ploegsteert Wood during the period 10th/18th April, 1918, for extreme bravery.

This N.C.O., during the whole of this period, was in charge of all the Lewis guns in the battalion, no officer being available.

He displayed the utmost fearlessness and courage in visiting his guns under the heaviest shell fire, and on no less than three occasions succeeded in getting into action guns temporarily knocked out and their crews put out of action. On one occasion he single-handed repaired and brought into action again a gun and put out of action a party of 12 Germans coming round his flank. His bravery and personal example were beyond all praise.

Awarded . . . . **M.M.**

Major A. Reade, M.C., 2nd South Lancashire Regt., attd. 10th Cheshire Regt.

For most conspicuous gallantry and leadership from 13th to 15th April, 1918, whilst in command of the composite battalions formed from the Brigade at Crucifix Corner, west of Neuve Eglise.

On the 14th inst. the enemy, succeeding in breaking through a portion of the line, reached Crucifix Corner. This officer called on 30 men to follow him in a counter-attack which he led himself, driving the enemy back to his original position, capturing 20 prisoners, machine guns, and killing about 60 Germans. His own losses were 4 killed and 6 wounded.

It was mainly owing to this officer's gallantry and leadership that the position was handed over intact upon relief on the night of the 15th/16th April.

Awarded .... **D.S.O.**

No. 65178 Sergt. W. Sanders, M.M., 106th Field Coy., R.E.

On the 9th April, when his section was holding the right flank of the line behind Le Bizet with enemy fire converging from three sides his conduct in visiting posts under a hail of bullets inspired his men with his own cheerful gallantry. He assisted materially in getting two machine guns into action, thereby arresting the enemy's advance. Later, when the line had to be withdrawn, the orderly nature of the withdrawal was largely due to his organising capacity, and the successful evacuation of one of the machine guns and of all our wounded was due to his utter disregard of personal danger and coolness under devastating fire. During the succeeding eight days of fighting his conduct was distinguished by the same high attributes which won him at once the loyal respect of all ranks under him and inspired them with the same spirit of devotion to duty.

Awarded .... **D.C.M.**

2nd Lieut. M. D. Walker, 11th Lancashire Fusiliers.

At Kemmel Village, on 26th April, 1918, this officer took command of " A " Coy. of his battalion on the Coy. Commander becoming a casualty at the commencement of our attack on the village. With his company and men from a number of units which he had found without leaders, he fought his way right through the village into the open country beyond and occupied an old dilapidated British strong point. He held this for over an hour against large numbers of the enemy on whom he inflicted large numbers of casualties. He eventually discovered that he was not in touch with our troops on his flanks and as the mist was rising and his party was almost surrounded he withdrew to the remainder of the attacking force. His skilful leadership and the cool manner in which he conducted himself during this operation, won the admiration of all ranks, and his holding the post in front of the village contributed largely to the subsequent operations.

Awarded .... **M.C.**

No. 31104 Pte. G. Wells, 3rd Battn. Worcester Regt.

On the 13th April at the Mont De Lille, and during the whole of the operations 9th to 20th April, 1918, Pte. Wells repeatedly took messages under very heavy fire. He showed the greatest determination, devotion to duty and contempt of danger.

Awarded .... **M.M.**

Honours and Awards from 9th April to 5th May, 1918.

BAR TO THE DISTINGUISHED SERVICE ORDER.

Lt.-Col. C. W. H. Birt, D.S.O. .. 8th Border Regt.
Lt.-Col. J. D. Deane-Drummond, 25th Battn. M.G. Corps.
D.S.O., M.C.

THE DISTINGUISHED SERVICE ORDER.

Lt.-Col. J. B. Allsopp .. .. 2nd South Lancs. Regt.
Lieut. A. B. Miller .. .. .. Attd. 4th South Staffords.
Major E. P. Nares, M.C. .. .. Cheshire Regt., attd. 9th L.N. Lancs.
Major N. G. Pearson, M.C. .. 6th South W. Borderers.
Major A. Reade, M.C. .. .. 2nd South Lancs., attd. 10th Cheshires.
Major J. A. Simmons, M.C. .. Cheshire Regt.
Major R. F. Traill .. .. .. 3rd Worcesters.
Major E. W. Denny.. .. .. Attd 75th Bde., H.Q.

SECOND BAR TO THE MILITARY CROSS.

Lieut. R. Strong, M.C. .. .. 8th Borders.

BAR TO THE MILITARY CROSS.

Lieut. H. B. Brown, M.C. .. .. 1st Wiltshire Regt.
Lieut. K. M. Bourne, M.C. .. .. 2nd South Lancs. Regt.
Capt. W. F. Bryden, M.C. .. .. 2nd South Lancs. Regt.
Capt. R. K. Beswick, M.C. .. .. 11th Lancs. Fusiliers.
Capt. A. H. Huycke, M.C. .. .. R.A.M.C.
Lieut. J. M. Marsh, M.C. .. .. 9th Loyal North Lancs.

MILITARY CROSS.

2nd Lieut. A. L. Armstrong.. .. 105th Field Coy. R.E.
2nd Lieut. R. F. Ackerley .. .. 11th Lancs. Fusiliers.
Lieut. A. C. Amos .. .. .. 6th South W. Borderers.
2nd Lieut. C. Bates .. .. .. 4th South Staffords.
Capt. A. J. Bentley .. .. .. 8th Borders.
Major A. M. Bellingham .. .. Attd. 25th Battn. M.G. Corps.
Lieut. F. Brittorous .. .. .. Attd. 9th Loyal N. Lancs.
Capt. C. C. Chance .. .. .. R.A.M.C. 76th Field Amb.
Capt. L. G. Carr .. .. .. London Regt., attd. 4th S.Staffs.
2nd Lieut. F. W. Darvell .. .. 8th Border Regt.
Lieut. D. H. Doherty .. .. M.O.R.C., U.S.A., attd. 3rd Worcester Regt.
Lieut. J. F. Duggan, D.C.M. .. 8th Borders.

2nd Lieut. F. K. Dyson	.. ..	Attd. 25th Battn. M.G. Corps.
Lieut. C. W. Ellen ..	.. ..	106th Field Coy. R.E.
2nd Lieut. E. Foulkes	.. ..	2nd South Lancs. Regt.
Capt. C. H. Haddow ..	.. ..	R.A.M.C., attd. 9th Loyal N. Lancs.
Capt. W. S. Hartley ..	.. ..	9th Manchesters, attd. 9th L.N. Lancs.
Capt. H. A. Hutson ..	.. ..	11th Lancs. Fusiliers. South Staffords.
2nd Lieut. D. P. C. Imrie	.. ..	1st London Regt., attd. 4th.
Major S. O. Jones ..	.. ..	"A" Battery, 112th Bde., R.F.A.
2nd Lieut. J. S. Kennedy	.. ..	106th Field Coy. R.E.
Capt. E. Lattey ..	.. ..	3rd Worcester Regt.
2nd Lieut. O. H. Mason	.. ..	Attd. 4th South Staffords.
Capt. A. C. Mann ..	.. ..	R.A.M.C., attd. 6th S.W.B.
Lieut. A. B. Miller ..	.. ..	4th South Staffords.
Capt. F Priestley ..	.. ..	1st Wiltshire Regt.
2nd Lieut. A. A. Rice	.. ..	106th Field Coy. R.E.
Capt. S. B. Schwabe ..	.. ..	Attd. 2nd South Lancs.
2nd Lieut. K. T. Stephens ..	.. ..	3rd Worcester Regt.
2nd Lieut. W. Stelfox	.. ..	11th Lancs. Fusiliers.
Capt. D. H. Stickler ..	.. ..	6th South W. Borderers.
Capt. E. O. Underhill	.. ..	Attd. 3rd Worcesters.
Lieut. N. Walker ..	.. ..	Cheshires, attd. Bde. H.Q.
2nd Lieut. M. D. Walker	.. ..	11th Lancs. Fusiliers.
2nd Lieut. N. E. Ward	.. ..	11th Lancs. Fusiliers.
2nd Lieut. R. Wilson	.. ..	9th Loyal N. Lancs.
Lieut. L. F. Williams	.. ..	8th Border Regt.
2nd Lieut. J. J. Woolley	.. ..	4th South Staffords.

BAR TO THE DISTINGUISHED CONDUCT MEDAL.

18327 Corpl. A. Burnett, D.C.M., M.M.	25th Battn. M.G. Corps.
45530 Sergt. H. Edgar, D.C.M., M.M.	Attd. 7th Bde. Signals, R.E.
33896 B.S.M. F. Howes, D.C.M. ..	"A" Battn. 112th Bde., R.F.A.
8368 C.S.M. J. Trowbridge, D.C.M.	Cheshire Regt.

THE DISTINGUISHED CONDUCT MEDAL.

275 C.S.M. R. Abbott	11th Lancs. Fusiliers.
72528 L./Corpl. A. E. F. Blake ..	25th Battn. M.G. Corps.
67008 Sgt. W. Barker, M.M.	130th Field Coy. R.E.
16897 Sergt. J. Bertenshaw	Cheshire Regt.
8963 Sergt. J. F. Bridges, M.M., Bar	1st Wiltshire Regt.
40458 Pte. W. L. Cross, M.M. ..	R.A.M.C. 75th Field Amb.
19967 C.S.M. J. Croll	9th Loyal N. Lancs.
6847 L./Corpl. A. Corlett	11th Lancs. Fusiliers.
65638 Sergt. J. Foley, M.M., Bar ..	106th Field Coy. R.E.
5869 C.S.M. J. M. J. Gent	8th Border Regt.
53080 C.S.M. (A/R.S.M.) A. Greenhalgh.	10th Cheshire Regt.

43881 C.S.M. H. E. P. Goodwin	25th Battn. M.G. Corps.
39213 Staff Sergt. J. Ingram, M.M., Croix de Guerre.	R.A.M.C. 77th Field Amb.
19702 Sergt. A. E. Kay	3rd Worcesters.
97475 Pte. A. Mabson	25th Battn. M.G. Corps.
032977 Pte. W. H. Middlemass	A.S.C. (M.T.) 76th Field Amb.
6/17090 Sergt. (A/C.S.M.) J. Pearson	6th South W. Borderers.
7427 C.S.M. S. Pearce, M.M., Bar	1st Wiltshire Regt.
65178 Sergt. W. Sanders. M.M.	106th Field Coy., R.E.
6770 Corpl. E. Simpson	25th Battn. M.G. Corps.
13323 Sergt. H. Smith	3rd Worcesters.
12895 Sergt. J. Wilson	10th Cheshires.

BAR TO THE MILITARY MEDAL.

15091 Sergt. M. Crayston, M.M.	8th Border Regt
17094 Sergt. D. Cook, M.M.	3rd Worcesters.
6/17154 Corpl. J. Elsdon, M.M.	6th South W. Borderers.
44495 Sergt. T. Green, M.M.	6th South W. Borderers.
7780 Corpl. J. Joll, M.M.	11th Lancs. Fusiliers.
15153 Pte. J. R. Jones, M.M.	8th Borders.
17395 Pte. D. Misell, M.M.	2nd South Lancs.
10085 Pte. E. Roberts, M.M.	8th Border Regt.
203060 Pte. H. Todkill, M.M.	8th Border Regt.
71737 Gnr. J. Pinkey, M.M.	"A" Battery, 112th Bde., R.F.A.

THE MILITARY MEDAL.

360018 Sapper W. Aspinall	25th Div. Sig. Coy., 7th Bde. Sig. Sec.
81717 Pte. T. Atkins	25th Battn. M.G. Corps.
W/606 Pte. H. Ashley	10th Cheshire Regt.
35804 Pte. E. Allsworth	3rd Worcester Regt.
16738 L./Corpl. C. E. Atkinson	11th Cheshire Regt.
64610 L./Bomb. F. G. Blackwell	"C" Battery, 112th Bde., R.F.A.
104620 Sapper E. Barwick	106th Field Coy. R.E.
177218 Sapper G. A. Burgess	105th Coy. R.E.
65610 Corpl. L. P. Burles	106th Field Coy. R.E.
66594 L./Corpl. H. Bangay	25th Div. Sig. Coy. R.E.
36708 Pte. A. B. Bromage	25th Div. Sig. Coy. R.E. (Wireless Sect.).
6/17159 Corpl. B. Bishop	6th S.W.B.
55234 Corpl. W. T. Barnett	25th Battn. M.G. Corps.
78400 Pte. W. C. Bissmire	R.A.M.C. 76th Field Amb.
13616 Pte. E. H. Burry	1st Wiltshire.
49430 Pte. W. Bailey	10th Cheshire, attd. 7th Bde. Sigs.
14271 Pte. W. Bradbury	10th Cheshire Regt.
15795 Pte. W. Dunbebin	10th Cheshire Regt.
45336 Pte. S. J. Barty	4th South Staffs.
34706 Pte. H. Barker	1st Wiltshires.
12945 Pte. J. Bromley	9th Loyal N. Lancs.

8793 Pte. J. Bennett..	3rd Worcester Regt.
8576 Pte. T. Bullivant	3rd Worcester Regt.
39982 Pte. A. Blackburn	11th Lancs. Fusiliers.
35203 Pte. E. W. Brocklehurst	11th Lancs. Fusiliers.
10271 Pte. H. Bimpson	2nd South Lancs. Regt.
235167 Pte. J. Brady	2nd South Lancs. Regt.
203133 L./Corpl. W. Bray	8th Border Regt.
13513 Pte. J. Bell	8th Border Regt.
23097 Pte. F. Babington	11th Cheshire Regt.
241042 L./Corpl. W. Bradshaw	11th Cheshire Regt.
266492 Pte. T. B. Bearchill ..	11th Cheshire Regt.
30440 2/Corpl. F. H. Croucher	130th Field Coy. R.E.
86891 Corpl. G. Carr ..	25th Div. Sig. Coy. R.E.
6/19225 Pte. J. Cassidy	6th South W. Borderers.
6/16470 Sergt. T. Chattington	6th South W. Borderers.
82068 Corpl. H. Cotterill	25th Battn. M.G. Corps.
42310 Pte. H. Chilton	R.A.M.C. 76th Field Amb.
38050 Pte. H. Cragg ..	R.A.M.C. 77th Field Amb.
235260 L./Corpl. E. Coppock	4th South Staffs.
7692 L./Corpl. S. Clare	1st Wiltshire Regt.
25489 L./Corpl. E. C. Colbourne	1st Wiltshire Regt.
29819 Corpl. H. E. Cole	1st Wiltshire Regt.
29266 Pte. H. Cobbold	9th Loyal N. Lancs.
39678 Pte. A. J. Cotterill	3rd Worcesters.
17684 Pte. A. Cooper	2nd South Lancs. Regt.
31988 Pte. H. Collins	2nd South Lancs. Regt.
244415 Pte. J. Christian	11th Cheshire Regt.
52546 L./Corpl. A. Costello ..	11th Cheshire Regt.
14972 L./Corpl. J. Cheshire ..	11th Cheshire Regt.
15795 Pte. W. Dunbebin	10th Cheshire Regt.
60932 L./Bomb. F. A. J. Dyer	"A" Battery, 112th Bde. R.F.A.
145100 Sapper N. Davy	106th Field Coy. R.E.
186814 Sapper S. Dovaston ..	106th Field Coy. R.E.
6/17152 L./Corpl. E. Davies..	6th South W. Borderers.
M2/116640 Pte. A. E. Dawson	A.S.C. (M.T.) 75th Field Amb.
30232 L./Corpl. J. Diggle	9th L.N. Lancs.
36984 L./Corpl. A. E. Dodd..	9th L.N. Lancs.
47742 Sergt. H. Duffill	No. 2 Sect. 25th Div. Sigs. R.E. 74th Bde.
33981 L./Corpl. R. Dugdale..	11th Lancs. Fus.
31639 L./Corpl. W. Didsbury	2nd South Lancs.
203842 Pte. H. Darby	2nd South Lancs.
50166 Dr. F. Cooper ..	"B" Batt., 110th Bde., R.F.A.
27452 Sergt. W. Crew	"B" Batt., 110th Bde., R.F.A.
9226 Corpl. C. Elliman	3rd Worcesters.
85245 Sapper H. A. Freeman	106th Field Coy. R.E.
6/17106 Corpl. J. Fellows	6th S.W.B.
28082 Pte. E. Fray ..	R.A.M.C. 77th Field Amb.
13563 Pte. W. Forsbury	4th South Staffs.
33433 Pte. F. Foulder	11th Lancs. Fus.
241660 Pte. D. Fearnside	9th L.N. Lancs.
72393 Pte. H. Facey ..	11th Cheshires.

44047 Sapper J. R. Gibbs	..	..	130th Field Coy. R.E.
11622 Pte. A. Gallent		..	..	6th S.W.B.
18193 Sergt. W. Graham	..	..	25th Battn. M.G. Corps.
129680 Pte. F. C. Graham	..	..	25th Battn. M.G. Corps.
142952 L./Corpl. R. Greenhalgh	..	25th Battn. M.G. Corps.
W/1079 Sergt. L. Goodwin	..	..	10th Cheshires.
11674 Pte. F. Gee	..	..	10th Cheshires.
30226 L./Corpl. J. Glover	..	..	9th L.N. Lancs.
47738 L./Corpl. A. Gray	..	..	No. 2 Sect. 25th Div. Sig. Coy. 74th Bde.
8230 Corpl. F. Greaves	..	..	11th Lancs. Fus.
34136 Sergt. P. Graff.	..	..	2nd South Lancs. Regt.
15037 Pte. J. George..	..	..	8th Border Regt.
14455 Sergt. R. F. Graham	..	..	8th Border Regt.
260155 Pte. W. Gelling	..	..	8th Border Regt.
65937 L./Corpl. A. J. Harding	..	130th Field Coy. R.E.
57306 Corpl. F. Henderson	..	..	106th Field Coy. R.E.
65050 Sergt. E. Hodgson	..	..	105th Coy. R.E.
65355 Spr. F. Horrod	..	..	106th Field Coy. R.E.
65109 Corpl. F. Hudghton	..	..	106th Field Coy. R.E.
95411 L./Corpl. E. Hurley	..	..	106th Field Coy. R.E.
89503 Corpl. E. J. Hillson	..	..	25th Battn. M.G. Corps.
6934 Pte. S. Hughes ..	..	..	25th Battn. M.G. Corps.
5111 Sergt. F. Haylor	..	..	25th Battn. M.G. Corps.
49724 Pte. J. Hall ..	..	..	R.A.M.C. 75th Field Amb.
12845 Pte. H. Hitchen	..	..	10th Cheshire Regt.
88025 2/Corpl. F. Hawkesley	..	No. 2 Sect. 25th Div. Sigs., 74th Bde.
31088 Corpl. W. Hailey	..	..	2nd South Lancs.
14077 Pte. J. W. Hooper	..	..	Attd. H.Q., 75th Bde. (2nd South Lancs.)
28895 Pte. W. Hewitt	..	..	8th Borders.
13548 Pte. J. Hird ..	..	..	8th Borders.
84868 Gnr. V. Ingles..	..	..	"A" Bty., 112th Bde., R.F.A.
20482 Pte. W. Ingram		..	10th Cheshires.
216413 Spr. A. L. James	..	..	130th Field Coy. R.E.
140159 Spr. E. Jones..	..	..	130th Field Coy. R.E.
67009 Corpl. R. Jopling	..	..	130th Field Coy. R.E.
90097 L./Corpl. H. W. Jones	..	25th Battn. M.G. Corps.
122732 Pte. S. Jaines	..	..	25th Battn. M.G. Corps.
42231 Pte. J. Jones ..	..	..	R.A.M.C. 76th Field Amb.
266298 Corpl. R. Jones	..	..	10th Cheshires.
26279 Corpl. H. Jobber	..	..	11th Lancs. Fus.
15138 Corpl. W. Jones	..	..	9th L.N. Lancs.
26595 Pte. W. D. Jones	..	..	8th Border, attd. 75th T.M.B.
25923 Pte. W. Kitchener	..	..	1st Wiltshires.
27875 Pte. W. Kay ..	..	..	9th L.N. Lancs.
14830 L./Corpl. W. Kirkham	..	2nd South Lancs.
90019 Bty. Q.M.-Sergt. R. H. Looney	"C" Bty., 112th Bde., R.F.A.
84467 Spr. B. Lack ..	..	..	130th Field Coy. R.E.
313154 L./Corpl. W. Liddell..	..	25th Div. Sigs. R.E.
6/16794 Pte. B. Lewis	..	..	6th S.W.B.
73796 Corpl. A. Liggett	..	..	25th Battn. M.G. Corps.

22128 Sergt. S. Lewis	25th Battn. M.G. Corps.
5179 Pte. H. Lord	11th Lancs. Fus.
35208 L./Corpl. B. Lake	9th L.N. Lancs.
30152 Pte. F. Lewis	3rd Worcester.
41404 Pte. L. Lamport	3rd Worcester.
28271 L./Corpl. E. Latham	2nd South Lancs.
67026 Sergt. J. Miller	130th Field Coy. R.E.
164726 2/Corpl. S. Mogridge	130th Field Coy. R.E.
178358 Spr. E. D. Moir	130th Field Coy. R.E.
49495 Spr. R. Morgan	106th Field Coy. R.E.
75839 Spr. E. Milnes	25th Div. Sig. Coy. R.E.
229147 Pte. W. Martin	6th South W. Borderers.
6/17203 Pte. R. Maybury	6th South W. Borderers.
102672 Pte. F. Miller	R.A.M.C. 75th Field Amb.
24649 Pte. H. Moore	4th South Staffs.
24030 Pte. J. Mellor	10th Cheshire Regt.
53529 Pte. G. H. Morris	10th Cheshire Regt.
2568 Corpl. J. McConnell	11th Lancs. Fus.
28561 Pte. J. McFarland	3rd Worcs.
26458 Pte. T. Murphy	9th L.N. Lancs.
8238 Cropl. T. Morris	2nd South Lancs. (attd. 75th T.M.B.)
15754 Pte. T. McGuinness	8th Borders.
27959 Pte. J. Maylor	11th Cheshires.
11668 Corpl. A. Newsham	9th L.N. Lancs.
16229 Pte. R. Nicholas	11th Lancs. Fus. (25th Div. Sigs. R.E.)
240251 Pte. G. Nevitt	2nd South Lancs.
31600 Bomb. J. Orford	No. 2 Sect. D.A.C.
331027 Pte. W C. Oliver	11th Lancs. Fus.
25420 Corpl. J. O'Connell	8th Border Regt. (75th T.M.B.)
40019 Pte. J. Owen	3 Worcester Regt.
169214 L./Corpl. W. D. Poole	105th Field Coy. R.E.
58215 Spr. H. Pigg	25th Div. Sig. Coy. R.E.
142952 Pte. P. Parr	25th Battn. M.G. Corps.
17535 Sergt. W. Powell	25th Battn. M.G. Corps.
22100 Pte. W. Powell	25th Battn. M.G. Corps.
24186 Pte. J. W. Pears	R.A.M.C. 76th Field Amb.
10890 Corpl. P. W. Puddick	1st Wiltshire.
50875 Corpl. F. Perrin	10th Cheshires.
45493 Pte. A. Pennifold	11th Lancs. Fus.
29341 Pte. C. Parker	9th L.N. Lancs.
23742 Pte. H. Prescott	9th L.N. Lancs.
12588 Sergt. A. Pugh	3rd Worcesters.
49014 Corpl W. Pearson	11th Cheshires.
45304 Pte. F. Rose	4th South Staffs.
326325 Pte. E. Roberts	3rd Worcesters.
10136 Sergt. J. Rowe	9th L.N. Lancs.
9987 Sergt. B. J. Rimmer	2nd South Lancs.
72067 Pte. I. Rees	11th Cheshire.
56978 L./Corpl. C. Sayles	105th Coy. R.E.
145035 2/Corpl. A. J. Smart	105th Coy. R.E.
122646 Pte. J. Scouler	25th Battn. M.G. Corps.

63963 Sergt. H. J. Smith	..	..	25th Battn. M.G. Corps.
39191 Pte. W. Spencer	..	..	4th South Staffs.
26541 Pte. R. Stubbs	..	..	10th Cheshire.
14058 Pte. G. Stevens	..	..	4th South Staffs.
37160 Pte. H. Stebbings	..	..	11th Lancs. Fus.
206040 L./Corpl. J. Spragg	..	..	3rd Worcesters.
8958 Sergt. E. Stanbridge	..	..	9th L.N. Lancs.
14659 Pte. W. J. Stafford	..	..	8th Borders.
50989 Pte. K. J. Strachan	..	..	11th Cheshires.
45872 Sergt. A. Smith	..	..	"B" Battn., 110th Bde., R.F.A.
155675 Spr. A. D. Thwaites	..	..	106th Field Coy. R.E.
97578-L./Corpl. L. Thomas	..	..	130th Field Coy. R.E.
65087 2/Corpl. W. Tingay	..	..	106th Field Coy. R.E.
82080 Spr. R. Townend	..	..	106th Field Coy., attd. H.Q. 25th Div.
143123 L./Corpl. W. J. Turner	..	..	130th Field Coy. R.E.
6/14504 Pte. D. Thomas	..	..	6th South Wales Borderers.
38000 Pte. C. Taylor	..	..	25th Battn. M.G. Corps.
133 Pte. J. Tovey	..	..	1st Wiltshires.
36197 Pte. B. Tate	..	..	4th S. Staffs. (7th Bde. Sig. Sect.)
18418 Corpl. W. J. Taylor	..	..	1st Wiltshires.
10343 Pte. P. F. Taylor	..	..	4th South Staffs.
35243 Pte. G. Taylor	..	..	3rd Worcesters.
330120 Pte. C. R. Tabrum	..	..	11th Lancs. Fus.
37264 Sergt. J. W. Tonkin	..	..	2nd South Lancs.
178050 L./Corpl. H. Wilson	..	..	106th Field Coy. R.E.
54375 Corpl. N. Willoughby		..	25th Div. Sigs.
51465 L./Corpl. S. Wells	..	..	No. 2 Sect. Div. Sig. Coy. R.E.
50817 Pte. J. R. Whittle	..	..	R.A.M.C. 76th Field Amb.
60482 Pte. W. Wiggins	..	..	10th Cheshires.
30867 L./Corpl. G. Wallis	..	..	3rd Worcs.
31104 Pte. G. Wells	..	..	3rd Worcs.
9373 Corpl. F. Wilson	..	..	3rd Worcs.
204873 L./Corpl. J. Watson	..	..	9th L.N. Lancs.
18206 Pte. W. Watkins	..	..	2nd South Lancs.
15482 Sergt. W. Wilkinson	..	..	2nd South Lancs.
52445 Pte. H. Widdows	..	..	11th Cheshires.
52507 Sergt. J. Wildgoose	..	..	11th Cheshires.
6/17353 Pte. L. Young	..	..	6th S.W. Borderers.
30255 Sergt. L. Lee	..	..	25th Divisional Train, A.S.C.
16017 Pte. S. Hayward	..	..	9th L.N. Lancs.

25th Division.

SUMMARY OF CASUALTIES REPORTED SUFFERED BY THE DIVISION FROM 9th APRIL, 1918, TO 4th MAY, 1918.

Unit.	Officers.			Other Ranks.		
	K.	W.	M.	K.	W.	M.
25th Div. H.Q.	—	2	—	—	1	—
R.A.H.Q.—						
110th Bde.	—	1	—	16	54	—
112th Bde.	—	3	—	9	57	—
25th D.A.C.	—	—	—	—	1	—
X/25 T.M.B.	—	—	—	—	21	—
Y/25 T.M.B.	—	—	1	—	19	13
R.E.H.Q.—						
105th Field Coy.	1	2	—	5	27	—
106th Field Coy.	1	1	—	6	34	1
130th Field Coy.	—	1	1	16	44	3
25th Sig. Coy. R.E...	—	1	—	3	23	5
7th Brigade H.Q.—						
10th Cheshire	3	9	5	32	295	336
4th S. Staffords	4	12	8	20	213	481
1st Wiltshires	5	5	6	24	173	482
7th T.M.B.	—	1	—	—	7	16
74th Brigade H.Q.	—	—	—	—	—	—
11th Lancs. Fus.	4	22	3	29	274	212
3rd Worcesters	6	11	3	49	296	172
9th L.N. Lancs.	5	15	1	26	333	328
74th T.M.B.	—	2	—	1	7	15
75th Brigade H.Q.—						
11th Cheshires	2	11	7	32	305	532
8th Borders	4	16	3	44	331	288
2nd S. Lancs.	3	15	2	87	495	197
75th T.M.B.	—	1	—	—	15	4
6th S.W.B.	—	15	1	32	293	82
25th Battn. M.G. Corps.	3	17	10	34	207	167
25th Div. Train	—	—	—	—	5	—
R.A.M.C.	—	3	6	—	—	—
75th Field Amb.	2	—	—	16	28	6
76th Field Amb.	—	—	—	1	8	—
77th Field Amb.	—	—	—	4	29	10
225th Emp. Coy.	—	—	—	—	1	—
	43	170	57	486	3596	3350

STATEMENT OF OFFICER CASUALTIES DURING PERIOD 9th APRIL, 1918, TO 3rd MAY, 1918.

7th Brigade.
10th Cheshires.

Killed.

2nd Lieut. E. H. Simpson.
2nd Lieut. A. Pumphrey.

2nd Lieut. W. A. Willmore.

Wounded.

2nd Lieut. E. Webster.
Capt. S. Cheetham.
2nd Lieut. E. J. Higson.
2nd Lieut. N. H. Robertson.
2nd Lieut. G. R. Montague.

2nd Lieut. A. W. Hunt.
Major A. Reade.
2nd Lieut. S. Makin.
2nd Lieut. B. W. Bill.

Missing.

Col. W. E. Williams (Prisoner of war.)
Capt. G. C. Meredith (Prisoner of war.)
Lieut. E. A. Saunders (Died of wounds.)
2nd Lieut. K. B. Ralston (Wounded and prisoner.)

2nd Lieut. E. M. Gibson.
Lieut. M. S. Redmond, M.O., R.C. U.S.A. (attached.)
Lieut. Evans, R.W. Kent (attd. 10th Ches.). (Prisoner.)

4th South Staffords.

Killed.

2nd Lieut. E. L. Stiles.
Capt. O. Barlow, M.C. (Died of wounds.)
2nd Lieut. E. Pepper.

2nd Lieut. H. W. Wheeler.
Lt.-Col. J. E. Stewart (8th Borders.)

Wounded.

Lieut. C. G. Hancock.
2nd Lieut. A. E. Collins.
Major R. A. T. Rees.
2nd Lieut. C. Bates.
2nd Lieut. A. H. Nutt.
Capt. L. G. Carr (Died of wounds.)

2nd Lieut. I. M. L. Oliver.
2nd Lieut. A. Moorcroft.
2nd Lieut. W. B. Brown.
2nd Lieut. J. Mc. P. McKenzie.
2nd Lieut. H. W. Webb.
Lieut. H. J. Bristol (Died of wounds.)

Missing.

Lt.-Col. L. H. K. Finch, D.S.O. (Prisoner of war.)
Lieut. F. R. Laver (Wounded.)
2nd Lieut. L. R. J. Tonks (Wounded.)
2nd Lieut. A. P. Walker.
2nd Lieut. S. K. Morey.

Capt. F. C. Nichols, R.A.M.C., attached. (Prisoner of war.)
2nd Lieut. A. H. Nutt (Wounded and missing.)
2nd Lieut. H. R. Webb (Wounded and missing.)
2nd Lieut. A. T. Kingsley.

1st Wiltshire Regt.

Killed.

Major F. G. Wynne, D.S.O.
Lieut. F. Naylor.
Lieut. H. W. B. Burkett.

Lt.-Col. A. G. Cade.
2nd Lieut. C. E. Blencowe.
Major G. D. Brown, M.C.

Wounded.

Capt. G. K. Wait.
Lieut. F. Priestley.

2nd Lieut. B. Burton.
2nd Lieut. W. E. Walker.

Missing.

Lt.-Col. S. S. Ogilvie, D.S.O.
  (Prisoner of war.)
Capt. F. Smith (Prisoner of war.)
Lieut. C. H. G. Thomas.
2nd Lieut. S. J. Parker, M.C.,
  D.C.M. (Prisoner of war.)

Lieut. L. M. Edens, M.C., R.C.,
  U.S.A. (attd. 1st Wilts.)
Capt. S. V. Pill, R.A.M.C. (attd.
  1st Wilts.)
2nd Lieut. W. A. Pritchard.

7th T.M. Battery.

Wounded.

Capt. L. H. Cecil.

74th Infantry Brigade—
Headquarters.

Wounded.

Capt. J. C. O. Marriott, D.S.O., M.C.

11th Lancashire Fusiliers.

Killed.

2nd Lieut. M. L. Bernstein, M.C.
2nd Lieut. H. C. Cotter.

2nd Lieut. J. V. Blackwell.
Capt. T. Rufus.

Wounded.

2nd Lieut. R. Milne.
2nd Lieut. J. H. Drinkwater.
2nd Lieut. S. Torrance.
2nd Lieut. R. F. Ackerley.
2nd Lieut. T. G. Preston.
2nd Lieut. O. T. Brown.
2nd Lieut. G. W. Talbot.
Capt. M. A. Ward, M.C. (Died of
  wounds.)
2nd Lieut. F. E. Baker.
2nd Lieut. K. E. A. Spafford.
2nd Lieut. F. A. Timson.
Capt. H. W. J. Lermit.
2nd Lieut. J. A. Houghton.

2nd Lieut. H. Skelton.
2nd Lieut. K. A. Saffery.
2nd Lieut. A. Lee.
Major E. Munday.
Capt. G. A. Potts, M.C.
Capt. C. M. Newman.
Lieut. E. A. R. Ash. (Died of
  wounds.)
Lt.-Col. J. F. T. P. Ward-McQuaid.
2nd Lieut. J. E. Littler (Died of
  wounds.)
Capt. T. C. D. Watt, R.A.M.C.
  (attd. 11th Lancs. Fus.)[1]

Missing.

2nd Lieut. I. J. Challis. (Died.)
Lieut. A. Merchant. (Wounded and missing.)

Lt.-Col. E. C. de R. Martin, D.S.O., M.C. (Prisoner of war.)

3rd Worcester Regt.

Killed.

2nd Lieut. J. A. Bomber.
Lieut. J. W. R. Campbell, M.C.
2nd Lieut. H. Chignell.

2nd Lieut. W. H. Parker.
2nd Lieut. A. E. Braggins.
Lieut. W. G. Round, M.C.

Wounded.

2nd Lieut. L. R. Whittingham (Died of wounds.)
Capt. F. A. Reading, M.C.
Capt. A. Brewer, M.C.
2nd Lieut. A. B. Rowe.
2nd Lieut. A. V. P. Rowlands.
Lieut. R. P. Giles.
2nd Lieut. P. H. C. Constable.

2nd Lieut. F. Carr.
Capt. M. Hardman.
2nd Lieut. B. J. Mason.
2nd Lieut. H. L. S. Savory. (Died of wounds.)
2nd Lieut. I. G. N. Fothergill.
Rev. A. M. Milne, C.F. (attd. 3rd Worcs.)

Missing.

2nd Lieut. H. U. Richards.

Capt. E. V. P. Parsons.

9th Loyal North Lancs.

Killed.

2nd Lieut. J. G. Barrett, M.C.
2nd Lieut. T. F. McCarthy.
Lieut. A. A. Baldwin.

Lieut. W. K. Tydesley.
2nd Lieut. J. C. Lancaster.

Wounded.

2nd Lieut. H. J. E. Sloane.
Lt.-Col. W. H. M. Weinholt, D.S.O.
Lieut. B. J. Edward (Died of wounds.)
2nd Lieut. R. Wilson.
2nd Lieut. H. W. Summerson.
2nd Lieut. W. Mohr.
Capt. L. C. Rice.
Capt. B. A. D. Leverson.
2nd Lieut. W. Ashworth.
2nd Lieut. E. S. Morris.

2nd Lieut. R. L. Isherwood.
2nd Lieut. G. Wolstonholme.
Capt. W. H. Cullen (York and Lancs.)
Capt. W. S. Hartley.
Rev. M. S. Evers, C.F. (attd. 9th L.N.L.)
Capt. F. Smith.
Capt. P. R. Shields.

Missing.

Lieut. H. G. Evans.

74th T.M. Battery.

Wounded.

2nd Lieut. J. N. Giddings.

2nd Lieut. H. Brighton.

75th Inf. Brigade.
11th Cheshires.

Killed.

Capt. G. R. Barton.

2nd Lieut. R. P. Greg (Died of wounds.)

Wounded.

2nd Lieut. D. A. Poole.
Lt.-Col. G. Darwell, M.C.
Capt. W. S. Syme, M.C.
2nd Lieut. E. Thomas.
2nd Lieut. E. C. L. Hilder.
2nd Lieut. F. T. Woodcock.

2nd Lieut. W. Crute.
2nd Lieut. J. Goodwin.
2nd Lieut. A. W. Bytheway.
2nd Lieut. A. Mayor.
Capt. H. G. Oliver, R.A.M.C. (attd. 11th Cheshires.)

Missing.

Lieut. H. R. Wall.
Lieut. C. A. Beard.
Lieut. J. A. Snape (Prisoner of war.)

Lieut. F. W. Harvey.
2nd Lieut. J. T. Hassell.
2nd Lieut. F. Hammond (Prisoner of war.)
2nd Lieut. A. Taylor.

8th Battn. Border Regt.

Killed.

Capt. P. H. Coxon, M.C.
Lieut. G. G. R. Bott, M.C.

2nd Lieut. F. C. Corley.
2nd Lieut. W. J. Crookson.

Wounded.

Lieut. M. C. Clodd.
2nd Lieut. C. A. Watts.
2nd Lieut. J. Grellis, M.C.
Lieut. A. K. Lister.
2nd Lieut. T. C. Vaughan.
Lieut. R. Strong, M.C.
Capt. J. Dawson, M.C.
2nd Lieut. H. T. Lay.

2nd Lieut. T. F. Middleton.
Major T. S. Wilkinson.
2nd Lieut. J. W. Rogers.
2nd Lieut. J. Gibson.
Lt.-Col. C. W. H. Birt, D.S.O.
2nd Lieut. J. H. Mackie.
2nd Lieut. J. T. R. Verel.
Capt. H. E. William, R.A.M.C. (attd. 8th Borders.)

Missing.

2nd Lieut. A. Cameron, M.M. (Wounded and missing.)
2nd Lieut. J. W. A. Allan. (Wounded.)

2nd Lieut. G. F. Hook.
2nd Lieut. W. C. Preston.
Capt. W. J. Isbister, R.A.M.C. (attd. 8th Borders.)

2nd South Lancashire Regt.

Killed.

Lieut. H. S. Coppock.
2nd Lieut. J. R. Dow.

Capt. R. Nevill, M.C.

Wounded.

2nd Lieut. A. Craven.
2nd Lieut. F. Halhead.
Capt. B. Harris, M.C.
Lieut. L. F. Edwards. (Died of wounds.)
2nd Lieut. J. H. Tilley.
Capt. H. L. Ross. (Died of wounds.)
2nd Lieut. D. Webster.
2nd Lieut. R. M. Douglas.

Capt. T. C. Eckenstein.
Capt. W. F. Bryden, M.C.
2nd Lieut. E. Williams.
Lieut. K. M. Bourne, M.C.
Capt. G. T. McLean, R.A.M.C. (attd. 2nd S. Lancs.)
2nd Lieut. E. G. L. Marshall.
2nd Lieut. A. M. Gregg.
Lieut. R. S. Johnson.

Missing.

2nd Lieut. A. J. C. Walters.

Capt. A. G. Clark, R.A.M.C. (attd. 2nd S. Lancs.)

75th T.M. Battery.

Wounded.
Capt. T. L. David.

25th Battn. M.G. Corps.

Killed.

Capt. W. W. Ashcroft.
2nd Lieut. W. Weldrick.
Lieut. E. W. Brutton, M.C.

Lieut. H. A. Collymore.
2nd Lieut. D. Carmichael.

Wounded.

Lt.-Col. J. D. Deane-Drummond, D.S.O., M.C.
2nd Lieut. L. A. Kingscote.
2nd Lieut. A. E. Harwood.
2nd Lieut. T. R. Franklin.
2nd Lieut. C. Hartley.
Lieut. A. E. Woodruff.
Major A. M. Bellingham.

2nd Lieut. T. S. Rees.
2nd Lieut. W. Wilkins.
2nd Lieut. G. F. Stocks.
2nd Lieut. A. H. Hind, M.C.
2nd Lieut. T. A. Harries.
2nd Lieut. A. R. Soar.
Lieut. C. W. Soutar, M.C.
Lieut. E. H. Tyacke.

Missing.

Lieut. E. J. C. Maddison. (Prisoner of war.)
Lieut. F. W. Jacob. (Prisoner of war.)
Lieut. S. Morrison. (Prisoner of war.)
Lieut. F. H. C. Redington, M.C. (Prisoner of war.)

2nd Lieut. H. M. Perryman. (Prisoner of war.)
2nd Lieut. J. C. Roberts.
2nd Lieut. R. F. Hitchcock. (Wounded.)
Lieut. H. E. Hayes. (Prisoner of war.)
2nd Lieut. T. J. Kemp. (Wounded.)

6th South Wales Borderers (Pioneers).

Wounded.

2nd Lieut. T. R. Jones
2nd Lieut. P. Butterworth.
2nd Lieut. E. W. S. Kite.
Capt. J. C. Owen, M.C.
Capt. D. Jenkins, M.C.
Lieut. C. McRigg.
2nd Lieut. A. L. Clough.
Lt.-Col. N. T. Fitzpatrick, D.S.O., M.C.

2nd Lieut. L. Petts.
2nd Lieut. I. K. Fraser.
Lieut. G. H. Tayler.
Lieut. J. H. Richards, M.C. (Died of wounds.)
2nd Lieut. W. T. Davies. (Died of wounds.)
Major N. G. Pearson, M.C.
Lieut. W. E. Hanna.

Missing.
2nd Lieut. A. Jenkins.

5th Divisional Artillery.
10th Brigade, R.F.A.
Wounded.
2nd Lieut. H. V. Barrett.

12th Brigade, R.F.A.
Wounded.
2nd Lieut. H. Gooch.   2nd Lieut. H. S. Gordon.
2nd Lieut. H. R. Goodman.

Y/25 T.M. Battery.
Missing.
2nd Lieut. W. E. Green.

105th Field Coy. R.E.
Killed.
Lieut. F. W. Cooper, M.C.

Wounded.
Lieut. F. H. Ridge.   Capt. W. B. H. Carr.

106th Field Coy. R.E.
Killed.
Capt. E. P. D. Cator.

Wounded.
Lieut. C. W. Ellen.

130th Field Coy. R.E.
Wounded.
Lieut. V. Harbord.

Missing.
Lieut. B. L. Rigden.

25th Divisional Signal Co. R.E.
Wounded.
Lieut. F. Nicholls.

76th Field Ambulance.
Killed.
Capt. R. S. Kennedy.

75th Field Ambulance.
Killed.
Capt. I. K. F. McLeod.

CHAPTER VIII.

Battle of the Aisne, 27th May, 1918.

The 9th of May, the 25th Division entrained at Rexpoede and other small sidings N.W. of Poperinghe, and commenced its long journey of about thirty hours to the district near Fismes, about 20 miles S.E. of Soissons in Champagne. Here the Division learned that it once more came under the leadership of the IXth Corps.

To the few in the 25th Division who had served with the original British Expeditionary Force in August and September, 1914, the district brought memories of the Battle of the Marne and the subsequent advance to the Aisne ; but no hint was given of the extent of the tragedy shortly to be enacted over this historic ground.

The 50th, 8th, and 21st Divisions had all reached the new area a few days previous to the arrival of the 25th Division and were gradually relieving French Divisions of the VIth French Army, in the sector east of the Chemin des Dames and on both banks of the Aisne. All four Divisions had recently been engaged in the fighting, both in Flanders and on the Somme, from the commencement of the great German offensive and all were urgently in need of a period of training or at any rate the opportunity to recuperate in a quiet sector of the line before taking part in any further fighting. This rest was promised to the troops in the sector east of Craonne, now taken over by the IXth Corps. Very little artillery activity was displayed by either side and the troops both on the British and the neighbouring French front appeared to have settled down to a period of peaceful trench warfare.

The front, of about 24,000 yards, held by the IXth British Corps ran along the high ground about four miles north of the Aisne for the first 16,000 yards, gradually bending back S.E. on its right to the important point of Berry-au-Bac, where the line crossed the river and continued on S.E. in the direction of Rheims for another 8,000 yards.

The right sector, south of the Aisne, was held by the 21st Division, in touch with the 36th French Division on its right ;

he 8th Division in the centre, and the 50th Division to the
eft, joining up with the 22nd French Division of the XIth
'rench Corps, north of Craonne. From this point the French
ront lay along the important and commanding ridge known
.s the Chemin des Dames, captured by the French troops in
\pril, 1917.

Whether the subsequent attack on the 27th May was part
)f a deliberate policy to attack and destroy exhausted British
Divisions in whatever sector of the line they might be found,
)r whether these sectors were chosen for attack irrespective
)f their defenders, is a point known only to the Germans them-
;elves. But there 's no doubt that these few British Divisions,
n their exhausted, untrained and unwelded state, both
)ut-numbered, out-gunned, and practically unprovided with
aeroplanes, were totally unable to withstand the shock of the
German assaults and successfully defend the sector of the line
assigned to them along the Aisne.

Divisional Headquarters were established at Arcis-le-Ponsart,
about midway between the Aisne and the Marne, with the
7th, 74th and 75th Brigades at Arcis, Coulonges and Vandeuil
and the Divisional Artillery at Crugny and the neighbouring
villages. The weather was glorious, and this famous district
of Champagne, with its steep valleys and wooded hillsides, was
looking its very best and provided a very pleasant change
after the flat and dull monotony of Flanders. Billets were
scarce, but the troops of the Division found ample and
extremely comfortable accommodation in the very excellent
hutted camps erected by the French in their back areas. All
units at once settled down to a good three weeks training, and
events, it was hoped, would allow of sufficient time to train and
absorb the reinforcements who were daily arriving in large
numbers for the Division. The Divisional School was opened
at Coulorges, and classes of instruction for junior officers and
non-commissioned officers in musketry, Lewis guns, trench
mortars and the various French bombs and grenades were
started with the help of instructors from the IXth Corps School
and some French instructors kindly lent by the French Army.

The 25th Division, during the battle of the Lys and the
fighting round Kemmel, between 9th April and 4th May,
had lost over 7,000 men or two-thirds of its fighting strength,
including no less than nine of its commanding officers and
275 other officers. These heavy losses, coming on the top

of the casualties sustained by the Division in the battle of Bapaume between the 21st and 26th March (175 officers and 3,179 other ranks), made it imperative in the interests of the fighting efficiency of the Division for the new commanding officers and the large number of junior officers to have suitable opportunity to get an intimate knowledge of their men before taking part in any further fighting.

It had been abundantly proved during the recent battle, that the units with their abnormal proportion of boys under 20 years of age and older men over 35 were not up to the previous standard. The scarcity of men of the best fighting ages between 21 and 28 was most noticeable in every unit. The older men, largely men combed out from administrative employment and past the best fighting age, proved the fallacy of the theory that it is possible to make a fighting soldier of the man of 35 equal to the continental soldier of the same age, who has performed military service in his youth.

About the middle of May reports were received from escaped French prisoners that immense dumps of ammunition had been formed behind the German front, telephone cable and field guns dug in ; all of which went to prove that the enemy were making deliberate preparations for an attack, although there was no sign of any concentration of troops. Quiet artillery registration was also noticed and reported to the IXth Corps. This, however, was quite in accordance with the German method, employed so successfully in March and April. With every preparation complete as regards supply of ammunition, trench mortars, new roads, railways, sidings, trolley lines, telephone cable dug in, so that at the last moment troops and more artillery could be swiftly moved up to the line, which it was intended to attack.

The VIth French Army Commander about this time gave instructions for the 25th Division to move up nearer the line, across the river Vesle. Accordingly the 22nd May, Divisional Headquarters moved to Montigny, with the 7th, 74th and 75th Brigades at Montigny, Vendeuil, and Romain respectively. The Divisional School and Divisional Ammunition Column were stationed at Baslieux, north-east of Fismes.

The afternoon of the 26th May, definite information was received that the enemy intended to deliver an attack the following morning on both the French front along the Chemin des Dames, and that of the British IXth Corps, and possibly the French front on our right.

At 9.15 p.m. the same evening the Brigades moved up in close support of the 21st, 8th, and 50th Divisions, and before daybreak the 7th, 74th and 75th Brigades had reached Guyencourt, Muscourt, and Ventelay respectively, between two and three miles south of the Aisne. The 110th and 112th Brigades R.F.A. moved forward by order of the IXth Corps and came under the orders of the 8th and 21st Divisions respectively, but owing to the late issue of the order by the IXth Corps half the field guns were unable to get into position in time to lay off their angles before the enemy bombardment began. The "B" Teams and Brigade Instructional Platoons were sent to join the Divisional School at Baslieux.

At 1 a.m., 27th May, the Germans commenced a heavy bombardment with gas shells of every description and H.E. The villages in the back areas as far as Fismes, as well as the front and support lines were deluged with shells from upwards of a thousand guns, to which we were able to reply with four Divisional Artillery's, totalling 144 field guns and 48 howitzers and 118 medium and heavies, chiefly French. A very inadequate supply of gas shells was available with which to reply to the enemy's intense bombardment. This lasted to 4 a.m., when the German infantry delivered their attack.

The artillery bombardment was accompanied by an intense trench mortar bombardment. The great development of this weapon by the Germans in range, accuracy and portability has undoubtedly provided an effective answer to the elaborate and well-wired system of trenches on which both sides have been accustomed to rely. These trench mortars, used in large numbers, are able to blow away with equal ease thick or narrow belts of wire and render any trench system within their range quite untenable. Fire trenches and communication trenches are blown in ; all movement or reinforcement of the men in the bombarded zone is quite impossible and troops holding these lines whether in small or large numbers, are practically destroyed or so dazed that there can be no effective resistance to any subsequent infantry attack. The most effective reply to these hurricane trench mortar bombardments undoubtedly consists in a withdrawal just before the attack from the front system of defence to a main battle line at least two miles behind, leaving only a thin line of outposts in the original front line. Owing to their portability these weapons can also be moved forward along with the infantry in advance of and over ground impracticable for Field Artillery.

Five German Divisions, the 5th Guards, 58th, 52nd, 7th Reserve, and 33rd Reserve Divisions with three in reserve (the 213th, 88th and 232nd Divisions) took part in the assault on the IXth Corps front, though their attack on the right sector, south of the Aisne, held by the 21st Division was not serious or pushed home to the same extent as against the 8th and 50th Divisions. Thirteen German Divisions, with another eight Divisions behind, were employed against the French front of about 30 miles. The enemy, assisted by a few tanks, were quickly through the first and second lines of defence, and by 7 a.m. had gained possession of the Californe Plateau and Ville au Bois. Further to the left the French troops had been forced back from the Chemin des Dames. The German advance was now so rapid that by 8 a.m. the whole of the 50th and 8th Divisional Artillery north of the Aisne was in their hands and a little later half of that of the 25th Division. The battalions holding the front line were swept away and the remnants were falling back on the river.

The 25th Division, which was in Corps reserve, was instructed to hold the second line of defence south of the Aisne along the heights south of the Maizy-Cormicy Road, thence bending back south-east to Trigny, a line of about 12 miles ; at the same time sending one battalion forward to guard the bridges between Concevreux and Pontavert. The 8th Border Regiment of the 75th Brigade, who moved off at 9.30 a.m. to defend the eight bridges between Pontavert and Concevreux, received information that the enemy were across the canal before the battalion could get into position.

By 10 a.m. the 25th Division was in position with the 7th Brigade on the right holding a line from Cormicy to Bouffignereux, 75th Brigade in the centre, continuing the line to Roucy, and the 74th Brigade on the left from Concevreux to Maizy, who now passed under the command of the 21st, 8th, and 50th Divisions respectively, so that the Division now ceased to command any of its fighting troops.

7th Infantry Brigade ...	Brig.-Gen. C. J. GRIFFIN,C.M.G. D.S.O. (wounded).
1st Battn. Wiltshire Regt.	Lt.-Col. E. K. B. Furze, D.S.O., M.C. (wounded).
10th Cheshire Regt.	Lt.-Col. E. C. Cadman (killed).
4th S. Staffords ...	Lt.-Col. A. M. Morris, D.S.O.
74th Infantry Brigade	Brig.-Gen. H. M. CRAIGIE-HAL-KETT, D.S.O.
9th L. N. Lancs. Regt.	Major C. S. Darby-Griffiths, M.C. (killed). Lt.-Col. A. M. Tringham, D.S.O. (wounded).
3rd Worcester Regt.	Major R. F. Traill, D.S.O.
11th Lancs. Fus. ...	Lt.-Col. G. P. Pollitt, R.E., D.S.O. (wounded and missing).
75th Infantry Brigade	Brig.-Gen. A. A. KENNEDY, D.S.O.
11th Cheshire Regt.	Lt.-Col. E. R. S. Prior, D.S.O., M.C. (died of wounds).
8th Border Regt. ...	Lt.-Col. J. N. de La Parrelle, D.S.O., M.C.
2nd S. Lancs. Regt.	Lt.-Col. J. B. Allsopp, D.S.O. (killed).
25th Bn. Machine Gun C.	Lt.-Col. W. T. RAIKES, M.C.
6th S.W.B. (*Pioneers*)	Lt.-Col. L. C. W. DEANE, D.S.O., M.C. (killed).
25th Divisional Artillery	Brig.-Gen. K. KINCAID-SMITH, C.M.G., D.S.O.
110th Brigades R.F.A.	Lt.-Col. H. R. Phipps, D.S.O.
112th Brigade R.F.A.	Lt.-Col. E. V. Sarson, D.S.O. (prisoner of war).

From right to left the 7th Brigade had the 10th Cheshires on the right with A, B, C, and D Companies, commanded by Capt. W. Yates, 2nd Lieut. Moulton, Capt. Deane (killed), succeeded by Lieut. Cotterill, and 2nd Lieut. Cookson. The 4th S. Staffords in the centre with A, B, C and D Companies, commanded by 2nd Lieut. Bates, Capt. G. L. Kelsey, Lieut. Miller (wounded), succeeded by 2nd Lieut. Lloyds and 2nd Lieut. Davies. The 1st Wilts Regiment on the left with A, B, C, and D Companies commanded by Lieut. Anderson,

2nd Lieut. Howe, Capt. Arnott (wounded), and Capt. Priestley.

The 75th Brigade in the line with the 2nd S. Lancs on the right of Roucy, with A, B, C, and D Companies, commanded by Capt. K. M. Bourne, M.C., Capt. T. Sweet-Escott, 2nd Lieut. J. Acheson, and Capt. S. B. Schwabe, M.C. The 8th Border Regiment, 2nd Lieut. J. Bell, Capt. C. W. McCallon, Capt. F. L. Williams, and 2nd Lieut. C. Spence, commanding their companies. The 11th Cheshire Regiment on the left, between Concevreux and Roucy, with A, B, C, and D Companies, commanded by 2nd Lieut. W. Tooker, Capt. J. A. Warrilow, 2nd Lieut, Woodcock, and 2nd Lieut. T. H. Richards.

On the left the 74th Brigade with the 11th Lancashire Fusiliers on the right, A, B, C, and D Companies commanded by 2nd Lieut. L. Shipman (wounded), succeeded by Lieut. G. H. Broadbent (missing), Capt. C. Newman (missing), and Lieut. F. A. H. Graham, (missing) The 9th L.N. Lancs, on the left with A, B, C, and D Companies' commanded by Capt. W. F. Loudon (wounded), succeeded by Lieut. H. J. Sanderson, Capt. A. Sumner (wounded), succeeded by Lieut. W. Readman, Capt. R. P. Shields (wounded, missing) succeeded by 2nd Lieut. E. M. Morrison and Capt. C. Marshall, The 3rd Worcester Regiment with A, B, C, and D Companies, commanded by Capt. E. L. Armstrong, Capt. E. Lattey, Capt. E. A. Humphries (missing) succeeded by 2nd Lieut. B. H. Newcombe, and Capt. T. Grant (wounded) succeeded by 2nd Lieut. V. B. Wosley (missing), took up a position covering the bridgehead at Concevreux.

The position was now becoming critical. By mid-day the Germans had succeeded in crossing the river and canal both at Maizy on our left and at Pontavert, in front of the centre of our position, their advance being facilitated by the failure to destroy the bridges. On the left, the 74th Brigade were unable to gain touch with the French troops who had fallen back south of the river, and a gap of about two miles was left practically undefended, between Maizy and the French right at Villers-en-Prayeres.

Early in the afternoon, 100 men of the 74th Brigade Instructional Platoon, under Capt. R. J. P. Hewetson, were sent forward to help fill the gap. When approaching Glennes, they encountered the enemy in large numbers. The platoon, a body of picked men, fought most gallantly against overwhelming odds, and succeeded in delaying the enemy's advance for over an hour. Ultimately, after the majority had become casualties, the remainder, when nearly surrounded, were forced to retire, and only one officer and two men succeeded in rejoining their Brigade.

At about three in the afternoon the enemy, who had crossed the river and canal at Maizy, were reported to be advancing in force down the val ey towards Muscourt, and in addition large bodies were seen coming from the direction of Pontavert. The attack developed along the line between 3 and 4 p.m. Bouffignereux, held by the 1st Wilts Regt., was captured early in the fight ; the battalion H.Q. were rushed, Capt. Brookes, R.A.M.C., being killed and Lt.-Col. Furze severely wounded. Col. Furze had recently been promoted to the command of the battal on from G.S.O.2 of the Div sional Staff ; an excellent appointment, fully in accord with public opinion of the New Armies, which is wholly in favour of a frequent interchange between the Staffs and the fighting units. The battalion suffered heavy casualties and was now forced to retire. Capt. Parkes, M.C., won a bar to his M.C. for his excellent work throughout the battle. Sergt. Bray, R.S.M. Clarke and Cpl. White, received decorations for the skill with which they commanded their men, when all officers had become casualties.

The 10th Cheshires and 4th S. Staffords were then heavily attacked from their left flank. The position of the trenches was very unsatisfactory and the " Field of Fire " was very poor. Lt.-Col. Cadman was killed almost at once, and about 7.30 p.m. the line was gradually withdrawn, pivoting on the 6th S. Wales Borderers, who were continuing the line to the right of the 7th Brigade.

Capt. Huffam, Capt. Yates, 2nd Lieut. Boyes, 10th Cheshires, and 2nd Lieut. Hawkins, Acting Adjutant 4th S. Staffords, did good work during the battle. 2nd Lieut. Lloyds, 4th S. Staffords, commanded his company with great dash and skill during the retirement and all received the Military Cross.

2nd Lieut. Davies, 4th S. Staffords, was invaluable ; when the battalion was nearly surrounded he successfully covered their retirement with a few men of his company and afterwards received the D.S.O. Cpl. Pearce did useful work in going forward and getting valuable information. Pte. Shaw,

10th Cheshires, Pte. Bates, Pte. Edwards, 4th S. Staffords, as stretcher bearers ; Pte. Wiggins, 10th Cheshires, Pte. Rhodes, Pte. Sedgeley and Pte. Skidmore, 4th S. Staffords, as runners were all conspicuous for their courage and received the Military Medal.

In the centre of our line the 75th Brigade of which Brig.-Gen. Kennedy had on arrival, about mid-day, assumed command, was now disposed with two companies of the 8th Border Regt. at Roucy ; remnants of the 23rd and 24th Brigades of the 8th Division to the right and left of the village respectively; the 2nd S. Lancs on the extreme right, and the 11th Cheshires on the left towards Concevreux, with B and D Companies of the 8th Borders in Brigade Reserve, near the Bois de Rouvroy.

The attack at once developed on the left and large numbers of the enemy were seen moving across the open and massing in the wood about 500 yards N.W. of Bouffignereux, and also on the front of the 2nd S. Lancs. Splendid long range targets were offered, but without artillery little impression could be made, though, later on, great execution was inflicted with machine guns and rifle fire. Unfortunately Lt.-Col. J. B. Allsopp, 2nd S. Lancs., was killed early in the battle, and Lt.-Col. E. R. S. Prior, 11th Cheshire Regt., was severely wounded. The latter died soon afterwards of his wounds, at the dressing station. Both these officers had served for some time with the Division and their death was a great loss to their units. Capt. Wilkinson, 11th Cheshires, succeeded Col. Prior in command, but was killed the following morning.

Pte. Dickenson, 2nd S. Lancs., did good work with a Lewis gun. Sergt. Mitchell took command of his company with great ability when all officers had become casualties. Pte. Huxley and Pte. Warwick managed to carry ammunition to the front line when urgently required, and Pte. Andrews and Pte. Atherton as runners, all won decorations for their services.

The left of the Brigade now began to retire, and a new position was taken up along the top of the ridge to the left of the line held by B and D Companies, of the 8th Borders, south of the Bois de Rouvroy and astride the Roucy-Ventelay Road. Between 5 and 8 p.m. the Germans attempted several attacks on the new line. Emerging from the wood cheering and shouting, they were quickly mown down by machine-gun fire, and driven back with heavy casualties ; foiled in this attempt to drive in the line by a frontal attack, the enemy now commenced an encircling movement round the right flank, at the same time bringing up trench mortars with which to bombard the front. One company of German infantry, who were at first mistaken for the S. Lancs., succeeded in establishing themselves so far to the right rear as to command any retirement along the road towards Ventelay.

A further retirement was now imperative, and about dusk the remnants of the Brigade were successfully withdrawn across the valley to the next ridge south of Ventelay, A and D Companies of the 8th Borders covering the retirement. A small party of Germans, who had by this time obtained a footing in the village of Ventelay itself, managed to cut off a few men in the dark.

Lieut. Beckett and Capt. Bentley commanded their companies with great skill, the former beating off no less than six German attacks during the afternoon. Cpl. Booth and L.-Cpl. Tattersall did excellent work with their Lewis guns. Pte. Bell, D.C.M., Pte. Vaughan and Cpl. Robinson, D.C.M., during the night 27th/28th went forward on patrol and obtained valuable information as to the position of the enemy. L.-Cpl. Wilkie, in charge of a listening post, and Pte. Dixon, for his work as a stretcher bearer, all received well-earned decorations.

The 8th Borders by 10.30 p.m. were now practically surrounded. The road through Ventelay was blocked by the enemy, who were also established in small bodies on either flanks. At 1.30 a.m. 27th/28th the remainder of the battalion determined to fight its way back in the dark, and started off with advance and flank guards along the spur running south between Ventelay and Romain. The flank guard became engaged with the enemy in the outskirts of Ventelay, but the remainder of the battalion were enabled to get through to Romain, which they found occupied by the 21st French Infantry Regt. From this time on the 8th Borders remained with the 3rd Battalion 21st French Regt., and took up successive positions with the French troops along the Aerodrome to the north of Courville, then to the north and finally to the south of Crugny. The morning of the 30th the battalion, now commanded by Major Fraser, finally joined up with the 74th Brigade near Romigny.

(12064) I 2

Meanwhile, on the left, strong attacks had developed against the battalions of Gen. Craigie-Halkett's Brigade About 4 p.m. the 3rd Worcesters, with two companies covering the bridgeheads in front of Concevreux, found that the enemy had forced their way into the village behind them. This necessitated a withdrawal to the high ground south of the village. 2nd Lieut. Armstrong commanded his company with great skill, covering the retirement of the battalion. Capt. Grant and 2nd Lieut. Pickles led counter-attacks at a critical moment and succeeded in checking the enemy. Cpl. Oakley, as a stretcher-bearer, attended the wounded under heavy fire. Sergt. Webber commanded his platoon with great abilty, and all received decorations.

During the afternoon the enemy offered excellent targets to the 9th L. N. Lancs. and 11th Lancashire Fusiliers, and heavy casualties were inflicted by our machine gun and rifle fire. With the Lancashire Fusiliers L.-Cpl. Halliwell won the admiration of all ranks by riding out nine times, under heavy machine gun fire, to bring in wounded men. In this way he succeeded in rescuing one officer and eight men, and for his gallant conduct afterwards received the V.C. Cpl. Garfat and Pte. Walne did excellent work with their Lewis guns ; Cpl. Greenwood and L.-Cpl. Thompson showed great courage in collecting and re-organising men during the retirement ; Sergt. Barnett, Transport Sergt., managed to deliver stores and ammunition under most difficult circumstances, and Pte. Mansell for his work as a stretcher-bearer, all received decorations which they richly deserved.

During their retirement the 3rd Worcesters suffered heavily, and early in the battle Major Darby-Griffiths, commanding the 9th L.N. Lancs., was killed. Major Lloyd, 105th Field Company R.E., at once took over the command of the battalion. 2nd Lieut. Baines handled his men with great skill, and held on until nearly surrounded, ably assisted by L.-Cpl. Blodwell, when all other N.C.Os. had become casualties. Pte. Still did excellent work with his Lewis gun until nearly surrounded. Cpl. Farnworth, and Cpl. Wood were conspicuous for their courage in attending wounded under heavy fire, also Pte. Cartwright and Pte. Lane as stretcher-bearers ; Pte. Lever, in spite of his knee being smashed by a bullet, successfully delivered a message entrusted to him. Sergt. Carr, with complete disregard of danger, repaired telephone wires under heavy machine gun fire.   Capt. Stead, with men of the T.M. Battery, at a critical moment formed a defensive flank, assisted by Cpl. Nelson and all received decorations.

Before dark the line gradually retired to new positions about 1½ miles north of Romain, with its left well thrown back   Small bodies of the French troops were now gradually coming up to reinforce the left flank   Before midnight a further withdrawal across the valley to the high ground west of the Ventelay-Montigny Road was ordered, and the new positions were reached before dawn.

It is difficult to write of the events of the 27th May, with reserve.   The three Brigades of the 25th Division were placed by the IXth Corps, early in the fight, under the command of the 21st, 8th and 50th Divisions ; no reserves of either infantry or artillery were kept in hand, whilst a big gap of at least two miles was left undefended between the 74th Brigade and the right flank of the XIth French Corps.   The 50th and 8th Divisions were practically destroyed before 8 a.m. in their positions on the north of the Aisne, and but few managed to escape across the river.   Important bridges at Pontavert, Concevreux and to the west of Maizy were not blown up, allowing the enemy to cross the river without difficulty.   Expected to check an enemy flushed with initial success, and overwhelming in numbers, the 25th Division never had the remotest chance of holding the German divisions for any appreciable time, over the wide stretches of country between the right of the XIth French Corps and the 21st Division.

Enemy aeroplanes during the whole day were able to fly low and observe every movement of the British troops, guide the attacking infantry and direct the German artillery fire and themselves attack our infantry with bombs and machine guns.   There was no gun of any description behind our Brigades with which to reply.   The 110th Brigade, R.F.A., of the Divisional Artillery had been sent up to positions in the Bois de Gernicourt, along the low ground south of the Aisne, and had lost 14 of its guns before 9 a.m., with many of its officers and personnel.   The 112th Brigade, R.F.A., sent up the evening of the 26th, was more fortunate, and remained in action with some of its guns till late in the afternoon of the 27th.

The Germans employed the same methods as had proved so successful up north during their attacks.   After their capture of our first system of defence, the advance was made by trickling forward all along the front with small columns which wormed their way through cover and folds in the ground with great skill, and, what is perhaps more important, with great determination. These small columns were invariably accompanied by light machine guns, which were used with great skill. Also, during an attack, these light machine guns were usually used to cover the short rushes forward of each group of men, and proved most successful in obtaining a superiority in the volume of fire, whilst the infantry whom they were covering were getting forward. To their skill in the employment of the light machine gun must be attributed a large share of the German success.

The morning of the 28th found the 7th Brigade along the high ground east of Prouilly, with troops of the 62nd Brigade, 21st Division, on its right.

Capt. Farmer, 10th Cheshires, with a few men of his Company, held his position south of Prouilly with great skill. 2nd Lieut. Siddons did excellent work during a surprise attack, and Lieut. Hull, M.O.R.C., U.S.A., was conspicuous for his bravery in attending to the wounded under heavy fire ; all received the M.C. Cpl. Gilbert, 4th S. Staffords, commanded his platoon with great dash, and Pte. Thompson, 4th S. Staffs, did wonderful work with his Lewis gun throughout the battle, receiving a well-earned D.C.M. for his services.

A composite battalion of about 300 men, which had been formed the previous evening from parties of the 1st Wilts, 4th S. Staffs, and 10th Cheshire Regts., under Major Cannon, 1st Wilts Regt., with some machine guns and 40 men of the 130th Field Company R.E., held their position all night on the high ground south of Bouvencourt. The enemy attempted a surprise attack about 2.30 a.m. in the morning, but were beaten off. A little way to the left, the 75th Brigade, which had been re-inforced during the night by 600 details, was not seriously engaged. C.-Q.-M.-Sergt. Tellett and C.-Q. M. Sergt. Yates, 11th Cheshire Regt., showed great enterprise in getting rations safely delivered to the men of their battalion during the night, and received the Military Medal.

Across the valley to the left the 74th Brigade held the high ground N.W. of Montigny. The battalions without exception had now become very reduced in numbers. Every unit had been engaged in severe fighting without cessation for nearly 24 hours, and with the exception of the 6th S. Wales Borderers, the approximate strength was about 100 men per battalion.

About 4 a.m. the enemy attacked all along the line. Trench mortars had been brought up, and the positions were heavily shelled. The line was now gradually withdrawn across the valley to the southern bank of the river, still pivoting on its right flank. During its retirement the composite battalion of the 7th Brigade, under Major Cannon, held up the enemy south of Pevy, and again to the N.W. of Prouilly, inflicting very heavy casualties with machine gun and rifle fire, and 2nd Lieut. Kennedy, 9th L. N. Lancs., with a few men successfully held a bridge-head near Joncherry against repeated attacks.

By 9 a.m. the whole of the 75th Brigade was south of the river. On the left the 11th Lancashire Fusiliers of the 74th Brigade won immortal fame by their heroic defence of the high ground north of the river, covering the retirement of the 3rd Worcesters and L.N. Lancs., and enabling the latter to reach the southern bank of the Vesle River. Two men got away, and when last heard of Lt.-Col. Pollitt and the remainder of the 11th Lancashire Fusiliers were practically surrounded, but making the Germans pay heavily for their advance.

The following was issued by Gen. Jackson, commanding the 50th Division, under whose orders the 74th Brigade was acting :—

> " The 11th Battalion Lancashire Fusiliers took up a position on the left of the Brigade in the early hours of the morning and maintained its ground to the end, although enveloped on both flanks. Very few men, if any, of this battalion crossed the Vesle, and there is little doubt that the commanding officer carried out his orders to the letter in maintaining his position to the last."

Hitherto it has not been customary with the British Army to reward units for gallant actions of this description. As a powerful aid to that priceless quality of *esprit de corps*, the bestowal of a collective reward for great gallantry cannot be surpassed ; and as an incentive to collective endurance in battle, its value cannot be over-estimated.

The policy of granting immediate rewards to individual officers and men has proved of the very greatest value to all ranks, but the truly immediate bestowal on the actual field of battle of those lesser decorations by Brigadiers would undoubtedly still further increase its effect. Events move so fast during active operations that the action which has gained a reward is often forgotten in the turmoil of modern warfare before the award is announced. Moreover, as not infrequently happens, those whose gallantry merit an immediate reward very often become casualties before the decorations are awarded.

The remains of the 7th Brigade, who had successfully held their position on the high ground east of Prouilly, throughout the 28th, although subjected to a very heavy shelling and machine gun fire, were withdrawn at dusk across the valley to the south of the River Vesle and about 1½ miles east of Joncherry. The crossings over the Vesle east and west of Joncherry had been successfully defended till about 2 p.m., when the line was gradually retired, on the left, to the high ground north of Vendeuil, and later north of Serzy. During the defence of these bridges across the Vesle, very heavy casualties were inflicted by machine gun fire on the attacking infantry. Trench mortars were, however, quickly got up by the enemy, and these bombarded our machine gunners at the bridge-heads ; and at the same time strong forces of the enemy crossing the river about two miles up at Les Venteaux, threatened to envelop our small forces on the river. The line swung back in the general direction of Branscourt-Serzy.

The morning of the 28th the 1/6th Cheshire Regt. detrained at Fere-en-Tardenois and marched to Faverole, headquarters of the 8th Division, and were attached to the 23rd Brigade, 8th Division. At the same time a composite force under Major Charrington was sent up as reinforcements for the units of the 25th Division. These small bodies of unorganised men from " B " teams, reinforcements, stragglers and such like, proved a sad waste of material, and would have been more useful if taken further back behind the line and carefully organised into a fighting unit.

By the evening of the 28th the line had been forced still further back on the left. The 7th Brigade kept their positions during the night of the 28th/29th and most of the following

day along the railway, and then bending back south to Branscourt, having on their left the remains of the 75th Brigade,
with the details of the 21st Division joining up with the remains
of the 23rd Brigade of the 8th Division. Fresh French
reinforcements were dug in west of the Sapigncourt-Treslonne
Road, connected up with the 74th Brigade, holding the high
ground north of Savigny. During the retirement Cpl. Smith
and Sergt. Stokes, M.M., 3rd Worcesters, distinguished
themselves by their energy in collecting and organising
stragglers. With these men they were able to cover the
retirement of the companies and do excellent work until
they themselves were both wounded later on.

The same evening the remains of the 50th Division were
finally withdrawn, and the 74th Brigade came under the
command of the 8th Division, who now assumed command
of the sector.

The night of the 28th/29th was fairly quiet, but early the
next morning a bombardment started and became extremely
violent by about 8 a.m. The German attack soon developed on
the left. The French troops held their ground splendidly
and all attacks were beaten off. The same afternoon between
3 and 4 p.m. the line was again heavily shelled with H.E.,
and soon afterwards another infantry attack developed along
the whole front. Some units of the 7th Brigade, from the
high ground east of Savigny, did excellent work in covering
the retirement of the 414th French Regt. on the right and
the remainder of the 23rd Brigade on the left, to their new
positions north of Bouleuse. Casualties were rather severe
during the retirement. On the right, Brig.-Gen. Griffin had
been wounded and Capt. Hawkins (Staff Capt.), 7th Brigade,
had been killed by the same shell. The 7th Brigade was now
left without any Staff, as Capt. Perrin, the Brigade Major,
had been killed during the fighting on the 27th. Towards
the evening of the 29th the remains of the 7th Brigade withdrew to the high ground south of Rossigny.

The 19th Division, who had de-'bused the morning of the
29th at Charmbracy, came up along the line Tramery-Lery
and also some more French Colonial troops. By 10.30 p.m.
the 7th Brigade, reinforced by the inclusion of the 1/6th
Cheshires and also one company of the D.L. Infantry, were now
covering the Lhery-Romigny Road in touch with the 19th
Division on the right and French troops on the left.

L.-Cpl. Asher and Cpl. Carter, 1st Wilts, did excellent work with a French machine gun whose team had become casualties, and succeeded in inflicting heavy casualties on the attacking infantry. Lieut. and Qmr. Fairfax and C.Q.M.-Sergt. Worrall, 10th Cheshires, showed great enterprise in delivering the rations to their unit under great difficulties. 2nd Lieut. Appleby did most useful work near Romigny; going forward on patrol he was able to obtain valuable information as to the enemy's movements.

French reinforcements were now rapidly coming up. The 28th and 40th French Divisions took over the line on the right and left respectively of the 19th Division, which also the morning of the 30th relieved the 8th Division, in command of all the troops in that sector.

The 21st Division was also relieved by the 45th French Division during the night 29th/30th, and the 7th and 75th Brigades were at the same time withdrawn and marched next day to Mery-Premacy and Bligny, respectively. From these places they were withdrawn to the south of the Marne and joined the 25th Divisional Headquarters near Etoges and Loisy.

The morning of May 30th the 74th Brigade Headquarters retired to Ville-en-Tardenois. About 9 a.m. German infantry were reported advancing on Romigny in large numbers. To meet them a composite battalion of the 50th Division, which had just been formed and sent up to reinforce the 74th Brigade, was ordered up to the high ground N. and E. of Romigny. These were unable to push back the German infantry, and by mid-day the Brigade was falling back on the line Sarcy Ville-en-Tardenois with the 3rd Worcesters on the right and the 9th L.N. Lancs. on the left, in touch with troops of the 19th Division on their right. Three companies of the 6th S. W. Borderers also joined the Brigade during the morning and were placed in support to the composite battalion of the 50th Division. By noon the enemy had got possession of the village of Romigny and the neighbouring high ground, and the left flank was now forced back to the high ground S.W. of Ville-en-Tardenois.

2nd Lieut. Morrison, 9th L.N. Lancs., commanded his company with great skill. During the attack he re-organised his men and formed at a critical moment a defensive flank. L.-Cpl. Wass with his Lewis gun team and Pte. Bailey as a runner were conspicuous for their courage, and all received decorations.

During the afternoon, in conformity with the 56th Brigade of the 19th Division on the left and the 30th French Regt. on the right, the 74th Brigade withdrew to the high ground west of Aubilly. From this position all attempts by the enemy to advance were beaten off.

About 11 a.m. the 31st, a German attack began to develop on the line held by the remnants of the 74th Brigade, whose headquarters had previously moved to Nappes. This was beaten off, and later in the afternoon the Brigade and details attached to it, moved to hold a short front west of Champlace with the remainder of the Worcesters and North Lancs. in support.

The following morning the remains of Gen. Craigie-Halkett's 74th Brigade and other attached units were withdrawn to re-organise and to be in reserve to the 19th Division. The Brigade had fought without a break for five days, and although terribly reduced in numbers was always an organised body of men. With good signal communications, excellent administrative arrangements, the Brigade had admirably acquitted itself during a most difficult retirement in face of overwhelming odds.

A composite battalion 25th Division was now organised under Major Traill, 3rd Worcesters, and in the afternoon the 1st composite battalion of the 8th Division was organised under Col. James, 22nd D.L. Infantry ; the same night a second composite battalion was sent up composed of " B " teams and stragglers under Major Mott, 2nd S. Lancs.

During the morning of the 1st June a strong German attack on the 50th Division composite battalion and troops of the 40th French Division had been driven off, but about 4 p.m. a second attack was more successful, and the French line on the left was forced back. Brigade Headquarters retired about a mile back to Boullin, and early the following morning a line was dug from the village of La Neuville to the southern end of the Bois d'Eglise, the remainder of the 2nd June was quiet. The morning of the 3rd June, the second composite battalion of the 8th Division arrived and came under the orders of Brig.-Gen. Craigie-Halkett, and the 50th Division composite battalion and 1/6th Cheshires were transferred to the 57th Brigade, 19th Division. The troops under the

74th Brigade were now composed of two composite battalions of the 25th Division and two composite battalions of the 8th Division.

The night of the 3rd/4th June the line on the left flank was advanced a few hundred yards, but in all other respects the night was quiet. On the 4th June Brig.-Gen. C. Hickie, commanding the 7th Brigade, exchanged duties with Brig-. Gen. Craigie-Halkett, who returned to 25th Divisional Headquarters.

The 4th and 5th June passed quietly, but on the 6th June the Germans began a heavy bombardment along the line with gas shells and H.E. On our immediate front the infantry attack was smashed up by artillery fire. On the right the enemy was more successful, but were driven back by a counter-attack.

The 6th June a third composite battalion, formed from the 7th Brigade, was sent up in 'buses under Lt.-Col. Morris, 4th S. Staffs. The same day the enemy attacked from Champlat to north of Rheims, gaining a temporary footing on the Montagne de Bligny ; from this important position they were at once ejected by an energetic counter-attack of the K.S.L.I. Another attack three days later, on the 9th June, met with no better result, the Germans being immediately thrown back from any position of our line which they may have temporarily captured.

The 9th June the Divisional Headquarters moved a few miles further south, from Etoges to Allemant, and the 14th June to Pleurs. To the regret of all ranks it was now learnt that the infantry of the Division would be broken up and the Service battalions used as reinforcements for other units. This decision, though a great blow to the Division, was inevitable owing to the scarcity of reinforcements and the policy of keeping Regular and Territorial Divisions up to strength rather than Divisions of the New Army. The 17th/18th June the three composite battalions were withdrawn from the line, and the following day the 19th Division was relieved by an Italian Division. Shortly afterwards the 1st Wilts, 3rd Worcesters and 2nd S. Lancs., all old Regular battalions, entrained to join the 21st, 19th, and 30th Divisions ; at the same time a composite Brigade was made from the remainder of the infantry units for service with the 50th Division, until they were finally disbanded a few weeks later, to provide reinforcements for their sister units.

In the neighbourhood, American troops were seen marching up towards the Marne. Of fine physique, fresh, vigorous, well trained, brimful of enthusiasm, national pride and *esprit de corps*, unhampered by too hard-bound a tradition, these soldiers of the New World were soon to show that in common with the Canadians and Australians they were the equal to the best that Europe could produce.

The 24th June, Divisional Headquarters with the artillery and other Divisional troops entrained for Hesdin in the 1st Army Area.

25th BATTALION MACHINE GUN CORPS.

The evening of the 26th May, the 25th Machine Gun Battalion was ordered to proceed to the forward area from its billets in Hourges ; the companies marching independently to the Brigades to which they were attached.

" A " Company, commanded by Major S. L. Courtauld, M.C., to 7th Brigade at Guyencourt (right).

" B " Company, commanded by Major D. Campbell, to 74th Brigade at Muscourt (left).

" C " Company, commanded by Capt. T. C. B. Udall, to 75th Brigade at Ventelay (centre).

" D " Company, commanded by Major G. McCree, in reserve at Romain.

The companies arrived early the 27th after the German bombardment had commenced and A, B, and C companies immediately reconnoitred positions in their respective areas and in the second line of defence, along the ridges south of the Maizy-Cormicy Road. Major Campbell, M.C., used his machine guns with great skill both along the Aisne and later during the successive retirements.

About 8.30 a.m. the enemy was engaged all along the front from Bouffignereux-Roucy-Concevreux to Maizy. Four machine guns of B Company under 2nd Lieut. W. L. Johnstone did great execution at the bridges at Maizy, but were eventually, about mid-day, forced to retire and fell back to Muscourt. Sergt. Graham, M.M., and L.-Cpl. McGava did excellent work, the latter, though seriously wounded, refusing to leave his machine gun until completely exhausted.

Two sections of D Company in reserve were now sent to reinforce the 74th and 75th Brigades and later the remaining two sections of D Company were also sent to the 74th Brigade on the left flank where the situation appeared to be most serious.

About 6 p.m. the 27th, a strong enemy attack was completely broken up along the Muscourt-Romain Road by the concentrated fire of seven machine guns at point-blank range. On the right, however, the enemy, working well through the woods east and west of Guyencourt, cut off and destroyed by close range sniping several machine guns belonging to A and C Companies. Great execution was done by these guns before they were knocked out or captured. Capt. Udall, commanding C Company, with his headquarters at Roucy, was surrounded and probably captured. About midnight the 27th the enemy were reported in Courlandon and Ventelay, and a retirement was then made to the high ground north of Montigny. In all eleven machine guns out of the 64 were still working under the orders of the Battalion Headquarters, though several others were known to have attached themselves to infantry units south of Bouvencourt.

Cpl. Bashforth, Cpl. Gosling and Pte. Knight fought their guns most gallantly and in every case only retired when nearly surrounded. Pte. Keyes, when the gun team was knocked out, still kept his machine gun in action. Pte. Gough, in a gallant attempt to rescue his company officer, was himself captured by the enemy, but later was successful in escaping to our lines. As runners Pte. Glynn, Pte. Perrie and Pte. Smith were conspicuous for their courage in taking messages through heavy fire, and Pte. Simm made several journeys with belt boxes for the machine guns, under similar conditions. All received decorations which they thoroughly deserved.

Very early the next morning the enemy attacked and drove back the whole line to the River Vesle, where positions were taken up about 9.15 a.m. Four machine guns under 2nd Lieut. Coleman fought to the last, covering the retirement from the high ground east of Montigny, and none came back. This gallant officer was last seen wounded in the hip and encouraging his gun crews. A line was then taken up along the southern bank of the Vesle from Joncherry, and a stand was made at the bridges across the river at midday. Here heavy casualties were inflicted on the attacking infantry who came on in large numbers and gave splendid targets at short ranges to the machine gunners. The enemy then brought up light trench mortars with extraordinary speed and whilst bombarding the garrisons at the bridge-heads succeeded in crossing the river further west near Les Venteaux, evidently with the object of getting round behind the small parties along the river. To avoid capture a general retirement was made during the afternoon to a line Branscourt-Serzy, where touch was gained with the French troops on the left and the line maintained during the night 28th/29th. British units of the three divisions were now all mixed up and as far as could be ascertained only four machine guns remained with the battalion.

The following morning reports were received that the enemy had worked further round the left flank to Largery and were moving towards Lhery. The 19th Division, de-bussing a short distance further back, were now reinforcing the line Tramery-Lhery, which later on in the evening became the front line. At daybreak the 30th the enemy again succeeded in pressing back the left flank and coming through from Aougny and Aiguizy forced our line back to the high ground north of Bois de Bouvaville-Ville en Tardenois-Sarcy. 2nd Lieut. Bolam, who had arrived the previous day, did splendid work with two machine guns from the high ground near Romigny and inflicted heavy casualties.

From this point the line remained fairly steady and opportunity was taken to re-organise the battalion and to give some rest to the four remaining machine gun teams. Major McCree, who had been fighting with two machine guns with details of the 50th Division, rejoined the battalion, also some other machine gun teams, whose guns had been destroyed, and who had remained fighting as infantry with the units of their brigades. Casualties had been heavy ; five officers and 10 other ranks killed, including Lieut. Coston, Lieut. Tyacke, Lieut. Willson, 2nd Lieut. Reay and 2nd Lieut. Hughes, 10 officers and 120 other ranks wounded, 5 officers and 108 other ranks missing.

R.E. AND 6th SOUTH WALES BORDERERS (PIONEERS).

On their arrival in the Fismes area the three Field Companies and the 6th S.W. Borderers (Pioneers) were at once employed in making rifle ranges and other facilities for training. This work was barely finished when the 25th Division was moved up nearer the line across the River Vesle, and the work was again started on the construction of new rifle ranges.

The evening of the 26th May the 130th, 106th, and the 105th Field Companies R.E., under Major F. E. B. Musgrave, M.C., R.E., Major C. G. Lynam, M.C., R.E., and Major J. W. Lloyd, R.E., moved up with the 7th, 75th and 74th Brigades to Guyencourt, Ventelay and Muscourt, respectively. The 6th S.W. Borderers, under Lt.-Col. Deane, D.S.O., M.C. marched about six miles to Vaux Varennes, where it came under the orders of Brig.-Gen. Griffin, commanding 7th Infantry Brigade. About 8.30 a.m. the battalion began to occupy the second line of defence extending from the right of the 7th Brigade to about 600 yards west of Trigny. Along this line, approximately about 4 miles in length, there was a fairly good traversed trench 2 feet in depth and strongly wired in front. During the afternoon stragglers from the front line were collected and re-organised for the defence of this second line, which was heavily attacked about 7 p.m. The enemy were, however, beaten off by Lewis gun and rifle fire, also a second attack about 8.30 p.m. The night was fairly quiet, but by 7 a.m. the morning of the 28th it was found that parties of German machine guns had worked round the flanks of our detached companies, especially D Company. Heavy casualties were inflicted by the Lewis guns, and four machine guns of A Company, 25th Machine Gun Battalion, which were, however, eventually knocked out by shell fire.

French troops of the Colonial Division put up a splendid fight against heavy odds on the right. During the early morning of the 28th A and C Companies, commanded by Capt. Stickler and Lieut. Amos, with D Company commanded by Lieut. Davies, respectively, retired to the Trigny-Prouilly line, a few men of D Company being cut off and captured. From there a further retirement was made to the line Rheims-Joncherry railway, with their left on the tile works.

Lieut. Bowen did good work collecting and re-organising scattered units, and 2nd Lieut. Parry, at a critical moment with about 60 men, covered the retirement of other troops with great coolness and ability. Sergt. Edwards and C.-S.-M. Ricketts, D.C.M., commanded their men with great skill when all officers had become casualties. Pte. Beard, Pte.

Elvin, Cpl. Goth, Pte. Nethercote, and Pte. Thompson did great execution with their Lewis guns, whilst Pte. Capewell and Pte. Prince were conspicuous for their courage as runners and Pte. Walkins for his work as a stretcher-bearer under heavy fire. Capt. Mann, R.A.M.C., with great coolness attended the wounded and organised bearer parties under most difficult conditions. Sergt. Cooper, D.C.M., set an example of cheerfulness to the men ; and all won well-earned decorations.

At 10 a.m. orders were received that the 6th S. Wales Borderers were transferred to the 62nd Brigade, 21st Division, and were required to reinforce the line further south in front of Rosnay and Hill 202. On arrival this position was found to be held by French troops, and the battalion was then placed by the French commander in support about half a mile behind. During the afternoon the battalion lost its commanding officer, who was killed by a shell in Rosnay Village : Lt.-Col. Deane, D.S.O., M.C., a young mining engineer in civil life, had received a commission from the Yeomanry in the early days of the war, and had shown remarkable gifts of leadership during his service with the battalion. His death was a great loss to the Division.

Early on the 29th, under orders from the G.O.C. 45th French Division, the 6th S.W. Borderers, now much reduced in numbers, marched to Meiz Preveny and Marfaux for a short rest before continuing to Loisy, south of the Marne, where they rejoined their transport with the Headquarters, 25th Division. Meanwhile, the 130th, 105th and 106th Field Companies R.E. had moved up with their respective infantry brigades, though with the understanding that they were not to be used as infantry. Attached to the Brigades to improve and strengthen the defences, it was never intended that they should be used as infantry, but the inevitable happened, and by 10 a.m., 27th, the Field Companies were all being employed as infantry, and were continually so employed throughout the battle. On the right about 7 p.m., the 27th, the 130th Field Company R.E. held a line forming a left flank defence to the 7th Brigade, retiring later with the other troops of the Brigade to the south of Bouvencourt, where it remained all night with Major Cannon's force, and successfully repulsed two heavy attacks. From 9 a.m., 28th, the Field Company was continuously engaged during the retirement across the Vesle river and at positions south of Branscourt, north of Bouleuse, and finally along the hills west of Aubilly, when it was withdrawn on the 30th and rejoined the Divisional Headquarters.

About 5.30 p.m., the 27th, the 106th Field Company attached to the 75th Brigade, lined the ridge ¾ mile N.E. of Ventelay, and later the same night south of Bouvencourt ; here the Field Company was able to do good work collecting and organising stragglers and beat off several attacks.

Lieut. Saxon, R.E., did excellent work, and won the Military Cross. During the night Cpl. Garrahy, M.M., volunteered to go forward to find out the situation, and managed to penetrate 500 yards beyond the enemy's out-posts. L.-Cpl. Bray and Sapper Thwaites, 106th Field Company, showed great initiative in command of isolated parties. Sapper Robinson did splendid work in charge of a Lewis gun team, covering the retirement of other troops. Later on, at a critical moment, L.-Cpl. Dawson rallied a party of stragglers and held the northern outskirts of Romigny, where they were heavily attacked, and enabling our troops to withdraw. All these subsequently received the Military Medal. On the 29th, along with the 1/6th Cheshires, 8th Borders and a composite battalion, the 106th Field Company R.E. dug a line north of Romigny, where they were heavily attacked the following morning. Retiring with other troops, the Field Company then came under the orders of the 74th Brigade, with whom they remained until relieved by the 130th Field Company on the 10th June. The Grand Pont Chatillon and other bridges across the Marne were prepared for demolition on the 31st and subsequently handed over to the French Engineers.

The 105th Field Company R.E., about 10.30 a.m., 27th, was in the support position on Muscourt Hill alongside the 74th T.M. Battery and a party of L.N. Lancs. During the retirement an attack was beaten off the same evening from the high ground between the Montigny and Ventelay, and the following morning the Field Company assisted in holding the bridges east of Joncherry across the Vesle. Here Major Lloyd, R.E., was wounded and taken prisoner, and the remains of the Field Company fell back with other troops of the Brigade.

Casualties were heavy, and there is no doubt that these technical troops might have been much better employed in the destruction of bridges, roads, railways, and other technical duties than as infantry, useful as they proved themselves in this rôle. The arrangements for the demolition of all bridges over the Aisne were directly under the control of the Army authorities, who had given orders that no bridges were to be destroyed without direct instructions from their Headquarters.

Events moved too fast for orders to reach the troops responsible, and although 34 bridges out of 42 were blown up on the initiative of the local commander on the spot, yet 8 were left intact, including two important bridges at Pontavert and Concevreux and several to the west of Maizy, where the enemy were enabled to cross the river without opposition. The failure to destroy these bridges made the defence of the Aisne a hopeless task.

ARTILLERY.

The Divisional Artillery, which had been in action with only a few days' rest since 21st March, reached Champagne the 11th May, and at once settled down to a fortnight's Brigade Training in camps mid-way between the Aisne and the Marne. This much-needed rest and training was interrupted 10 days later, when the artillery was ordered up along with the remainder of the Division across the Vesle river.

The 25th May, the 110th and 112th Brigades R.F.A. were placed at the disposal of the 8th and 21st Divisions, and the following morning the 110th Brigade marched up to positions in the Bois de Gernicourt along the low ground south of the Aisne between Bouffignereux and the river. The 112th Brigade, under the orders of the 21st Division, left its camp at Baslieux about 7.30 p.m., the 26th, for positions in a wood south-west of Cormicy, about 3 miles south of the Aisne.

110th Brigade R.F.A.			Lt.-Col. H. R. PHIPPS, D.S.O.
A/110	...	...	Major J. Watson, M.C.
B/110	...	...	Major A. L. Harman, M.C.
C/110	...	...	Major D. C. Wilson, D.S.O. (P. of W.)
D/110	...	...	Major A. P. Evershed, M.C.

112th Brigade R.F.A.			Lt.-Col. E. V. Sarson, D.S.O.
A/112	...	...	Major W. Swinton, M.C.
B/112	...	...	Major H. T. Vincent (Sick).
			Major Dean, M.C.
C/112	...	...	Major W. E. Mackay, M.C.
D/112	...	...	Major G. Sumpter, D.S.O., M.C.

Ill luck attended the batteries from the very beginning. The positions chosen by the IXth Corps for the 110th Brigade lay in the wood along the low ground south of the Aisne. The field of fire was very bad ; the batteries were now committed to a definite position from which, should a withdrawal become necessary, they would be obliged to retire up the front of a steep range of hills, and in addition they could no longer be regarded as a reserve.

By 8 a.m., the 27th, the 8th Division, with its Divisional artillery, north of the Aisne, was practically destroyed, and the 110th Brigade now found itself without infantry protection, with the enemy swarming in large numbers across the Aisne even before the news arrived concerning the fate of the troops north of the river. By mid-day A, B, and C batteries, 110th Brigade, had lost 14 guns, and D/110 its 4 howitzers. Major Wilson and Major Evershed were both captured, with many of the personnel of the four batteries. Later a composite battery was formed consisting of 4 18-pounders and 2 howitzers, commanded by Capt. Watts and then by Capt. Radcliffe, which subsequently joined up with the 112th Brigade, R.F.A.

2nd Lieut. Keniston, B/110, did excellent work with his battery ; Sergt. Francis D.C.M., and Battery Sergt.-Major Johnson, A/110, were conspicuous for their coolness whilst getting the wagons up to the battery positions, and later when the batteries were nearly surrounded, and it was necessary to retire under heavy machine gun fire. Gunner Morrisey, B110, won a D.C.M. for his wonderful good work as a linesman. Driver English, A/110, and Gunner Nutman, as orderlies, never failed to deliver messages entrusted to them. Bombr. Trussler, A/110, in charge of his battery signallers, did excellent work, and all received well-earned decorations.

The 112th Brigade began to arrive at their position S.W. of Cormicy at 1 a.m., the 27th, just as the preliminary bombardment commenced. All roads leading to the position were heavily shelled with gas and H.E. shells, with the result that many horses were killed and the roads were badly blocked for two hours or more. All the batteries, however, were in action by 6 a.m. the 27th and continuous and steady fire was kept up all day. Lieut. Williams, C/112, won the Military Cross for his coolness under most difficult conditions.

During the morning from the commencement of the bombardment the battery positions were heavily shelled, and soon after mid-day the artillery of the 21st Division retired, covered by the 112th Brigade. Casualties were naturally heavy, 2nd Lieut. J. P. Morgan, B/112, being killed ; and later in the afternoon great difficulty was experienced in getting ammunition along the roads in rear of the battery positions. Lieut. Jones, B/112, did splendid work bringing up teams and getting the wagons away under heavy fire. He afterwards received the Military Cross, and Major Mackay, C/112, a Bar.

At about 5 p.m. considerable rifle and machine gun fire appeared to be coming from the left rear of the battery positions, but orders were received to hang on to 8 p.m. before retiring. At 7.10 p.m. a patrol reported the enemy in rear of the batteries and working through the wood about 200 yards behind. Lt.-Col. Sarson was successful in collecting sufficient infantry, who were now retiring through the guns, to hold up the enemy for a short time, but was finally compelled to order the guns of C battery to be destroyed. Hand-to-hand fighting took place round the gun-pits, but A and B/112 successfully withdrew to Prouilly, and D/112 to south of Bouvencourt. B/112 whilst galloping back came under machine gun fire at short range, and owing to casualties among the horses was compelled to abandon three guns. Lt.-Col. Sarson, 2nd Lieut. Standen and a small party of gunners on their way back ran into a party of German infantry and were unfortunately captured.

From their wagon lines the Brigade then marched to Savigny during the night, and came into action the following day, being joined by the composite battery from 110th Brigade in place of C/112, and reinforced by a few guns from the 8th Division R.A. The Brigade now fought under Lt.-Col. Phipps. During the night of 28th/29th the Brigade again retired to a position east of Brouillet, and successively during the next few days to positions near Lhery, Ville en Tardenois, Chaumuzy and behind Champlat.

The D.A.C., commanded by Lt.-Col. C. S. Hope-Johnstone, was equally unlucky during its movements on the 27th May. No. 1 and No. 2 Sections successfully delivered ammunition to the guns of the 110th and 112th Brigades along roads heavily shelled all day, and it was only when the guns were actually captured that the wagons were withdrawn from the forward area. Great credit is due to the drivers for their coolness and bravery in sticking to a very difficult task in spite of heavy casualties both to personnel and horses. Driver Maharaj Singh and Driver Nathan Singh, two Indian drivers attached to the D.A.C., set a fine example by their courage when conveying ammunition to the batteries.

The S.A.A. Section came under heavy shell fire in the wagon lines at Romain during the early morning, but ammunition was supplied to all infantry units of the Division during the day, and it was not until the evening that the section received orders to fall back on Unchair, south of the Vesle. During the march back it was discovered too late that the line of retreat through Courlandon had been cut ; the enemy being stationed on three sides with machine guns at close range. An attempt was made to get across country, but this eventually became impossible for a large convoy of some 40 wagons. Driver Holloway was conspicuous for his coolness in taking the lead and getting his teams away. Three officers, 67 other ranks and about 100 horses together with the wagons, fell into the hands of the enemy. On the 3rd June, Col. Ballard, 8th Divisional Artillery took over the group which remained in its position until relieved by Italian batteries on the 17th June, when the Brigade rejoined the 25th Division Headquarters.

CASUALTIES AND MEDICAL ARRANGEMENTS.

The evening of the 26th May the 75th, 76th and 77th Field Ambulances under Lt.-Col. H. A. Davidson, D.S.O., Lt.-Col. W. Tyrrell, D.S.O., M.C., and Lt.-Col. H. B. Kelly, D.S.O., became responsible for clearing all casualties of the 74th, 75th, and 7th Brigades respectively, and advanced dressing stations were at once formed at Muscourt, Ventelay, and Guyencourt. From 1 a.m. the 27th May, a few casualties were sustained by units of the Division from gas and H.E. shells, and some damage was caused to the H.Q. and Transport of the 76th Field Ambulance in their camp two miles further back at Courlandon. Later on during the morning many casualties were treated from the 21st, 8th, and 50th Divisions, and during the afternoon in accordance with the situation and retirement of our troops, the advanced dressing stations were moved further back.

Unfortunately the advanced dressing station at Bouvencourt was captured about dusk by the enemy together with Lt.-Col. Kelly, D.S.O., Major Lescher, M.C., Capt. C. Witts, M.C., Lieut. Findlay and 27 other ranks of the 77th Field Ambulance. By this time the 76th and 77th Field Ambulance had fallen back to Montigny where at 8.30 p.m. there were as many as 800 wounded awaiting to be evacuated. With the exception of 35 cases, all were successfully cleared during the night by 100 motor lorries, a very creditable performance. During the day Capt. Brooke, R.A.M.C., attached to the 1st Wilts, was killed at the same time as Lt.-Col. Furze was wounded when their Battalion Headquarters was surrounded by the enemy.

Early the 28th May, Montigny was captured by the Germans and advanced dressing stations were formed by the 75th, 76th Field Ambulances at Largery and Thiery respectively The 77th Field Ambulance being held in reserve and retiring with Divisional Headquarters. Many narrow escapes were experienced by the ambulance cars during the evacuation of the wounded. One Sunbeam car of the 76th Field Ambulance was captured and remained in German hands for several hours before it escaped. In the case of another car belonging to the 76th Field Ambulance the car full of wounded was fired on by German machine guns at close range, and though the orderly was killed the car and driver managed to escape. Throughout the fighting the cases were most successfully dealt with, especially having regard to the fact that the casualty clearing stations were out of action and in the hands of the enemy early the 28th ; this involved long journeys of nearly 20 miles to the French hospitals at Epernay, Verneuil and Dormans on the Marne.

From the 29th to the 31st May, as the troops retired southeast, advanced dressing stations were successively formed by the 75th Field Ambulance at Passy, Cuisles and Nappes, and by the 76th Field Ambulance at Olizy St. Violaune, Nanteuil la Fosse and St. Denis. On the 1st June, owing to the small number of troops of the 25th Division remaining in the line, the 76th Field Ambulance was withdrawn and the 75th Field Ambulance remained under the orders of the 19th Division to clear any cases of the 74th Brigade and attached troops.

The following is a list of those who received rewards for services during the operations, with details of the more notable acts of gallantry for which the award was granted :—

9860 L./Corpl. J. Halliwell, 11th Lancashire Fusiliers.

For conspicuous and unflinching gallantry in the field. At Muscourt on the 27th May, 1918, during the withdrawal of the remnants of the battalion during a heavy engagement with the enemy, this N.C.O. captured a stray German horse, mounted it and rode out under heavy rifle and machine gun fire and rescued a wounded man from " No Man's Land." He repeated this performance and succeeded in rescuing one officer and nine other ranks. In each case he rode out, picked up the wounded man and rode back with him. He made another effort to reach a wounded man but was driven back by the very close advance ot the enemy. This man's conduct was magnificent throughout. He set a splendid example to all who saw him.

Awarded . . . . V.C.

19111 Pte. (L./Corpl.) A. Asher, 1st Wiltshire Regt.

For most conspicuous and gallant conduct during the hostile operations between May 27th and June 8th, during which time this N.C.O. was continuously in the line. He at all times set a magnificent example ot cheerfulness and courage, even under the most trying conditions.

On one occasion at Tramery when the enemy were attacking in great force, this N.C.O. observed a French machine gun well in front of our line, the team having become casualties. On his own initiative he at once rushed out under heavy rifle and machine gun fire, and manned the gun, and, after finding out how to fire it, he, together with Corpl. Carter, opened fire, and inflicted heavy casualties on the enemy. When a withdrawal became necessary, he brought the gun out of action and took up another position, covering the withdrawal in a most effective manner.

This courageous action was performed at a most opportune time, as our troops, operating with the French, were very short of S.A.A. ; and the behaviour of L./Corpl. Asher at this time had a wonderful steadying effect upon all the men.

Throughout the operations the magnificent example of courage, dash and cheerfulness set by this N.C.O. was most inspiring, and beyond all praise.

Awarded . . . . D.C.M.

2nd Lieut. (A./Lieut.) F. Baines, 9th L.N. Lancs (attd. 74th T.M. Battery).

For conspicuous gallantry and devotion to duty. On 27th May, near Muscourt, this officer was in command of a small composite force.

and by his ability, and the skill with which he handled his force, they were able to hold up the enemy's advance for a considerable time. The enemy repeatedly attacked his right flank but was driven back on each occasion. Although his force suffered many casualties he carried on in a very cool and courageous manner, and held on to his position until it was almost surrounded.

Awarded .... M.C.

33978 L./Corpl. E. Blodwell, 9th L.N. Lancs (attd. 74th T.M.B.).

On the 27th May, 1918, in the vicinity of Muscourt, this N.C.O. was with Lieut. Baines' party, and when both sergeants had been wounded and the two corporals killed, L./Corpl. Blodwell continued to assist Lieut. Baines in controlling and encouraging his men. To do this he continually moved along the line, although exposed to heavy rifle and machine gun fire at close range, and inspired the men by his coolness and disregard of danger. When the party was almost completely surrounded and the order to withdraw was given, he was the last to leave and remained to help a wounded man to cover about 500 yards distant over open ground swept by rifle and machine gun fire.

Awarded .... M.M.

Lieut. W. Beckett, D.C.M., 8th Border Regt.

On the 27th May, 1918, in the vicinity of Roucy, this officer was ordered to take forward his company to reinforce another battalion of the Brigade. Having reconnoitred the approaches under heavy artillery and machine gun fire, he coolly led his men forward to the required position. On reaching this he discovered that the battalion had been driven back and withdrawn to the flank, and the position occupied by the enemy. He immediately engaged them, but was obliged to withdraw to his original post. His skilful handling of his men on this occasion was the means of reducing considerably the numbers of casualties in his company.

Later in the day this officer held with his company the right of a position which had both flanks in the air. In this position he was, during a period of six hours, repeatedly attacked by the enemy, but he repulsed them on all occasions, continually up and down the line and steadying his men.

His magnificent courage and utter disregard of personal safety was a splendid example to his men.

Awarded .... M.C.

31512 Pte. W. Dickenson, 2nd South Lancashire Regt.

During operations in the Roucy Sector.

For conspicuous gallantry and devotion to duty whilst in charge of a Lewis gun team on 27th May, 1918. When most of his men had become casualties he continued to serve his gun in the open, inflicting heavy loss on the enemy, retired in good order, eventually bringing his gun intact out of the fight.

Awarded .... M.M.

2nd Lieut. F. Davis, 4th South Staffordshire Regt. (Wounded.)

On the 27th May, 1918, in the wood south-west of Cormicy, this officer showed great ability as a leader, and gallant conduct of the very highest order.

When the left flank of the batatlion was completely in the air, with the enemy working round in great strength, he kept his men steady, and by his coolness enabled an orderly withdrawal to be effected.

Shortly afterwards, when the battalion was almost completely surrounded, he formed a rearguard with the remaining men of his company, and through his very skilful leadership, and by engaging his men at close quarters, he enabled the remainder of the battalion to withdraw through a bottle-neck position. He then succeeded in extricating his own men.

On the following day, south of Prouilly, he hung on to a very important tactical position with the utmost resolution, though he lost the greater number of his men from heavy and direct shell fire, he himsel f b ng wounded.

Throughout these two days of fighting, his personal disregard for danger was an example to everyone, and his skilful handling of his men saved the battalion on two occasions.

Awarded ..........D.S.O.

40851 Pte. W. Elvin, 6th South Wales Borderers (Pioneers).

On May 28th, 1918, for conspicuous gallantry and coolness on the high ground north-west of Hermonville, while in charge of a Lewis gun, on the left flank of the forward half company.

He displayed conspicuous devotion to duty in warding off repeated attempts of the enemy to work round the left flank. Several of the enemy were killed, but by making a long detour they eventually got round the flank and almost surrounded the half company.

Even when knowing that the enemy had got to the flank and to the rear, he continued to keep up a fire to cover the withdrawal of the remainder of his platoon. He then successfully got his gun away.

Awarded ..........M.M.

65948 Pte. A. Gough, 25th Battn. Machine Gun Corps.

During the operations near Roucy on 27th May, 1918, this man was the servant of Capt. T. E. B. Udall and acted as his runner. Hearing that this officer had been captured by the enemy, he went back to try and rescue him, although the village was then in possession of the enemy. He failed in this, but managed to secure Capt. Udall's pack which contained maps and papers which might have been useful to the enemy. He was captured by the enemy whilst returning to our lines. but managed to escape with the documents and rejoined our lines.

Pte. Gough has on many occasions shown great courage, resourceful-ness and the utmost contempt for danger.

Awarded ..........D.C.M.

Lieut. A. J. Hull, M.O.R.C., U.S.A., attd. 4th South Staffs.

On the 27th May, 1918, this officer showed gallantry of a very high order. Being without stretcher bearers, he himself helped to carry several wounded down a road near Cormicy that was being heavily shelled.

He went several times to the front line to attend to wounded. He made a gallant effort later to rescue an ambulance car which had been abandoned owing to the driver being killed.

On the same day when forced to withdraw his aid post, he turned back to attend to a severely wounded man. He succeeded in getting his case away with the enemy only 50 yards away at the time.

Awarded .... **M.C.**

Lieut. P. L. Jones, " B " Battery, 112th Brigade, R.F.A.

Near Gernicourt wood, on the 27th May, 1918, while the battery was pulling into action, very heavy casualties were sutained in men and horses. Later Lieut. Jones brought up teams under the most intense shell fire, collected such wagons as could be removed, took away harness and cleared the roads of dead horses and damaged vehicles, during which his teams again suffered heavy casualties. In spite of this Lieut. Jones persisted till he had removed all the serviceable ammunition wagons, which subsequently proved invaluable in keeping the battery in action.

The work done by this officer was of the utmost value, the clearing of the roads alone, later enabling the batteries to move unhampered, was entirely due to the bravery, resource and gallantry of this officer and to the manner in which he inspired his men.

Awarded .... **M.C.**

770051 Bty. Sergt.-Major E. Johnson, A/110th Bde., R.F.A.

At Gernicourt Wood on May 27th, 1918, just before the battery withdrew, four horses of one gun team were killed by machine gun fire. B.S.M. Johnson at once set about organising a composite team and was still engaged in hooking in outriders when the battery withdraw. Being a limber short, two guns were taken away by one limber, the muzzles being lashed together. Whilst galloping over the open the leaders were killed and guns stuck. B.S.M. Johnson galloped after them with his composite team, unlashed the second gun, limbered it up and brought both guns safely away. Under very great difficulties he showed great initiative and powers of leadership.

Awarded .... **D.C.M.**

2nd Lieut. W. L. Johnstone, 25th Battn. Machine Gun Corps.

For gallantry, skill and devotion to duty in handling his four machine guns, when in action on the Aisne.

This officer placed his guns so as to cover the open plain, north of the Aisne, and two bridges in the vicinity of Muscourt. He was able to inflict heavy losses on large bodies of the enemy advancing across the plain and later completely held up the enemy on the bridges, doing great execution at the range of 100 yards and under. He fought his guns in these positions until the enemy, working round the flanks, had overwhelmed his two left guns, who continued firing to the end, and only withdrew his two remaining guns when the enemy were within 50 yards of them. He succeeded in getting into action again on the high ground a little distance behind, from which position he again held up the enemy on the Maixy-Muscourt Road.

Awarded ..........M.C.

130214 Pte. E. G. Keyes, 25th Battn. Machine Gun Corps.
(Wounded.)

For conspicuous bravery on May 27th, 1918, north of Romain, during a heavy enemy attack. The gun to which this man belonged was subjected to severe enemy machine gun and rifle fire, and both the Nos. 1 and 2 were wounded.

Pte. Keyes, without the slightest hesitation, immediately rushed forward and after drawing his wounded comrades clear of the gun and under cover, manned the gun and kept it in action for several hours, although continually harassed by snipers ; causing severe casualties to the enemy.

His conduct was beyond praise and his action undoubtedly saved a critical situation.

He was wounded on the 29th May, while covering an Infantry withdrawal.

Awarded ..........D.C.M.

10119 Sergt. C. Mitchell, 2nd South Lancs Regt.

For conspicuous gallantry and devotion to duty during recent operations in the Roucy Sector, on 27th May. When all his company officers had become casualties, he assumed command and reorganised the company, holding on to his position until forced to withdraw to conform with the flanks.

This N.C.O. has done generally good work and by his cheerful disposition inspired all ranks.

Awarded ..........M.M.

5334 Gnr. J. Morrisey, B/110th Brigade, R.F.A.

On May 27th, 1918, in Gernicourt Wood, Gnr. Morrisey, on the conclusion of his tour of duty as operator, volunteered to act as linesman at a time when the line was being continually cut by the enemy's bombardment. On six different occasions he went along the line running through the wood, which was being heavily shelled and gassed. Working in the dark and with his gas helmet on the whole time, Gnr. Morrisey showed the greatest determination, and it was owing to his efforts that the communications were maintained.

Awarded ..........D.C.M.

Lieut. (A/Capt.) T. G. Parkes, M.C., 1st Wiltshire Regt.
(Wounded.)

This officer did very good work throughout the fighting south of the Aisne from May 27th to June the 8th.

On May 27th, at Bouffignereux, when Bn. H.Qrs. was surprised, it was largely due to his quickness and good shooting that anyone got away.

From then onwards he fought a consistently good rearguard action, collecting men wherever he saw stragglers, collecting ammunition and food for his men from several battalions and brigades.

He was wounded by a splinter of shell, but continued to carry on, and by his energy, cheerfulness and determination succeeded in keeping any men he had with him in good heart and fighting spirit, and generally helped considerably in his portion of the battlefield.

Awarded .... **Bar to M.C.**

2nd Lieut. E. W. Pickles, 3rd Worcester Regt.

On 27th May, 1918, at Concevreux, this officer displayed great gallantry and devotion to duty. His battalion was retiring and closely followed by the enemy, and it seemed just possible that heavy casualties would be inflicted before another position could be taken up. Grasping the situation, 2nd Lieut. Pickles collected some 20 men, turned and attacked the enemy with such effect that the whole advance in that neighbourhood was checked for at least half an hour.

Awarded .... **M.C.**

65525 Spr. R. W. Robinson, 106th Field Coy. R.E.

On the night of the 27th/28th May, near Ventelay, there being no N.C.O. left in his section, he took command of a Lewis gun team and covered the withdrawals of our forces remaining there till practically surrounded. Throughout the operations his initiative, cheerfulness and personal gallantry were conspicuous; he has previously done very fine work at Dranoutre in April, 1918.

Awarded .... **M.M.**

26637 Driver Maharaj Singh, 19638 Driver Nathan Singh ; No. 1 Section, 25th D.A.C.

These drivers were conveying ammunition to a battery in action on the 26th/27th May in Gernicourt Wood.

One wagon load was successfully delivered under heavy enemy shelling and the wagon returned to the dump and refilled, an endeavour being made later to deliver a further wagon load. This, owing to the intense enemy fire, was found to be impracticable, and the convoy had to be turned back. The animals of the wagon in question became unmanageable, due to bursting shells, and the wagon, badly ditched, was abandoned. These drivers were found to be absent later, and it was not until they returned to the column, with the salved wagon, that it was realised that they had voluntarily gone back into the wood under fire at a great personal risk and brought the wagon loaded with ammunition, which otherwise would have fallen into the hands of the enemy. Their conduct was most commendable and constituted a splendid example not only to the other natives but also the whole personnel of the section.

Awarded .... **M.M.**

2nd Lieut. J. Siddons, D.C.M., M.M., 10th Cheshire Regt.

For conspicuous gallantry in action.

During the operations south of the Aisne from May 27th to June 8th, this officer displayed, at all times, the greatest disregard of personal safety. This was particularly conspicuous on the night 27th/28th

May, south of Bouvancourt, when the enemy made a surprise attack on the position.

2nd Lieut. Siddons got into action a machine gun which had been left without a crew, and with it materially assisted in the repulse of the enemy.

During the enemy attack on the 28th, and again on the 30th, at Bouleuse, when the position was under heavy machine gun fire and artillery fire, which was causing many casualties, this officer fearlessly went along the line (only a series of holes) encouraging the men and improving their morale.

Throughout the whole of the operations, carried out under the most adverse conditions, the bearing of 2nd Lieut. Siddons was always most courageous. He was invaluable in rallying the men after a withdrawal, and collecting them when scattered, and his demeanour and cheerfulness throughout did much to keep up the spirit and morale of the men.

Awarded .... M.C.

44192 Pte. P. Shaw, 10th Cheshire Regt.

During the battle north-east of Guyencourt, and the subsequent retirement.

On May 27th, 1918, after the order to withdraw had been given and the company was withdrawing, Pte. Shaw, stretcher bearer, remained tending the wounded under intense rifle and machine gun fire. He actually fell into the hands of the enemy whilst so engaged, but he eventually succeeded in rejoining, and brought a wounded man along with him.

Awarded .... M.M.

22220 Pte. A. Still, 9th L.N. Lancashire Regt.

For conspicuous gallantry on the 27th May, 1918, at Muscourt.

This man kept his Lewis gun in action and inflicted many casualties, although practically surrounded by the enemy. He only withdrew when all his ammunition was expended.

Awarded .... M.M.

42811 Pte. W. Thompson, 4th South Staffordshire Regt.

For most conspicuous gallantry during four days' fighting near the Aisne, from the 27th to 30th May, 1918.

He was one of a Lewis gun team, and during the first day's fighting the remainder of his team became casualties, and all the magazines were lost with the exception of the one on the gun. During each withdrawal that was ordered he stayed behind with his gun, firing and reloading his one magazine himself, until every one was clear.

His gallantry was particularly noticeable on the 29th May, near Branscourt, when he took forward his gun, and by enfilade fire prevented the enemy for a whole day from concentrating and organising an attack on the battalion, which he repeatedly tried to do.

Awarded .... D.C.M.

18117 L./Corpl. H. Thompson, 11th Lancashire Fusiliers.

For conspicuous gallantry and devotion to duty. During the whole of 27th May at Muscourt, whilst the enemy were heavily attacking the battalion, this N.C.O. showed great courage and coolness under fire of heavy artillery, machine gun and rifles, and continually collecting and organising men and inspiring them with courage ; he also made several journeys out into " No Man's Land " and brought in wounded men. He set a very fine example of coolness and courage, and did much to stiffen the resistance.

Awarded .........M.M.

39777 Sergt. R. Webber, 3rd Worcester Regt.

On the 27th May, at Concevreux, this N.C.O. displayed great bravery and coolness. When his platoon commander became a casualty he assumed command and reorganised the platoon. In spite of heavy casualties he held his position against overwhelming numbers of the enemy. By his fine example he instilled confidence into his men under most trying conditions. Eventually he had to retire to conform with the general line.

Awarded .........M.M.

2nd Lieut. E. G. Wylie, M.C., Durham Light Infantry, attd. 11th Lancashire Fusiliers.

On 29th May, near Joncherry, this officer was Brigade Intelligence Officer, and during the crossing of the Vesle he collected parties of men who were without leaders and held up the advancing enemy who had broken through and crossed the river on the left flank. These parties and a few machine guns under 2nd Lieut. Wylie held up the enemy for four hours, thereby enabling our troops to take up a position on the high ground. Throughout the day this officer rendered most valuable service and was an example to the troops.

Awarded ....Bar to M.C.

33468 L./Corpl. R. Wilkie, 8th Border Regt.

On the evening of the 27th May, at Roucy, this N.C.O. showed conspicuous gallantry and untiring devotion to duty. He was out in front in a listening post. He sent back valuable information that the enemy were about to attack.

Heedless of all personal danger under heavy machine gun fire, this N.C.O. stuck to his post and kept the enemy back until he was reinforced by a Lewis gun team from his company.

Throughout the operations his great coolness inspired his comrades and set them a fine example.

Awarded .........M.M.

17514 Pte. T. Watkins, 6th South Wales Borderers.   (Pioneers.)

On May 27th/28th, north-west of Hermonville, and near Rosnay.

His great devotion to duty as a stretcher bearer deserve the highest praise.   On several occasions under heavy shell fire he attended to the wounded regardless of personal danger.

On one occasion when the company was withdrawing to a new position and was being shelled, and sustaining heavy casualties, this man attended to the wounded, dressed their wounds under heavy machine gun and shell fire.

On another occasion he attended to a wounded French soldier who was being heavily sheiled.

Awarded ..........M.M.

Honours and Awards.

VICTORIA CROSS.

9860 L./Corpl. J. Halliwell ... ... 11th Lancashire Fusiliers.

DISTINGUISHED SERVICE ORDER.

2nd Lieut. F. Davis ... ... 4th South Staffords.

BAR TO MILITARY CROSS.

Capt. A. J. Bentley, M.C.	8th Border Regt.
Capt. A. C. Mann, M.C., R.A.M.C. ...	Attd. 6th S.W.B.
Capt. (A./Major) W. G. MacKay, M.C.	C/112 Bde., R.F.A.
Lieut. (A./Major) D. Campbell, M.C. ..	25th Battn. M.G. Corps.
Lieut. (A./Capt.) T. G. Parkes, M.C. ..	1st Wilts Regt.
2nd Lieut. (A./Capt.) G. Rowley, M.C.	1/6th Cheshire Regt.
2nd Lieut. (A./Capt.) G. H. Stead, M.C.	Cheshire Regt., attd. 74th T.M.B.
2nd Lieut. E. G. Wylie, M.C.	D.L.I., attd. 11th L. Fus.

MILITARY CROSS.

2nd Lieut. H. Appleby	4th South Staffords.
2nd Lieut. (A./Lieut.) F. Baines ...	9th L.N. Lancs., attd. 74th T.M.B.
Lieut. W. Beckett, D.C.M.	8th Border Regt.
Lieut. W. L. Bowen	Mon. Regt., attd. 6th S.W.B.
2nd Lieut. T. Bolam	25th Battn. M.G. Corps.
Lieut. (A./Capt.) O. Behrendt, R.E. ...	Divl. Gas Officer.
2nd Lieut. R. J. Boyes..	10th Cheshire Regt.
Hon. Lieut. and Qr.M. R. I. Fairfax ..	10th Cheshire Regt.
Lieut. (A./Capt.) W. S. Farmer ...	10th Cheshire Regt.
Capt. T. Grant	3rd Worcester Regt.
2nd Lieut. H. A. Hawkins	4th South Staffords.
Lieut. (A./Capt.) R. E. Huflum ...	10th Cheshire Regt.
Lieut. A. J. Hull, M.O.R.C., U.S.A. ...	Attd. 4th South Staffs.
Lieut. P. L. Jones	B/112th Bde., R.F.A.
2nd Lieut. W. L. Johnstone	25th Battn. M.G. Corps.
2nd Lieut. W. H. Kennedy	1st Wilts Regt., attd. 74th Bde. Signals.
2nd Lieut. J. R. Keniston	B/110th Bde., R.F.A.
2nd Lieut. W. H. R. Lloyds	4th South Staffords.
2nd Lieut. D. M. Morrison	4th (attd. 9th) Battn. L.N.L.
2nd Lieut. J. I. Parry	3rd Cheshire Regt.
2nd Lieut. E. W. Pickles	3rd Worcester Regt.
2nd Lieut. J. Siddons, D.C.M., M.M. ..	10th Cheshire Regt.
T./Lieut. F. C. Saxon, R.E.	106th Field Coy. R.E.
T./Lieut. S. Williams	C/112th Bde., R.F.A.
2nd Lieut. (A./Capt.) W. Yates ...	10th Cheshires.

BAR TO DISTINGUISHED CONDUCT MEDAL.

6/17085 C.S.M W. H. Ricketts, D.C.M. 6th S.W. Borderers.

DISTINGUISHED CONDUCT MEDAL.

19111 Pte. (L./Corpl.) A. Asher	1st Wiltshires.
9129 Sergt. (A./R.S.M.) C. Clarke ..	8th Borders, attd. 1st Wilts.
9053 Sergt. G. Bray	1st Wilts.
770051 Batty. Sergt.-Major E. Johnson	A/110th Bde., R.F.A.
5334 Gnr. J. Morrisey	B/110th Bde., R.F.A.
131449 L./Corpl. A. McGava	25th Battn. M.G. Corps.
22745 Corpl. (A./Sergt.) A. Myers ..	25th Battn. M.G. Corps.
8672 Corpl. J. T. Nelson	11th Lancs. Fus., attd. 74th T.M.B.
26095 Sergt. W. Barnett	11th Lancs. Fus.
130214 Pte. E. G. Keyes	25th Battn. M.G. Corps.
42811 Pte. W. Thompson	4th South Staffords.
60482 Pte. W. Wiggins, M.M.	10th Cheshires.

BAR TO MILITARY MEDAL.

51157 Pte. A. Gadd, M.M.	1/6th Cheshires.
145887 Corpl. J. T. Garrahy, M.M. ..	106th Field Coy. R.E.
18193 Sergt. W. Graham, M.M. ..	25th Battn. M.G. Corps.
10293 Sergt. J. Stokes, M.M.	3rd Worcester Regt.

MILITARY MEDAL.

39975 Pte. F. Andrews	2nd South Lancs.
582 Pte. J. Atherton	2nd South Lancs.
17410 Sergt. T. Atkinson	8th Border Regt.
145273 L./Corpl. C. A. Bray	106th Field Coy. R.E.
67610 Corpl. J. T. Bashforth	25th Battn. M.G. Corps.
36030 Pte. (L./Corpl.) M. L. Bates ..	4th South Staffs.
46286 Pte. H. W. Bailey	3rd Worcester Regt.
17177 Pte. A. Beard	6th S.W.B.
27963 Pte. T. Bell, D.C.M.	8th Border Regt.
19778 Corpl. J. Booth	8th Border Regt.
33978 L. Corpl. E. B. Blodwell ..	9th L.N. Lancs.
50749 Pte. E. Churms	10th Cheshire Regt.
53956 Sergt. J. Cooper, D.C.M. ..	6th S.W.B.
17086 Pte. F. Capewell..	6th S.W.B.
29032 Corpl. H. Carter	1st Wilts Regt.
264896 Sapper E. T. Carr	25th Div. Signal Co., R.E.
36925 Pte. J. Cartwright	9th L.N. Lancs.
266767 L./Corpl. W. Beswick	1/6th Cheshire Regt.
266284 Pte. L. Blackwell	1/6th Cheshire Regt.
74238 L./Bomb. E. Davies	B/110th Bde., R.F.A.
57280 L./Corpl. F. Dawson	106th Field Coy. R.E.
9100 Pte. R. Dixon	8th Border Regt.
31512 Pte. W. Dickenson	2nd South Lancs.
182258 Driver W. G. English	A/110th Bde., R.F.A.
12735 Pte. W. Edwards	4th South Staffords.

39139 Pte. W. H. Edwards	6th South Wales B.
40851 Pte. W. Elvin	6th South Wales B.
23807 Sergt. C. Francis, D.C.M.	A/110th Bde., R.F.A.
24c78 Corpl. R. Farnworth	9th L.N. Lancs.
65948 Pte. A. Gough	25th Battn. M.G. Corps.
34064 Pte. T. Glynn	25th Battn. M.G. Corps.
108135 L./Corpl. (A./Corpl.) P. S. Gosling.	25th Battn. M.G. Corps.
241259 Corpl. W. H. Gilbert	4th South Staffords.
6/19383 Corpl. W. Goth	6th S.W.B.
28437 Corpl. T. Garfat	11th Lancs. Fus.
26224 Corpl. S. Greenwood	11th Lancs. Fus.
6679 Pte. (A.L./Corpl.) G. Gumm	1st Wilts Regt.
120161 Drv. G. R. Holloway	25th Div. Amm. Col.
1366 Pte. G. Hartless	2nd South Lancs.
26403 Pte. W. Huxley	2nd South Lancs.
123546 L./Corpl. W. Knight	25th Battn. M.G. Corps.
13205 Corpl. J. H. Lloyd	3rd Worcester Regt.
27081 Pte. H. Lever	9th L.N. Lancs.
30276 Pte. F. Lane	9th L.N. Lancs.
9591 Pte. H. Mansell	11th Lancs. Fus.
10119 Sergt. C. Mitchell	2nd South Lancs.
17506 Pte. W. Nethercote	6th S.W.B.
15593 Pte. A. Newton	8th Borders.
120831 Gnr. M. Nutman	H.Q. 110th Bde., R.F.A.
7358 L./Corpl. H. Oakley	3rd Worcester Regt.
42771 Corpl. H. Pearce	4th South Staffs.
129675 Pte. W. Perrie	25th Battn. M.G. Corps.
6/29040 Pte. I. Prince	6th South W. Bord.
10175 Pte. W. Rhodes	4th South Staffords.
65525 Spr. R. Robinson	106th Field Coy. R.E.
38714 Pte. T. Regan	10th Cheshire Regt.
23903 Corpl. W. Robinson, D.C.M.	8th Border Regt.
55204 Pte. R. Simm	25th Battn. M.G. Corps.
90536 Pte. A. G. Smith	25th Battn. M.G. Corps.
44192 Pte. P. Shaw	10th Cheshire Regt.
11341 Pte. (L./Corpl.) J. Sedgley	4th South Staffords.
266582 Sergt. H. Skermer	1/6th Cheshires.
267996 Pte. R. Siddall	1/6th Cheshires.
30594 Pte. (L./Corpl.) J. Skidmore	4th South Staffs.
17120 Corpl. F. Stemp	6th South W. Bord.
12914 Corpl. A. E. Smith	3rd Worcester Regt.
8778 Sergt. S. Steadman	3rd Worcester Regt.
22220 Pte. A. Still	9th L.N. Lancs.
155675 Spr. A. D. Thwaites	106th Field Coy. R.E.
11667 Pte. S. Thompson	6th S.W. Bord.
16799 C.Q.M.S. W. Tellett	11th Cheshires.
25618 L./Corpl. J. Tattersall	8th Border Regt.
18117 L./Corpl. H. Thompson	11th Lancs. Fus.
9484 Bomb. A. Trussler	A/110th Bde., R.F.A.
6580 L./Corpl. R. Toggart	2nd South Lancs.
33265 Pte. H. Vaughan	8th Border Regt.

K 2

17514 Pte. T. Watkins ..	..	..	6th S.W. Bord.
15352 C.Q.M.S. T. S. Worrall ..		..	10th Cheshire Regt.
33468 L./Corpl. R. Wilkie	..	..	8th Border Regt.
39777 Sergt. R. Webber	..	..	3rd Worcesters.
15532 Corpl. (A./Sergt.) F. Wood		..	9th L.N. Lancs.
24088 L./Corpl. E. M. Wass	..	..	9th L.N. Lancs.
35232 Pte. R. Walne ..	..	..	11th Lancs. Fus.
22908 Corpl. H. T. White	..	..	1st Wilts. Regt.
8812 Pte. T. Warwick ..	..	..	2nd South Lancs.
13247 C.Q.M.S. A. Yates	..	..	25th Divl. Signals R.E.
19638 Drv. Nathan Singh	..	..	25th Divl. Amm. Col.
26637 Drv. Maharaj Singh	..	..	25th Divl. Amm. Col.

SUMMARY OF CASUALTIES.

NOON, 26th MAY, TO NOON, 14th JUNE, 1918.

Unit.	Officers.			Other Ranks.		
	K.	W.	M.	K.	W.	M.
Divl. H.Qrs.	—	—	1	—	—	—
H.Qrs. Div. R.A.	—	—	—.	—	—	—
110th Bde., R.F.A.	—	1	6	7	33	37
112th Bde., R.F.A.	2	4	2	13	87	34
25th Div. Amm. C.	—	—	3	1	6	68
H.Qrs. R.E.	—	—	—	—	—	—
105th Field Coy.	—	1	3	10	36	25
106th Field Coy.	—	—	—	1	20	7
130th Field Coy.	—	3	—	4	28	21
25th Div. Sig. Co.	—	—	—	1	5	5
H.Qrs. 7th Inf. Bde. ..	1	1	1	—	—	—
10th Cheshires	3	3	5	9	92	188
4th South Staffs.	1	9	4	14	111	186
1st Wilts.	2	6	6	8	106	181
7th T.M. Battery	—	1	—	1	2	12
H.Qrs. 74th Inf. Bde. ..	—	—	—	—	—	—
11th Lancs. Fus.	—	7	13	12	93	317
3rd Worcesters	—	6	6	10	60	244
9th L.N. Lancs.	2	6	3	6	220	139
74th T.M. Battery	—	—	—	3	16	11
H.Qrs. 75th Inf. Bde. ..	—	1	—	—	—	—
11th Cheshires	1	6	10	7	67	329
8th Borders..	3	2	9	9	79	169
2nd South Lancs.	3	11	1	18	169	161
1st/6 Cheshires	—	—	—	5	56	1
75th T.M. Battery	—	1	1	—	10	11
6th S.W. Borderers	1	3	4	18	110	111
25th Bn. M.G. Corps ..	5	11	6	9	119	108
25th Div. Train, A.S.C. ..	—	—	1	—	—	4
R.A.M.C.	1	1	1	—	—	—
75th Field Amb.	—	1	—	—	4	14
76th Field Amb.	—	1	—	1	—	—
77th Field Amb.	—	—	4	3	12	38
225th Div. Emp. Co. ..	—	—	—	—	3	—
Total	25	86	90	172	1544	2421

STATEMENT OF OFFICER CASUALTIES.

1st Wiltshire Regt.

Killed.

Capt. F. A. Brooke, R.A.M.C., attd. 1st Wilts.
2nd Lieut. F. E. Turnbull.

Wounded.

2nd Lieut. H. J. Anderson.
2nd Lieut. A. M. Reid.
2nd Lieut. E. W. J. Duley.

Lieut. G. T. Sands.
Lieut. H. C. Reid.
Capt. T. G. Parkes, M.C.

Missing.

Lt.-Col. E. K. B. Furze, D.S.O.,
M.C. (Wounded and prisoner of
war.)
2nd Lieut. O. L. Desages.
2nd Lt. J. D. Parkin. (Wounded
and prisoner of war.)

Capt. F. Priestley, M.C.
(Wounded.)
Capt. J. F. Arnott, M.C.
(Wounded.)
2nd Lieut. J. B. Stanley.

10th Cheshire Regt.

Killed.

Lt.-Col. E. C. Cadman.
Capt. J. E. H. Dean, M.C.

2nd Lieut. P. A. Francis.

Wounded.

2nd Lieut. A. H. J. Jones.
2nd Lieut. A. Douglas.

2nd Lieut. J. G. Haggart.

Missing.

2nd Lieut. S. A. Ellis.
2nd Lieut. G. B. Gordon.
2na Lieut. T. Moulton.

2nd Lieut. H. J. Hollamby.
2nd Lieut. P. Cookson. (Wounded.)

4th South Staffords.

Killed.

2nd Lieut. L. H. Lycett.

Wounded.

Lieut. A. B. Milner, M.C.
2nd Lieut. T. Cartwright.
2nd Lieut. A. Moorcroft.
2nd Lieut. H. J. Foley.
2nd Lieut. F. Davis.
2nd Lieut. H. B. Lacey.

Capt. L. J. Kelsey, M.C.
2nd Lieut. W. R. Jones.
2nd Lieut. J. A. Greatorex.
Capt. J. D. Hewetson.
Lieut. A. J. Hull, M.O.R.C.,
U.S.A., attd. 4th S. Staffs.

Missing.

2nd Lieut. L. Paramore.

2nd Lieut. A. St. Leger.
(Wounded.)

9th Loyal N. Lancs.

Killed.

Major O. S. Darby-Griffiths, M.C.   2nd Lieut. H. W. Summerson.

Wounded.

Capt. W. F. Loudon, M.C.   Lt.-Col. A. M. Tringham, D.S.O.
2nd Lieut. J. B. M. Lightbody.   2nd Lieut. W. Readman.
Lieut. A. Sumner.   2nd Lieut. A. McGregor.

Missing.

2nd Lieut. A. E. Downing.   Capt. P. R. Shields.
(Wounded.)   Capt. R. J. P. Hewetson.

3rd Worcester Regt.

Wounded.

Lieut. J. T. Milner.   Capt. E. Lattey.
Capt. T. P. Muspratt.   (Died.)   2nd Lieut. E. W. Pickles.
2nd Lieut. G. E. Clay.

Missing.

Lieut. A. J. Sinclair.   Capt. T. Grant.
2nd Lieut. R. O. Goulden.   2nd Lieut. E. V. Matthews.
(Wounded.)   2nd Lieut. V. B. Wasley.
Capt. E. A. Humphries, M.C.   Lieut. W. B. J. Will. (Wounded.)
(Wounded.)   2nd Lieut. W. H. Todhunter.

11th Lancashire Fusiliers.

Wounded.

Lieut. J. A. Nathan.   2nd Lieut. A. J. Gifford.
2nd Lieut. L. Shipman.   Capt. S. J. Gowland.
2nd Lieut. E. S. Gardner.   2nd Lieut. T. D. A. Micklethwaite.
2nd Lieut. L. E. Appleyard.

Missing.

Lt.-Col. G. Pollitt, D.S.O., R.E.   2nd Lieut. G. A. Broadbent.
Lieut. F. Eyre.   2nd Lieut. D. R. Auty.
Capt. H. A. Hutson.   (Killed.)   2nd Lieut. J. H. Smith.
Capt. C. M. Newman.   Capt. R. M. Colebank, R.A.M.C.,
Lieut. J. W. Bottomley.   attd. 11th Lancs. Fus.
2nd Lieut. A. Jones.   2nd Lieut. F. H. Graham.
2nd Lieut. W. Dale.   2nd Lieut. J. A. Pighills.
2nd Lieut. E. A. North, D.C.M.

75th Infantry Brigade H.Q.

Wounded.
Capt. W. K. Innes.

11th Cheshire Regt.

Killed.

Capt. H. M. Wilkinson, M.C.

Wounded.

Lt.-Col. E. R. S. Prior, D.S.O., M.C.
  (Died of wounds.)
Lieut. T. Blackburn.
Lieut. C. Wright, M.C.

2nd Lieut. J. West.
2nd Lieut. K. E. Peters.
2nd Lieut. T. Davies.
2nd Lieut. T. B. Roberts.

Missing.

Capt. C. de W. Woodyer, M.C.
2nd Lieut. C. F. M. Barrett.
2nd Lieut. A. Mayor.
2nd Lieut. W. Ryden.
2nd Lieut. A. E. Bytheway.

2nd Lieut. H. R. Carson.
2nd Lieut. F. W. James.
2nd Lieut. J. S. Burgoyne.
2nd Lieut. A. C. Unwin.

8th Border Regt.

Killed.

2nd Lieut. J. J. Bell.
2nd Lieut. J. K. Mackenzie.

2nd Lieut. H. G. Machell.

Wounded.

2nd Lieut. H. W. S. Young.

Capt. F. L. Williams. (Died.)

Missing.

Capt. A. Miscampbell. (Prisoner
  of war.)
Lieut. H. Lansley. (Prisoner of
  war.)
2nd Lieut. W. T. Thornton.
  (Prisoner of war.)
2nd Lieut. J. Brown. (Prisoner
  of war.)

2nd Lieut. D. Phillip. (Prisoner of
  war.)
2nd Lieut. C. Spence.
2nd Lieut. E. A. Jackson.
  (Wounded.)
2nd Lieut. G. A. Sutcliffe.
2nd Lieut. F. W. Darvell.

2nd South Lancashire Regt.

Killed.

Lt.-Col. J. B. Allsopp, D.S.O.

Lieut. F. J. Cooper.

Wounded.

2nd Lieut. W. T. Allen.
Capt. K. M. Bourne, M.C.
Capt. J. R. Beall, M.C.
Capt. A. R. O. Manning.
2nd Lieut. T. E. Starkey.
2nd Lieut. J. Acheson. (Died of
  wounds.)

2nd Lieut. H. Gidman.
2nd Lieut. W. Napier.
2nd Lieut. G. Parkin.
Lieut. A. L. Claydon.
2nd Lieut. G. Gething.
Lieut. S. J. Jones. (Died of
  wounds.)

Missing.

2nd Lieut. R. W. Simpson. (Prisoner of war.)

7th T.M. Battery.

Wounded.

Capt. A. Harrison, D.S.O.

75th T.M. Battery.

Wounded.

Lieut. J. I. Blackburne.

Missing.

Capt. A. C. Devlin. (Prisoner of war.)

110th Bde., R.F.A.

Wounded.

Lieut. R. E. C. Escombe.

Missing.

Major A. P. Evershed.
2nd Lieut. D. H. Thompson.
2nd Lieut. E. J. Curphey.
Lieut. J. Kane-Smith.

Major D. C. Wilson, D.S.O., M.C.
(Prisoner of war.)
2nd Lieut. W. Graham.

112th Bde., R.F.A.

Killed.

2nd Lieut. J. P. Morgan.

2nd Lieut. C. F. Butler.

Wounded.

2nd Lieut. M. E. Ross.
2nd Lieut. G. M. Scrutton.

2nd Lieut. F. C. Bent.
Lieut. S. Williams, M.C.

Missing.

Lt.-Col. E. V. Sarson. (Prisoner of war.)

2nd Lieut. A. O. Standen.

25th Divl. Ammn. Col.

Missing.

Lieut. E. G. Attenborough.
(Prisoner of war.)
2nd Lieut. W. Joyes. (Prisoner of war.)

2nd Lieut. C. L. F. Platt.
(Prisoner of war.)

25th Battn. Machine Gun Corps.

Killed.

Lieut. E. B. Willson.
2nd Lieut. F. Hughes.

2nd Lieut. W. R. Reay.
Lieut. E. H. Tyacke.

Wounded.

2nd Lieut. J. M. Lawther.
2nd Lieut. R. J. Webb.
Lieut. W. R. Fisher.
2nd Lieut. F. I. B. Parry.
2nd Lieut. G. L. Robbins.

2nd Lieut. H. P. Gardiner.
2nd Lieut. P. W. Moss.
Capt. C. G. W. Mackrell.
Lieut. G. D. Herron.

Missing.

Lieut. T. C. B. Udall. (Prisoner of war.)
2nd Lieut. R. H. Cocksedge. (Wounded and prisoner of war.)
Lieut. D. J. Coleman. (Prisoner of war.)

2nd Lieut. H. A. Wharton. (Wounded.)
2nd Lieut. A. S. Calvert. (Prisoner of war.)
Lieut. G. H. Coaton. (Prisoner of war.)

105th Field Coy. R.E.

Wounded.

2nd Lieut. A. L. Armstrong.

Missing.

2nd Lieut. R. H. Walmesley. (Prisoner of war.)
2nd Lieut. A. Atkinson.

Major V. W. Lloyd. (Wounded and prisoner of war.)

130th Field Coy. R.E.

Wounded.

2nd Lieut. J. S. Kennedy.

Missing.

2nd Lieut. W. L. Lax. (Wounded and prisoner of war.)

2nd Lieut. J. D. Eddy.

6th S.W. Borderers.

Killed.

Lt.-Col. L. C. W. Deane, D.S.O., M.C.

Wounded.

2nd Lieut. J. I. Parry.
Lieut. W. J. Kendrick.

Qr.-Mr. and Hon. Capt. A. Case.

Missing.

Lieut. H. Davies. (Prisoner of war.)
2nd Lieut. G. Carlyle. (Prisoner of war.)

2nd Lieut. H. R. Murray. (Prisoner of war.)
2nd Lieut. F. T. Kitchen.

R.A.M.C.

Wounded.

Lieut. W. J. Daly, M.O.R.C., Capt. A. H. Huycke, attd. 75th U.S.A., attd. 76th Field Amb.   Field Amb.

Missing.

Lt.-Col. H. B. Kelly, D.S.O.   Capt. C. Witts.
Major F. G. Lescher, M.C.   Lieut. A. S. Findlay.

25th Divl. Train, A.S.C.

Missing.

2nd Lieut. W. L. Mallarbar.

25th Divl. H. Qrs.

Missing.

Capt. G. Jennings. (Prisoner of war.)

7th Bde. H. Qrs.

Killed.

Capt. S. Hawkins, M.C.

Wounded.

Brig.-Gen. C. J. Griffin, D.S.O.

Missing.

Capt. R. P. Perrin, M.C. (Wounded and missing.)

Birthday Honours and Awards, June, 1918.

C.M.G.

Capt. and Bt. Lt.-Col. (T./Brig.-Gen.) H. K. Bethell, D.S.O. — 7th Hussars and Staff Commanding 74th Inf. Bde.

Major, Bt. Lt.-Col. (T./Brig.-Gen.) C. J. Griffin, D.S.O. — Lancashire Fus., Commanding 7th Inf. Brigade.

Major and Bt. Col. (T./Lt.-Col.) O. H. L. Nicholson, D.S.O. — G.S.O. 1, Staff, and W. Yorks. Regt.

D.S.O.

Capt. (A./Lt.-Col.) W. E. Williams .. — Middlesex Regt., attd. Cheshires.

MILITARY CROSS.

Lieut. T. Blackburn	11th Cheshire Regt.
2nd Lieut. (A./Lieut.) H. C. Briggs ..	R.F.A., attd. X/25 T.M.B.
P2nd Lieut. S. W. Boast	2nd South Lancs. Regt.
T./Lieut. (A./Capt.) C. A. Butcher, R.E.	H.Q., R.E., 25th Division.
T./Capt. K. D. Falconer, R.A.M.C. ..	Attd. 110th Bde., R.F.A.
Capt. C. A. Godfrey	9th Loyal N. Lancs. Regt.
Lieut. (T./Capt.) M. F. Horton, R.A...	H.Q. R.A., 25th Division.
T./Capt. A. H. Huycke, R.A.M.C. ..	75th Field Ambulance.
T./Capt. G. C. Meredith	10th Cheshire Regt.
T./Lieut. L. Nicholls, R.E.	25th Divl. Signal Coy.
Lieut. H. D. H. Padwick	9th Loyal N. Lancs. Regt.
2nd Lieut. E. G. Pullan	3rd Worcester Regt., attd. 25th Divl. Signal Coy.
Lieut. R. V. Reid	5th Battn., attd. 9th L.N. Lancs. Regt.
T./Lieut. (A./Capt.) S. F. Terry ..	1st Wiltshire Regt.
8198 T/R.S.M. T. S. Ross	2nd South Lancs. Regt.
T./Lieut. A. Tyler	25th Divl. Train, A.S.C.
Lieut. H. P. White	10th Cheshire Regt.

D.C.M.

52761 Sergt. (A./C.S.M.) F. Allen ..	11th Cheshire Regt.
50121 Sergt. J. Attridge	R.F.A., attd. X/25 T.M.B.
95926 C.S.M. H. Breeze, R.E.	106th Field Coy. R.E.
12882 C.S.M. J. F. Davies	3rd Worcester Regt.
16457 Btty. S.M. C. Ellis	" C " Bty., 110th Bde., R.F.A.
24595 Pte. W. D. Jones	8th Border Regt., attd. 75th T.M.B.
51326 L./Corpl. W. J. Lawson.. ..	25th Divl. Signal Coy. R.E.
12017 C.S.M. W. Lewis	1st Wiltshire Regt.
16441 Pte. (L./Corpl.) R. Morris ..	8th L.N. Lancs. Regt.
28147 R.S.M. W. G. Newton	9th L.N. Lancs. Regt.

MERITORIOUS SERVICE MEDAL.

313140 Spr. F. Allen, R.E.	25th Divl. Signal Coy.
T.S/7674 Whr. S. Sgt. W. Anwyl	25th Divl. Train, A.S.C.
T/19072 Whr.S.Sergt. J. Armitage	25th Divl. Train, A.S.C.
26908 Sergt. W. Barnett	11th Lancs. Fusiliers.
14605 Sergt. W. Bennett	10th Cheshire Regt.
7310 Sergt. (A./R.Q.M.S.) W. Bickley	3rd Worcesters, attd. 7th Bde. H.Q.
51282 Sergt. F. Birch	No. 3 Sect. 25th Divl. Signal Coy. R.E., attd. 75th Bde. H.Q.
30538 Staff-Sergt. F. G. Boxhall, R.A.M.C.	75th Field Ambulance.
235168 Pte. R. H. Burton	2nd South Lancs. Regt.
9362 Bty. Q.M.S. J. McCamley, M.M.	R. Irish R., attd. 74th T.M.B.
55004 Bomb. (A./Sergt.) G. Cockburn	R.A. (Clerks Section, R.G.A.), attd. H.Q. 25th D. Art.
50971 S./Sergt. J. Dale, R.A.M.C.	76th Field Ambulance.
6/17128 Sergt. D. Davies	6th South Wales Borderers.
6792 Sergt. A. Feltham..	1st Wiltshire Regiment.
71505 Bomb. (A./Sergt.) J. R. Forsyth	R.A. (Clerks Section, R.G.A.), attd. 25th Div. Art.
S/232705 Sergt. G. A. Griffin	A.S.C., Clerical Section, attd. 74th I. Bde.
56936 Corpl. G. Hodgkins	R.F.A., attd. Y/25 T.M.B.
65050 Sergt. E. Hodgson, R.E.	105th Field Coy. R.E.
18157 Corpl. S. Hughes..	R.F.A., attd. X/25 T.M.B.
30623 Sergt.-Major R. J. Ivins, R.A.M.C.	77th Field Ambulance.
T3/029815 Wheeler S/Sergt. W. Jones	25th Divl. Train, A.S.C.
9181 R.Q.M.S. F. V. Kearns	6th S.W. Borderers.
5793 R.Q.M.S. J. Knight	8th Border Regt.
16691 Sergt. T. H. Lea..	11th Cheshire Regt.
90019 Bty. Q.M.S. R. H. Looney	"C" Bty., 112th Bde., R.F.A.
S/19420 T/SSS.M. F. C. Manley, M.M.	A.S.C., attd. H.Q. 25th Div.
6727 C.S.M. W. Martin..	74th M.G. Coy.
164726 Spr. (A./2nd Corpl.) S. Mogridge	130th Field Coy. R.E.
2689 C.Q.M.S. T. B. Newton	2nd South Lancs. Regt.
8248 R.Q.M.S. G. Nuttall	11th Lancashire Fusiliers.
10271 R.Q.M.S. J. Quinn	3rd Worcesters.
23769 Sergt. L. Riggs	112th Bde. R.F.A., H.Q.
37583 Sergt. H. Smith	11th Lancashire Fusiliers.
12942 Sergt. W. Swinburne	8th Border Regt.
313146 2nd Corpl. (A./Corpl.) J. W. Taylor.	25th Div. Signal Coy., R.E.
63157 B.S.M.G. Theaker	"D" Bty., 110th Bde., R.F.A.
5526 Sergt. J. Walker	8th Border Regt.
9003 Sergt. G. Walters	1st Wiltshire Regt.
50815 Pte. J. White	11th Cheshire Regt.
4439 Sergt. G. Wicks	A.V.C., attd. 7th Bde.
14344 R.Q.M.S. H. Wood	10th Cheshire Regt.

MENTIONED IN DISPATCHES.

Lieut. (A./Major) A. Anderton, M C. .. 110th Bde., R.F.A.
2nd Lieut. (A./Capt.) G. R. G. Alston 112th Bde. R.F.A.
T./Lieut. (A./Capt.) W. W. Ashcroft .. 25th Battn. M.G. Corps.
Major (T./Lt.-Col.) J. B. Allsopp .. 8th South Lancs., attd. 2nd Battn.

14489 Corpl. J. Atherton .. .. 9th L.N. Lancs. Regt.
7721 Corpl. J. Airey .. .. .. 11th Lancashire Fusiliers.
Capt. (A./Lt.-Col.) C. W. Blackall .. 3rd Battn. E. Kent Regt., attd. 4th South Staff. Regt.
Capt. and Bt. Lt.-Col. (T./Brig.-Gen.) H. K. Bethell, D.S.O. 7th Hussars and Staff. Commanding 74th Inf. Bde.
14869 L./Sergt. J. Berry .. 8th Battn. Border Regt.
19843 Pte. (L./Corpl.) H. Carney .. 2nd South Lancs. Regt.
2nd Lieut. (A./Capt.) L. H. Cecil .. 11th K.R.R.C., attd. 7th T.M.B.)
Capt. J. D. Crichton .. .. .. 9th L.N. Lancs. Regt.
4959 R.Q.M.S. (A./R.S.M.) J. Crowe .. 3rd Worcester Regt.
2nd Lieut. (A./Capt.) T. L. David .. Yorks. and Lancs. (75th T.M.B.)
T./Capt. (A./Major) L. C. W. Deane, M.C. 6th S.W. Borderers.
2nd Lieut. A. W. Dean.. .. .. A.S.C. 25th Divl. Train.
Major (T./Lt.-Col.) R. J. Done, D.S.O., R.E. C.R.E., 25th Division.
2nd Lieut. A. Elliott, R.E. .. .. 105th Field Coy. R.E.
T./Lieut. (A./Capt.) P. A. Foy, M.C. .. 25th Div. Signal Coy. R.E.
S4/248429 Corpl. R. H. Gardner .. A.S.C., 25th Div. H.Q.
101765 Engr.-Clerk 2nd Corpl. (A./ Sergt.) G. E. Gardiner. R.E., H.Q., 25th Division, Lancs. Fusiliers.
Major, Bt. Lt.-Col. (T./Brig.-Gen.) C. J. Griffin, D.S.O. Commdg. 7th Inf. Bde.
Lieut. R. G. Goldie .. .. .. 1st L.N. Lancs., attd. 8th Battn.
Major Hon. W. E. Guinness, D.S.O. .. Suffolk Yeo. and Staff.
Capt. (A./Major) A. L. Harman, M.C. 110th Bde., R.F.A.
8542 Sergt. E. G. Harris .. .. 1st Wiltshire Regt.
6/19227 Sergt. G. Hemmings .. .. 6th S.W. Borderers.
Lieut. H. E. Howse .. .. .. 2nd South Lancs. Regt.
2nd Lieut. W R. Holmes .. .. 1st Wiltshire Regt.
S/26825 Corpl. (A./Sergt.) W. Hull, M.M. A.S.C., 25th D.H.Q.
51397 Sergt. C. H. Jefferson .. .. R.E. (H.Q. 25th Division).
5712 T./Sub-Condr. (A./Condr.) C. G. Journeaux A.O.C. H.Q. 25th Division.
T./Capt. S. O. Jones .. .. .. 112th Bde., R.F.A.
Lieut. (A./Major) F. G. Massey, M.C... 2nd New Zeal. R. Bde. (11th L. Fus.)
Major R. K. A. Macaulay, D.S.O. .. R.E., Commanding 130th Field Coy. R.E.
S.S. 6573 S.Q.M.S. A. E. Mirfin .. A.S.C., 25th D.H.Q. G.S.O. 1.

Major and Bt. Col. (T./Lt.-Col.) O. H.   Staff and W. Yorks. Regt.
  L. Nicholson, D.S.O.
2nd Lieut. W. A. Okes-Voysey   ..   A.S.C. 25th Div. Train.
Lieut. (A./Capt.) E. V. P. Parsons   ..   5th Battn. attd. 3rd Worcs.
                                     Regt.
7406 Sergt. W. Prior ..   ..   ..   1st Wilts., attd. 7th Bde. H.Q.
Lieut. S. E. Rumsey, M.C.   ..   ..   6th S.W. Borderers.
Capt. T. Rufus ..   ..   11th Lancs. Fus.
5701 Sergt. (A./C.S.M.) A. F. Sheppard   1st Wilts. (7th Bde. H Q.)
6877 Sergt. J. Smith ..   ..   ..   25th M.G. Corps.
8118 Sergt. R. C. Storey   ..   ..   25th Divl. Ammn. Col.
18129 Sergt. J. Thompson   ..   ..   25th Battn. M.G. Corps.
430266 Spr. P. Turner ..   ..   ..   25th Divl. Sig. Coy. R.E.
2nd Lieut. S. F. Trusler   ..   ..   6th South W. Borderers.
89850 R.S.M. E. Whitbread ..   ..   25th Divl. Ammn. Col.
Lieut. (A./Capt.) H. M. Wilkinson   ..   11th Cheshire Regt.
13247 C.Q.M.S. A. Yates   ..   ..   11th Cheshire Regt.
2nd Lieut. J. H. B. Young, M.C.   ..   10th Cheshire Regt.

PROMOTION TO THE RANK OF HONORARY MAJOR.

Qr.-Mr. and Hon. Capt. S. T. Boast,   2nd South Lancs. Regt.
  M.C., D.C.M.

French Honours.

LEGION D'HONNEUR (COMMANDEUR).
Major-General Sir E. G. T. Bainbridge, K.C.B.

LEGION D'HONNEUR (CHEVALIER).
Major (Brevet Lieut.-Col.) R. J. C.R.E., 25th Division.
Done, D.S.O.
T./Capt. (A./Major) A. R. Moir, 25th Batt., M.G. Corps.
M.C.
T./Major C. J. Lynam, M.C. .. R.E.

MÉDAILLE MILITAIRE.
16214 Pte. E. G. Keyes .. .. 25th Batt., M.G. Corps.

MÉDAILLE D'HONNEUR.
73408 Pte. H. Thackray .. .. 25th Batt., M.G. Corps.

CROIX DE GUERRE (WITH PALM).
Capt. (A./Major) A. L. Harman, R.F.A.
M.C.
Major (T./Lieut.-Col.) J. N. De la Royal Fusiliers, attd. Border Regt.
Perrelle, D.S.O., M.C.
40189 Pte. W. Hartwell .. .. Worcester Regt.
17177 Pte. A. Beard .. .. S.W. Borderers.
16214 Pte. E. G. Keyes .. .. M.G. Corps.
N2/153312 Pte. W. H. Campbell.. A.S.C., attd. R.A.M.C.
27963 Pte. T. Bell, D.C.M. .. Border Regt.
33263 Pte. H. Vaughan .. .. Border Regt.

CROIX DE GUERRE (WITH GOLD STAR).
T./Major A. Reid-Kellett .. S.W. Borderers.
Capt. W. B. Bagshawe, M.C. .. Bde. Major, 74th Bde.
17528 Pte. A. Pearce .. .. 6th Batt., S.W. Borderers.
73408 Pte. H. Thackray .. .. 25th Batt., M.G. Corps.
9100 Pte. R. Dixon .. .. Border Regt.
95203 Spr. R. Morton .. .. Royal Engineers.
15802 Q.M.S. J. A. Haddock .. Cheshire Regt.
15119 Pte. (A./Cpl.) R. Martin .. L.N. Lancs. Regt.

CROIX DE GUERRE (WITH SILVER STAR).
Capt. Sir F. V. L. Robinson, Bart., A.P.M., 25th Division.
M.C.
Capt. (A./Major) R. W. Cooper, M.C. D.A.Q.M.G., 25th Division.
Major (T./Lieut.-Col.) R. A. David- R.A.M.C.
son, D.S.O.
2nd Lieut. W. J. Bullock, M.M. .. Wilts Regt.
Major E. de W. H. Bradley, M.C... K.O.Y.L.I. (O.C. Signals).
43035 Pte. (A./Sgt.) D. J. James.. R.A.M.C.
39901 Pte. W. Lamb .. .. Cheshire Regt.
8298 A./C.S.M. F. Jowett.. .. Worcester Regt.

CROIX DE GUERRE (WITH BRONZE STAR).
S/19420 T./S.M. F. C. Manley, M.M. A.S.C., attd. H.Q., 25th Div.
5712 T./Sub-Cond. (A./Cond.) C. G. A.O.C., attd. H.Q., 25th Div.
Joirneaux.
24827 Sergt. W. G. Tallowin .. R.F.A.
13358 Sergt. W. O. Smith .. R.F.A.
56220 Sergt. T. W. Williams .. Sig. Coy.

PART II.

PART II.

THE middle of September the Divisional and Brigade Headquarters returned from England, and the 25th Division was reformed at St. Riquier, near Abbeville, with nine battalions from the British Divisions on the Italian front. The Divisional troops who had been attached to other formations from time to time during July, August, and September, also rejoined.

Towards the end of the month the Division moved by rail and route march to the 4th Army area near Amiens, and joined the XIIIth Corps in time to take part, on the 3rd and 4th October, in the hard fighting connected with the capture of the Beaurevoir position and the subsequent advance to Le Cateau. The 23rd and 24th October the Division was engaged in the capture of Pommereuil and the clearing of the Bois l'Eveque east of Le Cateau, and on the 4th November it carried through with brilliant success the passage of the Sambre Canal and the capture of Landrecies. The Divisional Artillery were in action almost continuously from the 8th August until the 11th November, covering in turn the 12th, 47th British, and 27th American Divisions until the arrival of the 25th Division with the XIIIth Corps.

In recognition of their services during these operations, officers and men of the Division have received :—

2 V.C.	113 M.C.
1 C.B.	56 D.C.M.
6 C.M.G.	448 Military Medals.
6 O.B.E.	75 Meritorious Service Medals.
26 D.S.O.	173 Mention in Despatches.

making a total since July, 1916, of 3,379 honours, including—

6 V.C.	517 M.C.
1 K.C.B.	310 D.C.M.
1 C.B.	1,742 Military Medals.
12 C.M.G.	124 Meritorious Service Medals.
6 O.B.E.	533 Mention in Despatches.
117 D.S.O.	

The losses during these latter operations had been comparatively slight—officers : 41 killed, 208 wounded, and 3 missing ; other ranks, 729 killed, 3,880 wounded, and 428 missing—making a very heavy total (excluding sick) since July, 1916, of 45,803 casualties, including officers : 413 killed, 1,427 wounded, and 234 missing ; other ranks, 5,354 killed, 28,290 wounded, and 10,085 missing, of whom the majority, especially during the Somme battles, are believed to have been either killed or wounded.

After the signing of the Armistice the Division moved back to billets in the Le Cateau area, and a fortnight later to an area east of Cambrai, where it was employed in salvage work. Demobilisation was in full swing by the middle of January, and by the end of March the despatch to England for discharge of all men enlisted before the 1st January, 1916, and the transfer of the remainder to other Divisions for the Army of Occupation had been completed. Later the cadres of all units returned to England to hand in their equipment.

So near the time it may be difficult to write of events in their true perspective. Due credit may have been omitted to some, and bare justice done to others. However, it is sincerely hoped that this very imperfect record of the wonderful achievements of both the old and new 25th Division may supply a connected account of the combined efforts of the many units and services concerned, and at the same time bear some testimony to the gallant conduct of all ranks and their fallen comrades of the 25th Division.

M. K.-S.

CAMBRAI,

5th March, 1919.

NOTE:—The establishment of the Division in July, 1916, was approximately 18,000, including—

12 battalions of infantry	12,000
R.F.A.	3,000
R.E., R.A.M.C., A.S.C., Pioneer Battalion ..	3,000

All Units were maintained at their full strength by means of reinforcement during 1916 and 1917. In December, 1917, the infantry were reduced by three battalions, and in February, 1918, the establishment of the remaining nine battalions was further reduced from 1,000 to 750 men. There are no figures available to show the exact number of reinforcements received by the Division during its service in France, but about 65,000 joined the Division to replace casualties and sick.

25th DIVISION.

Battle Order, 15th September, 1918.

COMMANDER..	..	MAJOR-GENERAL J. R. E. CHARLES, C B., D.S.O.
A.D.C. ..	..	Capt. Hon. G. St. V.-Harris, M.C. (wounded).
		2nd Lieut. G. A. C. Peter, R.F.A. 8.10.15.
A.D.C. ..	..	Capt. J. A. Reiss.
G.S.O. 1 ..	..	Lt.-Col. D. F. Anderson, D.S.O.
G.S.O. 2 ..	..	Major G. R. Dubs, M.C.
G.S.O. 3 ..	..	Capt. C. de Gaussen, R.E.
A.A. and Q.M.G.	..	Lt.-Col. Hon. E. P. J. Stourton, D.S.O.
D.A.A.G. ..	..	Major J. S. Fulton, M.C.
D.A.Q.M.G...	..	Major R. W. Cooper, M.C.
		Major H. M. Greenhill. 1.11.18.
A.D.M.S. ..	..	Col. H. N. Dunn, C.M.G., D.S.O., R.A.M.C. (wounded).
		Lt.-Col. A. E. Hamerton, C.M.G., D.S.O., R.A.M.C. 1.11.18.
D.A.D.M.S.	..	Major T. E. Dun, M.C., R.A.M.C.
D.A.D.V.S.	..	Major G. D. Norman, A.V.C.
D.A.D.O.S.	..	Major A. C. H. Eagles, M.C.
A.P.M. ..	..	Capt. Sir F. V. L. Robinson, Bart., M.C.

H.Q., R.A.—

COMMANDER	..	Brig.-Gen. K. J. KINCAID-SMITH, C.M.G., D.S.O., R.A.
Bde. Major	..	Major N. M. McLeod, D.S.O., M.C., R.A.
Staff Captain	..	Capt. M. F. Horton, M.C., R.A.
Staff Lieutenant..		Lieut. G. A. Keay, R.A.

H.Q., R.E.—

COMMANDER	..	Lt.-Col. R. S. DONE, D.S.O., R.E.
Adjutant	..	Capt. C. A. Butcher, M.C., R.E.
O.C. 25th Div. Sig. Co.		Major W. M. Keasey, M.C., R.E.
110th Brigade, R.F.A.	..	Lt.-Col. K. E. Milford, D.S.O., R.A.
112th Brigade, R.F.A.	..	Lt.-Col. L. H. Queripel, C.M.G., D.S.O., R.A.
Divl. Ammn. Col. ..	..	Lt.-Col. C. S. Hope-Johnson.
H.Q., T.M. Group ..	..	Capt. G. W. Nowell Usticke, M.C.
105th Field Coy., R.E.	..	Major F. W. Richards, M.C.
106th Field Coy., R.E.	..	Major C. G. J. Lynam, M.C
130th Field Coy., R.E.	..	Major F. E. Musgrave, M.C.
75th Field Ambulance	..	Lt.-Col. H. A. Davidson, D.S.O.
76th Field Ambulance	..	Lt.-Col. D. Large, D.S.O., M.C.
77th Field Ambulance	..	Lt.-Col. H. H. Leeson, M.C.
25th Bn. M.G. Corps	..	Lt.-Col. W. T. Raikes, M.C.
H.Q., Divl. Train ..	..	Lt.-Col. F. B. Lord, D.S.O.
Senior Supply Officer	..	Major C. V. Ewart.
11th Bn. S. Lancs. (Pioneers)		Major C. C. Champion, D S.O

T/MAJOR-GENERAL J. R. E. CHARLES, C.B , C.M.G.,
D.S.O., R.E.

7th INFANTRY BRIGADE.

COMMANDER	..	Brig.-Gen. C. J. HICKIE.
Brigade Major	..	Capt. R. M. Burmann, D.S.O., M.C. (killed).
		Capt. W. G. P.dsley. 29.10.18.
Staff Captain	..	Capt. H. P. White, M.C.
9th Devons	.. ..	.. Lt.-Col. H. I. Storey, D.S.O.
20th Manchesters	..	.. Lt.-Col. C. S. Burt, D.S.O. (wounded).
21st Manchesters	..	.. Lt.-Col. C. E. N. Lomax, M.C.

74th INFANTRY BRIGADE.

COMMANDER	..	Brig.-Gen. H. M. CRAIGIE HALKETT, D.S.O.
Brigade Major	..	Capt. W. B. Bagshaw, M.C.
Staff Captain	..	Capt. C. A. Godfrey, M.C.
9th Yorks.	.. ..	.. Lt.-Col. R. S. Hart, D.S.O.
11th Notts and Derbys		.. Lt.-Col. H. N. Young, D.S.O. (killed).
13th Durham L.I.	..	.. Lt.-Col. D. H. Clarke, D.S.O., M.C. (wounded).

75th INFANTRY BRIGADE.

COMMANDER	..	Brig.-Gen. M. E. RICHARDSON, D.S.O.
		Brig.-Gn. C. W. Frizell, D.S.O., M.C. 12.10.18.
Brigade Major	..	Capt. I. S. O. Playfair, D.S.O., M.C., R.E.
Staff Captain	..	Capt. F. Treacher, M.C.
1/8th Warwicks	..	.. Lt.-Col. P. H. Whitehouse.
1/5th Gloucesters	..	.. Lt.-Col. D. Lewis, D.S.O., M.C.
1/8th Worcesters	..	.. Lt.-Col. H. T. Clarke.

CHAPTER I.

Battle of the 100 Days.

LE CATEAU.

A FEW days after their arrival in the new area, north-west of Hesdin, the Divisional and Brigade Head-quarters, with cadres of their respective battalions, proceeded to Aldershot with a view to the Infantry units being more speedily provided with reinforcements direct from the training centres in England. The Divisional troops, including the Artillery, 25th Battn. Machine Gun Corps, Engineers, Signal Company, Field Ambulances, and the Divisional Train, A.S.C., remained behind with Headquarters at Royon, the majority of these units being attached from time to time, to other formations in the front line.

From about the middle of July, the Infantry units of the Division now in England began to receive a steady stream of recruits and reinforcements, so that it was hoped that within a few weeks the Division would once more be fit to take the field. Large numbers of these men were subse-quently rejected by the medical authorities as unfit for service in the field, with the result that the beginning of September found the battalions with a strength considerably below their full establishment. A few days later the 75th Infantry Brigade was made up to full strength by transferring men from other units; its number was changed to the 236th Infantry Brigade, and it was warned for service in North Russia. On the 15th September, the Divisional and Brigade Headquarters (7th and 74th Brigades) returned to France.

In the area a few miles east of Abbeville, with Divisional Headquarters at St. Riquier, the 25th Division was now re-formed under the command of Major-General J. R. E. Charles, C.B., D.S.O. All Divisional troops which had been tem-porarily attached to other formations were gradually brought back, except the Divisional Artillery, who were in action with the IIIrd Corps and the 25th Battn. Machine Gun Corps, who were with the 59th Division. These rejoined the 25th

Division in the line later on in October. On the 17th, 18th, and 19th September, nine battalions arrived from the British Corps on the Italian front. The 9th Devons, 20th and 21st Manchesters from the 7th Division formed the 7th Brigade. The 9th Yorks, 11th Sherwood Foresters, and 13th Durham Light Infantry from the 23rd Division formed the 74th Brigade, and the 1/8th R. Warwicks, 1/5th Gloucesters, and 1/8th Worcesters from the 48th Division formed the 75th Brigade, for which a new Headquarters was provided.

Fortunate indeed was the 25th Division to be made up with such splendid battalions. After taking part in the severe fighting, along the British front in 1916 and 1917, these battalions had been transferred with their Divisions to the Italian front in November, 1917. On the 15th June they helped to break up the Austrian attacks on the Asiago plateau, but otherwise trench warfare on the Italian front had been comparatively quiet. With men of the best fighting age, and led by experienced officers, these battalions were able to take part with conspicuous success in the heavy fighting during October, and fully justified the high reputation which they held amongst their old friends in the Divisions with whom they had been associated so long and whom they were naturally loath to leave.

The situation on the Western front had undergone a remarkable change since the anxious days of the German offensive in March and April. On the 26th March, stress of battle had produced unity of command of the Allied Forces, and Marshal Foch henceforth controlled operations along the whole front. The great and increasing stream of American troops allowed training divisions to be formed as a support behind the thin British line, and by the middle of August the American Armies had successfully redressed the balance of man power in favour of the Allied powers.

The great German attacks south of Arras, between the Lys and La Bassee and along the Aisne in Champagne, though spectacular in effect and costly in men and material to British and French troops (including 180,000 British and French prisoners and over 2,000 guns), had been brought to a standstill, and had failed to produce any decisive results. In all these battles, the part played by the 25th Division has been briefly recorded in previous chapters ; very severe casualties were sustained by the Division, but the Germans in every case were forced to pay an equally heavy price for their successes.

Here it may be of interest to quote the words of Captain von Schwink, Staff Officer with the 17th German Army. This officer had been with General von Below in Italy, and accompanied him to France, where he took over command of the German Army on the Arras front. Captain von Schwink in his lecture is reported to have said " that they were all much impressed by the fighting qualities of the 3rd British Army, especially of the 25th Division, which had successfully held up five German divisions on the 21st March."

The failure of the German attempt to broaden their salient south-west of Soissons and their attack east and west of Rheims on the 15th July, marked clearly the turning point in the fortunes of the Allied armies. The successful defence of the line east of Rheims, by General Gouraud's French army, left at the disposal of Marshal Foch, troops with which he was able to carry out a few days later the great counter-attack along the western flank of the German salient stretching to the Marne. On a front of 27 miles, the main attack of French divisions with two British divisions and American troops came as a complete surprise to the enemy, who by the end of July were once more back on the Aisne. This success was quickly followed by other blows, and the great German reserves massed in the north for their final effort to capture the Channel ports were used up piecemeal against the Allied attacks.

On the 8th August the 4th British Army delivered a most successful surprise attack north-east of Amiens, taking 21,850 prisoners and 400 guns. Troops were brought up with the greatest possible secrecy. Of the Canadian Corps, probably the finest shock troops in the world, two battalions were put in the line on the Ypres sector for a night, their arrival being no doubt duly chronicled by the enemy ; at the same time the remainder of the Canadian Corps was concentrated behind Amiens moving only by night, so that the Germans were totally unaware of their presence on this sector until the attack actually took place. A few days later the 1st French Army attacked on the right, and the 21st August the 3rd British Army on the left towards Bapaume, capturing another 34,250 prisoners and 270 guns. On the 26th August the 1st British Army attacked east of Arras, and by the middle of September the Germans were back on the Hindenburg line. Meanwhile, the American troops drove in the famous salient of St. Mihiel, and continued their advance in the Argonne. On the 18th September the 3rd and 4th British Armies captured the line running through Epehy in front of the main Hindenburg line, which now ran through Cambrai and along the Canal du Nord, taking 18,850 prisoners and 200 guns. On the 27th September a further advance was made by the 1st, 3rd, and 4th British Armies on a 50-miles front from the Sensee to St. Quentin, capturing 36,500 prisoners and 380 guns, and a few days later, the 2nd Army, with the Belgians to the north, cleared the sector from Ypres to the sea.

In the meantime, the 25th Division, which had completed its reorganisation and been joined by the Divisional troops in the St. Riquier area near Abbeville, now moved by rail on the 24th September to the XIIIth Corps, 4th Army, and was billeted in the area midway between Albert and Amiens on the right bank of the Ancre, with Divisional Headquarters at Hennencourt. In this area the villages had suffered considerably during the recent fighting, but a few remained habitable and offered some sort of accommodation and cover for the troops. Nearer Albert and in the town itself no roof remained, and everywhere was to be seen the same scenes of utter desolation as throughout the old Somme battlefields.

During the next few days the Division moved up by route march to Templeux le Guerrard, just behind the front line, and along with the 66th, 50th and 18th Divisions of General Morland's XIIIth Corps, relieved Divisions of the IIIrd Corps, on the left of the 4th Army. Operations by the 4th Army on the 27th September with the IXth Corps, 2nd American Corps, the 3rd Corps and the Australians had carried the British advance on this front still further; from the north of St. Quentin the line ran west of the village of Beaurevoir, joining up with the Vth Corps 3rd Army west of Le Catelet; on the right it was in touch with troops of the 1st French Army near St. Quentin.

The main Hindenburg line, running north and south through Bellicourt had been the scene of heavy fighting in which British, American and Australian troops had all rendered fine service. The 2nd Australian Division had successfully forced the Maisnieres-Beaurevoir line 4 to 5 miles behind the main Hindenburg line, but had not secured the village of Beaurevoir or the high ground beyond the Guisancourt Farm, about 2 miles to the north-west.

The capture of these positions was necessary to enable artillery to be brought up and preparations to be made for another advance along the British front. This was the first task allotted to the 25th Division.

On the 3rd October, the 7th, 74th and 75th Infantry Brigade were concentrated at Ronssoy, Moislains and Nurlu respectively, with Divisional Headquarters at Combles. The same afternoon, Brig.-Gen. Hickie's 7th Brigade marched up to Quennimont Farm and after dark relieved the 5th and 7th Australian Brigades in the line several hundred yards west of Beaurevoir village. Brig.-Gen. Craigie Halkett's 74th Brigade marched up to Mont St. Martin in support with Brig.-Gen. Frizell's 75th Brigade at St. Emilee, a few miles behind in reserve. The 21st Battalion Manchesters (7th Brigade) was placed temporarily at the disposal of the 50th Division on the left, but rejoined its own brigade the same evening. Late in the afternoon, orders were received to continue on 4th October the attack started by the Australians on the 3rd and to complete the capture of Beaurevoir and the high ground beyond it.

The relief was somewhat difficult owing to the uncertainty as to the exact position of the front line held by the Australian troops after the fighting the previous day, and also the unavoidable lack of time for reconnaissance of the ground to be taken over. It was, however, finally completed before daybreak along a line from the Canal des Torrens to southwest of Guisancourt Farm, altogether about 3,800 yards. The Brigade attacked at once, with the 20th Manchesters on the right, the 9th Devons on the left, and 21st Manchesters in support.

The German position was very strong and well chosen, giving excellent command over absolutely open and exposed ground with facilities for hiding large numbers of machine guns in farm buildings, houses and along the railway, and was defended by the 121st Division and troops of the 204th, 119th and 2nd Guard Divisions. It was intended to capture the high ground by working round Beaurevoir village, which was to be continuously bombarded and then subsequently mopped up. The 20th Manchesters attacked with A, B, C and

D) companies, commanded by Lieut. H. S. Painter, M.C.;
Captain F. Nicholls, M.C.; Captain A. G. N. Dixey, M.C.;
and Captain C. A. Forsyth, M.M. (wounded), succeeded by
Captain J. Waring, M.C. The battalion started off well
and made good progress, but were soon held up by very
heavy machine-gun fire from Beaurevoir Cemetery to
Beaurevoir Mill.

Lt.-Col. C. S. Burt, D.S.O., was wounded early in the
fight and Major Gemmell took command. Captain Dempsey
as adjutant and Captain Nicholls did splendid work in a very
difficult situation ; the latter led his company to their objective
and later, finding both flanks unprotected, he effected a
most skilful withdrawal. C.S.M. Perry, when all his officers
had become casualties, commanded his Company with great
skill, and Corpl. Mills did most effective work with his Lewis
gun section, both during the attack and also whilst covering
the withdrawal, until he himself was wounded. Pte. Summer-
scales distinguished himself by going back to Beaurevoir
village, through the enemy's barrage, in order to gain information, and Private Shaw as a stretcher-bearer was conspicuous for his courage in attending to the wounded under
heavy fire. All received decorations.

The 9th Devons on the left attacked with the 1st, 2nd, 3rd
and 4th Coys., commanded by Capt. C. Stewart, Capt. J. W.
Palmer, Capt. R. O. Schuh, M.C., and Lieut. H. C. Wilson.
Owing to the greater difficulty attending the relief of the
Australians the previous night, on this portion of the line,
and the lateness of the receipt of the orders for the attack,
the battalion did not move forward before 7.30 a.m. It soon
gained a footing in Bellevue Farm, but was driven back by
a German counter-attack.

Sergt. Wood led his platoon with great skill and gallantry.
Pte. Vigg did excellent work with his Lewis gun, and it was
largely owing to his covering fire that two platoons, which
were in danger of being cut off, managed to withdraw.
Pte. Hooper, both on this and other occasions performed
fine service as a stretcher-bearer under heavy fire.

During the day casualties were heavy, especially on the
left, but the difficulties of the task allotted to the Division
and the importance of the position to the German defence
made them inevitable. Orders were received to continue
operations on the 5th October, as the early capture of

Beaurevoir was essential as a preliminary to an attack on a very large scale which was contemplated for 7th October.

Accordingly, the 74th Brigade moved up during the evening and took over half the front now held by the battalion of the 7th Brigade with the intention of resuming the attack the next morning. The 75th Brigade also moved up to Quennemont Farm, sending the 1/8th Warwicks to Lormisset.

At 6 a.m., the 5th October, the two Brigades went forward. On the right, the 21st Manchesters with A, B, C and D Coys., commanded by 2nd Lieut. R. A. Tresise, D.C.M., Major E. W. Walker, M.C. (wounded), Captain J. W. Bell, M.C., and Lieut. G. H. Tomkinson, M.C. (wounded), respectively. On the left, the 74th Brigade had all three battalions in the front line. The 9th Yorks attacked with A, B, C and D Coys., commanded by Capt. W. L. Blow, M.C., Lieut. G. M. Wolstenholme, M.C. (killed), Capt. W. F. Greenwood, M.C. (wounded), and Lieut. C. Read (killed). The 13th Durham Light Infantry attacked with A, B, C and D Coys., commanded by Capt. I. Bewley, M.C., Capt. C. R. Chapman (wounded), succeeded by Lieut. R. S. F. Mitchell, M.C., 2nd Lieut. R. H. Farrier, M.C., and Lieut. F. L. F. Rees, M.C. (wounded).

The 11th Sherwood Foresters attacked with A, B, C and D companies, commanded by Lieut. O. R. Orchard, Capt. C. W. Bartlets, M.C., Capt. H. A. Watts, M.C. (wounded), succeeded by Lieut. C. H. Rose and Capt. R. W. Clark, M.C. (wounded), succeeded by Lieut. W. A. Wilson.

The attack commenced well, especially on the flanks where good progress was made north of the village of Beaurevoir. The Germans at once launched a strong counter-attack, supported by large numbers of machine guns, and succeeded in forcing back our troops once more to their original line, except in the centre at Bellevue Farm which was successfully held by men of " A " Coy., 9th Yorkshire Regiment. Two tanks gave some assistance in Beaurevoir village, which was entered by a party of men under Lieut. Redhead, M.C., 21st Manchesters, but who were eventually forced to withdraw to the railway cutting south of the village. Later, he joined a second attack by the 75th Brigade and did some splendid work with his men. Sergt. Fitzpatrick, when his platoon commander was wounded, led an attack on a German machine gun and killed the crew. L./Corpl. Carr was badly wounded whilst carrying an important message, but gallantly crawled along for another 1,000 yards until able to deliver it, whilst Pte. Wood, Pte. Mason and Pte. Edwards on this and other occasions showed great courage as runners under heavy fire. Pte. Hudson, employed as a stretcher-bearer, repeatedly attended to the wounded with a complete disregard for his own safety, and all received decorations.

Throughout the morning the difficulties of communication, the uncertainty of the situation as regards the progress and exact position of the attacking troops, rendered the task of the Artillery extremely difficult and made it impossible for the guns to give the Infantry adequate support owing to the danger of shelling our own men. Captain Blow, 9th Yorks, led " A " Company with great skill and gallantry, capturing Bellevue Farm and 30 prisoners ; 2nd Lieut. Sutliff, 2nd Lieut. Taylor and C.S.M. Goodison, when their company commanders were killed, themselves took command and showed fine qualities of leadership in the handling of their respective companies. Corpl. Connell, with a party of men attacked and captured a strong point, whilst Pte. Cannings himself captured a machine gun which was holding up the advance, being wounded during the fight. With the 13th Durham Light Infantry, Lt.-Col. Clarke was unfortunately wounded early in the fight and Capt. Greenwood assumed command. 2nd Lieut. Farrier led " C " Company throughout the attack, and on several occasions saved the situation by his prompt action. 2nd Lieut. Bannerman and 2nd Lieut. Dewar also displayed good leadership when their company commanders were wounded. Pte. Clark, M.M., employed as a stretcher-bearer, was conspicuous for his bravery in bringing back wounded when his company temporarily retired, whilst Pte. Crossley with his Lewis gun and Pte. Russell as a runner, showed a fine example to the other men of their unit. All received decorations.

At 11 a.m., A and C Coys., 1/8th R. Warwicks, commanded by Capt. E. S. C. Vaughan and Capt. J. Richards, made a second attempt to capture Guisancourt Farm. B and D Coys., commanded by 2nd Lieut. P. Lowe, M.C., and Capt. C. W. McFarlane, being in reserve about a mile behind. The attacking companies were at once met with heavy machine-gun fire and were unable to get across the open ground where every movement was in full view of the enemy.

During the afternoon the remainder of the 75th Brigade was brought up, and at 6.30 p.m., launched a third and successful attack against Beaurevoir village. The 1/5th Gloucesters with A, B, C and D companies, commanded by Lieut. G. W. E. Seago, Capt. R. de W. Rogers, Capt. F. G. Hill, M.C., and Lieut. P. A. Morfey, M.C., and the 1/8th Worcesters on the left with A, B, C and D companies, commanded by Capt. G. L. Watkinson, M.C., Capt. G. H. Smith, M.C., Capt. J. O. Walford and Lieut. T. L. Jones, M.C. (wounded), succeeded by 2nd Lieut. E. Wedgbury, M.C., D.C.M., M.M., went through the front line of the 7th and 74th Brigades on a front of about 2,000 yards. The Artillery barrage was good and the enemy were completely taken by surprise. The village was quickly over-run and the 1/5th Gloucesters, not waiting for the barrage to lift, got right through, taking most of the garrison prisoners. Lt.-Col. Lewis, D.S.O., M.C., gained the distinction of a Bar to his D.S.O., for the able manner in which he organized and carried out the attack. Capt. R. de W. Rogers led " B " Coy. with great dash and successfully organized a defensive position on the far side of the village. Later on, during the advance to Le Cateau, he was severely wounded whilst commanding his Company. Capt. Hill and Lieut. Morfey with their companies rendered splendid service throughout the attack and 2nd Lieut. Cox took over a patrol in the face of heavy machine-gun fire. Pte. Iles, as a Ground Scout for his platoon, behaved in a most gallant manner and L./Sergt. Hewson, though wounded, rushed a house with his section and captured a machine gun and its crew. Sergt. Edwards and Sergt. Packer, when their officers were wounded, commanded their men with great ability, the former being in charge of a post on the right flank during the night.

On the left, the 1/8th Worcesters, whilst waiting for the Artillery bombardment to lift, came under heavy machine-gun fire from some pits and houses on the western side of the village. This was dealt with, however, by the prompt action of 2nd Lieut. Wedgbury who worked round the right flank with his platoon and attacked the enemy from the rear, capturing a machine gun and 36 prisoners. 2nd Lieut. Barber also led his platoon with great skill and dash through the village. Lieut. Watkinson with " A " Coy. captured a hundred prisoners and two machine guns and later, when the other Company Commanders were wounded, he took command and organized the defence of the far side of the village. C.S.M. Leighton showed the greatest coolness and bravery throughout. Corpl. Coleman, M.M., in command of his platoon, and Sergt. Timmins rendered splendid service in consolidating along their objective, and Pte. Turner, when his platoon was held up by a hidden machine gun, scouted forward regardless of danger. L./Corpl. Smith did valuable work in leading forward patrols whilst the situation on the flanks was still uncertain, and Pte. Steer as a runner carried several messages under heavy shell fire. All received decorations.

Meanwhile, troops of the 7th Brigade had captured the whole of Beaurevoir Cemetery on the right, though their further advance was rendered impossible (without artillery preparation) by machine-gun fire from Ponchaux village, about 2,000 yards to the north-east. It was remarkable how rapidly the troops " dug themselves in," showing that trench warfare had at any rate taught the value of getting cover as quickly as possible. On the left, troops of the 74th Brigade made another attempt to reach the high ground of Guisancourt Farm, but were again unsuccessful.

At 4.10 a.m., the following morning, the 6th October, A and C Coys., 1/8th R. Warwicks, commanded by Captain Richards, and A and D Coys., 11th Sherwood Foresters, made a final attack on the Farm. Brig.-Gen. Craigie Halkett personally directed the attack until his men were finally established in possession of the farm, and secure against any counter-attack. Posts were soon established north and east of the farm, and at the same time the line was straightened out, and parties pushed forward in the valley between Beaurevoir and Guisancourt Farm. 2nd Lieut. Brown, with two sections, rushed one of the main defences of the farm, capturing 3 machine guns and 17 prisoners ; subsequently, he beat off several determined counter-attacks. Pte. Hazeldon did excellent work with some German bombs during the morning, and Pte. Swift, Pte. Sharp and Pte. Reeves as runners, performed their duties with the greatest gallantry, the former being wounded a few days later whilst carrying a message. Pte. Hedges and Cpl. Harris did excellent work with their Lewis guns, the latter successfully driving off a counter-attack. L./Cpl. Gardiner led his section with great dash throughout, and Sergt. Moulding, after the Coy. Sergt.-Major had been killed, set a splendid example to his men, and all received decorations. With the 11th Sherwood Foresters, Capt. Bird, as Adjutant, did useful work in establishing a strong point on the flank of the battalion at a critical moment. Capt. Watts led " C " Coy. to their final objective with great skill and energy ; later on, he reconnoitred, with a patrol, some high ground about 800 yards in front of the line, and succeeded in getting back with valuable information. Pte. Sutherland and Pte. Swindle did splendid work on this and other occasions with their Lewis guns, whilst Sergt. Moss, in charge of his two Lewis guns, held his ground at a critical moment on the flank of the battalion. Cpl. Collins won his D.C.M. for a fine display of initiative and leadership ; being with a carrying party and seeing the situation rather critical, he rushed forward to the firing line with all the men he could get together. Pte. J. Smith gallantly fetched in two wounded men who were lying only 50 yards from a German machine-gun post, and Pte. Whitlock, another stretcher bearer, was conspicuous for his courage in attending to the wounded under fire. Pte. Horner, Pte. Heath and Pte. N. S. Smith on several occasions took messages of great importance, through machine-gun fire, the latter being wounded during the journey, and all received well earned decorations.

During the 6th and 7th October, the line was perceptibly advanced to the north of Beaurevoir, but no further major operations took place, though preparations were made for a further advance along the whole British front on the 8th October. In the meantime, the 2nd Australian Division on the right, and the 50th Division on the left, had pushed well forward, encountering but little opposition in their advance. The artillery moved up to positions in the valley east of Guisancourt Farm and Beaurevoir, and the troops were rested as much as possible after their strenuous fighting of the past few days, though those actually in the line were heavily shelled during these two days, and consequently had very little opportunity for rest before continuing operations.

About this time, old members of the Division received a visit from their former chief, Maj.-Gen. Sir Guy Bainbridge, K.C.B., who, through two years of strenuous war, had won the esteem and affection of all ranks under his command.

Constant and unfailing efforts to promote the welfare of his troops had led both officers and men to regard their Commander as a personal friend, and all were unfeignedly glad to welcome him.

The advance made by the Division, though only some 3,000 yards in depth, had been in face of great difficulties, considerably increased by the lack of time for previous reconnaissance of the ground by the Regimental Officers, which proved a serious handicap in organizing the attack. The German position was extremely strong and well chosen, and had also been strongly wired. It was stubbornly defended by troops provided with quantities of machine guns, and whose morale, though somewhat weakened by their defeat in the Hindenburg line the previous week, was still good. Casualties sustained by the Division were heavy, but were inevitable under the circumstances; 508 Germans, including 5 officers were taken prisoners.

8th OCTOBER.

The evening of the 7th October, the Division held the line with all three brigades in the front line in touch on the right with the 30th American Division of the 2nd American Corps, who had just finished their relief of the Australian Corps. The 7th Brigade had 9th Devons in front, 21st Manchesters in support, and 20th Manchesters in reserve, with one company on the right of the 21st Manchesters acting as liaison troops with the Americans. The 75th Brigade in centre, with 1/5th Gloucesters and 1/8th Worcesters in front, and 1/8th R. Warwicks in support, and the 74th Brigade, with all 3 Battalions, 9th Yorks, 13th Durham L.I. and 11th Sherwood Foresters in the front line, joining up with the 50th Division just north of Guisancourt Farm.

Before daybreak, the 8th October, the 9th Devons extended their front to the south, and took over about 200 yards from the 30th American Division; at the same time the 66th Division, under Maj.-Gen. Bethell, lately commanding the 74th Brigade, passed through the 75th and 74th Brigades and formed up on the left of the 9th Devons, the two brigades marching back to their assembly positions about 2½ miles behind the front line, the 75th Brigade in support in Assegai Valley, and the 74th Brigade in Corps reserve. The transport

L

of all three brigades was brought up so as to be able to march immediately in rear of its brigade.

At 5.10 a.m., the 4th Army moved forward to the attack ; IXth Corps on the right, 2nd American Corps and XIIIth Corps joining up with Vth Corps, 3rd Army on the left ; the XIIIth Corps with 25th, 66th and 50th Divisions in front, and troops of the 1st Cavalry Division in close support. The 25th Division went forward with the 9th Devons (7th Brigade) on a front of about 1,000 yards, followed by the 21st Manchesters in support about 800 yards behind, and the 20th Manchesters another 800 yards behind in reserve. The advance was covered by an overhead machine gun barrage, and the 25th Divisional Artillery, with 2 Army Brigades (the 86th and 104th Army Brigades, R.F.A.), making 72 field guns and 18 howitzers, whilst the heavy artillery bombarded selected points. The artillery barrage crept forward at the rate of 100 yards per 3 minutes for the first 1,200 yards, and then slowed down to 100 yards per 4 minutes.

Across undulating down land, with practically no wire or other obstacles, the attack went well and by 7.20 a.m., the 9th Devons had advanced about $2\frac{1}{2}$ miles and reached the first objective. During the early morning the mist was very thick which caused some difficulty in keeping direction, but on the whole was undoubtedly in favour of the British troops. The enemy in Ponchaux did not give much trouble, whilst two machine guns from Bronx Farm were quickly rushed ; tanks gave great assistance, including an American tank from the right flank which had been clearing up machine gun posts in Sonia Wood with much success. About 500 prisoners were captured and large numbers of dead Germans were lying about, whilst our own casualties were comparatively slight. On the right and left, the 30th American and 66th Divisions reached their first objective about the same time. Lt.-Col. Storey, D.S.O., won a bar to his D.S.O., for the fine qualities of leadership which he displayed in carrying through the attack. 2nd Lieut. Manley, in command of No. 2 Coy., led his men with great skill to their final objective, whilst Capt. Schuh, M.C., in support with No. 1 Coy., successfully cleared up several machine gun posts during the advance. 2nd Lieut. Jacob set a fine example to his men, whilst Corpl. Phelps and Corpl. Pearson both won the D.C.M. for the manner in which they rallied and commanded their companies when all the Officers and other N.C.Os. had become casualties. Sergt. de Att and Sergt. Pike, M.M., did fine work in command of their platoons, the former being wounded three times during the day. Pte. Attis organized a small party on his own account, and whilst mopping up the village, captured 2 machine guns and 27 prisoners. Pte. Brice, Pte. Courtney, L./Cpl. Meagre and Pte. Osmond all did most effective work with their Lewis guns, the latter practically clearing the way for his platoon which ultimately captured 2 machine guns and about 100 prisoners, whilst L./Cpl. White and Corpl. Cockran led their platoons with great dash when their commanders became casualties. All received decorations.

After the capture of their first objective, the artillery barrage halted for half-an-hour on a line about 300 yards in front of the Devons ; the further advance to their second objective was not made under a regular barrage, but the leading battalion was covered by the 112th Brigade, R.F.A. Of four whippet tanks, which during the early morning had kept well up with the attacking infantry, two were blown up by a German field gun, but the others were most useful. The brigade continued its advance with the 21st Manchesters and the 20th Manchesters in support, the Devons remaining for the present on the first objective for its defence in case of a counter-attack. A section of heavy tanks, which had moved about 1,500 yards in rear of the attacking infantry, now pushed on to Serain Farm and north-west into Serain, where they did splendid work in helping to clear the village. The 20th Manchesters throughout kept close touch with the 30th American Division on the right flank, providing liaison posts at all important points, especially on the northern edge of Premont village. The advance was well maintained, and by 9.30 a.m., the 21st Manchesters had reached the second objective, roughly a distance of 4½ miles in 4½ hours, in touch with the 66th Division who had been equally successful in maintaining their advance on the left. Lt.-Col. C. E. Lomax, M.C., displayed great gallantry at the head of his battalion, and it was largely owing to his leadership that the second objective was reached with so little loss. Capt. Bell, M.C., with " C " Coy., was responsible for the right flank of the battalion during the advance, and very skilfully organized an attack on a machine gun post which was causing much trouble, whilst Capt. Orgill, M.C., as Adjutant, was invaluable in the organization and arrangements for the battalion on this and many other occasions. C.S.M. Smith, M.M., showed the greatest gallantry when his company was held up by a machine gun post on the flank, and it was mainly owing to him that his company was able to get into touch with the Americans on the right, and eventually capture the post. Pte. Flood and Corpl. Graham did good work with their men in face of heavy machine gun fire, whilst C.S.M. Lucy, M.C., D.C.M., Sergt. Hayward, M.M., and Sergt. Longson all set a splendid example of cheerfulness and courage to their companies throughout, and all received well-earned decorations

With the 20th Manchesters, Maj. J. S. Gemmell, M.C., showed great initiative in dealing with machine gun posts on the right flank of the brigade during the advance, whilst Capt. Llewellyn and Capt. Nicholls both did excellent work in command of their companies. Pte. Cassidy distinguished himself by rushing a machine gun and taking 7 prisoners, whilst Pte. Betteley invariably did most effective work with his Lewis gun ; on this occasion he successfully covered the advance of his company and enabled them to rush Foal Copse. Sergt. Evans and Sergt. Bradbury as Coy. Sergt. Major, were invaluable in carrying out re-organization of their men during the advance near Bronx farm. Pte. Ellis, Pte. S. Taylor and Pte. H. Taylor were all conspicuous for their courage in taking messages across ground swept by fire, and Pte. Bradley, when his company was held up from Foal Copse, gallantly went out to explain the situation to a " tank " commander, and to guide the tank to their assistance.

During the morning, the 1/8th R. Warwicks (75th Brigade) marched up to Ponchaux and relieved the 20th Manchesters holding liaison points with the American troops, whilst early in the afternoon the remainder of the 75th Brigade moved to Ponchaux along with Divisional Headquarters.

At 4 30 p.m., the 66th Division pushed out posts another mile in advance of the original objective in order to occupy the high ground in front of Serain, the 7th Brigade conforming to their advance. By evening, the Divisional front was held by the 7th Brigade with the 21st Manchesters and 20th Manchesters in front with the 9th Devons in support ; at the same time the 7th Brigade front was extended on the right by taking over about 1,000 yards from the Americans. The 75th Brigade, with its Headquarters at Ponchaux, had the

1/5th Gloucesters at Sonia Wood some 2½ miles behind the front with the 1/8th R. Warwicks spread out in depth on the right flank and the 1/8th Worcesters at Ponchaux. The 74th Brigade had not yet moved from its position, now some 6 miles in rear. Most valuable work had been performed during the day's operations by a detachment of Corps Cyclists. One party was attached to the 7th Brigade, and the remainder worked from Divisional Headquarters, and were able to bring back most useful information. In this way, they were largely responsible for communication during the day between the units in front and Headquarters behind.

The day's fighting was eminently successful ; all objectives had been gained without much difficulty, and with trifling losses. The spirit and morale of the troops was as high as could be desired, and all ranks felt that the back of the German resistance, at any rate in this particular sector, of the British advance, was gradually crumbling. During the night 8th/9th, German aeroplanes were particularly active in bombing our lines and back areas ; all telephone lines were broken and quick communication became a matter of some difficulty, and in fact, could only be maintained by Motor Cyclists, who, owing to the congestion of troops and traffic on the roads, were obliged to move at a very slow pace. In Serain, Premont and other villages on the line of advance, many French civilians were liberated.

9th to 12th OCTOBER.

Owing to the breakdown of telephonic communication with Corps Headquarters, it had not been possible to receive or issue definite orders for the further advance of the Division until very late at night. The 74th Brigade moved up soon after midnight, and during the early hours of the morning of the 9th it was possible to issue definite instructions as regards the plan of operations for the day.

At 6 a.m., the 75th Brigade passed through the two Battalions of the 7th Brigade, and advanced from the cross-roads between Serain and Premont, with the 1/8th R. Warwicks on the right, 1/5th Gloucesters on the left, and 1/8th Worcesters in support. The artillery barrage crept forward at the rate of 100 yards per 3 minutes. The attacking troops advanced on a front of about 3,000 yards, meeting with very little resistance, though some casualties were caused from the wood on the flank ; it was soon clear that the Germans had retired during the night, leaving only weak rearguards, which caused but little delay. A few casualties to our men were caused by our own Artillery barrage, owing to the rapidity of their advance in the fog. The first objective, along a line about 1,000 yards north-west of Maretz, was reached by 7.30 a.m., where a few prisoners were captured, and many French civilians released.

The 74th Brigade now came up and in the further advance became responsible for the attack on the right half of the second objective. The two Brigades continued their advance at 8 a.m., with Brigade transport immediately in rear and each supported by a Battery of Field Artillery. The 74th Brigade had the 11th Sherwood Foresters in front, 9th Yorks and 13th Durham Light Infantry in support.

Everything went well, and the Brigades met with no resistance for about 2½ miles. The country was undulating down land, free from wire or other obstacles and progress was comparatively easy for the troops. Artillery was moving up rapidly in rear of the Infantry Brigades, and the 1st Cavalry Division was advancing towards the front line in expectation of a favourable opportunity being afforded them to break through the retreating German lines. About 9 a.m. resistance was encountered along the railway line running north and south-west of Honnechy village. Vigorous attacks were organised by the 74th Brigade and the 1/8th Worcesters (75th Brigade) dealing direct with their Artillery ; after a short rest, the advance was resumed at 2 p.m., against the German rear-guards, who were here provided with numerous machine guns, and some batteries of Field Artillery. The enemy offered considerable resistance at first, but as our troops pressed on his resistance suddenly broke, and the line retired rapidly before becoming engaged at close quarters. The village of Honnechy was soon passed, and the line established a few hundred yards east and south-east, linking up with the Americans on the right, and troops of the 66th Division on the left. Fortunately the railway bridge was reached by the Worcesters in time to prevent its destruction, and a great deal of rolling stock and railway material was captured. Many civilians were also released, who spoke in praise of the rapidity of the British advance, which they said had prevented the evacuation of the women and children by the Germans. During the morning, Sergt. Stone, 1/8th R. Warwicks Regt., set a fine example in rushing a German post and capturing three prisoners, and all ranks of the Battalion appreciated the energy displayed by C.Q.M.S. Jay and C.Q.M.S. Brahan in the preparation and delivery of the rations the previous night, near Bronx Farm, when the locality was being heavily bombed by German aeroplanes. With the 1/5th Gloucesters, Pte. Cobb won a D.C.M. for the greatest gallantry in rushing a house near Maretz, and capturing, single-handed, a German officer with a machine gun and about 15 other prisoners. He had been previously wounded, but refused to go to the Dressing Station. L/Corpl. Ireland led parties against machine-gun posts in Maretz, and alone attacked and captured three snipers, who were causing a lot of trouble. Pte. Thomas and Pte. Cole did wonderful good work with their Lewis guns, and Sergt. Stephens and two Lewis Gunners rushed a house and captured 16 Germans. Lt.-Col. H. T. Clarke of the 1/8th Worcesters organised and carried through the attack on Honnechy with the greatest ability. Sergt. Atkinson, M.M., and Corpl Prince, M.M., when their Companies were temporarily held up, did excellent work in getting communication with the units on the flanks; Corpl. Prince though wounded, still carrying on in charge of the leading wave of the attacking troops. Pte. Wisdom showed wonderful fighting spirit in charge of his Lewis Gun section, and Pte. Ruggles, when the advance was held up, went forward alone, killed a German officer and came back with useful information as to the whereabouts of the German machine-gun posts. All received decorations.

With the 11th Sherwood Foresters, 2nd Lieut. Sallmayer, M.C., greatly distinguished himself when the line came under heavy machine gun fire south of Honnechy. With a complete disregard for his own safety he rallied the men and led them to the successful capture of the first objective. Sergt. Beecroft and Pte. Ainsworth pushed forward alone and captured a machine gun and it's crew which was holding up the advance, whilst Corpl. Wynne, M.M., and Sergt. Wilkes displayed the greatest gallantry in leading their men, the latter taking command of his Company when his Company Commander was killed. C.S.M. Coleman, M.M., 9th Yorks, did very useful work with his Company south of Honnechy, and L/Corpl. Oliver was most energetic in going forward to gain information about the enemy's machine-gun posts. L/Corpl. Sutton did wonderful good work with his Lewis gun against an awkward machine-gun post ; L/Corpl. Clark and Pte. Kidson showed the greatest gallantry throughout ; the latter, employed as a stretcher bearer, repeatedly bringing in wounded men under machine-gun fire. Pte. Leete was the first to reach the objective, and at all times set a very fine example to the others of his unit. All received decorations.

Troops of the 1st Cavalry Division passed through the infantry line north and south-east of Honnechy about 2.30 p.m., and one party captured Reumont village, about three miles to the north before dark, patrols reaching the Selle River about four miles beyond. Although unable to make very much headway the appearance of the cavalry gave great encouragement to the tired infantry. To the south of Honnechy some German field guns and machine guns prevented their advance, and they were also attacked by German aeroplanes, who used their machine guns with considerable effect. Their failure to break through the retiring German line was a great disappointment to the cavalry, but must not be regarded in any way as proof that mounted troops are no longer required in European warfare. The frantic appeals on all sides for mounted troops, and the invaluable work done by the few available during the retirement in March, can never be forgotten or over-estimated. Intelligence reports indicated that the enemy would probably make a stand on the Selle River to the south and south-east of Le Cateau, and that a line of defence with strong belts of wire was in progress of construction on the east bank of the river. Information was, however, very scanty, and the exact position and strength of the German line on the Divisional and neighbouring front was somewhat uncertain.

At 5.30 a.m., the 10th October, the Division moved forward on a 3,000 yards front in the same order as the preceding day, with the 74th Brigade on the right, 75th on the left, and 7th Brigade in Divisional Reserve about 2,000 yards behind ; each Brigade supported by its own Brigade of Field Artillery, acting directly under the orders of the Brigadier. The 74th Brigade had the 13th Durham Light Infantry in front, 9th Yorks about 300 yards behind in support, and 11th Sherwood Foresters about 500 yards behind in reserve. The 75th

Brigade, with the 1/8th R. Warwicks in front, 1/5th Gloucesters in support, and the 1/8th Worcesters in reserve. For the first two miles there was no opposition of any sort, but at about 8 a.m., the leading platoons came under heavy machine-gun fire from the railway embankments south of Le Cateau, and from St. Benin, a suburb of Le Cateau, situated about 1½ miles to the south of the town, and on the rising ground west of the river Selle. This opposition, especially from the high ground on the right flank, gradually intensified as the attack was pressed forward. A few German guns, firing over open sights, were silenced by the 110th Brigade, R.F.A., supporting the Warwicks, which enabled the battalion to push on another half mile. 2nd Lt. Hunt and C.S.M. Whitehouse, of the 1/8th R. Warwicks, did splendid work with Lewis guns when the advance was held up. 2nd Lt. Prince, as a liaison Officer, was invaluable, continually bringing back information under machine-gun fire. C.S.M. Yates was excellent with his men, and on several occasions, his fine example had great effect on his Company. With the 1/5th Gloucesters Sergt. Derrick did excellent work with his platoon ; when the officers were wounded he took command and organised a defensive flank with great skill. All received decorations for their gallantry.

At 2.30 p.m., the 74th Brigade launched their attack on St. Benin. This was successfully carried through, and the enemy gradually withdrew from the village without offering much opposition. Further to the left, the situation was more complicated, and it was impossible for the 75th Brigade to cross the river and break through the German lines, without careful preparations and more Artillery support. Its further advance was therefore countermanded. On the right, the Division had maintained contact with the Americans, who now had posts in St. Benin, and with the 66th Division, which had got well forward on the left, and had a few advanced patrols in Le Cateau itself.

Sergt. Sledge, M.M., 13th Durhams, won a D.C.M. for his splendid work during the fight. When his Company Commander was killed, he took command, and though himself wounded, he successfully led his men to their objective. Pte. Powell, Pte. Shelley and Pte. Beatie did splendid work with their Lewis guns ; the latter, when all the others in his gun team were wounded, managed to collect a few more men, and still carried on with his gun. Sergt. Heatherington and Sergt. Hammond, in command of platoons, led their men forward under very difficult circumstances. Pte. Horne and Pte. Dyer, when all the N.C.Os. had been wounded, collected parties of men and successfully carried on the attack. L/Corpl. Barron led a patrol forward when the advance was held up, and got back with valuable information ; L/Corpl. Smith as a stretcher bearer on many occasions was conspicuous for his courage in attending the wounded under heavy fire, and Pte. Bews never failed to deliver messages entrusted to him, often through heavy fire. With the 9th Yorks, Lt.-Col. R. S. Hart, D.S.O., won a Bar to his D.S.O. for his fine leadership throughout the attack. Sergt. Smith, Sergt. Dawson and Corpl. Shields did very useful work with their men, the latter going through the village with patrols to gain information as to the enemy's position on the river bank. Sergt. Collinson, M.M., organised and led a party against a German strong point which was holding up the advance from the flank, and won a second bar to his M.M.

During the 11th October, there was no further advance, but the German Artillery continued to display activity from their position east of the Selle, which was now held in considerable strength with a series of trench and rifle pits protected by strong wire entanglements. The night of the 11th/12th October, the Division was relieved in the line by the 50th Division, and the three Brigades found good accommodation, about 6 miles behind, in the villages of Serain, Premont and Ellincourt, with the Divisional Headquarters at Serain. These villages, situated on the edge of the battle area, had received but little damage from the fighting, which in most cases had quickly passed over them. A great many French civilians were released, giving the British troops a most enthusiastic welcome after their four years under the harsh and rigid regulations of the German Commandants in the areas behind the front line.

The battalions were now considerably below their full strength, but large numbers of reinforcements, of exceptionally good material, were arriving daily ; young men of the best fighting age, from the coal mines and agricultural life, who had only recently been withdrawn from their civil employment.

The rapid advance of the army had left the railheads

for the supply of rations, ammunition stores and reinforcements some distance behind ; with a systematic destruction of the majority of the railway bridges and the line, it was found impossible to repair and reconstruct the railway at such a rate as would keep pace with the forward movements of the troops. The situation, though mitigated by the rapid construction of narrow 2-feet trolley lines, threw a great strain on the motor lorry transport service in the delivery of supplies and ammunition to the troops, now 20 to 25 miles in advance of the railheads.

Casualties sustained by the Division during this period were :—

	Killed.	Wounded.	Missing.
Officers ...	23 ...	98 ...	2
Other ranks ...	342 ...	1905 ...	236

ARTILLERY.

On its arrival in the Royon area the 25th Divisional Artillery was at once fitted out with any new guns, horses, material and reinforcements required to replace the serious losses incurred on the Marne. By the first week of July this work was nearly complete, and the two Brigades (110th and 112th) R.F.A. marched to the Doullens area in 3rd Army reserve, and the 28th July further south to the IIIrd Corps, 4th Army area, east of Amiens, where they remained in Corps reserve until moved into action with the 12th Division, IIIrd Corps, the beginning of August. It was not until the 3rd October that the Divisional Artillery once more joined up with the 25th Division during its attack on the Beaurevoir position.

The 1st August the 112th Brigade, R.F.A., went into action behind the 58th Division, relieved next day by the 12th Division, and on the 4th August Brig.-General Kincaid Smith, the C.R.A., 25th Division, took over command of the Artillery, which now consisted of the 25th Divisional Artillery (110th and 112th Brigades), R.F.A., and the 169th, commanded by Lieut.-Col. Rainsford Hannay, D.S.O., and 232nd Army Brigades, R.F.A., commanded by Lieut.-Col. G. S. Tovey, D.S.O. Their front ran from Albert to Morlancourt, on the left of the IIIrd Corps.

110th Brigade, R.F.A.			Lt.-Col. S. G. R. Willis, D.S.O.
A/110	...	...	Major J. W. Watson, M.C.
B/110	...	...	Major A. L. Harman, D.S.O., M.C.
C/110	...	...	Major E. M. Watts, M.C.
D/110	...	...	Major P. C. L. Williams, M.C.
112th Brigade, R.F.A.			Lt.-Col. L. H. Queripel, C.M.G., D.S.O.
A/112	...	...	Major W. Swinton, M.C.
B/112	...	...	Major S. O. Jones, M.C.
C/112	...	...	Major W. C. Mackay, M.C.
D/112	...	...	Major D. D. Pole-Evans, M.C.

Preparations for the great attack on the 8th August had been carried out with the greatest secrecy, and only at the last moment was its scope made known to the troops engaged. On the 6th August the Germans attacked the 18th Division on the right of the 12th Division, penetrating to the support line, but were ejected by a counter-attack the next day, assisted by the 110th, 169th Brigades, R.F.A., and 47th Brigade, R.G.A. During the night the 112th Brigade and D/232 had been heavily gassed, and sustained a few casualties. At 4.20 a.m., the 8th August, the Divisions launched their attack, and met with immediate success all along the line. A thick mist at the time rendered observation from the air and ground observation posts extremely difficult, but this improved later in the day, and good targets were obtained on retreating bodies of the enemy. Trench mortars under Capt. N. Usticke did useful work bombarding the German trenches in front of Morlancourt, particularly X/25T.M. Battery, which carried out their programme in spite of several gas cylinders being exploded in their trench by German shells. Major Mackay, C/112, was unfortunately gassed and wounded during the attack, but refused to leave his battery until ordered to do so. Here as on every other occasion he showed the greatest gallantry, and received a second bar to his Military Cross. 2nd Lieut. Nurcombe, A/112, went with the Infantry attack, and by visiting the advanced posts was able to give great assistance to the battalion covered by his battery. Sergt. Gillies and Corpl. Atkinson, A/112, set a fine example to men of their unit, the former following up the

Infantry with his section of guns with great dash and gallantry. Sergt. Motion, C/112, at great risk from exploding ammunition, succeeded in extinguishing a fire in his gun pit, and Sergt. Ransome, B/112, with remarkable coolness, extricated some ammunition wagons as they came under heavy shelling near the gun position. Driver Scott and Driver Graham, D/112, showed great courage and presence of mind when their wagons, with ammunition for the battery, were hit by a shell. Corpl. Lieper, B/112, and Bdr. Blezard, D/112, were conspicuous for their courage in mending lines under heavy fire and keeping up communications. All received decorations as well as Corpl. Allan, D/112, for his fine example to the men of his battery when heavily shelled with mustard gas. Corpl. Wyvill and Sergt. Palmer, D.C.M., of X/25 T.M. Battery, did excellent work bombarding the German trenches with their mortars, and Bdr. Slater showed great coolness and bravery in collecting wagons and teams which had been stampeded by shelling on their way up to the guns. All received Military Medals.

The attack was continued the evening of the 9th August. All went well, and visibility was excellent for the Artillery. The 82nd and 83rd Brigades, R.F.A. (18th Divisional Artillery), in action south of the Ancre River, were now placed under the C.R.A., 25th Division. Small local attacks were carried out the afternoon of the 10th August, and excellent shooting was made by all batteries on parties of retiring Germans, especially by the 112th Brigade, R.F.A., from their positions west of the Ancre. The German retaliation was feeble, but the Morlancourt area was heavily shelled day and night. The 47th Brigade, R.G.A., commanded by Lieut.-Col. Andrews, D.S.O., was affiliated to the 25th Division Artillery during the operations; two batteries of 60-pounders (25th H.B. and 144th H.B.), knows as Gough's group, now joined the Field Artillery covering the 12th Division, and preparations were made for a further advance.

At 4 55 a.m., the 13th August, the 12th Division attacked, supported by all available Field and Heavy Artillery, comprising 96 18-pounders, 24 4·5-inch howitzers, 32 6-inch howitzers, and 6 8·2-inch howitzers. The barrage and artillery bombardment were excellent, and all objectives were quickly reached. Later, a counter-attack drove our Infantry back on the right, but this was rectified next day. The 17th

August large movements of troops and transport eastwards, behind Fricourt and Mametz, indicated that the enemy were withdrawing, and all roads were subjected to increased bombardment. The 18th August the 82nd Brigade, R.F.A., was transferred to the 18th Division on the right, which left the 12th Division covered by four brigades—the 110th Brigade, with two batteries south of Mametz Wood and two batteries in Ville, the 112th Brigade north of the Ancre, the 83rd Brigade north of and the 169th west of Morlancourt ; these were reinforced two days later by the 77th and 179th Army F.A. Brigades. Preparations were now made for a further advance on a large scale, large quantities of ammunition—500 rounds per 18-pounder and 400 rounds per 4·5-inch howitzer—being dumped in the gun positions on the night 19th/20th and 20th/21st. Single guns from all batteries of the 110th Brigade and A and B/112th Brigade were also moved forward.

At 4.45 a.m., the 23rd August, the attack was launched. It was expected by the enemy, but by 9.30 a.m. the 12th Division, with the 47th and 18th Divisions on right and left, had gained all their objectives. The Cavalry with the 179th Brigade, R.F.A., were, however, unable to push through, and the same evening a German counter-attack forced back the 47th Division on the right. L.-Bdr. Allen, B/110, set a very fine example to the other men of his section when their gun position was being heavily shelled, and Fitter Perkins gallantly continued to attend to the guns under similar condition. Sergt. Steadman, B/110, as Batt. Sergt.-Major, displayed great coolness in getting the teams away from the battery position, whilst Bdr. Beynon, A/110, gallantly delivered a message across ground swept by fire, his companion being killed. Signaller Fitton, A/112, and Signaller Robinson, D/112, were at all times conspicuous for their courage in laying and mending lines to the forward observation posts. All were awarded Military Medals for their gallantry. The six Brigades R.F.A. were now re-grouped ; the 77th and 110th Brigades, commanded by Lieut.-Col. Gosling, D.S.O., forming right group ; 179th Brigade and one battery 169th Brigade, the centre group, commanded by Lieut.-Col. Gley, C.M.G., D.S.O., the 169th Brigade and 83rd Brigade, the left group, commanded by Lieut.-Col. Rainsford Hannay, D.S.O., with the 112th Brigade acting independently nnder the C.R.A.

Early the 24th August, the 83rd Brigade pulled out of action, and along with the 169th Brigade, remained in mobile reserve ready to move forward in case of any advance, and the 112th Brigade, R.F.A., moved up east of Meaulte in close support of the Infantry of the 12th Division. The same night the final objectives of the previous day were successfully reached by the Infantry, and preparations pushed on for a further advance the next day. Major Pole Evans, M.C., D/112, was with the first Infantry patrols to enter Mametz, and registered his battery whilst under heavy machine-gun fire ; on all occasions he showed the greatest gallantry, and received a second bar to his Military Cross. L./Bdr. Ford, Gnr. Meehan and Gnr. Moore, B/110, when their gun pit was set on fire by a 5-inch shell, jumped in regardless of their danger, and succeeded in putting it out ; whilst L./Bdr. Weller, C/112 maintained a line through to the front observation posts under constant machine-gun fire. Gnr. Colenutt and Gnr. Fawcett were both conspicuous for their courage in getting back with messages from the front when communication broke down, the latter being wounded during the journey. All received Military Medals.

The 25th August, the enemy were found to have withdrawn during the night. The 12th Division was at once formed into three brigade groups with the 169th Brigade, R.F.A., attached to the 35th Infantry Brigade, forming the advance guard, the 112th Brigade attached to the 36th Infantry Brigade, and the 179th Brigade attached to the 37th Infantry Brigade ; all three Artillery Brigades acting directly under the Infantry Brigadier, and the remaining three Artillery Brigades, 110th, 8th, and 97th, being required to assist in the supply of ammunition.

Late the 26th August, the 83rd Brigade, R.F.A., was ordered to rejoin the 18th Division on the right and the 62nd and 63rd Brigades, R.F.A. (the 12th Divisional Artillery), arrived in the neighbourhood, relieving the 179th and 169th Brigades the next day, whilst the 77th Brigade was also withdrawn for rest and placed in G.H.Q. reserve. The 37th Infantry Brigade made a successful advance early the 27th August, but was counter-attacked, and compelled to relinquish the high ground later in the day. The 62nd Brigade, R.F.A., now acted with the 35th Infantry Brigade group, the 63rd Brigade, R.F.A., with the 37th Infantry Brigade, and the 112th Brigade,

R.F.A., with the 36th Infantry Brigade group, whilst the 110th Brigade acted independently under the C.R.A. Major Williams, D/110, did excellent work with his battery during the attack, and 2nd Lieut. Scrotton, D/112, by visiting advanced posts of the Infantry, was able to gain valuable information for his battery. Capt. Stirling, R.A.M.C., attached 112th Brigade, R.F.A., on this and many other occasions, was conspicuous for his courage in attending to the wounded under heavy fire. These officers received the Military Cross. Dvr. Turton, D/110, won the Military Medal for his coolness and pluck in extricating his ammunition wagon when some of the horses were killed at the battery position, as well as Dvr. Rose, C/112, for his courage in repairing telephone lines under heavy shell fire.

A further advance was made by the 12th Division, early the 28th August, and some of the guns had good targets over open sights against parties of retiring Germans and their field batteries. The enemy again withdrew during the night 28th/29th, and in the morning the 37th Infantry Brigade formed the advance guard, with the 63rd and 110th Brigade, R.F.A., in close support. B/110, under Major Harman, went in front with some cavalry, and the line was successfully carried beyond Maurepas and Combles, the former leading his battery with great energy and determination. 2nd Lieut. Walder, B/110, led his section with great boldness, completely de stroying a German battery at point-blank range, and 2nd Lieut. Norton, C/112, behaved with great coolness when his battery was badly shelled whilst coming into action. All were awarded the Military Cross for their gallantry. Batt. Sergt.-Major Theaker, D/110, and Farrier-Sergt. Cusick, A/110, showed great courage when sudden shelling of the lines caused many casualties amongst the drivers and horses, and Corpl. Cuthbertson, D/110, Dvr. Hoy, B/110, and Sergt. Richards, D/110, distinguished themselves by their gallant behaviour when in charge of ammunition wagons for the batteries, the latter being wounded during the action. Sergt. Daws, D.C.M., D/112, and Batt. Sergt.-Major Wilson, D.C.M., C/112, on this and several occasions, set a splendid example to the others when their batteries were heavily shelled. Bdr. Blezard, M M. D/112, as a signaller, and Dvr. Darlington, B/112, when in charge of some ammunition wagons, did good work; all receiving Military Medals for their gallantry.

Sergt. Rayner, B/112, won his D.C.M. for gallantly working his gun for five hours under heavy shelling, inflicting considerable loss on the retiring Infantry.

The 30th August, the 47th Division relieved the 12th Division, and the C.R.A., 47th Division, took over command of the four brigades R.F.A. Capt. Horton, Staff Captain, 25th Divisional Artillery, remained behind with the C.R.A., 47th Division, to superintend the administrative work of the 110th and 112th Brigades, R.F.A., whilst H.Q., 25th Divisional Artillery, moved back to St. Gratien. During this period the Artillery had very heavy fighting in close support of the Infantry, and sustained heavy casualties, although all the batteries vied with each other in getting as close to the front line as possible. Major Dean, M.C., C/112, gallantly led his battery into action within 800 yards of our Infantry front line at a time when the advance was temporarily held up, and Capt. Alston, with A/112, also brought his guns close up to the front line. Gnr. Speak, 112th Brigade, R.F.A., repeatedly carried messages across ground swept by fire, and both L./Corpl. Dempsey and Spr. Preston, R.E., attached 112th Brigade, distinguished themselves by mending wires under most difficult conditions. Dr. Barber and Dr. Berry, A/112, did good service getting their ammunition wagons up to the battery positions under fire, and Sergt. Donnachie, A/110, though wounded, was excellent with his gun teams. All received decorations.

On the 6th September the 47th Division was relieved by the 58th Division, and two days later the 110th and 112th Brigades were pulled out of action into mobile reserve under the 74th Division, ready for action in case of any attack by the enemy. On the 14th September the 112th Brigade, R.F.A., was placed under the 12th Division, the 110th Brigade, R.F.A., under the 18th Division. Large quantities of ammunition were dumped in the gun positions, and all preparations were made for another attack on a large scale. Lieut.-Col. Willis, D.S.O., commanding 110th Brigade, went sick on the 6th September, his place being taken by Major Macleod, D.S.O., M.C., the Brigade Major, until the arrival of Lieut.-Col. R. E. Milford, D.S.O., a little later.

The 18th September, the 18th and 12th Divisions attacked the ridge running through Ronssoy and Epehy. The night before the attack the 110th and 112th Brigades, R.F.A., took up their battle positions north of Villers Faucon. The attack by the 18th Division covered by the 110th Brigade, R.F.A., went well, and the village was captured by a flank attack from the south, but some machine guns held out in the village and wood, which caused the batteries trouble when they advanced. At Epehy, on the 12th Division front, the Germans retook the village and the advance of the artillery north of the St. Emilie-Ronssoy ridge was delayed. B/110 suffered severely from shelling whilst firing its barrage, but completed the programme and carried out a skilful advance. All batteries came in for heavy shelling and machine-gun fire, which caused considerable casualties in their forward positions. Capt. C. M. Duncan, C/110, took his section forward in close support of the Infantry, and at one time actually got his guns in action in front of the Infantry and in full view of the enemy. Here he was able to deal with remarkable success with a German battery and some machine-gun nests. Lieut. Melly, A/110, though wounded, gallantly kept up the fire of his guns, and 2nd Lieut. Peter, B/110, as F.O.O. for the 110th Brigade, R.F.A., did good work keeping touch with the leading Infantry.

On the 21st September, the attack was resumed by the 18th and 12th Divisions, with the 112th Brigade, R.F.A., in action south of Epehy, and the 110th Brigade, R.F.A., behind Ronssoy. The battle swayed backwards and forwards through the maze of trenches which the Germans had dug for themselves, and consequently called for the utmost activity and vigilance on the part of the Artillery; ultimately the enemy were driven back. Major Swinton, M.C., A/112, and Major Pole Evans, D/112, greatly distinguished themselves by bringing their batteries into action so far forward that they were able to knock out the German machine guns and thus help the Infantry advance.

Corpl. Saunders and Gnr. Hawkesworth, A/110, gallantly kept on working their guns under heavy fire though they were both wounded, and Bdr. Benson and Dr. Gray, C/110, did splendid work keeping the batteries supplied with ammunition; L/Corpl. Kearns, A/110, constantly repaired the telephone line under heavy fire. All received well-earned decorations.

The 24th September, the 27th American Division relieved the 18th Division, and the following day the 110th and 112th Brigades joined the centre and left group respectively, covering the Americans. Both Brigades came under the command of the 4th Australian Divisional Artillery, whose C.R.A. was acting as C.R.A. to the American Division. The 27th September the 27th and 30th American Divisions attacked and captured the preliminary line of trenches, in front of the main Hindenburg line, a strongly prepared position running at this point east of the village of Bellicourt. The bombardment was carried out for two days with all available artillery, and during the night 28th/29th all batteries moved forward to battle positions east of Ronssoy and Epehy under heavy shell and machine-gun fire, suffering many casualties, but successfully occupying their prearranged positions. The 29th September, the 27th and 30th American Divisions (2nd American Corps) attacked and captured the portion of the Hindenburg line along their front, the Australian Divisions passing through to reach the final objectives, though great difficulty was experienced by the latter, owing to large parties of German machine-gunners being overrun by the leading troops in their advance.

The 110th and 112th Brigades remained in action under the 2nd Australian Division until the 3rd October, when the 25th Division came up and relieved the Australians in front of Beaurevoir and now formed the right Division of the XIIIth Corps, with the 60th Division on the left. The Artillery covering the 25th Division now consisted of two groups ; the 104th and 108th Army F.A. Brigades under Lt.-Col. L. H. Ward, D.S.O., forming the right group with the 110th and 112th Brigades, R.F.A., forming the left group, and the 86th Army F.A. Brigade in mobile reserve. After two unsuccessful attacks, the strong position in front of Beaurevoir and Guisancourt Farm was finally captured by troops of the 25th Division, and the way opened for a further advance on a large scale. On the 7th October the 108th Army F.A. Brigade was transferred to the 18th Division, and the following morning the British attacked all along their line. Everything went well, and all objectives were reached up to time. The Americans captured Premont on the right, the 25th Division the village of Serain with the 60th Division well up on the left. The Artillery Brigades pushed on north and east of Ponchaux, except the 104th Army F.A. Brigade, which remained behind resting in action. Capt. Chamier, Adjutant, 110th Brigade, R.F.A., was invaluable on this and many other occasions, and 2nd Lt. Briggs, A/112, did splendid work for his battery by reconnoitring the front line at a critical moment ; Sergt. Agnew, D.C.M., D/112, won a bar to his D.C.M., for his courage and coolness in extinguishing a fire at a dump of shells. Sergt. Jones, D/112, set a fine example to all ranks when his battery was heavily bombed, and Gnr. Weall, D/112, was conspicuous for his courage in taking urgent messages across ground swept by fire. Dr. Hargreaves maintained a line up to the forward O.P., though constantly broken by shelling, and Gnr. Franklin, 112th Brigade, R.F.A., though wounded, succeeded in getting rations up to the batteries.

The attack was resumed early on the 9th October ; Maretz was occupied, and the troops reached the outskirts of Honnechy and Maurois. The Artillery Brigades moved forward to position in vicinity of Maretz in the evening. Brigade groups were formed, and the Artillery Brigades were placed directly under the Infantry Brigadiers ; the 110th Brigade with the 75th Infantry Brigade, the 112th Brigade with the 7th Infantry Brigade, and the 86th Brigade with the 74th Infantry Brigade. The morning of the 10th October, Honnechy, Maurois and Reumont were successfully reached, but the advance failed to reach the high ground east of Le Cateau, and was held up along the River Selle, and in the western outskirts of the town. Major Williams, D/110, did excellent work with the advanced guard of the 75th Brigade, and 2nd Lt. Allan, D/110, took his section of guns along with the Infantry, and came into action at close range in full view of the German machine guns, and both received the Military Cross.

No moves took place during the next few days, but preparations were made for an attack on a large scale along the line of the Selle River. The 50th Division relieved the 25th Division on the 11th/12th October, but the C.R.A. remained with the former in command of the Artillery covering their front. This now consisted of the 110th, 112th, 86th, 104th and 150th Brigades, and the 27th Brigade, R.G.A., commanded by Major Armstrong, D.S.O. This Brigade of heavy artillery rendered very valuable service during the subsequent operation. At 5.20 a.m., the 17th October, the attack was launched in a very thick mist, and the river crossed successfully by St. Benin Ford, though not without some difficulty. On the left, at the Le Cateau Railway triangle, resistance was stronger, and it was not until evening that the situation was finally cleared up. This was practically the last well-organised line of resistance, and provided the enemy with a very strong position along the railway with complete command of the River Selle, covering their front. The artillery programme was extremely complicated, owing to the fact that the attacking troops were restricted to the use of this one ford. 2nd Lt. Scattergood, B/112, and 2nd Lt. Thorpe, D/112, gallantly pushed forward to find a crossing for their guns. Corpl. Dyer, M.M., and Gnr. Stafford, A/112, though the former and several others of the party were wounded, carried on with their work to prepare the crossing in spite of the heavy fire. Marechal des Logis P. Quehen, of the French Mission, attached 112th Brigade, R.F.A., with great courage reconnoitred the line of the river in spite of heavy machine-gun fire, and Corpl. Robinson, B/112, repeatedly carried messages under similar conditions. All received decorations for their gallantry.

The evening of the 18th the attack was resumed with complete success, and the 112th and 86th Brigades moved forward and crossed the river. The next day the 25th Division relieved the 50th Division, and the remainder of the Artillery moved forward; the 86th and 112th Brigades covering the right sector, and the 104th and 110th Brigades the left sector of the Divisional front with the 150th Brigade in mobile reserve.

Large quantities of ammunition were now dumped in the gun positions, and all preparations made for another attack on a large scale. The attack was postponed for 24 hours, but at 1.20 a.m., the 23rd October, the Infantry advanced. The country was much intersected, and all communication very difficult and progress slow. The 112th Brigade moved forward at 2.30 a.m. to cross the Richemont Brook, but owing to a temporary check in front, came into action near the Bazuel-Le Cateau Road, until the crossing at Garde Mill was clear. Later, during the day, it finally occupied positions in the northern edge of Bois L'Eveque, to support the 74th Infantry Brigade with observed fire. The 110th Brigade, R.F.A., moved up to the neighbourhood of Pommereuil, and were in action south of the village, with the 104th and 150th Brigades in mobile reserve. The following morning the attack was resumed, and the final objectives reached.

L./Bdr Claney, B/112, showed remarkable coolness and bravery when a shell wounded nearly all the men and horses of his sub-section. Corpl. Morton, D/110, and L./Bdr. Dutton, A/112, did splendid work when badly bombed, and Signaller Parker, A/112, was conspicuous for his courage in mending lines under shell fire to keep up communication. They were all awarded Military Medals.

During the nights 25th/26th and 26th/27th, the 110th and 112th Brigades, R.F.A., were relieved by the 66th Divisional Artillery, and moved back for a rest at Honnechy, after having been in action almost continuously since the commencement of the battle on the 8th August.

R.E. AND PIONEERS.

On their arrival in the Royon area, the three Field Companies R.E., which had lost more than half their personnel, were gradually made up to strength, reorganised and refitted. Several weeks were spent in musketry training, and on various constructional works in the neighbourhood. Practice in pontooning and spar bridging at Beaurainville proved of the greatest value in the subsequent operations round Le Cateau and Landrecies. For about a month the 106th Field Company, R.E., were employed on the defences of the G.H.Q. line ; the 105th Field Company, R.E., in the construction of a tank bridge at Arras, and the 130th Field Company, R.E., in building a school at Maresquel.

The middle of September, the 105th, 106th and 130th Field Companies, under Major F. W. Richards, M.C., Major C. G. Lynam, M.C., and Major F. E. Musgrave, M.C., rejoined the Division at St. Riquier. For the moment, the Division was without any pioneer battalion, as the 6th S.W. Borderers had been transferred to the 30th Division in July, and it was not until the second week in October that the 11th South Lancs (Pioneers) arrived from England to take their place. This was unfortunate, as the Infantry units during the advance were unable to spare the large working parties required for the repair of roads and bridges, and the Field Companies themselves were at times hard pressed to find the necessary labour.

From the 3rd to 7th October, during the fighting at Beaurevoir, the three Field Companies, R.E., were employed in opening, repairing and clearing roads and tracks within the Divisional boundaries and the erection of water points, No. 1 and 4 Sections of the 130th Field Company, R.E., being placed at the disposal of the Artillery, to give technical advice and assistance in the preparation of gun pits, shelters, etc. Near Geneve Corpl. Webb, 106th Field Coy., R.E. though himself wounded by a shell, refused to leave his section until all the other wounded sappers had been attended to and received a Military Medal for his gallantry. During the next three days, the construction of water points, and repair of wells along the line of advance at Ponchaux, Sonia Wood, Bronx farm, Serain, Premont and Honnechy became the most pressing duty. The difficulties of water supply for men and animals at short notice, in a district where running streams and other sources of supply were very scanty, were considerably increased by the presence of large bodies of Cavalry, close up behind the Infantry. Quick repair of roads for lorries, the filling up of shell holes, and the construction of diversions round the enormous craters, blown by the retreating Germans at convenient cross roads, had also to be undertaken, and it was in this work that the absence of a pioneer battalion was keenly felt. Fine weather, however, made it possible for the horse transport to go across the open and relieved the pressure on the roads. On the 10th October, the advance was held up at the Selle River, and after the relief of the 25th Division, the 11th/12th the Field Companies went back to the Serain-Ellincourt area for a few days' rest, although a considerable amount of work in connection with billets, sanitation and water supply required attention within the Divisional area.

The discovery and removal of "booby traps," mines and charges in dugouts, railway bridges, embankments and buildings was not the least important work performed by the R.E. during the advance. At Bousigny Station, no less than 80 charges and 200 detonators were discovered and withdrawn. This at all times is a very delicate operation, requiring some skill and courage, but if left in unskilled hands such work was apt to lead to unpleasant surprises with disastrous results. In fact, along the line of advance, every village had quite a quarter of its buildings fitted out with some sort of ingenious booby trap, which had to be very carefully handled. Very good work was done by a Section of No. 182 Tunnelling Coy. (attached to the Division) in dealing with these cunning devices.

The 11th South Lancs (Pioneers) arrived from England the 13th October, under Lt.-Col. C. C. Champion, D.S.O., with its three Companies commanded by Capt. Taylor, Capt. Boulton and Capt. Askew. Newly formed at home, and with a large proportion of its men of B2 category, and others who had had no Pioneer training of any sort, the Battalion acquitted itself remarkably well during the next three weeks.

After reaching the line of the Selle River, all difficulties regarding water supply for the troops practically ceased. The country from now on was well watered, and the repair and construction of roads and railway bridges was the chief task to be performed by the R.E. On the 14th October, the three Field Companies and the Pioneer battalion commenced the repair of the bridges blown up by the enemy near Le Cateau. Most of this work had to be carried out under more or less continuous shelling, which caused a considerable number of casualties amongst the working parties. On the 17th October, the 105th Field Coy, R.E., at the cost of a good many casualties, did some work on preparing the site for the bridge, south of Le Cateau, but the 106th and 130th Field Coys., R.E., were unable to do little more than reconnoitre during the night the site of their bridges, north and south of the town, as they were still under machine-gun fire. On the 18th October, the attack by the Infantry was resumed, the bridge sites became quieter, and it was then possible to get up lorries and push on with the work.

The 130th Field Coy., R.E., completed in 5½ hours a 22-ft. span tank bridge over the Selle, south of Le Cateau. The 105th Field Coy., R.E., working in shifts throughout the night, completed a 30-ft. span traffic bridge, as well as a smaller bridge a little further south, both being ready for traffic the following day. The 106th Field Coy., R.E., at their bridge north of Le Cateau, were unable to work before 2 p.m., the 18th October, owing to machine-gun fire and were stopped by bursts of gas and shelling during the night, losing two officers and 11 other ranks. Work was resumed next day, and by evening the 50-ft span bridge was nearly complete, when it was taken over by the 50th Division, R.E. The three Field Companies then went back to rest for a few days near Honnechy. The Pioneer battalion supplied large working parties to assist the engineers in the construction of these bridges.

SIGNAL COMMUNICATIONS.

Soon after the departure of Divisional Headquarters to England, the 25th Division Signal Coy., R.E., was sent from Royon to Samer, near Boulogne, to assist in training the 27th American Division. The beginning of August it returned to the Royon area for a short time, and then moved to the 1st Army H.Q. at Ranchicourt, and its linesmen were temporarily attached for duty to the 51st and 46th Divisions, near Arras. The 15th September, the Signal Coy. rejoined the Divisional Headquarters at St. Riquier.

In the meantime Major E. de W. Bradley, M.C., had been promoted to Chief Signal Officer, IInd Corps, and was succeeded in command of the 25th Divisional Signal Coy. by Major W. M. Keasey, R.E., M.C. The former had been in charge of the Signal Coy. for nearly three years, and it was largely owing to his knowledge, keenness and energy that the Divisional communications had been so successful in the past, and the Signal Coy. had attained such a high state of efficiency. The Signal School established under Capt. Belcher, M.C., at Meteren in October, 1916, had been successful in turning out large number of officers and men who were subsequently of the utmost value to their units in maintaining efficient forward communications. After a long stay at Meteren, Couin and Monnecove, near St. Omer, during 1917 and 1918, the school moved to Rimboval, near Royon, the beginning of August, 1918, and Domqueur the end of September, where it remained until it was disbanded. The object of the school was not only to give technical instruction in all the different branches of communications, but also to impress on all ranks that good communications were not merely to satisfy the curiosity of the Staff and others behind the battle-front, but that early and accurate information as to the progress of the troops in the battle was absolutely necessary so that the Commander should be able to give instructions for the movement of other troops, perhaps held in reserve. The development of contact aeroplanes has done a great deal towards keeping a Commander informed as to the situation in the front line, but nothing can lessen the vital importance for good arrangements for communications within the Division. For the Field Artillery, communications between the forward observation posts and their batteries is essential, and is work which requires courage and a cool head, whilst for the linesmen it is particularly arduous owing to the continual breaking of the line by shelling.

Communications in the battles of 1916 and 1917 had been maintained by buried cable routes, but from the 3rd October, 1918, there commenced the most difficult work that the Signal Coy. had been called upon to perform during the war. The state of the country between Divisional and Brigade Headquarters was bad for good communications. Cables had to be run along the ground at the side of the roads, and it was impossible to protect them from transport or tanks. There was no time or opportunity to select "safe" routes, and as the advance continued, and mobile and semi-mobile warfare became an accomplished fact, the work became more difficult. This entailed very hard work for the linesmen, who were continually out mending broken lines under heavy fire, and performed their work with the greatest gallantry.

Lieut. Pullan, M.C., Lieut. Ingleson, and Lieut. Kennedy, M.C., were responsible for the communications of the 7th, 75th, and 74th Brigades respectively, with Capt. Goddard, M.C., in charge of the Artillery Signals. The Brigades were usually able to keep telephone communications through to their battalions, and No. 1 Section (Cable Section) did its best to maintain communication with the Brigades. This was rendered more difficult by the continual passage of the tanks, the natural enemy of all ground cables.

When the Division moved forward beyond the Hindenburg line at Bellicourt, communications improved. A Divisional Advanced Exchange was established close up behind the Infantry Brigades, and all the main trunk lines were laid from the Division to this Advanced Exchange, and from there radiated to the Brigades. "Wireless" proved to be of great value, and was ably controlled by Lieut. C. A. Oliver. Visual signalling was also made use of, and worked well in this area.

With the Artillery, communications between Divisional Artillery H.Q., Brigades and batteries was excellent throughout ; occasionally the lines to units were broken, but never for long. One main line was as a rule laid to a forward exchange from Divisional Artillery H.Q. ; this exchange was close to the Artillery Brigade H.Q., which were generally not far from the batteries ; all the energies of the Artillery signals were concentrated on keeping this line through. Lines were successfully laid from Templeux le Guerrard to Bellicourt, Bellicourt to Ponchaux, Ponchaux to Trou-au-Soldats, and from there to Honnechy, and so on during the advance. These were long lines, which needed much maintenance, but their great value amply repaid the hard work expended on them.

SUPPLIES.

After its arrival in the Royon area the Divisional Train A.S.C., with the exception of No. 1 Coy., which accompanied the 25th Divisional Artillery, did a great deal of useful work for the local French civilians. Assistance with wagons and horses during the harvest was very welcome to these people, whose transport facilities were extremely limited. The 16th September, the Divisional Train joined up with the Division at St. Riquier, and moved the end of September via Flexicourt, St. Gauveur, Warloy, Montauban, Moisleins, and Ronsoy, when the Division went into action at Beaurevoir and where No. 1 Coy. rejoined.

During the advance great credit was due to the Divisional Train A.S.C., under Lt.-Col. F. B. Lord, D.S.O., and the Senior Supply Officer, Major C. V. Ewart, in their successful efforts to keep the Division supplied with rations.

No. 1 Coy. (198th Coy., R.A.S.C.) Major G. E. Hodder.
No. 2 Coy. (199th Coy., R.A.S.C.) Capt. K. Kennard,M.C.
No. 3 Coy. (200th Coy., R.A.S.C.) Capt. R. G. Finch.
No. 4 Coy. (201st Coy., R.A.S.C.) Capt. C. H. R. Brown

Transportation difficulties very soon became acute, owing to explosions on the railway from delay action mines, left by the Germans in their retreat. These mines were continually destroying the railway, and each one as a rule caused a delay and block on the line of anything from six to twelve hours or more. It therefore became extremely difficult to forecast the time of arrival of any supply train, which led to increased strain on both men and horses. During the battle at Beaurevoir, and also for the few days from the 12th to the 19th October, whilst the Division was resting in the Serain-Ellicourt area, the lorries were required for the transport of ammunition, and all supplies were loaded up by horse transport from the supply trains and delivered direct to the Brigade refilling points. This procedure, especially during the later period, entailed a daily average of about 25 miles for the horses. During the advance, however, the lorries again loaded up from the supply train at railhead.

From Roisel, the railhead for the broad gauge, a light 2-ft. railway was opened to Joncourt, Bellicourt, and Montbeehain. The line, however, was extremely fragile, and continual upsets rendered the hour of arrival of these trains somewhat uncertain. On the 7th November, when the Division was finally relieved by the 66th Division, the supply railhead was no less than 33 miles behind the fighting troops, from which it will be readily understood how important a factor in the advance of the Army was the repair and rebuilding of the railways and bridges.

An epidemic of influenza claimed several victims amongst the personnel of the A.S.C., including Capt. A. Fenner, M.C., who had been with the Division from its earliest days. At one time so many men were in hospital that it was necessary to call upon the Infantry to provide drivers temporarily in their place.

CASUALTIES AND MEDICAL ARRANGEMENTS.

Along with other units of the Division the 75th, 76th, and 77th Field Ambulances had suffered considerable losses in personnel and material on the Marne ; these were, however, soon replaced during their stay in the Royon area. The middle of July, the 77th Field Ambulance, under Lt.-Col. H. H. Leeson, M.C., was attached to the 16th Division in the line, but returned in time to rejoin the Division at St. Requier the middle of September. In the meantime Lt.-Col. Tyrrell, D.S.O., M.C., who by his untiring energy and personal bravery had won the admiration of all ranks throughout the Division, had been succeeded by Lt.-Col. D. Large, D.S.O., M.C., in command of the 76th Field Ambulance.

Proceeding with the Division to the XIIIth Corps, the end of September, the 75th, 76th, and 77th Field Ambulances were responsible for clearing the wounded of the 74th, 75th, and 7th Infantry Brigades respectively. Although a far smaller number of wounded were treated by the Ambulances than during previous operations, yet the difficulties were great owing to the rapid advance after the battle at Beaurevoir, and the necessity for keeping in close touch with the Brigades.

Blowing of large craters along the main roads and the destruction of bridges often made it impossible to get the motor ambulances up to the main dressing stations, and it was therefore necessary to rely more on horse ambulances for the work until the roads were made passable for motor transport.

During October influenza was very prevalent amongst the troops as well as the personnel of the R.A.M.C. ; in fact, amongst the stretcher-bearers nearly half were laid up at the same time, returning German prisoners being extensively used in their place.

The 4th October a main dressing station was established by the 75th Field Ambulance at Ronssoy, with an advanced dressing station near 74th Brigade H.Q., to deal with its casualties during the battle at Beaurevoir. Major Sullivan, R.A.M.C., won his Military Cross for his services whilst in charge of the advanced dressing station during the battle, and it was largely owing to his energy that about 300 cases were successfully evacuated under heavy shelling. Pte. Hart, R.A.M.C., and Pte. Hoodless, R.A.M.C., rendered fine service in continually guiding bearer squads to the Regimental Aid Posts, and assisting in the evacuation of the wounded under fire. Both received Military Medals.

As the advance continued, the advanced dressing station and bearers were pushed up to Serain Farm and a collecting post formed at Ponchaux, and the following days to Maretz, Trous-les-Soldats, and Honnechy Station, where continual gas shelling necessitated its removal to the higher ground in the village. For the attack, the 23rd October, and the subsequent advance, the Bearer Division, under Capt. A. H. Huycke, M.C., was lent to the 76th Field Ambulance ; collecting posts were established successively at Pommereuil, in an old German dressing station at the north-west corner of the Bois L'Eveque, and at the cross roads south of Boursis. A great many French civilians suffering from gas poisoning and unable to walk, were treated and evacuated from this district. Sergt. Timm, R.A.M.C., displayed great coolness when the car loading post at Tilleul Farm was heavily shelled, and Pte. Forde distinguished himself by extricating wounded men from the wreckage of limbers, and animals wounded by heavy shelling. Pte. Kelly worked incessantly for two days attending to the wounded under fire.

On the 5th October the 76th Field Ambulance constructed

a main dressing station near Malakoff Farm, in an old support line trench, and an advanced dressing station in a trench on the Railway Ridge near Beaurevoir, working in conjunction with the 75th Field Ambulance. Sergt. Fishwick, R.A.M.C. did splendid work visiting the Regimental Aid Posts and relay posts during the afternoon and night, and Pte. Wyatt was conspicuous for his courage whilst acting as a runner and stretcher bearer under constant and heavy machine-gun fire. Two days later, at Ponchaux, Pte. Jamieson, R.A.M.C., and Pte. Jenkins, R.A.M.C., for six hours on end during a very bad bombing air attack, searched for wounded and dressed them quite regardless of their own personal safety. They were all awarded the Military Medal.

As the 75th Brigade advanced, dressing stations were opened at Serain and Honnechy, the 9th October. It was now decided to establish a Corps main dressing station half way to the C.C.S., at Roisel, and during the next ten days the 76th Field Ambulance fulfilled this role at Honnechy until relieved, the 19th October, by the 66th Divisional Field Ambulance. Casualties from all divisions in the XIIIth Corps were received at Honnechy, and from the 12th to the 19th October, between 2,500 and 3,000 cases passed through the dressing station. On the 20th October, the 76th Field Ambulance relieved the 77th Field Ambulance at St. Benin and became responsible for evacuating casualties from the line held by the 25th Division. Shelling the same night caused several casualties amongst the horses and personnel of the A.S.C. Pte. White, R.A.M.C., and Pte. Gregory, R.A.M.C., carried many wounded men back to safety under constant and heavy machine-gun fire, whilst Pte. Bishop, A.S.C., M.T., drove his ambulance with great coolness along shelled roads, and all received Military Medals for their gallantry.

The 23rd October, the 76th Field Ambulance moved back to Le Cateau, receiving wounded from at least three divisions, and on the 24th, as the advance continued, it moved on to Pommereuil, with a collecting post at Foresters House. During the next few days many French civilians in a very feeble condition from age, sickness, and gas poisoning, were evacuated through the Ambulance.

The 77th Field Ambulance established its main dressing station at Hargicourt with advanced dressing station at Bellicourt the 4th October. Pte. Davis, R.A.M.C., and Pte.

Burgess, R.A.M.C., won Military Medals for their incessant work for nearly 48 hours, evacuating wounded from the Regimental Aid Posts to the advanced dressing station, the former being wounded whilst trying to reach the 21st Manchesters Aid Post. Later on, near Bazuel, Capt. Haddow, M.C., won a bar to his M.C. for his gallantry in attending to wounded at the Regimental Aid Posts under heavy fire; whilst Pte. Smith, Pte. Armitage and Pte. Gee set a fine example to all ranks, the latter saving the lives of many French civilians who had been gassed. On the 7th, 8th, and 9th October, as the advance continued, the advanced dressing station was pushed forward to Mint Copse, between the village of Geneve and later to Maretz, with main dressing station at Bellicourt and Estrees. At Geneve, considerable damage was caused by German aeroplanes during the night 8th/9th; about 60 bombs were dropped in the vicinity of the dressing station between 7 p.m. and 1 a.m., Capt. Wells, R.A.M.C., being wounded, together with several others amongst the R.A.M.C. personnel and transport. From the 10th to the 12th October the advanced dressing station remained at Honnechy, with the main dressing station at Busigny, and relay posts in cellars at Le Cateau and St. Souplet, where the ambulance was relieved and returned to Elincourt for a few days' rest.

On the 18th October, the 77th Field Ambulance became responsible for clearing the 75th Brigade, temporarily attached to the 50th Division, and opened an advanced dressing station at the Busigny-Le Cateau-St. Souplet cross-roads. Owing to heavy shelling the advanced dressing station was moved during the afternoon to the village of St. Souplet, and next day to St. Benin. On the 20th October the 77th Field Ambulance was relieved by the 76th Field Ambulance, and remained in its transport lines until the 28th October, when owing to heavy shelling at Le Cateau, it was decided to move the Divisional Rest Station and establish it under the 77th Field Ambulance at Honnechy, where a great many cases of influenza were treated.

CHAPTER II.

Battle of the 100 Days.

LANDRECIES.

FROM the 12th to the 16th October, the 25th Division remained in the Serain-Premont-Ellincourt area in corps reserve for a short rest after the strenuous work of the previous eight days. Since the assault and capture of the German position at Beaurevoir, the Division during four days fighting had advanced across 16 miles of country, always in touch with the German rearguards, who were not only well provided with quantities of machine guns and batteries of Field Artillery, but also had the advantage of a retirement across undulating down land, well suited to the skilful employment of their weapons. The fullest use was invariably made of all sunken roads, isolated farms, houses, railway tracks and natural features of the ground along their line of retreat.

The majority of the casualties had been sustained during the battle at Beaurevoir, otherwise losses had been comparatively slight, which, in itself, constitutes an eloquent testimony to the skill displayed by subordinate and battalion commanders in the handling of their men. About 850 unwounded German prisoners, with 30 guns and Howitzers, had been captured, besides large numbers of machine guns, which, for the moment, could not be collected and counted. Reinforcements were now arriving in a steady stream, but all three Brigades were still considerably below their normal strength.

The 16th October Brig.-Gen. Frizell's 75th Brigade moved up to Honnechy, under the orders of the 50th Division. At 5.20 a.m., the 17th October, the XIIIth Corps, with the 18th and 50th Divisions, attacked along the line of the River Selle, south of Le Cateau, and during the morning the 75th Brigade moved up from Honnechy, and concentrated about a mile west of St. Benin, in order to cross the river the following morning and carry·on the attack to the next objective. The crossing of the river between St. Benin and Le Cateau, early the 18th October, was greatly hindered by thick mist and severe shelling immediately west of the railway, where most of the bridges had also been destroyed. At 7.30 a.m., the Brigade advanced from their assembly position along the railway embankment east of St. Benin, with the 1/8th Worcesters Regt. on the right, 1/5th Gloucesters on the left, 1/8th R. Warwicks in support. A, C and D Coys, 1/8th Worcesters, commanded by Capt. G. L. Watkinson, M.C., Capt. J. O. Walford and 2nd Lt. E. Wedgbury, M.C., D.C.M., M.M. A, B, C and D Coys, 1/5th Gloucesters, commanded by Lt. F. J. Lovell, Capt. V. B. Bingham-Hall, Capt. F. S. Hill, M.C., and Lt. P. A. Morfey, M.C. A, B, C and D Coys., 1/8th R. Warwicks, commanded by Lt. W. R. Pratt, 2nd Lt. C. F. Hunt, M.C., Lt. A. P. Hack, and 2nd Lt. W. H. Fawke, The attack was successful in every way ; the 50th Division, with a Brigade of the 66th Division on the left, and the 54th American Brigade on the right, reached the first objective up to time, and at 8.45 a.m., the leading Companies of the 75th Brigade passed through the 50th Division for their attack on the second objective, which was practically the line of the Bazuel-Le Cateau main road. Owing to the heavy mist and fog, there was some difficulty in keeping direction ; cn the right C and D Coys., 1/8th Worcesters, were held up by heavy machine-gun fire from the right front, but A Coy., on the left, in touch with the Gloucesters, managed by skilful use of their Lewis Guns, to push on in spite of the stiff resistance put up by the German machine guns and their Field guns, now firing over open sights.

C Coy., of the Warwicks, now reinforced the Worcesters on the right, who, in the meantime, had succeeded after heavy fighting, in reaching the outskirts of Bazuel, capturing a battery of 4.2-in. Howitzers. By 3 p.m., the whole line of the objectives had been successfully consolidated, and touch gained with the Americans and 66th Division on the flanks. Capt. Walford, 1/8th Worcesters, commanded C Coy. with great ability during the attack, and later on organised the line of defence east of the village of Bazuel, whilst Lt. Reynolds was most successful in capturing, with his platoon, a 77-mm. gun, which was firing at them from about 400 yards range. Sergt. Turner, M.M., Sergt. Faulkner, Sergt. Jones and Sergt. Hodgetts led their platoons with great courage and dash, the latter going forward alone to locate a German machine gun which was causing trouble. Pte. Day and Pte. Plumb repeatedly carried messages across ground swept by machine-gun fire, whilst Pte. Fellows distinguished himself in reconnoitring ahead of his section. Pte. Wainwright, employed as a Signaller, mended under fire at least 40 breaks in the line, and enabled communications to be kept through at a critical time. With the Gloucesters, Capt. Bingham Hall did excellent work, leading his company some distance beyond their objective, in order to assist troops on his right who were temporarily held up. 2nd Lt. Scroggie, entirely on his own account, attacked and captured with his platoon a ridge which dominated his line. Later, he successfully beat off several counter-attacks by the Germans. Corpl. Peacey set a wonderful example of courage and leadership when he captured, along with Pte. Bullock and his section, two machine guns and several prisoners. Pte. Jarvis did wonderfully effective work with his Lewis gun, whilst Pte. Williams, L./Cpl. Fletcher and L./Cpl. Pugh never failed to deliver messages entrusted to them under the most difficult conditions. Sergt. Smart, when his platoon officer was severely wounded, at once took command and led his platoon right through the fight, capturing several prisoners. Sergt. Owen, L./Cpl. Vosper and Corpl. Fowler, at the head of their sections, rushed several posts, capturing machine guns and several prisoners, whilst Corpl. Swanborough was severely wounded whilst leading an attack on another machine-gun post. Pte. Proudfoot and Pte. Webber in a most gallant manner rescued 2nd Lt. Woodward when he was severely wounded, and exposed to heavy machine-gun fire. 2nd Lt. Hughes, 1/8th R. Warwicks, when employed as Brigade Intelligence Officer, went out on this and other occasions beyond the front line, and invariably returned with valuable information. L./Corpl. Amey did most effective work with his Lewis gun when in charge of an isolated post, and L./Corpl. Crannage set a fine example to his men when their platoon commander was wounded. Pte. Whitehead on this and several other occasions delivered messages under extremely heavy fire. All received well-earned decorations.

Many prisoners and machine guns were captured during the day, and after dark a German ammunition convoy, unaware of the capture of its batteries, drove into Bazuel and was added to the bag. During the night there were indications that seemed to point to a general retirement of the German line, and arrangements were therefore made for a further advance early the morning of the 19th, with the 75th Brigade as advance guard to the 50th Division. This belief proved to be premature, and it soon became evident that the enemy had no intention of retreating until forced to do so.

The 25th Division, during the day, relieved the 50th Division. 7th and 74th Brigades moving up nearer the front, and the same night, 19th/20th, the 7th Brigade took over the left half of the Divisional sector from the 75th Brigade, with two battalions, 20th Manchesters, commanded by Lt.-Col. C. Pilkington, C.M.G., and 21st Manchesters in the front line, and the 9th Devons in close support. With the object of securing a better starting point for future operations, which were known to be imminent, the four battalions in the front line, by means of small patrols of eight men each, attempted to capture early the 20th October the line of the Richemont Brook, about 500 to 600 yards in front of our advanced posts. On the right and centre these patrols met with complete success, capturing about 50 prisoners, but on the left no advance was possible. 2nd Lt. Preston, 21st Manchesters, led his men with irresistible dash, and it was largely owing to his leadership that a mill which was strongly held by infantry with five machine guns was captured. Sergt. Wilkinson, M.M., in charge of one of the parties also did splendid work, and received a bar to his M.M. The weather had also broken, and incessant rain for three or four days increased the difficulties of transport, and led to great discomfort amongst the troops who were in battle order, without blankets or great coats.

During the 20th October and the night 20th/21st a series of reliefs and readjustments of boundaries with the flank Divisions took place : the 7th Brigade took over the whole Divisional front of about 2,500 yards ; the 6th Division of the IXth Corps relieved the 2nd American Corps, who were withdrawn for rest, and the 18th Division relieved the 66th Division on the left. The two American Divisions (the 27th and 30th) of the 2nd American Corps had had a very hard time whilst fighting with the 4th British Army. Forming part of the newly-raised American Armies, they had been in Europe only a few months carrying on with their training behinp the British line, combined with a few weeks' experience in a quiet sector further north. Their length of service and training was, therefore, somewhat similar to that of the new British Divisions employed at the battle of Loos in September, 1915, and the splendid spirit with which they helped to smash the Hindenburg line near Bellicourt will never be forgotten by the British troops.

23rd to 24th OCTOBER.

The 23rd October the 4th Army attacked with the IXth and XIIIth Corps in order to form a defensive flank facing south-east for the protection of the 3rd Army during its operations further north and, at the same time, the XIIIth Corps, with the 25th and 18th Divisions, was required to advance its line sufficiently to the east to admit the 6-in. guns being able to shell the important railway junction at Leval. The task allotted to the 25th Division was somewhat ambitious ; an advance of about 8,000 yards on a 2,000 yards front, including the capture of the village of Pommereuil and clearing of the Bois L'Eveque to a line east of the villages of Fontaine and Malgarni on the edge of the forest of Mormal, across a tract of country much intersected by thick hedges and covered by orchards. This advance was a totally different proposition from that successfully carried between Beaurevoir and Le Cateau. In the wood itself, felled trees and thick undergrowth made the going extremely difficult, increased by the swampy nature of the ground from the recent rains. This gave the Germans excellent cover for their nests and pockets of machine guns. Observation over the wood and line of advance was also in favour of the Germans from the high ground east of Malgarni, and for the present the line was well supported by field guns and Howitzers of various calibre.

The capture of Pommereuil and a line a few hundred yards east of the village was the task of the 7th Brigade, but owing to the numerical weakness of its three battalions, whose combined fighting strength hardly reached 700 rifles, the 1/8th R. Warwicks (75th Brigade) were attached in Brigade Reserve. The fighting strength of the infantry of the Division was 3,290 rifles. Between the first and second objectives, the 18th Division was to push forward on the left with a view to out-flanking the Bois L'Eveque from the north, with the

1/8th Worcesters (75th Brigade) protecting their right flank along the northern edge of the wood. The 1/5th Gloucesters (75th Brigade) being told off to " mop up " the north-eastern portion, and the 1/8th R. Warwicks the southern half of the Bois L'Eveque, and then to establish themselves along its north-western border. Touch during their advance was to be maintained by the 7th and 75th Brigades, with the 6th Division on the right flank. In the meantime the 74th Brigade was to move up during the morning along the north-west edge of the wood and ultimately to form up under cover of the wood for a further advance to the line east of the villages of Fontaine and Malgarni. As things turned out, however, the latter were unable, owing to opposition on the way up, to get into their assembly position in time to carry on the attack the same day.

The 7th Brigade attacked at 1.20 a.m., with all three battalions in the front line ; 21st Manchesters, 9th Devons and 20th Manchesters on the left. A, B and C Coys., 21st Manchesters, commanded by 2nd Lt. J. D. Preston, Capt. W. H. Cox, and Capt. J. H. Miller, M.C ; Nos. 1, 2 and 3 Coys., 9th Devons, commanded by Capt. R. O. Schuh, M.C. (wounded), Capt. A. J. F. Prynne and 2nd Lt. L. Elwood. A, B and C Coys., 20th Manchesters, commanded by Capt. G. W. L. Pritchard, M.C. (killed) succeeded by 2nd Lt. J. T. Walley, Capt. F. Nicholls, M.C., and Capt. H. S. Bagshaw, M.C. (wounded).

At the moment of the attack there was bright moonlight, but the night was rather misty ; white armlets were worn to distinguish between friend and foe. The battalions sustained some casualties whilst forming up in their assembly positions, but the leading waves made fairly good progress once the assault was launched. The artillery barrage crept forward at the rate of 100 yards per four minutes. The troops were soon across the Richemont Brooke, but the mist, combined with the smoke of the bursting shells and the inter-sected nature of the country, increased the difficulties of keeping close contact and direction in their advance to the village of Pommereuil. A good many pockets and isolated groups of Germans were overrun in the dark. Brig.-Gen. Hickie, 7th Brigade, riding with his groom into the village of Pommereuil before dawn, himself captured several Germans. Two tanks gave assistance to the Infantry in clearing the village. As soon, however, as it became daylight, local commanders were able to organise "mopping up" parties, which soon overcame all resistance, and the battalions were established by 11.15 a.m. along the line of their first objective east of Pommereuil.

Major Murray, 21st Manchesters, did excellent work in command of the battalion during the morning. When the units had got rather mixed up in the mist, he re-organised the attack with complete success. 2nd Lt. Best was invaluable to the battalion as Signalling Officer, keeping up communications under most difficult conditions. On this occasion he not only did his own work, but also took command of No. 1 Coy. when its Officers were wounded. Pte. Rutter won his D.C.M. for the courageous way in which he successfully mended 15 breaks along 800 yards of telephone cable at a time when it was very doubtful whether a runner could get through. Sergt. Hayward and Sergt. Smith, when their platoon officers were wounded, led their men with great skill and dash throughout the fight; the former rushed a machine gun and killed its crew. Pte. Shepherd, with a small party, captured another machine gun ; Pte. Deans did useful work in getting touch with troops on the flank and Pte. Knowles managed to guide a tank to the assistance of his Company, which was held up by uncut wire. With the 9th Devons Capt. Pridham did excellent work in command of the battalion during the fight. 2nd Lt. Cox was extremely quick in dealing with four machine-gun posts which were holding up the advance, and Pte. Courtney won a D.C.M. for a wonderful display of courage when he rushed a machine-gun post alone, and accounted for the whole crew with his fists and revolver. L./Corpl. Matthews, D.C.M., and Pte. Radmore did most effective work with their Lewis guns, and Corpl. Roberts led his platoon with great skill and judgment against a machine-gun post. Pte. Tuckerman distinguished himself by collecting a few men and attacking a house where he captured eight prisoners. Pte. Baker and Pte. Newman were conspicuous for their courage in attending to the wounded under heavy fire, whilst Pte. Eamer and Pte. Venning managed to carry most important messages to their destination under similar conditions. Sergt. Harper did useful work in getting touch with units on the flank, and all received decorations. With the 20th Manchesters, 2nd Lt. Isherwood and 2nd

Lt. Elder displayed considerable skill in leading their platoons on the right of the battalion in spite of the strong machine-gun opposition. L./Corpl. Crompton won his D.C.M. for the effective way in which he covered the advance of the Company on his right with his Lewis guns. Sergt. Sherry and Pte. Doherty, when their Officers were wounded, led their platoons with the greatest gallantry, whilst Pte. Hammond did most excellent work as a runner. Pte. Johnson, employed as a linesman, had a very difficult task to perform in mending the lines which were continually being broken during these two or three days. C.Q.M.S. Cadman and C.Q.M.S. Phipper earned the gratitude of all ranks by the way in which they prepared and delivered rations to the troops in the front line under extremely difficult conditions. All received decorations.

The 1/8th R. Warwicks with A, B, C and D Coys, commanded by Lieut. R. W. Pratt, 2nd Lieut. C. F. Hunt, M.C., Lieut. A. P. Hack and Capt. E. S. C. Vaughan, had been attached to the 7th Brigade and had been employed in clearing up these small parties of Germans overrun in the dark. At 9 a.m. they pushed on through the wood for another 2,000 yards, though not without considerable opposition. Capt. Mortimer, M.C., did excellent work in command of the battalion clearing up the machine gun posts which had been overrun in the dark. 2nd Lieut. Scrivener lead a party against a machine gun post which was holding up the advance, and captured 30 prisoners, including 4 officers and 8 machine guns ; a very fine performance. Corpl. Hall gallantly led his section against a machine gun nest and Pte. Eldred put another machine gun out of action with hand grenades and wounded the crew. Sergt. Lovett, when his Coy. Sergt.-Major was wounded, took on the duties with great success. Pte. Rubeley, Pte. Smith, M.M., Pte. Williams and Pte. Crowe, at a time when runners were having a very difficult time, never failed to deliver any messages entrusted to them, whilst Pte. McCarthy invariably showed the greatest courage in attending to the wounded under heavy fire. All received well earned decorations for their gallantry.

In the meantime, the 1/8th Worcesters with A, C and D Coys, commanded by Capt. G. L. Watkinson, M.C., Capt. J. O. Walford and 2nd Lieut. Wedgbury, M.C., D.C.M., M.M., and 1/5th Gloucesters with A, B, C and D Coys. commanded by 2nd Lieut. W. H. Robbins, Capt. V. B. Bingham Hall, 2nd Lieut. H. A. Cooke and Lieut. P. A. Morfey, M.C., had left their assembly positions at 1.20 a.m. Their subsequent advance was somewhat hindered by the thick mist, but on the other hand it facilitated their attack on several German machine gun posts which were giving trouble. The 1/8th Worcesters moving along the north-western edge of the Bois L'Eveque on the right of the 18th Division, successfully established posts at the north-west corner of the wood ; several prisoners, machine guns and 3 howitzers being captured during the morning. As it grew light, heavy casualties were inflicted on large parties of the enemy retiring from Pommereuil. Maj. Bate, M.C., 1/8th Worcesters, commanded the battalion with considerable skill during the fight, during which it captured several guns and about 200 prisoners ; 2nd Lieut. Wedgbury, M.C., D.C.M., M.M., showed remarkable qualities of leadership when he managed with only 17 men to penetrate about 2 miles behind the enemy's main line of resistance and captured a battery of howitzers with its detachments. Further on he captured Tilleuls farm with it's garrison of 150 men and 5 machine guns ; Corpl. Owers was the only N.C.O. of the party and performed fine service. Capt. Watkinson did splendid work with his company clearing part of Pommereuil where he secured many prisoners. Sergt. Sherwood, D.C.M., won a bar to his D.C.M. for his gallantry in attacking, with three other men, a machine gun post and so clearing a way for his company. Pte. Clift was excellent as a scout for his company, and Pte. Rowbottom at all times searched cellars and dugouts with the greatest courage and energy. For $1\frac{1}{2}$ hours Pte. Wood attended a severely wounded man under fire and Pte. Pitt performed fine service as a runner and scout. Pte. Knight did most effective work with his Lewis gun and Sergt. Slader led his platoon with conspicuous success. Sergt. Atkinson, M.M., in the advance through Pommereuil, led parties with the greatest determination and all received decorations.

The 1/5th Gloucesters encountered considerable opposition from the outset. Pte. Miles gained the V.C. for his great gallantry in clearing the way for his company. Quite alone he rushed forward 150 yards ahead of his men, captured 2 machine guns, killed their detachments and enabled his company to work round in the rear of the enemy and capture

16 more machine guns. On the right, A Coy. was unable to advance more than about 2,000 yards, until troops of the 71st Brigade, 6th Division resumed the attack later in the afternoon. To the left, B and C Coys. entering the wood at Flaquet Brefaut, gradually worked forward in a north-easterly direction so that by dusk the whole wood had been finally cleared and "mopped up"; a defensive flank was then formed, as a precaution facing south-east, along the Bazuel-Malgarni road. Throughout the fighting great success was invariably achieved by small parties with Lewis guns pushing on without reference to what was happening on their flanks; in fact these were the identical methods which had been employed so successfully by the Germans against the 25th and other Divisions during their offensives on the Lys and the Aisne the previous May; but only after they had succeeded in breaking the front line. During the early morning, 2nd Lieut. Ovenden, 1/5th Gloucesters, went out with a patrol of 4 men, all of whom became wounded; he then returned for his platoon, attacked and captured two machine guns with their detachments. Pte. Williams, Pte. Chedgery and Pte. Woodman carried messages through machine-gun fire, and L./Corpl. Payne did wonderful good work with his Lewis gun. Corpl. Edgeworth and Sergt. Niblett led patrols on several occasions, and in spite of opposition managed to return with valuable information.

Brig.-Gen. Craigie Halkett's 74th Brigade moved out of Honnechy at midnight 22nd/23rd, and thence to the northern edge of the wood to carry on the attack and push the line further east before dusk. Unexpected opposition however, was encountered from a party of Germans with machine guns in a sunken road about a mile east of Le Cateau, where in the initial stages of the attack, a gap existed between the 25th and 18th Divisions, which had not been searched by the preliminary bombardment. The 9th Yorks deployed and with the help of the Stokes mortars soon cleared the road, but only after considerable delay. The brigade then moved along the north-western edge of the wood, and at dusk the three battalions were approximately along the north-eastern edge in touch with the 18th Division at the northern corner, and in position for a further advance practically due east the next morning. The artillery also moved forward during the day to positions near Bois l'Eveque, to cover the advance next day. Sergt. Collins and Corpl. Hewgill, 9th Yorks, led their men with great determination, the latter with his section capturing a machine-gun post. Pte. Dyson, when his platoon officer was wounded, gallantly went forward to reconnoitre a way for his unit. L./Corpl. Stead did valuable work as a runner under heavy fire, and Pte. Brown under similar conditions showed great bravery in attending to his Company Commander who was severely wounded. All received Military Medals.

At 4 a.m., the 24th October, the line again moved forward ; the 74th Brigade reinforced by the 1/8th Worcesters with the 6th Division on the right, the 18th Division on the left. The 6th Division which had had heavy fighting the previous day, made rapid progress on the right, and the troops of the 7th and 75th Brigade who had formed the defensive flank the previous evening, were now withdrawn to Pommereuil. On the right of the 74th Brigade, the 9th Yorks with A, B and C Coys., commanded by Capt. W. R. Knott, 2nd Lieut. J. S. Wood and 2nd Lieut. W. Littlefair. The 13th Durham L.I. with their 2 Coys. commanded by Lieut. R. S. F. Mitchell and 2nd Lieut. H. Gardner, and on the left the 11th Sherwood Foresters with A and B Coys., commanded by Capt. W. A. Clifton, M.C., and Capt. H. H. Spicer, M.C. (wounded), succeeded by Lieut. A. D. Parkin, M.C. As the attacking waves came in to the open ground, east of the wood, they were met by heavy machine gun and rifle fire from a prepared position west of Malgarni, known as the Herman Stellung II line. Nothing had been previously known of this line of trenches which was found to be protected by two strong belts of wire. Opposition was, however, soon overcome, and except for some hand to hand fighting in the village of Malgarni, there was little further resistance, the line of the objective, south-east of Fontaine being in our hands by 10 a.m. The Worcesters on the left had a hard day's fighting, and captured Fontaine au Bois with a group of houses beyond known as " Les Grandes Chenes," with about 375 prisoners. Capt. Walford did remarkably well with his company. 2nd Lieut. Bateman, M.M., and 2nd Lieut. Gordon also pushed on with the greatest energy and determination to their objectives in spite of opposition from machine gun posts ; unfortunately, the former was wounded early in the fight, but still carried on. At 2 p.m., the brigade moved forward to its final objective about 2,000 yards further east. This line was successfully reached by 6 p.m. ; at the same time the 1/8th Worcesters worked along the left flank, linking up with the 18th Division, who had met with considerable resistance and did not quite reach their final objective before dark. Capt. Knott, 9th Yorks, and 2nd Lieut. Wood led their men during the attack with great skill and determination. Pte. Gilmore did most effective work with his Lewis gun team, and Pte. Muller with his section attacked and captured a machine gun post which was holding up the advance. Pte. Adams, Pte. Guest, Pte. Stendall and L./Corpl. Copley successfully delivered several messages under heavy fire, and Pte. Glennell gallantly went forward alone to cut some wire which was holding up the advance of his unit. Sergt. Smith, M.M., did fine service at the head of his platoon against a machine gun post. With the 11th Sherwood Foresters, Capt. Clifton, M.C., was wounded early in the attack but continued to lead his company. Sergt. Johnson was invaluable in command of his platoon, and later as Coy. Sergt. Major, whilst Pte. Smith, Pte. Nicholson and L./Cpl. Frisby were conspicuous for their courage as stretcher-bearers, they attended the wounded in the open and the latter though himself wounded, still carried on with his work. L/Corpl. Chappin and Pte. Walmsley did wonderful good work with their Lewis guns, and Sergt. Richardson set an example of the highest courage to his men. Pte. Blow did splendid work as a runner, and Pte. Wardle though himself wounded succeeded in collecting the mules carrying his Lewis guns which had been stampeded by shelling. Capt. Lawrie, R.A.M.C., attached to the battalion, was conspicuous for his bravery in attending to the wounded under heavy fire. With the 13th Durham L.I., Lt.-Col. Hone, M.C., was unfortunately hit by a sniper when reconnoitring in front ; he had led the battalion throughout the operations with great skill, and was a great loss to his unit. 2nd Lieut. Willey as Adjutant, did valuable work during the fight, and both Lieut. Gardner and Lieut. Mitchell, M.C., led their companies with the greatest determination. Pte. Winter went forward alone and managed to find a gap in the wire for his party. L./Corpl. Armstrong, M.M., and Pte. Jones for several days mended wires and maintained communication under most difficult conditions, and all received decorations.

During the night 24th/25th, the 7th Brigade took over the

left half of the Divisional front, and the 75th Brigade went back to Pommereuil in Divisional reserve. During the next few days, the 74th and 7th Brigades held the front with two Battalions in the front line, and one in support, with Headquarters at Pommereuil, and Divisional Headquarters at Le Cateau Station.

Preparations were now made for another attack on a large scale. Patrols were constantly active, and posts were pushed forward whenever possible in order to improve our line and gain better observation, which at the best, however, was extremely difficult owing to the enclosed nature of the country. It soon became apparent that ready made gaps through the hedges in this closely intersected country should be carefully avoided, as they were usually commanded by machine guns. In spite of the extra time and trouble involved, many casualties were saved by cutting new gaps. Unfortunately, Lt.-Col. Young, D.S.O., 11th Sherwood Foresters was killed the morning of the 25th, and Capt. R. M. Burmann, D.S.O., M.C., Brigade Major of the 7th Brigade, who had served throughout the war, was also killed by a shell on the 27th October, whilst reconnoitring near Fontaine au Bois. Pte. Holding, 21st Manchesters as a runner, and Corpl. Alcock did extremely useful work, the latter continually leading patrols and procuring valuable information. 2nd Lieut. Allison, 13th Durham L.I., led his platoon in an attempt to capture a German post near Fontaine in a most gallant manner and though nearly surrounded, managed to fight his way back. C.S.M. Hammond, M.M., and C.S.M. Thomson, D.C.M., were invaluable with their companies in re-organizing and encouraging their men, and Pte. Poulter did splendid work with his Lewis gun in covering the temporary retirement of his company. Sergt. Walton, Sergt. Killeen and Pte. Robinson went out in charge of patrols, and returned with valuable information, whilst Pte. Jackson successfully kept the battalion supplied with bombs and ammunition under very difficult conditions, and all received decorations.

The German artillery was not very active, though on several occasions villages in the forward area were bombarded with gas shells. This proved a great hardship to any French civilians who had been left behind in the villages, and were naturally unprovided with gas masks. Five hundred and forty-six unwounded prisoners, including 17 Officers were captured, and many machine guns and guns of every description. Casualties were heavy ; 67 Officers and 1,386 other ranks.

	Killed.		Wounded.		Missing.
Officers... ...	9	...	55	...	3
Other Ranks ...	192	...	974	...	220

NOVEMBER 4th to 8th.

During the concluding days of October, and the first few days of November, preparations were pushed on for what proved to be the final advance of the 4th, 3rd, and 1st Armies, which carried the British line to the east of Maubeuge and Mons, roughly an advance of about 25 miles, along a front of 30 miles. Railways were repaired, bridges re-built, and the railheads gradually advanced close up to the fighting troops. Thousands of prisoners and men from the Labour Coys. were employed on this work, which became the main factor governing the advance of the armies. After the capture of Landrecies most of the German artillery was either captured, destroyed or withdrawn, and resistance by the German rearguards dwindled to what was necessary to gain sufficient time to blow up the bridges and craters at cross roads. On the XIIIth Corps and 3rd Army front, the forest of Mormal was the chief obstacle with the River Sambre to the east. This great stretch of forest land, covering about 50 square miles, had provided the Germans with a vast supply of timber for the construction of their dugouts, huts, trenches and the humble duckboard ; many saw mills had been erected, and numerous light trolley lines had been laid for the transport of the timber. The forest had also been successfully used for the assembly and concealment of the German Divisions prior to their attack the 21st March on the British line in front of St. Quentin, Bapaume and Arras.

The task before the 25th Division was to assault the German position along a front of about 2,000 yards, and to advance through a very intricate and enclosed country to the banks of the Sambre Canal, about 1½ miles from the starting point. The crossing of the canal, about 55 feet wide and 6 to 7 feet deep, the capture of Landrecies and the establishment of a line east of the town completed the first objective. An advance of a further two miles was given as a second objective, so as to bring the Divisional front about a mile beyond the Petite Helpe River. This last move was, however, contingent on the successful advance on the right by the 32nd Division, who had relieved the 6th Division on the IXth Corps front. The 50th Division was in touch on the left. During the night, October 30th/31st, the 50th Division took over the portion of the 25th Division front held by the 7th Brigade, which withdrew to billets in Le Cateau. The night of the 31st/1st November, the 75th Brigade relieved the 74th Brigade, which moved back to Pommereuil and St. Benin. To the 75th Brigade was entrusted the task of the crossing of the Canal and the capture of Landrecies with two Companies of the 21st Manchesters (7th Brigade) responsible for " mopping up " the area on the right flank. The two leading battalions, 1/5th Gloucesters and 1/8th R. Warwicks were to cross the canal and make good the far bank, after which the other battalion of the Brigade, the 1/8th Worcesters, would pass through and complete the capture of the town. The 74th Brigade was to move in rear of the 75th Brigade, ready to force their way across the canal should the leading brigade require assistance, and ultimately to pass through the battalions of the 75th Brigade beyond the town, and carry on the advance. The 7th Brigade was held in Divisional reserve ready to move at 15 minutes notice. The fighting strength of the infantry of the Division was now 4,190 rifles.

At 6.15 a.m., the 4th November, the 75th Brigade attacked, with the 1/5th Gloucesters on the right, the 1/8th R. Warwicks on the left, and the 1/8th Worcesters in support. The 105th Field Coy., R.E., under Major F. W. Richards, M.C., R.E., and one company of the 11th South Lancs. (Pioneers), commanded by Capt. S. E. Boulton, M.C., came immediately behind the leading wave of infantry, carrying up rafts made out of petrol tins, in case all bridges were destroyed by the Germans in their retreat. The Infantry were also provided with life belts. A and B Coys., 21st Manchesters, under Capt. Miller, M.C., reinforced the 75th Brigade on the right of the Gloucesters. A, B, C and D Coys., 1/5th Gloucesters, commanded by 2nd Lt. W. H. Robbins, Capt. V. B. Bingham Hall, 2nd Lt. G. H. West, and Capt. G. E. Ratcliffe, M.C. A, B, C and D Coys., 1/8th R. Warwicks, commanded by 2nd Lt. H. Fawke, Lt. J. G. Eccles, Capt. E. S. C. Vaughan and Lt. A. P. Hack. A, C and D Coys.,

1/8th Worcesters, commanded by Capt. L. R. Bomford, M.C. (wounded), Capt. J. O. Walford (wounded), and 2nd Lt. Wedgebury, M.C., D.C.M., M.M. (wounded), succeeded by 2nd Lt. P. N. Coleman.

The attack started well up behind the artillery barrage, and though isolated machine-gun posts interfered with the advance to a certain extent, the troops were able to push on and capture them by getting round their flanks. The 1/8th R. Warwicks encountered rather more opposition on the left. L./Corpl. Amey, 1/8th R. Warwicks won a V.C. for his work during the morning. With his section he first of all captured a German strong point with several machine guns and about 50 prisoners; then successfully attacked another machine-gun post, finishing up with the capture, single-handed, of a Chateau in the village of Faubourg Soyers, with its garrison of about 20 Germans. This gallant action practically cleared away the last of the opposition in the neighbourhood, though great assistance was given by a tank, No. 9107, under 2nd Lt. Knowles, in clearing machine guns out of this village, a small suburb of Landrecies, situated on the west side of the canal. Lt. Eccles was taken prisoner when separated from his Company early in the advance, but appeared three hours later at his Battalion Headquarters, with a party of eight Germans. 2nd Lt. Brundrett, 21st Manchesters, led his men with conspicuous success during the fight. Pte. Harris, single-handed, captured 30 prisoners, including eight officers, whilst Pte. Williams did splendid work with his Lewis gun.

Prisoners began to arrive early, and continued to come back in increasing numbers. By 9.20 a.m., the leading men of both battalions had reached the canal, and were ready to force their way across. Fortunately the foot bridges put up by the Germans, and a temporary wooden bridge about 1,000 yards north-east of the lock were reached before the enemy had had time to destroy them; whilst although the main road bridge at Landrecies lock was blown up about 10.30 a.m., the lock gates themselves were not destroyed, and were available for the Infantry. The Artillery halted their barrage along a line 300 yards east of the Canal, and machine guns were pushed forward as soon as possible to cover the crossing by direct and indirect fire. Smoke shells were fired on the high ground east and south of the canal, and large numbers of smoke bombs were also dropped by aeroplanes to assist and conceal the movements of the troops. Four tanks came along with the Infantry as far as the Canal, and four supply tanks were put at the disposal of the engineers to carry up any bridging material required. Worcesters, Gloucesters and Warwicks crossed almost simultaneously along the Divisional front, though each unit as well as the Engineers, claimed that their men were the first to reach the opposite bank, and the town of Landrecies. The houses on the far side of the Canal had been well prepared for its defence with plenty of machine guns and garrisoned by men of the 1st Guards Reserve Division, Jager Division, and a Cyclist Brigade, but there is no doubt that our Artillery was so effective that the defence was fairly swept away. On the left, C Coy., 1/8th Worcesters, crossed over by means of the rafts carried along for the purpose. As soon as it became evident that the rafts were no longer required as ferries, the Engineers quickly formed them into floating bridges, so that by mid-day there were more than half a dozen crossings fit for Infantry. The 105th Field Coy., R.E., were responsible for this work, which was very well done. Pontoon bridges were then erected on each side of the lock, and though the work was somewhat delayed by shelling, yet both bridges were ready for horse transport soon after dark. Many prisoners and much material and stores were captured in Landrecies, including a Regimental Commander and his Staff, whilst at the Hospital, a Sick Parade of German invalids were surprised by a party of Worcesters. Some wagons belonging to the Divisional Ammunition Column, which had been captured by the Germans on the Aisne in May, were also recovered. The troops were received with great enthusiasm by the French civilian inhabitants, and a few days later, after a ceremonial march through the streets, it was announced that one of the Boulevards would be renamed the "Boulevard Charles," as a compliment to the Division and its Commander. The following message was also received from the Army Commander :—"Please convey to the 25th Division my congratulations and warm thanks for their gallantry and determination in forcing the passage of the canal and capturing Landrecies. It was a very difficult operation requiring great skill and dash. The success of these efforts is most creditable to all ranks, especially to the Engineers, who constructed the bridges."

By noon the troops had gained their first objective east

of the town, and the 112th and 150th Brigades, R.F.A., had moved up to cover the further advance. 2nd Lt. West, 1/5th Gloucesters, collected and reorganised the men of his Company with great coolness when the other officers were wounded, and Capt. Bingham Hall displayed remarkable powers of leadership throughout the fight and the crossing of the canal. C.S.M. Bromage and Sergt. Hobbs, M.M., did splendid work in reorganising their Companies during the advance to the canal, and in getting the men across, the latter being the first man in the Company to reach the other side. L./Corpl. Hornigold, though wounded, and Corpl. Gillies led their platoons with great dash, the latter capturing two German Officers and 40 prisoners. Pte. Matthews did very fine work as a Stretcher Bearer, attending to the wounded under heavy fire, and both Pte. Davis and L./Corpl. Curry did wonderful good work with their Lewis guns, covering the crossing of the Canal. L./Corpl. Clee, M.M., and Corpl. King, M.M., led their platoons throughout with great dash, and Corpl. Coulson, in charge of a platoon, managed to obtain valuable information prior to the attack. L./Corpl. Trigg carried out his duties as linesman, keeping communication through and mending wires under heavy fire, whilst Pte. Scanlon and L./Corpl. Lewis did splendid work as runners under similar conditions. With the 1/8th R. Warwicks, Lt.-Col. Whitehouse gained the D.S.O. for his work throughout the fighting. Under his leadership, the battalion fought its way to and crossed the canal, capturing about 200 prisoners and several guns. Lt. Vaughan, by his energetic action, managed to reach the canal with his men and capture the bridge before the Germans had time to destroy it, whilst 2nd Lt. Bradley did splendid service as Signal Officer in keeping up communications. Sergt. Wootton, M.M., Pte. Ellaway, Corpl. Kirby, L./Corpl. Rushbrook and Pte. Hill were most effective with their Lewis guns against machine-gun posts, the latter, though wounded, still gallantly carried on until relieved. Sergt. Lissaman, when his platoon officer was wounded, took command, and managed to capture a bridge before it could be destroyed. Pte. Caudle and L.-Corpl. Fourt, as Signallers, repaired the lines under most difficult conditions, whilst Pte. Hirst repeatedly carried messages under heavy fire. L./Corpl. Rolfe, M.M., in charge of a patrol, and Pte. Laity as a Scout, did very good work. L./Corpl.

Gilbert, when all other N.C.Os. were wounded, reorganised and led his platoon, and Sergt. Harvey, when his Company Commander, Lt. Eccles, was taken prisoner, took command with complete success. All received decorations. With the Worcesters, Lt.-Col. Clarke, D.S.O., won the distinction of a bar to his D.S.O. for his services in command of his battalion, which captured about 375 prisoners and several guns during the day. Capt. Bomford, M.C., and Capt. Walford, M.C., led their companies to the canal in spite of strong opposition from machine-gun posts and superintended the crossing with great coolness. Later on in the day both were unfortunately wounded. After the capture of the town, 2nd Lt. Coe attacked and captured two batteries with about 40 prisoners. L./Corpl. Stokes, Pte. Beasant and L./Corpl. Bowler did wonderful good work with their Lewis guns, and Pte. Adams delivered messages on several occasions through machine-gun fire. Sergt. Roberts and Sergt. Hodgetts, M.M., both rendered splendid service in command of their platoons during the difficulties in crossing the canal, whilst Sergt. Jennings, as Company-Sergeant-Major, was invaluable to his Company. Pte. Dale, as a Scout, Corpl. Somers and Pte. Hodges, in charge of patrols, gained valuable information, and all received decorations.

At 9.10 a.m., the 11th Sherwood Foresters (74th Brigade) moved up to follow the 75th Brigade across the canal, and by 2 p.m. the 9th Yorks and 13th Durham Light Infantry, who had been kept back until the 32nd Division on the right flank had reached the canal, began to cross over. On the left the 50th Division had been equally successful, and had reached their first objective.

At 3.30 p.m., the 74th Brigade moved forward through the 75th Brigade, with the 11th Sherwood Foresters on the right, 9th Yorks on the left, and 13th Durham Light Infantry in support. A, B and C Coys., 11th Sherwood Foresters, commanded by Capt. W. A. Clifton, M.C., Lt. O. R. Orchard, and Lt. A. D. Parkin, M.C. A, B, C and D Coys., 9th Yorks, commanded by Capt. W. L. Blow, M.C., Lt. R. J. Darvall, Capt. W. R. Knott, and Capt. A. B. H. Roberts, M.C. A and B Coys., 13th Durham Light Infantry, commanded by 2nd Lt. R. H. Farrier, M.C., and 2nd Lt. H. Gardner. By 6.45 p.m., the battalions had reached a line running through Le Preseau, about 3,000 yards beyond the first objective. On the way, several large guns and howitzers were captured, and a certain amount of fighting took place with German rear-guards in the various houses and farm buildings. Troops of the 75th Brigade meanwhile formed a defensive flank to the south-east in touch with the 32nd Division on the right, where they remained during the night. During the afternoon the 7th Brigade moved up to the canal, sending the 9th Devons to reinforce the line east of Landrecies.

Sergt. Caygill, 9th Yorks, led his platoons with great skill and courage, whilst Sergt. Wilkinson did splendid work in repairing wires and keeping up communications during the advance. Pte. Saint and Sergt. Stephenson were at all times conspicuous for their courage in attending to the wounded under heavy fire. Pte. Watts, 11th Sherwood Foresters, crawled forward with his Lewis gun and silenced a machine gun which was holding up the advance, and all received Military Medals. Sergt. Garfoot won a D.C.M. for the gallant way in which, with only two men, he rushed another machine gun post and captured the gun with 20 prisoners.

At 6.15 a.m., 5th November, the 74th Brigade group continued their advance with the 11th Sherwood Foresters in front, followed by 9th Yorks and 13th Durham Light Infantry, with one Coy., 25th M.G. Corps, 110th Brigade, R.F.A., and the 130th Field Coy., R.E. One troop of the 12th Lancers was attached as advance guard. The 75th Brigade kept pace with the 74th Brigade ; the 1/8th R. Warwicks being responsible for protection of the right flank until the 32nd Division, who had encountered more opposition, got level and straightened out the line. Very little opposition was encountered, and by 9.40 a.m. the advance guard had crossed the Petite Helpe River west of Maroilles, and was pushing on through the village. At 9.55 a.m., the 75th Brigade moved forward from their position west of Landrecies, and marching through Le Preseau, came up in support of the 74th Brigade. At 10.20 a.m. the 75th Brigade began to concentrate in order to follow on behind the 7th Brigade in the main body of the Division. Soon after midday the 11th Sherwood Foresters reached Rue du Faux village, and continued their advance eastwards. Fortunately, one bridge over the Petite Helpe River was left standing and here armoured cars, lorries and heavy guns were able to cross the river without delay ; the German sentry guarding the demolition charge being captured. As a rule, the scheme of demolition of important bridges, railways, etc., had been very thoroughly carried out by the enemy, at any rate in front of the 25th Division, and their neglect to destroy this particular bridge was a piece of unexpected good fortune for the Division, as otherwise lorries would have been unable to cross the river for two or three days. At 2 p.m. the 7th Brigade was crossing the river, and by 3.15 p.m. the leading battalion, the 21st Manchesters, were through Maroilles and pushing on to the village of Basse Noyelles to fill the gap between the 74th Brigade and 50th Division. By 4.40 p.m. A Coy. were in touch with the 50th Division in Noyelles, where a few prisoners were captured. Pte. Stallebras, 11th Sherwood Foresters, did most effective work with his Lewis gun, and Pte. Percival, when the advance was held up near a bridge, rushed forward under heavy machine-gun fire and prevented its destruction, though unfortunately he received two wounds during the performance of this gallant action. L./Corpl. Geggie later on gallantly searched for a wounded comrade under heavy fire, and all received Military Medals.

Fighting went on all the afternoon on the eastern side of Maroilles, and by dark the outpost line along the Divisional front was held by the 11th Sherwood Foresters and 9th Yorks, with the 13th Durham Light Infantry in support, and on the left, 21st Manchesters and 20th Manchesters, with 9th Devons in support. Divisional Headquarters moved to Landrecies during the afternoon.

The advance continued at 6.30 a.m., the 6th November, with the 74th Brigade on the right and the 7th Brigade on the left. Each Brigade group was complete with its brigade of Field Artillery, one company of the 25th M.G. Corps, one Field Company R.E., and one troop 12th Lancers. Armoured cars were also attached to the Division. The 32nd Division commenced their advance somewhat later, but their mounted troops were under way soon after daybreak. This time the 9th Yorks led the 74th Brigade with 13th Durham Light Infantry and 11th Sherwood Foresters in the main body. The 20th Manchesters formed the advance guard to the 7th Brigade, with the 9th Devons and 21st Manchesters behind. A, B, C and D Companies, 20th Manchesters, commanded by 2nd Lt. S. T. Walley, Capt. F. Nicholls, M.C., 2nd Lt. D. Kitchen, and 2nd Lt. I. Iserwood. Nos. 1, 2 and 3 Coys., 9th Devons, commanded by 2nd Lt. R. Cox, Capt. J. W. Palmer, Lt. H. C. Wilson. A, B, C and D Coys., 21st Manchesters, commanded by Capt. G. Langdon, M.C., Capt. J. W. Bell, M.C. (killed), Capt. S. H. Miller, M.C., and 2nd Lt. J. D. Preston. Little resistance was met with at first, as the German rearguard appeared to have been withdrawn during the night. Cavalry patrols covered the front, and although fired at by machine guns, the advance was not seriously contested. By 10 a.m. the 20th Manchesters were at Taisnieres, and pushing on to the Grande Helpe River, beyond the village. On the right, about mid-day, the 9th Yorks were held up about a mile west of Marbaix by machine-gun posts. With artillery support, these posts were soon rushed and captured, and by 2 p.m. Marbaix had been occupied. By 6 p.m. the 20th Manchesters had reached the village of Dompierre, and the Divisional front for the night, 6th/7th November, was held by the 9th Yorks on the right, 11th Sherwood Foresters on the left, with the 13th Durhams in support. The 20th Manchesters (7th Brigade) maintained their outpost line on the eastern outskirts of Dompierre, linking up with the 50th Division on the left. During the night patrols from both Brigades were sent out and communication was established between them at Baptiste, a small village midway between Marbaix and Dompierre. Capt. Nicholls, 20th Manchesters, commanded the two companies, forming the advance guard, and organised the attack on machine-gun posts at Dompierre and Taisnieres, with considerable skill. 2nd Lt. Branham and 2nd Lt. Kitchen handled their men with great determination, capturing two strong points near Dompierre, with several machine-guns and their detachments. Corpl. Barton and Corpl. Burgam rendered excellent service with their Lewis gun, and Pte. Waterhouse on this and other occasions was conspicuous for his courage in attending to the wounded under fire. Pte. Leigh showed great fighting spirit in charge of a section with whom he attacked and captured a machine-gun post. Pte. Duncan, 11th Sherwood Foresters, when his platoon was held up by a machine gun, gallantly crept forward by himself, captured the gun and killed its detachment. All received military medals. •

Cavalry patrols pushed forward early the 7th November, and at 8 a.m., the 75th Brigade, with 1/5th Gloucesters leading, 1/8th R. Warwicks, and 1/8th Worcesters in rear, passed through the 74th Brigade, and, together with the 7th Brigade on the left, continued the advance across the Petite Helpe River. All bridges were destroyed, but the whole brigade managed to cross over on a fallen tree. German rearguards had been again withdrawn during the night, and no opposition was encountered for about two miles. By 9.30 a.m., Cavalry patrols had reached St. Hilaire, and the leading battalions of the 75th and 7th Brigades, the 1/5th Gloucesters, and the 21st Manchesters were pushing on rapidly towards the Avesnes-Maubeuge mainroad. Capt. J. W. Bell, M.C., 21st Manchesters, was unfortunately killed whilst leading his Company, probably the last officer casualty in the whole Division. By mid-day the 21st Manchesters had reached a point about 2,000 yards short of the main road, but further to the right considerable opposition was encountered by the 75th Brigade. Fighting continued all the afternoon on the right and by dusk the battalions were still about one mile short of the main road.

During the night the 66th Division relieved the 25th Division along their front, all three Brigades marching back to the Landrecies-Preux-Bousies area with Divisional Headquarters at Landrecies, the Machine Gun Battn. and Field Coys., R.E., being relieved the following night. The Divisional Artillery and all other attached troops remained with the 66th Division.

Since leaving Le Cateau, the Division, during the two days' fighting on the 23rd and 24th October, had advanced about 4½ miles through very difficult country, including the Bois L'Évesque, a small wood half way between Le Cateau and the Forest of Mormal. Between the 4th and 8th November it had covered another 12 miles, including the passage of the Sambre Canal in the face of a strong defence by numerous machine guns and heavy artillery. Its success was undoubtedly due to the splendid co-operation of all ranks of the various services of the Division, the finely developed esprit de corps of all units, and their determination to carry through an operation which required the greatest initiative on the part of the Company and local Commanders on the spot. The Artillery was most effective throughout the advance ; its bombardment to cover the passage of the canal not only broke down the defence, but by its accuracy assisted the Infantry to carry through, with comparatively slight losses, what must always be a most complicated and difficult military operation. The work of the Field Companies, R.E., in the repair of the numerous bridges, roads, and the manufacture of rafts, meant a sustained effort over many days, with very little sleep and rest, by every man in the unit, for which they cannot be too highly praised. Administrative arrangements, both as regards ordnance stores and supplies, were excellent ; long distances and damaged roads undoubtedly put a severe strain both on men and horses, yet on very rare occasions were the troops unprovided with food. Throughout the operations great credit is due to the regimental transport for their prompt delivery of rations to the troops in the firing line.

During the subsequent stages of the advance there was no prepared line of defence. Most of the German artillery had been either captured, destroyed, or withdrawn, and any opposition came from rearguards entirely composed of machine-gun detachments. Prisoners numbered 889, including 26 officers, with large quantities of material, machine guns and guns of every description. Our casualties amounted to 32 officers and 608 other ranks.

	Killed.	Wounded.	Missing.
Officers	5	27	—
Other ranks	78	469	61

The 12th November, the Division moved back to billets in the Le Cateau area, and the beginning of December to an area east of Cambrai, with Divisional Headquarters at Avesnes-les-Aubert, where it was employed in salvage work in the surrounding country. On the 4th December the Division received a visit from the King and the Prince of Wales, who passed through the villages of Carnières, Boussieres, St. Hilaire, and Quiévy, where several units of the Division were billeted.

Demobilisation was in full swing by the middle of January, and worked quite smoothly in spite of the unfortunate " pivotal " system which was wisely abolished the beginning of February. Of the 14,000 men, roughly the strength of the Division at Christmas, 1918, about 3,000 men who had joined after the 1st January, 1916, were transferred to other divisions forming the Army of Occupation on the Rhine ; about 300 releasable men re-engaged for service in the postbellum army, and the remainder, with the exception of those required for the cadres, had all been despatched to England for their discharge by the end of March. All arrangements at Cambrai for the XIIIth Corps demobilisation camp were excellent, and men were despatched down the line with a minimum of delay, across the Channel, and through their dispersal stations in England. A few weeks later the cadres of all units of the Division returned to England, and handed in their equipment and stores on demobilization.

ARTILLERY.

During the few days that the Divisional Artillery was out at rest at Honnechy, preparations had been completed along the British front for another attack on a large scale by the 4th, 3rd, and 1st Armies, with the first French Army on the right, along a 50-mile front. 400 rounds per 18-pounder and 250 rounds per 4·5-inch howitzer were dumped at the gun positions and, on the night of the 2nd/3rd November, the 110th and 112th Brigades, R.F.A., moved into positions along the eastern edge of the Bois L'Eveque, and the following night all batteries not already forward took up their battle positions. The crossing of the Sambre Canal and the capture of Landrecies was the task allotted to the 25th Division covered by the 110th, 112th, and the 330th and 331st Brigades R.F.A., of the 66th Divisional Artillery.

The Divisional Artillery had been very fortunate as regards casualties during the last two months, and changes in the command had been few.

110th Brigade, R.F.A.	Lt.-Col. K. E. Milford, D.S.O.	
A/110	Major J. W. Watson, M.C.	
B/110	Major A. L. Harman, D.S.O.,M.C.	
C/110	Major E. Sherlock.	
D/110	Major P. C. L. Williams, M.C.	
112th Brigade, R.F.A.	Lt.-Col. L. H. Queripel, C.M.G., D.S.O.	
A/112	Major W. Swinton, M.C.	
B/112	Major C. M. Duncan, D.S.O.	
C/112	Major H. V. Dean, M.C.	
D/112	Major D. D. Pole Evans, M.C.	

At 6.15 a.m., the 4th November, the attack commenced with an excellent barrage and bombardment; good progress was made by the Infantry, especially on the right. All resistance was eventually overcome; by midday the canal had been crossed under a most effective bombardment by all the available artillery, and Landrecies captured by the 75th Infantry Brigade. Two sections of 6-inch trench mortars followed in close support of the Infantry. The 150th and 110th Brigade, R.F.A., moved forward to cover the 74th Infantry Brigade on the left, and the 112th Brigade covered the 75th Infantry Brigade, with the 330th and 331st Brigades protecting their right flanks. Many prisoners, machine guns, and one 8-inch howitzer, and about 42 field guns were captured during the day. Lieut. Lane, D.C.M., did most effective work with his trench mortars, and Capt. Radcliffe, M.C., A/110, after the capture of Landrecies, pushed on ahead of his battery with one gun, which he brought into action at very close range. Sergt. Agathe, M.M., D/110, as Batt. Sergt.-Major, set a very fine example in maintaining the fire of his battery, and Spr. Webb displayed great endurance in keeping up communications when the lines were continually broken by the shelling. All received decorations.

The advance continued the 5th November, with the 74th Infantry Brigade in front, supported by the 110th Brigade, R.F.A., as far as Maroilles. The 330th and 331st Brigades remained in mobile reserve, whilst the 150th and 112th Brigades, R.F.A., concentrated south of the canal.

The 6th November, brigade groups were formed, and the advance was continued on a two-brigade front, with the 74th Infantry Brigade on right and 7th Infantry Brigade on left, supported by the 110th and 150th Brigades, R.F.A., with the 112th attached to the 75th Brigade in reserve, all brigades being directly under the orders of the Infantry Brigadiers. In the evening the two leading brigades were in action near Marbaix and Dompierre, but by this time most of the German artillery had either been captured, destroyed, or withdrawn, and the greater part of the opposition encountered was from machine-gun posts.

The 7th November the advance reached to within a mile of the Avesnes-Maubeuge main road, when the 66th Division relieved the 25th Division during the night 7th/8th, and the following day the Divisional Artillery moved back to the west of Landrecies, with the exception of the 112th Brigade, R.F.A., which accompanied the 66th Division beyond Avesnes.

On the 4th November, R.A. Headquarters moved back to Le Cateau with the brigades at St. Benin, and during the next fortnight the whole were engaged in salvage work along with the Infantry of the Division. On the 1st December the Artillery accompanied the Division to the area east of Cambrai, with Headquarters at Avesnes-Les-Aubert, the 110th Brigade at St. Hilaire, the 112th Brigade at Carnières, and D.A.C. at Quiévy.

During the whole period the work of the Divisional Ammunition Column, under Lt.-Col. C. S. Hope Johnstone, with Capt. Webb, Capt. Tacon, and Capt. Flowers in command of No. 1, No. 2, and No. 3 Section, had been most arduous and severe. Long distances, continual moves, and large quantities of ammunition required at the gun positions entailed a heavy strain of the personnel and horses of this most important branch on the Artillery. On no occasion did they fail to keep the batteries supplied with ammunition and the work of the drivers, very often carried out under most difficult conditions, usually at night and along heavily shelled roads, was beyond all praise.

R.E. AND PIONEERS.

The 25th Division relieved the 50th Division on the 20th October, the Field Companies and the Pioneers being employed during the next three days on the roads, which required continual attention with so much traffic by lorries, heavy guns, and tractors.

Very early the 23rd October the Division attacked. To cross the Richemont Brook, which was reported to be from 5 feet to 12 feet wide and 3 or 4 feet deep, and which lay almost at right angles to our own line of advance, 14 light bridges, about 20 feet long, were made. The 130th Field Coy., R.E., went forward with the Infantry behind the Artillery barrage, and no difficulties were experienced on the right ; the stream was narrow and the bridges were soon in position. On the left, the enemy held up the advance with machine-gun posts from the Garde Mill and along the high ground to the east ; in the end, three out of seven bridges were placed in position, with a loss of two sappers killed and eleven wounded. 2nd

Corpl. Foster, R.E., and 2nd Corpl. Hunter, R.E., in charge of parties carrying the bridges along with the attacking Infantry, did splendid service during the morning, the former being badly wounded when quite near the stream. L./Corpl. Meredith, R.E., was conspicuous for his courage when the majority of his party were wounded, and all received decorations for their gallantry, as well as L./Corpl. Caffyn, R.E., for coolly riding through an artillery barrage with some arm bands urgently needed by the Sappers with the Infantry.

The 106th Field Coy. made a crossing for the Artillery over the Le Cateau-Bazuel railway the night 22nd/23rd, when L./Corpl. Stratton, Dvr. Payne, Dvr. Mayes, Dvr Sumner, Dvr. Nurse, Dvr. Hamilton and Dvr. Crawford all showed remarkable pluck in driving up to within easy reach of the enemy with the necessary material, in spite of shelling and machine-gun fire, and were awarded Military Medals. It then concentrated on the removal of a railway bridge from the Le Cateau-Bazuel main road. This steel bridge, about 70 feet long and weighing about 400 tons, had been cleverly blown lengthways into the main road below, forming an immense obstacle to all traffic. For four days, from the 24th to the 28th, day and night shifts of Sappers and a company of the Pioneers were working at this job, which in the end required about 12,000 lbs. of explosives and quantities of German shells to effect its removal.

The 105th Field Company, R.E., after the Infantry had gone beyond Richemont Brook, were able to put up a trestle bridge for the Artillery, and then worked on water points in Pommereuil and the neighbourhood. 2nd Lieut. Gurnhill, R.E., and Spr. Brown, R.E., won the Military Cross and Military Medal respectively for their gallant attempt to reconnoitre the line of the river whilst held by German machine-gun posts, the former being severely wounded during the attempt. From the 27th to the 29th, a support line of short lengths of fire trench, machine-gun emplacements, and a certain amount of wire was constructed with the help of two companies of Pioneers; also communications up to the front line across the small fields, orchards, and thick hedges, so as to avoid the roads, which were being occasionally shelled. On the 30th the Field Companies and Pioneers were withdrawn for a few days' rest to Le Cateau, Honnechy, and St. Benin.

On the 4th November the 25th Division again attacked with the object of crossing the Sambre-Oise Canal, about 3,000 yards in front of our line, and the capture of Landrecies on the far side. Most careful organisation in every detail was necessary to ensure that there should be some means of getting the front waves of the attacking Infantry across the canal on as wide a front as possible both without delay and without getting wet, and also that some sort of light bridge should be thrown across as quickly as possible. The canal itself was about 55 feet wide and 6 or 7 feet deep, and several small bridges put up by the Germans, as well as the main steel girder bridge and lock, were reported to be standing. Before reaching the canal, the troops in our right sector had to cross the "Ancient River," about 20 feet wide and 3 or 4 feet deep. Pontoons and bridging materials could neither be driven up in wagons with the attacking Infantry nor carried by hand for so long a distance as $1\frac{1}{2}$ miles, so it was decided to make 80 rafts of petrol tins, for ferrying the Infantry across. For the design Major Richards, R.E., 105th Field Coy., R.E., was responsible. Each raft with a buoyancy of about 230 lbs. was able to take one soldier; made from 16 petrol tins with a light superstructure, it weighed 95 lbs., and could be carried by two pioneers and one sapper. Later on, when sufficient men to secure the far bank had been ferried across, the rafts could be formed into permanent floating bridges.

Time was short, as only three days remained in which to complete all arrangements. By midday, the 2nd November, the rafts and superstructure were finished by the 105th and 106th Field Coys., and a demonstration in their use was given on the Selle River for the instruction of the Infantry, which was extremely useful, though it left some of the spectators rather sceptical as to the utility of these frail rafts under machine-gun fire; however, each Infantry soldier was to be supplied with a life-belt in case of accidents. During the night 2nd/3rd November, the rafts were all got up in wagons to the assembly positions just behind the front line and, with the help of "A" Company, 11th South Lancs, three dumps were formed by Capt. Ridge, R.E., 105th Field Coy. Five rafts were damaged by shelling during the night, but these were replaced before daylight. The superstructure for the rafts and other heavy bridging material was loaded up on three "supply tanks," which were to move forward four hours behind the Infantry.

During the 3rd November, the 105th Field Coy., R.E., with the 11th South Lancs (Pioneers) moved up to Pommereul and after dusk to their assembly positions, where they drew and distributed the rafts from the dumps. Three bridging parties had been formed, each in charge of an officer, each party being subdivided into groups of five rafts, which were to advance in single file until near the canal, when the groups were to spread out so that the rafts would be about 20 yards apart along the whole front of the canal. The 130th Field Coy. had also made two portable bridges, for the lock at Landrecies, which were also got into their assembly positions with their carrying parties of six sappers each. By midnight, 3rd/4th, all parties were in position and everything was ready.

The attack started at 6.15 a.m. in a thick fog, with the R.E. and Pioneer parties just behind the leading Infantry and close up to the Artillery barrage, which crept forward at 100 yards per 6 minutes. Owing to the fog and enclosed nature of the ground, with its thick hedges, the carrying parties got somewhat mixed up with the Infantry and some took a hand in the fighting, capturing some Germans and machine guns. At the railway embankment the advance was held up for a short time until the arrival of two tanks, which gave good assistance in clearing out the German rearguards. The "Ancient River" was soon reached, and Sergt. Wood, R.E., and Spr. Barbour, R.E., 105th Field Coy., R.E., managed to withdraw the mine charges from the large bridge before it could be blown up by the Germans, an action requiring great coolness and presence of mind. Two more floating bridges were at once put across the river by 2nd Lieut. Armstrong R.E., 105th Field Company, R.E., and No. 1 Bridging Party. The Infantry quickly got across and the advance continued to the canal. Here one plank bridge was found intact and, as rafting across was unnecessary, two light bridges were at once thrown across.

No. 2 Bridging Party, under 2nd Lieut. Wells, R.E., 130th Field Coy., R.E., reached the canal with 17 rafts intact, and two floating bridges were quickly made. The large steel bridge was still standing, and some of the Gloucesters managed to use it before it was blown up at about 10.30 a.m., the German who touched off the mine managing to gallop off on a black horse. Desperate efforts were made to save the bridge, but the machine-gun fire was too heavy. The lock, however, was intact, and the 130th Field Coy. soon got two plank bridges in position. 2nd Corpl. Hunter, R.E., M.M., Spr. Martyn, R.E., Spr. Hackett, R.E., Spr. Mann, R.E., and Corpl. Thomas, R.E., M.M., all rendered the greatest service during the advance to the canal bank, and it was largely owing to their efforts that the passage of the canal at this point was so successful. All received decorations for their gallantry as well as 2nd Lieut. Wells, R.E., in command of the party.

On the left, No. 3 Bridging Party, under Lieut. Petty, R.E., M.M., 105th Field Coy., R.E., had further to go than the others, through very difficult country. Five of the rafts went astray, and a few more were destroyed, but about a company of the Warwicks and Worcesters were successfully ferried across in about 10 minutes. Two floating bridges were then made for the remainder of the Infantry. On the whole, casualties were very light, eight sappers wounded, and of the Pioneer Battn., four officers wounded, six other ranks killed, and 30 other ranks wounded. 2nd Lieut. Petty, M.M., and 2nd Lieut. Armstrong, R.E., 105th Field Coy., R.E., did splendid service in command of the bridging parties, whilst 2nd Corpl. Shuttleworth, R.E., Corpl. Garden, R.E., 2nd Corpl. Andrew, R.E., Spr. Berry, R.E., Spr. Inston, R.E., Corpl. Thomson, R.E., Spr. Bird, R.E., and Corpl. Smith, R.E., all won Military Medals for their gallantry during the whole operation. Close up with the attacking Infantry, they were not only taking part in the fighting, but able to give valuable assistance in cutting gaps through wire and hedges. Spr. Burton, R.E., and Spr. Wilson, R.E., were invaluable in taking messages under fire. Sergt. Shepherd, M.M., R.E. won his D.C.M. for his fine leadership in the attack and capture of a machine-gun post with about 20 prisoners, and his coolness during the ferrying across of the Infantry. Capt. Boulton, M.C., commanded, with conspicuous success, the company of the 11th South Lancs. (Pioneers) working with the 105th Field Coy., R.E., during the crossing of the canal. Lieut. Henshaw was wounded early in the attack, but gallantly carried on whilst the Infantry were being ferried across. Pte. Redstone set a fine example when his party was held up by a machine-gun post, capturing several prisoners single-handed, whilst Sergt. Owen and Sergt. Ions led their sections with great skill and dash. Pte. Eglington and Pte. Dawson were invaluable as runners under most difficult conditions, the latter being wounded whilst helping to ferry the Infantry across, and Pte. Rundle rendered his section valuable assistance by volunteering to go forward and gather information about the other parties. All received well-earned decorations.

The success of the operation was remarkable, and was due in no small degree to the excellent arrangements in all technical details made by Lt.-Col. R. J. Done, D.S.O., C.R.E., 25th Division, combined with the drive and keenness of the Infantry and of their platoon and subordinate commanders, the close co-operation of all arms, and the very effective artillery barrage, which fairly smothered the German defence along the canal bank.

About 4 p.m., the 106th Field Coy., R.E., commenced work on their two pontoon and trestle bridges, which were open to horse traffic by 10.30 p.m. the same night. 2nd Corpl. Hitchen, R.E., Corpl. Smith, R.E., Spr. O'Halloran, Spr. Stapleton, Spr. Howarth, and Spr. Ford all worked with splendid energy, and received Military Medals for their gallantry, as well as Spr. Howells, for continually carrying messages under machine-gun fire.

On the 5th November the advance continued with the 130th Field Coy. attached to the 74th Brigade in front ; a pontoon bridge near the Old Mill Depres, and two cork bridges were put up without much difficulty. On the 6th November the advance continued on a two-brigade front, the 105th Field Coy., R.E., with the 7th Brigade, and the 130th Field Coy. with the 74th Brigade. The Pioneers did excellent work on the roads and filling in craters. At Taisnieres the 105th Field Coy. completed a pontoon bridge over the Grande Helpe River, replaced afterwards by a trestle bridge. Between the 7th and 10th November, the 106th Field Coy. launched and completed an 84-feet span Inglis rectangular bridge at Maroilles, and the 130th Field Coy. an " A " traffic bridge at Taisnieres. From the 11th to the 17th November the three Field Companies, R.E., and the Pioneer Battalion continued to work under the 66th Division (who had relieved the 25th Division on the 7th/8th November), improving the bridges, roads, diversions, and repairing damage done by delayed explosions, and on the 17th November, marched back to join the Division in the area round Le Cateau.

25th BATTALION M.G. CORPS.

The 25th Battn. M.G. Corps, commanded by Lt.-Col. W. T. Raikes, M.C., returned from Champagne with the remainder of the 25th Division the end of June, and during the first fortnight of July its energies were directed towards reorganising and training the new drafts from England. The 17th July, the Battalion left Crequy, near Royon, for the 1st Corps area, moving up in lorries to the Bois-des-Dames, and on the 24th it was attached to the 59th Division, relieving the 3rd Canadian M.G. Battn. in the Mercatel sector east of Arras.

The 21st August the Machine Gun Battn. participated in the opening stages of the attack by the 3rd and 4th armies, with indirect covering fire on the front of the Guards Division, the extreme left of the attack.

A Coy. commanded by Major S. L. Courtauld, M.C.
B ,, Major Roscoe.
C ,, Major A. H. W. Sime, D.S.O., M.C.
D ,, Major A. R. Moir, M.C.

The 23rd August it covered a successful attack by a Brigade of the 32nd Division, and the same night was relieved in the line, and entrained along with the 59th Division for Lillers, where it went into the line again the night 26th/27th August, in front of Robecq. The German withdrawal along the Lys was now in progress, and the line taken over by the 59th Division gradually advanced until the old lines were reached. During September the usual inter-company reliefs were carried out, and on the 2nd/3rd October, the Machine Gun Battn. was finally relieved by the 47th Battn. Machine Gun Corps, and entrained two days later to rejoin the 25th Division down south. Detraining at Tincourt, it at once joined the 66th Division, with which it remained from the 6th to the 19th October, whilst the 25th Division retained for the present the services of the 100th Battn. Machine Gun Corps in its place. The 8th October and the following days, the battalion took part in the fighting and the subsequent advance to Serain, Meretz and Le Cateau ; A Coy. attached to the 198th Infantry Brigade 66th Division, B Coy. to the South African Brigade, C Coy. to the 199th Brigade, and D Coy. in reserve. Pte. Cooper won a Military Medal for gallantly going out under machine-gun fire to rescue his Section Officer, who was lying badly wounded in the open. On the 10th October a main line of resistance was taken up by the 66th Division on the high ground west of Le Cateau, with A and D Coys. in the forward area, and B and C Coys. in reserve. Inter-company reliefs were carried out during the next two days and on the 17th October the Machine Gun Battn. took part in the successful attack along the line of the River Selle by the 66th Division, with the 50th Division on their right. Pte. Hollingworth displayed great courage and though wounded refused to leave his gun. The machine-gun barrage was most effective, but the battalion sustained considerable casualties during the next morning in Le Cateau. Later in the day the 18th Battn. Machine Gun Corps arrived to take its place with the 66th Division, and the 25th Battn. Machine Gun Corps rejoined its own Division on the right with C and B Coys. in the front line and A and D Coys. in reserve. During the last two days fighting, the battalion had lost so many men through sickness and casualties, that it was only possible to man 48 guns instead of 64 guns even with minimum teams.

Arrangements were now made for the further advance on the 23rd October. A Coy. with its two sections was to go forward in close support of the 7th and 75th Brigades, whilst the remaining 40 machine guns reinforced by 24 machine guns from the 50th Division, were to support the attack by barrage fire. The attack started at 1.20 a.m. with a good machine gun barrage, during which 150,000 rounds were fired by the 40 guns of the 25th Battn. alone ; one Section, A Coy., moved in support of the 20th Manchesters and the other section with the 1/8th Worcesters to Tilleuls farm. Here three guns were knocked out by shell fire, and the section sustained considerable casualties. At 5 a.m., two Sections of D Coy., under 2nd Lt. Murray, did excellent work in helping the advance of the 74th Brigade. The same afternoon A and B Coys. assisted in forming a defensive flank facing south-east, the machine guns being placed in position so as to command tracks through the Bois L'Eveque. Capt. Bartholomew, in charge of a group of barrage machine guns, set a splendid example of courage and physical endurance during the attack, and 2nd Lt. Anderson, when the Infantry were held up, boldly moved eight guns across ground swept by fire. 2nd Lt. Murray did wonderful good work against some field guns, which were firing point blank at a British tank, and all received the Military Cross for their gallantry. Corpl. Wales was conspicuous for his courage in mending telephone lines under fire, and L./Corpl. Brownhill and Corpl. Morris both showed great resource and daring in getting their own guns into action against German machine gun nests and helping the Infantry to advance. The following night at Pommereuil, C.Q.M.S. Ellis showed great courage and presence of mind in extricating some horses and clearing the billets which were being shelled at the time. All received Military Medals for their services, as well as Pte. Paterson for excellent work with his gun on the 25th October.

The 24th October Lt. Murray covered the flank of the advance with indirect fire from his two sections, and during the afternoon Lt. Anderson, with two sections of D Coy., supported the further advance of the 7th Brigade. The 25th October three sections relieved D Coy. in the forward area, and the following day, owing to casualties, it was found necessary to amalgamate C and D Coys. into one Company of four Sections, under Major A. W. H. Sime, D.S.O., M.C., and A and B Coys. into one Company of four Sections under Major Roscoe.

From the 26th October to 3rd November inter-company reliefs took place. During the temporary lull in the advance, Corpl. Atkinson, whilst in charge of an advanced post near Malgarni, had both of his machine guns knocked out by shelling, but gallantly carried on with rifles and Dvr. Cox also distinguished himself by his coolness in getting his limbers up to the line under constant shelling. Both received Military Medals. Arrangements were also made for the crossing of the Sambre Canal. To carry out this operation four Sections (32 machine guns), reinforced by 24 machine guns of the 100th Battn. Machine Gun Corps, were to cover the advance by indirect machine-gun barrage whilst the remainder, consisting of four Sections, were to move behind the attacking infantry to positions close to the canal from which they could cover the crossing with direct fire. Of these the two sections of D Coy., under 2nd Lt. Parker and 2nd Lt. Allison, had no opportunity of direct fire owing to the mist, and in the evening they were employed to protect the right flank of the Division ; 2nd Lt. Allison was unfortunately wounded during the advance. Another section under Lt. Dalton got into position near the canal, crossed over with the infantry and took up positions south and south-east of Landrecies. The remaining section, under 2nd Lt. Murray, succeeded in reaching the canal behind the Infantry, and caused considerable damage to the enemy on the far bank. Of those sections which had been covering the advance by machine-gun barrage, three sections were ordered forward at 7 a.m., to assist the crossing of the canal, from pre-arranged positions. Some German machine-gun nests were, however, still holding out, and Major Sime and Lt. Hill were both wounded whilst getting their guns into action. Lt. Ross was wounded and taken prisoner, but persuaded his captors to surrender and carry him back. Sergt. Smith, Pte. Hatherley and Corpl. Goodwin rendered splendid service with their guns in covering the advance of the Infantry from a position which was constantly shelled for over two hours. L./Sergt. Waterson set a fine example of courage and determination throughout the attack, and Pte. Arthur, Pte. Vickers and Pte. Tyrer worked with splendid energy to get their guns across the canal, the latter doing fine service in silencing some German machine guns. Sergt. Tulley, assisted by Pte. Poole, distinguished themselves by the capture of two machine guns and several prisoners, and all were awarded Military Medals. A few days later Corpl. Kerwin rushed up his guns when the Infantry were checked near St. Hilaire, and did fine work against some German snipers and machine gunners.

At 5 p.m., three sections A Coy. moved forward with the 74th Brigade, and continued with them during the advance the following day. C Coy. moved with the 7th Brigade, though neither came into action. The 7th November, good work was done by C Coy. in support of the 7th Brigade, and D Coy. with the 75th Brigade. The night 7th/8th the Infantry of the Division were relieved by the 66th Division, and the 9th and 10th the Machine Gun Battn. was finally relieved by the 100th Machine Gun Battn., and moved back to Bousies, and later to Le Cateau.

SIGNAL COMMUNICATIONS.

After the capture of Le Cateau and the crossing of the Selle River, signal communications became somewhat easier and more satisfactory. The XIIIth Corps Signals opened an advanced exchange at Pommereuil, and erected an air line oute, which was most useful, as our lines were now free from the danger of being continually damaged by transport. Whilst at Pommereuil the 74th Brigade Signal Section unfortunately sustained heavy casualties at its advanced Brigade Headquarters at Tilleul Farm. Lt. Kennedy was wounded and Capt. West became responsible for the 74th Brigade Signal communications. Sergt. Goodwin, M.M., won a D.C.M. for his splendid work during the attack east of Pommereuil, the 23rd October. The lines were continually broken, and it was largely owing to his fine example of gallantry that communications were kept through to the battalions. Pte. Chilton, M.M., Sapper Hensby, M.M., and Sapper Mather, M.M., also distinguished themselves repairing lines under fire, with a complete disregard for their own safety, and each received a Bar to his Military Medal. L./Corpl. Weston, in charge of the 74th Brigade Wireless Section, did good work in keeping up communications with the "wireless" when other lines were broken. On the night 3rd/4th November, previous to the crossing of the Canal, Spr. Morris and Pnr. Beer, R.E., rendered splendid service mending lines through to the battalions of the 75th Brigade, under constant shelling, the latter being wounded during the night. Pte. Clarke, 1/8th Worcesters, and Pte. Coles, 1/5th Gloucesters, attached Signal Coy., also distinguished themselves carrying messages on the same occasion. 2nd Corpl. Ward, Signal Coy., R.E., though much interfered with by the shelling, was very successful with his wireless signal station, keeping up continuous communication with Brigades and flanking Divisions, and all received well-earned Military Medals.

For the crossing of the Sambre Canal, two main trunk lines were laid as far forward as possible ; a wireless station was also sent forward, and proved most useful throughout the attack. As soon as Landrecies was captured, the cable pairs were laid over the canal, No. 1 Section Cable wagon being amongst the first horsed vehicles to cross the canal by the pontoon bridge. 2nd Lt. H. B. Rishworth did good work in charge of the cable section and received a Military Cross for his services. Corpl. Lyall, in charge of the forward detachment. with Spr. Chatwin, Spr. Harries and Spr. Main, 25th Division Signal Coy., R.E., distinguished themselves by their energy and courage in laying and mending forward cables very often under heavy fire, and all received Military Medals for their gallantry.

From Landrecies, signal communications were much simplified, owing to the limited amount of transport on the roads, and the absence of shelling. Ground lines could now be put down with some certainty that nothing would happen to them and that they would not be broken. Towards the end of the advance, field cables became very scarce, and wireless was relied upon to an increasing extent for the transmission of messages.

CASUALTIES AND MEDICAL ARRANGEMENTS.

During the crossing of the Sambre Canal, the capture of Landrecies and the subsequent advance, the 75th and 76th Field Ambulances formed collecting posts close to their Infantry Brigade Headquarters and went forward with them. With the 75th Field Ambulance, Pte. Howocks, R.A.M.C., and Pte. Erskine, R.A.M.C., did splendid work, leading their stretcher squads and keeping touch with the advancing units under machine gun fire. Pte. Todd, A.S.C., M.T., and Pte. Westlanke, A.S.C., M.T., with the 76th Field Ambulance, drove their ambulances with great coolness along the shelled roads throughout the operations. Pte. Godart, R.A.M.C., and Pte. Barker, M.M., 76th Field Ambulance, were conspicuous for their gallantry in assisting the regimental aid posts to evacuate the wounded, and acting as runners through machine gun fire. Pte. Laing, R.A.M.C., and Pte. Chaplin, R.A.M.C., 76th Field Ambulance, on several occasions set a fine example whilst in charge of bearer squads, searching for wounded and bringing them back, and all received Military Medals for their gallantry.

The 75th Field Ambulance moved to Landrecies on the 4th November, Rue des Juifs on the 5th November, Maroilles on the 6th November, and Marbaix on the 7th with the 76th Field Ambulance at Landrecies on the 5th November, Maroilles the 6th, and Dompierre the 7th November. Casualties were few, and at times it was possible to bring a small motor ambulance right up to the regimental aid posts, and evacuate direct to the Corps main dressing station in rear.

The 77th Field Ambulance remained at Honnechy as a Divisional Rest Station until the 6th November, when it was moved up to Le Cateau; to Landrecies the 9th, and the Chateau at Bousies the 10th November. The rest station did useful work, and many men were retained with the Division who would otherwise have been evacuated to the base.

Lt.-Col. A. E. Hammerton, C.M.G., D.S.O., R.A.M.C., succeeded Col. H. N. Dunn, A.D.M.S. of the Division, at the beginning of November, the latter having been severely wounded by a shell and unfortunately losing an eye.

Casualties incurred by the Division since the 3rd October, were :—

	Killed.	Wounded.	Missing.
Officers	41	208	3
Other ranks ...	729	3,880	428

making a total (excluding sick) since July, 1916, of 45,803.

	Killed.	Wounded.	Missing.
Officers	413	1,427	234
Other ranks ...	5,354	28,290	10,085

Of the missing, a large proportion, especially during the Somme battles in 1916, are believed to have been either killed or wounded.

The following is a list of those who received rewards for services during the operations, with details of the more notable acts of gallantry for which the award was granted :—

No. 307817 L./Corpl. W. Amey, 1/8th Royal Warwickshire Regt.

For conspicuous and outstanding gallantry on November 4th, 1918, during the attack on Landrecies.

The attack commenced in the fog resulting in many hostile machine-gun nests not being " mopped up " by the leading troops. This N.C.O., with his Section, having lost touch with his Company, attached himself to another Company which was held up by heavy machine-gun fire, and carried out the following deeds of gallantry :—

1. On his own initiative, he led his Section to attack a machine-gun nest in the face of heavy fire. With great bravery, he forced the garrison to retire to a neighbouring farm, finally causing them to capitulate, and capturing about 50 prisoners and several machine guns.

2. Later, single handed, he attacked a hostile machine-gun post situated in a farm-house. Exposed to heavy fire, he advanced unhesitatingly, killed two of the garrison and drove the remainder into a cellar until assistance arrived.

3. Again later and unaided, he attacked a Chateau in Faubourg Soyers, which was strongly held, and holding up the line of advance. With determination and disregard to personal safety, he rushed the Chateau, killing two Germans and holding up the remainder until reinforced.

This gallant act was instrumental in the capturing of a further 20 prisoners, and cleared away the last of the opposition in this Sector.

Throughout the day, the conduct of Lance-Corporal Amey, in the face of such opposition and danger, was of the highest type and beyond all praise. The work done by him not only resulted in clearing up a critical situation, but was instrumental in the saving of many lives.

Awarded.........V.C.

No. 17324 Pte. F. G. Miles, 1/5th Bn. Gloucestershire Regt.

For conspicuous gallantry and splendid initiative in attack. On the 23rd October, 1918, during the advance against the Bois L'Eveque, his Company was held up by a line of machine guns in the sunken road near the Moulin L. Jacques. Pte. Miles alone, and on his own initiative, made his way forward for a distance of 150 yards under exceptionally heavy fire, located one machine gun and shot the man firing the gun. He then rushed the gun, and kicked it over, thereby putting it out of action. He then observed another gun firing from 100 yards further forward ; he then advanced alone, shot the machine-gunner, rushed the gun and captured the team of eight. Finally, he stood up and beckoned on his Company, who, following his signals, were enabled to work round the rear of the line, and capture 16 machine guns, one officer and 50 other ranks.

The courage, initiative and entire disregard of personal safety shown by this very gallant private soldier, was entirely instrumental in enabling his Company to advance at a time when any delay would have seriously jeopardised the whole operation in which it was engaged.

Awarded.........V.C.

No. 241001 Sergt. R. Atkinson, M.M., 1/8th Worcester Regt.

During operations of 23rd and 24th October, 1918, his conduct was beyond all praise ; he continually searched houses in the advance through Pommereiul, helped to maintain fire on numerous enemy parties who impeded our advance, especially one party of about 150, whom we drove out of the village with loss. He assisted to reorganize the Company, and form posts in the face of numbers of the enemy.

On the 24th, he again displayed great initiative and leadership, and, in the final advance, when our left was held up by the enemy's machine-gun fire, he established his posts according to orders after a stiff fight. During both days his conduct and leadership were most marked ; he was worth a platoon.

Awarded.........D.C.M.

No. 4794 L./Corpl. T. Armstrong, M.M., 13th Durham Light Infantry.

For conspicuous bravery and devotion to duty during the operations of 23rd October to the 30th, between Le Faux and Tilleuls Fm. This N.C.O., during very heavy shell fire, repaired the telephone wires on several occasions, so keeping the Battalion in communication with the Battalions on left and right, and also with Brigade.

Awarded.........Bar to M.M.

Capt. S. E. Boulton, M.C., 11th South Lancs. (Pioneers).

For conspicuous gallantry and devotion to duty, displayed in building operations, near Landrecies, on the 4th November, 1918. His Company, together with a Field Company R.E., were responsible for getting the first line of Infantry across the Sambre-Oise Canal. For the fact that this was quickly and efficiently done under shell and heavy machine-gun fire, Capt. Boulton's skill, energy and determination was largely responsible.

Awarded..........**Bar to M.C.**

No. 82034 Pioneer E. Beer, R.E., attached 75th Brigade. (Wounded.)

For conspicuous gallantry and devotion to duty at Malgarai on the 4th November, 1918, in laying out and mending telephone lines under heavy shell fire. He was stunned and wounded by a shell, but before going to a dressing station he made certain that the line was in working order. On all occasions he has shown great devotion to duty and disregard of risk.

Awarded..........**M.M.**

No. 40388 Pte. (L./Corpl.) T. Betteley, 20th Manchester Regt. (Wounded.)

For devotion to duty and the splendid example he sets his men. This N.C.O. is in charge of a Lewis Gun Section, and his work is always characterized by absolute fearlessness. At Beaurevoir on 4th October he brought his gun into action against enemy machine guns with great effect. During the attack, 8th and 9th October, he did splendid work against hostile machine guns in front of Broux farm, and later, when under accurate fire from Foal Copse, he kept his gun in action, so that the Company was able to rush the Copse. He was slightly wounded on 10th October, but did not leave the Company until he knew that it would shortly be relieved. His conduct throughout won the admiration of all the officers and men of his Company.

Awarded..........**D.C.M.**

Lieut. (A./Capt.) W. L. Blow, 9th Batt. Yorkshire Regt.

At Belle Vue Farm on 5th October, 1918, this officer led his Company with the greatest skill and gallantry, capturing the farm and taking 30 prisoners. On 9th October, at St. Benin, he made a most daring and valuable reconnaissance of the line, getting across and only retiring when held up by an enemy post.

Awarded..........**M.C.**

No. 20959 Pte. J. Clark, M.M., 13th Durham Light Infantry:

For conspicuous bravery and devotion to duty during the advance on Beaurevoir on 5th October, 1918. This man is a stretcher-bearer and performed excellent work. When his Company partially withdrew, with complete disregard to personal safety, he went forward and brought in many of our wounded. At another time during the advance, he carried many of the wounded out of a valley which was being shelled by mustard gas shells risking his own life and saving many others.

Awarded..........**Bar to M.M.**

No. 325019 Pte. C. S. Crowe, 1/8th Royal Warwickshire Regt.

During the operations near Bazuel and Pommereuil, on 23rd and 24th October, 1918, this man, whilst acting as a Company runner, did excellent work and showed untiring energy and courage. Although often required to run messages over a dangerous zone, he fulfilled his duties with ability and intelligence and with disregard for personal safety. His conduct throughout was most praiseworthy and of great value to his Company Commander, who was thus able to keep touch with the situation.

Awarded...........**M.M.**

No. 35898 Pte. H. Clennell, 9th Yorkshire Regt.

On 24th October, 1918, at Malgarni, when his platoon was held up by machine-gun fire, in front of a strong belt of wire, this man volunteered to go forward and cut the wire. He accomplished this lying on his back under very heavy machine-gun fire.

Awarded..........**M.M.**

T./2nd Lieut. (A./Capt.) W. A. Clifton, 11th Sherwood Foresters. (Wounded.)

During the advance east of Le Cateau, on the 23rd and 24th October, 1918, this officer showed marked courage and ability, when in command of a Company. On the 24th instant, during the attack on Fontaine au Bois, the attack was temporarily checked by enemy wire. He rushed forward with a small party and succeeded in cutting a gap in the face of heavy Artillery and machine-gun fire. During this operation he received a wound, from a bullet, in the arm, but continued to lead his men forward. His personal example and total disregard for personal danger were mainly instrumental in the capture and consolidation of the final objective.

Awarded..........**Bar to M.C.**

No. 19116 Corpl. W. H. Collins, 11th Sherwood Foresters.

On the 5th October, 1918, in the attack and capture of Guisancourt Farm, this N.C.O. was one of the carrying party. Noticing that the line was held up by very heavy machine-gun fire, he rallied all the men near him and rushed forward into the firing line, thus materially assisting the advance and capture of the objective. Again, on the 9th October, when the leading line had been held up by very heavy machine-gun fire and artillery fire over open sights, in the railway cutting south of Honnechy, he rushed forward alone, and then by crawling reached an enemy machine gun, which he captured single-handed.

Awarded..........**D.C.M.**

No. 10091 Pte. N. Courtney, 9th Devonshire Regt.

On the 23rd October, during the attack on Pommereuil, Pte. Courtney, who was in charge of a Lewis Gun Section, attacked an enemy machine-gun post, but finding that some of his company had advanced beyond the hostile machine gun and would consequently suffer from the fire of his Lewis gun, he ordered the gun to cease fire, and then he immediately rushed the post, accounting for the whole crew with his fists and revolver. This total disregard for his personal safety and his coolness and quickness of action were the means of preventing many casualties, and was the finest example he could set his men.

Awarded..........D.C.M.

Capt. C. M. Duncan, C/110th Brigade, R.F.A.

On the 18th September, 1918, near Ronssoy, Capt. Duncan was in command of a section of guns acting in close support of our Infantry attack. In the first phase of the attack he took his guns forward with the Infantry, and engaged parties of the enemy and hostile machine guns with great effect over open sights, from positions close up to our Artillery barrage. We then advanced with the Infantry over the Ronssoy ridge, until they were held up by heavy machine-gun fire.

Seeing the situation, he led his guns up, through the Infantry, over ground which was being swept by machine-gun fire, and with the utmost coolness and determination brought them into action in front of the Infantry.

While coming into action he was seen and fired on by a section of 77-mm. guns and 4·2-inch howitzers, but in spite of the greatest difficulties, he got his guns into action, silencing the section of 77-mm. guns, and by his rapid and accurate fire on hostile machine-gun posts, enabled the Infantry to advance. We remained in action with his section in this position for the rest of the day and all the next day, under frequent machine-gun fire, engaging enemy guns and machine-gun posts, rendering the greatest assistance to the Infantry throughout the operation. Capt. Duncan displayed the greatest courage and dash.

Awarded..........D.S.O.

No. 54816 Pte. J. P. Forde, R.A.M.C., 76th Field Ambulance.

Whilst the 74th Infantry Brigade were marching through Le Cateau, in the morning of the 23rd October, they were heavily shelled on the Landrecies Road. This man extricated many wounded men from the wreckage of overturned limbers and wounded animals, and his conduct undoubtedly saved many lives. During the subsequent operations before Fontaine his behaviour was of the same high standard.

Awarded..........M.M.

L./Corpl. (A./2nd Corpl.) G. H. Foster, 130th Field Coy., R.E.
(Wounded.)

This N.C.O. was in charge of a party of ten men, carrying a footbridge to form a crossing over the Richemont River for the Infantry, during the attack south-east of Le Cateau, on the 23rd October.

The attack was made in the dark in a thick fog, and there were numerous thick hedges and sunken roads to cross. The bridge had to be carried 1,500 yards, and along with the first wave of the attacking Infantry.

Under extremely heavy machine-gun fire at close range and the enemy barrage, this N.C.O. guided his party. When about 200 yards from the river he was badly wounded, and fell, but seeing his party waver, and realising the importance of his task, he got up and pushed on, successfully throwing his bridge across the stream. He then collapsed, and had to be carried back to our lines. He showed throughout the greatest determination and pluck, and set a very fine example to his men.

Awarded..........D.C.M.

No. 39849 Pte. R. Gee, 77th Field Ambulance, R.A.M.C.

Throughout operations on the 22nd and 23rd October, leading to capture of Fontaine-au-Bois, performed splendid work in charge of a stretcher squad, evacuating civilians who had been gassed on the morning of the attack. Through his courage and fine example a large number of cases were got away which would otherwise have been left behind, owing to the heavy bombardment.

Awarded..........M.M.

No. 47257 Sergt. J. Goodwin, M.M., 25th Div. Sig. Coy., R.E.

For conspicuous gallantry during the operations commencing on the 23rd October, 1918, east of Le Cateau. This N.C.O. was in charge of Brigade Report Centre, situated in a village that was continually shelled. From three hours before zero until three hours after zero, the lines back to brigade and forward to battalions were constantly being cut by shell fire. During this time Sergt. Goodwin was in the open the whole time, repairing these lines, which unavoidably ran along roads that were constantly shelled. It was entirely due to his splendid example to other men that communication was maintained. On one occasion the house, in the cellar of which they had a signal office, was hit by a shell, cutting all the lines. This N.C.O. remained in the roadway for a whole hour, sorting out the lines and repairing them, although the road was being heavily barraged. Throughout the operations the work done by this N.C.O. has been magnificent, both in repairing lines and running forward communications.

Awarded..........D.C.M.

No. 67268 Dvr. J. Graham, 112th Brigade, R.F.A.

On the night 6th/7th August, 1918, the two centre horses behind this driver were killed by a high-explosive shell on the Albert Road. Owing to the fact that the vehicles were marching with a big interval to avoid shell fire, this driver had to act for himself. He acted in the most admirable manner. He got the lead driver of an empty wagon to unhook his two horses and come to his assistance. These two drivers then extricated the dead horses and shaken centre driver, hooked in their lead horses, and then brought the full wagon up to the battery. All this they did under shell fire, and in spite of being told that the shell fire was too bad for them to reach the battery.

The conduct of Dvr. Graham under these circumstances was of the best. He showed courage, determination, and leadership.

Awarded..........M.M.

No. 242501 Sergt. G. W. Hobbs, M.M., 1/5th Battn. Gloucester Regt.

For conspicuous gallantry near Landrecies on the 4th November, acting as C.S.M. when his Company Commander was wounded, and his company much disorganised in the mist, he showed the greatest courage and determination in collecting his men and in dealing with two hostile machine guns, which were holding up the company. Upon reaching the Sambre Canal he again reorganised his company, leading them across the Canal under heavy enemy fire, being the first man in his company across the Canal.

Throughout the operation he set a magnificent example to his company.

Awarded..........D.C.M.

No. 97152 Spr. M. O'Halloran, 106th Field Coy., R.E.

For conspicuous courage throughout, especially on the 4th November, 1918, when engaged on the construction of a pontoon bridge at Landrecies. The site of the bridge was being subjected to heavy bursts of shell fire. Under these trying circumstances Spr. O'Halloran, by his cheerfulness and solid work, set an example that materially assisted the progress of the work.

Awarded..........M.M.

No. 3529, Pte. J. Jamieson, R.A.M.C., 76th Field Ambulance.

For conspicuous gallantry and devotion to duty at Ponchaux, on the night of the 8th October, 1918. The advanced dresssing station was heavily and continually bombed for seven hours, but he searched for wounded and dressed them and evacuated them, utterly regardless of his personal safety, inspiring everyone by his coolness and courage.

Awarded..........M.M.

No. 306759, Sergt. D. H. Lissaman, 1/8th R. Warwick Regt.

For conspicuous gallantry displayed on the 4th November, 1918, during the attack on Landrecies.

His platoon was detailed to rush and capture one of the bridges crossing the Canal.

During the advance, his platoon commander was wounded, but he immediately took charge and by great dash and leadership, led his men forward to their objective, and succeeded in capturing the bridge before it could be destroyed.

Awarded..........D.C.M.

2nd Lieut. G. Murray, 25th Battn. M.G. Corps.

On the 23rd October, at the quarry near Bousies, this officer acted with exceptional bravery and carried out some fearless and valuable reconnaisances.

He located an enemy field gun firing at one of our tanks over open sights, got a Vicker's gun in action against it, thereby causing the crew to run away from the gun which was captured later. Afterwards his guns silenced a machine gun nest which was holding up our advance under intense machine gun and shell fire.

His fine example and endurance inspired the whole of his section to do most excellent and vital work throughout the whole action.

Awarded..........**M.C.**

Lieut. (A./Major) W. G. Mackay, M.C. and Bar, C/112th Brigade R.F.A.

On the night of the 7th/8th August, near Bresle, his battery was heavily shelled with gas shell. Major Mackay was conspicuous in looking after his men without any thought for himself, this being the cause of there being so few gas casualties in his battery.

During the operations on the 8th and 9th August, his energy, initiative and disregard to danger were very conspicuous in looking after his men, personally observing shoots and sending in valuable information, some of which he had to join the infantry attack to collect.

Though he was several times requested to send his officers on the above duties, as he was suffering from the effects of mustard gas, he persisted in carrying out his duties with his accustomed splendid coolness, energy and devotion to duty till the afternoon of the 9th August, when he became blind from the effects of the gas and had to be taken to the Aid Dressing Station.

Awarded..........**Second Bar to M.C.**

Lieut. (T./Capt.) E. F. Orgill, M.C., 21st Battn Manchester Regt.

For consistent gallantry and devotion to duty displayed during the operations from the 4th to 11th October, 1918. Capt. Orgill, as Adjutant to this battalion, made all the arrangements for the supply and maintenance of S.A.A., Grenades, &c., during the operations. During the actual fighting he personally accompanied the first line of the Battalion, greatly inspiring all ranks by his calmness and contempt of danger. During the advance, the line came under direct fire from a battery of field guns on the high ground between Sonia Farm and Serain. Capt. Orgill organized an attack on these guns which effectually put them out of action, and resulted in the gun crews being killed. The continuous services of this officer in reconnoitring and reporting on the situation were of the very greatest value to his Commanding Officer, while his courage and determination were a magnificent example to all troops with whom he came in contact.

Awarded..........**Bar to M.C.**

No. 17459, C.S.M. H. Perry, 20th Battn. Manchester Regt.

On the 4th October, when his company was attacking Ponchaux, all his officers becoming casualties, he took charge and carried on, constantly patrolling his line under heavy machine gun fire and sniping, ensuring that his company kept in touch with its flanks and inspiring his men, who were lying in a very exposed position to maintain their line.

Awarded..........**D.C.M.**

2nd Lieut. J. M. Petty, M.M., 105th Field Coy., R.E.

On the 4th November, 1918, during the advance to and the crossing of the Sambre Canal at Landrecies, this officer was in command of a large party of over 100 Sappers and Pioneers carrying 35 floats. He had first to assemble these men in the front line with the floats, advance under the barrage, and then ferry the first wave of infantry across the canal.

The operation was a complete success (the crossing of the first company north-east of main bridge at Landrecies being effected by ferrying) very largely due to the drive and initiative of 2nd Lieut. Petty. During the advance, the party besides clearing gaps for the infantry, did a considerable amount of mopping up and took many prisoners. The actual ferrying was done under heavy machine gun fire along the canal, and 2nd Lieut. Petty was responsible for the success of the operation.

2nd Lieut. Perry with his bridging section and a small party of infantry, were the first to arrive at the Canal.

Awarded..........**M.C.**

No. 61090, Pte. V. Redstone, 11th South Lancs. (Pioneers).

For conspicuous gallantry and devotion to duty on the 4th November, 1918, at Landrecies.

This man was with a bridging party and throughout the day displayed great courage and disregard for his own safety when under artillery and machine gun fire. His conduct and example was invaluable to the men about him. At one period when the bridging party was held up through machine gun fire due to Faubourg Soyeres not being cleared of the enemy, this man, at great personal risk went forward into several houses and secured a number of prisoners. Later be collected several of our infantry together and went forward and cleared further houses of the enemy.

At all times, this man has shewn great coolness under heavy enemy shell and machine gun fire.

Awarded..........**D.C.M.**

Capt. R. de W. Rogers, Leinster Regt. attd. 1/5th Gloucestershire Regt. (Wounded).

Conspicuous gallantry in leading his company during the attack on Beaurevoir, the 5th October, and Maretz the 6th October, and during the advance on Le Cateau, the 10th October. At Beaurevoir, he led his company throughout the attack, and successfully organized a defensive position on the further edge of the village, thereby enabling the battalion on the left to carry their portion of the village, where they had previously been held up.

At Maretz, finding that the Division on the left had not come up, he cleared their portion of the village, and formed a defensive flank under heavy fire from snipers and machine guns, materially assisting their subsequent advance.

During the advance on Le Cateau on the 10th October, although wounded on the 9th October, he again led his company forward. When the leading battalion was held up by heavy machine gun fire, he made a most gallant attempt to assist them by pushing on until both he and all his officers were casualties. Although too severely wounded to speak, he insisted upon writing down a clear report of the situation and his dispositions before going to the dressing station. His conduct throughout was a magnificent example of dash and courage.

Awarded.........**D.S.O.**

No. 19071, Pte. A. E. Rutter, 21st Battn. Manchester Regt.

For conspicuous gallantry and devotion to duty whilst employed as a Linesman on the Signal Section during the operations from the 19th/30th October, 1918. During this period, telephone communications were extremely difficult to maintain, on account of exceptionally heavy shell fire which was continually cutting the wires. Pte. Rutter invariably volunteered to go out and repair the wires, although frequently not on duty at the time, and in spite of the fact that the shelling was of the most severe description. On the night of the 22nd/23rd October, the enemy put down an S.O.S. barrage between Battalion Headquarters at Basuel and one of our advanced companies which was about 800 yards in front of the general line. A few hours before zero, for a general attack when the necessity of maintaining communications between Battalion Headquarters and Company Headquarters was absolutely imperative, the wires were found to be cut, and the shelling was so intense as to make it impossible for runners to get through. Pte. Rutter at once volunteered to repair the line, and with one of the men went along the whole 800 yards of line, mending it in no less than 15 places. On arrival at Company Headquarters, he found that the wire had again been broken. He immediately went out again and repaired a further large number of breaks. Throughout the whole of these operations, Pte. Rutter's absolute contempt of danger was most marked, and the instance of his incomparable devotion to duty recorded above is by no means isolated.

Awarded.........**D.C.M.**

No. 17368 Signaller J. J. Robinson, " D " Battery, 112th Brigade, R.F.A.

On the 22nd August, 1918, near Morlancourt, this Signaller went forward with the F.O.O. in close touch with the Infantry. He showed great courage in the face of hostile rifle fire, going from one post to another to obtain information.

He showed very great determination in collecting his information and carrying out his orders, and did not allow himself to be prevented from doing so by anything.

On the 4th September, 1918, near Bouchavesnes, this Signaller again went forward with an officer to reconnoitre a position. He pushed ahead of our outposts and discovered the whereabouts of the enemy by drawing their fire. He came under heavy shell fire and rifle fire as a result of this, but he replied to the enemy's fire with a rifle, and although he was half buried by a shell, he went and brought some Lewis Gunners to the spot and pointed out where the enemy were.

This Signaller is a fearless and determined soldier.

Awarded.......... **M.M.**

Lieut. (A./Capt.) R. O. Schuh, M.C., 9th Bn. Devonshire Regt.

On the 8th October, 1918, in the attack on Ponchaux, this officer showed great skill and gallantry. His Company had been detailed to " mop up " the village of Ponchaux. This task he most successfully carried out, he being the only officer left with it. He advanced close behind the attacking Companies and was personally responsible for clearing several hostile machine-gun posts during the advance to the final objective. His skill, coolness and disregard for his personal safety was a fine example to all ranks.

Awarded.......... **Bar to M.C.**

No. 68600 Sergt. L. Steadman, " B " Battery, 110th Brigade, R.F.A.

On the night of 21st August, when the Battery was moving into action in front of Morlan-Court, the enemy commenced to shell the position. Sergt. Steadman, who was acting as B.S.M., displayed great gallantry and disregard of personal danger in getting the teams away. During the early hours of the morning the enemy shelled the position heavily with gas and H.E. just prior to the attack. Sergt. Steadman continued the making of arrangements for opening the barrage with the greatest coolness. It was largely due to his maintenance of gas discipline that no gas casualties occurred.

Awarded.......... **M.M.**

No. 81232 Sergt. J. Tully, 25th Bn. Machine Gun Corps. (Wounded.)

For conspicuous bravery and initiative. On the 4th November, 1918, at Landrecies, after his officer had been wounded, this N.C.O. took charge of four Vickers guns. On encountering an enemy machine-gun nest holding out, he rushed forward alone and engaged the enemy with his revolver. A few men coming to his assistance enabled him to capture two machine guns and several prisoners, in addition to inflicting casualties.

Later in the day, whilst carrying out a fearless reconnaissance, he was wounded by a sniper.

Awarded.......... **D.C.M.**

No. 63198 Gunner W. Weall, " D " Battery, 112th Brigade, R.F.A.
(Attached Headquarters.)

On the night of 7th/8th October, 1918, near Beaurevoir, before our attack was launched, urgent despatches had to be taken to the Batteries. Intense hostile shelling both H.E. and gas was being maintained in the area of the Batteries. In spite of this, Gunner Weall delivered his despatches in the shortest possible time, and on returning to Brigade Headquarters, hearing that further despatches had to be delivered, he immediately volunteered to go himself to avoid the risk of another runner losing his way in the dark.

Altogether during the night Gunner Weall made three consecutive journeys to the Batteries, on two occasions wearing his mask the whole way.

Awarded.........M.M.

2nd Lieut. E. Wedgbury, M.C., D.C.M., M.M., Gloucester Regt., attached 1/8th Worcesters.

For most conspicuous gallantry and leadership when commanding a Company during the operations resulting in forming a defensive flank along north-west edge of Eveque Wood, 23rd October, 1918.

He advanced three miles through country held by the enemy, the whole of which time he was out of touch with British troops. He took command of two platoons which had lost direction, carrying them forward to their objective, and afterwards pushing on towards his own objective, Tilleals Farm, which was two miles behind the enemy's main line of resistance and on which they were still in position and sending up S.O.S. signals. At this time, having only 17 men with him, he encountered a battery of three 4·2 Hows., two of which were in action. These he charged, himself killing the battery commander in a hand-to-hand fight and captured two other officers, the guns and crews. He then carried Tilleuls Farm, which was held with machine guns, one of which he put out of action and captured several others.

His courage and coolness inspired all under him, and it was due to his splendid leadership that the defensive flank was formed, enabling troops on the flank to come up. He captured 5 officers and 156 other ranks.

Awarded.........D.S.O.

Awards and Honours.

VICTORIA CROSS.

307817 L./Corpl. W. Amey ..	1/8th R. Warwickshire Regt.
17324 Pte. F. G. Miles	1/5th Gloucester Regt.

BAR TO THE D.S.O.

Major (A./Lt.-Col.) H. T. Clarke, D.S.O.	1/8th Worcester Regt.
Major (T./Lt.-Col.) R. S. Hart, D.S.O.	Notts. and Derby Regt., attd. Yorks. Regt.
T./Major (A./Lt.-Col.) D. Lewis, D.S.O., M.C.	Yorks. and Lancs. Regt., attd Gloucester Regt.
Major (T./Lt.-Col.) H. I. Storey, D.S.O.	9th Devon Regt.

D.S.O.

Capt. (A./Major) J. P. Bate, M.C.	1/8th Worcester Regt.
Lt. (A./Capt.) L. R. Bomford, M.M.	1/8th Worcester Regt.
Major (A./Lt.-Col.) H. T. Clarke..	1/8th Worcester Regt.
T./Major J. S. Gemmell, M.C. ..	20th Manchester Regt.
T./Capt. (A./ Lt.-Col.) P. F. Hone, M.C.	13th Durham Light Infantry.
Capt. (T./Lt.-Col.) G. E. N. Lomax, M.C.	Welsh Regt., attd. Manchester Regt.
T./Major D. Murray	21st Manchester Regt.
T./Capt. F. Nicholls	20th Manchester Regt.
T./Capt. (A./Major) F. G. Richards, M.C.	R.E.
Capt. R. de W. Rogers	Leins. Regt., attd. 1/5th Gloucester Regt.
Lt.-Col. P. H. Whitehouse ..	1/8th R. Warwickshire Regt.
Capt. C. M. Duncan	R.F.A.
2nd Lieut. E. Wedgbury, M.C., D.C.M., M.M.	Gloucester Regt., attd. 1/8th Worcesters.

2nd Bar to the M.C.

Lieut. (A./Major) W. G. Mackay, M.C.	R.F.A.
T./Capt. (A./Major) D. D. Pole Evans, M.C.	R.F.A.
Capt. (A./Major) W. Swinton, M.C.	R.F.A.

Bar to M.C.

2nd Lieut. A. L. Armstrong, M.C.	R.E.
Capt. (A./Major) J. H. Bayley, M.C.	R.A.M.C.
Lieut. J. W. Bell, M.C.	21st Manchester Regt.

Lieut. (A./Capt.) V. B. Bingham-Hall, M.C.	1/5th Gloucester Regt.
Capt. B. W. Bird, M.C.	Notts. and Derby Regt.
Capt. S. E. Boulton, M.C. ..	11th Sth. Lancs. Regt.
T./2nd Lieut. (A./Capt.) W. A. Clinton, M.C.	Notts. and Derby Regt.
Capt. G. B. Dempsey, M.C. ..	20th Manchester Regt.
Lieut. (T./Capt.) E. F. Orgill, M.C.	21st Manchester Regt.
T./Capt. L. M. Greenwood, M.C...	13th Durham Light Infantry.
T./Capt. (A./Major) C. H. Haddow, M.C.	R.A.M.C.
Lieut. (A./Capt.) S. F. Hill, M.C.	1/5th Gloucester Regt.
Lieut. H. M. Lane, M.C., D.C.M.	Attd. Y 25th T.M.B.
Lieut. R. S. F. Mitchell, M.C. ..	13th Durham Light Infantry.
Lt. (A./Capt.) H. Mortimore, M.C.	Seaforth Highlanders, attd. 1/8th R. Warwickshire Regt.
T./Lieut. (A./Major) H. V. Dean, M.C.	R.F.A.
Capt. (A./Major) A. L. Harman, M.C.	R.F.A.
Lieut. (A./Major) D. D. Pole Evans, M.C.	R.F.A.
T./Capt. R. P. Pridham, M.C. ..	9th Devonshire Regt.
Lt. (A./Capt.) C. G. Ratcliffe, M.C.	R.F.A.
Lieut. T. J. Redhead, M.C. ..	21st Manchester Regt.
2nd Lieut. C. L. J. M. Sallmayer	Notts. and Derby Regt.
2nd Lieut. (A./Capt.) R. O. Schuh, M.C.	9th Devon Regt.
Capt. J. O. Walford, M.C. ..	1/8th Worcester Regt.
T./Lieut. (A./Capt.) G. L. Watkinson, M.C.	1/8th Worcester Regt.
Lieut. (A./Major) P. C. L. Williams, M.C.	R.F.A.

MILITARY CROSS.

Lieut (A./Major) G. R. G. Alston	R.F.A.
2nd Lieut. T. H. Allen	R.F.A.
T./2nd Lieut. J. A. B. Allinson ..	13th Durham Light Infantry.
T./Lieut. M. L. Anderson	25th Batt. M.G. Corps.
2nd Lieut. W. Bannerman ..	13th Durham Light Infantry.
2nd Lieut. G. H. Barber	1/8th Worcester Regt.
2nd Lieut. S. T. Bateman, M.M.	1/8th Worcester Regt.
T./2nd Lieut. D. A. Best	20th Manchester Regt.
Lieut. (A./Capt.) V. B. Bingham-Hall.	1/5th Gloucester Regt.
Lieut. (A./Capt.) W. L. Blow ..	9th Yorkshire Regt.
2nd Lieut. H. Branham	20th Manchester Regt.
2nd Lieut. H. Briggs, M.M. ..	R.F.A.
2nd Lieut. A. J. Brown	1/8th R. Warwickshire Regt.
2nd Lieut. H. Brundrett ..	21st Manchester Regt.
Lieut. (A./Capt.) S. E. Chamier	R.F.A.
2nd Lieut. A. Coe	1/8th Worcester Regt.

2nd Lieut. A. J. Cox	1/5th Gloucester Regt.
2nd Lieut. R. Cox	9th Devon Regt.
2nd Lieut. W. R. Dewar	13th Durham Light Infantry.
2nd Lieut. J. E. Elder	20th Manchester Regt.
Lieut. F. J. Emson	Notts. Yeo., attd. M.G. Corps.
2nd Lieut. R. H. Farrier	13th Durham Light Infantry.
2nd Lieut. H. Gardner	13th Durham Light Infantry.
2nd Lieut. D. Gordon	1/8th Worcester Regt.
Lieut. (A./Major) J. E. H. Griffin	1/8th R. Warwickshire Regt.
Lieut. L. Hensham	11th South Lancs Regt.
2nd Lieut. L. D. C. Hughes	1/8th R. Warwickshire Regt.
2nd Lieut. C. F. Hunt	1/8th Warwickshire Regt.
2nd Lieut. J. Isherwood	20th Manchester Regt.
T./2nd Lieut. D. Kitchen	20th Manchester Regt.
T./Capt. W. R. Knott	9th Yorkshire Regt.
Lieut. H. M. Lane, D.C.M.	X/25 T.M. Batt.
T./Capt. F. W. K. Lawrie, R.A.M.C.	Attd. 11th Sherwood Foresters.
2nd Lieut. W. E. Manley	9th Devon Regt.
Lieut. P. A. Morley	Hunts Cyclists Corps, attd. 1/5th Gloucester Regt.
2nd Lieut. A. J. M. Melly	R.F.A.
T./2nd Lieut. G. Murray	25th Batt. M.G. Corps.
Capt. F. Nicholls	20th Manchester Regt.
2nd Lieut. F. M. Norton	R.F.A.
2nd Lieut. F. C. J. Nurcombe	R.F.A.
T./2nd Lieut. C. L. Ovenden	1/5th Gloucester Regt.
2nd Lieut. C. A. Oliver,	R.E., attd. Div. R.A. Sig.
2nd Lieut. J. M. Petty, M.M.	R.E.
T./2nd Lieut. J. D. Preston	21st Manchester Regt.
2nd Lieut. C. V. Prince	1/8th R. Warwickshire Regt.
Lieut. (A./Capt.) G. W. L. Pritchard	20th Manchester Regt.
2nd Lieut. G. A. C. Peter	R.F.A.
Lieut. W. H. Reynolds	1/8th Worcester Regt.
2nd Lieut. H. B. Rishworth	25th Div. Sig. Co., R.E.
T./Lieut. (A./Major) W. Roscoe	25th Batt. M.G. Corps.
2nd Lieut. J. H. Scattergood	R.F.A.
2nd Lieut. A. Scrivener	1/8th R. Warwickshire Regt.
2nd Lieut. V. Scroggie	1/5th Gloucester Regt.
Capt. J. Stirling	R.A.M.C., attd. 112th Brigade, R.F.A.
2nd Lieut. G. M. Scrutton	R.F.A.
T./Capt. (A./Major) C. J. Sullivan	R.A.M.C.
2nd Lieut. G. W. Sutcliff	9th Yorkshire Regt.
2nd Lieut. L. J. Taylor	9th Yorkshire Regt.
2nd Lieut. E. Thorpe	R.F.A.
Lieut. E. S. C. Vaughan	1/8th R. Warwickshire Regt.
Capt. J. O. Walford	1/8th Worcester Regt.
T./Lieut. (A. Capt.) W. N. Wallis	25th Batt. M.G. Corps.
Lieut. G. L. Watkinson	1/8th Worcestershire Regt.
2nd Lieut. (A./Capt.) H. A. Watts	Notts. and Derby Regt.
2nd Lieut. G. G. Weaving	Notts. Yeo., attd. M.G. Corps.
2nd Lieut. E. Wedgbury, D.C.M., M.M.	Gloucester Regt., attd. 1/8th Worcester Regt.

2nd Lieut. G. S. Wells .. .. R.E.
2nd Lieut. G. H. West .. .. 1/5th Gloucester Regt.
T./2nd Lieut. J. W. Willey .. 13th Durham Light Infantry.
Lieut. (A./Major) P. C. L. Williams R.F.A.
T./2nd Lieut. J. S. Wood .. 9th Yorkshire Regt.
2nd Lieut. A. E. W. Walder .. R.F.A.

BAR TO D.C.M.

67143 Sergt. A. Agnew, D.C.M. R.F.A.
240119 Sergt. A. J. T. Sherwood, 1/8th Worcester Regt.
   D.C.M.

D.C.M.

31109 Sergt W. J. Brown .. R.F.A.
241001 Sergt. R. Atkinson, M.M. 1/8th Worcester Regt.
40388 Pte. (L.Corpl.) T. Betteley 20th Manchester Regt.
240665 C.S.M. W. Bromage .. 1/5th Gloucester Regt.
28074 Private G. Cobb .. .. 1/5th Gloucester Regt.
19116 Corpl. W. H. Collins .. 11th Sherwood Foresters.
13055 C.S.M. W. Coleman, M.M... 9th Yorkshire Regt.
10091 Pte. N. Courtney .. .. 9th Devon Regt.
20552 L./Corpl. J. E. Crompton .. 20th Manchester Regt.
240126 Sergt. H. Faulkner .. Worcester Regt.
18575 Sergt. F. Fitzpatrick .. 21st Manchester Regt.
38591 2nd Corpl. G. H. Foster .. R.E.
73189 Sergt. J. R. Garfoot .. Notts and Derby Regt.
8899 C.S.M. J. A. Goodison .. 9th Yorks.
47257 Sergt. J. Goodwin, M.M. .. 25th Div. Sig. Corpl., R.E.
16010 Sergt. G. M. Green .. 9th L. N. Lancs., attd. 75th
   Brigade H.Q.
P3 Sergt. (a./S.S.M.) S.W. Halliway, M.M.P.
   M.M.
57408 Pte. G. Harris .. .. 21st Manchester Regt.
242501 Sergt. G. W. Hobbs, M.M. 1/5th Gloucester Regt.
11749 L./Corpl. A. J. Hornigold .. 1/5th Gloucester Regt.
305649 Sergt. G. A. Johnson .. Notts and Derby Regt.
8899 C.S.M. J. Leighton .. .. 1/8th Worcester Regt.
306759 Sergt. D. H. Lissaman .. 1/8th R. Warwickshire Regt.
240079 Corpl. W. Peacey .. 1/5th Gloucester Regt.
12585 Corpl. H. E. Pearson .. 9th Devon Regt.
17459 C.S.M. H. Perry .. .. 20th Manchester Regt.
14448 Corpl. T. Phelps .. .. 9th Devon Regt.
95759 Sergt. W. F. Rayner .. R.F.A.
61090 Pte. V. Redstone .. .. 11th South Lancs. Regt.
240220 Corpl. (A./Sergt.) W. 1/8th Worcester Regt.
   Roberts.
306573 L./Corpl. Wl Rushbrook.. 1/8th R. Warwickshire Regt.
19071 Pte. A. E. Rutter .. .. 21st Manchester Regt.
68600 Sergt. L. Steadman, M.M... R.F.A.
65249 Sergt. G. Shepherd, M.M. .. R.E.
18483 Sergt. A. Sledge, M.M. .. 13th Durham Light Infantry.
18071 Sergt. M. Smith. M.M. .. 9th Yorkshire Regt.

18279 C.S.M. J. B. Smith, M.M...	21st Manchester Regt.
81232 Sergt. I. J. Tully	25th Batt. M.G. Corps.
305960 C.S.M. H. Whitehouse ..	1/8th Warwickshire Regt.
137986 Sergt. A. Wood	R.E.

SECOND BAR TO M.M.

19788 Sergt. J. Collinson, M.M. ..	9th Yorks.
66797 Spr. C. H. Hensby, M.M. ..	Signal Coy., R.E.

BAR TO M.M.

246853 Sergt. L. H. Agathe, M.M.	R.F.A.
24794 L./Corpl. T. Armstrong, M.M.	13th Durham Light Infantry.
241001 Sergt. R. Atkinson, M.M.	1/8th Worcesters.
405142 Pte. S. W. Barker, M.M.	R.A.M.C.
57013 Bdr. J. Blezard, M.M. ..	R.F.A.
60028 Sergt. A. S. Bradley, M.M.	R.E., attd. Div. Art. Sig.
8036 L./Corpl. G. F. Cannings, M.M.	9th Yorks.
23818 Pte. H. Chilton, M.M. ..	Loyal North Lancs., Sig. Coy.
20959 Pte. J. Clark, M.M. ..˙	13th Durham Light Infantry.
240596 Sergt. T. H. C. Coleman, M.M.	1/8th Worcesters.
60932 Corpl. F. Dyer, M.M. ..	R.F.A.
203696 L./Corpl. W. Glee, M.M. ..	1/5th Gloucesters.
18067 Sergt. (A.C.S.M.) T. S. Hammond, M.M.	13th Durham Light Infantry.
40644 Sergt. A. E. Hodgetts, M.M.	1/8th Worcesters.
9704 Corpl. F. King, M.M. ..	1/5th Gloucesters Regt.
360024 Spr. J. Mather, M.M. ..	Signal Coy., R.E.
48998 Spr. E. Perris, M.M. ..	R.E. (H.Q., 75th Brigade).
201348 Corpl. (L./Sergt.) C. Prince, M.M.	1/8th Worcesters.
25824 Sergt. W. Pike, M.M. ..	9th Devons.
33789 L./Corpl. C. J. Rolfe, M.M.	1/8th Royal Warwicks.
30274 Pte. A. Smith, M.M. ..	1/8th Royal Warwicks.
242592 Pte. H. Turner, M.M. ..	1/8th Worcesters.
240817 Sergt. E. Turner, M.M. ..	1/8th Worcesters.
51465 L./Corpl. S. Wells, M.M. ..	R.E.
92104 Pte. G. Whitlock, M.M. ..	11th Sherwood Foresters.
241284 L./Corpl. G. Wisdom, M.M.	1/8th Worcesters.
19327 Sergt. C. Wilkinson, M.M...	21st Manchester Regt.
241719 Pte. F. Wood, M.M. ..	1/8th Worcesters.
307788 Sergt. F. G. Wootton, M.M.	1/8th Royal Warwicks.
50584 Corpl. E. Wynne, M.M. ..	11th Sherwood Foresters.

MILITARY MEDAL.

176726 L.-Corpl. (A./2nd Corpl.) W. H. Andrews.	R.E.
237675 Spr. M. Ashcroft	25th Div. Sig. Co., R.E.
34466 Pte. A. Austen	20th Manchesters.
60575 Corpl. J. C. Allan	R.F.A

96133 Corp. H. Atkinson ..	.. R.F.A.
33143 L./Sergt. E. de Atk	.. 9th Devons.
16462 Pte. G. Attis ..	.. 9th Devons.
48401 Corp. F. Atkinson ..	.. 25th Batt. M.G. Corps.
137323 Pte. G. Arthur ..	.. 25th Bn. M.G. Corps.
50197 Pte. W. Armitage ..	.. R.A.M.C.
11728 Corpl. W. D. Alcock	.. 21st Manchester Regt.
34370 Pte. W. J. Adams ..	.. 9th Yorkshire Regt.
307817 L.-Corpl. W. Amey	.. 1/8th Warwicks.
59399 Pte. A. E. Adams ..	.. 1/8th Worcester Regt.
705552 Sergt. H. Brassington	.. R.F.A.
65104 Spr. T. Barbour ..	.. R.E.
62190 Spr. H. H. Bird ..	.. R.E.
66090 Spr. H. Brown ..	.. R.E.
242533 (L-Corpl.) L. Bowler	.. 1/8th Worcester Regt.
65103 Spr. A. O. Burton ..	.. R.E.
74189 Dvr. W. Barber ..	.. R.F.A.
836809 Dvr. W. Benjamin	.. R.F.A.
76164 Bdr. H. Benson ..	.. R.F.A.
211356 Fitter S. W. Baker	.. R.F.A.
31991 Pte. T. H. Briggs ..	.. R.A.M.C.
71914 Dvr. J. Bradbury ..	.. R.F.A.
51013 Bdr. J. Blezard ..	.. R.F.A.
44550 Pte. J. Beattie ..	.. 13th Durham Light Inf.
18135 L./Corpl. T. W. Barron	.. 13th Durham Light Inf.
6936 Sergt. L. Beecroft ..	.. 11th Sherwood Foresters.
305069 C.Q.M.S. H. Brahan	.. 1/8th R. Warwicks.
305569 Corpl. E. Beard ..	.. 1/8th R. Warwicks.
16594 Pte. G. Bews ..	.. 13th Durham Light Inf.
47044 Pte. A. Burgess ..	.. R.A.M.C.
45564 Spr. J. W. Berry ..	.. R.E.
39666 Pte. F. Bradley ..	.. Manchester Regt.
40420 Sergt. W. Bradbury	.. Manchester Regt.
66809 Pte. H. A. Brice ..	.. 9th Devons.
3249 Bdr. J. E. Beynon ..	.. R.F.A.
67004 Dr. F. Berry ..	.. R.F.A.
90137 L.-Corpl. E. Brownbill	.. 25th Bn. M.G. Corps.
35894 Pte. T. Brown ..	.. 9th Yorks Regt.
71786 Pte. J. N. Blow ..	.. 11th Sherwood Foresters.
82034 Pnr. E. Beer ..	.. R.E. (75th Inf. Bde.).
M2/074090 A. E. Bishop ..	.. A.S.C. (M.T.). R.A.M.C.
31467 Pte. H. E. Baker ..	.. 9th Devon Regt.
40519 A./Corpl. A. Burgum	.. 20th Manchester Regt.
31352 Pte. A. Bullock ..	.. 1/5th Gloucester Regt.
51028 L./Corpl. J. Beasent	.. 1/8th Worcesters.
40206 Cpl. W. Barton ..	.. 20th Manchester Regt.
404112 Dvr. T. A. Crawford	.. R.E.
32709 Spr. J. Chatwin ..	.. Signal Coy., R.E.
90140 Dvr. A. E. Cox ..	.. 25th Bn., M.G. Corps.
9971 Pte. H. Cooper ..	.. 25th Bn., M.G. Corps.
31650 Pte. H. J. Chaplin ..	.. R.A.M.C.
17842 C.Q.M.S. H. Cadman	.. 20th Manchester Regt.
38192 L./Cpl. G. F. Codley	.. 9th Yorks. Regt.

35898 Pte. H. Clennell	9th Yorks. Regt.
13501 Pte. G. Cassidy	20th Manchester Regt.
10091 Pte. N. Coutney	9th Devon Regt.
16012 Corpl. G. Cockran	9th Devon Regt.
52869 Pte. T. Crossley	13th Durham Light Inf.
33058 L./Corpl. D. B. Clark ..	9th Yorks. Regt.
57197 Pte. J. Corson	11th Lancs. Fusiliers.
266698 Pte. R. Cole	1/5th Gloucester Regt.
242267 L./Corpl. F. Cleaver ..	1/5th Gloucester Regt.
55036 L./Corpl. R. Carr	21st Manchester Regt.
23257 Corpl. H. Connell	9th Yorks. Regt.
12840 Corpl. G. Cuthbertson ..	R.F.A.
851250 Gnr. T. H. Colenutt ..	R.F.A.
15272 Farr.-Sergt. T. Cusick ..	R.F.A.
48993 Sergt. H. McCoy	11th South Lancs. Regt.
235473 Sgt. R. Caygill	9th Yorks. Regt.
25942 Sergt. C. Collins	9th Yorks. Regt.
203193 L.-Corpl. H. T. Chappin ..	11th Sherwoods.
325619 Pte. C. S. Crowe	1/8th Warwicks.
242357 Pte. A. Clarke	Worcs. (att. 75th Inf. Bde.)
38781 Pte. W. Coles	1/5th Gloucester Regt.
306560 Pte. A. Caudle	1/8th Warwicks.
305473 L.-Cpl. W. Crammage ..	1/8th Warwicks.
262264 Pte. E. Chidgey	1/5th Gloucester Regt.
240339 L.-Cpl. F. Curry	1/5th Gloucester Regt.
260089 Cpl. W. Coulson	1/5th Gloucester Regt.
242356 Pte. G. H. Cleft	1/8th Worcester Regt.
64717 L.-Bbr. T. Dutton	R.F.A.
46064 Pte. A. Dawson	11th South Lancs.
1313 Pte. D. Doherty	20th Manchester Regt.
9081 L./Corpl. T. Dickinson ..	Army Cyclist Corps.
28275 Sergt. B. Dawson	9th Yorks. Regt.
17317 Pte. F. Dyer	13th Durham Light Inf.
39030 Pte. J. Davis	R.A.M.C.
240159 Sergt. H. S. Derrick ..	1/5th Gloucester Regt.
242547 Pte. W. Dauncey	1/5th Gloucester Regt.
13358 Sergt. L. Dawe, D.C.M. ..	R.F.A.
57036 Dvr. G. Darlington.. ..	R.F.A.
313150 L./Corpl. A. Dempsey, R.E.	Attd. R.F.A.
121012 Sergt. R. J. Donnachie ..	R.F.A.
10666 Sergt. T. Daley	11th Sherwood Foresters.
35050 Pte. W. Deans	21st Manchester Regt.
17783 Pte. A. E. Dyson	9th Yorks. Regt.
108447 Pte. G. A. Duncan ..	11th Sherwoods.
260244 Pte. J. S. Davies	1/5th Gloucesters.
202644 Pte. R. Dale	1/8th Worcesters.
294272 Pte. W. Day	1/8th Worcesters.
46349 Pte. J. Eglinton	11th South Lancs.
6773 C.Q.M.S. H. Ellis	25th Bn. M.G. Corps.
81242 Pte. W. Erskine	R.A.M.C.
23742 L.-Corp. R. Easton ..	1/8th Worcester Regt.
48966 Pte. A. Ellis	20th Manchester Regt.
19110 Sergt. F. Evans	20th Manchester Regt.

39757 Sergt. E. T. Edwards	1/5th Gloucester Regt.
3929 Pte. G. Edmonds	20th Manchester Regt.
31491 Pte. A. Eamer	9th Devon Regt.
242984 Pte. J. Eldred	1/8th Warwick Regt.
41539 Pte. L. G. Ellaway	1/8th Warwick Regt.
200094 Corpl. W. T. Edgeworth	1/5th Gloucesters.
240017 C.S.M. F. Finch	1/5th Gloucesters.
178987 Spr. J. M. Ford	R.E.
200895 L.-Corpl. F. C. Frisby	11th Sherwoods.
305057 L.-Corpl. F. Fourt	1/8th Warwicks.
240310 L.-Corpl. W. C. Fletcher	1/5th Gloucesters.
40208 L.-Corpl. T. Fothergill	21st Manchester Regt.
39919 Gnr. J. Franklin	R.F.A.
240297 Sergt. L. Fletcher, D.C.M.	1/5th Gloucester Regt.
23634 Pte. E. G. Flood	21st Manchester Regt.
15568 Corpl. E. H. Fowler	1/5th Gloucesters.
240126 Sergt. H. Faulkner	1/8th Worcesters.
73519 Sergt. J. M. Fishwick	R.A.M.C.
13271 Pte. J. Fellows	1/8th Worcesters.
54816 Pte. J. P. Forde	R.A.M.C.
221230 Sig. S. Fitton	R.F.A.
761430 Gnr. J. P. Fawcett	R.F.A.
51306 Corpl. W. French	R.E., attd. R.F.A.
45518 Batt. S. Maj. J. Froggart	R.F.A.
122235 L.-Bdr. A. Ford	R.F.A.
400570 A./Corpl. Gardner	R.E.
132424 Cpl. J. Goodwin	25th Bn., M.G. Corps.
170177 Dvr. A. B. Gray	R.F.A.
90185 L.-Corpl. G. W. Gaffin	R.E.
55060 Corp. J. Graham	21st Manchester Regt.
307885 L.-Corpl. A. Gardiner	1/8th R. Warwick Regt.
67268 Dvr. J. Graham	R.F.A.
45733 Sergt. J. C. Gillies	R.F.A.
42940 Pte. A. W. Godart	R.A.M.C.
40660 Pte. T. Gregory	R.A.M.C.
39849 Pte. R. Gee	R.A.M.C.
29729 Pte. G. H. Gilmore	9th Yorks. Regt.
38954 L.-Corpl. E. Gegie	9th Yorks. Regt.
53584 Pte. C. Guest	9th Yorks. Regt.
249870 L.-Cpl. A. Gilbert	1/8th Warwicks.
241962 Corpl. H. J. Gillies	1/5th Gloucesters.
65192 A./Corpl. T. Hitchen	R.E.
18135 Spr. H. Howells	R.E.
95229 2nd Corpl. M. Hunter	R.E.
90989 Dvr. E. Hamilton	R.E.
22491 A./Corpl. S. Hackett	R.E.
51213 Spr. W. Howarth	R.E.
4368 L.-Bdr. S. H. Hawksworth	R.F.A.
56330 Dvr. C. W. Hoy	R.F.A.
91130 Spr. G. Harris	Signal Coy., R.E.
20738 Pte. J. F. Hooper	9th Devon Regt.
57073 Dvr. J. Hargreaves	R.F.A.
26505 Pte. A. Horner	11th Sherwood Foresters.

306619 Pte. J. Hedges	1/8th R. Warwick Regt.
306567 Corp. A. Harris	1/8th R. Warwick Regt.
325041 Pte. F. Hazeldon	1/8th R. Warwick Regt.
39945 L.-Sergt. C. Hewson	1/5th Gloucester Regt.
25834 Pte. L. W. Hudson	21st Manchester Regt.
9513 Pte. J. W. Hoodless	R.A.M.C.
63543 Pte. W. Hall	R.A.M.C.
17398 Pte. W. Horn	13th Durham Light Inf.
18067 Sergt. P. F. Hammond	13th Durham Light Inf.
241609 Corpl. C. Henderson	1/8th Worcester Regt.
9662 Sergt. H. Heatherington	13th Durham Light Inf.
19463 Pte. F. Heath	11th Sherwood Foresters.
17843 Pte. A. Hainsworth	11th Sherwood Foresters.
142093 Pte. D. Hollingworth	25th Bn., M.G. Corps.
132539 Pte. N. Hatherley	25th Bn. M.G. Corps.
49728 Pte. W. Horrocks	R.A.M.C.
14340 Sergt. S. J. Harper	9th Devon Regt.
4122 Pte. A. G. Hammond	20th Manchester Regt.
4176 Pte. W. J. Holding	21st Manchester Regt.
18608 Sergt. E. Hayward	21st Manchester Regt.
28109 Pte. J. W. Huller	9th Yorks. Regt.
397762 Pte. W. Hill	1/8th Warwicks.
33258 Pte. F. Hirst	1/8th Warwicks.
305988 Sergt. T. Harvey	1/8th Warwicks.
305539 Corpl. G. C. L. Hall	1/8th Warwicks.
18311 L.-Sergt. F. Hodges	1/8th Worcesters.
40644 Sergt. A. E. Hodgetts	1/8th Worcesters.
140236 Spr. J. Inston	R.E.
240192 Pte. J. Iles	1/5th Gloucester Regt.
240641 L.-Corpl. P. W. Ireland	1/5th Gloucester Regt.
204895 Sergt. J. Ions	11th South Lancs.
44601 Corpl. C. Jackson	13th Durham L.I.
7680 Pte. C. C. Johnson	20th Manchester Regt.
45008 Pte. L. Jones	Manchester Regt.
127504 Spr P. W. Jiggins	25th Div. Sig. Co., R.E.
240747 A./Sergt. J. Jones	1/8th Worcesters.
305463 C.Q.M.S. A. Jay	1/8th R. Warwick Regt.
71979 Sergt. J. F. Iones	R.F.A.
3529 Pte. J. Jamieson	R.A.M.C.
7075 Pte. H. Jenkins	R.A.M.C.
240045 Sergt. W. Jennings	1/8th Worcesters.
39200 Pte. S. Jarvis	1/5th Gloucester Regt.
102517 Corpl. G. Kerwin	25th Bn., M.G. Corps.
81864 Pte. J. O. Kelly	R.A.M.C.
400462 Pte. A. Knowles	21st Manchester Regt.
40092 Pte. J. Kidder	20th Manchester Regt.
38026 Pte. G. W. Kidson	9th Yorks. Regt.
215140 L.-Bdr. W. Kearns	R.F.A.
13869 Sergt. J. Killeen	13th Durham L.I.
306568 Corpl. W. H. Kirby	1/8th Warwicks.
242590 Pte. F. Knight	1/8th Worcesters.
96449 Corpl. G. Lyall	Signal Coy., R.E.
512358 Pte. R. Laing	R.A.M.C.

;50487 Pte. W. Leigh	20th Manchester Regt.
;0595 Corpl. R. Lieper	R.F.A.
;981 Dvr. C. Lingwood	R.F.A.
;8476 Pte. F. Leete	9th Yorks. Regt.
;1061 Corpl. G. Laking	1/8th Worcester Regt.
;00320 Sergt. T. Longson.. ..	21st Manchester Regt.
;9442 C.S.M. J. Lucy, M.C., D.C.M.	21st Manchester Regt.
305290 Sergt. W. Lovatt	1/8th Warwicks.
267178 Pte. E. Laity	1/8th Warwicks.
29516 L.-Corpl. G. Lewis	1/5th Gloucesters.
33793 Corpl. J. Morton ..	R.F.A.
146424 L.-Corpl. G. E. Meredith..	R.E.
90997 Dvr. A. Mayes	R.E.
82317 Spr. A. G. Mann	R.E.
463119 Spr. R. Main	Signal Coy., R.E.
122137 Corpl. G. Morris	25th Bn., M.G. Corps.
101554 Pte. W. H. Mealing ..	R.A.M.C.
644584 Sergt. R. Motion	R.F.A.
71790 Corpl. C. W. Miller ..	D.A.C.
79771 Gnr. P. Meehan	R.F.A.
250611 Gi.r. A. Moore	R.F.A.
241631 Pte. L. Morris	1/8th Worcester Regt.
45955 Pte. F. Malloy	13th Durham Light Inf.
40314 Pte. T. McLynn	20th Manchester Regt.
44482 Pte. A. Morris	20th Manchester Regt.
161022 Corpl. J. McKean ..	25th Div. Sig. Co., R.E.
44454 Corpl. A. Mills	20th Manchester Regt.
42663 L.-Corpl. S. A. J. Meagre ..	9th Devon Regt.
40645 Pte. J. Mason	21st Manchester Regt.
26280 Sergt. J. C. Moss ..	11th Sherwood Foresters.
307650 Sergt. W. H. Molding ..	1/8th R. Warwick Regt.
122137 Corpl. G. Morris	25th Batt. M.G.C.
305657 Pte. J. McCarthy	1/8th R. Warwick Regt.
57322 L.-Corpl. J. P. Matthews, D.C.M.	9th Devon Regt.
360017 Spr. J. Morris	R.E., att. 75 Bde.
242470 Pte. J. Mathews	1/5th Gloucesters.
97152 Spr. M. O'Hallaron ..	R.E.
162962 Dvr. J. A. Nurse	R.E.
15807 Pte. W. Newman	9th Devon Regt.
33690 Pte. G. E. Neeves	1/8th R. Warwick Regt.
28122 Corpl. G. Newgill	9th Yorks. Regt.
241300 Sergt. W. Niblett	1/5th Gloucesters.
58534 Pte. G. Nicholson	11th Sherwoods.
20350 Sergt. W. Owen	11th South Lancs.
17804 Sergt. H J. Owen	1/5th Gloucesters.
33538 Pte. J. Osmond	9th Devon Regt.
34493 L.-Corpl. G. Oliver	9th Yorks. Regt.
260170 Corpl. A. P. Owers ..	1/8th Worcesters.
741649 Sgnr. A. E. Parker ..	R.F.A.
808984 Dvr. R. E. Payne	105th Fld. Co., R.E.
145474 Pte. T. Poole	25th Batt. M.G. Corps.
10869 Fitter R. Perkins	R.F.A.

31819 Sergt. T. P. Palmer, D.C.M.	X/25th T.M. Batt.
242307 Sergt. F. Packer	1/5th Gloucester Regt.
19226 Sergt. J. Palin	21st Manchester Regt.
78422 Pte. S. Powell	13th Durham Light Inf.
930264 Spr. H. Preston	R.E., attd. R.F.A.
89108 Pte. J. Paterson	25th Bn., M.G. Corps.
260625 Pte. H. Percival ..	11th Sherwoods.
78424 Pte. H. Poulter ..	13th D.L. Infantry.
240292 L.-Corpl. F. E. Pugh ..	1/5th Gloucesters.
28323 L.-Corpl. C. G. Payne ..	1/5th Gloucesters.
39229 Pte. E. Proudfoot	1/5th Gloucesters.
241589 Pte. H. J. Paggett ..	1/8th Worcesters.
240665 Pte. W. E. Pitt	1/8th Worcesters.
240940 L.-Corpl. C. Plumb ..	1/8th Worcesters.
17195 C.Q.M.S. A. F. Phippen ..	20th Manchesters.
60516 A.-Cpl. A. W. Robinson ..	R.F.A.
31753 Corpl. P. Roberts	9th Devons.
148588 Dvr. H. Rose	R.F.A.
17368 Sig. J. J. Robinson.. ..	R.F.A.
57357 Sergt. W. G. Ransome ..	R.F.A.
43440 Pte. G. Russell ..	13th Durham Light Inf.
26328 Pte. R. Rawnsley	21st Manchester Regt.
204863 Pte. S. Rumble	11th South Lancs. Regt.
242536 Pte. A. Ruggles	1/8th Worcester Regt.
740739 Sergt. J. Richards ..	R.F.A.
43235 Pte. T. Radmore	9th Devons.
53960 Sergt. S. B. Richardson ..	11th Sherwood Foresters.
307569 Pte. A. E. Rubeley ..	1/8th Warwicks.
67407 Pte. E. Rowbottom ..	1/8th Worcesters.
96073 Pte. J. Robinson	13th Durham Light Inf.
242432 Sergt. F. W. Slader ..	1/8th Worcesters.
263025 Pte. J. T. Scanlon ..	1/5th Gloucesters.
39829 Pte. G. W. Snowling ..	1/5th Gloucesters.
240991 Corpl. A. F. Swanborough	1/5th Gloucesters.
240236 Sergt. G. C. Smart ..	15th Gloucesters.
73015 Pte. J. Smith	11th Sherwoods.
14472 L.-Corpl. J. Smith ..	R.E.
199265 L.-Corpl. F. Stratton ..	R.E.
61177 Dvr. W. Sumner	R.E.
240224 L.-Corpl. E. Stokes ..	1/8th Worcesters.
65512 2nd Corpl. D. Shuttleworth	R.E.
158934 Sergt. W. Smith	25th Bn., M.G. Corps.
113840 Spr. F. Stapleton	R.E.
164897 Corpl. F. Sanders	Notts. Yeomanry.
44483 Pte. H. Shaw	20th Manchester Regt.
34433 Gnr. H. Stafford	R.F.A.
14065 Pte. W. Summerscales ..	20th Manchester Regt.
34518 L.-Corpl. T. Sutton ..	9th Yorks. Regt.
13274 Corpl. R. Shields	9th Yorks. Regt.
34942 Sergt. H. Smith	9th Yorks. Regt.
242348 L.-Corpl. W. H. Smith ..	1/8th Worcester Regt.
241865 Pte. F. Steer	1/8th Worcester Regt.
305078 Pte. R. N. Swift	1/8th R. Warwick Regt.

306511 Sergt. E. G. Stone	..	1/8th R. Warwick Regt.
307776 Pte. F. Sharp	..	1/8th R. Warwick Regt.
73376 Pte. G. Spruce	..	11th Sherwood Foresters.
3461 Pte. H. Swindle	..	11th Sherwood Foresters.
17905 Pte. N. S. Smith	..	11th Sherwood Foresters.
245250 Pte. A. E. Shelley	..	13th Durham Light Inf.
241865 Pte. F. Steer	..	1/8th Worcesters.
24826 L.-Corpl. J. W. Smith	..	13th Durham Light Inf.
240530 Sergt. W. A. Stephens	..	1/5th Gloucester Regt.
47291 Pte. M. Smith	..	R.A.M.C.
200762 Sergt. J. Sherry	..	20th Manchester Regt.
36381 Col. F. Stafford	..	11th Sherwood Foresters
306021 Sergt. W. Sheffield	..	1/8th R. Warwicks.
136384 Pte. G. Scorer	..	25th Batt. M.G. Corps.
35267 Bdr. A. T. Spencer	..	R.F.A.
12974 Bdr. J. R. Slater	..	X/25th T.M. Batt.
63157 Dr. R. J. Scott	..	R.F.A.
68600 Sergt. L. Steadman	..	R.F.A.
127988 Gr. H. Speak	..	R.F.A.
32733 Spr. G. W. Salter	..	R.E., att. R.F.A.
17064 Corp. J. W. E. Saunders	..	R.F.A.
15620 Sergt. T. W. Stainton	..	9th Yorks.
49945 Pte. C. Shepherd	..	21st Manchester Regt.
240290 L.-Corpl. C. L. Somers	..	1/8th Worcesters.
18727 Sergt. H. Smith	..	21st Manchesters.
14321 L.-Corpl. F. Stead	..	9th Yorks.
34514 Pte. J. T. Stendall	..	9th Yorks.
34278 Pte. G. J. Saint	..	9th Yorks.
15985 Sergt. R. Stevenson	..	9th Yorks.
36190 Pte. H. Stellabras	..	11th Sherwoods.
73119 Pte. J. A Sutherland	..	11th Sherwoods.
57993 Pte. J. Tyrer	..	25th Bn. M.G. Corps.
402431 Corpl. C. G. Thomson	..	R.E.
30411 A./Sergt. G. Timm	..	R.A.M.C.
M2/116936 Pte. J. Todd	..	A.S.C., M.T., attd. R.A.M.C.
9458 Pte. C. Tuckerman	..	9th Devons.
240287 L.-Corpl. L. D. Trigg	..	1/5th Gloucesters.
240298 Pte. E. F. Tilley	..	1/5th Gloucesters.
61357 B.S.M. G. F. Theaker	..	R.F.A.
52647 C.S.M. G. Thomson, D.C.M.		13th Durham Light Inf.
242307 Sergt. F. Thacker	..	1/5th Gloucester Regt.
203664 Pte. W. Thomas	..	1/5th Gloucester Regt.
40714 L.-Sergt. J. Timmins	..	1/8th Worcester Regt.
40333 Pte. H. Taylor	..	20th Manchester Regt.
39762 Pte. S. Taylor	..	20th Manchester Regt.
22067 Sergt. H. J. Tipper	..	R.E., attd. R.F.A.
25755 Dvr. J. Turton	..	R.F.A.
240671 Sergt. E. N. Turner	..	1/5th Gloucester Regt.
8858 C.S.M. W. T. Tait	..	9th Yorks. Regt.
126364 Pte. J. T. Vickers	..	25th Bn., M.G. Corps.
23157 Pte. H. C. Venning	..	9th Devons.
26786 Pte. J. Vigg	..	9th Devon Regt.
240163 L.-Corpl. W. Vesper	..	1/5th Gloucesters.

127273 2nd Corpl. J. H. Ward ..	Signal Coy., R.E.
22280 L.-Corpl. A. Weston ..	1/8th Worcesters.
87489 Corpl. W. Halles	Signal Coy, attd. 25th M.G. Bn.
73516 Pte. H. White	R.A.M.C.
M2/116576 A./Corpl. R. F. West-lake	A.S.C. (M.T.), R.A.M.C.
44886 Pte. H. Waterhouse ..	20th Manchester Regt.
19303 Pte. J. Williams ..	21st Manchester Regt.
38092 L.-Corpl. H. White.. ..	9th Devon Regt.
63198 Gnr. W. Weall	R.F.A.
65611 Corpl. E. C. Webb	R.E.
38189 L /Sergt. J. H. Waterson ..	25th Bn. M.G.C.
240458 Corpl. A. J. Wood ..	1/8th Worcester Regt.
43646 Pte. H. Wood	21st Manchester Regt.
13814 Sergt. F. Wood	9th Devon Regt.
305490 Sergt. G. Wilkes	11th Sherwood Foresters.
60910 Corpl. E. C. Wyvill ..	X/25th T.M. Batt.
2326 Batt. S.M. W. J. Wilson, D.C.M.	R.F.A.
8149 L.-Bdr. A. F. Weller ..	R.F.A.
45772 Gnr. P. Wilkie	R.F.A.
8470 Sergt. W. H. Wilkinson ..	9th Yorks.
118230 Pte. J. J. Wardle ..	11th Sherwood Foresters.
92098 Pte. J. Walmsley ..	11th Sherwood Foresters.
76538 Pte. F. Watts	11th Sherwood Foresters.
18/1488 Sergt. I. B. Walton ..	13th Durham Light Inf.
54317 Pte. H. W. Winter ..	13th Durham Light Inf.
33630 Pte. A. Williams	1/8th Warwicks.
57308 Pte. F. Whitehead	1/8th Warwicks.
260297 Pte. T. Williams	1/5th Gloucesters.
242530 Pte. F. Webber	1/5th Gloucesters.
242356 Pte. J. Woodman ..	1/5th Gloucesters.
202772 Pte .A R. Wainwright ..	1/8th Worcesters.
568425 Spr. H. J. Webb, R.E. ..	R.F.A.
62253 Pte. S. R. Wyatt	R.A.M.C.
267818 C.S.M. W. H. Yates ..	1/8th Warwicks.
48902 Spr. G. McK. Young ..	25th Div. Sig. Co., R.E.
1708 M. des Logis P. Quehen ..	French Mission, attd. 112th Brigade, R.F.A.

25th Division.

SUMMARY OF CASUALTIES REPORTED FROM
3rd OCTOBER TO 11th NOVEMBER, 1918.

Divisional Artillery and 25th Battalion M.G. Corps from 8th August to 11th November.

Unit.	Officers.			Other Ranks.		
	K.	W.	M.	K.	W.	M.
25th Div. H.Q.	..	3	..	1	5	..
110th Bde., R.F.A.	..	9	..	20	99	..
112th Bde., R.F.A.	2	14	..	34	150	2
25th D.A.C.	..	1	..	..	4	..
X/25th T.M. Batty.	..	1	..	..	7	..
105th Field Coy., R.E.	..	1	..	1	36	..
106th Field Coy., R.E.	..	3	..	3	26	..
130th Field Coy., R.E.	..	1	..	6	36	..
25th Div. Sig. Coy.	..	1	..	5	20	2
R.A.M.C.	..	3	..	..	..	..
75th Field Amb.	..	..	..	..	11	..
76th Field Amb.	..	..	..	2	9	..
77th Field Amb.	..	1	..	2	5	..
225th Div. Emp. Coy.	..	1	..	1	4	..
H.Q. 7th Inf. Bde.	1	1	..	1	3	..
9th Devons	5	11	..	60	326	..
20th Manchesters	5	15	..	80	251	34
21st Manchesters	4	15	..	64	342	80
7th T.M. Batty.	..	..	..	..	6	..
H.Q. 74th Inf. Bde.	..	..	..	3	10	..
9th Yorks.	5	18	..	69	359	106
11th Sherwood Foresters	4	19	..	62	385	56
13th Durham L.I.	5	21	1	107	526	80
74th T.M. Batty.	..	1	..	..	7	..
H.Q. 75th Inf. Bde.	..	..	..	1	..	..
1/8th R. Warwick. Regt.	2	14	..	53	313	24
1/5th Gloucester Regt.	3	17	..	51	300	14
1/8th Worcester Regt.	3	18	..	53	377	19
75th T.M. Batty.	..	..	..	..	2	..
25th Bn. M.G. Corps	2	14	1	40	250	..
100th Bn. M.G. Corps	..	..	..	4	34	..
11th S. Lancs. (Pioneers)	..	5	1	6	35	1
	41	208	3	729	3,880	428

STATEMENT OF OFFICER CASUALTIES.

25th D.H.Q.

Wounded.

Capt. G. St. V. Harris, M.C., East Kent Yeo.
Capt. Murray, U.S.A., 2nd American Corps, attd. Div. H.Q.

110th Bde., R.F.A.

Wounded.

2nd Lieut. C. A. Gell-Woolley.
Capt. P. Kent, Dragoons, attd.
  110th Bde.
2nd Lieut. A. J. M. Melly.
Lieut. E. A. Hassard, M.C. (died)

2nd Lieut. A. W. Smith.
Lieut. E. G. Murdock.
2nd Lieut. J. P. G. Magwood (died)
2nd Lieut. A. E. Walder, M.C.
Major P. C. L. Williams, M.C.

112th Bde., R.F.A.

Killed.

2nd Lieut. P. Padley.
Lieut. W. R. Johnston.

Wounded.

Major W. Swinton, M.C.
2nd Lieut. F. C. B. Wheeler (2)
Lieut. C. F. A. Dobson (2)
2nd Lieut. G. R. Trustum.
Major W. G. MacKay, M.C. (2)
2nd Lieut. W. M. Upton.
2nd Lieut. H. R. Goodman.

Lieut. J. Moresby White.
Major S. O. Jones, M.C.
2nd Lieut. J. W. Hudson, M.C.
2nd Lieut. P. R. Mead.
2nd Lieut. E. W. Cormack.
Major D. D. Pole Evans, M.C.
Lieut. C. J. Nurcombe, M.C.

25th Div. Amm. Col.

Wounded.

2nd Lieut. A. St. John Sibborn.

X 25 T.M. Battery.

Wounded.

Lieut. H. M. Lane, M.C., D.C.M.

105th Field Coy., R.E.

Wounded.

2nd Lieut. J. B. Curnhill.

106th Field Coy., R.E.

Wounded.

2nd Lieut. A. H. Turner.
2nd Lieut. G. B. Kellagher.

Lieut. F. C. Saxon.

130th Field Coy., R.E.

Wounded.

2nd Lieut. C. G. Milligan.

R.A.M.C.

Wounded.

Capt. G. Moore, attd. 1/8th Warwick Regt.

Col. H. N. Dunn, C.M.G., D.S.O.
Capt. D. G. Gardiner, attd. 9th
  Devon Regt.

77th Field Ambulance.

Wounded.

Capt. W. W. Wells.

225th Div. Emp. Coy.

Wounded.

Lieut. H. Pomeroy, Cheshire Regt.

H.Q. 7th Inf. Bde.

Killed.

Capt. R. M. Burmann, D.S.O., M.C., East Lanc. Regt., Bde. Major.

Wounded.

Lieut. N. Walker, Cheshire Regt.

9th Devons.

Killed.

Lieut. S. P. Tozer.   2nd Lieut. M. W. Higgs.
2nd Lieut. A. S. Bridgewater.   Lieut. B. P. Yeatman.
Lieut. W. J. Hyatt.

Wounded.

2nd Lieut. S. C. Holman.   2nd Lieut. C. Sutton, M.C.
2nd Lieut. T. H. Haine, M.C.   Capt. N. C. Wilson.
2nd Lieut. L. McW. Easterbrook.   Lieut. R. M. Haswell.
2nd Lieut. J. Geddes.   2nd Lieut. H. Arnold (died).
2nd Lieut. H. H. H. de la Cour.   Lieut. C. H. Brock (died).
Capt. A. G. Gardner, R.A.M.C., attd. 9th Devon Regt.

20th Manchesters.

Killed.

Capt. J. Waring, M.C.   Capt. G. W. L. Pritchard.
Lieut. K. R. Woollaston.   2nd Lieut. G. S. Walker.
2nd Lieut. A. Hulme.

Wounded.

Lieut. C. A. Forsyth.   2nd Lieut. Earle.
Lieut.-Col. C. S. Burt, D.S.O. S.   Capt. J. Waring, M.C.
    Staff.   Lieut. J. Charlesworth.
2nd Lieut. H. G. Poulton.   2nd Lieut. E. M. Wright.
2nd Lieut. J. J. Wilkinson.   Capt. H. S. Bagshaw, M.C.
2nd Lieut. C. J. D. Seddon.   2nd Lieut. L. J. Poynter (died).
2nd Lieut. J. Lea.   2nd Lieut. J. Elder.
2nd Lieut. R. O. Garside.   Capt. W. H. Bowsher, M.C. (died).

21st Manchesters.

Killed.

Capt. J. C. Richardson.   2nd Lieut. J. H. Webb, M.C.
2nd Lieut. E. F. Ponting.   Capt. J. W. Bell, M.C.

Wounded.

Major H. W. Walker, M.C.
Lieut. G. H. Tomkinson, M.C.
2nd Lieut. R. G. Rogers.
2nd Lieut. C. Hewitt.
2nd Lieut. F. Dunn.
2nd Lieut. J. E. Thompson, M.C.
2nd Lieut. R. A. Tresise (died).

2nd Lieut. T. W. Thurley.
2nd Lieut. R. W. Bertenshaw.
Capt. H. Ingham.
2nd Lieut. D. A. Best.
2nd Lieut. F. Schofield.
2nd Lieut. T. W. Bellis.

9th Yorks.

Killed.

Lieut. G. M. Wolstenholme, M.C.
Lieut. G. Read.
Major G. N. Hunnybun, M.C.

Lieut. H. Dixon.
Lieut. W. H. Grimsley.

Wounded.

2nd Lieut. R. H. Akers.
Capt. C. H. B. Botting, M.C.
Capt. W. F. Greenwood, D.S.O.,
   M.C.
Lieut. R. Ward.
2nd Lieut. P. Helms (died).
2nd Lieut. H. H. Ransome.
2nd Lieut. J. F. Guttridge.
Revd. W. E. Jones, C.F., attd.
   9th Yorks.
2nd Lieut. W. A. Sharpe.

2nd Lieut. H. D. Foster.
2nd Lieut. I. R. Edwards-Grate.
   (died).
2nd Lieut. T. F. Day.
Lieut. G. H. V. Saunders.
2nd Lieut. C. L. Porter.
Lieut. A. R. Porter.
2nd Lieut. T. Narrow.
2nd Lieut. J. G. Anderson.
2nd Lieut. J. A. Pomfrey (died).

11th Sherwood Foresters.

Killed.

2nd Lieut. W. R. Branker,
   K.R.R.C.
2nd Lieut. W. A. Powell.

Capt. C. W. Bartlett, M.C.
Lieut.-Col. H. N. Young, D.S.O.,
   Royal Inniskilling Fus.

Wounded.

2nd Lieut. W. R. Garrett.
Lieut. A. D. Swale (died).
Lieut. C. G. Mc C. Kemball.
Capt. R. W. Clark, M.C.
2nd Lieut. H. G. Whittington.
2nd Lieut. T. Cheetham, M.C.
Capt. H. A. Watts.
Lieut. O. R. C. Orchard.
Major L. H. Gibson, M.C. (2)
2nd Lieut. R. L. Swire, M.C.

2nd Lieut. C. J. Bond.
Capt. J. H. Spicer, M.C.
2nd Lieut. J. Pickard, Ox. and
   Bucks. Light Inft.
2nd Lieut. W. A. Wilson.
Capt. B. W. Bird, M.C. (died).
Capt. W. A. Clifton, M.C.
2nd Lieut. L. J. Goossens.
2nd Lieut. R. W. Tomkins.

13th Durham Light Infantry.

Killed.

Lieut. H. P. Hart.
Lieut. H. Golder.
2nd Lieut. C. Dodds.

2nd Lieut. P. G. Smith.
Capt. I. Bewley, M.C.

Wounded.

Lieut.-Col. D. H. Clarke, D.S.O., M.C.
Capt. C. R. Chapman.
Lieut. F. L. F. Rees, M.C.
2nd Lieut. N. H. Willis, M.C.
2nd Lieut. G. E. Jackson.
2nd Lieut. J. D. Inches.
2nd Lieut. W. Bannerman (2)
Lieut.-Col. P. F. Hone, M.C.
2nd Lieut. C. H. Bishop (died of wounds).

2nd Lieut. H. C. Geipel.
Lieut. A. C. Hales.
2nd Lieut. E. C. Forrest.
2nd Lieut. R. W. Robinson.
2nd Lieut. T. Bolton.
2nd Lieut. R. T. Aitkenhead
2nd Lieut. W. R. Dewar.
2nd Lieut. E. H. Callow.
Lieut. R. Skelton.
2nd Lieut. A. Holmes (died).
2nd Lieut. W. E. Walker.

Missing.

2nd Lieut. F. Audas (P. of W.).

74th T.M. Battery.

Wounded.

2nd Lieut. O. F. Woodcock, Bedford Regt.

1/8th R. Warwick Regt.

Killed.

2nd Lieut. B. J. Young.

Capt. J. Richards.

Wounded.

2nd Lieut. C. A. Cox.
Lieut. J. Harris.
Capt. C. W. McFarlane.
2nd Lieut. W. H. Fawke.
2nd Lieut. A. L. Chick.
2nd Lieut. C. C. Middleton.
2nd Lieut. C. F. Hunt.

2nd Lieut. H. L. Morgan.
2nd Lieut. W. F. Lee.
2nd Lieut. F. J. Hassall.
2nd Lieut. C. J. Miller.
Capt. G. G. Bowerman, M.C.
2nd Lieut. R. Craigan

1/5th Gloucester Regt.

Killed.

2nd Lieut. C. F. Hussey.
2nd Lieut. V. Scroggie.

Capt. S. F. Hill, M.C

Wounded.

Lieut. G. W. E. Seago, E. Kent Regt. (died).
2nd Lieut. A. J. Cox.
Lieut. J. A. Carroll, Glos. Yeo.
Capt. C. R. de W. Rogers, Leinster Regt. (2).
2nd Lieut. H. J. Northcott, Dorset Regt. (2) (died).
2nd Lieut. H. R. H. Morris.

Capt. G. Hawkins.
2nd Lieut. C. L. P. Gilshenan.
2nd Lieut. W. L. Pålmer.
2nd Lieut. H. H. Searle.
2nd Lieut. S. F. Woodward (died).
Lieut. F. J. Lovell.
2nd Lieut. H. Busby.
2nd Lieut. H. G. Powell.
2nd Lieut. A. T. Jackson (died)

1/8th Worcester Regt.

Killed.

Capt. H. G. C. Carter, M.C.
2nd Lieut. H. D. King.

Lieut. C. A. Connor.

Wounded.

Lieut. E. Stainton.
Capt. J. O. Walford.
Lieut. T. L. Jones, M.C. (died).
2nd Lieut. L. Goodyear.
Lieut. R. J. C. W. Hawtrey.
Capt. G. H. Smith, M.C.
Lieut. W. S. Gundrey, M.C.
Lieut. F. W. Wiles.
2nd Lieut. F. H. Astill.
2nd Lieut. G. Hales.

2nd Lieut. C. Brown (died).
Lieut. A. R. Watson.
Lieut. R. S. Miller (P. of W.)
Lieut. W. H. Reynolds.
2nd Lieut. S. T. Bateman, M.M.
2nd Lieut. J. H. Greenaway.
Capt. L. R. Bomford, M.C.
2nd Lieut. E. Wedgbury, D.C.M.,
   M.M.
2nd Lieut. D. A. Franks.

25th Battalion M.G. Corps.

Killed.

2nd Lieut. P. W. Moss.

2nd Lieut. W. E. Belschner.

Wounded.

Lieut. A. A. Hill.
2nd Lieut. S. Gray, Worcester
   Regt.
2nd Lieut. W. F. Gardner.
2nd Lieut. W. A. Costley.
2nd Lieut. A. E. Williams.
2nd Lieut. E. E. Shorthouse.
2nd Lieut. J. Bolam, M.C.
2nd Lieut. F. Aulton, S. Staff.

Major A. W. H. Sime, D.S.O.,
   M.C.
Lieut. P. A. Ross.
2nd Lieut. J. Allison.
2nd Lieut. A. E. Hill, Sherwood
   Foresters.
2nd Lieut. A. Turnbull.
Lieut. J. Melville.

Missing.

2nd Lieut. R. J. Roberts.

11th S. Lancs. (Pioneers).

Wounded.

Lieut. H. V. Worrall, Lancs. Fus.
Capt. M. D. Robinson.
Lieut. L. Henshaw

2nd Lieut. H. Jones (died)
2nd Lieut. J. Kirkpatrick.

Missing.

2nd Lieut. R. Carr (P. of W.).

25th Div. Signal Coy.

Wounded.

2nd Lieut. W. E. H. Kennedy, Wilts Regt.

Honours and Awards, New Year's List, 1919.

C.B.

Bt. Col. (T./Brig.-Gen.) K. J. Kincaid Smith, C.M.G., D.S.O. — C.R.A. 25th Div.

C.M.G.

Capt. and Bt. Maj. (T./Lt.-Col.) E.C. de L. Martin, D.S.O., M.C. — Yorks. Light Inf., attd. 11th Lancs. Fus.

Bt. Lt.-Col. R. T. Lee, D.S.O. .. — G.S.O.I., 25th Div.

Major Bt. Lt.-Col. (T./Brig.-Gen.) H. M. Craigee Halkett, D.S.O. — Comdg. 74th Brigade.

BREVET LIEUT.-COL.

Major (A./Lt.-Col.) R. J. Done .. — C.R.E. 25th Div.

ORDER OF THE BRITISH EMPIRE.

Major R. W. Cooper, M.C. .. — D.A.Q.M.G., 25th Div.

SECOND BAR TO D.S.O.

T./Lt.-Col. H. G. Pollitt, D.S.O., R.E. — Comdg. 11th Lancs. Fus.

BAR TO D.S.O.

Major A. Reade, D.S.O., M.C. .. — 11th Cheshires.

Major W. H. M. Weinholt, D.S.O. — 9th L.N. Lancs.

Major (A./Lt.-Col.) J. N. de la Perrelle, D.S.O., M.C. — 6th Royal Fus., attd. 8th Border Regt.

Major (T./Lt.-Col.) C. W. H. Birt, D.S.O. — 8th Bn. Border Regt.

D.S.O.

Capt. (A./Major) E. D. W. H. Bradley, M.C. — Comdg. 25th Div. Sig. Coy.

T./Major A. Reid-Kellett, M.C. .. — 6th Bn. S.W. Borderers.

Capt. (A./Major) T. I. Dun, M.C., R.A.M.C. — D.A.D.M.S. 25th Div.

MILITARY CROSS.

Lieut. (A./Capt.) A. Flowers .. — R.F.A.

2nd Lieut. G. Macdonald .. — R.F.A.

2nd Lieut. E. J. S. Dalton .. — 25th Bn. M.G. Corps.

D.C.M.

63428 Sergt. H. Ellis .. .. — R.F.A.

71737 Sig. Bomdr. J. Pinkney, M.M. — R.F.A.

120896 Sergt. J. H. C. Limbfield — R.F.A.

62963 Sergt. F. M. Keogan .. — R.F.A.

134132 Sergt. J. Boyle .. .. — R.E.

MILITARY MEDAL.

40695 Corpl. J. A. Leach .. .. — 6th Bn. S.W. Borderers

57334 Dvr. J. W. Blackwell .. — R.F.A.

30637 Sergt. H. Huntlea .. — R.F.A.

8188 B.S.M. R. Storey .. .. — R.F.A.

56220 Sergt. T. W. Williams .. — 25th Div. Sig. Coy.

54209 Sergt. H. L. Pennington .. — 25th Div. Sig. Coy.

MERITORIOUS SERVICE MEDAL.

S./248429 Corpl. R. H. Gardner ..	A.S.C.
24893 Sergt. W. T. Hunn ..	Lancs. Fus.
P./1845 L./Corpl. D. Clear ..	M.M.P.
P./797 L./Corpl. A. W. Petch ..	M.M.P.
5821 B.S.M. J. J. Bennett ..	R.F.A.
M.T./105942 Pte. T. E. Goode ..	A.S.C., attd. R.F.A.
2nd Corpl. (A./Sergt.) G. E. Gardner	R.E.
57341 C.Q.M.S. T. H. Pearson ..	R.E.
65614 Farr.-Sergt. F. Hodges ..	R.E.
161553 2nd Corpl. T. McKail ..	25th Div. Sig. Coy.
15577 Sergt. W. L. Hitchings ..	6th Bn. S.W. Borderers
39665 Corpl. W. Swain	6th Bn. S.W. Borderers.
36903 C.Q.M.S. J. Massey ..	25th Bn. M.G. Corps.
6889 C.Q.M.S. W. A. Graham ..	25th Bn. M.G. Corps.
122317 Corpl. G. Morris	25th Bn. M.G. Corps.
6773 C.Q.M.S. H. Ellis	25th Bn. M.G. Corps.
T.3/029937 Corpl. (A./C.Q.M.S.) W. V. S. Angel.	R.A.S.C.
T.4/144293 Dvr. W. Hawkins ..	R.A.S.C.
T.3/028993 C.S.M. A. A. Cooper	R.A.S.C.
M.2/115415 Sergt. W. E. Day ..	R.A.S.C.
M.2/100119 M.S. S. F. Skinner ..	R.A.S.C.
38595 A./Q.M.S. F. D. Grahame..	R.A.M.C.
T.1/S.R./290 T.S. M. J. Beaumont	R.A.M.C.
57848 Corpl. W. F. Dobson ..	R.A.M.C.
T.3/026832 S.S. M. J. Johnston ..	R.A.S.C., attd. R.A.M.C.
S.E. 8343 Sergt. J. Pickup ..	R.A.V.C.
9647 C.Q.M.S. J. Turner, M.M. ..	2nd R.I.R., attd. 74th Bde. H.Q.
W./326 Sergt. W. H. Gray ..	Cheshire Regt., attd. 74th Bdr., H.Q.
27649 Pte. (A.Corpl.) J. Griffin ..	Cheshire Regt., attd. 74th Bdr. H.Q.
14430 C.Q.M.S. H. Malley ..	8th Border Regt.
14869 Sergt. J. Berry	8th Border Regt.
7903 Sergt. Cook S. Bardell ..	2nd South Lancs.
29906 Sergt. H. C. Hudson ..	2nd South Lancs.

MENTIONS.

Major C. W. O. Jenkyn, M.C. ..	Army Chaplains Dept.
Major (Lt.-Col.) R. T. Lee, D.S.O.	G.S.O.I. 25th Div.
Major R. W. Cooper, M.C. ..	D.A.Q.A.G. 25th Div.
Major J. S. Fulton, M.C. ..	D.A.A.G. 25th Div.
Lieut. H. Pomeroy	Cheshire Regt. and Labour Corps.
Capt. R. A. R. Spread	Army Chaplains Dept.
S./26825 Corpl. (A./S. Sergt.) W. Hull, M.M.	A.S.C.
223142 Corpl. W. Balmire ..	Labour Corps.
Bt. Col. (T./Brig.-Gen.) K. J. Kincaird-Smith, C.M.G., D.S.O., R.A.	C.R.A. 25th Div.
Major (A. Lt.-Col.) E. V. Sarson, D.S.O.	R.F.A.

4558 B.S.M. J. Froggatt .. .. R.F.A.
Major (A./Lt.-Col.) D. J. Done, C.R.E. 25th Div.
D.S.O., R.E.
T./Capt. (A./Major) C. G. J. R.E.
Lynam, M.C.
T./Capt. (A./Major) F. E. Mus- R.E.
grave, M.C.
45076 C.Q.M.S. T. W. Andrews .. R.E.
Capt. A./Major E. de W. H. V. K.O.Y.L.I., comdg. 25th Div. Sig.
Bradley, M.C. Co.
Lieut. (A./Capt.) J. C. R. Dallas.. Middlesex Regt., attd. 25th Div.
Sig. Co.
Lieut. E. T. Sandiford .. .. Sth. Lancs., attd. 25th Div. Sig.
Co.
5271 Sergt. (A./C.S.M.) R. Sutton 25th Div. Sig. Co.
58208 Spr. A. S. H. White .. 25th Div. Sig. Co.
T./Major A. Reid-Kellett, M.C. .. 6th Bn. S.W. Borderers.
Bt. Major (T./Lieut.-Col.) N. T. R.E., attd. 6th S.W. Borderers.
Fitzpatrick, M.C.
Lieut. S. E. Runsey, M.C. .. 6th Bn S W Borderers.
T./2nd Lieut. S. Kelly .. .. 6th Bn. S.W. Borderers.
6/17092 Pte. G. Meredith .. 6th Bn. S.W. Borderers.
Lieut. (A./Capt.) C. G. W. Mackrell 25th Bn. M.G. Corps.
T./Lieut. (A./Capt.) W. M. Wallis 25th Bn. M.G. Corps.
T./Lieut. and Q.M. C. Laycock .. 25th Bn. M.G. Corps.
36247 Pte. N. Andrews .. .. 25th Bn. M.G. Corps.
Capt. R. J. Finch .. .. R.A.S.C.
T./Capt. J. Poyser .. .. R.A.S.C.
T. 3/029551 Dvr. J. Tanser .. R.A.S.C.
S. 4/084615 S./Sergt. D. Wright R.A.S.C.
Capt. (A./Maj.) S. G. Spoor .. R.A.S.C.
M./18478 L./Corpl. (A./C.S.M.) P. R.A.S.C.
Glynn.
Capt. (A./Major) J. H. Bayley, M.C. R.A.M.C.
7732 Pte. L. Thompson .. .. R.A.M.C.
41694 Sergt. (A./S./Sergt.) D. Lyons R.A.M.C.
Capt. L. A. Donovan .. .. R.A.V.C.
Lieut. W. J. E. Ross .. .. 1st Wilts.
Major A. Reade, D.S.O., M.C. .. 10th Cheshires.
Major (Bt. Lieut.-Col.) (T./Brig.- Comdg. 74th Brigade.
Gen.) H. M. Craigie-Halkett,
D.S.O.
Capt. J. C. O. Marriott, D.S.O., M.C. Staff Capt. 74th Brigade.
Lieut.-Col. The Hon. W. R. Guin- Brigade Major 74th Brigade.
ness, D.S.O.
2nd Lieut. S. W. Boast, M.C. .. 2nd Sth Lancs.
2nd Lieut. J. Blackburn .. .. 2nd Sth. Lancs.
29631 Corpl. L. Aspin .. .. 2nd Sth. Lancs.
Major T./Lieut.-Col. C. W. H. Birt, 8th Bn. Border Regt.
D.S.O.

HIGHER RATE OF PAY.

Capt. and Q.M. B. Bartholomew, L.N.L. Regt. and General List.
M.C.

Birthday Honours, June, 1919.

C.M.G.

T./Maj.-Gen. J. R. E. Charles, Comdg. 25th Div.
C.B., D.S.O., R.E.
Major (Bt. Lt.-Col.) (T./Brig.-Gen.) Comdg. 7th Brigade.
C. J. Hickie.
Major (T./Lt.-Col.) D. F. Ander- G.S.O. 1, 25th Div.
son, D.S.O.

O.B.E.

Major (A./Lt.-Col.) C. S. Hope- Comdg. 25th D.A.C.
Johnstone, R.F.A.
T./Capt. J. Poyser..   ..   ..   R.A.S.C.
Capt. (A./Major) S. G. S, o⸱ r   ..   Comdg. 25th Div. M.T. Coy.
T./Major G. V. Ewart   ..   ..   R.A.S.C.
Capt. (T./Major) J. S. Fulton, M.C.   D.A.A.G., 25th Div.

D.S.O.

T./Lt.-Col. W. T. Raikes, M.C. ..   25th Batt. M.G. Corps.

BREVET LIEUT.-COL.

Major (T./Lt.-Col.) Hon. E. P. J. A.A. & A.M.G. 25th Div.
Stourton, D.S.O.
Major N. M. McLeod, D.S.O., M.C. Brigade Major 25th Div. Artillery.
(on completion of 15 years' ser-
vice).
Capt. (Bt. Major) (T./Brig.-Gen.) Comdg. 75th Brigade.
C. W. Frizell, D.S.O., M.C.
Major (T./Lt.-Col.) R. S. Hart, 9th Yorks.
D.S.O.

BREVET MAJOR.

Lieut. (T./Lt.-Col.) W. R. Corrall, 11th Sherwood Foresters.
M.C. (on promotion to Captain).
Capt. S. O. Playfair, D.S.C., M.C., Brigade Major 75th Brigade.
R.E.
T./Capt. A. G. Dean, M.C.   ..   11rh South Lancs.
Capt. F. Treacher, M.C. ..   ..   Staff Capt. 75th Brigade.
T./Capt. G. A. Godfrey, M.C.   ..   Staff Capt. 74th Brigade.
Lieut. (T./Capt.) H. P. White, Staff Capt. 7th Brigade.
M.C. (on promotion to Capt.)

M.C.

Lt. (A./Capt.) J. C. Dallas   ..   25th Div. Sig. Coy. R.E.
Lieut. (T./Capt.) C. de L. Gaussen, G.S.O. 3, 25th Div.
R.E.
Lieut. (A./Capt.) E. Gilbert   ..   1/8 Worcester Regt.
240005 T./R.S. Major H. Heath ..   1/8 Worcester Regt.
Capt. D. G. Gardiner, R.A.M.C. ..   Att. 9th Devons.
Lieut. (A./Capt.) F. H. Ridge   ..   R.E.

Lieut. C. S. Salmon   ..   ..   25th Batt. M.G. Corps.
T./2nd Lt. T. W. Thurley   ..   21st Manchesters.
T./Capt. S. A. Webb, R.F.A.   ..   25th D.A.C.
T./Lieut. (A./Major) F. W. Bar-   25th Butt. M.G. Corps.
   tholomew.
Capt. (A./Major) G. R. Crouch   ..   1/5th Gloucesters.
Lieut. G. A. Keay   ..   ..   R.F.A.
2nd/Lt. W. Y. Gow   ..   ..   1/8th R. Warwick Regt.

D.C.M.

21460 Sergt. W. Allen   ..   ..   25th Batt. M.G. Corps.
65610 Sergt. L. P. Burles, M.M...   R.E.
24825 L./Cpl. R. Bell   ..   ..   13th Durham L. Inf.
4186 C. S. Maj. J. Clark   ..   R.E.
5407 R.S. Major W. Manley   ..   9th Devons.
15748 C.S. Major L. W. Pollard ..   11th Sherwood Foresters.
8618 C.S. Major A. S. Ryan   ..   11th South Lancs.
63189 Sergt. J. Thorpe   ..   ..   R.F.A.
52012 Sergt. J. Wilkinson, R.F.A.   25th D.A.C.

M.S.M.

T.4/040225 Wheeler Sergt. J. T.   R.A.S.C.
   Allen.
18819 R.Q.M. Sergt. L. Barrie   ..   21st Manchesters.
17024 Sergt. R. J. Broadsmith   ..   20th Manchesters.
240692 L./Cpl. S. G. Brunsdon ..   1/5th Gloucesters.
20056 C.Q.M. Sergt. G. M. Board-   11th South Lancs.
   man.
90391 Cpl. J. Broadhurst   ..   R.F.A.
81649 Cpl. (A./Sergt.) J. A. Baker   R.F.A.
M.S./789 Pte. N. W. G. Collins ..   R.A.S.C.
37317 Sergt. (A./S. Sergt.) A. Cur-   R.A.M.C.
   rell.
39999 Pte. (A./Sergt.) C. Collinge..   R.A.M.C.
47245 Sergt. H. Demay, M.M.   ..   25th Div. Sig. Coy., R.E.
223141 Cpl. J. E. Ellis   ..   ..   Labour Corps, att. 225th Div.
     Employ.
12340 Sergt. E. S. Eden   ..   ..   9th Devons.
305094 C. S. Major A. Flowers   ..   1/8th R. Warwick Regt.
39752 R.S. Major J. Gardiner   ..   1/5th Gloucesters.
43399 Sergt. H. Garnett   ..   ..   13th Durham L. Inf.
31811 Pte. (A./Sergt.) O. Hopkins   R.A.M.C.
40037 Cpl. (A./Sergt.) P. Heyes ..   R.A.M.C.
S./19420 Cpl. (T./S.-Sergt.) W. Hull,   R.A.S.C.
   M.M.
D.M2/151477 Pte. W. A. Kidd   ..   R.A.S.C.
205171 Cpl. G. King   ..   ..   25th D.A.C.
17892 C.S.-Major J. W. Lyall,   9th Yorks.
   M.M.
M2/104485 Cpl. W. F. Lucas   ..   25th Div. M.T. Coy.
T1/4621 Cpl. C. W. Legge   ..   R.A.S.C.

6945 Pte. J. Lethaby	25th Batt. M.G. Corps.
67407 Bmdr. O. Leeke	R.F.A.
583810 Pte. H. Miller	Labour Corps, att. 225th Div. Employ.
M2/153930 Cpl. G. Minney ..	25th Div. M.T. Coy.
249477 Cpl. R. A. Newth.. ..	1/8th Worcesters.
22257 T./Farr.-Sergt. A. Newbury	R.E.
D./924 Sergt. A. New	M.M.P., att. H.Q. 25th Div.
74312 Sergt. F. Olive ..	11th Sherwood Foresters.
18960 C.R.M.-Sergt. C. H. Pearson	21st Manchesters.
15728 T./C.S.-Major A. J. Poulter, M.M.	R.E.
20064 R.Q.M.-Sergt. P. F. Routley	11th South Lancs.
21169 C.Q.M.-Sergt. J. Roberts ..	11th South Lancs.
M2/049537 M.S.-Sergt. F. E. Sadler	25th Div. M.T. Coy.
T1/5216 Sergt. W. Shaw	R.A.S.C.
88216 Farr. Q.M.-Sergt. H. Vance	R.F.A.
305670 Sergt.-Master Cook W. W. Walliter.	1/8th R. Warwick Regt.
S.4/084640 S.-Sergt. F. Wilkinson	R.A.S.C.
143045 Sergt. W. A. Walker ..	25th Batt. M.G. Corps.

MENTIONS.

14491 Corpl. E. Abbott	25th Batt. M.G. Corps.
A/3015 A./Staff-Sergt. R. Aytoun	R.A.O.C., attd. 1/5th Gloucesters.
276733 Pte. (A./Corpl.) G. V. Allen	13th Durham L.I.
7310 Sergt. (A./Q.M.S.) W. Beckley	Worcester Regt., attd. H.Q., 7th Bde.
33580 Pte. G. Browning	9th Devons.
40158 Sergt. W. Brown	21st Manchesters.
Capt. R. M. Burmann, D.S.O., M.C.	Bde. Major, 7th Bde.
6867 C.S.M. P. Brailsford ..	11th Sherwood Foresters.
Capt. W. B. Bagshaw, M.C. ..	Bde. Major, 74th Bde.
305212 Pte. (A./Sergt.) G. Bradshaw.	1/8th R. Warwick Regt.
48920 Corpl. F. Bailey	25th Divnl. Sig. Coy., R.E.
305299 L.-Corpl. W. E. Beatson ..	1/8th R. Warwick Regt.
S.4/O.39170 S.-Sergt. C. J. Buxton	25th Divnl. Train.
T. 4/O.38192 Dvr. A. Binks ..	198th Coy., R.A.S.C.
S. 4/O.72691 Sergt. J. Birdsall ..	R.A.S.C.
398610 Spr. H. Buchan	R.E.
SC/5796 Sergt. O. Brooker ..	R.A.V.C., attd. 110th Bde., R.F.A.
T./Lt. (A./Capt.) T. D. Barnes ..	25th D.A.C.
Bt. Col. (T./Major-Gen.) J. R. E. Charles, C.B., D.S.O., R.E.	Commanding 25th Division.
P. 1802 L.-Corpl. G. Coates ..	M.M.P., attd. 25th Divnl. H.Q.
223169 Pte. W. Cole	Labour Corps, attd. 225th Divnl. Emp. Coy.
41664 B.S.M. W. J. Corless ..	R.F.A.
40305 Sergt. W. Covell	R.E.
Lt. (A./Major) S. L. Courtauld, M.C.	25th Batt. M.G. Corps.
11272 C.S.M. H. Cheney	25th Batt. M.G. Corps.

T./Major (A./Lt.-Col.) C. C. Champion, D.S.O.	11th South Lancs.
TS/1554 SS.-Farrier W. Cockburn	R.A.S.C.
T. 3/O.28941 Dvr. F. G. Chennell	R.A.S.C.
S. 3/O.27908 C.Q.M.S. W. H. Carter	25th Divnl. Train.
M. 2/113998 Corpl. J. Cairns ..	25th Divnl. M.T. Coy.
M. 2/O.9607 Sergt. A. R. Cross ..	25th Divnl. M.T. Coy.
Major (Bt. Lt.-Col.) (T./Brig.-Gen.) H. M. Craigie Halkett, C.M.G., D.S.O.	Commanding 74th Bde.
T./2nd Lt. W. Carpenter	1/8th R. Warwick Regt.
240036 C.Q.M.S. T. E. Churchill..	1/8th Worcester Regt.
16017 Corpl. S. G. Cuthbert ..	11th Sherwood Foresters
Lt. J. Charlesworth	20th Manchesters.
P. 856 L.-Corpl. G. Dale	M.M.P., attd. H.Q., 25th Divn.
43460 Corpl. J. Drummond ..	21st Manchesters.
40810 Corpl. C. Dudnie	9th Yorks.
M. 2/100114 C.Q.M. Sergt. S. T. Divers	25th Div. M.T. Coy.
T. 3/O.28896 L.-Corpl. W. Dell ..	R.A.S.C.
5215 C.S.M. E. Driscoll	11th South Lancs.
Capt. (Bt. Major) (T./Major) G. R. Dubs, M.C.	G.S.O. 2, 25th Div.
Major (Bt. Lt.-Col.) R. J. Done, D.S.O., R.E.	C.R.E., 25th Div.
Col. H. N. Dunn, C.M.G., D.S.O., R.A.M.C.	A.D.M.S., 25th Div.
T./Capt. (A./Major) A. C. H. Eagles, M.C.	D.A.D.O.S., 25th Div.
34502 Sergt. J. Edmunds ..	R.F.A.
152214 L.-Corpl. J. Elder ..	25th Divnl. Sig. Coy., R.E.
Major H. G. Faber	13th Durham L.I.
240177 C.S.M. F. Finch	1/5th Gloucesters.
325026 L.-Corpl. F. Fox	1/8th R. Warwick Regt.
38592 Pte. (L.-Corpl.) P. Forkin..	R.A.M.C.
Capt. (A./Major) F. G. Foster ..	R.A.M.C.
2nd Lt. L. Goodyear	1/8th Worcesters.
2nd Lt. J. B. Gurnhill	R.E.
134081 Sapper P. Glasgow ..	R.E.
56642 L.-Corpl. W. Gush.. ..	25th Div. Sig. Coy., R.E.
43891 C.S.M. H. E. P. Goodwin, D.C.M.	25th Batt. M.G. Corps.
116574 L.-Corp. H. Geach ..	25th Batt. M.G. Corps.
T./Capt. (A./Major) H. Goodman	R.A.M.C.
49243 Pte. J. Gill	20th Manchesters.
34367 Pte. F. Haddock	9th Yorks.
18359 L.-Corpl. H. Heaton ..	13th Durham L. Inf.
M2/114072 Corpl. E. J. V. Hallett	25th Div. M.T. Coy.
T./Lieut. M. T. Hincks	25th Div. M.T. Coy.
41428 Corpl. W. A. Hoyer ..	R.A.M.C.
20180 Sergt. W. J. Hignett ..	11th South Lancs.
20719 Sergt. J. T. Halton ..	11th South Lancs.
67363 L.-Bdr. F. Hampson ..	25th D.A.C.

47052 Corpl. P. Jenks	R.A.M.C.
12037 Corpl. V. Jones	9th Devons.
63285 Dvr. M. Jackson	R.F.A.
42033 Sergt. P. H. Kirkup ..	9th Yorks.
T./Capt. M. Kennard, M.C. ..	R.A.S.C.
90892 2nd Corpl. F. Kerry ..	R.E.
17835 Corpl. H. Knott	R.F.A.
214582 L.-Bdr. J. Kent	25th D.A.C.
21638 Dvr. T. S. C. Lawson ..	R.F.A.
Capt. (A./Lieut.-Col.) H. H. Leeson, M.C.	R.A.M.C.
T./Lieut. T. M. Lewin	20th Manchesters.
2232 Sergt. J. Morley	20th Manchesters.
240490 C.Q.M.-Sergt. M. McHugh	1/8th Worcester Regt.
T/3 O.28524 Dvr. F. B. Mitchell..	25th Divl. Train.
T./2nd Lieut. R. Mackenzie ..	R.A.S.C.
152257 Pte. J. Marchant	25th Batt. M. G. Corps.
Lieut. (A./Capt.) D. J. Murmane, M.C.	R.E.
Major (A./Lieut.-Col.) K. E. Milford, D.S.O.	Comdg. 110th Bde., R.F.A.
88319 Sergt. A. L. Moulton ..	R.F.A.
T./Capt. (T./Major) G. D. Norman	D.A.D.V.S., 25th Div.
240121 Corpl. W. A. Nicholls ..	1/5th Gloucesters.
10887 Pte. R. Naven	9th Yorks.
T./Lieut. C. A. Oliver	25th Div. Sig. Coy., R.E.
14363 Sadd.-Sergt. C. H. Peach ..	25th D.A.C.
11730 Gnr. H. W. Pomroy ..	R.F.A.
65595 Sap. C. Poulter	R.E.
TS/8654 S.S. Saddler G. E. Pywell	R.A.S.C.
240487 Sergt. A. G. Pritchard ..	1/8th Worcester Regt.
40350 Pte. A. Parkinson	20th Manchesters.
Major (Bt. Lieut.-Col.) L. H. Queripel, C.M.G., D.S.O.	Comdg. 112th Bde., R.F.A.
T./Capt. J. A. Reiss	Camp Comdt. 25th Div.
311130 Sapper T. Reilly	25th Div. Sig. Coy., R.E.
S4/O.86953 Sergt. J. Rayson ..	25th Div. M. T. Coy.
2nd Lieut. H. N. Ransome ..	9th Yorks.
10452 L.-Corpl. E. Standen ..	20th Manchesters.
307853 Pte. H. J. Sherman ..	1/8th R. Warwick Regt.
Capt. L. R. C. Sumner, M.C. ..	1/5th Gloucesters.
M2/100148 Corpl. H. Steere ..	25th Div. M. T. Coy.
1099 Sergt. H. Smith	R.A.V.C., attd. 74th Bde.
T2/SRO. 1811 Sergt. W. H. Sargent	R.A.S.C., attd. 77th Fld. Amb.
T/26110 Wheeler-Corpl. G. Sheppard	R.A.S.C.
T./Capt. (A./Major) J. C. Sullivan	R.A.M.C.
204896 Sergt. S. T. Smith ..	11th South Lancs.
46522 C.Q.M. Sergt. C. S. W. Saunders	25th Div. Sig. Coy., R.E.

6547 T./Sub. Conductor J. A. R.A.O. Corps.
Salter
eut. (A./Capt.) D. G. Tacon   ..   25th D.A.C.
ıpt. J. Taylor, M.C.   ..   ..   11th South Lancs.
2860 Pte. E. Taylor   ..   ..   11th South Lancs.
128 L.-Corpl. H. Vayro..   ..   13th Durham L. Inf.
610 Corpl. J. C. Walker   ..   21st Manchesters.
265 Sergt. W. Walker :.   ..   11th Sherwood Foresters.
047 Pte. T. Wheeler   ..   ..   R.A.M.C.
ıpt. Rev. H. Wilcox   ..   ..   C.F.
519 Pte. H. Wedgbury   ..   25th Batt. M.G. Corps.
0476 S.C. Sergt. J. P. Williams..   R.E.
254 S. Sergt. H. P. Williams ..   R.A.V.C., attd. R.F.A.

Printed and bound by Antony Rowe Ltd, Eastbourne

19903025R00258

Printed in Poland
by Amazon Fulfillment
Poland Sp. z o.o., Wrocław